ISBN 978-0-260-69850-6
PIBN 11115622

UNITED STATES DEPARTMENT OF THE INTERIOR, Oscar L. Chapman, *Secretary*

FISH AND WILDLIFE SERVICE, Albert M. Day, *Director*   DANIEL M. COHEN

Statistical Digest 25

FISHERY STATISTICS
OF THE UNITED STATES
1949

BY

A. W. ANDERSON and C. E. PETERSON

UNITED STATES GOVERNMENT PRINTING OFFICE, WASHINGTON : 1952

For sale by the Superintendent of Documents, U. S. Government Printing Office, Washington 25, D. C.   -   :   -   Price $1.25 (paper)

Fishery Statistics of the United States and Alaska are compiled and published annually to make available information on both the economic and biological aspects of the domestic commercial fisheries.

Data on the economic aspects are necessary to persons engaged in the commercial fishery and to governmental agencies concerned with its regulation and protection. Those here given cover the total catch and value by species, the yield and value of manufactured products and byproducts, the employment of men, craft, and gear in the capture of fishery products; and related information.

From the biological standpoint these data are important to sound fishery management in providing detailed information on fluctuations in the commercial catch by species, locality and gear; and on the type of gear and boats operated. They assist conservation agencies in regulating the commercial fisheries so as to produce maximum yields without depletion.

Previous statistical reports on the fishery industries were issued under the Department of the Interior in the Administrative Report series for 1938 and in the Statistical Digest series for succeeding years. Reports for preceding years were issued in the Administrative Report series of the former Bureau of Fisheries.

The following is a listing of the various Statistical Digests issued since 1939:

No. 1 Fishery Statistics of the United States, 1939
     2 Alaska Fishery and Fur Seal Industries, 1940
     3 Propagation and Distribution of Food Fishes, Fiscal year, 1941
     4 Fishery Statistics of the United States, 1940
     5 Alaska Fishery and Fur Seal Industries, 1941
     6 Propagation and Distribution of Food Fishes, 1941
     7 Fishery Statistics of the United States, 1941
     8 Alaska Fishery and Fur Seal Industries, 1942
     9 Propagation and Distribution of Food Fishes, 1942
    10 Alaska Fishery and Fur Seal Industries, 1943
    11 Fishery Statistics of the United States, 1942
    12 Propagation and Distribution of Food Fishes, 1943
    13 Alaska Fishery and Fur Seal Industries, 1944
    14 Fishery Statistics of the United States, 1943
    15 Alaska Fishery and Fur Seal Industries, 1945
    16 Fishery Statistics of the United States, 1944
    17 Alaska Fishery and Fur Seal Industries, 1946
    18 Fishery Statistics of the United States, 1945
    19 Fishery Statistics of the United States, 1946
    20 Alaska Fishery and Fur Seal Industries, 1947
    21 Fishery Statistics of the United States, 1947
    22 Fishery Statistics of the United States, 1948
    23 Alaska Fishery and Fur Seal Industries, 1948
    24 Propagation and Distribution of Food Fishes, 1944-1948
    25 Fishery Statistics of the United States, 1949

FISHERY STATISTICS OF THE UNITED STATES: 1949

By A. W. ANDERSON, *Chief Branch of Commercial Fisheries*

and C. E. PETERSON, *Chief, Statistical Section*

Fish and Wildlife Service

CONTENTS

INTRODUCTION

This report contains a review of the fishery statistics for the year 1949, collected by the Branch of Commercial Fisheries during 1950. These include data on the volume of the catch of fishery products and their value, employment in the fisheries, quantity of gear operated, the number of fishing craft employed in the capture of fishery products, and certain information on the volume and value of the production of manufactured fishery products and byproducts.

Statistical surveys for the 1949 data were conducted in all sections except the South Atlantic and the Mississippi River States. Statistics on the various fisheries were collected by the following field agents: R. Balkovic, B. F. Greer, H. Haberland, C. H. Lyles, D. A. McKown, R. H. Marchant, C. B. Tendick, J. P. Wharton, R. H. Wilson, and F. M. Wood. The surveys in Washington and Oregon were supervised by F. C. Hinsdale. Data for the Great Lakes were assembled by the staff of Dr. John Van Oosten of the Branch of Fishery Biology; and those for the fisheries of Alaska were collected by the Branch of Alaska Fisheries of the Service.

Information on landings at Massachusetts ports was collected in cooperation with the Market News Section and the Branch of Fishery Biology. Data on the Hawaiian Fisheries were furnished by the Division of Fish and Game, Board of Commissioners of Agriculture and Forestry of the Territory of Hawaii.

The statistical surveys conducted during 1950, for 1949 data, were under the general direction of E. A. Power, Chief, Statistical Section, assisted by C. E. Peterson, Statistician. The survey material was assembled, tabulated, and prepared for publication by the staff of the Statistical Section under the direction of B. E. Finley, Fishery Marketing Specialist. He was assisted by Mary Donahue, Elsie English, Evelyn Hecht, Alice Hnatiw, Delia Ridge, Dorothy Stein, and Melissa Tinkey. Operation of the tabulating unit was directed by Mabel Swart, assisted by Barbara Fair, Adele Marshall and Marie Voigt. G. I. Sundstrom prepared many of the illustrations contained in the report.

In assembling the data on the fisheries, all appropriate records collected by the various State fishery agencies were used. In the Great Lakes and the Pacific Coast States, these records were such that it was necessary for the Service personnel to conduct only partial surveys. Statistics on the imports and exports of fishery products were furnished by the Bureau of the Census.

Information on the means of collecting the data and an explanation of terms used may be found in Section 13 of this publication.

Grateful acknowledgment is extended to the State and Federal agencies and to the various individuals who cooperated in furnishing portions of the data contained in this volume.

SECTION 1.- GENERAL REVIEW

Surveys covering the catch of fish and shellfish for the year 1949 were made in all areas of the United States and Alaska with the exception of the South Atlantic States and the Mississippi River and its tributaries. The South Atlantic States were last canvassed in 1945, and detailed data published in "Fishery Statistics of the United States, 1945". (Statistical Digest No. 18). The most recent complete data for the Mississippi River and its tributaries are for 1931. However, catch statistics for the Upper Mississippi area for 1949 were made available by the Upper Mississippi River Conservation Commission and are shown in Section 9 of this publication. In the following tables, the most recent employment, operating unit, and catch statistics are shown for each section of the country.

It is estimated that the 1949 catch of fishery products in all sections of the United States and Alaska totaled 4,796,000,000 pounds, valued at $339,000,000 to the fishermen. This was an increase of 5 percent in quantity compared with the previous year. The value of the 1949 catch declined 8 percent compared with the record high of 1948. The fisheries of the United States and Alaska experienced a general decrease in prices during 1949, and values for a number of items declined sharply. The price of fish oil, which reached a peak of 24 cents per pound in 1947, fell to as low as 5-1/2¢ per pound. Sharp declines also occurred in the amount received by canners for their production of canned Maine sardines, California pilchards, tuna, and most species of salmon. Despite general price declines in other products, the price of fish meal was maintained at a high level because of the recognized value of this product in animal feeding. Prices averaged somewhat over $150 per ton --nearly four times the amount received in 1940.

Outstanding developments during the year were the record landings of tuna and tuna-like fishes; the record landings of menhaden; the continued success of the ocean perch (rosefish) fishery; and the marked gains recorded by the Pacific salmon and pilchard fisheries. During 1949, the production of tuna and tunalike fishes on the Pacific Coast set a new record with landings totaling over 332,000,000 pounds. This catch exceeded the previous high established in 1948 by over 7 million pounds. The catch of menhaden off the Atlantic and Gulf States during 1949 broke all previous records with landings of 1,081,000,000 pounds, valued at over $11,500,000 to the fishermen. The catch was far greater than that of any other species taken by United States and Alaska fishermen. The Atlantic Coast catch of ocean perch (rosefish) during 1949 totaled almost 237,000,000 pounds -- a decrease of less than 1 percent in quantity but an increase of 2 percent in value compared with the previous year. The United States and Alaska catch of salmon totaled over 484,000,000 pounds in 1949 -- an increase of over 80,000,000 pounds compared with 1948. Salmon landings in the Pacific Coast States increased over 30,000,000 pounds compared with the previous year while those in Alaska gained almost 50,000,000 pounds. The Pacific Coast pilchard catch during 1949 amounted to 633,500,000 pounds, valued at $10,800,000 to the fishermen. This represented an increase of 70 percent in quantity and a decrease of 2 percent in value compared with 1948. The mackerel catch on the Atlantic Coast decreased 18 percent in volume compared with the previous year while the catch of Pacific mackerel gained 26 percent in poundage during the same period.

The per capita consumption of fishery products in the United States in 1949 totaled 11.4 pounds, edible weight basis. This was considerably above the wartime level of 9 pounds when a large portion of the canned pack was allocated to the armed forces and to lend-lease distribution.

The total catch of fishery products in the United States, as based on the most recent surveys for each section through 1949, amounted to 4,791,000,000 pounds, valued at $329,700,000 to the fishermen. The difference between these figures and the estimated totals listed above are due to the inclusion of estimates on the 1949 landings for the South Atlantic area and the Mississippi River and its tributaries. The following table which contains recorded production for the areas in which surveys were made for the years shown and estimates for other regions, indicates the trend of the yield and value of the domestic catch during recent years.

Year	Pounds	Value to the fishermen	Average price per pound
1939	4,443,328,000	$96,532,000	2.17¢
1940	4,059,524,000	98,957,000	2.44
1941	4,900,000,000	129,000,000	2.63
1942	3,876,524,000	170,338,000	4.39
1943	4,202,000,000	204,000,000	4.85
1944	4,500,000,000	213,000,000	4.73
1945	4,575,500,000	269,900,000	5.82
1946	4,456,000,000	310,000,000	6.96
1947	4,344,000,000	307,600,000	7.08
1948	4,575,000,000	367,000,000	8.02
1949	4,796,000,000	339,000,000	7.06

GENERAL REVIEW

A total of 1,002 vessels of 5 net tons and over received their first documents as fishing craft in 1949. This was 8 percent less than the number entering the fleet the previous year, but between three and four times the number documented annually prior to 1943. In the five years ending with 1949, a total of 5,312 vessels had been documented as fishing craft. In 1940, the entire fleet in the United States and Alaska totaled only 5,562 vessels. Despite the large increase in the size of the fleet, the annual catch has not increased proportionately compared with the prewar production. This has been due largely to the low yields of salmon in Alaska and pilchards in California.

Vessels obtaining their first documents as fishing craft, 1936 - 1949:

Year	Number	Year	Number
1936	1/ 435	1943	358
1937	335	1944	635
1938	1/ 376	1945	741
1939	357	1946	1,085
1940	320	1947	1,300
1941	354	1948	1,184
1942	358	1949	1,002

1/ Data are partly estimated.

San Pedro, California, continued to be the nation's leading fishing port, with landings of over 553,000,000 pounds, valued at $27,000,000 to the fishermen. Monterey, California, was in second place, with approximately 285,000,000 pounds followed by Gloucester, Massachusetts with 251,000,000 pounds. While San Diego, California -- with landings of almost 205,000,000 pounds -- occupied fourth place with respect to the volume of the landings, it was first in importance as far as value was concerned. Landings at that port had a value of $32,500,000.

It is estimated that the 1949 catch was marketed as follows: 1,629 million pounds (round weight basis) as fresh and frozen products; 1,663 million pounds were used for canning; 1,404 million pounds for bait and byproducts; and 100 million pounds for cured products.

The 1949 production of canned fishery products in the United States and Alaska amounted to 855,000,000 pounds, valued at $295,500,000 at the processors' level. The output of fishery byproducts was valued at $78,500,000. Compared with 1948, the value of canned products decreased 12 percent while the value of the byproducts decreased only 2 percent.

Almost 286,000,000 pounds of fishery products were frozen during 1949. This was a decrease of over 6,000,000 pounds or 2 percent compared with the record figure established during 1948.

The value of foreign trade in fishery products (imports and exports combined) by the United States during 1949 amounted to over $186,500,000. Of this amount, $151,600,000 represented the value of products entered for consumption and $34,900,000 the value of exports of domestic fishery products. Import items which were received in a considerable greater volume during 1949 were fresh and frozen tuna; shrimp; fillets, other than groundfish; and salted herring. Items showing large declines compared with the previous year were fresh sea herring, groundfish fillets, canned sardines and tuna, and sperm oil.

A review of the fisheries of each geographical area will be found at the beginning of each section in this volume. Summaries of the more important specific fisheries will be found in Section 12. Summarized data of the operating units and catch for all areas have been previously published in Current Fishery Statistics No. 703.

GENERAL REVIEW

DISPOSITION OF CATCH, 1931 - 1949

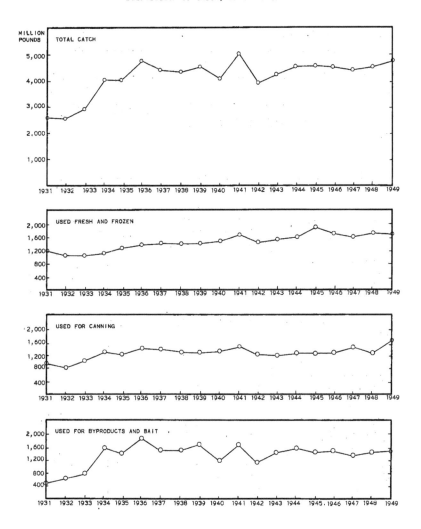

UNITED STATES AND ALASKA SUMMARIES

SUMMARY OF CATCH

(EXPRESSED IN THOUSANDS OF POUNDS AND THOUSANDS OF DOLLARS)

PRODUCT	NEW ENGLAND, 1949 AREA XXII		MIDDLE ATLANTIC, 1949 AREA XXIII		CHESAPEAKE, 1949 AREA XXIII		SOUTH ATLANTIC, 1945 AREA XXIV		GULF, 1949 AREA XXV	
	QUANTITY	VALUE	QUANTITY	VALUE	QUANTITY	VALUE	QUANTITY	VALUE	QUANTITY	VALUE
FISH.	931,433	38,577	473,274	10,830	232,781	9,037	339,577	9,514	355,948	13,686
SHELLFISH, ETC. . .	68,543	19,960	47,702	16,288	101,875	16,146	65,369	5,618	168,640	36,019
TOTAL . . .	999,976	58,537	520,976	27,118	334,656	25,103	404,946	15,132	524,588	49,705

PRODUCT	PACIFIC, 1949		LAKES, 1949		MISSISSIPPI RIVER AND TRIBUTARIES, 1931		ALASKA, 1949		TOTAL, VARIOUS YEARS	
	QUANTITY	VALUE	QUANTITY	VALUE	QUANTITY	VALUE	QUANTITY	VALUE	QUANTITY	VALUE
FISH.	1,311,479	93,375	85,691	11,458	44,062	2,257	466,261	38,759	4,240,506	227,493
SHELLFISH, ETC. . .	52,250	6,930	2	(1)	38,321	640	6,628	540	549,330	102,141
WHALE PRODUCTS. .	790	68	-	-	-	-	-	-	790	68
TOTAL . . .	1,364,519	100,373	85,693	11,458	82,383	2,897	472,889	39,299	4,790,626	329,702

NOTE: THE ROMAN NUMERALS APPEARING UNDER THE NAMES OF THE SECTIONS ARE THE NUMBERS GIVEN THE AREAS BY THE NORTH AMERICAN COUNCIL ON FISHERY INVESTIGATIONS. IT SHOULD BE EXPLAINED THAT THERE ARE INCLUDED IN THE OPERATING UNIT TABLES FOR THE AREAS, CRAFT WHOSE PRINCIPAL PORTS ARE IN THE RESPECTIVE AREAS BUT WHICH MAY AT TIMES FISH ELSEWHERE.

SUMMARY OF OPERATING UNITS

ITEM	NEW ENGLAND, 1949	MIDDLE ATLANTIC, 1949	CHESAPEAKE, 1949	SOUTH ATLANTIC, 1945 AND 1940	GULF, 1949
	NUMBER	NUMBER	NUMBER	NUMBER	NUMBER
FISHERMEN:					
ON VESSELS.	6,385	3,433	2,150	2,455	7,396
ON BOATS AND SHORE.	18,454	11,738	16,196	10,414	15,465
TOTAL	24,839	15,171	18,346	12,869	22,861
VESSELS:					
STEAM	5	-	-	-	-
NET TONNAGE	513	-	-	-	-
MOTOR	943	590	393	614	2,244
NET TONNAGE	31,607	14,109	5,385	6,960	34,680
SAIL.	-	-	111	45	-
NET TONNAGE	-	-	1,227	595	-
TOTAL VESSELS	948	590	504	659	2,244
TOTAL NET TONNAGE	32,120	14,109	6,612	7,555	34,680
BOATS:					
MOTOR	8,836	5,702	8,122	3,096	6,474
OTHER	5,003	1,364	3,867	2,860	4,694
ACCESSORY BOATS	241	183	73	236	276
APPARATUS:					
HAUL SEINES	15	217	590	514	295
PURSE SEINES AND LAMPARA NETS . .	187	55	18	45	53
STOP SEINES	136	-	-	-	-
OTTER TRAWLS.	900	272	64	1,119	5,483
BEAM TRAWLS	-	21	-	-	-
GILL NETS	1,349	2,271	2,153	3,940	1,964
TRAMMEL AND BAR NETS.	-	-	-	8	1,089
POUND NETS, TRAP NETS, AND W ldS.	303	260	1,878	2,520	1
FLOATING TRAPS.	86	-	-	-	-
STOP NETS	11	18	6	-	4
FYKE NETS	35	863	2,202	353	1,065
BAG NETS.	40	-	-	-	-
OTHER NETS 2/	542	50	1,176	309	7,014
HOOKS, BAITS OR SNOODS. . .	1,167,279	269,912	1,130,340	866,620	838,238
EEL POTS AND TRAPS.	1,222	2,285	24,054	535	-
BRUSH TRAPS	-	-	-	-	88,500
LOBSTER POTS AND TRAPS. . .	601,786	9,786	-	5,900	11,840
CRAB, CRAWFISH, AND TURTLE					
POTS AND TRAPS	1,482	955	71,335	7,330	4,020
HARPOONS AND SPEARS	213	5	-	49	132
CLAM DREDGES.	35	129	-	-	3
CRAB DREDGES.	-	38	369	-	-
OYSTER DREDGES.	116	376	836	349	393
SCALLOP DREDGES	5,734	126	-	-	36
MUSSEL AND OTHER DREDGES. . . .	-	-	7	-	-
SCRAPES	-	-	517	-	-
TONGS, RAKES, SHOVELS, HOES, FORKS, PICKS AND ORABS	6,019	8,661	7,754	647	2,193
DIVING OUTFITS.	-	-	-	-	40
OTHER APPARATUS 5/.	300	17,470	2,418	10,857	267

SEE FOOTNOTES AT END OF TABLE

(CONTINUED ON NEXT PAGE)

SUMMARY OF OPERATING UNITS - Continued

ITEM	PACIFIC, 1949	LAKES, 1940	MISSISSIPPI RIVER AND TRIBUTARIES, 1931	ALASKA, 1949	TOTAL, VARIOUS YEARS
	NUMBER	NUMBER	NUMBER	NUMBER	NUMBER
FISHERMEN:					
ON VESSELS	15,579	1,694	-	1/ 10,757	49,849
ON BOATS AND SHORE	16,215	3,448	15,884	-	107,814
TOTAL	31,794	5,142	15,884	10,757	157,663
VESSELS:					
STEAM	-	30	-	-	35
NET TONNAGE	-	646	-	-	1,159
MOTOR	3,232	469	-	1,597	10,082
NET TONNAGE	84,178	5,427	-	19,861	202,207
SAIL	-	-	-	-	156
NET TONNAGE	-	-	-	-	1,822
TOTAL VESSELS	3,232	499	-	1,597	10,273
TOTAL NET TONNAGE	84,178	6,073	-	19,861	205,188
BOATS:					
MOTOR	7,082	1,186	4,426	1,790	46,714
OTHER	824	599	10,120	1,683	31,214
ACCESSORY BOATS	1,193	-	-	-	2,202
APPARATUS:					
HAUL SEINES	187	169	1,013	132	3,132
PURSE SEINES AND LAMPARA NETS	884	-	-	701	1,943
STOP SEINES	-	-	-	-	136
OTTER TRAWLS	326	-	-	4	8,168
BEAM TRAWLS	25	-	-	7	53
GILL NETS	6,845	106,031	101	4,934	129,588
TRAMMEL AND BAR NETS	54	75	518	-	1,744
POUND NETS, TRAP NETS, AND WEIRS	43	8,336	374	353	14,068
FLOATING TRAPS	-	-	-	-	86
STOP NETS	-	-	-	-	39
FYKE NETS	1,600	1,787	32,541	-	40,446
BAG NETS 2/	1	-	-	-	41
OTHER NETS 2/	2,636	-	191	-	11,918
HOOKS, BAITS OR SNOODS	1,186,930	615,839	2,459,179	(3)	8,534,337
EEL POTS AND TRAPS	-	-	-	-	28,096
BRUSH TRAPS	-	-	-	-	88,500
LOBSTER POTS AND TRAPS	6,348	-	-	-	635,660
CRAB, CRAWFISH, AND TURTLE POTS AND TRAPS	78,903	700	456	1,337	166,518
HARPOONS AND SPEARS	120	-	-	-	519
CLAM DREDGES	-	-	-	-	167
CRAB DREDGES	-	-	-	-	407
OYSTER DREDGES	(4)	-	-	-	2,070
SCALLOP DREDGES	-	-	-	-	5,896
MUSSEL AND OTHER DREDGES	-	-	440	-	447
SCRAPES	-	-	-	-	517
TONGS, RAKES, SHOVELS, HOES, FORKS, PICKS AND GRABS	4/ 4,194	13	3,994	289	33,764
DIVING OUTFITS	-	-	-	-	40
CROWFOOT BARS	-	22	4,480	-	4,502
OTHER APPARATUS 5/	625	-	3,781	-	35,718

1/ INCLUDES PERSONS IN BOAT AND SHORE FISHERIES.
2/ INCLUDES CAST, DIP, LIFT, REEF, AND BRAIL OR SCOOP NETS.
3/ NUMBER NOT DETERMINED.
4/ OYSTER DREDGES ARE INCLUDED WITH TONGS ON PACIFIC COAST.
5/ INCLUDES FISH, PERIWINKLE AND COCKLE, AND CONCH POTS; BOX, SLAT, SHRIMP AND OCTOPUS TRAPS; LOBSTER AND SPONGE HOOKS; AND COQUINA SCOOPS.
NOTE:--DATA FOR THE SOUTH ATLANTIC STATES ARE FOR 1945 EXCEPT FOR THE EAST COAST OF FLORIDA WHICH ARE FOR 1940.

. GREAT LAKES FISHING TUG

GENERAL REVIEW

UNITED STATES AND ALASKA: CATCH BY REGION

(EXPRESSED IN THOUSANDS OF POUNDS AND THOUSANDS OF DOLLARS)

SPECIES	NEW ENGLAND, 1949		MIDDLE ATLANTIC, 1949		CHESAPEAKE, 1949		SOUTH ATLANTIC, 1945		GULF, 1949	
FISH	QUANTITY	VALUE	QUANTITY	VALUE	QUANTITY	VALUE	QUANTITY	VALUE	QUANTITY	VALUE
ALEWIVES.	5,067	57	144	4	26,969	504	8,450	186	-	-
AMBERJACK	(1)	(1)	-	-	-	-	108	2	103	6
ANGLERFISH.	7	(1)	58	3	-	-	-	-	-	-
BARRACUDA	-	-	-	-	-	-	41	2	43	2
BLUEFISH.	61	12	1,369	168	392	50	1,912	304	578	77
BLUE RUNNER OR HARDTAIL. . . .	-	-	-	-	-	-	91	6	1,136	34
BOWFIN.	-	-	-	-	(1)	(1)	-	-	-	-
BUFFALOFISH	-	-	-	-	-	-	-	-	794	64
BUTTERFISH.	2,704	216	3,089	323	1,097	73	57	3	-	-
CABIO OR CRAB EATER .	-	-	-	-	-	-	32	2	28	2
CARP.	42	3	122	8	1,282	72	883	27	24	2
CATFISH AND BULLHEADS	8	1	153	10	2,018	136	10,890	1,141	3,636	817
CERO.	-	-	-	-	-	-	-	-	2	(1)
CIGARFISH	-	-	-	-	-	-	-	-	4	(1)
COD	58,795	3,377	3,743	365	37	2	-	-	-	-
CRAPPIE	-	-	-	-	2	(1)	933	205	-	-
CREVALLE.	2	(1)	-	-	-	-	122	6	421	14
CROAKER	-	-	173	16	14,733	2,109	4,472	366	231	15
CUNNER.	9	(1)	3	(1)	-	-	-	-	-	-
CUSK.	3,620	133	-	-	-	-	-	-	-	-
DOLPHIN	2	(1)	(1)	(1)	(1)	(1)	80	8	(1)	(1)
DRUM:										
BLACK	-	-	13	1	69	3	679	49	1,231	104
RED OR REDFISH. .	-	.	-	-	77	6	1,043	117	2,858	464
EELS:										
COMMON.	119	21	415	74	1,318	159	181	9	(1)	(1)
CONGER.	16	1	52	1	30	1	-	-	-	-
FLOUNDERS	66,847	6,355	10,644	1,485	3,144	422	2,086	243	821	160
FRIGATE MACKEREL. . .	44	2	91	3	-	-	-	-	-	-
GARFISH	-	-	-	-	-	-	-	-	182	10
GIZZARD SHAD.	-	-	-	-	204	4	558	11	-	-
GRAYFISH.	625	6	56	2	-	-	-	-	-	-
GROUPERS.	-	-	2	(1)	-	-	1,417	138	8,397	835
GRUNTS.	-	-	-	-	-	-	76	5	84	7
HADDOCK	133,765	9,170	1,206	80	-	-	-	-	-	-
HAKE:										
RED	41,666	393	944	33	2	(1)	-	-	-	-
WHITE	14,213	531	116	5	18	1	4	1	-	-
HALIBUT	473	106	3	1	(1)	(1)	-	-	-	-
HARVESTFISH OR STARFISH.	-	-	-	-	601	33	812	49	-	-
HERRING, SEA.	168,413	2,677	2,181	32	86	2	-	-	-	-
HICKORY SHAD.	(1)	(1)	3	(1)	247	11	969	75	-	-
HOGCHOKER	-	-	-	-	3	(1)	-	-	15	1
HOGFISH	-	-	-	-	-	-	15	1	-	-
JEWFISH	-	-	-	-	-	-	216	30	187	10
KING MACKEREL	-	-	34	3	-	-	2,782	396	1,419	185
KING WHITING OR "KINGFISH" . . .	87	7	34	5	194	18	3,286	145	636	44
LAUNCE.	15	1	23	2	-	-	-	-	-	-
MACKEREL.	17,916	1,276	20,953	704	3,201	329	-	-	-	-
MENHADEN.	12,566	134	392,410	4,256	137,812	1,552	256,279	1,715	276,506	3,248
MINNOWS	100	7	-	-	-	-	-	-	514	31
MOJARRA	-	-	-	-	-	-	-	-	32	2
MOONFISH.	-	-	31	2	60	4	11,957	962	31,893	3,282
MULLET.	-	-	-	-	-	-	208	37	45	7
MUTTONFISH.	-	-	-	-	-	-	-	-	-	-
OCEAN PERCH (ROSEFISH)	236,987	9,820	-	-	-	-	-	-	-	-
OCEAN POUT.	5	(1)	-	-	-	-	-	-	-	-
PADDLEFISH OR SPOONBILL CAT. . . .	-	-	-	-	-	-	-	-	48	8
PERMIT.	-	-	-	-	-	-	1	(1)	20	1
PIGFISH	-	-	-	-	12	1	522	36	50	4
PIKE OR PICKEREL. . .	-	-	-	-	22	5	-	-	-	-
PILOTFISH	-	-	17	1	-	-	-	-	-	-
PINFISH	-	-	-	-	-	-	13	1	10	(1)
POLLOCK	28,789	806	42	2	-	-	-	-	-	-
POMPANO	-	-	-	-	(1)	(1)	356	137	646	338
SALMON:										
ATLANTIC.	1	1	-	-	-	-	-	-	-	-
TOTAL SALMON. .	1	1	-	-	-	-	-	-	-	-
SAND PERCH.	-	-	-	-	30	1	-	-	-	-
SAWFISH	-	-	-	-	-	-	-	-	35	1
SCUP OR PORGY	4,644	181	16,805	1,113	7,509	477	113	9	-	-
SEA BASS, BLACK (ATLANTIC) . .	302	37	5,061	685	4,680	466	454	66	-	-

SEE FOOTNOTES AT END OF TABLE   (CONTINUED ON NEXT PAGE)

UNITED STATES AND ALASKA: CATCH BY REGION - Continued

(EXPRESSED IN THOUSANDS OF POUNDS AND THOUSANDS OF DOLLARS)

SPECIES	NEW ENGLAND, 1949		MIDDLE ATLANTIC, 1949		CHESAPEAKE, 1949		SOUTH ATLANTIC, 1945		GULF, 1949	
FISH - CONTINUED	QUANTITY	VALUE	QUANTITY	VALUE	QUANTITY	VALUE	QUANTITY	VALUE	QUANTITY	VALUE
SEA CATFISH	-	-	-	-	-	-	11	1	1,372	62
SEA ROBIN	128	2	41	1	15	1	-	-	-	-
SEA TROUT OR WEAKFISH:										
GRAY.	19	3	4,013	413	6,676	463	4,770	529	-	-
SPOTTED	-	-	-	-	109	15	1,580	307	5,832	1,207
WHITE	-	-	-	-	-	-	-	-	657	51
SHAD.	490	74	2,363	402	3,884	591	2,065	423	-	-
SHARKS.	359	12	43	2	471	14	2,029	32	68	2
SHEEPSHEAD:										
FRESH-WATER. . . .	-	-	-	-	-	-	162	13	902	71
SALT-WATER.	-	-	-	-	-	-	13	1	466	45
SILVERSIDES	2	(1)	220	13	-	-	-	-	-	-
SKATES.	154	2	60	3	1	(1)	-	-	-	-
SMELT	162	41	-	-	-	-	-	-	-	-
SNAPPER:										
MANGROVE.	-	-	-	-	-	-	113	14	162	19
RED	-	-	-	-	-	-	250	55	7,888	1,864
WHITE	-	-	-	-	-	-	-	-	31	3
SNOOK OR SERGEANTFISH	-	-	-	-	-	-	205	27	662	88
SPADEFISH	-	-	-	-	-	-	-	-	(1)	(1)
SPANISH MACKEREL. . . .	-	-	-	-	15	2	5,979	721	3,876	419
SPOT.	(1)	(1)	49	5	8,659	553	7,510	399	266	18
STRIPED BASS.	162	31	902	229	4,542	774	609	122	-	-
STURGEON, COMMON. . .	10	1	25	9	16	4	42	15	5	1
SUCKERS	19	1	8	1	13	1	7	(1)	-	-
SUNFISH	5	(1)	1	(1)	1	(1)	1,256	238	-	-
SWELLFISH	11	(1)	881	60	424	13	(1)	(1)	-	-
SWORDFISH	944	340	22	11	17	1	-	-	-	-
TAUTOG.	101	6	71	3	17	1	-	-	-	-
TENPOUNDER.	-	-	-	-	-	-	-	-	701	22
TILEFISH.	271	20	964	69	4	(1)	-	-	14	1
TRIGGERFISH	-	-	-	-	-	-	-	-	14	1
TRIPLETAIL.	-	-	-	-	-	-	41	3	23	3
TUNA AND TUNALIKE FISHES:										
BLUEFIN	2,674	196	64	11	-	-	-	-	-	-
BONITO.	5	1	17	2	61	7	60	5	-	-
LITTLE.	(1)	(1)	705	51	25	1	-	-	(1)	(1)
TOTAL TUNA . . .	2,679	197	786	64	86	8	60	5	(1)	(1)
WHITEBAIT	-	-	28	4	-	-	-	-	-	-
WHITE PERCH	24	3	132	11	1,801	128	501	60	-	-
WHITING	90,036	1,920	1,578	74	6	(1)	-	-	-	-
WOLFFISH.	2,327	155	7	(1)	-	-	-	-	-	-
YELLOW PERCH.	10	1	5	1	189	28	10	1	-	-
YELLOW PIKE	-	-	-	-	(1)	(1)	-	-	-	-
YELLOWTAIL, ATLANTIC.	-	-	-	-	-	-	266	58	174	35
UNCLASSIFIED.	35,610	437	1,085	68	2	(1)	-	-	-	-
TOTAL. . . .	931,433	38,577	473,274	10,830	232,781	9,037	339,577	9,514	355,948	13,686
SHELLFISH, ETC.										
CRABS:										
BLUE:										
HARD.	3	1	4,227	393	62,785	3,133	17,018	588	26,595	982
SOFT AND PEELERS.	-	-	70	23	4,841	817	187	56	455	192
ROCK.	2,608	122	-	-	-	-	-	-	-	-
STONE	-	-	-	-	-	-	81	21	53	27
TOTAL CRABS . .	2,611	123	4,297	416	67,626	3,950	17,286	665	27,103	1,201
CRAWFISH, FRESH-WATER	-	-	630	3	-	-	-	-	40	1
HORSESHOE CRAB. . . .	-	-	630	3	-	-	-	-	-	-
LOBSTERS:										
NORTHERN.	23,994	8,594	660	309	2	(1)	-	-	-	-
SPINY	-	-	-	-	-	-	572	116	1,482	188
SHRIMP.	10	2	90	45	(1)	(1)	43,581	3,984	126,514	29,207
CLAMS:										
COQUINA	-	-	-	-	-	-	-	-	(1)	(1)
HARD.	4,536	1,160	11,588	3,967	1,733	736	506	153	85	29
OCEAN QUAHOG. . . .	63	5	-	-	-	-	-	-	-	-
RAZOR	74	8	-	-	-	-	-	-	-	-
SOFT.	10,195	1,950	1,012	192	1	(1)	-	-	-	-
SURF.	18	4	5,311	510	-	-	-	-	-	-
TOTAL CLAMS . .	14,886	3,127	17,911	4,669	1,734	736	506	153	85	29
CONCHS.	41	4	132	31	159	11	4	(1)	(1)	(1)

SEE FOOTNOTES AT END OF TABLE

(CONTINUED ON NEXT PAGE)

UNITED STATES AND ALASKA: CATCH BY REGION - Continued

(EXPRESSED IN THOUSANDS OF POUNDS AND THOUSANDS OF DOLLARS)

SPECIES	NEW ENGLAND, 1949		MIDDLE ATLANTIC, 1949		CHESAPEAKE, 1949		SOUTH ATLANTIC, 1945		GULF, 1949	
	QUANTITY	VALUE	QUANTITY	VALUE	QUANTITY	VALUE	QUANTITY	VALUE	QUANTITY	VALUE
SHELLFISH, ETC. - CONTINUED										
MUSSELS, SEA. . . .	769	52	126	26	-	-	43	5	-	-
OYSTERS, MARKET:										
EASTERN, PUBLIC .	486	232	540	336	16,914	6,343	1,822	423	6,557	2,086
EASTERN, PRIVATE.	3,515	1,241	16,872	8,736	14,863	5,031	999	222	6,564	2,753
TOTAL OYSTERS.	4,003	1,473	17,412	9,072	31,777	11,374	2,821	645	13,121	4,839
PERIWINKLES AND COCKLES.	140	20	-	-	-	-	-	-	-	-
SCALLOPS:										
BAY	1,310	923	23	28	-	-	22	8	136	58
SEA	13,980	5,168	4,307	1,593	9	4	-	-	-	-
SQUID	4,635	125	2,095	92	193	10	2	(1)	9	(1)
SEA URCHINS	80	2	-	-	-	-	-	-	-	-
TERRAPIN,										
DIAMOND-BACK . . .	-	-	4	(1)	253	51	16	8	16	1
TURTLES	-	-	15	4	122	10	256	21	22	3
FROGS	-	-	-	-	-	-	-	-	43	21
IRISH MOSS.	1,625	28	-	-	-	-	-	-	-	-
ROCKWEED.	-	-	-	-	-	-	260	13	-	-
SPONGES	-	-	-	-	-	-	-	-	69	471
BLOODWORMS.	402	297	-	-	-	-	-	-	-	-
SANDWORMS	37	22	-	-	-	-	-	-	-	-
TOTAL. . . .	68,543	19,960	47,702	16,288	101,875	16,146	65,369	5,618	168,640	36,019
GRAND TOTAL. .	999,976	58,537	520,976	27,118	334,656	25,183	404,946	15,132	524,588	49,705

SPECIES	PACIFIC, 1949		LAKES, 1949		MISSISSIPPI RIVER & TRIBUTARIES, 1931		ALASKA, 1949		TOTAL, VARIOUS YEARS	
FISH	QUANTITY	VALUE	QUANTITY	VALUE	QUANTITY	VALUE	QUANTITY	VALUE	QUANTITY	VALUE
ALEWIVES.	-	-	-	-	-	-	-	-	40,630	751
AMBERJACK	-	-	-	-	-	-	-	-	211	8
ANCHOVIES	3,724	62	-	-	-	-	-	-	3,724	62
ANGLERFISH.	-	-	-	-	-	-	-	-	65	3
BARRACUDA	2,456	366	-	-	-	-	-	-	2,542	370
BLACK BASS.	-	-	-	-	14	2	-	-	14	2
BLUEFISH.	-	-	-	-	-	-	-	-	4,312	611
BLUE PIKE	-	-	14,085	1,568	-	-	-	-	14,085	1,568
BLUE RUNNER OR HARDTAIL	-	-	22	1	428	9	-	-	1,227	40
BOWFIN.	-	-	22	1	428	9	-	-	450	10
BUFFALOFISH	-	-	6	1	15,773	687	-	-	16,573	752
BURBOT.	-	-	841	25	-	-	-	-	841	25
BUTTERFISH.	-	-	-	-	-	-	-	-	6,947	615
CABEZONE.	16	1	-	-	-	-	-	-	16	1
CABIO OR CRAB EATER	-	-	-	-	-	-	-	-	60	4
CABRILLA.	210	28	-	-	-	-	-	-	210	28
CARP.	406	12	4,568	151	11,891	456	-	-	19,218	731
CATFISH AND BULLHEADS.	202	39	1,415	250	10,267	878	-	-	28,789	3,272
CERO.	-	-	-	-	-	-	-	-	2	(1)
CHUB.	-	-	7,732	1,294	-	-	-	-	7,732	1,294
CIGARFISH	-	-	-	-	-	-	-	-	4	(1)
CISCO	-	-	134	37	-	-	-	-	134	37
COD	6,251	231	-	-	-	-	2,186	55	71,012	4,030
CRAPPIE	-	-	-	-	41	3	-	-	976	208
CREVALLE.	-	-	-	-	-	-	-	-	545	20
CROAKER	-	-	-	-	-	-	-	-	19,609	2,506
CUNNER.	-	-	-	-	-	-	-	-	12	(1)
CUSK.	-	-	-	-	-	-	-	-	3,620	133
DOLLY VARDEN TROUT.	-	-	-	-	-	-	15	1	15	1
DOLPHIN	-	-	-	-	-	-	-	-	82	8
DRUM:										
BLACK	-	-	-	-	-	-	-	-	1,992	157
RED OR REDFISH. .	-	-	-	-	-	-	-	-	3,979	587
EELS:										
COMMON.	-	-	20	2	6	(1)	-	-	2,059	265
CONGER.	-	-	-	-	-	-	-	-	98	3
FLOUNDERS	42,165	2,302	-	-	-	-	-	-	125,707	10,967
FLYING FISH	34	3	-	-	-	-	-	-	34	3
FRIGATE MACKEREL. .	-	-	-	-	-	-	-	-	135	5
GARFISH	-	-	(1)	(1)	72	1	-	-	254	11
GIZZARD SHAD. . . .	-	-	32	1	-	-	-	-	794	16
GOLDFISH.	-	-	170	9	-	-	-	-	170	9
GRAYFISH.	2/14,068	2/739	-	-	-	-	-	-	14,749	747
GROUPERS.	291	50	-	-	-	-	-	-	10,107	1,023
GRUNTS.	-	-	-	-	-	-	-	-	160	12

SEE FOOTNOTES AT END OF TABLE   (CONTINUED ON NEXT PAGE)

UNITED STATES AND ALASKA: CATCH BY REGION - Continued

(EXPRESSED IN THOUSANDS OF POUNDS AND THOUSANDS OF DOLLARS)

SPECIES	PACIFIC, 1949		LAKES, 1949		MISSISSIPPI RIVER & TRIBUTARIES, 1931		ALASKA, 1949		TOTAL, VARIOUS YEARS	
FISH - CONTINUED	QUANTITY	VALUE	QUANTITY	VALUE	QUANTITY	VALUE	QUANTITY	VALUE	QUANTITY	VALUE
HADDOCK.	-	-	-	-	-	-	-	-	134,971	9,250
HAKE:										
PACIFIC.	141	1	-	-	-	-	-	-	141	1
RED.	-	-	-	-	-	-	-	-	42,612	426
WHITE.	-	-	-	-	-	-	-	-	14,351	538
HALIBUT.	14,243	2,556	-	-	-	-	35,196	5,158	49,915	7,821
HARDHEADS. . . .	17	5	-	-	-	-	-	-	17	5
HARVESTFISH OR STARFISH.	-	-	-	-	-	-	-	-	1,413	82
HERRING:										
LAKE	-	-	21,934	788	-	-	-	-	21,934	788
SEA.	1,289	52	-	-	-	-	33,061	414	205,030	3,177
HICKORY SHAD . . .	-	-	-	-	-	-	-	-	1,219	86
HOGCHOKER.	-	-	-	-	-	-	-	-	18	1
HOGFISH.	-	-	-	-	-	-	-	-	15	1
JACK MACKEREL. . .	51,250	1,111	-	-	-	-	-	-	51,250	1,111
JEWFISH.	-	-	-	-	-	-	-	-	403	40
KINGFISH (CALIFORNIA). . .	764	40	-	-	-	-	-	-	764	40
KING MACKEREL. . .	-	-	-	-	-	-	-	-	4,235	584
KING WHITING OR "KINGFISH". . . .	-	-	-	-	-	-	-	-	4,237	219
LAKE TROUT	-	-	3,309	1,355	-	-	-	-	3,309	1,355
LAMPREY.	370	9	-	-	-	-	-	-	370	9
LAUNCE	-	-	-	-	-	-	-	-	38	3
LINGCOD.	8,009	737	-	-	-	-	179	10	8,188	747
MACKEREL	49,771	1,285	-	-	-	-	-	-	91,841	3,594
MENHADEN	-	-	-	-	-	-	-	-	1,075,573	10,905
MINNOWS.	-	-	-	-	1	(1)	-	-	101	7
MOJARRA.	-	-	-	-	-	-	-	-	514	31
MOONEYE.	-	-	8	(1)	3	(1)	-	-	11	(1)
MOONFISH	-	-	-	-	-	-	-	-	32	2
MULLET	72	5	-	-	-	-	-	-	44,013	4,255
MUTTONFISH	-	-	-	-	-	-	-	-	253	44
OCEAN PERCH (ROSEFISH). . .	-	-	-	-	-	-	-	-	236,987	9,820
OCEAN POUT	-	-	-	-	-	-	-	-	5	(1)
PADDLEFISH OR SPOONBILL CAT . .	-	-	-	-	951	44	-	-	999	52
PERCH.	485	67	-	-	-	-	-	-	485	67
PERMIT	-	-	-	-	-	-	-	-	21	1
PIGFISH.	-	-	-	-	-	-	-	-	584	41
PIKE OR PICKEREL .	-	-	166	15	5	(1)	-	-	193	20
PILCHARD	633,540	10,760	-	-	-	-	-	-	633,540	10,760
PILOTFISH.	-	-	-	-	-	-	-	-	17	1
PINFISH.	-	-	-	-	-	-	-	-	23	1
POLLOCK.	-	-	-	-	-	-	-	-	28,832	808
POMPANO.	89	25	-	-	-	-	-	-	1,091	500
QUILLBACK.	-	-	2	(1)	269	11	-	-	271	11
RATFISH.	1,472	13	-	-	-	-	-	-	1,472	13
ROCK BASS.	192	26	41	3	-	-	-	-	233	29
ROCKFISHES	23,958	1,097	-	-	-	-	13	3	23,971	1,100
SABLEFISH.	6,076	553	-	-	-	-	5,754	428	11,830	981
SALMON:										
ATLANTIC	-	-	-	-	-	-	-	-	1	1
CHINOOK OR KING.	25,512	5,286	-	-	-	-	14,076	2,219	39,588	7,505
CHUM OR KETA . .	5,940	715	-	-	-	-	46,734	2,484	52,674	3,199
PINK	44,215	4,421	-	-	-	-	228,950	19,533	273,165	23,954
RED OR SOCKEYE .	7,058	1,503	-	-	-	-	70,929	5,607	77,987	7,110
SILVER OR COHO .	13,134	2,109	-	-	-	-	27,657	2,819	40,791	4,928
TOTAL SALMON .	95,859	14,034	-	-	-	-	388,346	32,662	484,206	46,697
SAND PERCH	-	-	-	-	-	-	-	-	30	1
SAUGER	-	-	507	60	3	(1)	-	-	510	60
SAWFISH.	-	-	-	-	-	-	-	-	35	1
SCULPIN.	148	27	-	-	-	-	-	-	148	27
SCUP OR PORGY. . .	-	-	-	-	-	-	-	-	29,071	1,780
SEA BASS:										
BLACK (ATLANTIC)	-	-	-	-	-	-	-	-	10,497	1,254
BLACK (PACIFIC).	114	16	-	-	-	-	-	-	114	16
WHITE.	1,410	291	-	-	-	-	-	-	1,410	291
SEA CATFISH. . . .	-	-	-	-	-	-	-	-	1,383	63
SEA ROBIN.	-	-	-	-	-	-	-	-	184	4
SEA TROUT OR WEAKFISH:										
GRAY	-	-	-	-	-	-	-	-	15,478	1,408
SPOTTED.	-	-	-	-	-	-	-	-	7,521	1,529
WHITE.	-	-	-	-	-	-	-	-	657	51
SHAD	2,200	146	-	-	-	-	-	-	11,002	1,636

SEE FOOTNOTES AT END OF TABLE   (CONTINUED ON NEXT PAGE)

UNITED STATES AND ALASKA: CATCH BY REGION - Continued

(EXPRESSED IN THOUSANDS OF POUNDS AND THOUSANDS OF DOLLARS)

SPECIES	PACIFIC, 1949		LAKES, 1949		MISSISSIPPI RIVER & TRIBUTARIES, 1931		ALASKA, 1949		TOTAL, VARIOUS YEARS	
	QUANTITY	VALUE	QUANTITY	VALUE	QUANTITY	VALUE	QUANTITY	VALUE	QUANTITY	VALUE
SHARKS.	2/ 2,719	2/ 1,444	-	-	-	-	1,307	23	6,996	1,529
SHEEPSHEAD:										
FRESH-WATER . . .	-	-	3,127	127	3,905	143	-	-	8,096	354
SALT-WATER. . . .	62	5	-	-	-	-	-	-	541	51
SILVERSIDES	-	-	-	-	-	-	-	-	222	13
SKATES.	1,128	18	-	-	-	-	200	1	1,543	24
SMELT	4,642	319	1,557	148	-	-	-	-	6,361	508
SNAPPER:										
MANGROVE.	-	-	-	-	-	-	-	-	275	33
RED	-	-	-	-	-	-	-	-	8,136	1,919
WHITE	-	-	-	-	-	-	-	-	31	3
SNOOK OR										
SERGEANTFISH . . .	-	-	-	-	-	-	-	-	887	115
SPADEFISH	-	-	-	-	-	-	-	-	(1)	(1)
SPANISH MACKEREL. .	4	(1)	-	-	-	-	-	-	9,874	1,142
SPOT.	-	-	-	-	-	-	-	-	16,484	975
STEELHEAD TROUT . .	1,051	147	-	-	-	-	4	(1)	1,055	147
STRIPED BASS. . . .	25	1	-	-	-	-	-	-	6,240	1,157
STURGEON:										
COMMON.	452	81	-	-	-	-	-	-	550	111
SHOVELNOSE. . . .	-	-	22	22	87	8	-	-	109	30
SUCKERS	-	-	3,676	156	315	13	-	-	4,038	172
SUNFISH	-	-	8	1	22	1	-	-	1,293	240
SWELLFISH	-	-	-	-	-	-	-	-	1,316	73
SWORDFISH	199	87	-	-	-	-	-	-	1,165	438
TAUTOG.	-	-	-	-	-	-	-	-	189	10
TENPOUNDER.	-	-	-	-	-	-	-	-	701	22
TILEFISH.	-	-	-	-	-	-	-	-	1,239	89
TRIGGERFISH	-	-	-	-	-	-	-	-	14	1
TRIPLETAIL.	-	-	-	-	-	-	-	-	64	6
TULLIBEE.	-	-	810	47	-	-	-	-	810	47
TUNA AND										
TUNALIKE FISHES:										
ALBACORE.	54,794	10,039	-	-	-	-	-	-	54,794	10,039
BLUEFIN	4,390	713	-	-	-	-	-	-	7,128	920
BONITO.	1,830	178	-	-	-	-	-	-	1,973	193
LITTLE.	-	-	-	-	-	-	-	-	730	52
SKIPJACK.	80,512	11,923	-	-	-	-	-	-	80,512	11,923
YELLOWFIN	190,543	30,999	-	-	-	-	-	-	190,543	30,999
TOTAL TUNA . . .	332,069	53,852	-	-	-	-	-	-	335,680	54,126
WHITEBAIT	242	24	-	-	-	-	-	-	270	28
WHITE BASS.	-	-	807	102	4	(1)	-	-	811	102
WHITEFISH:										
COMMON.	-	-	8,837	3,040	-	-	-	-	8,837	3,040
MENOMINEE	-	-	144	26	-	-	-	-	144	26
OCEAN	31	3	-	-	-	-	-	-	31	3
WHITE PERCH	-	-	-	-	-	-	-	-	2,458	202
WHITING	-	-	-	-	-	-	-	-	91,620	1,994
WOLFFISH.	-	-	-	-	-	-	-	-	2,334	155
YELLOW PERCH. . . .	-	-	4,595	675	-	-	-	-	4,809	706
YELLOW PIKE	-	-	7,116	1,554	5	1	-	-	7,121	1,555
YELLOWTAIL:										
ATLANTIC.	-	-	-	-	-	-	-	-	440	93
PACIFIC	7,319	686	-	-	-	-	-	-	7,319	686
UNCLASSIFIED. . . .	242	19	-	-	-	-	-	4	36,939	528
TOTAL.	1,311,479	93,375	85,691	11,458	44,062	2,257	466,261	38,759	4,240,506	227,493
SHELLFISH, ETC.										
CRABS:										
BLUE:										
HARD.	-	-	-	-	-	-	-	-	110,628	5,097
SOFT AND										
PEELERS. . . .	-	-	-	-	-	-	-	-	5,553	1,088
DUNGENESS	33,605	3,462	-	-	-	-	1,429	81	35,034	3,543
KING.	-	-	-	-	-	-	1,207	72	1,207	72
ROCK.	(1)	(1)	-	-	-	-	-	-	2,608	122
STONE	-	-	-	-	-	-	-	-	134	48
TOTAL CRABS .	33,605	3,462	-	-	-	-	2,636	153	155,164	9,970
CRAWFISH,										
FRESH-WATER. . . .	46	10	2	(1)	29	(1)	-	-	117	11
HORSESHOE CRAB. . .	-	-	-	-	-	-	-	-	630	3
LOBSTERS:										
NORTHERN.	-	-	-	-	-	-	-	-	24,656	8,903
SPINY	834	284	-	-	-	-	-	-	2,888	588
SHRIMP.	872	66	-	-	49	4	2,268	181	173,384	33,489
ABALONE	714	398	-	-	-	-	-	-	714	398

SEE FOOTNOTES AT END OF TABLE   (CONTINUED ON NEXT PAGE)

UNITED STATES AND ALASKA: CATCH BY REGION - Continued

(EXPRESSED IN THOUSANDS OF POUNDS AND THOUSANDS OF DOLLARS)

SPECIES	PACIFIC, 1949		LAKES, 1949		MISSISSIPPI RIVER & TRIBUTARIES, 1931		ALASKA, 1949		TOTAL, VARIOUS YEARS	
SHELLFISH, ETC. CONTINUED	QUANTITY	VALUE	QUANTITY	VALUE	QUANTITY	VALUE	QUANTITY	VALUE	QUANTITY	VALUE
CLAMS:										
COQUINA	-	-	-	-	-	-	-	-	(1)	(1)
HARD.	394	126	-	-	-	-	14	1	18,856	6,172
OCEAN QUAHOG. . .	-	-	-	-	-	-	-	-	63	5
RAZOR	380	242	-	-	-	-	1,699	204	2,153	454
SOFT.	-	-	-	-	-	-	-	-	11,208	2,142
SURF.	-	-	-	-	-	-	-	-	5,329	514
MIXED	32	8	-	-	-	-	-	-	32	8
TOTAL CLAMS. .	806	376	-	-	-	-	1,713	205	37,641	9,295
CONCHS.	-	-	-	-	-	-	-	-	336	46
MUSSELS, SEA. . . .	-	-	-	-	-	-	-	-	958	83
MUSSEL SHELLS . . .	-	-	-	-	37,255	422	-	-	37,255	422
OCTOPUS	122	8	-	-	-	-	-	-	122	8
OYSTERS, MARKET:										
EASTERN, PUBLIC .	-	-	-	-	-	-	-	-	26,321	9,420
EASTERN, PRIVATE.	7	5	-	-	-	-	-	-	42,820	17,988
PACIFIC	8,164	1,849	-	-	-	-	11	1	8,175	1,850
WESTERN	203	278	-	-	-	-	-	-	203	278
TOTAL OYSTERS. .	8,374	2,132	-	-	-	-	11	1	77,519	29,536
PERIWINKLES AND COCKLES.	-	-	-	-	-	-	-	-	140	20
SCALLOPS:										
BAY	17	10	-	-	-	-	-	-	1,508	1,027
SEA	-	-	-	-	-	-	-	-	18,296	6,765
SQUID	6,860	184	-	-	-	-	-	-	13,794	411
SEA URCHINS	-	-	-	-	-	-	-	-	80	2
TERRAPIN, DIAMOND-BACK . . .	-	-	-	-	19	(1)	-	-	308	60
TURTLES	-	-	-	-	94	3	-	-	509	41
FROGS	-	-	-	-	875	131	-	-	918	152
IRISH MOSS.	-	-	-	-	-	-	-	-	1,625	28
ROCKWEED.	-	-	-	-	-	-	-	-	260	13
SPONGES	-	-	-	-	-	-	-	-	69	471
PEARLS AND SLUGS. .	-	-	-	-	-	80	-	-	-	80
BLOODWORMS.	-	-	-	-	-	-	-	-	402	297
SANDWORMS	-	-	-	-	-	-3	-	-	37	22
TOTAL.	52,250	6,930	2	(1)	38,321	640	6,628	540	549,330	102,141
WHALE PRODUCTS:										
LIVER	28	8	-	-	-	-	-	-	28	8
MEAL.	200	8	-	-	-	-	-	-	200	8
OIL	562	52	-	-	-	-	-	-	562	52
TOTAL.	790	68	-	-	-	-	-	-	790	68
GRAND TOTAL. . .	1,364,519	100,373	85,693	11,458	82,383	2,897	472,889	39,299	4,790,626	329,702

1/ LESS THAN 500 POUNDS OR 500 DOLLARS.
2/ THE CATCH OF GRAYFISH IN CALIFORNIA IS INCLUDED WITH SHARKS.

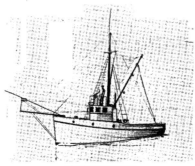

SWORDFISH HARPOONER

UNITED STATES AND ALASKA: CATCH BY STATES

STATES	MARINE WATERS & COASTAL RIVERS, 1949 & 1945		MISSISSIPPI RIVER AND TRIBUTARIES, 1931		LAKES, 1949 AND 1945 1/		TOTAL, VARIOUS YEARS	
	POUNDS	VALUE	POUNDS	VALUE	POUNDS	VALUE	POUNDS	VALUE
ALABAMA.	10,155,100	$1,973,751	1,822,153	$32,754	-	-	11,977,253	$2,006,505
ARKANSAS	-	-	15,732,507	411,451	-	-	15,732,507	411,451
CALIFORNIA . . .	1,129,261,300	72,504,719	-	-	-	-	1,129,261,300	72,504,719
CONNECTICUT. . .	24,194,800	2,157,545	-	-	-	-	24,194,800	2,157,545
DELAWARE	166,473,900	3,007,773	-	-	-	-	166,473,900	3,007,773
FLORIDA.	263,845,300	16,440,160	-	-	4,098,800	$526,628	267,944,100	16,966,788
GEORGIA.	21,397,700	1,349,536	-	-	-	-	21,397,700	1,349,536
ILLINOIS	-	-	14,262,630	367,238	1,496,600	285,936	15,759,230	653,174
INDIANA.	-	-	7,717,596	157,222	30,400	2,060	7,747,996	159,282
IOWA	-	-	7,777,967	302,395	-	-	7,777,967	302,395
KANSAS	-	-	455,421	16,673	-	-	455,421	16,673
KENTUCKY	-	-	1,621,751	60,882	-	-	1,621,751	60,882
LOUISIANA. . . .	288,587,200	27,403,637	19,213,368	994,374	-	-	307,800,568	28,398,011
MAINE.	294,297,200	14,988,040	-	-	-	-	294,297,200	14,988,040
MARYLAND	58,981,700	8,583,832	-	-	-	-	58,981,700	8,583,832
MASSACHUSETTS. .	647,612,900	38,991,476	-	-	-	-	647,612,900	38,991,476
MICHIGAN	-	-	-	-	25,533,900	4,116,398	25,533,900	4,116,398
MINNESOTA. . . .	-	-	3,498,280	137,656	6,603,100	455,490	10,101,380	593,146
MISSISSIPPI. . .	52,895,000	1,625,272	2,649,723	122,961	-	-	55,544,723	1,748,233
MISSOURI	-	-	927,636	76,981	-	-	927,636	76,981
NEBRASKA	-	-	145,310	16,253	-	-	145,310	16,253
NEW HAMPSHIRE. .	443,400	169,899	-	-	-	-	443,400	169,899
NEW JERSEY . . .	208,997,500	9,744,560	-	-	-	-	208,997,500	9,744,560
NEW YORK	145,505,000	14,364,800	-	-	2,304,700	402,923	147,809,700	14,767,723
NORTH CAROLINA .	198,168,800	5,495,252	-	-	-	-	198,168,800	5,495,252
OHIO	-	-	185,481	7,072	26,682,100	3,464,034	26,867,581	3,471,106
OKLAHOMA	-	-	39,640	4,145	-	-	39,640	4,145
OREGON	61,096,400	7,065,447	-	-	-	-	61,096,400	7,065,447
PENNSYLVANIA . .	-	-	-	-	4,436,000	712,532	4,436,000	712,532
RHODE ISLAND . .	33,428,000	2,229,916	-	-	-	-	33,428,000	2,229,916
SOUTH CAROLINA .	10,855,600	899,389	-	-	-	-	10,855,600	899,389
SOUTH DAKOTA . .	-	-	114,361	10,576	-	-	114,361	10,576
TENNESSEE. . . .	-	-	3,435,069	103,915	-	-	3,435,069	103,915
TEXAS.	79,530,800	9,124,500	138,500	6,368	-	-	79,669,300	9,130,868
VIRGINIA	275,674,800	16,598,481	-	-	-	-	275,674,800	16,598,481
WASHINGTON . . .	174,160,800	20,802,948	-	-	-	-	174,160,800	20,802,948
WISCONSIN. . . .	-	-	2,645,130	68,441	18,605,800	2,019,045	21,250,930	2,087,486
ALASKA	472,889,281	39,299,005	-	-	-	-	472,889,281	39,299,005
TOTAL . . .	4,618,452,481	314,819,938	82,382,523	2,897,357	89,791,400	11,985,046	4,790,626,404	329,702,341

1/ INCLUDES THE CATCH OF THE GREAT LAKES, RAINY LAKE, NAMAKAN LAKE, LAKE OF THE WOODS, AND LAKE OKEECHOBEE.

SEED OYSTER FISHERY, 1949

ITEM	NEW ENGLAND		MIDDLE ATLANTIC		CHESAPEAKE		TOTAL	
	NUMBER		NUMBER		NUMBER		NUMBER	
OPERATING UNITS								
FISHERMEN:								
ON VESSELS.	148		892		230		1,270	
ON BOATS AND SHORE:								
REGULAR	5		222		1,555		1,782	
CASUAL.	13		30		15		58	
TOTAL	166		1,144		1,800		3,110	
VESSELS:								
STEAM	3		-		-		3	
NET TONNAGE	437		-		-		437	
MOTOR	23		154		45		222	
NET TONNAGE	616		3,241		249		4,106	
SAIL.	-		-		29		29	
NET TONNAGE	-		-		462		462	
TOTAL VESSELS . . .	26		154		74		254	
TOTAL NET TONNAGE .	1,053		3,241		711		5,005	
BOATS:								
MOTOR	12		203		881		1,096	
OTHER	-		30		271		301	
APPARATUS:								
DREDGES	57		208		58		323	
YARDS AT MOUTH. . . .	85		208		77		370	
TONGS	15		222		1,325		1,562	
RAKES	-		-		26		26	
CATCH	BUSHELS	VALUE	BUSHELS	VALUE	BUSHELS	VALUE	BUSHELS	VALUE
OYSTERS, SEED:								
PUBLIC, SPRING.	730	$1,112	1,505,390	$1,505,080	2,022,668	$760,960	3,528,788	$2,267,152
PUBLIC, FALL.	11,493	14,721	389	778	906,500	497,950	918,382	513,449
PRIVATE, SPRING	298,760	692,760	32,500	32,500	165,125	59,100	496,385	784,360
PRIVATE, FALL	77,762	126,340	-	-	181,051	64,800	258,813	191,140
TOTAL.	388,745	834,933	1,538,279	1,538,358	3,275,344	1,382,810	5,202,368	3,756,101

UNITED STATES AND ALASKA: CATCH BY GEAR

GEAR	NEW ENGLAND, 1949		MIDDLE ATLANTIC, 1949		CHESAPEAKE, 1949	
	POUNDS	VALUE	POUNDS	VALUE	POUNDS	VALUE
PURSE SEINES	40,270,200	$888,555	397,553,600	$4,393,344	126,430,300	$1,466,592
HAUL SEINES	1,958,200	73,457	1,801,000	315,089	21,933,200	2,007,870
STOP SEINES	65,592,100	1,041,089	-	-	-	-
GILL NETS	12,812,100	599,975	3,226,800	461,269	7,340,500	888,932
LINES	25,958,100	1,475,832	8,296,700	864,786	25,008,600	1,316,166
POUND NETS	11,369,500	783,317	24,841,000	1,036,220	53,817,300	2,596,252
FLOATING TRAPS	8,905,900	346,719	-	-	-	-
OTHER TRAPS 3/	39,600	8,122	-	-	13,600	272
WEIRS	66,349,500	1,083,586	690,000	8,713	-	-
STOP NETS	4,600	725	81,800	4,522	71,000	3,580
FYKE AND HOOP NETS	55,200	3,197	384,000	36,041	3,059,100	297,154
DIP AND LIFT NETS	9,841,500	148,314	83,800	24,116	284,400	48,645
BAG, DRAG AND PUSH NETS	63,600	17,473	-	-	-	-
OTTER TRAWLS	691,848,000	31,935,664	40,021,900	3,839,429	19,118,200	1,726,116
BEAM TRAWLS	-	-	90,000	45,000	-	-
POTS	26,708,400	8,728,184	3,134,000	615,009	33,878,100	1,638,301
HARPOONS	1,103,600	354,856	21,900	10,900	-	-
SPEARS	10,800	2,020	-	-	-	-
SCRAPES	-	-	-	-	2,932,200	478,245
DREDGES	19,622,900	7,435,945	28,218,600	11,189,971	21,671,200	5,719,485
TONGS	2,038,300	505,545	9,910,600	3,504,113	16,908,000	6,248,266
RAKES	3,583,300	685,195	1,365,200	490,588	971,800	412,711
FORKS	143,900	23,155	-	-	-	-
HOES	11,686,700	2,392,765	937,500	164,062	-	-
BY HAND	10,300	3,186	318,000	113,961	1,219,000	333,746
TOTAL	999,976,300	58,536,876	520,976,400	27,117,133	334,656,500	25,182,313

GEAR	SOUTH ATLANTIC, 1945		GULF, 1949	
	POUNDS	VALUE	POUNDS	VALUE
PURSE SEINES	255,126,800	$1,722,037	276,486,900	$3,246,455
HAUL SEINES	26,561,500	2,415,658	15,881,700	1,709,906
GILL NETS	26,372,100	2,736,395	22,796,200	3,517,906
TRAMMEL NETS	178,500	34,333	11,297,800	538,621
LINES	20,147,500	1,417,152	52,151,800	5,276,145
POUND NETS	13,249,800	840,733	102,900	21,787
OTHER TRAPS 3/	-	-	212,600	90,324
STOP NETS	-	-	645,300	96,840
FYKE AND HOOP NETS	1,029,400	104,076	1,117,700	93,500
DIP AND LIFT NETS	290,300	73,557	820,600	125,171
CAST NETS	161,000	16,109	162,600	16,630
OTTER TRAWLS	49,758,400	4,314,673	127,354,000	29,292,968
POTS	7,955,700	568,313	1,975,900	244,129
SPEARS	451,800	63,314	160,600	36,424
DREDGES	1,486,700	356,130	5,780,900	1,773,756
TONGS	316,600	56,760	7,326,300	3,059,896
RAKES	820,800	179,602	45,600	19,152
GRABS	553,100	92,371	36,800	17,774
HOOKS	-	-	10,400	58,523
BRAIL OR SCOOP NETS	-	-	200	70
DIVING OUTFITS, ABALONE AND SPONGES	-	-	58,300	412,280
BY HAND	486,100	140,847	163,100	57,518
TOTAL	404,946,100	15,132,350	524,586,200	49,705,775

SEE FOOTNOTES AT END OF TABLE

(CONTINUED ON NEXT PAGE)

FISHING FOR TUNA

UNITED STATES AND ALASKA: CATCH BY GEAR - Continued

GEAR	PACIFIC, 1949		LAKES, 1949		MISSISSIPPI RIVER AND TRIBUTARIES, 1931	
	POUNDS	VALUE	POUNDS	VALUE	POUNDS	VALUE
PURSE SEINES	1/806,212,100	1/$24,423,869	-	-	-	-
HAUL SEINES	4,133,400	395,375	5,772,600	$325,003	13,739,657	$574,541
GILL NETS	2/36,982,200	2/6,164,428	41,026,700	5,738,172	166,598	6,547
TRAMMEL NETS.	(2)	(2)	-	-	1,134,206	75,615
LINES	343,800,800	56,305,612	590,800	227,083	10,140,037	772,245
POUND NETS.	1,108,000	149,291	8,320,300	1,239,262	224,275	9,541
TRAP NETS	-	-	28,200,500	3,733,159	-	-
OTHER TRAPS 3/.	34,533,900	3,758,554	-	-	-	-
WEIRS	173,800	8,688	-	-	-	-
FYKE AND HOOP NETS. . . .	222,100	39,386	1,780,600	195,640	18,507,204	797,130
DIP AND LIFT NETS	4,546,300	374,968	1,100	99	30,045	3,307
BAG, DRAG AND PUSH NETS .	41,300	2,455	-	-	-	-
REEF NETS	4,219,800	485,238	-	-	-	-
OTTER TRAWLS.	88,585,000	4,425,281	-	-	-	-
BEAM TRAWLS	799,100	60,943	-	-	-	-
POTS.	-	-	-	-	310,455	26,277
HARPOONS.	1,526,000	159,326	-	-	-	-
SPEARS.	-	-	-	-	2,250	270
DREDGES	4/8,373,500	4/2,131,953	-	-	3,699,100	40,958
CROWFOOT BARS	-	-	-	-	20,893,550	265,443
TONGS	(4)	(4)	-	-	1,601,876	21,091
RAKES	-	-	-	-	370,130	4,029
SHOVELS	806,100	375,820	-	-	-	-
FORKS	-	-	-	-	4,812,737	76,214
GRABS	-	-	-	-	873,099	130,621
BRAIL OR SCOOP NETS . . .	27,741,500	713,668	-	-	-	-
DIVING OUTFITS, ABALONE AND SPONGES.	713,600	398,259	-	-	-	-
BY HAND	(4)	(4)	-	-	5,877,304	93,528
TOTAL	1,364,518,500	100,373,114	85,692,600	11,458,418	82,382,523	2,897,357

GEAR	ALASKA, 1949		TOTAL, VARIOUS YEARS	
	POUNDS	VALUE	POUNDS	VALUE
PURSE SEINES.	160,421,101	$10,515,250	2,062,501,001	$46,656,102
HAUL SEINES	-	-	91,781,257	7,816,899
STOP SEINES	-	-	65,592,100	1,041,089
GILL NETS	67,784,759	5,656,605	218,507,957	25,770,229
TRAMMEL NETS.	-	-	12,610,506	648,569
LINES	69,791,010	8,608,127	554,885,347	76,263,158
POUND NETS.	169,264,154	13,979,076	282,297,229	20,655,479
TRAP NETS	-	-	28,200,500	3,733,159
FLOATING TRAPS.	-	-	8,905,900	346,719
OTHER TRAPS 3/.	-	-	34,799,700	3,857,272
WEIRS	-	-	67,213,300	1,100,987
STOP NETS	-	-	802,700	105,667
FYKE AND HOOP NETS. . . .	-	-	26,155,304	1,566,124
DIP AND LIFT NETS	-	-	15,898,045	798,177
CAST NETS	-	-	323,600	32,819
BAG, DRAG AND PUSH NETS .	-	-	104,900	19,928
REEF NETS	-	-	4,219,800	485,238
OTTER TRAWLS.	1,206,945	72,417	1,017,892,445	75,606,748
BEAM TRAWLS	2,267,934	181,434	3,157,034	287,377
POTS.	1,428,401	80,716	75,390,956	11,900,929
HARPOONS.	-	-	2,651,500	525,082
SPEARS.	-	-	625,450	102,028
SCRAPES	-	-	2,932,200	478,245
DREDGES	-	-	88,852,900	28,648,178
CROWFOOT BARS	-	-	20,893,550	265,443
TONGS	-	-	38,101,676	13,395,671
RAKES	-	-	7,156,830	1,791,277
SHOVELS	1,713,663	204,531	2,519,763	580,351
FORKS	-	-	4,956,637	99,369
HOES.	-	-	12,624,200	2,556,827
GRABS	-	-	1,462,999	240,766
HOOKS	-	-	10,400	58,523
BRAIL OR SCOOP NETS . . .	-	-	27,741,700	713,738
DIVING OUTFITS, ABALONE AND SPONGES.	-	-	771,900	810,539
BY HAND	11,314	849	8,085,118	743,635
TOTAL	472,889,281	39,299,005	4,790,626,404	329,702,341

1/ THE CATCH OF RING AND LAMPARA NETS IN CALIFORNIA HAS BEEN INCLUDED WITH PURSE SEINES.
2/ THE CALIFORNIA CATCH IN TRAMMEL NETS HAS BEEN INCLUDED WITH GILL NETS.
3/ INCLUDES CATCH BY BOX, BRUSH, SLAT, CRAB, OCTOPUS, LOBSTER, CRAWFISH, AND SHRIMP TRAPS.
4/ THE CATCH BY TONGS AND BY HAND HAS BEEN INCLUDED WITH DREDGES.

MANUFACTURED FISHERY PRODUCTS

. The output of manufactured products (canned, cured, packaged, and byproducts) in the United States and Alaska during 1949 had an estimated value of 550 million dollars. Canned products are estimated·to have accounted for 54 percent of the total; packaged shellfish, 18 percent; byproducts, 14 percent; packaged fish, 9 percent; and cured fish, 5 percent.

. The value of manufactured products as published in the following tables, which totals $453,754,857 represents the most recent figures collected by the Service, on the various segments of the manufactured fishery products industry. The variation between this figure and the estimated value mentioned in the first paragraph is due to the use of estimated 1949 values for cured fishery products and packaged shellfish in that paragraph.

The data listed in the following table are for 1949 for canned fish, fishery by-products, and packaged fish in the United States and for all products in Alaska; for 1940 for packaged shellfish and cured products in the United States except in the Mississippi River area; and for 1931 for cured products in the Mississippi River area. Data on manufactured fishery products processed by fishermen have been omitted. No data on this production are available for any year since 1940, when the total value of these products amounted to $2,343,798. Information on the production by fishermen in 1940 can be found in Manufactured Fishery Products, 1948, (C.F.S. No. 578) or in ''Fishery Statistics of the United States, 1948'' (Statistical Digest No. 22).

The pack of canned fishery products in 1949 amounted to 855,014,842 pounds, valued at $295,503,905 to the packers. This was an increase of 9 percent in volume, but a decline of 12 percent in value. The increase in volume resulted principally from larger packs of salmon, tuna, California sardines, and fish for animal food. The 1949 pack of canned salmon amounted to 265,196,448 pounds, valued at $103,439,983 to the canners. Compared with 1948 this was an increase of 15 percent in volume, but a decline of 14 percent in value.. Despite this decline of the price of canned salmon, the pack was the third most valuable in history. The tuna and tunalike fishes pack of 141,700,593 pounds, valued at $97,710,325 was the fifth consecutive record pack, and second largest value ever received by the processors. California sardines with a pack of 169,569,540 pounds, valued at $21,334,825 showed an increase of 42 percent in volume, but a decline of 3 percent in value when compared with the previous year.

The value of fishery byproducts processed was $78,472,495, a 2 percent decrease in comparison with the previous year. The principal byproducts were marine-animal oils, 17,695,833 gallons, valued at $17,364,977; marine-animal scrap and meal, 237,180 tons, valued at $35,652,142; marine and fresh-water shell buttons, valued at $10,478,733; and fish solubles valued at $5,144,111. A record production of menhaden scrap and meal continued while the production of menhaden oil decreased in volume and value.

The production of fresh and frozen packaged fish increased from 189,499,843 pounds, valued at $47,708,883, in 1948 to 194,215,265 pounds, valued at $48,389,905, in 1949.

FISH MEAL PLANT

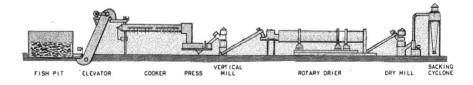

FISH PIT ELEVATOR   COOKER   PRESS   VERTICAL MILL   ROTARY DRIER   DRY MILL   SACKING CYCLONE

MANUFACTURED FISHERY PRODUCTS - VARIOUS YEARS 1/

ITEM	YEAR	UNIT	QUANTITY	VALUE
ALEWIVES:				
CANNED	1949	STANDARD CASES	111,994	$469,398
ROE, CANNED.	1949	DO	44,106	749,993
SALTED:				
ROUND.	1940	POUNDS	899,400	15,939
CORNEO	1940	DO	5,429,450	123,287
PICKLED 2/	1940	DO	4,851,500	176,819
SPICED	1940	DO	3,778,499	379,110
TIGHT-PACK, CUT.	1940	DO	280,100	12,698
WITH ROE	1940	DO	62,700	3,874
SMOKED, WHOLE AND FILLETS.	1940	DO	23,800	1,052
ANCHOVIES, CANNED.	1949	STANDARD CASES	3,757	34,184
BARRACUDA:				
SALTED, DRY.	1940	POUNDS	19,465	2,433
SMOKED	1940	DO	1,000	200
BLUE PIKE:				
FRESH FILLETS.	1949	DO	2,287,450	970,684
FROZEN FILLETS	1949	DO	628,223	249,225
BLUE RUNNERS, SALTED	1940	DO	250,000	10,000
BUFFALOFISH:				
SMOKED (U.S. EXCEPT MISSISSIPPI RIVER)	1940	DO	325,000	71,200
SMOKED (MISSISSIPPI RIVER)	1931	DO	25,700	3,245
BUTTERFISH:				
SMOKED (U.S. EXCEPT MISSISSIPPI RIVER)	1940	DO	478,300	111,750
SMOKED (MISSISSIPPI RIVER)	1931	DO	2,400	600
CARP:				
SMOKED (U.S. EXCEPT MISSISSIPPI RIVER)	1940	DO	168,550	49,575
SMOKED (MISSISSIPPI RIVER)	1931	DO	700	245
CHUB, CISCO, AND TULLIBEE:				
SMOKED (U.S. EXCEPT MISSISSIPPI RIVER)	1940	DO	5,008,672	1,549,519
SMOKED (MISSISSIPPI RIVER)	1931	DO	215,200	48,010
COD:				
FRESH FILLETS.	1949	DO	7,885,548	1,949,494
FROZEN FILLETS	1949	DO	5,766,217	1,282,127
LIVER OIL.	1949	GALLONS	283,028	483,845
SALTED:				
GREEN 2/	1940	POUNDS	374,802	15,685
DRY (ALASKA)	1949	DO	655,664	72,680
DRY (UNITED STATES).	1940	DO	2,644,732	225,800
BONELESS AND ABSOLUTELY BONELESS	1940	DO	8,574,007	1,387,954
TONGUES (ALASKA)	1949	DO	5,000	2,000
SMOKED, WHOLE, FILLETS, AND BONELESS	1940	DO	639,680	74,416
CUSK:				
FRESH FILLETS.	1949	DO	488,988	115,674
FROZEN FILLETS	1949	DO	125,280	24,960
SALTED	1940	DO	32,215	4,355
SMOKED WHOLE AND FILLETS	1940	DO	403,099	32,157
EELS, COMMON:				
SMOKED (U.S. EXCEPT MISSISSIPPI RIVER)	1940	DO	179,055	48,901
SMOKED (MISSISSIPPI RIVER)	1931	DO	31,300	8,138
FLOUNDERS:				
FRESH FILLETS.	1949	DO	16,718,255	5,598,252
FROZEN FILLETS	1949	DO	12,205,321	3,497,904
SMOKED	1940	DO	1,800	290
GROUPER:				
FRESH FILLETS.	1949	DO	375,767	160,687
FROZEN FILLETS	1949	DO	54,991	24,206
FRESH STEAKS	1949	DO	190,161	57,268
FROZEN STEAKS.	1949	DO	20,500	8,200
HADDOCK:				
FRESH FILLETS.	1949	DO	19,936,991	5,940,340
FROZEN FILLETS	1949	DO	22,202,805	5,904,431
SALTED	1940	DO	76,115	7,143
SMOKED:				
WHOLE.	1940	DO	29,200	5,808
FILLETS.	1940	DO	293,165	48,968
FINNAN HADDIE.	1940	DO	577,611	66,837
HAKE:				
FRESH FILLETS.	1949	DO	810,573	160,411
FROZEN FILLETS	1949	DO	559,655	74,443
SALTED:				
GREEN 2/	1940	DO	902,015	30,271
OTHER.	1940	DO	1,464,010	96,150
SMOKED FILLETS	1940	DO	39,400	1,227
HALIBUT:				
FRESH FILLETS.	1949	POUNDS	11,865	4,709
FROZEN FILLETS	1949	DO	376,148	122,097
FROZEN STEAKS.	1949	DO	3,445,773	1,295,656
FROZEN CHEEKS.	1949	DO	1,070	246
SMOKED	1940	DO	1,500	468

SEE FOOTNOTES AT END OF TABLE   (CONTINUED ON NEXT PAGE)

MANUFACTURED FISHERY PRODUCTS - VARIOUS YEARS 1/ - Continued

ITEM	YEAR	UNIT	QUANTITY	VALUE
HERRING, LAKE:				
FRESH FILLETS.	1949	POUNDS	257,600	$13,522
FROZEN FILLETS	1949	DO	127,768	19,503
SALTED	1940	DO	2,998,574	94,588
SMOKED	1940	DO	1,078,397	134,462
HERRING, SEA:				
SARDINES, CANNED	1949	STANDARD CASES	3,074,523	21,051,675
MEAL	1949	TONS	5,298	973,445
OIL.	1949	GALLONS	723,350	394,297
SALTED:				
BRINE SALTED . . . ;	1940	POUNDS	421,700	15,424
PICKLED IN VINEGAR	1940	DO	1,895,425	90,799
SPICED	1940	DO	1,637,869	173,251
SMOKED:				
BLOATERS:				
HARD	1940	DO	623,642	78,582
SOFT	1940	DO	8,066	403
UNCLASSIFIED	1940	DO	70,406	6,019
BONELESS	1940	DO	2,018,330	210,540
LENGTHWISE	1940	DO	68,517	3,862
MEDIUM SCALE	1940	DO	171,320	9,909
KIPPERED	1940	DO	489,500	52,113
UNCLASSIFIED	1940	DO	138,900	22,645
JEWFISH, DRY SALTED.	1940	DO	8,857	1,107
KING MACKEREL, SMOKED.	1940	DO	3,500	525
LAKE TROUT:				
FRESH FILLETS.	1949	DO	100,700	57,065
FROZEN FILLETS	1949	DO	1,600	935
SMOKED (U.S. EXCEPT MISSISSIPPI RIVER)	1940	DO	789,771	243,842
SMOKED (MISSISSIPPI RIVER)	1931	DO	2,100	315
LINGCOD:				
FRESH FILLETS.	1949	DO	564,427	96,100
FROZEN FILLETS	1949	DO	559,715	110,555
FROZEN STEAKS.	1949	DO	263,614	45,647
SMOKED	1940	DO	800	100
MACKEREL:				
FRESH FILLETS.	1949	DO	283,931	62,294
FROZEN FILLETS	1949	DO	553,057	142,456
CANNED	1949	STANDARD CASES	1,049,927	6,848,930
SAETEO:				
SPLIT AND BRINE SALTED	1940	POUNDS	1,904,900	160,370
DRY, WHOLE AND FILLETS	1940	DO	1,668,548	108,898
SMOKED, WHOLE AND FILLETS.	1940	DO	90,300	17,010
MENHADEN:				
ROE, SALTED.	1940	DO	1,000	250
MEAL AND DRY AND ACID SCRAP.	1949	TONS	113,399	17,813,339
OIL.	1949	GALLONS	8,293,911	3,407,510
MOONEYE, SMOKED.	1940	POUNDS	5,000	600
MULLET:				
SALTED	1940	DO	1,254,300	81,200
ROE, SALTED.	1940	DO	60,000	14,825
OCEAN PERCH (ROSEFISH):				
FRESH FILLETS.	1949	DO	639,061	138,956
FROZEN FILLETS	1949	DO	72,553,477	15,195,718
PADDLEFISH OR SPOONBILL CAT:				
SMOKED (U.S. EXCEPT MISSISSIPPI RIVER)	1940	DO	127,500	55,850
SMOKED (MISSISSIPPI RIVER)	1931	DO	20,000	5,000
PILCHARD:				
CANNED	1949	STANDARD CASES	3,768,212	21,334,825
DRY, SALTED.	1940	POUNDS	9,683	968
MEAL	1949	TONS	39,278	6,219,717
OIL.	1949	GALLONS	6,123,140	2,872,532
POLLOCK:				
FRESH FILLETS.	1949	POUNDS	2,718,923	424,978
FROZEN FILLETS	1949	DO	6,390,673	844,317
SALTED:				
GREEN 2/	1940	DO	184,772	5,665
DRY, WHOLE	1940	DO	262,335	12,069
SMOKED	1940	DO	40,000	960
ROCKFISHES:				
FRESH FILLETS.	1949	DO	3,148,194	443,895
FROZEN FILLETS	1949	DO	2,163,665	356,981
SABLEFISH:				
FROZEN FILLETS	1949	POUNDS	36,821	6,878
FROZEN STEAKS.	1949	DO	26,965	9,223
SALTED (ALASKA).	1949	DO	65,867	9,130
SALTED (UNITED STATES)	1940	DO	58,090	3,281
SMOKED (ALASKA).	1949	DO	5,458	1,364
KIPPERED OR SMOKED (U.S. EXCEPT MISSISSIPPI RIVER) .	1940	DO	1,145,864	265,885
KIPPERED OR SMOKED (MISSISSIPPI RIVER)	1931	DO	30,000	10,500

SEE FOOTNOTES AT END OF TABLE   (CONTINUED ON NEXT PAGE)

MANUFACTURED FISHERY PRODUCTS - VARIOUS YEARS 1/ - Continued

ITEM	YEAR	UNIT	QUANTITY	VALUE
SALMON:				
FROZEN STEAKS	1949	POUNDS	1,667,678	$703,725
CANNED:				
.CHINOOK OR KING	1949	STANDARD CASES	207,868	5,796,265
CHUM OR KETA	1949	DO	718,878	10,763,832
PINK	1949	DO	3,236,317	51,753,924
RED OR SOCKEYE	1949	DO	1,075,437	28,924,268
SILVER OR COHO	1949	DO	277,495	5,948,419
STEELHEAD	1949	DO	8,931	244,275
TOTAL CANNED SALMON			5,524,926	103,430,983
SMOKED, CANNED	1949	DO	275	11,243
EGGS FOR BAIT, CANNED	1949	DO	10,719	275,744
SALTED:				
HARD (ALASKA)	1949	POUNDS	278,725	88,582
HARD (UNITED STATES)	1940	DO	28,000	4,200
HILD-CURED (ALASKA)	1949	DO	3,675,294	1,469,451
MILD-CURED (UNITED STATES)	1940	DO	4,290,510	886,341
EGGS FOR CAVIAR	1940	DO	291,518	26,856
BELLIES	1940	DO	7,600	520
SMOKED:				
WHOLE AND FILLETS (ALASKA)	1949	DO	16,396	9,091
WHOLE (U.S. EXCEPT MISSISSIPPI RIVER)	1940	DO	8,113,086	2,770,902
WHOLE (MISSISSIPPI RIVER)	1931	DO	312,400	71,730
KIPPERED (ALASKA)	1949	DO	11,511	9,108
KIPPERED (UNITED STATES)	1940	DO	2,543,104	721,048
MEAL	1949	TONS	1,760	245,847
OIL:				
EDIBLE	1949	GALLONS	14,652	25,716
INDUSTRIAL	1949	DO	152,324	73,712
SAUGER:				
FRESH FILLETS	1949	POUNDS	743,738	326,703
FROZEN FILLETS	1949	DO	196,106	78,252
SEA BASS:				
FRESH FILLETS	1949	DO	53,100	14,220
FROZEN FILLETS	1949	DO	34,000	9,320
FRESH STEAKS	1949	DO	28,000	8,320
FRESH SPLIT "BUTTERFLY"	1949	DO	21,000	5,665
FROZEN SPLIT "BUTTERFLY"	1949	DO	4,500	1,290
DRY SALTED	1940	DO	11,531	1,441
SEA TROUT, GRAY:				
FRESH FILLETS	1949	DO	83,000	26,510
FROZEN FILLETS	1949	DO	39,258	11,852
FRESH SPLIT "BUTTERFLY"	1949	DO	37,000	10,480
FROZEN SPLIT "BUTTERFLY"	1949	DO	11,000	3,180
SALTED	1940	DO	3,000	649
SHAD:				
CANNED	1949	STANDARD CASES	13,835	106,194
ROE, CANNED	1949	DO	4,434	273,323
SMOKED	1940	POUNDS	127,400	25,344
SHARK LIVER OIL	1949	GALLONS	444,647	4,707,231
SHEEPSHEAD, SMOKED	1940	POUNDS	8,000	1,000
SNAPPER, RED:				
FRESH FILLETS	1949	DO	13,400	8,510
FROZEN FILLETS	1949	DO	7,300	4,645
FRESH STEAKS	1949	DO	29,500	14,445
FROZEN STEAKS	1949	DO	20,500	10,525
SNOOK, FRESH FILLETS	1949	DO	9,000	5,280
SPANISH MACKEREL:				
FRESH FILLETS	1949	POUNDS	84,000	34,280
FROZEN FILLETS	1949	DO	6,500	660
SPOT, SALTED	1940	DO	159,400	9,580
STURGEON:				
CANNED, SMOKED AND KIPPERED	1949	STANDARD CASES	363	20,319
SMOKED AND KIPPERED (U.S. EXCEPT MISSISSIPPI RIVER) . . .	1940	POUNDS	530,588	410,599
SMOKED AND KIPPERED (MISSISSIPPI RIVER)	1931	DO	183,300	46,595
ROE, SALTED	1940	DO	60	120
THIMBLE-EYED MACKEREL, SMOKED	1940	DO	100	20
TUNA AND TUNALIKE FISHES:				
CANNED:				
ALBACORE	1949	STANDARD CASES	1,466,849	21,750,314
YELLOWFIN	1949	DO	3,902,763	51,412,937
BLUEFIN	1949	DO	76,877	999,642
SKIPJACK (INCLUDES SOME LITTLE TUNA)	1949	DO	1,438,988	18,492,672
BONITO	1949	DO	33,734	365,444
YELLOWTAIL	1949	DO	126,133	1,305,084
MISCELLANEOUS SPECIES OF TUNA	1949	DO	76,334	804,289
TONNO	1949	DO	168,642	2,579,943
TOTAL CANNED TUNA AND TUNALIKE FISHES			7,290,320	97,710,325

SEE FOOTNOTES AT END OF TABLE   (CONTINUED ON NEXT PAGE)

MANUFACTURED FISHERY PRODUCTS - VARIOUS YEARS 1/ - Continued

ITEM	YEAR	UNIT	QUANTITY	VALUE
TUNA AND TUNALIKE FISHES - CONTINUED:				
OIL, LIVER	1949	GALLONS	12,384	$645,515
SALTED, DRY	1940	POUNDS	140,828	17,513
SMOKED OR KIPPERED	1940	DO	1,518	339
WHITE BASS, FRESH FILLETS.	1949	POUNDS	11,100	3,795
WHITEFISH, COMMON:				
FRESH FILLETS.	1949	DO	167,755	80,526
FROZEN FILLETS	1949	DO	16,300	7,410
CANNED CAVIAR.	1949	STANDARD CASES	2,558	113,160
SMOKED (U.S. EXCEPT MISSISSIPPI RIVER)	1940	POUNDS	2,347,669	817,368
SMOKED (MISSISSIPPI RIVER)	1931	DO	275,000	52,200
WHITEFISH, MENOMINEE, SMOKED . . . . : . . .	1940	DO	10,000	2,500
WHITINGS:				
FRESH FILLETS.	1949	DO	51,500	7,710
FROZEN FILLETS	1949	DO	1,119,513	198,727
FRESH SPLIT "BUTTERFLY".	1949	DO	22,500	3,375
FROZEN SPLIT "BUTTERFLY"	1949	DO	3,006,002	475,792
TOTAL PACKAGED WHITING			4,199,515	685,604
SMOKED	1940	DO	131,500	19,725
WOLFFISH:				
FRESH FILLETS.	1949	DO	52,266	16,006
FROZEN FILLETS	1949	DO	258,968	76,166
YELLOW PERCH:				
FRESH FILLETS.	1949	DO	361,582	177,929
FROZEN FILLETS	1949	DO	56,534	27,639
YELLOW PIKE:				
FRESH FILLETS.	1949	DO	631,005	314,738
FROZEN FILLETS	1949	DO	61,619	31,135
CRABS:				
BLUE, HARD:				
CANNED (INCLUDES ROCK CRABS)	1949	STANDARD CASES	46,975	943,120
FRESH COOKED MEAT.	1940	POUNDS	7,197,691	2,456,818
MEAL AND SCRAP	1949	TONS	6,906	431,106
DUNGENESS:				
CANNED	1949	STANDARD CASES	114,854	2,547,765
FRESH-COOKED MEAT (ALASKA)	1949	POUNDS	53,943	47,337
FRESH-COOKED MEAT (UNITED STATES).	1940	DO	1,380,318	412,437
FROZEN-COOKED MEAT (ALASKA).	1949	DO	39,510	19,755
MEAL AND SCRAP	1949	TONS	907	47,668
KING:				
FRESH-COOKED MEAT (ALASKA)	1949	POUNDS	34,500	37,950
FROZEN-COOKED MEAT (ALASKA).	1949	DO	129,708	117,520
ROCK, FRESH-COOKED MEAT.	1940	DO	295,694	107,881
CANNED SPECIALTIES (BLUE AND DUNGENESS).	1949	STANDARD CASES	4,469	92,974
LOBSTERS:				
NORTHERN, FRESH-COOKED MEAT.	1940	POUNDS	277,500	315,182
SPINY, FRESH-COOKED MEAT	1940	DO	49,000	16,400
CANNED SPECIALTIES (NORTHERN AND SPINY).	1949	STANDARD CASES	4,277	113,042
SHRIMP:				
CANNED:				
REGULAR WET PACK	1949	STANDARD CASES	664,721	11,203,325
SPECIALTIES.	1949	DO	4,066	121,105
PACKAGED, FRESH AND FROZEN (ALASKA).	1949	POUNDS	517,585	470,468
PACKAGED, FRESH AND FROZEN (UNITED STATES)	1940	DO	15,620,399	2,302,921
SUNDRIED	1940	DO	1,930,400	326,416
MEAL OR BRAN	1949	TONS	1,283	115,292
ABALONE STEAKS	1940	DO	333,991	126,716
CLAMS:				
HARD:				
CANNED:				
WHOLE	1949	STANDARD CASES	13,245	157,544
MINCED	1949	DO	87,946	831,122
CHOWDER.	1949	DO	704,583	4,542,760
JUICE, BROTH AND NECTAR.	1949	DO	14,111	40,154
FRESH-SHUCKED (UNITED STATES).	1940	GALLONS	138,691	170,226
FROZEN-SHUCKED (ALASKA).	1949	POUNDS	2,016	504
RAZOR:				
CANNED:				
WHOLE.	1949	STANDARD CASES	539	10,263
MINCED	1949	DO	41,118	734,685
FROZEN-SHUCKED (ALASKA).	1949	POUNDS	300	150
SOFT:				
CANNED:				
WHOLE AND MINCED	1949	STANDARD CASES	155,129 .	1,469,711
CHOWDER, JUICE, BROTH AND NECTAR	1949	DO	169,389	993,469
FRESH-SHUCKED.	1940	GALLONS	402,742	611,114
SURF, FRESH-SHUCKED.	1940	DO	9,080	11,132
MUSSELS, STEAMED, SHUCKED.	1940	POUNDS	901,978	187,354
MUSSEL-SHELL PRODUCTS:				
BUTTONS.	1949	GROSS	4,720,239	3,696,452
LIME, GRIT AND CUT SHELLS.	1949	TONS	4,155	71,251

SEE FOOTNOTES AT END OF TABLE   (CONTINUED ON NEXT PAGE)

MANUFACTURED FISHERY PRODUCTS - VARIOUS YEARS 1/ - Continued

ITEM	YEAR	UNIT	QUANTITY	VALUE
OYSTERS:				
EASTERN:				
CANNED:				
NATURAL.	1949	STANDARD CASES	338,929	$4,758,394
SOUP, STEW AND SMOKED.	1949	DO	577	19,050
FRESH-SHUCKED.	1940	GALLONS	6,506,292	8,722,971
SHELL PRODUCTS:				
CRUSHED SHELL FOR POULTRY FEED	1949	TONS	298,792	2,126,802
LIME, BURNED AND UNBURNED.	1949	DO	35,270	244,979
PACIFIC:				
CANNED:				
NATURAL.	1949	STANDARD CASES	113,989	1,766,813
SMOKED	1949	DO	1,977	176,396
COCKTAILS, SPREAD AND STEW	1949	DO	2,649	47,486
FRESH-SHUCKED (ALASKA)	1949	GALLONS	181	934
FRESH-SHUCKED (UNITED STATES).	1940	DO	478,402	599,661
SHELL PRODUCTS (INCLUDES SMALL AMOUNTS OF CLAM SHELL).				
CRUSHED SHELL FOR POULTRY FEED	1949	TONS	24,870	266,992
LIME UNBURNED.	1949	DO	3,096	23,479
WESTERN OR NATIVE, FRESH-SHUCKED	1940	GALLONS	28,167	215,786
SCALLOPS, BAY, FRESH-SHUCKED	1940	DO	23,088	65,369
SQUID, CANNED.	1949	STANDARD CASES	65,999	341,232
TERRAPIN AND TURTLE PRODUCTS:				
CANNED:				
MEAT	1949	STANDARD CASES	946	25,164
SOUP AND STEW.	1949	DO	17,585	202,473
MISCELLANEOUS:				
PACKAGED FISH, FRESH OR FROZEN 3/.	1949	POUNDS	823,269	281,058
CANNED:				
ANIMAL FOOD.	1949	STANDARD CASES	1,931,757	8,663,442
FISH CAKES	1949	DO	144,080	1,690,494
FISH FLAKES, GROUNDFISH.	1949	DO	32,365	506,224
ROE AND CAVIAR 4/.	1949	DO	24,642	557,778
PASTES AND SPREADS 5/.	1949	DO	594	22,520
SOUPS AND STEWS 6/	1949	DO	13,790	173,435
MISCELLANEOUS ITEMS 7/	1949	DO	14,872	322,359
PICKLED TONGUES AND SOUNDS	1940	POUNDS	17,900	1,613
BUTTONS, MARINE PEARL-SHELL.	1949	GROSS	4,089,712	6,782,281
FISH SOLUBLES.	1949	POUNDS	103,342,712	5,144,111
GLUE	1949	GALLONS	198,031	401,983
MEAL:				
GROUNDFISH ("WHITEFISH") INC. OCEAN PERCH (ROSEFISH) .	1949	TONS	31,425	5,221,652
TUNA AND MACKEREL.	1949	DO	19,139	3,073,742
FUR SEAL	1949	TONS	347	55,627
WHALE.	1949	TONS	117	16,088
MISCELLANEOUS MEAL AND SCRAP 8/.	1949	DO	17,327	1,438,619
OIL:				
BODY:				
TUNA AND MACKEREL.	1949	GALLONS	597,935	265,736
FUR SEAL	1949	GALLONS	49,253	20,592
WHALE:				
SPERM.	1949	GALLONS	47,000	38,500
OTHER.	1949	DO	27,950	13,975
MISCELLANEOUS 9/	1949	DO	831,961	406,952
LIVER AND VISCERA 10/.	1949	DO	94,298	4,008,864
OTHER BYPRODUCTS 11/	1949	-	-	6,697,046
TOTAL.	-	-	-	453,754,857
SUMMARY, 1949				
PACKAGED PRODUCTS:				
FISH, FRESH OR FROZEN (FILLETS, STEAKS, ETC.).	1949	POUNDS	194,215,265	48,389,905
SHELLFISH (ALASKA PRODUCTION).	1949	DO	779,146	694,618
CANNED FISH AND SHELLFISH PRODUCTS	1949	DO	855,014,842	295,503,905
CURED PRODUCTS:				
SALTED, DRIED, OR PICKLED (ALASKA PRODUCTION).	1949	DO	4,680,550	1,641,843
SMOKED (ALASKA PRODUCTION)	1949	DO	33,365	19,563
BYPRODUCTS:				
MEAL AND SCRAP	1949	DO	474,360,000	35,652,142
OIL.	1949	DO	134,966,420	17,364,977
SHELL PRODUCTS:				
LIME, POULTRY GRIT, AND CUT SHELLS	1949	DO	732,366,000	2,733,503
BUTTONS.	1949	GROSS	8,809,951	10,478,733
FISH SOLUBLES.	1949	POUNDS	103,342,712	5,144,111
OTHER.	1949	-	-	7,099,029
TOTAL.	1949	-	-	424,722,329

SEE FOOTNOTES AT END OF TABLE   (CONTINUED ON NEXT PAGE)

MANUFACTURED FISHERY PRODUCTS - VARIOUS YEARS 1/ - Continued

ITEM	YEAR	UNIT	QUANTITY	VALUE
SUMMARY, 1940				
PACKAGED SHELLFISH, FRESH OR FROZEN.	1940	POUNDS	94,349,263	$16,648,384
CURED PRODUCTS:				
SALTED, DRIED AND PICKLED. . . . . :	1940	DO	46,955,410	4,203,046
SMOKED AND KIPPERED.	1940	DO	28,868,886	7,934,520
TOTAL.	1940		-	28,785,950
SUMMARY, 1931				
SMOKED PRODUCTS.	1931	-	1,098,100	246,578
GRAND TOTAL.			-	453,754,857

1/ DATA ON THE PRODUCTION OF THE DIFFERENT PRODUCTS ARE FOR THE YEARS INDICATED.

2/ THIS ITEM IS USUALLY AN INTERMEDIATE PRODUCT, AND ALTHOUGH INCLUDED IN THE TOTAL, MAY BE SHOWN IN ITS FINAL STAGE OF PROCESSING IN THIS OR ANOTHER SECTION.

3/ INCLUDES FRESH OR FROZEN FILLETS, STEAKS, OR "BUTTERFLY" OF BLUEFISH, CROAKER, DRUM, OCEAN POUT, PICKEREL, PORGY, SEA ROBIN, SHEEPSHEAD, SMELT, STRIPED BASS, STURGEON, SWORDFISH, TRIGGERFISH, AND UNCLASSIFIED SPECIES.

4/ INCLUDES CANNED ROE OF HERRING, MACKEREL, MENHADEN AND DEEP SEA FISH, AND CAVIAR FROM SALMON AND STURGEON ROE.

5/ INCLUDES CANNED PASTES AND SPREADS FROM ANCHOVIES, HERRING, HALIBUT AND SALMON.

6/ INCLUDES CANNED BOUILLABAISSE, CRAWFISH BISQUE, CREOLE GUMBO, FISH CHOWDER, FROG LEGS NEWBURG, AND SHELLFISH NEWBURG.

7/ INCLUDES CANNED RED DRUM, HADDOCK, FINNAN HADDIE, MENHADEN, MULLET, BARBECUED SALMON, SALMON IN CHEESE SAUCE, SMOKED SHAD, KIPPERED SHAD, SWELLFISH, TUNAFISH FRANKFURTERS, CLAM CAKES AND LOAF, CONCHS, MUSSELS, AND SCALLOPS.

8/ INCLUDES THE PRODUCTION OF SCRAP AND MEAL FROM ANCHOVIES, HORSESHOE CRABS, SHARKS, SQUIDS, UNCLASSIFIED SPECIES; COD LIVER PRESS CAKE; AND FISH POMACE.

9/ INCLUDES THE PRODUCTION OF BODY OIL FROM ANCHOVIES, OCEAN PERCH (ROSEFISH), AND UNCLASSIFIED SPECIES.

10/ INCLUDES LIVER AND VISCERA OIL OF HALIBUT, LINGCOD, ROCKFISHES, SABLEFISH, SOLE, SWORDFISH, WHALE, AND UNCLASSIFIED SPECIES.

11/ INCLUDES THE PRODUCTION OF AGAR-AGAR, GLUE, KELP PRODUCTS, PEARL ESSENCE, ISINGLASS, IRISH MOSS, AND CRAB SHELLS.

NOTE:--SOME OF THE ABOVE PRODUCTS MAY HAVE BEEN MANUFACTURED FROM RAW PRODUCTS IMPORTED FROM ANOTHER COUNTRY; THEREFORE THEY CANNOT BE CORRELATED DIRECTLY WITH THE CATCH WITHIN THE UNITED STATES AND ALASKA. THE LIME AND POULTRY FEED MANUFACTURED FROM SHELL PRODUCTS WAS PRODUCED FROM OYSTER AND CLAM SHELLS WHICH ARE NOT INCLUDED IN THE CATCH STATISTICS FOR THESE SHELLFISH.

PRODUCTION OF CERTAIN MANUFACTURED FISHERY PRODUCTS, 1941 - 1949

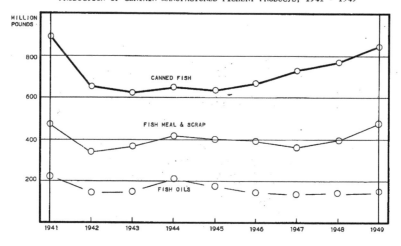

CANNED FISHERY PRODUCTS AND BYPRODUCTS

Canned fishery products and byproducts valued at $373,976,400 at the processor's level were produced in the United States and Alaska during 1949. This represented a decrease of 10 percent compared with the record year of 1948. The value of canned products decreased 12 percent while the value of the byproducts decreased only 2 percent.

The 1949 pack of canned salmon amounted to 5,524,916 standard cases (265,195,968 pounds), valued at $103,430,980 to the canners. Compared with 1948, this was an increase of 15 percent in volume, but a decline of 14 percent in value. Although the pack was the second largest in the past six years, it was far less than the 1935-39 average of 7,163,985 cases. Despite the sharp decline in the price of canned salmon in 1949, the pack was the third most valuable in history. There were two outstanding reasons for the comparatively successful 1949 season. The first was the exceptionally good run of pink salmon in southeastern Alaska; and second, the good run of pinks in Puget Sound. If these two areas had not been so productive, 1949 would have been an unusually poor year for the salmon industry.

The pack of tuna and tunalike fishes, which amounted to 7,290,320 cases (141,700,593 pounds), valued at $97,710,325, was 252,562 cases greater than the 1948 production. Although the 1949 pack of tuna established a new record for the fifth consecutive year, the canners received nearly 15 million dollars less for the pack than in the previous year. Two developments were responsible for this; first, there was a general decline in values of canned fish and this decline was accentuated in tuna by a record production; second, increased imports of canned tuna brought about increased competition. Production of tuna on the east coast, while minor compared with that of the west coast, was nearly 3 times that of the previous year. Although yellowfin continued to make up the bulk of the pack, the production of skipjack recorded a noticeable gain compared with the previous year.

The 1949 pack of California sardines (pilchards) amounted to 3,768,212 standard cases (169,569,540 pounds), valued at $21,334,825. Compared with the previous year, this was an increase of 42 percent in volume, but a decline of 3 percent in value. While the 1949 pack was the second largest in history, it was 1,238,942 cases less than the record 1941 production, but with canning being the most profitable method of processing during 1949, a much greater portion of the catch was canned during 1949 than in previous years. Export markets furnished a good outlet for part of the 1949 pack of California sardines.

California led in the production of canned fishery products with a pack of 385,583,894 pounds, valued at $119,497,465. Alaska was second with 211,646,994 pounds, valued at $82,225,067. These areas accounted for 70 percent of the volume of the 1949 pack and 68 percent of its value.

The 1949 production of fishery byproducts in the United States and Alaska was valued at $78,472,495 -- 2 percent less than in the previous year. The principal byproducts were marine-animal oils, 17,694,887 gallons, valued at $17,364,977; marine-animal scrap and meal, 237,180 tons, valued at $35,652,142; marine and fresh-water shell buttons, valued at $10,478,733; and fish solubles, valued at $5,144,111. Byproducts were produced in 314 plants in 24 states and Alaska in 1949.

MENHADEN REDUCTION PLANT

SUMMARY OF PRODUCTION: BY COMMODITIES, 1949

PRODUCT	NUMBER OF PLANTS	STANDARD CASES	POUNDS PER CASE	POUNDS	VALUE
CANNED PRODUCTS:					
SALMON:					
UNITED STATES	48	1,133,325	48	54,399,600	$22,167,812
ALASKA.	117	4,391,601	48	210,796,848	81,263,171
TOTAL SALMON.	165	5,524,926		265,196,448	103,430,983
SARDINES:					
MAINE	51	3,074,523	20.3	62,412,817	21,051,675
CALIFORNIA.	49	3,768,212	45	169,569,540	21,334,825
TUNA AND TUNALIKE FISHES:					
TUNA:					
SOLID		3,432,195	21	72,076,095	51,505,272
FLAKES AND GRATED		3,698,258	18	66,568,644	44,534,525
TOTAL TUNA.	56	7,130,453		138,644,739	96,039,797
TUNALIKE FISHES:					
SOLID		59,416	21	1,247,736	642,491
FLAKES AND GRATED		100,451	18	1,808,118	1,028,037
TOTAL TUNALIKE FISHES	21	159,867		3,055,854	1,670,528
TOTAL TUNA AND TUNALIKE FISHES. . .	56	7,290,320		141,700,593	97,710,325
ALEWIVES.	16	111,994	45	5,039,730	469,398
ANCHOVIES	6	3,757	48	180,336	34,184
MACKEREL (INCLUDING JACK MACKEREL). . . .	58	1,049,927	45	47,246,715	6,848,930
SALMON, SMOKED.	7	275	48	13,200	11,243
SHAD.	9	13,835	45	622,575	106,194
STURGEON, SMOKED.	6	363	48	17,424	20,319
FISH ANIMAL FOOD.	17	1,931,757	48	92,724,336	8,663,442
FISH CAKES.	9	144,080	48	6,915,840	1,690,494
FISH FLAKES, GROUNDFISH	4	32,365	42	1,359,330	505,224
FISH PASTE AND SPREAD	3	586	48	28,128	22,088
FISH MISCELLANEOUS.	8	18,854	48	904,992	259,644
ROE AND CAVIAR.	53	86,459	48	4,150,032	1,969,998
TOTAL FISH.		23,052,233		798,082,036	264,129,966
CLAM PRODUCTS:					
WHOLE AND MINCED.	38	297,977	15	1/ 4,469,655	3,203,325
CHOWDER	11	863,166	30	1/ 25,894,980	5,498,974
JUICE, BROTH, AND NECTAR.	13	24,917	30	1/ 747,510	76,719
TOTAL CLAM PRODUCTS	46	1,186,060		31,112,145	8,779,018
CRAB MEAT, NATURAL.	52	161,829	19.5	3,155,666	3,490,885
CRABS, MISCELLANEOUS PREPARATIONS	14	4,469	48	214,512	92,974
LOBSTER SOUP, STEW, AND OTHER SPECIALTIES	3	4,277	48	205,296	113,042
OYSTERS:					
NATURAL	62	452,918	14	2/ 6,340,852	6,525,207
SMOKED.	9	2,026	48	97,248	180,336
SOUP, STEW, AND OTHER SPECIALTIES . . .	7	3,177	48	152,496	62,596
SHRIMP:					
WET PACK.	57	664,721	15	2/ 9,970,815	11,203,325
MISCELLANEOUS SPECIALTIES	16	4,066	48	195,168	121,105
SQUID	10	85,999	48	4,127,952	341,232
TERRAPIN AND TURTLE:					
MEAT.	3	946	48	45,408	25,164
SOUP AND STEW	8	17,585	48	844,080	202,473
MISCELLANEOUS SHELLFISH SPECIALTIES . . .	10	9,816	48	471,168	236,582
TOTAL SHELLFISH		2,597,889		56,932,806	31,373,939
TOTAL CANNED FISH AND SHELLFISH . .	492	25,650,122		855,014,842	295,503,905

			UNIT	QUANTITY	VALUE
BYPRODUCTS:					
MARINE-ANIMAL SCRAP AND MEAL.	222		TONS	237,180	$35,652,142
MARINE-ANIMAL OILS:					
BODY OIL.	144		GALLONS	16,861,476	7,519,522
LIVER AND VISCERA OIL	23		DO	834,357	9,845,455
OYSTER AND MARINE CLAM-SHELL PRODUCTS . .	23		TONS	362,028	2,662,252
FRESH-WATER MUSSEL-SHELL PRODUCTS	16		-	-	3,767,703
MARINE PEARL-SHELL BUTTONS.	25		GROSS	4,089,712	6,782,281
LIQUID GLUE	5		GALLONS	198,031	401,983
FISH SOLUBLES	29		POUNDS	103,342,712	5,144,111
MISCELLANEOUS BYPRODUCTS.	16		-	-	6,697,046
TOTAL BYPRODUCTS.	319		-	-	78,472,495
GRAND TOTAL	3/ 739		-	-	373,976,400

1/ "CUT OUT" OR "DRAINED" WEIGHTS OF CAN CONTENTS ARE GIVEN FOR WHOLE OR MINCED CLAMS, AND THE GROSS CAN CONTENTS FOR OTHER CLAM PRODUCTS.
2/ DRAINED WEIGHT.
3/ EXCLUSIVE OF DUPLICATION.

NOTE:--LISTS OF CANNERS AND MANUFACTURERS OR FISHERY BYPRODUCTS BY INDIVIDUAL COMMODITIES MAY BE OBTAINED FROM THE FISH AND WILDLIFE SERVICE, WASHINGTON 25, D. C.

GENERAL REVIEW

SUMMARY OF PRODUCTION: BY STATES, 1949

STATE	CANNED		BYPRODUCTS	TOTAL
	POUNDS	VALUE	VALUE	VALUE
MAINE.	95,109,192	$26,680,616	$3,488,917	$30,169,533
MASSACHUSETTS.	35,807,848	4,965,276	7,976,235	12,941,511
CONNECTICUT, RHODE ISLAND, NEW HA PSHIRE	2,253,480	437,679	1/ 1,786,712	2,224,391
NEW YORK	5,055,159	1,573,139	4,091,491	5,654,630
NEW JERSEY	(2)	(2)	2/ 8,958,989	8,958,989
DELAWARE AND PENNSYLVANIA.	(2)	(2)	2/ 4,990,136	4,990,136
MARYLAND	5,700,884	1,109,487	1,896,420	3,005,907
VIRGINIA	3,763,662	706,578	3,300,586	4,00°,164
NORTH CAROLINA	647,336	397,912	3,896,130	4,294,042
SOUTH CAROLINA	1,460,720	1,401,211	146,653	1,547,864
GEORGIA.	(2)	(2)	2/401,400	401,400
FLORIDA.	(2)	(2)	2/1,890,805	1,890,805
ALABAMA.	(2)	(2)	2/702,571	702,571
MISSISSIPPI.	2,849,024	3,101,511	1,076,832	4,178,343
LOUISIANA.	10,465,646	11,270,778	4,853,704	16,124,482
TEXAS.	-	-	1,370,875	1,370,875
MINNESOTA.	-	-	7,402	7,402
IOWA	-	-	3,376,985	3,376,985
ARKANSAS, OHIO, WISCONSIN, MISSOU I.	(2)	(2)	2/ 173,030	173,030
WASHINGTON	53,895,059	23,009,231	6,218,436	29,227,667
OREGON	20,001,025	13,683,517	356,321	14,039,838
CALIFORNIA	385,583,894	119,497,465	21,713,110	141,210,575
ALASKA	211,646,994	82,225,067	1,253,193	83,478,260
ACTUAL POUNDS AND VALUES	855,014,842	295,503,905	78,472,495	373,976,400

1/ VALUE OF BYPRODUCTS IS FOR CONNECTICUT.
2/ CANNED AND BYPRODUCTS COMBINED WHEN LESS THAN THREE FIRMS IN A STATE REPORT.

FACTORS USED TO CONVERT STANDARD CASES TO POUNDS

PRODUCT	PRIOR TO 1938	1939 AND 1940	1941	1942	1943	1944 TO 1947	1948 AND 1949
	POUNDS PER CASE	POUNDS PER CASE	POUNDS PER CASE	POUNDS PER CASE	POUNDS PER CASE	POUNDS PER CASE	POUNDS PER CASE
SARDINES:							
MAINE.	25	25	25	20.3	20.3	20.3	20.3
CALIFORNIA	48	48	48	45	45	45	45
TUNA AND TUNALIKE FISHES:							
SOLID.	24	24	21	22.5	22.5	21	21
FLAKES	24	24	21	18	18	18	18
MACKEREL	48	48	48	45	45	45	45
ALEWIVES	48	48	48	48	45	45	45
SHAD	48	48	48	48	48	45	45
FISH FLAKES.	48	48	48	48	48	42	42
OYSTERS.	15	15	15	15	22.5	22.5	14
SHRIMP, WET PACK	17.25	17.25	17.25	21	21	21	15
CLAM PRODUCTS:							
WHOLE AND MINCED	15	15	15	15	15	15	15
JUICE, CHOWDER, BROTH, ETC.	30	30	30	30	30	30	30
CRABS.	48	39	39	39	39	39	19.5
ALL OTHER.	48	48	48	48	48	48	48

NOTE:--THE FACTORS LISTED ABOVE WERE USED IN CONVERTING THE STANDARD CASES REPORTED IN THE CANNED FISHERY PRODUCTS BULLETINS FOR THE YEARS INDICATED. THE CASES SHOWN FOR ALL YEARS LISTED IN THE HISTORICAL SECTION ON PAGE 1? REPRESENT THE SAME SIZED CASES REPORTED FOR 1949.

PLANTS ENGAGED IN THE PRODUCTION OF CANNED FISHERY PRODUCTS AND BYPRODUCTS, 1949

STATE	CANNED PRODUCTS	BYPRODUCTS	TOTAL PLANTS, EXCLUSIVE OF DUPLICATION	STATE	CANNED PRODUCTS	BYPRODUCTS	TOTAL PLANTS, EXCLUSIVE OF DUPLICATION
	NUMBER	NUMBER	NUMBER		NUMBER	NUMBER	NUMBER
NEW ENGLAND:				S. ATLANTIC AND GULF - CONT'D.:			
MAINE.	61	19	73	ALABAMA.	3	1	3
MASSACHUSETTS.	14	14	27	MISSISSIPPI.	20	4	24
CONNECTICUT.	1	3	4	LOUISIANA.	43	46	87
RHODE ISLAND	1	-	1	TEXAS.	-	5	5
NEW HAMPSHIRE.	1	-	1	TOTAL.	87	81	162
TOTAL.	78	36	106	GREAT LAKES AND MISS. RIVER:			
MIDDLE ATLANTIC:				ARKANSAS	-	1	1
NEW YORK	10	8	18	UHIO	1	-	1
NEW JERSEY	1	20	21	WISCONSIN.	1	-	1
DELAWARE	-	2	2	MINNESOTA.	-	4	4
PENNSYLVANIA	1	6	7	MISSOURI	-	1	1
TOTAL.	12	36	48	IOWA	-	11	11
CHESAPEAKE BAY:				TOTAL.	2	17	19
MARYLAND	12	9	19	PACIFIC COAST:			
VIRGINIA	14	15	27	WASHINGTON	69	12	80
TOTAL.	26	24	46	OREGON	24	8	28
S. ATLANTIC & GULF:				CALIFORNIA	65	94	112
NORTH CAROLINA	12	15	25	TOTAL.	158	114	220
SOUTH CAROLINA	6	3	8	ALASKA	129	11	138
GEORGIA.	2	1	3	GRAND TOTAL.	492	319	739
FLORIDA.	1	6	7				

PACK OF CANNED SALMON: STANDARD CASES, 1949

SPECIES AND CAN SIZE	ALASKA						TOTAL	
	SOUTHEASTERN		CENTRAL		WESTERN			
	CASES	VALUE	CASES	VALUE	CASES	VALUE	CASES	VALUE
CHINOOK OR KING:								
1-POUND TALL	541	$11,776	24,859	$556,858	2,610	$57,438	28,010	$626,072
1-POUND FLAT	-	-	383	9,192	444	9,324	827	18,516
1/2-POUND FLAT	474	11,964	9,776	283,609	10,920	318,302	21,170	613,875
TOTAL.	1,015	23,740	35,018	849,659	13,974	385,064	50,007	1,258,463
CHUM OR KETA:								
1-POUND TALL	239,998	3,528,758	200,614	2,990,972	35,473	549,518	476,085	7,069,248
1-POUND FLAT	-	-	270	5,705	-	-	270	5,705
1/2-POUND FLAT	3,168	56,165	18,743	415,964	826	23,311	22,737	495,440
4-POUND.	17	238	117	1,755	-	-	134	1,993
TOTAL.	243,183	3,585,161	219,744	3,414,396	36,299	572,829	499,226	7,572,386
PINK:								
1-POUND TALL	2,061,010	32,631,944	561,333	9,081,172	-	-	2,622,343	41,713,116
1-POUND FLAT	-	-	181	2,715	-	-	181	2,715
1/2-POUND FLAT	42,925	861,080	15,347	336,269	-	-	59,273	1,197,349
4-POUND.	46	736	487	7,792	-	-	533	8,528
TOTAL.	2,103,982	33,493,760	578,348	9,427,948	-	-	2,682,330	42,921,708
RED OR SOCKEYE:								
1-POUND TALL	15,294	381,068	274,544	6,821,956	494,606	12,623,047	784,444	19,826,961
1-POUND FLAT	-	-	9,016	245,180	23,272	631,791	32,288	876,971
1/2-POUND FLAT	23,538	681,872	109,143	3,536,661	17,497	565,066	150,178	4,783,599
4-POUND.	720	17,280	6	156	-	-	726	17,436
TOTAL.	39,552	1,080,210	392,709	10,603,953	535,375	13,820,804	967,636	25,504,967
SILVER OR COHO:								
1-POUND TALL	105,121	2,148,678	55,654	1,123,719	4,429	89,373	165,204	3,361,770
1-POUND FLAT	-	-	2,052	45,100	-	-	2,052	45,100
1/2-POUND FLAT	19,782	478,798	4,075	94,363	136	2,936	23,993	576,097
4-POUND.	16	240	1,087	21,740	-	-	1,103	21,980
TOTAL.	124,919	2,627,716	62,868	1,284,922	4,565	92,309	192,352	4,004,947
STEELHEAD:								
1-POUND TALL	50	700	-	-	-	-	50	700
TOTAL.	50	700	-	-	-	-	50	700
GRAND TOTAL.	2,512,701	40,811,287	1,288,687	25,580,878	590,213	14,871,006	4,391,601	81,263,171

PACK OF CANNED SALMON: STANDARD CASES, 1949 - Continued

SPECIES AND CAN SIZE	WASHINGTON CASES	WASHINGTON VALUE	OREGON CASES	OREGON VALUE	CALIFORNIA CASES	CALIFORNIA VALUE	UNITED STATES TOTAL CASES	UNITED STATES TOTAL VALUE	GRAND TOTAL, U.S. AND ALASKA CASES	GRAND TOTAL, U.S. AND ALASKA VALUE
CHINOOK OR KING:										
1-POUND TALL	15,496	$282,783	13,536	$237,638	1/ 1,113	1/ $21,240	30,145	$541,661	58,155	$1,167,733
1-POUND FLAT	-	-	2/ 4,511	127,018	-	-	4,511	127,018	5,338	147,534
1/2-POUND FLAT	18,366	469,246	3/ 98,322	3,145,798	-	-	116,688	3,615,044	137,858	4,228,919
1/4-POUND FLAT	-	-	6,489	253,513	-	-	6,489	253,513	6,489	253,513
OTHER	28	566	-	-	-	-	28	566	28	566
TOTAL	33,890	752,595	122,858	3,763,967	1,113	21,240	157,861	4,537,802	207,868	5,796,265
CHUM OR KETA:										
1-POUND TALL	198,642	2,845,116	8,540	136,039			207,182	2,981,215	683,267	10,070,463
1-POUND FLAT	8,910	158,320	2,257	31,692			11,167	190,012	270	6,705
1/2-POUND FLAT	-	-	-	-					33,904	685,452
4-POUND	-	-	-	-					134	1,993
THERD	1,303	20,219	-	-			1,303	20,219	1,303	20,219
TOTAL	209,855	3,023,655	10,797	167,791			219,652	3,191,446	718,878	10,763,832
PINK:										
1-POUND TALL	447,995	6,838,088	-	-			447,995	6,838,088	3,070,339	48,551,204
1-POUND FLAT	100,189	1,905,228	-	-			100,188	1,905,228	181	2,715
1/2-POUND FLAT	-	-	-	-					159,461	3,102,577
4-POUND FLAT	-	-	-	-					533	8,528
T ERHD	5,804	88,900	-	-			5,804	88,900	5,834	88,900
TOTAL	553,987	8,832,216	-	-			553,987	8,832,216	3,236,317	51,753,924
RED OR SOCKEYE:										
1-POUND TALL	12,363	315,618	-	-			12,398	315,618	796,832	20,142,579
1-POUND FLAT	-	-	-	-					32,288	876,971
1/2-POUND FLAT	92,347	2,973,326	235	7,473			92,582	2,980,799	242,760	7,764,398
1/4-POUND FLAT	2,723	118,141	106	4,693			2,829	122,834	2,629	122,834
4-POUND	-	-	-	-					726	17,436
OTHER	2	50	-	-			2	50		50
TOTAL	107,460	3,407,135	341	12,166			107,801	3,419,301	1,075,437	28,924,268
SILVER OR COHO:										
1-POUND TALL	43,035	836,256	740	14,627			43,775	850,883	209,379	4,212,653
1-POUND FLAT	-	-	-	-					2,062	45,100
1/2-POUND FLAT	23,024	541,151	5,936	147,596			28,960	688,747	52,953	1,264,844
1/4-POUND FLAT	1,890	54,587	8,919	315,568			10,809	370,155	10,809	370,155
4-POUND	-	-	-	-					1,103	21,90
OTHER	1,599	33,687	-	-			1,599	33,687	1,599	33,687
TOTAL	69,548	1,465,681	15,595	477,791			85,143	1,943,472	277,495	5,948,419
STEELHEAD:										
1-POUND TALL	-	-	4/ 1,624	4/ 26,533			1,624	26,533	1,674	27,233
1-POUND FLAT	-	-	3/ 5,671	3/ 156,981			5,671	156,981	5,671	156,981
1/2-POUND FLAT	-	-	1,586	60,061			1,586	60,061	1,586	60,061
1/4-POUND FLAT										
TOTAL	-	-	8,881	243,575			8,861	243,575	8,931	244,275
GRAND TOTAL	973,740	17,491,292	158,472	4,665,290	1,113	21,240	1,133,325	22,167,812	5,524,926	103,430,983

1/ INCLUDES A SMALL PACK OF 1/2-POUND FLATS.
2/ INCLUDES A SMALL PACK OF 1-POUND OVALS.
3/ INCLUDES A SMALL PACK OF 1/2-POUND OVALS.
4/ INCLUDES A SMALL PACK OF 1-POUND FLATS.

NOTE:-- "STANDARD CASES" REPRESENT THE VARIOUS SIZED CASES CONVERTED TO THE EQUIVALENT OF FORTY-EIGHT 1-POUND CANS, EACH CONTAINING 16 OUNCES OF SALMON. SALMON WERE CANNED IN 34 PLANTS IN WASHINGTON, 11 IN OREGON, 3 IN CALIFORNIA, AND 117 IN ALASKA.

SUPPLEMENTARY REVIEW OF THE PACIFIC COAST STATES SALMON PACK, 1949

BY DISTRICTS - STANDARD CASES

SPECIES	PUGET SOUND		COLUMBIA RIVER		COASTAL		TOTAL	
	CASES	VALUE	CASES	VALUE	CASES	VALUE	CASES	VALUE
CHINOOK OR KING. . . .	21,622	$417,972	133,073	$4,055,146	3,166	$64,684	157,861	$4,537,802
CHUM OR KETA	199,225	2,887,121	10,797	167,791	9,630	136,534	219,652	3,191,446
PINK	553,987	8,832,216	-	-	-	-	553,987	8,832,216
RED OR SOCKEYE	93,520	2,915,749	6,592	237,187	7,689	266,365	107,801	3,419,301
SILVER OR COHO	63,516	1,342,829	16,466	496,562	5,161	104,081	85,143	1,943,472
STEELHEAD.	-	-	8,881	243,575	-	-	8,881	243,575
TOTAL.	931,870	16,395,887	175,809	5,200,261	25,646	571,664	1,133,325	22,167,812

PACK OF MAINE SARDINES (INCLUDING SEA HERRING), 1949

STYLE OF PACK	STANDARD CASES	VALUE	CAN AND CASE SIZES	ACTUAL CASES	VALUE
NATURAL.	48,738	$105,000	3-1/4 OUNCES NET (100 CANS) . . .	2,941,454	$20,624,895
IN SOYBEAN OR			10 OUNCES NET (48 CANS)	20,164	139,211
OTHER VEGETABLE OIL.	2,760,926	19,199,855	15 OUNCES NET (48 CANS)	40,628	223,933
IN MUSTARD SAUCE . . .	174,777	1,237,962	OTHER SIZES (CONVERTED TO		
IN TOMATO SAUCE. . . .	52,346	175,225	3-1/4 OUNCES NET) (100 CANS). .	13,281	63,636
IN OLIVE OIL.	22,072	209,423			
OTHER 1/	15,664	124,210	TOTAL	3,015,527	21,051,675
TOTAL.	3,074,523	21,051,675			

1/ INCLUDES SPECIAL PACKS OF SARDINES (INCLUDING SEA HERRING) SMOKED AND KIPPERED; SMOKED IN SOY OIL; SMOKED
IN OLIVE OIL; AND FILLETS IN SOYA OIL.

NOTE:--"STANDARD CASES" REPRESENT THE VARIOUS SIZED CASES CONVERTED TO THE UNIFORM BASIS OF ONE HUMORED 1/4 OIL
CANS (3-1/4 OUNCES NET) TO THE CASE. SARDINES (INCLUDING SEA HERRING) WERE CANNED IN 47 PLANTS IN MAINE;
3 IN MASSACHUSETTS; AND 1 IN NEW HAMPSHIRE.

PACK OF CALIFORNIA SARDINES (PILCHARDS), 1949

STYLE OF PACK	STANDARD CASES	VALUE	CAN AND CASE SIZES	ACTUAL CASES	VALUE
NATURAL, WITHOUT			1-POUND CANS:		
SAUCE OR OIL	1,525,280	$7,003,531	15 OUNCES NET, TALL (48 CANS) .	1,517,609	$6,263,540
IN TOMATO SAUCE. . . .	1,986,444	12,743,787	15 OUNCES NET, OVAL (48 CANS) .	1,653,346	9,908,371
IN MUSTARD SAUCE . . .	217,915	1,156,589	1/2-POUND CANS:		
OTHER 1/	38,573	430,918	8 OUNCES NET, TALL (48 CANS). .	294,866	1,088,997
			8 OUNCES NET, OBLONG (48 CANS).	267,105	1,361,152
TOTAL.	3,768,212	21,334,825	5 OUNCES NET (100 CANS)	420,258	2,477,216
			OTHER SIZES (CONVERTED TO		
			15 OUNCES NET) (48 CANS). . . .	24,426	235,549
			TOTAL	4,177,610	21,334,825

1/ INCLUDES SPECIAL PACKS OF SARDINES (PILCHARDS) IN SOYBEAN OIL; IN OLIVE OIL, AND IN OLIVE OIL AND TOMATO
SAUCE; FILLETS WITHOUT SAUCE OR OIL AND FILLETS IN SOYBEAN OIL.

NOTE:--"STANDARD CASES" REPRESENT THE VARIOUS SIZED CASES CONVERTED TO THE UNIFORM BASIS OF FORTY-EIGHT
1-POUND OVAL CANS (15 OUNCES NET). SARDINES (PILCHARDS) WERE CANNED IN 49 PLANTS IN CLAIFORNIA.

PACK OF CANNED ALEWIVES: STANDARD CASES, 1949

STATE	CASES	VALUE
MARYLAND	67,828	$295,021
VIRGINIA	44,166	174,377
TOTAL.	111,994	469,398

NOTE:--"STANDARD CASES" REPRESENT THE VARIOUS SIZED CASES CONVERTED TO THE EQUIVALENT OF FORTY-EIGHT CANS OF
15 OUNCES EACH. PRACTICALLY THE ENTIRE PACK WAS CANNED IN 15 OUNCE CANS. ALEWIVES WERE CANNED IN 7 PLANTS
IN MARYLAND AND 9 PLANTS IN VIRGINIA.

PACK OF CANNED TUNA AND TUNALIKE FISHES: STANDARD CASES, 1949

SPECIES	CALIFORNIA		WASHINGTON AND OREGON		MAINE, MASSACHUSETTS, AND MARYLAND		TOTAL	
	CASES	VALUE	CASES	VALUE	CASES	VALUE	CASES	VALUE
TUNA:								
ALBACORE:								
SOLID.	749,419	$12,162,794	323,951	$5,198,781	-	-	1,073,369	$17,361,575
FLAKES	273,539	3,303,616	119,941	1,080,121	-	-	393,480	4,388,739
TOTAL. . . .	1,022,957	15,471,412	443,892	6,278,902	-	-	1,466,849	21,750,314
YELLOWFIN:								
SOLID.	1,510,543	21,932,854	103,034	1,554,829	-	-	1,613,577	23,487,683
FLAKES	2,243,363	27,341,076	45,823	584,178	-	-	2,289,186	27,925,254
TOTAL. . . .	3,753,906	49,273,930	148,857	2,139,007	-	-	3,902,763	51,412,937
BLUEFIN:								
SOLID.	36,331	497,934	-	-	-	-	36,331	497,934
FLAKES	40,546	501,708	-	-	-	-	40,546	501,708
TOTAL. . . .	76,877	999,642	-	-	-	-	76,877	999,642
SKIPJACK:								
SOLID.	1/ 481,159	1/ 6,841,594	26,814	416,083	-	-	1/ 507,973	1/ 7,257,677
FLAKES	1/ 902,860	1/10,866,470	28,155	368,525	-	-	1/ 931,015	1/11,234,995
TOTAL. . . .	1/1,384,019	1/17,708,064	54,969	784,608	-	-	1/1,438,989	1/18,492,672
TONNO, SOLID . .	168,642	2,579,943	-	-	-	-	168,642	2,579,943
MISCELLANEOUS:								
SOLID.	-	-	-	-	2/32,303	2/$320,460	2/ 32,303	2/ 320,460
FLAKES	-	-	-	-	2/44,031	2/ 483,829	2/ 44,031	2/ 483,829
TOTAL. . . .	-	-	-	-	2/76,334	2/ 804,289	2/ 76,334	2/ 804,289
TOTAL TUNA .	6,406,401	86,032,991	647,718	9,202,517	76,334	804,289	7,130,453	96,039,797
TUNALIKE FISHES:								
BONITO:								
SOLID.	21,698	235,107	-	-	-	-	21,698	235,107
FLAKES	12,036	130,337	-	-	-	-	12,036	130,337
TOTAL. . . .	33,734	365,444	-	-	-	-	33,734	365,444
YELLOWTAIL:								
SOLID.	37,718	407,384	-	-	-	-	37,718	407,384
FLAKES	88,415	897,700	-	-	-	-	88,415	897,700
TOTAL. . . .	126,133	1,305,084	-	-	-	-	126,133	1,305,084
TOTAL TUNA-LIKE FISHES	159,867	1,670,528	-	-	-	-	159,867	1,670,528
GRAND TOTAL TUNA AND TUNALIKE FISHES . .	6,566,268	87,703,519	647,718	9,202,517	76,334	804,289	7,290,320	97,710,325

1/ INCLUDES A SMALL PRODUCTION OF LITTLE TUNA.
2/ INCLUDES PACKS OF LITTLE, BLUEFIN, AND YELLOWFIN TUNA.

NOTE:--"STANDARD CASES" REPRESENT THE VARIOUS SIZED CASES CONVERTED TO THE EQUIVALENT OF FORTY-EIGHT NO. 1/2 TUNA CANS TO THE CASE, EACH CONTAINING 7 OUNCES NET WEIGHT OF SOLID MEAT OR 6 OUNCES NET WEIGHT OF FLAKES OR GRATED. THE TOTAL PACK IN WASHINGTON AMOUNTED TO 71,422 CASES OF SOLID PACK, VALUED AT $1,082,063 AND 36,332 CASES OF FLAKES, VALUED AT $332,225; WHILE THAT IN OREGON TOTALED 382,377 CASES OF SOLID PACK, VALUED AT.$6,087,630 AND 157,587 CASES OF FLAKES, VALUED AT $1,700,599. TUNA AND TUNALIKE FISHES WERE CANNED IN 31 PLANTS IN CALIFORNIA, 9 IN WASHINGTON, 10 IN OREGON, IN 2 PLANTS EACH IN MAINE, MASSACHUSETTS, AND MARYLAND.

SUPPLEMENTARY REVIEW OF THE PACK OF TUNA AND TUNALIKE FISHES BY CAN SIZES, 1949

CAN AND CASE SIZES		ACTUAL CASES	VALUE
1 POUNDS	(6 CANS)	10,190	$221,588
1-POUND FLATS.	(48 CANS)	88,891	2,293,795.
1/2-POUND FLATS.	(48 CANS)	6,863,959	91,651,983
1/4-POUND.	(48 CANS)	316,743	2,617,369
MISCELLANEOUS, STANDARD CASES.	(48 CANS)	63,906	925,590
TOTAL.		7,343,689	97,710,325

PACK OF CANNED MACKEREL, 1949 1/

STATE	STANDARD CASES	VALUE	CAN AND CASE SIZES	ACTUAL CASES	VALUE
MAINE.	19,021	$127,420	15 OUNCES NET, TALL (48 CANS). . .	962,688	$6,187,087
MASSACHUSETTS.	95,142	815,625	15 OUNCES NET, OVAL (48 CANS). . .	17,971	105,251
MARYLAND	18,954	139,470	15 OUNCES NET (24 CANS).	45,455	161,086
			4 OUNCES NET (24 CANS).	73,831	282,241
TOTAL.	133,117	1,082,515	OTHER SIZES (CONVERTED TO		
CALIFORNIA	916,810	5,766,415	STANDARD CASES).	12,087	112,265
GRAND TOTAL.	1,049,927	6,848,930	TOTAL.	1,112,032	6,848,930

1/ INCLUDES THE PACK OF JACK MACKEREL IN CALIFORNIA.

NOTE:--"STANDARD CASES" REPRESENT THE VARIOUS SIZED CASES CONVERTED TO THE EQUIVALENT OF FORTY-EIGHT 1-POUND CANS TO THE CASE, EACH CAN CONTAINING 15 OUNCES OF FISH. MACKEREL WERE CANNED IN 41 PLANTS IN CALIFORNIA, 7 IN MAINE, 6 IN MASSACHUSETTS, AND 4 IN MARYLAND.

PACK OF CANNED SHAD, 1949

STATE	STANDARD CASES	VALUE	CAN AND CASE SIZE	ACTUAL CASES	VALUE
MARYLAND 1/.	851	$10,000	15 OUNCES NET (48 CANS).	13,331	$98,090
WASHINGTON, OREGON, AND CALIFORNIA	12,984	95,194	OTHER SIZES CONVERTED TO 15 OUNCES NET (48 CANS)	504	8,104
TOTAL.	13,835	105,194	TOTAL.	13,835	105,194

1/ THE PRODUCTION IN MARYLAND WAS PRINCIPALLY FILLETS.

NOTE:--"STANDARD CASES" REPRESENT THE VARIOUS SIZED CASES CONVERTED TO THE UNIFORM BASIS OF FORTY-EIGHT NO. 1 TALL CANS TO THE CASE, EACH CAN CONTAINING 15 OUNCES OF FISH. SHAD WERE CANNED IN 5 PLANTS IN OREGON, 2 IN MARYLAND, AND 1 PLANT EACH IN WASHINGTON AND CALIFORNIA.

PACK OF CANNED GROUNDFISH FLAKES, 1949

STATES	STANDARD CASES	VALUE
MAINE AND MASSACHUSETTS.	32,365	$506,224

NOTE:--"STANDARD CASES" REPRESENT THE VARIOUS SIZED CASES CONVERTED TO THE EQUIVALENT OF FORTY-EIGHT CANS TO THE CASE, EACH CAN CONTAINING 14 OUNCES OF FISH. GROUNDFISH FLAKES WERE CANNED IN 2 PLANTS EACH IN MAINE AND MASSACHUSETTS.

PACK OF CANNED ANIMAL FOOD FROM FISHERY PRODUCTS, 1949

STATE	STANDARD CASES	VALUE	CAN AND CASE SIZE	ACTUAL CASES	VALUE
MAINE AND NEW YORK	537,188	$2,673,800	8 OUNCES NET (48 CANS)	1,824,580	$4,760,483
MASSACHUSETTS.	464,931	1,660,883	16 OUNCES NET (48 CANS).	1,000,662	3,816,495
VIRGINIA, MARYLAND, AND WASHINGTON	33,074	105,009	OTHER SIZES CONVERTED TO 16 OUNCES NET (48 CANS).	18,805	86,464
CALIFORNIA	896,489	4,222,300			
ALASKA	75	450			
TOTAL.	1,931,757	8,663,442	TOTAL.	2,844,047	8,663,442

NOTE:--"STANDARD CASES" REPRESENT THE VARIOUS SIZED CASES CONVERTED TO THE EQUIVALENT OF FORTY-EIGHT CANS, EACH CONTAINING 16 OUNCES. ANIMAL FOOD WAS CANNED IN 6 PLANTS IN MASSACHUSETTS, 4 IN CALIFORNIA, 2 IN MAINE, AND 1 PLANT EACH IN NEW YORK, MARYLAND, VIRGINIA, WASHINGTON, AND ALASKA.

GENERAL REVIEW
PACK OF CANNED FISH ROE AND CAVIAR, 1949

PRODUCT AND NUMBER OF PLANTS	STANDARD CASES	VALUE	STATES OF PRODUCTION AND NUMBER OF PLANTS
ROE:			
ALEWIFE (30)	44,106	$749,993	MARYLAND 7, VIRGINIA 14, NORTH CAROLINA 9.
DEEP SEA (3)	19,896	207,780	MASSACHUSETTS 3.
SHAD (11).	4,434	273,323	MARYLAND 1, NORTH CAROLINA 1, WASHINGTON 2, OREGON 5, CALIFORNIA 2.
HERRING (1), MACKEREL (2), MENHADEN (1)	2,311	35,930	CONNECTICUT 1, MASSACHUSETTS 1, MARYLAND 1, NORTH CAROLINA 1.
CAVIAR:			
SALMON (2), STURGEON (1), AND WHITEFISH (3).	4,993	427,228	NEW YORK 3, WISCONSIN 1.
TOTAL EDIBLE ROE AND CAVIAR (48) .	75,740	1,694,254	
SALMON EGGS FOR BAIT (5)	10,719	275,744	WASHINGTON 5.
GRAND TOTAL (53)	86,459	1,969,998	

NOTE:--"STANDARD CASES" REPRESENT THE VARIOUS SIZED CASES CONVERTED TO THE EQUIVALENT OF FORTY-EIGHT CANS, EACH CAN CONTAINING 16 OUNCES OF ROE.

SUPPLEMENTARY REVIEW OF PACK OF CANNED FISH ROE AND CAVIAR: BY STATES, 1949

STATE	NUMBER OF PLANTS (EXCLUSIVE OF DUPLICATION)	STANDARD CASES	VALUE	STATE - CONTINUED	NUMBER OF PLANTS (EXCLUSIVE OF DUPLICATION)	STANDARD CASES	VALUE
MASSACHUSETTS.	4 ⎤			N. CAROLINA.	9 ⎤		
CONNECTICUT.	1	21,066	$223,577	WISCONSIN. .	1	7,696	$176,400
NEW YORK	3	3,973	371,967	WASHINGTON .	7	10,847	283,544
MARYLAND	7	10,673	172,707	OREGON . . .	5 ⎤		
VIRGINIA	14	28,759	506,040	CALIFORNIA .	2 ⎦	3,445	235,763
				TOTAL.	53	86,459	1,969,998

PACK OF MISCELLANEOUS CANNED FISHERY PRODUCTS, 1949

PRODUCT	STANDARD CASES	VALUE	LOCATION AND NUMBER OF PLANTS
FISH:			
ANCHOVIES (NATURAL, SOYBEAN OIL, OLIVE OIL, AND TOMATO SAUCE)	3,757	$34,184	WASHINGTON 1, CALIFORNIA 5.
FISH CAKES	144,080	1,690,494	MAINE 4, MASSACHUSETTS 2, NEW YORK 1, VIRGINIA 1, CALIFORNIA 1.
FISH, SMOKED OR KIPPERED:			
SALMON	275	11,243	MASSACHUSETTS 1, WASHINGTON 1, OREGON 3, ALASKA 2.
STURGEON	363	20,319	WASHINGTON 3, OREGON 3.
MISCELLANEOUS (HADDOCK,HALIBUT PASTE AND SHAD).	327	10,193	MASSACHUSETTS 1, WASHINGTON 1, OREGON 1.
FISH PASTE AND SPREAD (ANCHOVY, HERRING, AND SALMON)	586	22,088	MASSACHUSETTS 1, MARYLAND 1, NEW YORK 1.
FISH SPECIALTIES (FISH CHOWDER, BARBECUED SALMON, SALMON AND CHEESE AND TUNA FRANKFURTERS)	14,441	201,037	MAINE 1, MASSACHUSETTS 3, ALASKA 1.
MISCELLANEOUS (HADDOCK, MENHADEN, MULLET, RED DRUM, AND SWELLFISH) . .	4,086	48,414	MASSACHUSETTS 1, MARYLAND 2, NORTH CAROLINA 1, CALIFORNIA 1.
SHELLFISH:			
CRAB SPECIALTIES:			
COCKTAILS.	544	16,317	OREGON 3, WASHINGTON 4.
DEVILED, SOFT-SHELL, SMOKED, IN SAUCE, SOUPS, AND STEWS	3,925	76,657	NEW YORK 1, N. CAROLINA 1, S. CAROLINA 1, ALABAMA 1, LOUISIANA 2, WASHINGTON 1.
LOBSTER SOUP AND STEW, AND LOBSTER THERMIDOR.	4,277	113,042	MAINE 1, NEW YORK 1, LOUISIANA 1.
OYSTER SPECIALTIES:			
SMOKED OYSTERS	2,026	180,336	LOUISIANA 1, WASHINGTON 8.
SOUP AND STEW.	3,051	56,514	NEW YORK 1, ALABAMA 1, LOUISIANA 2, WASHINGTON 2.
MISCELLANEOUS (COCKTAILS, DEVILED, PASTE, AND SPREAD)	116	6,082	LOUISIANA 1, WASHINGTON 6.
SHRIMP SPECIALTIES:			
CAKES, SMOKED, COCKTAILS, DEVILED, AND PASTE.	1,521	41,371	S. CAROLINA 1, MISSISSIPPI 1, LOUISIANA 3, WASHINGTON 3, OREGON 3.
SHRIMP IN SAUCES, SOUPS, AND STEWS .	2,545	79,734	NEW YORK 1, ALABAMA 1, S. CAROLINA 1, LOUISIANA 4.
SQUID.	85,999	341,232	CALIFORNIA 10.
TERRAPIN AND TURTLE PRODUCTS:			
HEAT	946	25,164	NEW YORK 1, GEORGIA 1, FLORIDA 1.
SOUP AND STEW.	17,585	202,473	NEW YORK 1, OHIO 1, GEORGIA 1, FLORIDA 1, LOUISIANA 4.
MISCELLANEOUS SHELLFISH (CONCHS AND MUSSELS)	3,230	47,098	MAINE 2, NEW YORK 1.
MISCELLANEOUS SHELLFISH SPECIALTIES (CLAM CAKES AND CLAM LOAF, FROG LEGS NEWBERG, SCALLOPS NATURAL AND IN SAUCE, CRAYFISH BISQUE, AND MISCEL- LANEOUS SHELLFISH STEWS)	6,586	189,484	MAINE 1, MASSACHUSETTS 2, NEW YORK 1,LOUISIANA 3.
TOTAL.	300,276	3,413,476	

NOTE:--"STANDARD CASES" REPRESENT THE VARIOUS SIZED CASES CONVERTED TO THE EQUIVALENT OF 48 CANS, EACH CONTAINING 16 OUNCES NET WEIGHT.

PACK OF CANNED CLAMS AND CLAM PRODUCTS, 1949

SPECIES, STATE, AND NUMBER OF PLANTS	STANDARD CASES					
	WHOLE AND MINCED		CHOWDER, JUICE, BROTH AND NECTAR		TOTAL	
	CASES	VALUE	CASES	VALUE	CASES	VALUE
SOFT CLAMS, MAINE (12).	155,129	$1,469,711	169,389	$993,469	324,518	$2,463,180
RAZOR CLAMS: WASHINGTON (4) AND OREGON (1)	3,847	75,619	-	-	3,847	75,619
ALASKA (13)	37,810	669,329	-	-	37,810	669,329
TOTAL RAZOR CLAMS	41,657	744,948	-	-	41,657	744,948
HARD CLAMS: 1/ RHODE ISLAND (1), NEW JERSEY (1), PENNSYLVANIA (1), AND MARYLAND (2).	-	-	699,719	4,520,981	699,719	4,520,981
NEW YORK (5).	74,027	684,798	14,775	45,190	88,802	729,988
WASHINGTON (4) AND CALIFORNIA (1) . .	26,943	300,883	4,088	15,753	31,031	316,636
ALASKA (3).	221	2,985	112	300	333	3,285
TOTAL HARD CLAMS.	101,191	988,666	718,694	4,582,224	819,885	5,570,890
GRAND TOTAL (46).	297,977	3,203,325	889,083	5,575,693	1,186,060	8,779,018

CAN CONTENTS AND NUMBER OF CANS TO CASE	ACTUAL CASES					
	WHOLE AND MINCED		CHOWDER, JUICE, BROTH AND NECTAR		TOTAL	
	CASES	VALUE	CASES	VALUE	CASES	VALUE
TIN: 3-1/2 OUNCES (48 CANS).	25,507	$260,958	-	-	25,507	$260,958
4 OUNCES (48 CANS)	53,461	718,623	-	-	53,461	718,623
5 OUNCES (48 CANS)	103,668	1,115,245	-	-	103,668	1,115,245
8 OUNCES (48 CANS)	31,275	352,356	104,727	$435,467	136,002	787,823
10 OUNCES (24 CANS)	8,772	95,612	111,820	422,041	120,592	517,653
10 OUNCES (48 CANS)	-	-	432,483	2,922,965	432,483	2,922,965
15 OUNCES (24 CANS)	-	-	239,683	1,073,946	239,683	1,073,946
20 OUNCES (24 CANS)	-	-	6,114	20,690	6,114	20,690
51 OUNCES (6 CANS)	40,857	490,408	3,146	9,200	44,003	499,608
51 OUNCES (12 CANS)	-	-	65,096	510,754	65,096	510,754
96 OUNCES (6 CANS)	-	-	2,286	10,485	2,286	10,485
OTHER SIZES (STANDARD CASES).	21,856	157,588	33,779	141,912	55,635	299,500
TOTAL	285,396	3,190,790	999,134	5,547,460	1,284,530	8,738,250
GLASS, MISCELLANEOUS SIZES (STANDARD CASES).	925	12,535	8,508	28,233	9,433	40,768
GRAND TOTAL	286,321	3,203,325	1,007,642	5,575,693	1,293,963	8,779,018

1/ INCLUDES THE PACK OF SURF CLAMS IN NEW YORK; PISMO CLAMS IN CALIFORNIA; AND COCKLES IN ALASKA.

NOTE:-- "STANDARD CASES" REPRESENT THE VARIOUS SIZED CASES CONVERTED TO THE EQUIVALENT OF 48 NO. 1 PICNIC CANS, EACH CAN OF WHOLE AND MINCED CLAMS CONTAINING 5 OUNCES OF MEAT, DRAINED WEIGHT; AND EACH CAN OF CHOWDER, JUICE, BROTH AND NECTAR, 10 OUNCES GROSS CONTENT.

SUPPLEMENTARY REVIEW OF CLAM PACK, 1949

PRODUCT	STANDARD CASES	POUNDS	VALUE
WHOLE CLAMS	66,754	1,001,310	$827,496
MINCED CLAMS.	231,223	3,468,345	2,375,829
CHOWDER	863,166	25,894,980	5,498,974
JUICE, BROTH AND NECTAR	24,917	747,510	76,719
TOTAL	1,186,060	31,112,145	8,779,018

GENERAL REVIEW

PACK OF CANNED CRABS, 1949

STANDARD CASES					ACTUAL CASES		
STATES	SPECIES	CASES	VALUE		CAN AND CASE SIZES	CASES	VALUE
EAST COAST:							
MAINE, MARYLAND,	ROCK AND				6-1/2 OUNCES NET (48 CANS) . . .	109,322	$2,435,575
AND GEORGIA.	BLUE	3,586	$76,773				
NORTH AND SOUTH					6-1/2 OUNCES NET (24 CANS) . . .	90,336	904,822
CAROLINA, ALABAMA,							
AND MISSISSIPPI. . .	BLUE	32,532	649,106				
LOUISIANA.	BLUE	10,857	217,241		13 OUNCE NET (24 CANS)	3,186	72,365
TOTAL.		46,975	943,120				
WEST COAST:					16 OUNCE NET (24 CANS)	1,490	34,038
WASHINGTON	DUNGENESS	65,004	1,434,938				
OREGON AND CALIFORNIA.	DUNGENESS	36,652	834,677				
ALASKA	DUNGENESS	13,198	278,150		OTHER SIZES CONVERTED TO 6-1/2		
					OUNCES NET (48 CANS)	2,320	44,085
TOTAL. . . .		114,854	2,547,765				
GRAND TOTAL. . . .		161,829	3,490,885		TOTAL.	206,654	3,490,885

NOTE:--"STANDARD CASES" REPRESENT THE VARIOUS SIZED CASES CONVERTED TO THE EQUIVALENT OF FORTY-EIGHT CANS TO THE CASE, EACH CAN CONTAINING 6-1/2 OUNCES OF CRAB MEAT. CRABS WERE CANNED IN 2 PLANTS IN MISSISSIPPI, 5 IN LOUISIANA, 18 IN WASHINGTON, 10 PLANTS EACH IN OREGON AND ALASKA, AND 1 PLANT EACH IN MAINE, MARYLAND, NORTH CAROLINA, SOUTH CAROLINA, GEORGIA, ALABAMA, AND CALIFORNIA.

PACK OF CANNED OYSTERS, 1949

STANDARD CASES				ACTUAL CASES		
STATE	CASES	VALUE		CAN AND CASE SIZES	CASES	VALUE
NORTH CAROLINA, GEORGIA, AND ALABAMA	23,094	$361,339		4-2/3 OUNCES NET (48 CANS) . . .	283,981	$4,175,746
SOUTH CAROLINA	66,336	862,641		5 OUNCES NET (48 CANS)	43,840	788,140
MISSISSIPPI.	72,142	1,042,959		6-1/2 OUNCES NET (48 CANS) . . .	61,410	996,829
LOUISIANA.	177,357	2,491,455		OTHER SIZES (STANDARD CASES) . .	36,430	564,492
WASHINGTON AND OREGON.	113,989	1,766,813				
TOTAL.	452,918	6,525,207		TOTAL.	425,661	6,525,207

NOTE:--"STANDARD CASES" REPRESENT THE VARIOUS SIZED CASES CONVERTED TO THE EQUIVALENT OF FORTY-EIGHT CANS TO THE CASE, EACH CAN CONTAINING 4-2/3 OUNCES DRAINED WEIGHT OF OYSTER MEATS. OYSTERS WERE CANNED IN 24 PLANTS IN LOUISIANA, 19 IN MISSISSIPPI, 8 IN WASHINGTON, 4 IN SOUTH CAROLINA, 2 PLANTS EACH IN NORTH CAROLINA, ALABAMA, AND OREGON, AND IN 1 PLANT IN GEORGIA.

PACK OF CANNED SHRIMP, 1949

STANDARD CASES				ACTUAL CASES		
STATE	CASES	VALUE		CAN AND CASE SIZES	CASES	VALUE
MISSISSIPPI.	116,314	$1,967,274		5 OUNCES NET (48 CANS)	645,116	$10,886,777
LOUISIANA.	495,800	8,371,199		7 OUNCES NET (48 CANS)	4,373	90,505
GEORGIA, ALABAMA, AND SOUTH CAROLINA	52,607	864,852		OTHER SIZES (STANDARD CASES) . .	13,483	225,043
TOTAL.	664,721	11,203,325		TOTAL.	662,972	11,203,325

NOTE:--"STANDARD CASES" REPRESENT THE VARIOUS SIZED CASES CONVERTED TO THE EQUIVALENT OF FORTY-EIGHT CANS OF 5 OUNCES EACH. SHRIMP WERE CANNED IN 17 PLANTS IN MISSISSIPPI, 35 IN LOUISIANA, 2 EACH IN ALABAMA AND SOUTH CAROLINA, AND 1 PLANT IN GEORGIA.

PRODUCTION OF MARINE-ANIMAL SCRAP AND MEAL, 1949

PRODUCT	ATLANTIC AND GULF COAST 1/		PACIFIC COAST (INCLUDING ALASKA)		TOTAL	
	TONS	VALUE	TONS	VALUE	TONS	VALUE
MEAL AND ORI'EO SCRAP:						
CRAB:						
BLUE.	6,906	$431,106	-	-	6,906	$431,106
DUNGENESS	-	-	907	$47,668	907	47,668
FUR-SEAL.	-	-	347	55,627	347	55,627
GROUNDFISH ("WHITE FISH") INCLUDING ROSEFISH.	31,425	5,221,652	-	-	31,425	5,221,652
HERRING	3,049	463,737	2,249	509,708	5,298	973,445
MENHADEN.	2/ 113,393	2/ 17,813,339	-	-	113,393	17,813,339
PILCHARD.	-	-	39,278	6,219,717	39,278	6,219,717
SALMON:	-	-	1,760	245,847	1,760	245,847
SHRIMP.	1,283	115,292	-	-	1,283	115,292
TUNA AND MACKEREL	-	-	19,139	3,073,742	19,139	3,073,742
WHALE . . . . . :	-	-	117	16,088	117	16,088
MISCELLANEOUS	3/ 12,522	3/ 795,964	4/ 4,805	4/ 642,655	17,327	1,438,619
TOTAL	168,578	24,841,090	68,602	10,811,052	237,180	35,652,142

1/ INCLUDES A SMALL PRODUCTION OF MISCELLANEOUS MEAL IN MINNESOTA.
2/ A SMALL PRODUCTION OF ACIDULATED SCRAP·HAS BEEN INCLUDED WITH DRY SCRAP AND MEAL.
3/ INCLUDES THE PRODUCTION OF COD LIVER PRESS CAKE, FISH POMACE, HORSESHOE CRAB AND MISCELLANEOUS SCRAP AND MEAL.
4/ INCLUDES THE PRODUCTION OF ANCHOVY, SHARK, SQUID, AND MISCELLANEOUS SCRAP AND MEAL.

PRODUCTION OF MARINE-ANIMAL OIL, 1949

PRODUCT	ATLANTIC AND GULF COAST		PACIFIC COAST (INCLUDING ALASKA)		TOTAL	
	GALLONS	VALUE	GALLONS	VALUE	GALLONS	VALUE
BODY OIL:						
FUR-SEAL.	-	-	49,253	$20,592	49,253	$20,592
HERRING	122,448	$61,574	600,902	332,723	723,350	394,297
MENHADEN.	8,293,911	3,407,510	-	-	8,293,911	3,407,510
PILCHARD.	-	-	6,123,140	2,872,532	6,123,140	2,872,532
SALMON:						
EDIBLE.	-	-	14,652	25,716	14,652	25,716
INDUSTRIAL.	-	-	152,324	73,712	152,324	73,712
TUNA AND MACKEREL	-	-	597,935	265,736	597,935	265,736
WHALE:						
SPERM	-	-	47,000	38,500	47,000	38,500
OTHER . . . . ,'	-	-	27,950	13,975	27,950	13,975
MISCELLANEOUS 1/.	573,069	306,511	258,892	100,441	831,961	406,952
TOTAL	8,989,428	3,775,595	7,872,048	3,743,927	16,861,476	7,519,522
LIVER AND VISCERA OIL:						
COD	283,028	483,845	-	-	283,028	483,845
SHARK	97,657	709,764	346,990	3,997,467	444,647	4,707,231
TUNA.	(2)	(2)	2/ 12,384	2/ 645,515	12,384	645,515
MISCELLANEOUS 3/.	3,356	190,823	90,942	3,818,041	94,298	4,008,864
TOTAL	384,041	1,384,432	450,316	8,461,023	834,357	9,845,455
GRAND TOTAL	9,373,469	5,160,027	8,322,364	12,204,950	17,695,833	17,364,977

1/ INCLUDES THE PRODUCTION OF ROSEFISH AND UNCLASSIFIED BODY OILS ON THE EAST COAST, AND ANCHOVY AND UNCLASSIFIED BODY OILS ON THE WEST COAST.
2/ EAST AND WEST COAST PRODUCTION COMBINED.
3/ INCLUDES THE PRODUCTION OF HALIBUT, ROCKFISH, SWORDFISH, WHALE, AND MIXED LIVER OILS ON THE EAST COAST, AND HALIBUT, LINGCOD, SABLEFISH, SOLE, ROCKFISH, AND WHALE LIVER OILS, VISCERA OILS AND MIXED LIVER OILS ON THE WEST COAST.

SUPPLEMENTARY REVIEW OF THE MENHADEN FISHERY, 1949 [1]

STATE	MENHADEN UTILIZED	DRY SCRAP AND MEAL		OIL		TOTAL
	POUNDS	TONS	VALUE	GALLONS	VALUE	VALUE
NEW JERSEY	157,582,459	16,620	$2,549,391	1,570,065	$714,605	$3,263,996
NEW YORK AND DELAWARE.	249,684,210	2/25,303	2/3,763,875	2,428,176	1,100,000	4,863,875
VIRGINIA	126,430,336	15,100	2,417,735	739,442	292,971	2,710,706
NORTH CAROLINA	227,679,400	2/23,016	2/3,421,841	751,687	259,901	3,681,742
FLORIDA.	54,919,900	6,070	1,006,765	259,834	93,262	1,100,027
MISSISSIPPI, SOUTH CAROLINA, LOUISIANA, AND TEXAS	256,333,960	27,284	4,653,732	2,544,707	946,771	5,600,503
TOTAL.	3/1,072,630,265	113,393	17,813,339	8,293,911	3,407,510	21,220,849

1/ DOES NOT INCLUDE THE PRODUCTION OF MENHADEN SOLUBLES.
2/ A SMALL PRODUCTION OF ACIDULATED SCRAP HAS BEEN INCLUDED WITH THAT OF DRY SCRAP AND MEAL.
3/ 1,600,940,694 FISH.

NOTE:--MENHADEN PRODUCTS WERE MANUFACTURED IN 9 PLANTS IN NORTH CAROLINA, 6 IN VIRGINIA, 4 IN FLORIDA, 3 IN NEW JERSEY, 2 EACH IN DELAWARE, MISSISSIPPI, AND LOUISIANA, AND IN 1 PLANT EACH IN NEW YORK, SOUTH CAROLINA, AND TEXAS.

PRODUCTION OF OYSTER AND MARINE CLAM-SHELL PRODUCTS, 1949 [1]

STATE	CRUSHED SHELL FOR POULTRY FEED		SHELL LIME, UNBURNED		TOTAL	
	TONS	VALUE	TONS	VALUE	TONS	VALUE
NEW JERSEY	3,701	$55,177	1,011	$4,685	4,712	$59,862
PENNSYLVANIA AND MARYLAND.	28,151	285,405	14,578	54,101	42,729	339,506
VIRGINIA, FLORIDA, LOUISIANA, AND TEXAS	266,940	1,786,220	2/19,681	186,193	286,621	1,972,413
WASHINGTON, OREGON, AND CALIFORNIA . .	24,870	266,992	3,096	23,479	27,966	290,471
TOTAL.	323,662	2,393,794	38,366	268,458	362,028	2,662,252

1/ MARINE CLAM-SHELL GRIT WAS PREPARED IN 1 PLANT IN WASHINGTON.
2/ INCLUDES A QUANTITY OF BURNED LIME PREPARED IN VIRGINIA.

NOTE:--CRUSHED SHELL PRODUCTS WERE PREPARED IN 4 PLANTS IN NEW JERSEY, 3 PLANTS EACH IN PENNSYLVANIA, MARYLAND, VIRGINIA, AND WASHINGTON, 2 PLANTS EACH IN TEXAS AND CALIFORNIA, AND 1 PLANT EACH IN FLORIDA, LOUISIANA, AND OREGON.

PRODUCTION OF FRESH-WATER MUSSEL-SHELL PRODUCTS, 1949

STATE	BUTTONS		LIME, GRIT, AND CUT SHELLS		TOTAL
	GROSS	VALUE	TONS	VALUE	VALUE
IOWA	4,293,600	$3,204,115	4,155	$71,251	$3,275,366
NEW YORK, PENNSYLVANIA, ARKANSAS, AND MISSOURI	426,639	492,337	-	-	492,337
TOTAL.	4,720,239	3,696,452	4,155	71,251	3,767,703

NOTE:--MUSSEL SHELL PRODUCTS WERE MANUFACTURED IN 11 PLANTS IN IOWA, 2 IN NEW YORK, AND IN 1 PLANT EACH IN PENNSYLVANIA, ARKANSAS, AND MISSOURI. MUSSEL SHELLS PURCHASED DURING THE YEAR AMOUNTED TO 5,628 TONS, VALUED AT $204,222. SHELLS WERE TAKEN IN 10 STATES IN THE MISSISSIPPI RIVER AND GREAT LAKES REGION. THE PRODUCING STATES IN THE ORDER OF THEIR IMPORTANCE WERE: TENNESSEE,WHICH CONTRIBUTED 31 PERCENT OF THE TOTAL QUANTITY; KENTUCKY, 30 PERCENT; ALABAMA, 17 PERCENT; INDIANA, 12 PERCENT; ILLINOIS, 6 PERCENT; ARKANSAS, 3 PERCENT; AND IOWA, MINNESOTA, MISSOURI, AND WISCONSIN, 1 PERCENT.

PRODUCTION OF MARINE PEARL-SHELL BUTTONS, 1949

STATE	GROSS	VALUE
CONNECTICUT.	1,118,060	$1,786,712
NEW YORK	559,339	1,272,226
NEW JERSEY	1,290,305	1,898,461
PENNSYLVANIA AND MARYLAND.	972,076	1,723,263
IOWA . . . . , ...	149,932	101,619
TOTAL.	4,089,712	6,782,281

1/ PRODUCED PRINCIPALLY FROM IMPORTED SHELLS.
NOTE:--MARINE PEARL-SHELL BUTTONS WERE MANUFACTURED IN 12 PLANTS IN NEW JERSEY, 4 IN NEW YORK, 3 PLANTS EACH
IN CONNECTICUT AND IOWA, 2 IN PENNSYLVANIA, AND 1 IN MARYLAND.

PRODUCTION OF MISCELLANEOUS BYPRODUCTS, 1949

PRODUCT	UNIT	QUANTITY	VALUE	LOCATION AND NUMBER OF PLANTS
GLUE	GALLONS	198,031	$401,983	MAINE 1, MASSACHUSETTS 3, CALIFORNIA 1.
FISH SOLUBLES. . .	POUNDS	103,342,712	5,144,111	MAINE 2, MASSACHUSETTS 5, NEW YORK 1, NEW JERSEY 2, DELAWARE 1, VIRGINIA 2, NORTH CAROLINA 1, SOUTH CAROLINA 1, MISSISSIPPI 2, FLORIDA 1, LOUISIANA 1, CALIFORNIA 10.
MISCELLANEOUS 1/ .	-	-	6,697,046	MAINE 5, MASSACHUSETTS 2, VIRGINIA 2, NORTH CAROLINA 2, SOUTH CAROLINA 1, CALIFORNIA 4.
TOTAL. . . .	-	-	12,243,140	

1/ INCLUDES THE PRODUCTION OF AGAR-AGAR, KELP PRODUCTS, PEARL ESSENCE, ISINGLASS, IRISH MOSS, AND CRAB SHELLS.

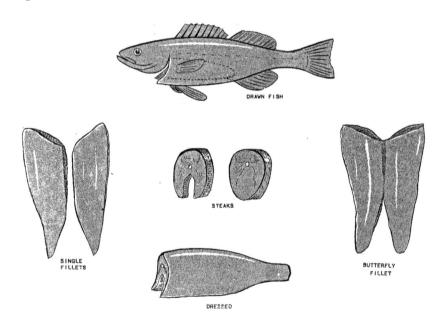

DRAWN FISH

SINGLE
FILLETS

STEAKS

DRESSED

BUTTERFLY
FILLET

GENERAL REVIEW

NUMBER OF PLANTS PRODUCING FISHERY BYPRODUCTS, 1949

PRODUCT	ATLANTIC AND GULF COASTS 1/	PACIFIC COAST AND ALASKA	TOTAL
	NUMBER	NUMBER	NUMBER
OYSTER AND MARINE CLAM-SHELL PRODUCTS:			
CRUSHED SHELL FOR POULTRY FEED	15	6	21
SHELL LIME:			
DURNED	2	-	2
UNBURNED	13	4	17
FRESH-WATER MUSSEL SHELL PRODUCTS:			
BUTTONS.	13	-	13
CRUSHED SNELL FOR POULTRY FEED	1	-	1
LIME, DUST AND SHELLS.	6	-	6
MARINE PEARL-SHELL BUTTONS	25	-	25
ACIDULATED SCRAP, MENHADEN	2	-	2
DRIED SCRAP AND MEAL:			
ANCHOVY.	-	2	2
CRAB:			
BLUE	11	-	11
DUNGENESS.	-	4	4
HORSESHOE.	1	-	1
FUR SEAL	-	1	1
GROUNDFISH (INCLUDING ROSEFISH).	10	-	10
HERRING.	6	4	10
MENHADEN	31	-	31
PILCHARD	-	76	76
SALMON	-	7	7
SHARK.	-	2	2
SHRIMP	46	-	46
SQUID.	-	1	1
TUNA AND MACKEREL.	-	38	38
WHALE.	-	1	1
MISCELLANEOUS DRIED SCRAP AND MEAL	20	17	37
BODY OIL:			
ANCHOVY.	-	2	2
FUR-SEAL	-	1	1
HERRING.	7	4	11
MENHADEN	29	-	29
PILCHARD	-	75	75
ROSEFISH	3	-	3
SALMON:			
EDIBLE	-	3	3
INDUSTRIAL	-	6	6
TUNA AND MACKEREL.	-	36	36
WHALE:			
SPERM.	-	1	1
OTHER WHALE.	-	1	1
MISCELLANEOUS BODY OIL	6	10	16
LIVER AND VISCERA OIL:			
COD.	8	-	8
HALIBUT.	3	3	6
LINGCOD.	-	1	1
ROCKFISH	1	1	2
SABLEFISH.	-	1	1
SHARK.	3	13	16
SOLE	-	1	1
SWORDFISH.	2	-	2
TUNA	2	4	6
WHALE.	1	1	2
VISCERA.	-	3	3
MISCELLANEOUS LIVER OIL.	1	5	6
AGAR-AGAR.	1	2	3
FISH SOLUBLES.	19	10	29
GLUE	4	1	5
PEARL ESSENCE.	6	-	6
KELP PRODUCTS.	2	2	4
IRISH MOSS	1	-	1
ISINGLASS.	1	-	1
CRAB SHELLS (FOR TABLE USE).	2	-	2
TOTAL EXCLUSIVE OF DUPLICATION	189	125	314

1/ INCLUDES FIRMS IN THE GREAT LAKES AND MISSISSIPPI RIVER STATES WHICH ENGAGED IN THE PRODUCTION OF FRESH-WATER MUSSEL-SHELL PRODUCTS, MISCELLANEOUS FISH MEAL AND CANNED TURTLE SOUP AND WHITEFISH CAVIAR.

NOTE:--LISTS OF CANNERS AND MANUFACTURERS OF FISHERY BYPRODUCTS BY INDIVIDUAL COMMODITIES MAY BE OBTAINED FROM THE FISH AND WILDLIFE SERVICE, WASHINGTON 25, D. C.

PACKAGED FISH

The production of fresh and frozen packaged fish (fillets, steaks, and split "butter-fly") in continental United States during 1949 totaled 194,011,159 pounds, valued at $48,338,569 to the processor. This represented an increase of 2 percent in volume and 1 percent in value compared with the previous year.

Ocean perch (rosefish) fillets, with a production of 73,192,538 pounds, was again the largest single item of packaged fish produced. Haddock fillets, with 42,139,796 pounds, and flounder fillets with 28,923,576 pounds, were second and third in importance. Ocean perch (rosefish) was also the most valuable species packaged during 1949 with a value of $15,334,674, followed by haddock ($11,844,771) and flounders ($9,096,156). Of the total packaged fish reported, 95 percent was filleted, 3 percent steaked, and the remaining 2 percent split "butterflied".

Because of the importance of the groundfish fishery in New England, that area continued to lead all others in the production of packaged fish and accounted for 80 percent (155,310,011 pounds) of the 1949 domestic production. The Pacific Coast States accounted for 11 percent; the Middle Atlantic States, 5 percent; the Great Lakes, 3 percent; and the Chesapeake, South Atlantic and Gulf States, the remaining 1 percent.

Data in this section cannot be correlated directly with that information published in the section on Manufactured Fishery Products, as that section included a small production in Alaska which is not included in the following tables. Data on the production of packaged fish during 1949 were previously published in "Current Fishery Statistics No. 579".

PRODUCTION OF PACKAGED FISH, 1949

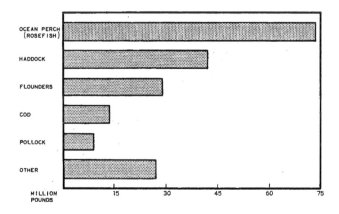

GENERAL REVIEW

SUMMARY OF PRODUCTION OF PACKAGED FISH, 1949

ITEM	FILLETS		STEAKS		SPLIT "BUTTERFLY"		TOTAL	
	POUNDS	VALUE	POUNDS	VALUE	POUNDS	VALUE	POUNDS	VALUE
FRESH. . . .	58,732,595	$17,203,495	697,661	$269,033	82,500	$19,970	59,512,756	$17,492,498
FROZEN	126,013,128	28,282,524	5,463,773	2,083,285	3,021,502	480,262	134,498,403	30,846,071
TOTAL . . .	184,745,723	45,486,019	6,161,434	2,352,318	3,104,002	500,232	194,011,159	48,338,569

PRODUCTION OF PACKAGED FISH: BY METHOD OF PREPARATION, 1949

SPECIES	FILLETS			
	FRESH		FROZEN	
	POUNDS	VALUE	POUNDS	VALUE
BLUE PIKE.	2,287,450	$970,684	628,223	$249,225
COD.	7,885,548	1,949,494	5,766,217	1,282,127
CUSK	488,988	115,674	125,280	24,960
FLOUNDERS.	16,718,255	5,598,252	12,205,321	3,497,904
GROUPERS	375,767	160,687	54,991	24,206
HADDOCK.	19,936,991	5,940,340	22,202,805	5,904,431
HAKE	810,573	160,411	559,655	74,443
HALIBUT.	11,865	4,709	173,112	71,007
HERRING, LAKE.	257,600	13,522	127,768	19,503
LAKE TROUT	100,700	57,065	1,600	935
LINGCOD	564,427	96,100	559,715	110,555
MACKEREL	283,931	62,294	553,057	142,456
POLLOCK.	2,718,923	424,978	6,390,673	844,317
ROCKFISHES	3,148,194	443,895	2,163,665	356,981
OCEAN PERCH (ROSEFISH) . .	639,061	138,956	72,553,477	15,195,718
SABLEFISH.	-	-	36,821	6,878
SAUGER	743,738	326,703	196,106	78,252
SEA BASS	53,100	14,220	34,000	9,320
SEA TROUT, GRAY.	83,000	26,510	39,258	11,852
SNAPPER, RED	13,400	8,510	7,300	4,645
SNOOK.	9,000	5,280	-	-
SPANISH MACKEREL	89,000	34,280	6,500	660
WHITE BASS	11,100	3,795	-	-
WHITEFISH	167,755	80,526	16,300	7,410
WHITING	51,500	7,710	1,119,513	198,727
WOLFFISH	52,266	16,006	258,968	76,166
YELLOW PERCH	361,582	177,929	56,534	27,639
YELLOW PIKE.	631,005	314,738	61,619	31,135
MISCELLANEOUS 1/	237,876	50,227	114,650	31,072
TOTAL	58,732,595	17,203,495	126,013,128	28,282,524

SPECIES	STEAKS				SPLIT "BUTTERFLY"			
	FRESH		FROZEN		FRESH		FROZEN	
	POUNDS	VALUE	POUNDS	VALUE	POUNDS	VALUE	POUNDS	VALUE
GROUPERS.	190,161	$57,268	20,500	$8,200	-	-	-	-
HALIBUT	-	-	3,445,773	1,295,656	-	-	-	-
LINGCOD	-	-	263,614	45,647	-	-	-	-
SABLEFISH	-	-	26,965	9,223	-	-	-	..
SALMON.	-	-	1,667,678	703,725	-	-	-	-
SEA BASS.	28,000	8,320	-	-	21,000	$5,665	4,500	$1,290
SEA TROUT, GRAY	-	-	-	-	37,000	10,480	11,000	3,180
SNAPPER, RED.	29,500	14,445	20,500	10,525	-	-	-	-
WHITING	-	-	-	-	22,500	3,375	3,006,002	475,792
MISCELLANEOUS 1/. . . .	450,000	189,000	18,743	10,309	2,000	450	-	-
TOTAL.	697,661	269,033	5,463,773	2,083,285	82,500	19,970	3,021,502	480,262

1/ INCLUDES BLUEFISH, CROAKER, DRUM, OCEAN POUT PICKEREL, PORGY, SEA ROBIN, SHEEPSHEAD, SMELT, STRIPED BASS, STURGEON, SWORDFISH, TRIGGERFISH, AND UNCLASSIFIED SPECIES.

PRODUCTION OF PACKAGED FISH: BY SECTIONS, 1949

SPECIES	NEW ENGLAND		MIDDLE ATLANTIC	
	POUNDS	VALUE	POUNDS	VALUE
COD.	9,120,249	$2,142,737	2,796,105	$820,755
CUSK	614,268	140,634	-	-
FLOUNDERS	16,697,600	5,341,330	3,946,650	1,587,278
HADDOCK.	39,931,382	11,149,573	2,209,414	695,198
HAKE	1,271,543	214,914	98,685	19,940
MACKEREL	830,088	202,168	6,900	2,582
POLLOCK.	9,092,896	1,265,595	16,700	3,700
OCEAN PERCH (ROSEFISH)	73,192,538	15,334,674	-	-
WHITING.	4,199,515	685,604	-	-
WOLFFISH	311,234	92,172	-	-
MISCELLANEOUS 1/	48,698	18,723	39,803	15,764
TOTAL.	155,310,011	36,588,124	9,113,257	3,145,217

SPECIES	CHESAPEAKE, SOUTH ATLANTIC, AND GULF		GREAT LAKES	
	POUNDS	VALUE	POUNDS	VALUE
BLUE PIKE.	-	-	2,915,673	$1,219,909
FLOUNDERS.	96,200	$30,198	-	-
GROUPERS	641,419	250,361	-	-
HERRING, LAKE.	-	-	385,368	33,025
LAKE TROUT	-	-	102,300	58,000
SALMON	-	-	200,300	90,182
SAUGER	-	-	939,844	404,955
SEA BASS	140,600	38,815	-	-
SEA TROUT, GRAY.	170,258	52,022	-	-
SNAPPER, RED	70,700	38,125	-	-
SNOOK.	9,000	5,280	-	-
SPANISH MACKEREL	95,500	34,940	-	-
WHITE BASS	-	-	11,100	3,795
WHITEFISH.	-	-	184,055	87,936
YELLOW PERCH	-	-	418,116	205,568
YELLOW PIKE.	-	-	692,624	345,873
MISCELLANEOUS 1/	130,225	34,130	588,788	209,106
TOTAL.	1,353,902	483,871	6,438,168	2,658,349

SPECIES	PACIFIC		TOTAL	
	POUNDS	VALUE	POUNDS	VALUE
BLUE PIKE.	-	-	2,915,673	$1,219,909
COD.	1,735,411	$268,129	13,651,765	3,231,621
CUSK	-	-	614,268	140,634
FLOUNDERS.	8,183,126	2,137,350	28,923,576	9,096,156
GROUPERS	-	-	641,419	250,361
HADDOCK.	-	-	42,139,796	11,844,771
HAKE	-	-	1,370,228	234,854
HALIBUT.	3,630,750	1,371,372	3,630,750	1,371,372
HERRING, LAKE.	-	-	385,368	33,025
LAKE TROUT	-	-	102,300	58,000
LINGCOD.	1,387,756	252,302	1,387,756	252,302
MACKEREL	-	-	836,988	204,750
POLLOCK.	-	-	9,109,596	1,269,295
ROCKFISHES	5,311,859	800,876	5,311,859	800,876
OCEAN PERCH (ROSEFISH)	-	-	73,192,538	15,334,674
SABLEFISH.	63,786	16,101	63,786	16,101
SALMON	1,467,378	613,543	1,667,678	703,725
SAUGER	-	-	939,844	404,955
SEA BASS	-	-	140,600	38,815
SEA TROUT, GRAY.	-	-	170,258	52,022
SNAPPER, RED	-	-	70,700	38,125
SNOOK.	-	-	9,000	5,280
SPANISH MACKEREL	-	-	95,500	34,940
WHITE BASS	-	-	11,100	3,795
WHITEFISH.	-	-	184,055	87,936
WHITING.	-	-	4,199,515	685,604
WOLFFISH	-	-	311,234	92,172
YELLOW PERCH	-	-	418,116	205,568
YELLOW PIKE.	-	-	692,624	345,873
MISCELLANEOUS 1/	15,755	3,335	823,269	281,058
TOTAL.	21,795,821	5,463,008	194,011,159	48,338,569

1/ INCLUDES BLUEFISH, CROAKER, DRUM, OCEAN POUT, PICKEREL, PORGY, SEA ROBIN, SHEEPSHEAD, SMELT, STRIPED BASS,
STURGEON, SWORDFISH, TRIGGERFISH, AND UNCLASSIFIED SPECIES.
NOTE:--PACKAGED FISH WERE PRODUCED IN THE FOLLOWING STATES IN THE SECTIONS INDICATED.
NEW ENGLAND--MAINE, MASSACHUSETTS, RHODE ISLAND AND CONNECTICUT.
MIDDLE ATLANTIC--NEW YORK AND NEW JERSEY.
CHESAPEAKE, SOUTH ATLANTIC AND GULF--MARYLAND, VIRGINIA, NORTH CAROLINA, ALABAMA AND FLORIDA.
GREAT LAKES--NEW YORK, PENNSYLVANIA, OHIO, MICHIGAN, WISCONSIN AND ILLINOIS.
PACIFIC--WASHINGTON, OREGON AND CALIFORNIA.

FROZEN FISH TRADE

FISH FROZEN

A total of 285,822,000 pounds of fishery products were frozen during 1949 by domestic freezing plants that reported their activities to the Fish and Wildlife Service. This was a decrease of over 6 million pounds or 2 percent compared with the record figure established during the previous year. However, the 1949 production of frozen fish was the third largest ever recorded. It is estimated that a catch of approximately 555 million pounds of fish and shellfish was required to yield the nearly 286 million pounds of round, dressed, and drawn fish, fish fillets, and shellfish frozen in 1949.

During the year, 82 percent of the freezings consisted of salt-water fish; 16 percent shellfish; and 2 percent, fresh-water fish. Compared with 1948, production of shellfish was relatively more important, while that of salt-water fish was less important. Five items accounted for 62 percent of the total poundage frozen. These were ocean perch (rosefish) fillets, which comprised 22 percent of the 1949 total; whiting in all its methods of preparation, 13 percent; halibut and shrimp, 11 percent each; and haddock, 5 percent. Substantial increases in the quantities of headed and gutted whiting, silver salmon, and shrimp frozen during 1949, were more than offset by declines in cod, flounder, haddock, pollock, and whiting fillets; mackerel; round whiting; and tuna.

According to geographical sections, the New England States led all other sections in the quantity of fishery products frozen, accounting for 51 percent of the total. Alaska ranked second with 15 percent, followed by the Pacific Coast States with 12 percent.

The increased development of cold storage space, coupled with the increased acceptance of frozen products by the public is believed to have been mainly responsible for the continued large freezings of fishery products during 1949.

COLD STORAGE HOLDINGS OF FISHERY PRODUCTS, 1942 - 1949

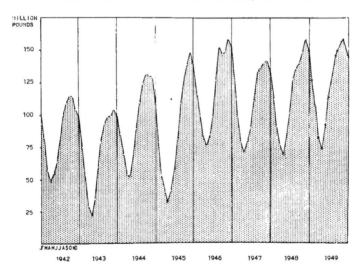

SUMMARY OF FREEZINGS: BY MONTHS, 1949

SPECIES	JANUARY	FEBRUARY	MARCH	APRIL	MAY	JUNE
SALT-WATER FISH:	POUNDS	POUNDS	POUNDS	POUNDS	POUNDS	POUNDS
BAIT AND ANIMAL FOOD	558,146	180,414	2,677,252	2,376,389	627,087	587,287
BLUEFISH	-	925	2,738	10,896	23,471	7,601
BUTTERFISH	23,576	35,005	8,532	7,431	20,554	14,122
COD, HADDOCK, HAKE AND POLLOCK						
(EXCEPT FILLETS)	48,796	52,113	40,026	130,440	137,208	69,712
CROAKERS	-	-	213,354	5,909	5,605	60,097
EELS	56,067	-	-	2,181	21,281	20,768
FILLETS:						
COD	217,142	237,410	368,450	503,015	482,663	396,256
FLOUNDER (INC. SOLE)	194,857	207,499	463,541	227,637	353,394	256,655
HADDOCK	263,511	980,544	970,096	2,737,603	2,128,966	2,436,254
LINGCOD	20,909	22,207	19,210	6,335	67,271	27,550
MACKEREL	2,969	26,328	8,460	71,199	8,773	72,699
POLLOCK	411,079	175,998	99,813	538,800	219,021	164,871
OCEAN PERCH (ROSEFISH)	2,470,864	2,896,816	3,146,957	4,705,123	7,627,316	7,916,944
WHITING (INC. SPLIT BUTTERFLY) . .	942	390	-	33,440	132,433	148,842
OTHER FILLETS	254,157	88,713	179,630	345,692	319,835	356,512
FLOUNDER (INC. SOLE, FLUKE AND						
CALIFORNIA HALIBUT	72,155	56,210	328,614	86,613	85,937	133,829
HALIBUT.	-	-	-	-	12,799,855	10,372,839
HERRING, SEA	187,710	86,276	230,029	359,455	334,955	130,312
MACKEREL (EX. FILLETS, SPANISH						
AND KING)	95,215	7,534	8,453	25,634	121,019	418,339
MULLET	157,120	56,688	7,166	11,775	12,269	9,106
SABLEFISH (BLACK COD)	19,010	9,200	512	111,548	232,976	381,203
SALMON:						
KING OR CHINOOK	-	-	1,003	660	573,155	856,912
SILVER OR COHO	-	-	-	-	3,145	229,862
FALL OR CHUM	-	-	-	-	16	2,472
STEELHEAD TROUT	-	-	-	4,601	6,743	2,506
UNCLASSIFIED	-	-	-	2,487	59,097	62,205
SCUP (PORGIES)	16,313	22,652	26,945	1,365	112,340	96,419
SEA TROUT (WEAKFISH, GRAY AND						
SPOTTED)	23,687	26,194	58,941	5,049	32,330	84,136
SHAD (INC. ROE SHAD)	-	-	1,846	4,344	53,827	38,345
SHAD ROE	-	-	-	14,396	39,885	6,694
SMELT.	40,153	23,618	461,373	204,470	8,094	35,308
SWORDFISH	-	-	-	-	-	2,912
TUNA	-	141,997	-	900	-	11,670
WHITING (SILVER HAKE):						
ROUND.	36,716	-	6,075	36,415	790,315	57,329
HEADED AND GUTTED (EX. FILLETS). .	15,640	45,974	29,460	42,172	1,975,244	6,681,745
UNCLASSIFIED SALT-WATER FISH	505,389	616,671	824,783	1,062,655	1,595,592	1,217,915
TOTAL SALT-WATER FISH	5,692,123	5,997,376	10,183,259	13,576,629	31,011,672	33,368,238
FRESH-WATER FISH:						
BAIT AND ANIMAL FOOD	18,802	-	257,000	-	-	-
BLUE PIKE AND SAUGER (EX. FILLETS).	335	-	-	747	43,136	7,635
CATFISH AND BULLHEADS.	68,781	11,996	12,535	18,861	94,575	43,023
CHUBS	9,470	5,296	2,469	4,295	12,469	93,618
FILLETS:						
BLUE PIKE AND SAUGER	-	-	-	22,082	15,500	3,575
LAKE HERRING	-	-	-	-	7,620	-
YELLOW PERCH	-	-	-	19,600	805	700
YELLOW PIKE	-	-	-	1,000	-	-
OTHER FILLETS	-	-	114	-	150	-
LAKE HERRING AND CISCO (EX. FILLETS)	110,310	-	1,802	8,053	23,174	6,989
LAKE TROUT	-	1,120	3,424	26,109	30,785	13,598
PICKEREL (JACKS OR YELLOW JACK). . .	976	406	2,072	43,738	1,200	30,038
STURGEON AND SPOONBILL CAT	1,321	1,474	4,641	10,346	33,082	64,744
SUCKERS	-	-	6,850	5,043	-	-
TULLIBEE . . . . :	-	5,010	-	-	-	-
YELLOW PERCH (EX.FILLETS).	255	-	-	15,879	1,145	-
YELLOW PIKE (EX. FILLETS).	3,682	753	275	61,461	32,084	8,723
WHITEFISH	22,698	7,519	2,034	6,421	8,144	29,157
UNCLASSIFIED FRESH-WATER FISH . . .	75,290	58,236	80,738	151,986	205,924	173,848
TOTAL FRESH-WATER FISH	311,920	91,810	373,954	395,621	509,793	475,648
SHELLFISH:						
CLAMS	9,734	24,589	10,360	91,197	64,936	39,077
CRABS (INC. CRAB MEAT)	37,183	20,690	28,740	86,535	303,234	89,201
LOBSTER TAILS (SPINY LOBSTER) . . .	69,358	85,153	61,619	34,911	1,685	39,266
OYSTERS	27,617	24,423	55,066	48,040	51,755	14,929
SCALLOPS	113,324	60,454	82,385	274,596	426,562	457,913
SHRIMP (INC. SHRIMP MEAT)	1,085,720	563,162	895,882	1,521,013	3,185,429	3,411,045
SQUID	40,445	20,437	159,260	336,432	2,115,843	940,600
UNCLASSIFIED SHELLFISH	47,139	25,426	22,642	20,950	103,979	64,054
TOTAL SHELLFISH	1,430,520	824,334	1,315,954	2,411,774	6,253,423	5,066,085
TOTAL FISH AND SHELLFISH	7,434,563	6,913,520	11,873,167	16,484,024	37,774,888	38,909,971

(CONTINUED ON NEXT PAGE)

SUMMARY OF FREEZINGS: BY MONTHS, 1949 - Continued

SPECIES	JULY	AUGUST	SEPTEMBER	OCTOBER	NOVEMBER	DECEMBER	TOTAL
	POUNDS	POUNDS	POUNDS	POUNDS	POUNDS	POUNDS	POUNDS
SALT-WATER FISH:							
BAIT AND ANIMAL FOOD . . .	648,486	703,125	442,905	385,717	698,269	861,190	10,746,267
BLUEFISH	12,909	175,932	52,141	98,120	32,783	19,815	437,331
BUTTERFISH	101,686	77,013	217,064	156,566	209,413	33,955	904,917
COD, HADDOCK, HAKE AND POLLOCK							
(EXCEPT FILLETS)	132,409	81,684	108,745	47,528	73,499	104,850	1,027,010
CROAKERS	192,327	216,277	76,390	39,953	-	18,078	827,990
EELS	6,351	11,624	45,536	26,739	3,085	10,571	204,203
FILLETS:							
COD	507,231	237,883	325,796	345,430	575,002	200,974	4,397,252
FLOUNDER (INC. SOLE) . .	442,244	1,267,559	982,355	657,255	774,305	292,185	6,119,486
HADDOCK	1,251,255	1,973,224	1,278,359	791,509	530,011	424,935	15,766,267
LINGCOD	31,036	58,617	50,456	73,990	1,202	-	378,793
MACKEREL	10,354	55,938	13,918	7,516	114,188	19,323	411,665
POLLOCK	162,143	157,667	74,011	358,562	695,783	1,009,343	4,067,091
OCEAN PERCH (ROSEFISH) .	7,262,340	7,615,104	6,159,408	4,935,674	4,387,594	2,935,791	62,059,931
WHITING (INC. SPLIT							
BUTTERFLY)	952,985	811,573	1,188,915	1,052,441	306,078	5,067	4,633,106
OTHER FILLETS	416,258	359,619	466,304	164,318	316,322	105,896	3,373,256
FLOUNDERS (INC. SOLE, FLUKE							
AND CALIFORNIA HALIBUT)	41,100	90,472	52,558	110,448	249,330	80,013	1,387,279
HALIBUT.	6,799,058	477,506	174,336	74,625	3,610	3,110	30,704,939
HERRING, SEA	74,558	71,677	75,515	84,967	137,357	1,095,455	2,868,266
MACKEREL (EX. FILLETS,							
SPANISH AND KING)	437,993	166,311	138,897	137,830	810,689	170,223	2,538,137
MULLET	2,808	49,535	111,533	125,302	395,841	259,250	1,198,393
SABLEFISH (BLACK COD) . .	899,992	1,935,120	1,323,138	622,418	149,595	14,281	5,698,993
SALMON:							
KING OR CHINOOK	955,450	953,086	913,942	217,854	48,017	763	4,520,842
SILVER OR COHO	1,953,499	3,351,185	2,140,171	521,369	129,174	2,241	8,330,646
FALL OR CHUM	13,252	330,539	220,178	521,494	531,522	823	1,620,296
PINK	114,505	1,373,282	497,224	-	-	-	1,985,011
STEELHEAD TROUT . .	10,158	24,140	10,786	1,702	5,799	925	67,360
UNCLASSIFIED	137,356	894,502	342,748	3,569	86	215	1,502,265
SCUP (PORGIES)	12,625	16,365	164,913	58,230	14,254	5,952	548,373
SEA TROUT (WEAKFISH, GRAY							
AND SPOTTED)	34,975	54,061	136,344	108,806	86,761	122,077	773,361
SHAD (INC. ROE SHAD) . . .	-	-	-	-	-	-	98,362
SHAD ROE	-	-	-	-	-	-	60,975
SMELT	95,213	75,324	21,805	13,445	23,885	4,689	1,007,377
SWORDFISH	42,651	78,689	19,531	25,413	890	-	170,086
TUNA	268,995	787,939	98,960	91,857	8,019	2,350	1,412,687
WHITING (SILVER HAKE):							
ROUND	392,019	146,674	271,184	121,321	105,278	21,613	1,984,939
HEADED AND GUTTED							
(EX. FILLETS)	5,161,890	8,755,126	7,527,001	3,857,477	621,321	14,100	34,727,150
UNCLASSIFIED SALT-WATER							
FISH	1,087,281	1,653,361	2,092,055	1,790,594	1,666,415	1,091,088	15,203,799
TOTAL SALT-WATER FISH .	30,665,392	35,087,733	27,815,122	17,630,039	13,705,377	8,931,141	233,764,101
FRESH-WATER FISH:							
BAIT AND ANIMAL FOOD . . .	-	-	-	-	-	750,000	1,025,802
BLUE PIKE AND SAUGER							
(EX. FILLETS).	325	3,485	-	8,682	145,560	13,228	223,133
CATFISH AND BULLHEADS . .	21,732	17,413	11,008	31,692	136,295	108,107	576,018
CHUBS	187,643	200,323	169,046	211,833	24,875	101,978	1,023,315
FILLETS:							
BLUE PIKE AND SAUGER . .	-	390	3,215	13,800	161,204	5,080	224,846
LAKE HERRING	-	-	-	169	-	29,510	37,299
YELLOW PERCH	620	34,694	20,405	9,705	920	6,939	94,388
YELLOW PIKE	182	8,569	1,310	6,377	945	-	18,383
OTHER FILLETS	-	-	-	3,536	2,608	41	6,449
LAKE HERRING AND CISCO							
(EX. FILLETS)	16,793	2,593	8,365	44,778	526,590	659,175	1,408,622
LAKE TROUT	45,482	57,890	19,536	48,326	9,842	3,650	259,762
PICKEREL (JACKS OR YELLOW							
JACK).	541	-	8,073	47,788	27,564	299	162,695
STURGEON AND SPOONBILL CAT	28,657	44,732	30,674	24,299	2,610	2,368	248,948
SUCKERS	1,000	-	-	1,205	1,050	490	15,638
TULLIBEE	2,000	2,000	3,000	1,100	35,000	-	48,110
YELLOW PERCH (EX. FILLETS)	3,719	200	11,746	25,431	32,033	32,157	122,565
YELLOW PIKE (EX. FILLETS).	1,316	645	9,135	47,249	20,181	1,264	186,768
WHITEFISH	133,546	41,420	64,001	80,949	3,035	25,778	424,702
UNCLASSIFIED FRESH-WATER							
FISH	57,043	80,911	64,746	175,492	165,923	51,003	1,341,140
TOTAL FRESH-WATER FISH.	500,599	495,265	424,260	782,411	1,296,235	1,791,067	7,448,583
SHELLFISH:							
CLAMS	13,955	22,548	58,295	13,734	10,232	7,296	365,913
CRABS (INC. CRAB MEAT) . .	227,166	214,353	187,089	123,094	42,206	46,961	1,406,452
LOBSTER TAILS (SPINY							
LOBSTER)	6,129	25,643	22,533	84,530	264,932	209,889	905,648
OYSTERS.	1,074	4,804	9,437	33,880	50,339	87,820	407,874
SCALLOPS	487,008	559,001	265,776	527,700	607,787	326,018	4,198,624
SHRIMP (INC. SHRIMP MEAT).	2,311,670	3,441,340	4,159,392	4,929,112	5,203,800	1,745,895	32,453,460
SQUID	197,552	65,572	26,400	98,139	122,516	5,289	4,128,485
UNCLASSIFIED SHELLFISH . .	58,662	129,969	126,955	85,663	32,312	25,127	742,878
TOTAL SHELLFISH . . .	3,303,216	4,463,320	4,855,837	5,895,852	6,334,724	2,454,295	44,609,334
TOTAL FISH AND SHELL-							
FISH	34,469,207	40,046,318	33,095,219	24,308,302	21,336,336	13,176,503	285,822,018

SUMMARY OF FREEZINGS: BY SECTIONS, 1949

SPECIES	NEW ENGLAND	MIDDLE ATLANTIC	SOUTH ATLANTIC	NORTH CENTRAL, EAST	NORTH CENTRAL, WEST
	POUNDS	POUNDS	POUNDS	POUNDS	POUNDS
SALT-WATER FISH:					
BAIT AND ANIMAL FOOD	586,411	2,571,007	353,368	-	-
BLUEFISH	17,862	398,270	15,004	2,562	-
BUTTERFISH	258,359	626,108	20,156	294	-
COD, HADDOCK, HAKE AND POLLOCK (EXCEPT FILLETS).	495,478	329,244	6,080	-	-
CROAKERS	1,290	132,388	674,980	-	-
EELS	36,905	149,150	15,163	2,985	-
FILLETS:					
COD.	4,022,209	118,711	350	-	-
FLOUNDER (INC. SOLE)	3,315,572	60,269	9,267	-	-
HADDOCK.	15,676,219	90,048	-	-	-
MACKEREL	303,507	900	-	-	-
POLLOCK.	4,064,619	2,472	-	-	-
OCEAN PERCH (ROSEFISH)	62,059,531	-	400	-	-
WHITING (INC. SPLIT BUTTERFLY) . . .	4,621,504	11,602	-	-	-
OTHER FILLETS.	1,278,456	5,204	31,447	1,770	15,915
FLOUNDERS (INC. SOLE, FLUKE AND CALIFORNIA HALIBUT)	410,832	521,438	139,793	537	-
HALIBUT.	217,789	29,464	-	-	-
HERRING, SEA	1,040,366	1,705,796	-	-	-
MACKEREL (EX. FILLETS, SPANISH AND KING)	1,782,599	599,559	400	-	-
MULLET	-	141,444	786,407	4,592	-
UNCLASSIFIED	100	11,421	-	-	-
SCUP (PORGIES)	124,415	211,320	212,638	-	-
SEA TROUT (WEAKFISH, GRAY AND SPOTTED)	-	130,111	506,411	-	-
SHAD (INC. ROE SHAD)	1,840	6,953	25,672	-	-
SHAD ROE	357	19,236	23,894	7,994	345
SMELT.	26,538	72,236	-	145,830	-
SWORDFISH.	161,956	1,795	-	-	-
TUNA	124,028	11,996	-	-	-
WHITING (SILVER HAKE):					
ROUND.	1,499,416	482,323	-	-	-
HEADED AND GUTTED (EX. FILLETS). . .	34,712,151	14,999	-	-	-
UNCLASSIFIED SALT-WATER FISH	2,188,995	1,820,569	2,479,258	868,125	108,476
TOTAL SALT-WATER FISH	139,031,304	10,276,033	5,300,688	1,034,689	124,736
FRESH-WATER FISH:					
BAIT AND ANIMAL FOOD	-	-	-	18,802	1,007,000
BLUE PIKE AND SAUGER (EX. FILLETS) . .	-	19,392	-	201,373	2,368
CATFISH AND BULLHEADS.	50,136	1,845	339,035	22,758	60,699
CHUBS.	43,861	151,293	940	817,221	-
FILLETS:					
BLUE PIKE AND SAUGER	-	51,866	-	172,470	510
LAKE HERRING	169	-	-	37,130	-
YELLOW PERCH	4,640	-	-	89,748	-
YELLOW PIKE.	-	818	-	15,791	1,774
OTHER FILLETS.	-	770	-	5,679	-
LAKE HERRING AND CISCO (EX. FILLETS) .	-	37,606	-	1,139,016	232,000
LAKE TROUT	5,962	101,731	-	109,107	42,337
PICKEREL (JACKS OR YELLOW JACK). . . .	-	46,104	-	82,091	34,500
STURGEON AND SPOONBILL CAT	-	227,148	14,119	7,681	-
SUCKERS.	-	-	-	15,638	42,000
TULLIBEE	-	2,160	3,950	-	-
YELLOW PERCH (EX. FILLETS)	491	2,129	-	119,945	-
YELLOW PIKE (EX. FILLETS).	197	128,687	280	55,649	-
WHITEFISH.	16,282	293,910	6,225	102,068	6,217
UNCLASSIFIED FRESH-WATER FISH.	2,051	716,472	36,998	373,658	101,025
TOTAL FRESH-WATER FISH.	123,789	1,791,931	401,547	3,385,825	1,530,430
SHELLFISH:					
CLAMS.	45,114	10,696	15,351	-	-
CRABS (INC. CRAB MEAT)	-	198,840	619,563	36	268
LOBSTER TAILS (SPINY LOBSTER).	45	58,296	219,661	5,545	3,689
OYSTERS.	33,809	400	109,549	-	-
SCALLOPS	3,647,684	400,521	147,079	2,340	-
SHRIMP (INC. SHRIMP MEAT).	95,975	1,442,706	3,698,313	12,184	-
SQUID.	2,262,697	1,251,024	64,083	-	-
UNCLASSIFIED SHELLFISH	128,027	485,322	39,770	347	400
TOTAL SHELLFISH	6,213,351	3,847,805	4,913,469	20,452	4,357
TOTAL FISH AND SHELLFISH.	145,368,444	15,915,769	10,615,704	4,440,966	1,659,523

NOTE:--THE SECTIONS INDICATED INCLUDE THE FOLLOWING STATES:
NEW ENGLAND--MAINE, MASSACHUSETTS, RHODE ISLAND AND CONNECTICUT.
MIDDLE ATLANTIC--NEW YORK, NEW JERSEY, AND PENNSYLVANIA.
SOUTH ATLANTIC--MARYLAND, DISTRICT OF COLUMBIA, VIRGINIA, SOUTH CAROLINA, GEORGIA, AND FLORIDA.
NORTH CENTRAL, EAST--OHIO, INDIANA, ILLINOIS, MICHIGAN, AND WISCONSIN.
NORTH CENTRAL, WEST--MINNESOTA, IOWA, MISSOURI, NORTH DAKOTA, NEBRASKA, AND KANSAS.

GENERAL REVIEW

SUMMARY OF FREEZINGS: BY SECTIONS, 1949 - Continued

SPECIES	SOUTH CENTRAL	PACIFIC	ALASKA	TOTAL
	POUNDS	POUNDS	POUNDS	POUNDS
SALT-WATER FISH:				
BAIT AND ANIMAL FOOD	119,418	3,560,539	3,556,524	10,746,267
BLUEFISH	3,633	-	-	437,331
BUTTERFISH	-	-	-	904,917
COD, HADDOCK, HAKE AND POLLOCK				
(EXCEPT FILLETS)	900	135,862	59,446	1,027,010
CROAKERS	19,332	-	-	827,990
EELS	-	-	-	204,203
FILLETS:				
COD	17,800	238,182	-	4,397,252
FLOUNDER (INC. SOLE)	-	2,732,129	2,250	6,119,485
HADDOCK	-	-	-	15,766,267
LINGCOD	-	377,954	839	378,793
MACKEREL	-	107,258	-	411,665
POLLOCK	-	-	-	4,067,091
OCEAN PERCH (ROSEFISH)	-	-	-	62,059,931
WHITING (INC. SPLIT BUTTERFLY)	-	-	-	4,633,106
OTHER FILLETS	6,786	1,992,843	40,835	3,373,256
FLOUNDER (INC. SOLE, FLUKE AND				
CALIFORNIA HALIBUT)	202,305	112,374	-	1,387,274
HALIBUT.	500	7,201,206	23,255,980	30,704,939
HERRING, SEA	-	32,104	90,000	2,868,266
MACKEREL (EX. FILLETS, SPANISH				
AND KING).	-	155,579	-	2,538,137
MULLET	265,950	-	-	1,198,393
SABLEFISH (BLACK COD)	-	1,992,572	3,706,421	5,698,993
SALMON:				
KING OR CHINOOK	-	2,483,396	2,037,446	4,520,842
SILVER OR COHO	-	2,548,118	5,782,528	8,330,646
FALL OR CHUM	-	785,066	835,230	1,620,296
PINK	-	51,081	1,933,930	1,985,011
STEELHEAD TROUT	-	52,074	15,286	67,360
UNCLASSIFIED	-	233,756	1,256,988	1,502,265
SCUP (PORGIES)	-	-	-	548,373
SEA TROUT (WEAKFISH, GRAY AND SPOTTED) .	136,839	-	-	773,361
SHAD (INC. ROE SHAD)	-	63,897	-	98,362
SHAD ROE	-	9,149	-	60,975
SMELT.	-	760,773	-	1,007,377
SWORDFISH	-	6,335	-	170,086
TUNA	-	1,276,663	-	1,412,687
WHITING (SILVER HAKE):				
ROUND	3,200	-	-	1,984,939
HEADED AND GUTTED (EX. FILLETS) . . .	-	-	-	34,727,150
UNCLASSIFIED SALT-WATER FISH	1,841,591	4,842,120	1,054,665	15,203,799
TOTAL SALT-WATER FISH	2,618,254	31,751,029	43,627,368	233,764,101
FRESH-WATER FISH:				
BAIT AND ANIMAL FOOD	-	-	-	1,025,802
BLUE PIKE AND SAUGER	-	-	-	223,133
CATFISH AND BULLHEADS	101,545	-	-	576,018
CHUBS.	-	-	-	1,023,315
FILLETS:				
BLUE PIKE AND SAUGER	-	-	-	224,846
LAKE HERRING	-	-	-	37,299
YELLOW PERCH	-	-	-	94,388
YELLOW PIKE	-	-	-	18,343
OTHER FILLETS	-	-	-	6,449
LAKE HERRING AND CISCO (EX. FILLETS) . .	-	-	-	1,408,622
LAKE TROUT	625	-	-	259,762
PICKEREL (JACKS OR YELLOW JACK)	-	-	-	162,695
STURGEON AND SPOONBILL CAT	-	-	-	248,948
SUCKERS.	-	-	-	15,638
TULLIBEE	-	-	-	48,110
YELLOW PERCH (EX. FILLETS)	-	-	-	122,565
YELLOW PIKE (EX. FILLETS).	1,955	-	-	186,768
WHITEFISH	-	-	-	424,702
UNCLASSIFIED FRESH-WATER FISH	107,789	3,147	-	1,341,140
TOTAL FRESH-WATER FISH.	211,914	3,147	-	7,448,583
SHELLFISH:				
CLAMS	-	267,029	27,723	365,913
CRABS (INC. CRAB MEAT)	54,731	416,144	116,770	1,406,452
LOBSTER TAILS (SPINY LOBSTER).	20,969	597,443	-	905,648
OYSTERS.	26,496	237,620	-	407,874
SCALLOPS	1,000	- -	-	4,198,624
SHRIMP (INC. SHRIMP MEAT)	25,983,598	1,220,684	-	32,453,460
SQUID	3,639	547,042	-	4,128,485
UNCLASSIFIED SHELLFISH	42,859	41,153	5,000	742,878
TOTAL SHELLFISH	26,133,292	3,327,115	149,493	44,609,334
TOTAL FISH AND SHELLFISH	28,963,460	35,081,291	43,776,861	285,822,018

NOTE:--THE SECTIONS INDICATED INCLUDE THE FOLLOWING STATES:
  SOUTH CENTRAL--KENTUCKY, TENNESSEE, ALABAMA, MISSISSIPPI, LOUISIANA, TEXAS, AND ARKANSAS.
  PACIFIC--WASHINGTON, OREGON, CALIFORNIA, COLORADO, UTAH, AND MONTANA.
  ALASKA

SUMMARY OF FREEZINGS: BY SECTIONS AND MONTHS, 1949

MONTH	NEW ENGLAND	MIDDLE ATLANTIC	SOUTH ATLANTIC	NORTH CENTRAL, EAST
	POUNDS	POUNDS	POUNDS	POUNDS
JANUARY	3,613,971	705,409	378,648	166,342
FEBRUARY	4,587,246	271,444	182,054	126,090
MARCH	5,369,048	775,688	447,225	23,745
APRIL	9,478,375	1,574,594	294,860	424,630
MAY	16,424,558	1,579,400	583,138	380,990
JUNE.	19,785,996	1,302,247	609,626	205,888
JULY.	17,363,973	1,349,344	777,195	208,156
AUGUST.	21,908,001	1,650,606	1,150,848	286,847
SEPTEMBER	18,514,098	1,462,738	1,868,053	313,777
OCTOBER	12,950,126	1,839,592	1,482,996	417,217
NOVEMBER.	9,779,860	1,534,816	1,573,365	1,110,530
DECEMBER.	5,593,190	1,869,891	1,267,696	775,752
TOTAL.	145,368,444	15,915,769	10,615,704	4,440,966

MONTH	NORTH CENTRAL, WEST	SOUTH CENTRAL	PACIFIC	ALASKA	TOTAL
	POUNDS	POUNDS	POUNDS	POUNDS	POUNDS
JANUARY.	4,970	952,193	1,613,030	-	7,434,563
FEBRUARY	9,911	554,184	1,182,591	-	6,913,520
MARCH.	259,221	676,247	2,420,393	1,901,600	11,873,167
APRIL.	12,404	1,681,750	1,669,551	1,347,860	16,484,024
MAY.	102,070	3,320,527	4,020,574	11,363,631	37,774,888
JUNE	25,057	3,213,955	3,919,983	9,846,217	38,909,971
JULY	24,406	1,969,651	5,320,249	7,456,231	34,469,207
AUGUST	15,288	2,893,479	4,805,251	7,335,998	40,046,318
SEPTEMBER.	19,897	3,187,158	4,254,986	3,474,512	33,095,219
OCTOBER.	136,995	4,131,175	2,758,918	591,283	24,308,302
NOVEMBER	179,236	4,621,843	2,443,345	93,341	21,336,336
DECEMBER	870,068	1,761,298	672,420	366,188	13,176,503
TOTAL	1,659,523	28,963,460	35,081,291	43,776,861	285,822,018

NOTE:--NEW ENGLAND INCLUDES MAINE, MASSACHUSETTS, RHODE ISLAND AND CONNECTICUT; MIDDLE ATLANTIC--NEW YORK, NEW JERSEY, AND PENNSYLVANIA; SOUTH ATLANTIC--MARYLAND, DISTRICT OF COLUMBIA, VIRGINIA, SOUTH CAROLINA, GEORGIA, AND FLORIDA; NORTH CENTRAL, EAST--OHIO, ILLINOIS, INDIANA, MICHIGAN, AND WISCONSIN; NORTH CAROLINA, WEST-- MINNESOTA, IOWA, MISSOURI, NORTH DAKOTA, NEBRASKA, AND KANSAS; SOUTH CENTRAL--KENTUCKY, TENNESSEE, ALABAMA, MISSISSIPPI, LOUISIANA, TEXAS, ARKANSAS; AND PACIFIC--WASHINGTON, OREGON, AND CALIFORNIA, COLORADO, UTAH, AND MONTANA. ALASKA.

HOLDINGS

Holdings of frozen fishery products in domestic cold storage plants reporting to the Fish and Wildlife Service on the first of each month during 1949 averaged a record 123,738,000 pounds. This monthly average is approximately 9 million pounds above the figure of the previous year, and nearly 4.5 million pounds above the average figure for the former high year of 1946. Ten years earlier in 1939, these holdings averaged 63,681,000 pounds. Holdings on January 1, which were a carry-over from the 1948 stocks, were 150,973,526 pounds. The peak, reached on December 1, amounted to almost 158 million pounds. The low point for holdings during the year was reached on May 1, when nearly 75 million pounds were in storage. According to the geographical distribution of average monthly holdings, the New England States ranked first, followed by the Middle Atlantic and Pacific Coast States.

SUMMARY OF COLD STORAGE HOLDINGS: BY MONTHS, 1949

SPECIES	JANUARY 1	FEBRUARY 1	MARCH 1	APRIL 1	MAY 1	JUNE 1
SALT-WATER FISH:	POUNDS	POUNDS	POUNDS	POUNDS	POUNDS	POUNDS
BAIT AND ANIMAL FOOD	1,817,251	2,085,208	2,126,323	3,976,775	4,977,578	3,490,658
BLUEFISH	336,925	333,964	187,930	141,380	144,050	158,095
BUTTERFISH	395,561	288,066	250,521	143,861	98,498	80,294
COD, HADDOCK, HAKE AND POLLOCK						
(EXCEPT FILLETS)	1,667,729	1,529,549	1,449,674	1,348,502	1,099,530	982,760
CROAKERS	313,842	174,101	94,533	241,037	123,231	106,389
EELS	195,242	238,398	181,145	114,273	79,370	115,962
FILLETS:						
COD	8,635,925	7,607,365	6,349,863	6,777,888	7,072,158	7,021,438
FLOUNDER (INC. SOLE)	4,698,786	4,081,606	3,129,865	2,368,373	2,240,068	1,834,697
HADDOCK	7,157,472	5,658,303	5,030,328	4,070,721	6,132,812	6,969,741
LINGCOD	131,178	150,437	143,992	121,205	110,230	159,296
MACKEREL	574,156	454,477	448,068	316,137	260,875	240,991
POLLOCK	3,972,769	3,999,220	3,380,155	2,528,413	2,614,537	2,447,431
OCEAN PERCH (ROSEFISH)	12,883,234	9,828,418	7,030,772	3,676,962	3,377,656	6,089,603
WHITING (INC. SPLIT BUTTERFLY) .	1,810,558	1,723,927	1,191,963	884,209	688,123	596,172
OTHER FILLETS	1,389,874	1,368,958	1,126,280	819,942	816,790	1,295,085
FLOUNDERS (INC. SOLE, FLUKE AND						
CALIFORNIA HALIBUT)	1,033,672	1,015,765	938,724	1,045,320	714,816	839,850
HALIBUT.	13,516,355	8,766,243	6,293,082	3,192,124	1,553,994	12,579,823
HERRING, SEA	1,231,265	1,120,658	825,866	841,820	1,115,374	1,138,736
MACKEREL (EX. FILLETS, SPANISH						
AND KING)	4,017,300	3,329,860	2,447,423	1,261,818	774,329	659,427
MULLET	723,666	744,536	624,539	601,841	426,275	318,507
SABLEFISH (BLACK COD)	4,674,840	5,539,581	3,684,309	3,033,990	2,669,066	2,325,167
SALMON:						
KING OR CHINOOK	4,167,289	3,206,030	2,531,395	1,901,337	1,529,864	1,768,957
SILVER OR COHO	3,743,984	2,738,982	2,206,414	1,432,897	924,042	817,693
FALL OR CHUM	1,899,568	1,672,105	1,363,252	1,073,055	1,023,992	844,355
PINK	159,014	144,021	126,409	118,880	112,583	10,615
STEELHEAD TROUT	73,083	40,656	67,183	91,317	69,221	92,638
UNCLASSIFIED	1,479,270	1,246,374	1,288,721	925,099	487,345	563,219
SCUP (PORGIES)	800,632	697,718	671,462	467,283	300,889	382,968
SEA TROUT (WEAKFISH, GRAY AND SPOTTED)	471,711	453,544	378,841	282,194	197,227	236,846
SHAD (INC. ROE SHAD)	229,402	184,564	151,740	93,323	80,155	156,514
SHAD ROE	59,118	59,542	47,891	28,481	39,216	76,039
SMELT.	1,430,634	1,353,363	1,956,704	2,215,950	1,830,198	1,474,208
SWORDFISH	1,690,924	1,896,711	1,807,408	1,554,532	1,025,050	806,907
TUNA	906,200	467,117	193,431	345,215	111,051	44,248
WHITING (SILVER HAKE):						
ROUND	5,164,531	4,189,643	1,862,421	1,058,630	1,247,744	1,221,020
HEADED AND GUTTED (EX. FILLETS). .	8,506,880	7,154,236	5,098,855	4,239,150	1,862,127	2,633,143
UNCLASSIFIED SALT-WATER FISH . . .	12,389,989	10,609,213	10,229,354	8,156,273	7,913,703	8,974,179
TOTAL SALT-WATER FISH	114,349,829	96,152,459	77,916,836	61,490,207	55,843,767	69,553,671
FRESH-WATER FISH:						
BAIT AND ANIMAL FOOD	2,732,795	2,433,171	2,073,906	2,312,205	2,270,855	2,152,880
BLUE PIKE AND SAUGER (EX. FILLETS) .	955,039	689,463	503,600	285,866	303,700	523,376
CATFISH AND BULLHEADS.	346,343	334,567	347,456	264,881	258,436	376,049
CHUBS.	1,028,571	798,003	633,067	402,842	287,986	246,088
FILLETS:						
BLUE PIKE AND SAUGER	502,725	243,458	292,074	380,297	369,810	156,681
LAKE HERRING	123,342	110,067	131,021	99,019	56,057	76,946
YELLOW PERCH	229,591	186,614	123,034	115,756	157,655	134,213
YELLOW PIKE	84,742	75,921	121,190	132,740	50,554	51,513
OTHER FILLETS	119,657	96,352	91,458	91,810	69,891	116,947
LAKE HERRING AND CISCO (EX. FILLETS)	1,806,814	1,067,190	965,650	656,514	544,350	550,890
LAKE TROUT	532,310	452,938	415,258	344,013	304,827	289,454
PICKEREL (JACKS OR YELLOW JACK) . .	146,929	317,559	108,383	93,011	138,847	122,472
STURGEON AND SPOONBILL CAT	490,230	420,066	383,904	313,210	281,002	304,821
SUCKERS.	20,694	15,624	12,534	19,999	23,924	23,774
TULLIBEE . . (EX. . . . .) . . .	218,148	182,111	167,419	42,444	27,802	31,902
YELLOW PERCH (EX. FILLETS).	608,759	535,625	400,088	326,270	258,932	301,429
YELLOW PIKE (EX. FILLETS).	191,387	196,811	211,198	260,867	263,920	290,906
WHITEFISH	1,677,397	1,372,222	1,346,241	1,091,691	746,970	570,231
UNCLASSIFIED FRESH-WATER FISH . . .	1,096,012	1,244,066	1,012,930	735,751	891,512	1,011,225
TOTAL FRESH-WATER FISH	12,911,485	10,771,628	9,340,411	7,969,186	7,307,030	7,331,797
SHELLFISH:						
CLAMS	330,461	243,549	165,088	142,764	258,815	275,573
CRABS (INC. CRAB MEAT)	563,350	472,685	455,405	337,740	339,526	599,625
LOBSTER TAILS (SPINY LOBSTER). . . .	780,738	723,746	613,816	754,923	529,007	740,137
OYSTERS	270,299	246,142	231,590	293,976	293,659	370,276
SCALLOPS	3,098,578	2,843,008	2,410,115	1,465,123	1,312,792	1,342,320
SHRIMP (INC. SHRIMP MEAT)	16,725,598	14,416,871	11,464,434	8,890,841	7,444,899	7,250,578
SQUID.	1,149,703	898,174	768,995	652,059	904,467	3,052,871
UNCLASSIFIED SHELLFISH	793,485	866,993	771,759	725,565	706,106	936,199
TOTAL SHELLFISH	23,712,212	20,711,168	16,881,202	13,262,991	11,789,271	14,567,579
TOTAL FISH AND SHELLFISH	150,973,526	127,635,455	104,138,449	82,722,384	74,940,068	91,453,047

(CONTINUED ON NEXT PAGE)

SUMMARY OF COLD STORAGE HOLDINGS: BY MONTHS, 1949 - Continued

SPECIES	JULY 1	AUGUST 1	SEPTEMBER 1	OCTOBER 1	NOVEMBER 1	DECEMBER 1	DECEMBER 31
	POUNDS	POUNDS	POUNDS	POUNDS	POUNDS	POUNDS	POUNDS
SALT-WATER FISH:							
BAIT AND ANIMAL FOOD..	3,567,400	3,466,412	2,895,573	2,436,020	2,067,767	2,089,844	2,140,915
BLUEFISH.........	146,703	124,568	271,359	311,367	390,261	388,366	370,890
BUTTERFISH........	74,252	157,839	223,921	415,037	558,008	768,666	752,465
COD, HADDOCK, HAKE AND POLLOCK, (EX.FILLETS)	1,069,200	941,866	903,391	911,526	1,116,151	1,075,082	1,349,381
CROAKERS.........	185,246	363,340	738,297	759,762	686,179	432,799	390,075
EELS...........	135,441	123,985	112,343	173,715	212,712	253,146	209,561
FILLETS:							
COD..........	6,563,496	7,685,418	8,039,267	7,058,124	6,657,698	6,836,302	6,351,265
FLOUNDER (IN. SOLE)	1,856,476	2,003,926	2,734,728	2,870,195	3,046,912	3,191,762	2,866,105
HADDOCK.......	7,615,363	7,773,241	7,921,560	6,561,990	5,265,924	4,563,437	3,696,058
LINGCOD.......	153,681	147,985	159,483	191,558	191,743	72,585	54,530
MACKEREL.......	284,571	224,473	221,738	183,805	204,218	213,011	201,196
POLLOCK.......	1,980,177	1,663,177	1,523,177	1,213,368	1,154,962	1,483,582	2,004,817
OCEAN PERCH (ROSEFISH)	8,626,015	11,515,766	14,025,581	14,075,356	13,853,533	14,475,792	14,141,844
WHITING(INC. SPLIT BUTTERFLY).....	598,378	2,264,961	3,096,199	4,022,166	3,987,135	3,747,649	3,573,433
OTHER FILLETS.....	1,500,082	1,585,100	1,999,241	2,614,553	2,578,532	2,715,862	2,371,905
FLOUNDERS(INC. SOLE, FLUKE, AND CAL.HALIBUT)	791,413	863,243	870,813	855,478	1,125,605	1,411,939	1,265,979
HALIBUT........	22,366,095	25,047,999	22,328,120	19,198,688	16,764,408	13,531,062	10,231,148
HERRING, SEA......	1,025,780	934,404	710,591	755,532	961,524	891,268	1,826,231
MACKEREL(EX. FILLETS, SPANISH, AND KING)...	1,160,232	1,398,918	1,121,223	1,168,726	1,064,026	1,979,718	2,110,263
MULLET.........	245,998	207,885	220,153	361,422	387,538	831,880	1,027,152
SABLEFISH (BLACK COD).	2,481,503	3,021,141	4,285,997	5,903,190	6,021,423	5,270,546	5,015,637
SALMON:							
KING OR CHINOOK...	2,286,137	3,111,717	4,331,757	5,265,574	5,344,355	4,540,978	3,643,172
SILVER OR COHO....	888,911	2,436,096	5,589,839	5,610,508	5,446,952	4,474,443	3,518,701
FALL OR CHUM....	757,540	692,072	984,993	808,544	1,120,079	1,702,018	1,843,921
PINK.........	14,141	144,600	1,407,347	125,980	110,090	73,227	69,796
STEELHEAD TROUT...	79,740	115,561	98,020	99,475	109,523	68,488	46,301
UNCLASSIFIED.....	890,854	826,097	1,717,384	1,299,649	1,469,993	1,308,530	1,272,200
SCUP (PORGIES).....	698,706	677,308	639,557	664,667	530,550	439,400	401,749
SEA TROUT (WEAKFISH, GRAY AND SPOTTED)...	259,763	244,952	282,981	526,012	515,717	620,680	852,559
SHAD (INC. ROE SHAD)..	235,195	245,597	214,170	185,189	181,769	169,919	157,767
SHAD ROE........	86,978	89,348	72,637	79,135	74,715	63,033	61,237
SMELT.........	1,374,348	1,336,716	1,557,558	1,311,797	1,077,576	935,557	755,936
SWORDFISH.......	1,005,629	1,036,982	1,093,140	1,183,985	1,124,180	1,376,865	1,264,215
TUNA.........	679,961	241,537	1,015,553	2,429,107		1,262,262	113,695
WHITING (SILVER HAKE):							
ROUND........	1,108,995	2,477,496	1,320,218	1,866,850	1,727,126	1,626,955	1,476,253
HEADED AND GUTTED (EX. FILLETS)...	7,766,491	8,717,659	16,359,297	19,947,903	21,961,130	20,403,361	18,271,261
UNCLASSIFIED SALT-WATER FISH.........	9,138,435	10,024,586	11,339,276	11,490,600	13,638,616	15,285,241	14,565,092
TOTAL SALT-WATER FISH	89,699,326	103,934,171	123,126,482	124,936,454	125,257,811	120,575,255	110,274,695
FRESH-WATER FISH							
BAIT AND ANIMAL FOOD..	2,058,375	1,865,030	1,539,964	1,042,774	720,320	729,495	1,631,043
BLUE PIKE AND SAUGER..	618,396	564,413	453,931	415,742	481,965	529,616	498,073
CATFISH AND BULLHEADS.	627,466	659,965	599,473	722,371	710,298	787,933	1,001,348
CHUBS.........	340,887	545,706	665,560	774,178	796,682	638,292	670,599
FILLETS:							
BLUE PIKE AND SAUGER.	222,693	172,119	77,497	114,629	161,459	376,369	560,899
LAKE HERRING.....	101,871	111,160	43,515	53,156	18,502	25,405	144,880
YELLOW PERCH.....	154,813	191,684	294,562	450,158	322,279	302,755	266,367
YELLOW PIKE.....	54,113	55,359	50,198	58,154	46,687	81,314	70,662
OTHER FILLETS....	151,692	129,453	186,697	161,477	220,531	190,983	168,729
LAKE HERRING AND CISCO (EX. FILLETS)....	420,427	362,266	330,208	307,273	365,371	906,070	1,358,239
LAKE TROUT......	317,158	348,956	510,917	617,759	795,080	714,092	646,133
PICKEREL (JACKS OR YELLOW JACK)....	140,422	123,690	109,354	108,476	172,795	219,338	127,783
STURGEON AND SPOONBILL CAT.........	356,783	372,431	391,251	422,576	436,128	392,991	294,889
SUCKERS........	25,574	26,574	25,769	25,769	26,974	25,771	19,709
TULLIBEE.......	17,845	103,569	174,828	176,335	165,757	240,901	226,903
YELLOW PERCH (EX. FIL.)	331,201	417,650	332,981	325,750	489,505	412,385	437,908
YELLOW PIKE (EX. FIL.).	281,845	229,291	208,896	195,404	279,686	292,043	273,351
WHITEFISH.......	571,736	836,522	1,326,899	2,026,242	2,505,486	2,171,871	1,707,413
UNCLASSIFIED FRESH-WATER FISH......	1,289,056	1,082,543	869,484	779,912	930,732	1,020,120	913,793
TOTAL FRESH-WATER FISH	8,082,353	8,198,381	8,191,949	8,778,335	9,646,237	10,057,744	11,018,721

(CONTINUED ON NEXT PAGE)

SPECIES	JULY 1	AUGUST 1	SEPTEMBER 1	OCTOBER 1	NOVEMBER 1	DECEMBER 1	DECEMBER 31
	POUNDS	POUNDS	POUNDS	POUNDS	POUNDS	POUNDS	POUNDS
SHELLFISH:							
CLAMS . . .	187,775	133,284	193,376	211,613	138,872	192,538	189,970
CRABS (INC. CRAB MEAT)	594,170	705,846	707,531	807,356	809,632	814,567	803,009
LOBSTER TAILS (SPINY LOBSTER)	937,283	806,000	774,729	1,067,128	951,150	1,289,488	1,676,415
OYSTERS	353,958	314,123	291,180	352,084	254,816	347,392	305,199
SCALLOPS	1,474,654	1,763,785	2,133,229	1,811,414	2,198,582	2,312,700	2,315,412
SHRIMP (INC. SHRIMP MEAT).	7,809,525	6,794,735	6,474,077	8,742,708	12,258,586	18,770,583	16,469,483
SQUID.	3,912,188	3,813,788	3,709,501	3,040,621	3,535,161	3,402,932	2,862,986
UNCLASSIFIED SHELLFISH	979,797	687,445	669,626	860,015	967,450	955,678	896,642
TOTAL SHELLFISH .	16,249,350	15,084,006	15,025,249	16,892,941	21,173,255	28,085,878	25,519,116
TOTAL FISH AND SHELLFISH . . .	114,031,029	127,216,559	146,343,680	150,607,730	156,077,303	158,718,877	148,812,532

SUMMARY OF HOLDINGS: BY SECTIONS AND MONTHS, 1949

DATE	NEW ENGLAND	MIDDLE ATLANTIC	SOUTH ATLANTIC	NORTH CENTRAL, EAST	NORTH CENTRAL, WEST	SOUTH CENTRAL	PACIFIC	ALASKA	TOTAL
	POUNDS	POUNDS	POUNDS	POUNDS	POUNDS	POUNDS	POUNDS	POUNDS	POUNDS
JANUARY 1	39,093,937	28,913,461	6,667,342	25,207,691	10,564,768	12,804,359	20,202,404	7,519,564	150,973,526
FEBRUARY 1	31,364,945	25,376,845	6,078,185	22,530,233	9,108,033	10,783,368	18,830,405	3,563,438	127,635,455
MARCH 1	23,697,352	22,418,988	5,061,010	19,635,929	7,226,417	9,358,285	15,401,693	2,338,775	104,138,449
APRIL 1	14,917,732	20,313,801	4,327,916	13,827,876	6,269,017	7,015,423	13,040,054	3,004,565	82,722,384
MAY 1	14,370,474	18,719,563	3,512,295	12,259,215	6,004,881	5,722,958	11,321,170	2,969,502	74,940,068
JUNE 1	21,178,764	16,906,950	3,515,553	13,419,558	6,215,812	5,972,886	12,954,641	11,287,883	91,453,047
JULY 1	28,302,667	19,495,825	3,700,413	15,125,437	6,745,450	6,145,447	16,484,720	18,031,070	114,031,029
AUGUST 1	34,457,240	20,423,577	4,374,916	15,082,231	7,801,278	5,890,808	18,958,353	20,228,155	127,216,558
SEPTEMBER 1	43,021,480	22,659,809	5,397,616	15,750,697	8,010,705	7,036,785	20,810,171	23,656,418	146,343,680
OCTOBER 1	43,945,385	24,751,416	7,128,078	16,485,408	6,802,624	8,730,015	23,968,261	18,796,543	150,607,730
NOVEMBER 1	44,016,542	25,062,996	8,313,052	19,676,668	8,371,962	11,004,197	26,268,559	13,363,327	156,077,303
DECEMBER 1	44,530,512	26,683,588	9,531,486	21,344,356	9,341,537	14,046,087	23,880,798	10,360,513	158,718,877
AVERAGE	31,908,086	22,561,068	5,639,072	17,445,442	7,705,207	8,709,213	18,510,103	11,259,980	123,738,176

NOTE: NEW ENGLAND INCLUDES MAINE, MASSACHUSETTS, RHODE ISLAND, AND CONNECTICUT; MIDDLE ATLANTIC--NEW YORK, NEW JERSEY, AND PENNSYLVANIA; SOUTH ATLANTIC--MARYLAND, DISTRICT OF COLUMBIA, VIRGINIA, SOUTH CAROLINA, GEORGIA, AND FLORIDA; NORTH CENTRAL, EAST--OHIO, ILLINOIS, INDIANA, MICHIGAN, AND WISCONSIN; NORTH CENTRAL, WEST-- MINNESOTA, IOWA, MISSOURI, NORTH DAKOTA, NEBRASKA, AND KANSAS; SOUTH CENTRAL--KENTUCKY, TENNESSEE, ALABAMA, MISSISSIPPI, LOUISIANA, TEXAS, ARKANSAS; AND PACIFIC--WASHINGTON, OREGON, AND CALIFORNIA, COLORADO, UTAH, AND MONTANA.

COLD-STORAGE HOLDINGS OF CURED FISH

During 1949, monthly cold storage holdings of cured herring averaged 11,638,011 pounds, while those of mild-cured salmon averaged 3,765,995 pounds. Compared with 1948, this represents an increase of 1,208,294 pounds or 12 percent in the average monthly holdings of cured herring, but a decrease of 978,621 pounds or 21 percent in average mild-cured salmon stocks. Cold storage stocks of cured herring were largest on July 1 when they reached slightly above 17 million pounds. The peak period for mild-cured salmon during 1949 was on October 1, when the stocks reached over 6 million pounds.

SUMMARY OF HOLDINGS OF CURED FISH: BY MONTHS, 1949

DATE	SALTED HERRING, CURED	SALTED SALMON, MILD-CURED	SALTED OTHER	SMOKED	TOTAL
	POUNDS	POUNDS	POUNDS	POUNDS	POUNDS
JANUARY 1	5,542,111	4,335,688	3,893,568	1,528,304	15,299,871
FEBRUARY 1	5,725,447	3,694,973	2,345,142	1,650,931	13,416,491
MARCH 1	7,879,345	2,715,606	3,783,893	1,421,886	15,801,730
APRIL 1	7,457,850	1,966,686	2,816,738	1,349,303	13,600,637
MAY 1	7,877,424	1,522,405	2,910,524	1,364,202	13,674,556
JUNE 1	12,661,277	888,271	4,697,539	1,510,648	19,757,735
JULY 1	17,259,332	2,475,434	5,424,108	1,369,465	26,528,339
AUGUST 1	16,081,443	4,150,863	5,929,991	1,312,959	28,275,256
SEPTEMBER 1	17,066,934	5,878,789	4,096,716	1,393,680	29,436,119
OCTOBER 1	16,524,491	6,420,325	5,347,255	1,398,886	29,695,957
NOVEMBER 1	13,337,365	5,892,960	4,767,059	1,567,414	25,564,788
DECEMBER 1	11,421,127	5,248,339	4,014,771	1,530,724	22,222,360
DECEMBER 31	10,909,999	4,998,049	3,305,061	1,564,280	20,467,047

FOREIGN FISHERY TRADE

During 1949, the value of United States foreign trade in fishery products amounted to $186,484,162, of which $151,609,793 represented the value of products imported for consumption and $34,874,369 the value of exports of domestic fishery products. The value of imports for consumption was 3 percent below the figure of the previous year, while the value of exports of domestic fishery products increased 43 percent.

Fishery imports during 1949 consisted of 470,517,127 pounds of edible products, valued at $113,752,823, and non-edible products valued at $37,856,970. Import items which were received in a considerable greater volume during 1949 were fresh and frozen tuna, shrimp, fillets other than groundfish, and salted herring. Items showing large declines compared with the previous year were fresh sea herring, groundfish fillets, canned sardines and tuna and tunalike fishes, and sperm oil.

Fishery exports during 1949 were made up of 146,660,030 pounds of edible products valued at $29,212,013, and non-edible products valued at $5,662,356. Exports of canned salmon increased from 2.6 million pounds in 1948 to 12.8 million pounds in 1949, while those of canned sardines increased from 29.3 million pounds to 106.8 million pounds. Exports of fish oils amounted to 38.6 million pounds--an increase of 228 percent compared with the previous year.

The data presented in the following tables are preliminary and are subject to minor revisions as they have been prepared for publication prior to the issuing of ''Foreign Commerce and Navigation of the United States, 1949'' by the Bureau of the Census.

These statistics have been furnished by the Bureau of Census, Department of Commerce.

EXPORTS OF DOMESTIC FISHERY PRODUCTS, 1949 [1]/

ITEM	POUNDS	VALUE
EDIBLE FISHERY PRODUCTS		
FRESH OR FROZEN:		
FISH:		
COD, HADDOCK, HAKE, POLLOCK AND CUSK.	344,068	$66,075
SALMON.	2,172,095	339,780
OTHER	2,138,694	279,082
TOTAL FISH, FRESH OR FROZEN	4,654,857	684,937
SHELLFISH:		
CLAMS	405,996	17,569
LOBSTERS.	164,950	78,732
OYSTERS, IN SHELL	75,203	16,138
OYSTERS, SHUCKED.	875,743	438,585
SHRIMP.	555,470	364,339
OTHER	110,829	48,018
TOTAL SHELLFISH, FRESH OR FROZEN.	2,188,191	963,381
TOTAL FRESH AND FROZEN FISH AND SHELLFISH	6,843,048	1,648,318
CANNED:		
FISH:		
COD, HADDOCK, HAKE, POLLOCK AND CUSK.	38,330	14,243
HERRING	780,921	106,806
MACKEREL.	2,235,503	429,541
SALMON.	12,831,631	6,041,257
SARDINES.	106,840,819	16,213,020
TUNA.	478,505	364,016
OTHER	3,414,586	656,843
TOTAL FISH CANNED	126,620,295	23,825,726
SHELLFISH: 1/		
CLAMS	19,651	8,472
CRABS AND CRAB MEAT	112,583	116,952
OYSTERS	88,030	75,912
SHRIMP.	1,645,013	1,342,837
OTHER	8,755,163	1,212,826
TOTAL SHELLFISH CANNED.	10,620,440	2,756,999
TOTAL FISH AND SHELLFISH CANNED	137,240,735	26,582,725

SEE FOOTNOTES AT END OF TABLE   (CONTINUED ON NEXT PAGE)

GENERAL REVIEW

EXPORTS OF DOMESTIC FISHERY PRODUCTS, 1949 [1]

ITEM	POUNDS	VALUE
EDIBLE FISHERY PRODUCTS - CONTINUED		
CURED:		
SALTED, PICKLED OR DRY-CURED:		
COD, HADDOCK, HAKE, POLLOCK AND CUSK.	1,024,726	$225,277
HERRING	206,807	42,402
SALMON.	157,738	57,927
OTHER FISH.	65,544	22,411
SHRIMP.	767,332	459,273
OTHER SHELLFISH	9,800	4,083
TOTAL FISH AND SHELLFISH, SALTED, PICKLED OR DRY-CURED. . .	2,231,947	811,373
SMOKED OR KIPPERED, MISCELLANEOUS FISH.	212,250	96,487
TOTAL CURED FISH AND SHELLFISH.	2,444,197	907,860
OTHER FISH AND SHELLFISH NOT ESPECIALLY PROVIDED FOR.	132,050	73,110
TOTAL EDIBLE PRODUCTS	146,660,030	29,212,013

NON-EDIBLE FISHERY PRODUCTS	UNIT	QUANTITY	VALUE
FISH AND MARINE ANIMAL OILS:			
FISH OILS	POUNDS	38,616,853	$4,153,504
FISH OILS, ETC., AND CONCENTRATES	DO	(2)	(2)
WHALE AND SPERM OIL	DO	255,892	27,113
TOTAL OIL.	DO	38,872,745	4,180,617
FUR, FUR SEAL, DRESSED OR DYED.	NUMBER	10,302	581,556
REPTILIAN AND AQUATIC LEATHER	POUNDS	42,518	288,466
OYSTER SHELLS FOR FEED.	TONS	26,581	377,851
SHELLS UNMANUFACTURED	POUNDS	2,907,797	233,866
BUTTONS OF PEARL OR SHELL	GROSS	(2)	(2)
TOTAL.	–	–	1,481,739
TOTAL NONEDIBLE PRODUCTS	–	–	5,662,356
GRAND TOTAL.	–	–	34,874,369

[1] CANNED LOBSTERS WHICH WERE FORMERLY SHOWN HAVE BEEN DELETED AS IT HAS BEEN FOUND THAT THIS ITEM IS NOT A U. S. EXPORT.

[2] DATA NOT AVAILABLE.

IMPORTS OF FISHERY PRODUCTS ENTERED FOR CONSUMPTION, 1949

ITEM	POUNDS	VALUE
EDIBLE FISHERY PRODUCTS		
FRESH OR FROZEN:		
FISH:		
WHETHER OR NOT WHOLE (EXCEPT FILLETS, STEAKS, ETC.):		
FRESH-WATER:		
BLUE PIKE	1,284,434	$154,997
CHUBS	484,750	103,622
EELS.	729,290	96,032
LAKE HERRING AND CISCOES.	727,942	243,089
LAKE TROUT.	3,495,048	1,035,409
MULLET (CATASTOMUS)	876,869	71,451
PIKE OR PICKEREL.	2,452,637	277,330
SAUGER.	2,723,211	337,061
TULLIBEES	1,726,670	165,682
WHITEFISH	13,738,000	3,991,601
YELLOW PERCH.	808,759	118,348
YELLOW PIKE	7,976,677	1,779,609
OTHER	15,265,791	2,947,785
TOTAL FRESH-WATER FISH.	52,290,078	11,322,016

(CONTINUED ON NEXT PAGE)

IMPORTS OF FISHERY PRODUCTS ENTERED FOR CONSUMPTION, 1949 - Continued

ITEM	POUNDS	VALUE
EDIBLE FISHERY PRODUCTS - CONTINUED		
FRESH OR FROZEN - CONTINUED:		
FISH - CONTINUED:		
WHETHER OR NOT WHOLE (EXCEPT FILLETS, STEAKS, ETC.) CONT'D.:		
SALT-WATER:		
COD, HADDOCK, HAKE, POLLOCK, AND CUSK	4,175,856	$369,195
HALIBUT	12,773,290	3,317,127
MACKEREL:		
FRESH	752,293	64,601
FROZEN	1,757,161	188,328
SALMON	24,746,701	5,658,217
SEA HERRING:		
FRESH	36,885,107	727,789
FROZEN	1,383,287	95,632
SHAD	244,897	26,163
SMELT	6,229,653	1,089,522
STURGEON:		
FRESH	354,084	261,895
FROZEN	47,487	40,227
SWORDFISH:		
FRESH	1,936,933	785,668
FROZEN	4,369,567	827,860
TOTUAVA (MEXICAN WHITE SEA BASS)	1,771,685	216,687
TUNA	20,606,381	2,921,551
OTHER	6,082,921	906,187
TOTAL SALT-WATER FISH	124,117,303	17,516,649
FILLETS, STEAKS, ETC:		
COD, HADDOCK, HAKE, POLLOCK, CUSK AND ROSEFISH	47,322,265	8,728,272
OTHER	18,496,757	5,085,033
TOTAL FILLETS, STEAKS, ETC.	65,819,022	13,813,305
TOTAL FISH FRESH OR FROZEN	242,226,403	42,651,970
SHELLFISH, ETC.:		
CLAMS (IN SHELL OR SHUCKED, MAY INCLUDE SOME PRESERVED OR PREPARED)	4,957,806	$853,198
CRABS:		
FRESH OR FROZEN	83,922	12,364
CRAB MEAT (FRESH-COOKED)	5,637	5,009
LOBSTERS:		
COMMON (INCLUDES FRESH-COOKED MEAT)	21,322,795	9,804,335
SPINY	9,356,052	5,109,015
OYSTERS:		
EXCEPT SEED OYSTERS	39,208	14,539
OTHER (PRINCIPALLY SEED OYSTERS)	3,092,243	270,789
SCALLOPS:		
FRESH	29,778	11,368
OTHER (PRINCIPALLY FROZEN)	369,908	192,472
SHRIMP AND PRAWN (MAY INCLUDE SOME DRIED AND CANNED)	1/ 29,673,205	1/13,606,057
FROGS LEGS	1,462,760	1,306,029
TURTLES (LIVE ONLY)	1,047,521	54,119
TOTAL SHELLFISH, ETC. FRESH OR FROZEN	71,440,835	31,239,294
TOTAL FRESH AND FROZEN FISH, SHELLFISH, ETC.	313,667,238	73,891,264
CANNED:		
FISH:		
ANCHOVIES:		
IN OIL	5,440,595	2,856,034
NOT IN OIL	823,387	219,227
SALMON, NOT IN OIL	917,786	254,863
SARDINES:		
IN OIL	16,207,305	6,033,018
NOT IN OIL (INCLUDES HERRING)	6,815,614	1,465,904
TUNA, IN OIL 2/	4,504,907	2,199,214
BONITO AND YELLOWTAIL 2/	8,053,940	3,106,523
OTHER:		
IN OIL	405,769	245,359
NOT IN OIL	1,076,849	412,749
TOTAL CANNED FISH	44,246,152	16,792,891

SEE FOOTNOTES AT END OF TABLE   (CONTINUED ON NEXT PAGE)

IMPORTS OF FISHERY PRODUCTS ENTERED FOR CONSUMPTION, 1949 - Continued

ITEM	POUNDS	VALUE
EDIBLE FISHERY PRODUCTS - CONT'D.		
CANNED - CONTINUED:		
SHELLFISH, ETC.:		
ABALONE (MAY INCLUDE FRESH AND DRIED AND CANNED PASTE AND SAUCE)	5,224,211	$1,768,764
CLAMS:		
RAZOR.	28,081	13,375
OTHER.	278,344	124,289
CHOWDER, JUICE, ETC.	16,510	3,540
CRAB MEAT (INCLUDES PASTE AND SAUCE)	2,306,794	1,959,604
LOBSTER MEAT:		
COMMON	1,409,585	2,088,586
SPINY.	696,073	520,955
OYSTERS AND OYSTER JUICE	336,282	303,012
OTHER.	1,223,088	484,953
TOTAL CANNED SHELLFISH.	11,518,968	7,267,078
MISCELLANEOUS:		
ANTIPASTO.	206,837	101,623
FISH CAKES, BALLS AND PUDDING.	965,506	183,577
CAVIAR AND OTHER FISH ROE (INCLUDES SOME NOT CANNED) . . .	417,129	558,252
PASTES AND SAUCES:		
FISH	75,079	51,259
LOBSTER.	44,078	25,594
SHELLFISH (EXCEPT LOBSTER AND CRABS)	141,610	69,096
TOTAL MISCELLANEOUS CANNED.	1,850,239	989,401
TOTAL CANNED FISH AND SHELLFISH	57,615,359	25,049,370
CURED:		
DRIED (UNSALTED):		
COD, HADDOCK, HAKE, POLLOCK AND CUSK.	688,589	204,266
SHARK FINS.	221,081	103,309
OTHER	429,646	161,958
TOTAL DRIED (UNSALTED).	1,339,316	469,533
PICKLED OR SALTED:		
ALEWIVES.	849,366	87,405
COD, HADDOCK, HAKE, POLLOCK AND CUSK:		
SKINNED OR BONED	5,937,743	1,407,304
OTHER.	43,398,498	6,591,835
HERRING	34,681,695	3,604,052
MACKEREL.	3,886,611	543,970
SALMON.	683,137	266,218
OTHER	1,101,702	319,651
TOTAL PICKLED OR SALTED	90,538,752	12,820,435
SMOKED OR KIPPERED:		
COD, HADDOCK, HAKE, POLLOCK AND CUSK:		
WHOLE, OR BEHEADED, OR EVISCERATED, OR BOTH.	253,425	53,821
FILLETS, STEAKS, ETC.	2,834,188	668,570
HERRING:		
WHOLE OR BEHEADED:		
HARD DRY-SMOKED.	1,041,768	100,564
OTHER.	181,901	23,362
BONED.	356,512	76,726
NOT BONED (EVISCERATED, SPLIT)	1,149,838	196,953
SALMON.	84,163	35,286
OTHER	30,154	8,349
TOTAL SMOKED OR KIPPERED.	5,931,949	1,163,631
TOTAL CURED	97,810,017	14,453,599
OTHER FISH AND SHELLFISH, NOT ESPECIALLY PROVIDED FOR	1,424,513	358,590
TOTAL EDIBLE FISHERY PRODICTS	470,517,127	113,752,823

SEE FOOTNOTES AT END OF TABLE   (CONTINUED ON NEXT PAGE)

IMPORTS OF FISHERY PRODUCTS ENTERED FOR CONSUMPTION, 1949 - Continued

ITEM	UNIT	QUANTITY	VALUE
NON-EDIBLE FISHERY PRODUCTS			
FISH AND MARINE ANIMAL OILS:			
COD:			
INDUSTRIAL.	GALLONS	663,512	$478,555
MEDICINAL	DO	1,496,101	2,843,279
HALIBUT LIVER	DO	1,978	105,885
HERRING	DO	2,119,650	1,290,708
SHARK, INCLUDING GRAYFISH:			
BODY.	DO	2,830	29,634
LIVER	DO	576,131	3,543,103
SOD	DO	13,869	10,396
WHALE:			
SPERM, REFINED.	DO	49,912	115,905
SPERM, CRUDE.	DO	1,104,411	1,275,608
OTHER	DO	758	1,542
SEAL.	DO	3,136	1,883
OTHER:			
BODY.	DO	21,762	77,619
LIVER	DO	72,469	2,803,826
TOTAL FISH AND MARINE ANIMAL OILS . .	DO	6,126,519	12,577,944
PEARLS:			
CULTIVATED.	-	-	1,733,698
NATURAL	-	-	532,310
TOTAL PEARLS.		-	2,266,008
SHELLS AND BUTTONS :			
SHELLS, UNMANUFACTURED:			
MOTHER-OF-PEARL	POUNDS	5,775,607	2,727,160
TORTOISE SHELL.	DO	2,784	3,998
OTHER	DO	2,989,813	439,820
SHELL AND MOTHER-OF-PEARL ORNAMENTED.	-	-	29,483
OCEAN PEARL OR SHELL BUTTONS AND BLANKS . . .	GROSS	844,197	580,683
TOTAL SHELL AND BUTTONS	-	-	3,781,144
SPONGES:			
HARDHEAD OR REEF.	POUNDS	778	5,287
SHEEPSWOOL.	DO	26,709	139,772
VELVET.	DO	179	1,436
YELLOW AND GRASS.	DO	8,838	25,041
OTHER	DO	231,551	1,765,538
TOTAL SPONGES	DO	268,055	1,937,074
OTHER:			
AGAR-AGAR	DO	313,098	471,036
AMBERGRIS	DO	157	10,148
AQUARIUM FISH (INCLUDING GOLDFISH).	-	-	25,599
AQUATIC LEATHERS:			
FISH:			
SHARK.	DO	122,777	19,989
OTHER.	DO	2,973,820	83,574
REPTILE SKINS, (RAW).	DO	4,545,943	2,074,389
REPTILIAN AND SHARK SKINS AND PRODUCTS. . .	-	-	3,422,552
SEAL SKINS:			
RAW (NOT FUR SKINS)	DO	1,302,575	411,052
FUR:			
NOT DRESSED	NUMBER	1,079	11,305
NOT DYED.	DO	50	1,012
DYED-DRESSED.	DO	1,940	35,411
WALRUS.	DO	8,988	15,668
BONES:			
CUTTLEFISH.	POUNDS	159,668	20,505
WHALE AND MANUFACTURES OF	-	-	7,383
COD LIVER OIL CAKE AND MEAL	POUNDS	2,118,810	115,700
FISH (OTHER THAN FOR HUMAN CONSUMPTION) . . .	-	-	906,950
FISH SOUNDS	POUNDS	147,133	53,774
GLUE.	DO	375,817	67,834
ISINGLASS	DO	16,520	10,906
KELP.	DO	2,190,257	65,895

SEE FOOTNOTES AT END OF TABLE   (CONTINUED ON NEXT PAGE)

IMPORTS OF FISHERY PRODUCTS ENTERED FOR CONSUMPTION, 1949 - Continued

ITEM	UNIT	QUANTITY	VALUE
NON-EDIBLE FISHERY PRODUCTS - CONTINUED			
OTHER - CONTINUED:			
LIVERS (EXCLUDING VISCERA, GLAMOS, ETC.) . .	POUNDS	3,061,954	$1,794,460
MOSS AND SEAWEEDS, DYEO OR MANUFACTURED. . .	DO	-	195,370
SCRAP AND MEAL:			
ANIMAL FEED.	TONS	46,985	6,954,997
FERTILIZER	DO	5,198	506,710
SODIUM ALGINATE.	POUNDS	9,270	8,092
SPERWICETTI WAX.	DO	19,380	4,489
TOTAL OTHER.	-	-	17,294,800
TOTAL NON-EDIBLE FISHERY PRODUCTS.	-	-	37,856,970
GRAND TOTAL.	-	-	151,609,793

1/ INCLUDES A SMALL QUANTITY PRESERVED.
2/ PRIOR TO 1948 IMPORTS OF BONITO AND YELLOWFIN WERE INCLUDED WITH THOSE OF TUNA. IN 1948 PART OF THE
   BONITO AND YELLOWTAIL RECEIVED WAS INCLUDED WITH TUNA.

NOTE: - THE DATA ARE PRELIMINARY AS THEY WERE COMPILED PRIOR TO THE ISSUING OF "FOREIGN COMMERCE AND
   NAVIGATION OF THE UNITED STATES, 1949". THE DATA INCLUDE IMPORTS TO UNITED STATES TERRITORIES AND
   POSSESSIONS. DATA ON THE FISHERIES OF THE UNITED STATES TERRITORIES AND POSSESSIONS, OTHER THAN ALASKA,
   ARE NOT INCLUDED IN THE OPERATING UNIT, CATCH, AND MANUFACTURED PRODUCTS TABLES.

IMPORTS OF FRESH AND FROZEN TUNA BY COUNTRY, 1949

COUNTRY	POUNDS	VALUE
COSTA RICA.	10,077,771	$1,527,297
JAPAN	2,839,298	442,272
PERU.	2,326,642	130,702
MEXICO.	1,990,098	323,342
CANADA.	1,234,246	217,319
ECUADOR	1,026,000	130,780
ALL OTHERS.	1,112,326	149,839
TOTAL.	20,606,381	2,921,551

IMPORTS OF FILLETS, STEAKS, ETC. BY COUNTRY, 1949

COUNTRY	POUNDS	VALUE
GROUNDFISH (INCLUDING OCEAN PERCH)		
CANADA (INCLUDING NEWFOUNDLAND).	41,685,312	$7,823,982
ICELAND.	5,130,528	801,442
NORWAY	506,425	102,848
TOTAL	47,322,265	8,728,272
OTHER THAN GROUNDFISH		
CANADA (INCLUDING NEWFOUNDLAND).	14,680,697	4,329,449
JAPAN.	1,727,917	495,550
NORWAY	1,030,358	158,121
ICELAND.	390,665	49,372
ALL OTHERS	667,120	52,541
TOTAL	18,496,757	5,085,033

IMPORTS OF SHRIMP BY COUNTRY, 1949 1/

COUNTRY	POUNDS	VALUE
MEXICO.	29,382,193	$13,450,481
ALL OTHERS.	291,012	155,576
TOTAL.	29,673,205	13,606,057

1/ PRIMARILY FRESH AND FROZEN.

IMPORTS OF CANNED SARDINES IN OIL BY COUNTRY, 1949

COUNTRY	POUNDS	VALUE
NORWAY.	9,697,262	$3,625,762
PORTUGAL.	4,020,208	1,717,206
CANADA.	1,496,338	267,543
ALL OTHERS.	993,497	422,507
TOTAL.	16,207,305	6,033,018

IMPORTS OF CANNED TUNA IN OIL BY COUNTRY, 1949

COUNTRY	POUNDS	VALUE
JAPAN	1,781,576	$883,742
PERU.	1,648,456	800,396
ANGOLA.	549,404	254,627
PORTUGAL.	298,898	140,288
ALL OTHERS.	226,573	120,161
TOTAL.	4,504,907	2,199,214

IMPORTS OF CANNED BONITO AND YELLOWTAIL BY COUNTRY, 1949

COUNTRY	POUNDS	VALUE
PERU.	7,971,852	$3,077,001
CHILE	76,863	25,056
ALL OTHERS.	5,225	4,466
TOTAL.	8,053,940	3,106,523

SECTION 2.- NEW ENGLAND FISHERIES

(Area XXII)[2]

During 1949, the demand for fresh fish at the docks in the New England Area was considerably lighter than in 1948 and the market was weaker. Keener competition from other protein foods, being offered at their lowest post war prices, brought about this weaker market condition. Demand was light at the start of the year and the market weak. There was a good recovery during the Lenten season although not as great as in the previous few years. During the late spring months, the demand slackened and the market weakened again. Excessively hot summer weather adversely affected the demand even more. Fall brought about a recovery and a stronger market, however the demand slowed down again during the last few months of the year with only brief rallies on occasions when supplies were very short.

The frozen fish market in New England started the year off slowly with some overstocked items on hand. It was not until the late winter that any appreciable improvement was noticed and, in the meantime, some inventories were moved at a sacrifice. The demand for frozen fish continued from fair to good until the late fall, with the poorest period during midsummer. At the end of the year, mostly due to the holiday season, the demand tapered off again. As the year closed, supplies of haddock and flounder fillets were light, but there were good supplies of cod and ocean perch (rosefish) fillets. Headed and gutted whiting was the only item in apparently heavy supply.

The offshore vessels out of Boston continued to fish on their usual grounds, varying little from their practice in recent years, and doing the greater part of their fishing on Georges Bank. However, when haddock became scarcer toward the end of the year, the number of trips to more distant grounds (Brown, La Have, Emerald, Western, and Middle Ground) were more numerous. Haddock was more plentiful on these more distant grounds and trips were more successful. The Gloucester ocean perch (rosefish) fleet operated on the grounds off Nova Scotia with increasing frequency during 1949. Generally, fishing conditions were good during most of the year, with the best catches during the early part of the year. However, fishing was spotty during some of the late fall and winter months, with the worst weather of the year coming in October, when high winds prevailed for several weeks hampering fishing operations considerably.

During 1949, the mackerel seiners had one of their poorest years in New England waters. Very few mackerel were located by the purse seiners during the year, apparently due to the scattering of the schools. By the end of August, all the vessels which had fitted out for purse seining in the spring, had ceased searching for mackerel. Most boats returned to otter trawling while a few turned to seining for menhaden, which was sold to reduction plants in Gloucester. The menhaden returned to this area in large quantities during 1949 after an absence of many years. Some vessels reoutfitted for mackerel purse seining in November and made a few successful trips off Cape Cod and Long Island. However, foul weather set in shortly thereafter and they put away their gear for the winter.

Swordfish harpooners had an average season. After a few good trips early in the season the remainder was no better than fair. These vessels were hampered a great deal by foggy weather which prevailed for lengthy periods during the middle of the summer.

The large otter trawl fleet, the backbone of the Boston fish-producing industry, was reduced in the spring of 1949 when twelve vessels were sold to the U. S. Army for use in Bizonal, Germany. These vessels represented about 25 percent of the large trawlers, and a conservative estimate places the loss in production at close to 20 million pounds in 1949. There were no adequate replacements for these vessels, and none were contemplated for the immediate future. Producers were reluctant to risk further investments, blaming high cost of production and reduced income due to lowered prices.

---

[2] *This number was assigned to this area by the North American Council on Fishery Investigations. It should be explained that there are included in this area craft whose principal fishing ports are in the area but at times fish elsewhere. A notable example is the southern trawl fishery which extends into Area XXIV.*

The New England Fisheries were handicapped during 1949 by several labor disputes. On May 2, 1949, lack of an agreement on terms for a new contract between the shore workers and the operators brought forth a period of about 4 months of confusion and uncertainty on the Boston Fish Pier. This resulted in a reduction in vessel landings there.

There was one minor controversy over the grading of fish while unloading, and the rules for the grading and reselling of fish were under heated debate but no definite action was taken to alter them. The major concern in the transportation field was the increased shipping costs. Movement of fish by truck continued to increase as it had in recent years.

Fishery leaders in New England continued their efforts to limit the increasing importation of groundfish fillets. Their request that the Government establish an absolute quota did not receive favorable action. A higher tariff rate was sought to offset the lower cost of producing foreign fillets, but this measure was also without success.

In the following tables, landings by certain types of gear may be shown in one state although the vessel, crew, and gear may be credited to another state. The catch is listed in the port where it is landed, while the operating units are credited to the port where the vessel landed the greatest portion of its catch.

The last complete survey of the fishery transporting, wholesaling and manufacturing industries was made for 1940. In that year, 186 men were employed in the operation of 84 vessels engaged in the transporting trade, and 12,650 persons were employed in wholesale and manufacturing establishments. The latter employees received $7,547,395 in salaries and wages during 1940. Detailed statistics on these branches of the industry for 1940 can be found in "Fishery Statistics of the United States, 1944" (Statistical Digest No. 16).

The following tables contain summarized and detailed information on the 1949 catch and operating units of the New England States. Condensed summary data on the operating units and catch by states of the New England States, appearing on the following pages, have been previously published in Current Fishery Statistics No. 692.

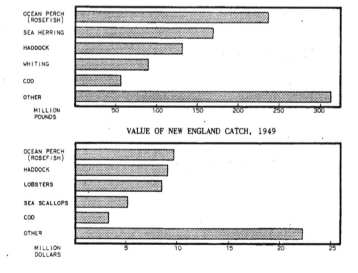

NEW ENGLAND CATCH, 1949

VALUE OF NEW ENGLAND CATCH, 1949

NEW ENGLAND FISHERIES

MAINE: CATCH BY GEAR, 1949

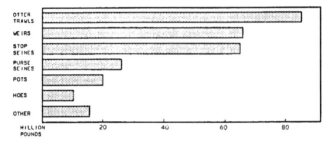

NEW HAMPSHIRE: CATCH BY GEAR, 1949

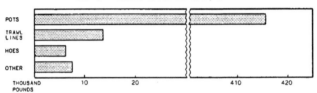

MASSACHUSETTS: CATCH BY GEAR, 1949

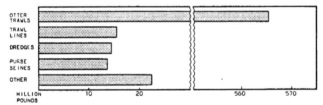

RHODE ISLAND: CATCH BY GEAR, 1949

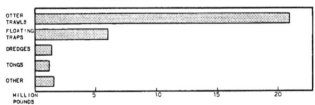

CONNECTICUT: CATCH BY GEAR, 1949

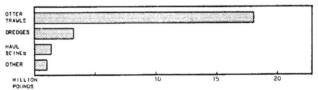

SECTIONAL SUMMARIES

SUMMARY OF CATCH, 1949

PRODUCT	MAINE		NEW HAMPSHIRE		MASSACHUSETTS	
	POUNDS	VALUE	POUNDS	VALUE	POUNDS	VALUE
FISH	262,501,600	$6,215,185	21,400	$1,588	621,691,400	$30,563,258
SHELLFISH, ETC.. .	31,795,600	8,772,855	422,000	168,311	25,921,500	8,408,218
TOTAL. . . .	294,297,200	14,988,040	443,400	169,899	647,612,900	38,991,476

PRODUCT	RHODE ISLAND		CONNECTICUT		TOTAL	
	POUNDS	VALUE	POUNDS	VALUE	POUNDS	VALUE
FISH	26,999,500	$841,331	20,219,700	$935,657	931,433,600	$38,577,019
SHELLFISH, ETC.. .	6,428,500	1,388,585	3,975,100	1,221,888	68,542,700	19,959,857
TOTAL. . . .	33,428,000	2,229,916	24,194,800	2,157,545	999,976,300	58,536,876

SUMMARY OF OPERATING UNITS, 1949

ITEM	MAINE	NEW HAMPSHIRE	MASSACHUSETTS	RHODE ISLAND	CONNECTICUT	TOTAL
	NUMBER	NUMBER	NUMBER	NUMBER	NUMBER	NUMBER
FISHERMEN:						
ON VESSELS.	477	-	5,155	286	467	6,385
ON BOATS AND SHORE:						
REGULAR	5,614	134	1,707	471	130	8,056
CASUAL.	3,199	112	5,294	1,075	718	10,398
TOTAL	9,290	246	12,156	1,832	1,315	24,839
VESSELS:						
MOTOR	111	-	639	85	108	943
NET TONNAGE	2,307	-	26,032	1,131	2,137	31,607
STEAM	-	-	-	-	5	5
NET TONNAGE	-	-	-	-	513	513
TOTAL VESSELS	111	-	639	85	113	948
TOTAL NET TONNAGE . . .	2,307	-	26,032	1,131	2,650	32,120
BOATS:						
MOTOR	5,200	101	2,655	529	351	8,836
OTHER	1,770	67	2,040	879	247	5,003
ACCESSORY BOATS	18	-	186	30	7	241
APPARATUS:						
PURSE SEINES:						
MACKEREL.	15	-	35	-	81	131
LENGTH, YARDS	5,150	-	17,120	-	13,288	35,558
OTHER	55	-	1	-	-	56
LENGTH, YARDS	16,780	-	39	-	-	16,819
HAUL SEINES, COMMON	3	-	5	7	-	15
LENGTH, YARDS	300	-	285	1,600	-	2,185
STOP SEINES	136	-	-	-	-	136
LENGTH, YARDS	41,850	-	-	-	-	41,850
GILL NETS:						
ANCHOR.	-	-	318	-	3	321
SQUARE YARDS.	-	-	162,133	-	1,100	163,233
DRIFT	354	-	545	30	99	1,028
SQUARE YARDS.	108,992	-	259,667	9,000	86,300	463,959
LINES:						
HAND.	1,717	37	757	221	73	2,805
HOOKS	3,300	74	895	221	219	4,709
TRAWL OR TROT WITH H OKS.	12,503	16	11,435	-	-	23,954
HOOKS	525,832	1,200	635,450	-	-	1,162,482
TROLL	-	-	-	88	-	88
HOOKS	-	-	-	88	-	88
POUND NETS.	-	-	81	-	5	86
FLOATING TRAPS.	24	-	46	16	-	86
STOP NETS	-	-	-	-	11	11
LENGTH, YARDS . . .	-	-	-	-	300	300
WEIRS	217	-	-	-	-	217
FYKE NETS, FISH	15	-	-	-	19	35
DIP NETS, COMMON.	150	8	246	-	93	497
BAG NETS.	40	-	-	-	-	40
LIFT NETS	45	-	-	-	-	45
OTTER TRAWLS, FISH. . . .	101	-	573	92	134	900
YARDS AT MOUTH.	2,686	-	15,574	2,339	1,773	22,372
TRAPS, BOX.	7	-	-	-	-	7
POTS:						
CRAB.	-	-	1,332	150	-	1,482
EEL	-	-	125	490	600	1,215
LOBSTER	461,675	11,750	98,309	17,443	12,609	601,786
PERIWINKLE AND COCKLE . .	-	-	-	300	-	300

(CONTINUED ON NEXT PAGE)

SUMMARY OF OPERATING UNITS, 1949 - Continued

ITEM	MAINE	NEW HAMPSHIRE	MASSACHUSETTS	RHODE ISLAND	CONNECTICUT	TOTAL
	NUMBER	NUMBER	NUMBER	NUMBER	NUMBER	NUMBER
APPARATUS - CONTINUED:						
HARPOONS.	89	-	79	21	7	196
SPEARS.	-	-	17	-	-	17
DREDGES:						
CLAM.	-	-	24	11	-	35
YARDS AT MOUTH.	-	-	22	11	-	33
OYSTER, COMMON.	-	-	15	16	1/ 85	116
YARDS AT MOUTH.	-	-	14	22	1/ 129	165
SCALLOPS.	57	-	4,342	1,329	6	5,734
YARDS AT MOUTH.	59	-	4,168	1,035	6	5,268
TONGS:						
OYSTER.	-	-	37	70	44	151
OTHER	-	-	357	963	48	1,368
RAKES, OTHER THAN FOR						
OYSTERS.	142	-	1,278	163	28	1,611
FORKS	-	-	119	-	-	119
HOES.	1,868	35	641	180	46	2,770

1/ INCLUDES 1 SUCTION DREDGE, 2 YARDS AT MOUTH.

CATCH BY STATES, 1949

SPECIES	MAINE		NEW HAMPSHIRE		MASSACHUSETTS	
FISH	POUNDS	VALUE	POUNDS	VALUE	POUNDS	VALUE
ALEWIVES	3,280,700	$31,157	4,500	$45	501,700	$7,937
AMBERJACK.	-	-	-	-	100	9
ANGLERFISH	-	-	-	-	1,500	54
BLUEFISH	-	-	-	-	25,400	5,050
BUTTERFISH	200	10	-	-	720,600	58,067
COD.	6,075,400	315,918	2,700	784	50,418,700	2,921,841
CREVALLE	-	-	-	-	1,100	31
CUNNER	-	-	-	-	200	7
CUSK	1,358,600	50,896	400	22	2,261,200	81,906
EELS:						
COMMON	41,800	8,672	-	-	40,500	6,627
CONGER	-	-	-	-	5,700	218
FLOUNDERS:						
GRAY SOLE.	761,000	34,848	-	-	7,380,400	509,007
LEMON SOLE	1,100	73	-	-	4,631,900	662,292
YELLOWTAIL	119,800	8,743	-	-	25,408,600	2,417,506
BLACKBACK.	832,800	39,774	-	-	14,399,200	1,555,852
DAB.	585,700	15,777	-	-	3,040,500	172,367
FLUKE.	-	-	-	-	1,786,700	337,869
UNCLASSIFIED	-	-	-	-	500	34
FRIGATE MACKEREL	-	-	-	-	1,300	55
GRAYFISH	587,000	4,802	-	-	32,900	763
HADDOCK.	7,184,800	468,765	1,400	142	126,496,700	8,697,596
HAKE:						
RED.	186,200	9,762	-	-	39,800,400	340,023
WHITE.	5,712,800	190,610	11,500	473	8,441,600	338,781
HALIBUT.	51,300	12,285	-	-	420,800	93,676
HERRING, SEA	149,894,000	2,408,383	-	-	11,593,900	143,455
LAUNCE	-	-	-	-	13,600	589
MACKEREL	3,351,900	157,569	-	-	13,969,400	1,065,480
MENHADEN	5,027,300	45,040	-	-	7,473,500	88,956
OCEAN PERCH (ROSEFISH)	55,502,600	2,014,071	-	-	181,484,100	7,805,195
OCEAN POUT	-	-	-	-	5,200	71
POLLOCK.	6,386,700	163,444	300	10	22,360,000	641,382
SALMON	1,000	507	-	-	300	116
SCUP OR PORGY.	-	-	-	-	465,900	15,824
SEA BASS	-	-	-	-	34,100	3,297
SEA TROUT OR WEAKFISH, GRAY. .	-	-	-	-	600	59
SHAD	4,900	206	-	-	11,100	769
SHARKS	71,400	7,173	-	-	238,100	3,842
SKATES	-	-	-	-	25,300	689
SMELT.	160,600	40,003	500	110	900	21
STRIPED BASS	-	-	-	-	71,800	11,071
STURGEON	500	69	-	-	6,700	740
SUCKERS.	9,300	651	-	-	-	-
SWORDFISH.	-	-	-	-	874,400	305,758
TAUTOG	-	-	-	-	49,500	2,864
TILEFISH	-	-	-	-	200,700	14,258
TUNA AND TUNALIKE FISHES:						
BLUEFIN.	159,600	15,134	-	-	2,461,000	175,665
TOTAL TUNA	159,600	15,134	-	-	2,461,000	175,665

(CONTINUED ON NEXT PAGE)

CATCH BY STATES, 1949 - Continued

SPECIES	MAINE		NEW HAMPSHIRE		MASSACHUSETTS	
FISH - CONTINUED	POUNDS	VALUE	POUNDS	VALUE	POUNDS	VALUE
WHITING.	12,580,200	$147,191	-	-	75,776,400	$1,726,618
WOLFFISH	190,800	4,295	100	$2	2,134,900	150,888
UNCLASSIFIED:						
FOR FOOD	2,381,600	19,357	-	-	4,222,700	101,778
OTHER.	-	-	-	-	12,399,100	116,305
TOTAL.	262,501,600	6,215,185	21,400	1,588	621,691,400	30,583,258
SHELLFISH, ETC.						
CRABS, ROCK.	734,400	20,217	-	-	1,765,400	98,455
TOTAL CRABS.	734,400	20,217	-	-	1,765,400	98,455
LOBSTERS, NORTHERN	19,272,700	6,696,961	415,900	166,360	3,563,000	1,405,385
SHRIMP	9,900	1,806	-	-	-	-
CLAMS:						
HARD, PUBLIC	589,800	98,483	-	-	1,665,300	537,488
HARD, PRIVATE.	-	-	-	-	132,000	48,575
RAZOR.	-	-	-	-	73,700	8,750
SOFT, PUBLIC	8,622,900	1,419,691	6,000	1,890	917,600	376,766
SOFT, PRIVATE.	-	-	-	-	800	369
SURF	-	-	-	-	10,600	2,617
TOTAL CLAMS.	9,212,700	1,518,174	6,000	1,890	2,800,000	974,565
MUSSELS, SEA	386,300	15,345	-	-	120,000	7,500
OYSTERS, MARKET:						
PUBLIC, SPRING	-	-	-	-	2,500	1,520
PUBLIC, FALL	-	-	-	-	13,000	5,750
PRIVATE, SPRING.	-	-	-	-	46,500	27,655
PRIVATE, FALL.	-	-	-	-	176,500	109,928
TOTAL OYSTERS.	-	-	-	-	238,500	144,853
PERIWINKLES AND COCKLES. . . .	10,300	3,186	-	-	41,500	1,860
SCALLOPS:						
BAY.	-	-	-	-	982,900	723,295
SEA.	509,000	179,845	-	-	13,468,900	4,987,202
SQUID.	20,100	395	-	-	2,436,100	53,227
SEA URCHINS.	79,500	2,291	-	-	-	-
IRISH MOSS	1,125,000	18,704	-	-	500,000	8,950
BLOODWORMS	401,800	297,021	100	61	-	-
SANDWORMS.	33,900	18,910	-	-	3,200	2,926
TOTAL.	31,795,600	8,772,855	422,000	168,311	25,921,500	8,408,218
GRAND TOTAL.	294,297,200	14,988,040	443,400	169,899	647,612,900	38,991,476

SPECIES	RHODE ISLAND		CONNECTICUT		TOTAL	
FISH	POUNDS	VALUE	POUNDS	VALUE	POUNDS	VALUE
ALEWIVES	133,700	$1,218	1,146,000	$16,699	5,066,600	$57,056
AMBERJACK.	-	-	-	-	100	9
ANGLERFISH	1,800	29	4,000	140	7,300	223
BLUEFISH	25,700	3,465	10,000	3,055	61,100	11,570
BUTTERFISH	1,279,400	86,263	704,300	71,369	2,704,500	215,709
CARP	-	-	42,200	3,438	42,200	3,438
CATFISH AND BULLHEADS.	-	-	7,800	395	7,800	395
COD.	1,707,300	78,586	590,700	60,121	58,794,800	3,377,250
CREVALLE	500	16	-	-	1,600	47
CUNNER	3,500	43	4,700	155	8,400	205
CUSK	-	-	-	-	3,620,200	132,824
DOLPHIN.	1,500	146	600	26	2,100	172
EELS:						
COMMON	16,100	2,369	20,500	3,637	118,900	21,305
CONGER	4,600	118	6,000	200	16,300	536
FLOUNDERS:						
GRAY SOLE.	9,500	820	6,200	545	8,157,100	545,220
LEMON SOLE	66,300	7,827	40,000	5,000	4,739,300	675,192
YELLOWTAIL	1,138,200	109,475	550,200	60,060	27,216,800	2,595,784
BLACKBACK.	1,301,900	68,683	3,909,200	201,894	20,443,100	1,866,203
DAB.	5,700	86	22,400	769	3,654,300	186,999
FLUKE.	469,600	75,158	371,700	70,401	2,628,000	483,428
UNCLASSIFIED	3,200	367	4,300	143	8,000	544
FRIGATE MACKEREL	43,100	1,888	-	-	44,400	1,943
GRAYFISH	-	-	5,300	153	625,200	5,718
HADDOCK.	69,600	3,407	12,100	1,000	133,764,600	9,170,910
HAKE:						
RED.	520,700	10,642	1,158,800	32,015	41,666,100	392,442
WHITE.	39,800	1,645	7,300	450	14,213,000	531,959
HALIBUT.	100	27	-	-	472,200	105,988
HERRING, SEA	4,256,700	70,707	2,668,600	54,000	168,413,200	2,676,545
HICKORY SHAD	400	43	-	-	400	43
KING WHITING OR "KINGFISH" . .	86,000	5,797	1,000	100	87,000	6,897
LAUNCE	1,500	45	-	-	15,100	634
MACKEREL	502,600	41,504	92,200	11,257	17,916,100	1,275,810

(CONTINUED ON NEXT PAGE)

NEW ENGLAND FISHERIES

CATCH BY STATES, 1949 - Continued

SPECIES	RHODE ISLAND		CONNECTICUT		TOTAL	
FISH - CONTINUED	POUNDS	VALUE	POUNDS	VALUE	POUNDS	VALUE
MENHADEN	38,100	$457	27,100	$247	12,566,000	$134,700
MINNOWS.	-	-	100,000	6,914	100,000	6,914
OCEAN PERCH (ROSEFISH)	-	-	-	-	236,986,700	9,819,265
OCEAN POUT	-	-	-	-	5,200	71
POLLOCK.	36,900	1,322	5,500	591	28,789,400	806,749
SALMON	-	-	-	-	1,300	623
SCUP OR PORGY.	2,416,800	73,497	1,761,900	91,517	4,644,600	180,838
SEA BASS	233,600	27,393	34,100	5,854	301,800	36,544
SEA ROBIN.	8,500	151	119,500	1,795	128,000	1,946
SEA TROUT OR WEAKFISH, GRAY. .	15,700	2,243	3,000	465	19,300	2,767
SHAD	3,200	131	470,700	73,191	489,900	74,297
SHARKS	11,700	601	37,400	520	358,600	12,136
SILVERSIDES.	-	-	1,500	25	1,500	25
SKATES	400	6	126,100	1,890	153,800	2,585
SMELT.	-	-	-	-	162,000	40,134
SPOT	300	13	-	-	300	13
STRIPED BASS	81,200	17,039	8,800	2,727	161,800	30,837
STURGEON	2,600	312	500	50	10,300	1,171
SUCKERS.	-	-	9,900	534	19,200	1,185
SUNFISH.	-	-	4,700	94	4,700	94
SWELLFISH.	1,900	221	9,300	265	11,200	486
SWORDFISH.	66,700	32,420	3,100	1,557	944,200	339,735
TAUTOG	27,300	1,152	24,200	2,209	101,000	6,225
TILEFISH	32,700	2,038	38,000	3,200	271,400	19,496
TUNA AND TUNALIKE FISHES:						
BLUEFIN.	17,900	1,928	35,400	3,730	2,673,900	196,457
BONITO	5,200	596	-	-	5,200	596
LITTLE	-	-	200	21	200	21
TOTAL TUNA	23,100	2,524	35,600	3,751	2,679,300	197,074
WHITE PERCH.	24,100	2,887	400	36	24,500	2,923
WHITING.	659,900	20,852	1,019,500	25,255	90,036,000	1,919,916
WOLFFISH	700	15	-	-	2,326,500	155,200
YELLOW PERCH	-	-	9,500	628	9,500	628
UNCLASSIFIED:						
FOR FOOD	15,200	304	547,500	25,320	7,167,000	146,759
OTHER.	11,609,900	84,379	4,433,800	90,000	28,442,800	290,684
TOTAL.	26,999,500	841,331	20,219,700	935,657	931,433,600	38,577,019
SHELLFISH. ETC.						
CRABS:						
BLUE, HARD	-	-	3,400	692	3,400	692
ROCK	108,000	3,250	-	-	2,607,800	121,922
TOTAL CRABS.	108,000	3,250	3,400	692	2,611,200	122,614
LOBSTERS, NORTHERN	354,600	155,859	388,300	169,058	23,994,500	8,593,523
SHRIMP	-	-	-	-	9,900	1,806
CLAMS:						
HARD, PUBLIC	2,135,100	469,343	13,300	5,897	4,403,500	1,111,211
HARD, PRIVATE.	-	-	-	-	132,000	48,575
OCEAN QUAHOG	62,800	5,232	-	-	62,800	5,232
RAZOR.	-	-	-	-	73,700	8,750
SOFT, PUBLIC	634,400	147,138	13,300	4,093	10,194,200	1,949,578
SOFT, PRIVATE.	-	-	-	-	800	369
SURF	7,300	1,824	-	-	17,900	4,441
TOTAL CLAMS.	2,839,600	623,537	26,600	9,990	14,884,900	3,128,156
CONCHS	-	-	41,500	4,379	41,500	4,379
MUSSELS, SEA	186,000	23,250	96,000	6,481	788,300	52,576
OYSTERS, MARKET:						
PUBLIC, SPRING	258,700	126,592	13,400	3,693	274,600	131,805
PUBLIC, FALL	152,100	75,728	48,700	18,799	213,800	100,277
PRIVATE, SPRING.	161,100	79,737	1,317,300	357,895	1,524,900	465,287
PRIVATE, FALL.	107,900	53,605	1,706,200	611,734	1,990,600	775,267
TOTAL OYSTERS.	679,800	335,662	3,085,600	992,121	4,003,900	1,472,636
PERIWINKLES AND COCKLES. . . .	88,000	14,600	-	-	139,800	19,646
SCALLOPS:						
BAY.	303,000	185,490	24,100	13,735	1,310,000	922,520
SEA.	-	-	2,100	1,000	13,980,000	5,168,047
SQUID.	1,869,500	46,937	307,300	24,210	4,635,000	124,769
SEA URCHINS.	-	-	-	-	79,500	2,291
IRISH MOSS	-	-	-	-	1,625,000	27,654
BLOODWORMS	-	-	-	-	401,900	297,082
SANDWORMS.	-	-	200	222	37,300	22,058
TOTAL.	6,428,500	1,388,585	3,975,100	1,221,888	68,542,700	19,959,857
GRAND TOTAL.	33,428,000	2,229,916	24,194,800	2,157,545	999,976,300	58,536,876

SUPPLEMENTARY REVIEW OF THE CATCH OF CERTAIN SHELLFISH, 1949

ITEM		MAINE		NEW HAMPSHIRE		MASSACHUSETTS	
		QUANTITY	VALUE	QUANTITY	VALUE	QUANTITY	VALUE
CRABS, ROCK.	NUMBER	2,203,200	$20,217	-	-	5,296,200	$98,455
CLAMS:							
HARD, PUBLIC	BUSHELS	53,618	98,483	-	-	151,391	537,488
HARD, PRIVATE.	DO	-	-	-	-	12,000	48,575
RAZOR.	DO	-	-	-	-	2,303	8,750
SOFT, PUBLIC	DO	574,860	1,419,691	.400	$1,890	70,585	376,766
SOFT, PRIVATE.	DO	-	-	-	-	62	369
SURF	DO	-	-	-	-	964	2,617
MUSSELS, SEA	DO	25,753	15,345	-	-	10,000	7,500
OYSTERS, MARKET:							
PUBLIC, SPRING	DO	-	-	-	-	384	1,520
PUBLIC, FALL	DO	-	-	-	-	2,000	5,750
PRIVATE, SPRING.	DO	-	-	-	-	7,154	27,655
PRIVATE, FALL.	DO	-	-	-	-	27,154	109,928
PERIWINKLES AND COCKLES. .	DO	572	3,186	-	-	2,306	1,860
SCALLOPS:							
BAY.	DO	-	-	-	-	167,150	723,295
SEA.	DO	84,833	179,845	-	-	2,244,817	4,987,202

ITEM		RHODE ISLAND		CONNECTICUT		TOTAL	
		QUANTITY	VALUE	QUANTITY	VALUE	QUANTITY	VALUE
CRABS:							
BLUE, HARD	NUMBER	-	-	13,600	$692	13,600	$692
ROCK	DO	324,000	$3,250	-	-	7,823,400	121,922
CLAMS:							
HARD, PUBLIC	BUSHELS	177,925	469,343	1,108	5,897	384,042	1,111,211
HARD, PRIVATE.	DO	-	-	-	-	12,000	48,575
OCEAN QUAHOG	DO	5,233	5,232	-	-	5,233	5,232
RAZOR.	DO	-	-	-	-	2,303	8,750
SOFT, PUBLIC	DO	31,720	147,138	665	4,093	678,230	1,949,578
SOFT, PRIVATE.	DO	-	-	-	-	62	369
SURF	DO	608	1,824	-	-	1,572	4,441
CONCHS	DO	-	-	2,075	4,379	2,075	4,379
MUSSELS, SEA	DO	15,500	23,250	9,600	6,481	60,853	52,576
OYSTERS, MARKET:							
PUBLIC, SPRING	DO	36,957	126,592	1,740	3,693	39,081	131,805
PUBLIC, FALL	DO	21,729	75,728	18,799		30,054	100,277
PRIVATE, SPRING.	DO	23,014	79,737	171,078	357,895	201,246	465,287
PRIVATE, FALL.	DO	15,414	53,605	221,584	611,734	264,152	775,267
PERIWINKLES AND COCKLES. .	DO	4,889	14,600	-	-	7,767	19,646
SCALLOPS:							
BAY.	DO	50,500	185,490	3,887	13,735	221,537	922,520
SEA.	DO	-	-	350	1,000	2,330,000	5,168,047

NOTE:--BUSHELS REPRESENT U.S. STANDARD BUSHEL OF 2,150.4 CUBIC INCHES CAPACITY

AVERAGE WEIGHTS OF CERTAIN SHELLFISH, 1949

ITEM		MAINE	NEW HAMPSHIRE	MASSACHUSETTS	RHODE ISLAND	CONNECTICUT
		QUANTITY	QUANTITY	QUANTITY	QUANTITY	QUANTITY
CRABS:						
BLUE, HARD	NUMBER PER POUND	-	-	-	-	4.00
ROCK	DO	3.00	-	3.00	3.00	-
CLAMS:	LBS. MEATS PER					
HARD, PUBLIC	U.S. STANDARD BUSHEL	11.00	-	11.00	12.00	12.00
HARD, PRIVATE. . . .	DO	-	-	11.00	-	-
OCEAN QUAHOG	DO	-	-	-	12.00	-
RAZOR.	DO	-	-	32.00	-	-
SOFT, PUBLIC	DO	15.00	15.00	13.00	20.00	20.00
SOFT, PRIVATE. . . .	DO	-	-	13.00	-	-
SURF	DO	-	-	11.00	12.00	-
CONCHS	DO	-	-	-	-	20.00
MUSSELS, SEA	DO	15.00	-	12.00	12.00	10.00
OYSTERS, MARKET:						
PUBLIC, SPRING . . .	DO	-	-	6.50	7.00	7.70
PUBLIC, FALL	DO	-	-	6.50	7.00	7.70
PRIVATE, SPRING. . .	DO	-	-	6.50	7.00	7.70
PRIVATE, FALL. . . .	DO	-	-	6.50	7.00	7.70
PERIWINKLES AND COCKLES	DO	18.00	-	18.00	18.00	-
SCALLOPS:						
BAY.	DO	-	-	5.88	6.00	6.20
SEA.	DO	6.00	-	6.00	-	6.00

NOTE:--BUSHELS REPRESENT U.S. STANDARD BUSHEL OF 2,150.4 CUBIC INCHES CAPACITY.

MANUFACTURED FISHERY PRODUCTS, VARIOUS YEARS 1/

ITEM	YEAR	UNIT	MAINE QUANTITY	VALUE	MASSACHUSETTS, RHODE ISLAND, CONNECTICUT AND NEW HAMPSHIRE QUANTITY	VALUE
BY MANUFACTURING ESTABLISHMENTS:						
ALEWIVES:						
SALTED, ROUND.	1940	POUNDS	839,400	$13,539	60,000	$2,400
SMOKED, WHOLE AND FILLETS.	1940	DO	18,500	515	300	37
BUTTERFISH, SMOKED	1940	DO	-	-	3,750	613
CARP, SMOKED	1940	DO	-	-	1,250	375
CHUBS, SMOKED.	1940	DO	-	-	10,000	3,500
CISCO, SMOKED.	1940	DO	-	-	50,000	13,500
COD:						
FRESH FILLETS.	1949	DO	226,445	42,200	3,656,543	922,951
FROZEN FILLETS	1949	DO	335,578	75,750	4,901,683	1,101,836
SALTED:						
GREEN 2/	1940	DO	374,802	15,685	-	-
DRY.	1940	DO	12,615	595	111,600	5,997
BONELESS AND ABSOLUTELY						
BONELESS	1940	DO	43,556	4,304	6,861,715	1,006,386
SMOKED:						
WHOLE.	1940	DO	73,500	3,140	-	-
FILLETS.	1940	DO	33,480	4,372	418,100	46,484
BONELESS	1940	DO	50,000	7,500	-	-
OIL, LIVER	1949	GALLONS	86,025	136,580	144,374	278,848
CUSK:						
FRESH FILLETS.	1949	POUNDS	164,999	38,820	323,989	76,854
FROZEN FILLETS	1949	DO	-	-	125,280	24,960
SALTED:						
GREEN 2/	1940	DO	5,800	157	-	-
DRY.	1940	DO	9,115	455	-	-
WHOLE.	1940	DO	-	-	15,700	3,467
BONELESS	1940	DO	-	-	1,600	276
SMOKED:						
WHOLE.	1940	DO	500	20	-	-
FILLETS.	1940	DO	8,740	874	393,859	31,263
EELS, SMOKED	1940	DO	-	-	2,000	300
FLOUNDERS:						
FRESH FILLETS.	1949	DO	102,073	30,585	9,300,824	3,151,479
FROZEN FILLETS	1949	DO	11,444	343	7,283,259	2,158,923
SMOKED	1940	DO	-	-	1,800	290
HADDOCK:						
FRESH FILLETS.	1949	DO	180,000	49,250	17,553,771	5,197,718
FROZEN FILLETS	1949	DO	821,418	219,589	21,376,193	5,683,016
SALTED:						
GREEN 2/	1940	DO	2,000	100	-	-
DRY.	1940	DO	12,615	595	100	7
WHOLE.	1940	DO	-	-	500	28
BONELESS AND ABSOLUTELY						
BONELESS	1940	DO	-	-	60,900	6,413
SMOKED:						
FINNAN HADDIE.	1940	DO	52,400	5,963	375,311	40,329
WHOLE.	1940	DO	-	-	500	68
FILLETS.	1940	DO	-	-	122,925	18,233
HAKE:						
FRESH FILLETS.	1949	DO	95,000	24,500	616,913	115,975
FROZEN FILLETS	1949	DO	36,900	4,461	522,730	69,978
SALTED:						
GREEN 2/	1940	DO	902,015	30,271	-	-
DRY.	1940	DO	9,115	455	384,050	10,933
WHOLE.	1940	DO	-	-	110,500	4,044
BONELESS AND ABSOLUTELY						
BONELESS	1940	DO	100,645	14,041	859,700	66,677
SMOKED FILLETS	1940	DO	39,400	1,227	-	-
HALIBUT, SMOKED.	1940	DO	-	-	1,500	468
HERRING, SEA:						
CANNED, SARDINES	1949	STANDARD CASES	2,977,817	20,720,506	96,706	331,169
SALTED:						
BRINE	1940	POUNDS	385,200	11,714	36,500	3,710
PICKLED IN VINEGAR	1940	DO	1,245,425	45,549	650,000	45,250
SMOKED:						
BLOATERS:						
HARD	1940	DO	93,942	4,703	39,200	824
SOFT	1940	DO	8,066	403	-	-
WHOLE.	1940	DO	4,500	125	-	-
KIPPERED	1940	DO	-	-	424,000	40,138
LENGTHWISE	1940	DO	68,517	3,862	-	-
MEDIUM SCALE	1940	DO	169,199	9,596	2,121	313
BONELESS	1940	DO	2,018,330	210,540	-	-
MEAL	1949	TONS	3,049	463,737	-	-
OIL.	1949	GALLONS	122,448	61,574	-	-

SEE FOOTNOTES AT END OF TABLE   (CONTINUED ON NEXT PAGE)

MANUFACTURED FISHERY PRODUCTS, VARIOUS YEARS 1/ - CONTINUED

ITEM	YEAR	UNIT	MAINE		MASSACHUSETTS, RHODE ISLAND, CONNECTICUT AND NEW HAMPSHIRE	
			QUANTITY	VALUE	QUANTITY	VALUE
BY MANUFACTURING ESTABLISHMENTS-CONTINUED:						
MACKEREL:						
FRESH FILLETS.	1949	POUNDS	-	-	280,631	$61,002
FROZEN FILLETS	1949	DO	-	-	549,457	141,156
CANNED	1949	STANDARD CASES	19,021	$127,420	95,142	815,625
SALTED:						
DRY FILLETS.	1940	POUNDS	-	-	1,660,000	108,300
SPLIT.	1940	DO	-	-	498,100	27,369
BRINE:						
WHOLE.	1940	DO	-	-	749,400	61,666
FILLETS.	1940	DO	-	-	657,400	71,335
SMOKED	1940	DO	-	-	26,100	3,960
OCEAN PERCH (ROSEFISH):						
FRESH FILLETS.	1949	DO	3,020	604	636,041	138,352
FROZEN FILLETS	1949	DO	15,825,064	3,222,757	56,728,393	11,972,961
POLLOCK: .						
FRESH FILLETS.	1949	DO	507,036	76,135	2,197,387	345,743
FROZEN FILLETS	1949	DO	759,947	91,758	5,628,526	751,959
SALTED:						
GREEN 2/	1940	DO	184,772	5,605	-	-
DRY.	1940	DO	9,115	455	248,620	11,293
WHOLE.	1940	DO	-	-	4,600	321
SMOKED	1940	DO	40,000	960	-	-
SALMON:						
SMOKED:						
WHOLE.	1940	DO	-	-	75,900	26,588
FILLETS.	1940	DO	-	-	2,000	500
SHAD,.SMOKED	1940	DO	-	-	400	94
SPOONBILL CAT, SMOKED.	1940	DO	-	-	2,500	2,000
WHITEFISH, SMOKED.	1940	DO	-	-	45,000	18,131
WHITING:						
FRESH AND FROZEN FILLETS . .	1949	DO	37,430	4,831	1,133,583	201,606
FRESH AND FROZEN SPLIT "BUTTERFLY"	1949	DO	-	-	3,028,502	479,167
WOLFFISH:						
FRESH FILLETS.	1949	DO	-	-	52,266	16,006
FROZEN FILLETS	1949	DO	-	-	258,383	75,952
CLAMS:						
HARD, FRESH-SHUCKED.	1940	GALLONS	120,000	136,500	2,500	3,663
SOFT:						
FRESH-SHUCKED.	1940	DO	29,100	29,420	373,642	581,694
CANNED:						
WHOLE AND MINCED	1949	STANDARD CASES	155,129	1,469,711	-	-
CHOWDER, JUICE BROTH, AND NECTAR. . . . : . . .	1949	DO	169,389	993,469	(3)	(3)
CRABS, ROCK, MEAT, PACKAGED, FRESH-COOKED	1940	POUNDS	52,172	25,915	243,522	81,966
LOBSTER MEAT, PACKAGED, FRESH-COOKED	1940	DO	16,300	19,300	261,200	295,882
OYSTERS, FRESH-SHUCKED	1940	GALLONS	-	-	262,487	591,277
SCALLOPS, BAY, FRESH-SHUCKED .	1940	DO	-	-	5,400	17,850
UNCLASSIFIED PRODUCTS:						
PACKAGED FISH.	1949	POUNDS	4/27,585	4/8,214	5/21,698	5/10,723
CANNED:						
ANIMAL FOOD.	1949	STANDARD CASES	(6)	(6)	464,931	1,660,883
FISH CAKES	1949	DO	37,375	350,031	(6)	(6)
FISH ROE	1949	DO	-	-	21,066	223,577
OTHER CANNED	1949	DO	7/529,053	7/3,019,479	8/210,799	8/2,371,701
TONGUES AND SOUNDS PICKLED . .	1940	POUNDS	-	-	17,900	1,613
BUTTONS, MARINE PEARL-SHELL. .	1949	GROSS	-	-	1,118,060	1,786,712
MEAL	1949	TONS	9/6,842	9/947,313	10/27,210	10/4,580,727
OILS, BODY AND LIVER	1949	GALLONS	11/75,926	11/31,343	12/454,675	12/395,509
MISCELLANEOUS.	1949	-	-	13/1,848,370	-	14/ 2,721,151
TOTAL			-	34,667,845	-	51,122,054

1/ DATA ON THE PRODUCTION OF THE DIFFERENT PRODUCTS ARE FOR THE YEARS INDICATED.
2/ THIS ITEM IS USUALLY AN INTERMEDIATE PRODUCT, AND ALTHOUGH INCLUDED IN THE TOTAL, MAY BE SHOWN IN ITS FINAL STAGE OF PROCESSING IN THIS OR ANOTHER SECTION.
3/ THIS ITEM HAS BEEN INCLUDED UNDER "UNCLASSIFIED PRODUCTS."
4/ INCLUDES FRESH AND FROZEN WOLFFISH AND UNCLASSIFIED FILLETS.
5/ INCLUDES FRESH AND FROZEN OCEAN POUT AND UNCLASSIFIED FILLETS, AND SWORDFISH STEAKS.
6/ THIS ITEM HAS BEEN INCLUDED WITH "OTHER CANNED".
7/ INCLUDES CANNED ANIMAL FOOD, TUNA, FISH CHOWDER, FISH FLAKES, CLAM CAKES, CRAB MEAT, SEA MUSSELS, AND LOBSTER NEWBURG.
8/ INCLUDES CANNED TUNA; FINNAN HADDIE, SMOKED SALMON; HADDOCK; SALMON AND CHEESE; FISH CHOWDER; SPREADS OF SALMON, HALIBUT, AND ANCHOVY; FISH CAKES; FISH FLAKES; SCALLOPS; CLAM LOAF; AND CLAM CHOWDER.
9/ INCLUDES GROUNDFISH (WHITE FISH) MEAL, COD-LIVER PRESS CAKE , FISH POMACE; AND UNCLASSIFIED SCRAP AND MEAL.
10/ INCLUDES GROUNDFISH (WHITE FISH), OCEAN PERCH (ROSEFISH) AND UNCLASSIFIED SCRAP AND MEAL.
11/ INCLUDES UNCLASSIFIED BODY AND LIVER OILS.
12/ INCLUDES OCEAN PERCH (ROSEFISH) AND UNCLASSIFIED BODY OILS, AND HALIBUT, SWORDFISH, AND TUNA LIVER OILS.
13/ INCLUDES GLUE, CONDENSED FISH SOLUBLES, ALGIN, IRISH MOSS EXTRACT, AND PEARL ESSENCE.
14/ INCLUDES GLUE, CONDENSED FISH SOLUBLES, SEAWEED EXTRACTIVES, AND ISINGLASS.
NOTE:—SOME OF THE ABOVE PRODUCTS MAY HAVE BEEN IMPORTED FROM ANOTHER STATE OR A FOREIGN COUNTRY; THEREFORE THEY CANNOT BE CORRELATED DIRECTLY WITH THE CATCH WITHIN THE STATE.

SUMMARY OF MANUFACTURED FISHERY PRODUCTS, VARIOUS YEARS

SUMMARY OF STATES STATE				VALUE
MAINE.				$34,667,845
MASSACHUSETTS.				48,198,996
RHODE ISLAND AND NEW HAMPSHIRE.				792,839
CONNECTICUT.				2,130,219
TOTAL				85,789,899

SUMMARY OF PRODUCTS ITEM	YEAR	UNIT	QUANTITY	VALUE
PACKAGED FISH	1949	POUNDS	155,310,011	$36,588,124
CANNED FISH AND SHELLFISH	1949	STANDARD CASES	4,776,428	32,083,571
FISHERY BYPRODUCTS.	1949	-		13,251,864
PACKAGED SHELLFISH.	1940	POUNDS	7,513,073	1,783,467
SALTED, DRIED AND PICKLED	1940	DO	17,125,075	1,581,065
SMOKED AND KIPPERED	1940	DO	4,677,590	501,808
TOTAL	-	-	-	85,789,899

FILLETING PLANT

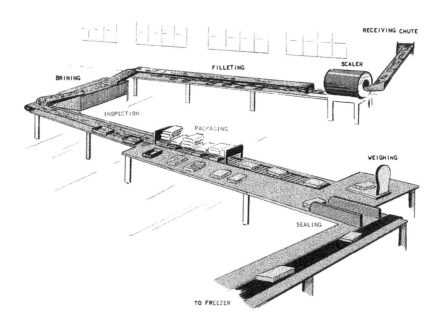

MAINE

OPERATING UNITS BY GEAR, 1949

ITEM	PURSE SEINES		HAUL SEINES, COMMON	STOP SEINES	GILL NETS, DRIFT	LINES	
	MACKEREL	OTHER				HAND	TRAWL OR TROT WITH HOOKS
	NUMBER	NUMBER	NUMBER	NUMBER	NUMBER	NUMBER	NUMBER
FISHERMEN:							
ON VESSELS	51	-	-	-	44	14	22
ON BOATS AND SHORE:							
REGULAR.	-	144	8	357	43	262	318
CASUAL	-	52	-	121	-	402	42
TOTAL.	51	196	8	478	87	678	382
VESSELS, MOTOR	15	-	-	-	8	11	5
NET TONNAGE.	136	-	-	-	133	74	80
BOATS:							
MOTOR.	-	55	3	136	13	225	225
OTHER.	-	55	3	132	1	67	-
ACCESSORY BOATS. . . .	15	-	-	-	-	-	-
APPARATUS:							
NUMBER	15	55	3	136	354	1,717	12,503
LENGTH, YARDS. . . .	5,150	16,780	300	41,650	-	-	-
SQUARE YARDS	-	-	-	-	108,992	-	-
HOOKS.	-	-	-	-	-	3,300	525,832

ITEM	FLOATING TRAPS	WEIRS	FYKE NETS, FISH	DIP NETS, COMMON	BAG NETS	LIFT NETS	OTTER TRAWLS, FISH	TRAPS, BOX
	NUMBER	NUMBER	NUMBER	NUMBER	NUMBER	NUMBER	NUMBER	NUMBER
FISHERMEN:								
ON VESSELS	-	-	-	-	-	-	335	-
ON BOATS AND SHORE:								
REGULAR.	41	323	4	26	18	-	138	-
CASUAL	8	163	-	124	26	45	-	12
TOTAL.	49	486	4	150	44	45	473	12
VESSELS, MOTOR	-	-	-	-	-	-	55	-
NET TONNAGE.	-	-	-	-	-	-	1,817	-
BOATS:								
MOTOR.	22	201	2	-	-	-	46	-
OTHER.	7	199	2	11	-	-	-	-
APPARATUS:								
NUMBER	24	217	15	150	40	45	101	7
YARDS AT MOUTH . . .	-	-	-	-	-	-	2,686	-

ITEM	POTS, LOBSTER	HARPOONS	DREDGES, SCALLOP	RAKES, OTHER THAN FOR OYSTERS	HOES	BY HAND, OTHER THAN FOR OYSTERS	TOTAL, EXCLUSIVE OF DUPLICATION
	NUMBER	NUMBER	NUMBER	NUMBER	NUMBER	NUMBER	NUMBER
FISHERMEN:							
ON VESSELS	51	3	16	-	-	-	477
ON BOATS AND SHORE:							
REGULAR.	4,339	60	77	67	816	9	5,614
CASUAL	1,012	82	7	75	1,052	26	3,199
TOTAL.	5,402	145	100	142	1,868	35	9,290
VESSELS, MOTOR	46	3	3	-	-	-	111
NET TONNAGE.	320	21	38	-	-	-	2,307
BOATS:							
MOTOR.	4,716	86	54	37	260	5	5,200
OTHER.	555	1	-	52	687	13	1,770
ACCESSORY BOATS. . . .	-	3	-	-	-	-	18
APPARATUS:							
NUMBER	461,675	89	57	142	1,868	-	-
YARDS AT MOUTH . . .	-	-	59	-	-	-	-

LOBSTER FISHING

NEW ENGLAND FISHERIES

MAINE: CATCH BY GEAR, 1949

SPECIES	PURSE SEINES POUNDS	VALUE	HAUL SEINES POUNDS	VALUE	STOP SEINES POUNDS	VALUE	GILL NETS POUNDS	VALUE
ALEWIVES	-	-	-	-	14,700	$194	-	-
BUTTERFISH	-	-	-	-	-	-	200	$10
COD	-	-	-	-	-	-	1,598,800	124,716
CUSK	-	-	-	-	-	-	29,500	897
FLOUNDERS:								
BLACKBACK	-	-	-	-	-	-	600	35
DAB	-	-	-	-	-	-	200	5
HADDOCK	-	-	-	-	-	-	186,400	16,077
HAKE:								
RED	-	-	-	-	-	-	154,200	8,693
WHITE	-	-	-	-	-	-	1,466,800	56,167
HALIBUT	-	-	-	-	-	-	1,000	238
HERRING, SEA	19,235,000	$309,700	-	-	65,515,500	1,037,798	-	-
MACKEREL	2,051,700	96,284	-	-	61,900	3,097	352,200	25,055
MENHADEN	5,019,000	44,942	-	-	-	-	-	-
OCEAN PERCH (ROSEFISH)	-	-	-	-	-	-	100	2
POLLOCK	155,700	1,786	-	-	-	-	3,162,900	89,947
SHAD	-	-	-	-	-	-	4,500	193
SHARKS	200	7	-	-	-	-	59,400	6,171
SMELT	-	-	7,100	$1,336	-	-	16,500	3,858
STURGEON	-	-	-	-	-	-	500	69
TUNA, BLUEFIN	1,000	101	-	-	-	-	700	102
WHITING	-	-	-	-	-	-	23,500	240
WOLFFISH	-	-	-	-	-	-	100	4
UNCLASSIFIED, FOR FOOD	-	-	-	-	-	-	16,800	318
SHRIMP	-	-	-	-	-	-	200	3
SQUID	500	10	-	-	-	-	7,500	153
TOTAL	26,463,100	452,830	7,100	1,336	65,592,100	1,041,089	7,082,600	332,953

SPECIES	LINES HAND POUNDS	VALUE	TRAWL OR TROT WITH HOOKS POUNDS	VALUE	FLOATING TRAPS POUNDS	VALUE	WEIRS POUNDS	VALUE
ALEWIVES	-	-	-	-	-	-	735,000	$6,350
COD	759,100	$25,653	1,392,600	$61,507	-	-	-	-
CUSK	12,300	321	659,600	31,033	-	-	-	-
FLOUNDERS:								
GRAY SOLE	-	-	800	29	200	$9	-	-
BLACKBACK	-	-	100	5	-	-	-	-
DAB	-	-	8,000	168	-	-	-	-
GRAYFISH	-	-	567,000	4,610	-	-	18,000	180
HADDOCK	40,000	2,322	484,100	33,803	-	-	-	-
HAKE:								
RED	-	-	11,500	439	-	-	-	-
WHITE	101,800	2,466	2,702,300	97,428	100	7	-	-
HALIBUT	8,700	2,094	15,800	4,018	-	-	-	-
HERRING, SEA	-	-	-	-	134,700	2,156	65,008,800	1,058,729
MACKEREL	6,900	517	-	-	334,500	16,427	544,700	16,189
MENHADEN	-	-	-	-	6,500	65	1,800	33
OCEAN PERCH (ROSEFISH)	-	-	400	11	-	-	-	-
POLLOCK	142,500	4,052	138,000	3,508	4,600	42	23,500	235
SALMON	-	-	-	-	1,000	507	-	-
SHARKS	600	67	7,400	428	-	-	200	8
SMELT	44,100	12,538	-	-	-	-	8,400	1,667
TUNA, BLUEFIN	13,600	1,142	-	-	-	-	-	-
WHITING	-	-	1,200	20	-	-	-	-
WOLFFISH	2,000	49	11,000	261	-	-	-	-
UNCLASSIFIED, FOR FOOD	-	-	341,000	3,156	-	-	9,100	195
SQUID	-	-	-	-	3,000	37	-	-
TOTAL	1,131,600	51,221	6,340,800	240,424	484,600	19,250	66,349,500	1,083,586

SPECIES	FYKE NETS POUNDS	VALUE	DIP NETS POUNDS	VALUE	BAG NETS POUNDS	VALUE	LIFT NETS POUNDS	VALUE
ALEWIVES	-	-	2,531,000	$24,613	-	-	-	-
EELS, COMMON	2,200	$550	-	-	-	-	-	-
POLLOCK	-	-	-	-	-	-	422,300	$4,636
SMELT	-	-	20,900	3,131	63,600	$17,473	-	-
SUCKERS	9,300	651	-	-	-	-	-	-
SEA URCHINS	-	-	79,500	2,291	-	-	-	-
TOTAL	11,500	1,201	2,631,400	30,035	63,600	17,473	422,300	4,636

(CONTINUED ON NEXT PAGE)

MAINE: CATCH BY GEAR, 1949 - Continued

SPECIES	OTTER TRAWLS		TRAPS, BOX		POTS		HARPOONS	
	POUNDS	VALUE	POUNDS	VALUE	POUNDS	VALUE	POUNDS	VALUE
COD.	2,324,900	$104,042	-	-	-	-	-	-
CUSK	657,200	18,645	-	-	-	-	-	-
EELS, COMMON	-	-	39,600	$8,122	-	-	-	-
FLOUNDERS:								
GRAY SOLE.	760,000	34,810	-	-	-	-	-	-
LEMON SOLE	1,100	73	-	-	-	-	-	-
YELLOWTAIL	119,800	8,743	-	-	-	-	-	-
BLACKBACK.	832,100	39,734	-	-	-	-	-	-
DAB.	577,500	15,604	-	-	-	-	-	-
GRAYFISH	2,000	12	-	-	-	-	-	-
HADDOCK.	6,474,300	416,563	-	-	-	-	-	-
HAKE:								
RED.	20,500	630	-	-	-	-	-	-
WHITE.	1,441,800	34,542	-	-	-	-	-	-
HALIBUT.	25,800	5,935	-	-	-	-	-	-
OCEAN PERCH (ROSEFISH)	55,502,100	2,014,058	-	-	-	-	-	-
POLLOCK.	2,337,200	59,238	-	-	-	-	-	-
SHAD	400	13	-	-	-	-	-	-
SHARKS	3,500	482	-	-	-	-	100	$10
TUNA, BLUEFIN.	100	6	-	-	-	-	144,200	13,783
WHITING.	12,555,500	146,931	-	-	-	-	-	-
WOLFFISH	177,700	3,981	-	-	-	-	-	-
UNCLASSIFIED, FOR FOOD	2,023,800	15,883	-	-	-	-	-	-
CRABS, ROCK.	-	-	-	-	734,400	$20,217	-	-
LOBSTERS, NORTHERN . .	2,700	1,075	-	-	19,270,000	6,695,886	-	-
SHRIMP	9,700	1,803	-	-	-	-	-	-
TOTAL	85,849,700	2,922,803	39,600	8,122	20,004,400	6,716,103	144,300	13,793

SPECIES	DREDGES		RAKES		HOES		BY HAND	
	POUNDS	VALUE	POUNDS	VALUE	POUNDS	VALUE	POUNDS	VALUE
CLAMS:								
SOFT, PUBLIC	-	-	-	-	8,622,900	$1,419,691	-	-
HARD, PUBLIC	-	-	-	-	589,800	98,483	-	-
MUSSELS, SEA	-	-	-	-	386,300	15,345	-	-
PERIWINKLES AND COCKLES	-	-	-	-	-	-	10,300	$3,186
SCALLOPS, SEA.	509,000	$179,845	-	-	-	-	-	-
IRISH MOSS	-	-	1,125,000	$18,704	-	-	-	-
BLOODWORMS	-	-	-	-	401,800	297,021	-	-
SANDWORMS	-	-	-	-	33,900	18,910	-	-
TOTAL	509,000	179,845	1,125,000	18,704	10,034,700	1,849,450	10,300	3,186

NEW HAMPSHIRE

OPERATING UNITS BY GEAR, 1949

ITEM	LINES		DIP NETS, COMMON	POTS, LOBSTER	HOES	TOTAL, EXCLUSIVE OF DUPLICATION
	HAND	TRAWL OR TROT WITH HOOKS				
	NUMBER	NUMBER	NUMBER	NUMBER	NUMBER	NUMBER
FISHERMEN ON BOATS AND SHORE:						
REGULAR.	1	2	-	131	3	134
CASUAL	9	-	8	63	32	112
TOTAL.	10	2	8	194	35	246
BOATS:						
MOTOR.	1	2	-	101	-	101
OTHER.	-	-	-	63	4	67
APPARATUS:						
NUMBER	37	16	8	11,750	35	-
HOOKS.	74	1,200	-	-	-	-

NEW ENGLAND FISHERIES

NEW HAMPSHIRE: CATCH BY GEAR, 1949

SPECIES	LINES				DIP NETS		POTS		HOES	
	HAND		TRAWL OR TROT WITH HOOKS							
	POUNDS	VALUE	POUNDS	VALUE	POUNDS	VALUE	POUNDS	VALUE	POUNDS	VALUE
ALEWIVES.	-	-	-	-	4,500	$45	-	-	-	-
COD	1,600	$112	1,100	$672	-	-	-	-	-	-
CUSK.	-	-	400	22	-	-	-	-	-	-
HADDOCK	100	12	1,300	130	-	-	-	-	-	-
HAKE, WHITE	1,000	43	10,500	430	-	-	-	-	-	-
POLLOCK	-	-	300	10	-	-	-	-	-	-
SMELT	500	110	-	-	-	-	-	-	-	-
WOLFFISH.	-	-	100	2	-	-	-	-	-	-
LOBSTERS, NORTHERN.	-	-	-	-	-	-	415,900	$166,360	-	-
CLAMS, SOFT, PUBLIC	-	-	-	-	-	-	-	-	6,000	$1,890
BLOODWORMS.	-	-	-	-	-	-	-	-	100	61
TOTAL.	3,200	277	13,700	1,266	4,500	45	415,900	166,360	6,100	1,951

MASSACHUSETTS

OPERATING UNITS BY GEAR, 1949

ITEM	PURSE SEINES		HAUL SEINES, COMMON	GILL NETS		LINES	
	MACKEREL	OTHER		ANCHOR	DRIFT	HAND	TRAWL OR TROT WITH HOOKS
	NUMBER	NUMBER	NUMBER	NUMBER	NUMBER	NUMBER	NUMBER
FISHERMEN:							
ON VESSELS.	401	-	-	42	18	17	122
ON BOATS AND SHORE:							
REGULAR	15	4	5	10	50	157	227
CASUAL.	5	-	11	12	31	453	81
TOTAL	421	4	16	64	99	627	430
VESSELS, MOTOR. . . .	31	-	-	7	3	4	14
NET TONNAGE	1,134	-	-	102	37	38	239
BOATS:							
MOTOR	4	-	-	11	35	261	114
OTHER	7	-	6	-	-	60	-
ACCESSORY BOATS . . .	62	-	-	-	-	-	12
APPARATUS:							
NUMBER.	35	1	5	318	545	757	11,435
LENGTH, YARDS . . .	17,120	39	285	-	-	-	-
SQUARE YARDS. . . .	-	-	-	162,133	259,667	-	-
HOOKS	-	-	-	-	-	895	635,450

ITEM	POUND NETS	FLOATING TRAPS	FYKE NETS, FISH	DIP NETS, COMMON	OTTER TRAWLS, FISH	POTS	
						CRAB	EEL
	NUMBER	NUMBER	NUMBER	NUMBER	NUMBER	NUMBER	NUMBER
FISHERMEN:							
ON VESSELS.	3	-	-	-	4,085	-	-
ON BOATS AND SHORE:							
REGULAR	115	41	-	56	72	16	5
CASUAL.	9	11	2	232	4	7	-
TOTAL	127	52	2	288	4,161	23	5
VESSELS, MOTOR. . . .	1	-	-	-	538	-	-
NET TONNAGE	5	-	-	-	23,041	-	-
BOATS:							
MOTOR	33	18	-	12	35	12	5
OTHER	42	25	1	242	-	4	-
ACCESSORY BOATS . . .	2	-	-	-	-	-	-
APPARATUS:							
NUMBER.	81	46	1	246	573	1,332	125
YARDS AT MOUTH. . .	-	-	-	-	15,574	-	-

(CONTINUED ON NEXT PAGE)

MASSACHUSETTS: OPERATING UNITS BY GEAR, 1949 - Continued

ITEM	POTS - CONT'D LOBSTER	HARPOONS	SPEARS	DREDGES CLAM	DREDGES OYSTER, COMMON	SCALLOP	TONGS OYSTER
	NUMBER	NUMBER	NUMBER	NUMBER	NUMBER	NUMBER	NUMBER
FISHERMEN:							
ON VESSELS.	-	340	-	-	-	897	-
ON BOATS AND SHORE:							
REGULAR	397	46	17	26	29	392	37
CASUAL.	1,240	7	-	22	-	2,238	-
TOTAL	1,637	393	17	48	29	3,527	37
VESSELS, MOTOR. . . .	-	53	-	-	-	110	-
NET TONNAGE	-	1,357	-	-	-	3,225	-
BOATS:							
MOTOR	1,042	26	-	24	14	1,172	-
OTHER	509	22	-	-	-	323	37
ACCESSORY BOATS . . .	-	110	-	-	-	-	-
APPARATUS:							
NUMBER.	98,309	79	17	24	15	4,342	37
YARDS AT MOUTH. . .	-	-	-	22	14	4,168	-

ITEM	TONGS - CONT'D, OTHER	RAKES, OTHER THAN FOR OYSTERS	FORKS	HOES	BY HAND, OTHER THAN FOR OYSTERS	TOTAL, EXCLUSIVE OF DUPLICATION
	NUMBER	NUMBER	NUMBER	NUMBER	NUMBER	NUMBER
FISHERMEN:						
ON VESSELS.	-	-	-	-	-	5,155
ON BOATS AND SHORE:						
REGULAR	153	368	32	253	87	1,707
CASUAL.	204	915	87	407	184	5,294
TOTAL	357	1,283	119	660	271	12,156
VESSELS, MOTOR. . . .	-	-	-	-	-	639
NET TONNAGE	-	-	-	-	-	26,032
BOATS:						
MOTOR	-	1	-	-	-	2,655
OTHER	357	848	12	19	-	2,040
ACCESSORY BOATS . . .	-	-	-	-	-	186
APPARATUS:						
NUMBER.	357	1,278	119	641	-	-

MASSACHUSETTS: CATCH BY GEAR, 1949

SPECIES	PURSE SEINES POUNDS	PURSE SEINES VALUE	HAUL SEINES POUNDS	HAUL SEINES VALUE	GILL NETS ANCHOR POUNDS	GILL NETS ANCHOR VALUE	GILL NETS DRIFT POUNDS	GILL NETS DRIFT VALUE
ALEWIVES.	252,900	$3,712	246,200	$4,158	-	-	-	-
BUTTERFISH.	1,200	86	-	-	-	-	-	-
COD	200	12	-	-	1,276,600	$89,502	-	-
CUSK.	-	-	-	-	7,000	243	-	-
FLOUNDERS:								
YELLOWTAIL.	-	-	-	-	200	15	-	-
BLACKBACK	-	-	-	-	1,900	127	-	-
DAB	-	-	-	-	800	36	-	-
HADDOCK	-	-	-	-	157,500	13,557	-	-
HAKE, WHITE	-	-	-	-	741,000	30,500	-	-
HALIBUT	-	-	-	-	100	25	-	-
HERRING, SEA.	364,200	4,651	-	-	-	-	8,900	$267
LAUNCE.	-	-	13,600	589	-	-	-	-
MACKEREL.	6,165,800	338,382	-	-	100	29	303,200	26,256
MENHADEN.	6,961,800	83,424	-	-	-	-	-	-
POLLOCK	100	3	-	-	2,820,400	64,813	-	-
SHAD.	-	-	-	-	3,300	162	1,500	13
SHARKS.	300	10	-	-	20,500	734	1,900	70
STURGEON.	-	-	-	-	200	34	-	-
TUNA, BLUEFIN	200	8	-	-	400	22	-	-
WHITING	-	-	-	-	900	24	113,000	1,833
UNCLASSIFIED, FOR FOOD.	-	-	-	-	100	8	-	-
TOTAL	13,746,700	430,288	259,800	4,747	5,031,000	199,831	428,500	28,439

(CONTINUED ON NEXT PAGE)

MASSACHUSETTS: CATCH BY GEAR, 1949 - Continued

SPECIES	LINES				POUND NETS		FLOATING TRAPS	
	HAND		TRAWL OR TROT WITH HOOKS					
	POUNDS	VALUE	POUNDS	VALUE	POUNDS	VALUE	POUNDS	VALUE
ALEWIVES	-	-	-	-	1,200	$16	-	-
AMBERJACK	-	-	-	-	100	9	-	-
ANGLERFISH	-	-	200	$5	200	41	200	$9
BLUEFISH	25,000	$5,000	-	-	-	-	91,500	2,412
BUTTERFISH	-	-	1,300	211	90,900	13,682	8,000	396
COD	379,400	22,727	6,503,900	408,872	13,700	511	-	-
CREVALLE	-	-	-	-	900	27	-	-
CUSK	2,400	57	1,004,800	33,818	-	-	-	-
EELS, CONGER	-	-	400	11	-	-	-	-
FLOUNDERS:								
GRAY SOLE	-	-	1,000	133	-	-	-	-
LEMON SOLE	400	19	105,200	11,337	-	-	-	-
YELLOWTAIL	-	-	93,800	7,778	-	-	-	-
BLACKBACK	5,600	231	46,900	3,610	2,800	230	-	-
DAB	200	7	4,200	299	-	-	-	-
FLUKE	-	-	-	-	4,400	661	-	-
FRIGATE MACKEREL	-	-	-	-	1,300	55	-	-
GRAYFISH	-	-	-	-	32,900	763	-	-
HADDOCK	28,500	1,720	4,623,700	354,120	-	-	-	-
HAKE:								
RED	-	-	1,200	79	-	-	-	-
WHITE	1,100	31	2,151,200	102,874	3,500	84	-	-
HALIBUT	500	114	101,900	32,536	-	-	-	-
HERRING, SEA	-	-	-	-	1,364,000	31,172	42,800	523
MACKEREL	-	-	-	-	5,674,400	580,957	1,540,800	80,755
MENHADEN	-	-	-	-	458,400	4,977	34,100	324
OCEAN PERCH (ROSEFISH)	-	-	6,500	487	-	-	-	-
POLLOCK	118,700	3,263	450,000	14,965	39,900	927	92,000	864
SALMON	-	-	-	-	-	-	300	116
SCUP OR PORGY	8,700	278	-	-	28,600	1,060	-	-
SEA BASS	1,100	99	-	-	2,500	248	-	-
SEA TROUT OR WEAKFISH:								
GRAY	-	-	-	-	600	59	-	-
SHAD	-	-	200	12	6,000	574	-	-
SHARKS	2,000	80	118,500	810	5,500	440	-	-
SKATES	-	-	21,100	536	-	-	-	-
STRIPED BASS	56,200	8,782	-	-	15,400	2,261	200	28
STURGEON	-	-	-	-	400	43	-	-
TAUTOG	37,400	2,163	-	-	2,800	203	-	-
TILEFISH	-	-	2,000	207	-	-	-	-
TUNA, BLUEFIN	1,393,000	85,913	-	-	1,037,700	87,053	7,000	503
WHITING	-	-	10,800	36	356,500	7,019	133,000	2,446
WOLFFISH	200	10	204,600	14,265	-	-	-	-
UNCLASSIFIED:								
FOR FOOD	-	-	5,300	216	78,200	1,210	100	8
OTHER	-	-	-	-	90,100	715	57,500	535
PERIWINKLES AND COCKLES	-	-	200	9	-	-	-	-
SQUID	-	-	-	-	2,009,100	43,509	322,900	5,712
TOTAL	2,060,400	130,494	15,458,900	987,226	11,322,000	778,506	2,330,400	94,632

SPECIES	FYKE NETS		DIP NETS		OTTER TRAWLS		POTS	
	POUNDS	VALUE	POUNDS	VALUE	POUNDS	VALUE	POUNDS	VALUE
ALEWIVES	1,400	$51	-	-	-	-	-	-
ANGLERFISH	-	-	-	-	1,300	$49	-	-
BUTTERFISH	-	-	-	-	535,700	41,676	-	-
COD	-	-	-	-	42,230,700	2,399,548	-	-
CREVALLE	-	-	-	-	200	4	-	-
CUNNER	-	-	-	-	200	7	-	-
CUSK	-	-	-	-	1,247,000	47,788	-	-
EELS:								
COMMON	700	57	-	-	-	-	29,000	$4,550
CONGER	-	-	-	-	5,300	207	-	-
FLOUNDERS:								
GRAY SOLE	-	-	-	-	7,379,300	508,871	-	-
LEMON SOLE	-	-	-	-	4,517,000	649,882	-	-
YELLOWTAIL	-	-	-	-	25,309,700	2,409,415	-	-
BLACKBACK	200	17	-	-	14,306,000	1,548,529	-	-
DAB	-	-	-	-	3,035,100	172,017	-	-
FLUKE	-	-	-	-	1,782,300	337,208	-	-
UNCLASSIFIED	-	-	-	-	500	34	-	-
HADDOCK	-	-	-	-	121,661,500	8,326,949	-	-
HAKE:								
RED	-	-	-	-	39,799,200	339,944	-	-
WHITE	-	-	-	-	5,544,700	205,291	-	-
HALIBUT	-	-	-	-	318,200	60,979	-	-
HERRING, SEA	-	-	6,700,800	$58,851	3,113,200	47,991	-	-

(CONTINUED ON NEXT PAGE)

MASSACHUSETTS: CATCH BY GEAR, 1949 - Continued

SPECIES	FYKE NETS POUNDS	FYKE NETS VALUE	DIP NETS POUNDS	DIP NETS VALUE	OTTER TRAWLS POUNDS	OTTER TRAWLS VALUE	POTS POUNDS	POTS VALUE
MACKEREL	-	-	-	-	285,100	$39,100	-	-
MENHADEN	-	-	-	-	19,200	231	-	-
OCEAN PERCH (ROSEFISH)	-	-	-	-	181,477,600	7,804,708	-	-
OCEAN POUT	-	-	-	-	5,200	71	-	-
POLLOCK	-	-	-	-	18,838,800	556,545	-	-
SCUP OR PORGY	-	-	-	-	428,600	14,486	-	-
SEA BASS	-	-	-	-	30,500	2,950	-	-
SHAD	-	-	-	-	100	8	-	-
SHARKS	-	-	-	-	89,300	1,694	-	-
SKATES	-	-	-	-	4,200	153	-	-
SMELT	-	-	-	-	900	21	-	-
STURGEON	-	-	-	-	6,100	663	-	-
SWORDFISH	-	-	-	-	600	314	-	-
TAUTOG	-	-	-	-	9,300	498	-	-
TILEFISH	-	-	-	-	198,700	14,051	-	-
TUNA, BLUEFIN	-	-	-	-	13,300	1,071	-	-
WHITING	-	-	-	-	75,162,200	1,715,260	-	-
WOLFFISH	-	-	-	-	1,930,000	136,611	-	-
UNCLASSIFIED:								
FOR FOOD	-	-	-	-	4,138,900	100,318	-	-
OTHER	-	-	-	-	12,251,500	115,055	-	-
CRABS, ROCK	-	-	-	-	-	-	1,765,400	$98,455
LOBSTERS, NORTHERN	-	-	-	-	1,500	288	3,561,500	1,405,097
PERIWINKLES AND COCKLES	-	-	-	-	41,300	1,851	-	-
SCALLOPS:								
BAY	-	-	54,800	$42,459	-	-	-	-
SEA	-	-	-	-	32,100	11,069	-	-
SQUID	-	-	-	-	106,100	4,006	-	-
TOTAL	2,300	$125	6,755,600	101,310	565,858,200	27,617,411	5,355,900	1,508,102

SPECIES	HARPOONS POUNDS	HARPOONS VALUE	SPEARS POUNDS	SPEARS VALUE	DREDGES POUNDS	DREDGES VALUE	TONGS POUNDS	TONGS VALUE
COD	-	-	-	-	6,200	$273	-	-
EELS, COMMON	-	-	10,800	$2,020	-	-	-	-
FLOUNDERS:								
GRAY SOLE	-	-	-	-	100	3	-	-
LEMON SOLE	-	-	-	-	9,300	1,054	-	-
YELLOWTAIL	-	-	-	-	4,900	298	-	-
BLACKBACK	-	-	-	-	35,800	3,108	-	-
DAB	-	-	-	-	200	8	-	-
HADDOCK	-	-	-	-	25,500	1,250	-	-
HAKE, WHITE	-	-	-	-	100	1	-	-
HALIBUT	-	-	-	-	100	22	-	-
POLLOCK	-	-	-	-	100	2	-	-
SHARKS	100	$4	-	-	-	-	-	-
SWORDFISH	873,800	305,444	-	-	-	-	-	-
TUNA, BLUEFIN	9,400	1,095	-	-	-	-	-	-
WOLFFISH	-	-	-	-	100	2	-	-
UNCLASSIFIED, FOR FOOD	-	-	-	-	100	18	-	-
CLAMS, HARD, PUBLIC	-	-	-	-	74,000	17,862	321,000	$96,258
MUSSELS, SEA	-	-	-	-	9,600	600	-	-
OYSTERS, MARKET:								
PUBLIC, SPRING	-	-	-	-	-	-	2,500	1,520
PUBLIC, FALL	-	-	-	-	-	-	13,000	5,750
PRIVATE, SPRING	-	-	-	-	2,200	1,100	-	-
PRIVATE, FALL	-	-	-	-	78,300	50,612	82,000	48,116
SCALLOPS:								
BAY	-	-	-	-	838,100	615,836	-	-
SEA	-	-	-	-	13,436,800	4,976,133	-	-
TOTAL	883,300	306,543	10,800	2,020	14,521,500	5,668,182	418,500	151,644

SPECIES	RAKES POUNDS	RAKES VALUE	FORKS POUNDS	FORKS VALUE	HOES POUNDS	HOES VALUE
CLAMS:						
HARD, PUBLIC	1,267,300	$422,130	-	-	3,000	$1,238
HARD, PRIVATE	132,000	48,575	-	-	-	-
RAZOR	-	-	-	-	73,700	8,750
SOFT, PUBLIC	-	-	-	-	917,600	376,766
SOFT, PRIVATE	300	138	-	-	500	231
SURF	5,100	1,617	5,500	$1,000	-	-
MUSSELS, SEA	-	-	110,400	6,900	-	-
OYSTERS, MARKET:						
PRIVATE, SPRING	16,300	11,300	28,000	15,255	-	-
PRIVATE, FALL	16,200	11,200	-	-	-	-
SCALLOPS, BAY	90,000	65,000	-	-	-	-
IRISH MOSS	500,000	8,950	-	-	-	-
SANDWORMS	-	-	-	-	3,200	2,926
TOTAL	2,027,200	568,910	143,900	23,155	998,000	389,911

RHODE ISLAND

OPERATING UNITS BY GEAR, 1949

ITEM	HAUL SEINES, COMMON	GILL NETS, DRIFT	LINES		FLOATING TRAPS	OTTER TRAWLS, FISH
			HAND	TROLL		
	NUMBER	NUMBER	NUMBER	NUMBER	NUMBER	NUMBER
FISHERMEN:						
ON VESSELS	-	-	9	-	58	174
ON BOATS AND SHORE:						
REGULAR	28	6	68	33	12	45
CASUAL.	-	-	74	-	-	16
TOTAL	28	6	151	33	70	235
VESSELS, MOTOR. . . .	-	-	4	-	6	63
NET TONNAGE	-	-	27	-	52	824
BOATS:						
MOTOR	4	3	83	22	3	29
OTHER	7	-	-	-	6	-
ACCESSORY BOATS . . .	-	-	-	-	15	-
APPARATUS:						
NUMBER.	7	30	221	88	16	92
LENGTH, YARDS	1,600	-	-	-	-	-
SQUARE YARDS.	-	9,000	-	-	-	-
HOOKS	-	-	221	88	-	-
YARDS AT MOUTH. . . .	-	-	-	-	-	2,339

ITEM	POTS				HARPOONS	DREDGES CLAM
	CRAB	EEL	LOBSTER	PERIWINKLE AND COCKLE		
	NUMBER	NUMBER	NUMBER	NUMBER	NUMBER	NUMBER
FISHERMEN:						
ON VESSELS	-	-	4	-	33	16
ON BOATS AND SHORE:						
REGULAR	2	6	76	4	22	12
CASUAL.	3	-	159	-	-	-
TOTAL	5	6	239	4	55	28
VESSELS, MOTOR. . . .	-	-	2	-	11	5
NET TONNAGE	-	-	12	-	150	127
BOATS:						
MOTOR	2	6	185	4	10	6
OTHER	-	-	-	-	6	-
ACCESSORY BOATS . . .	-	-	-	-	15	-
APPARATUS:						
NUMBER.	150	490	17,443	300	21	11
YARDS AT MOUTH. . . .	-	-	-	-	-	11

ITEM	DREDGES - CONT'D.		TONGS		RAKES, OTHER THAN FOR OYSTERS	HOES	TOTAL, EXCLUSIVE OF DUPLICATION
	OYSTER, COMMON	SCALLOP	OYSTER	OTHER			
	NUMBER	NUMBER	NUMBER	NUMBER	NUMBER	NUMBER	NUMBER
FISHERMEN:							
ON VESSELS.	35	8	-	-	-	-	286
ON BOATS AND SHORE:							
REGULAR	-	246	20	251	83	125	471
CASUAL.	-	323	50	712	80	55	1,075
TOTAL	35	577	70	963	163	180	1,832
VESSELS, MOTOR. . . .	8	4	-	-	-	-	85
NET TONNAGE	167	29	-	-	-	-	1,131
BOATS:							
MOTOR	-	250	-	101	25	-	529
OTHER	-	-	70	862	138	99	879
ACCESSORY BOATS . . .	-	-	-	-	-	-	30
APPARATUS:							
NUMBER.	16	1,329	70	963	163	180	-
YARDS AT MOUTH. . . .	22	1,035	-	-	-	-	-

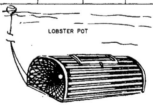

LOBSTER POT

RHODE ISLAND: CATCH BY GEAR, 1949

SPECIES	PURSE SEINES		HAUL SEINES		GILL NETS, DRIFT		LINES			
							HAND		TROLL	
	POUNDS	VALUE	POUNDS	VALUE	POUNDS	VALUE	POUNDS	VALUE	POUNDS	VALUE
ALEWIVES.	-	-	119,000	$1,057	-	-	-	-	-	-
COD	-	-	-	-	-	-	705,600	$34,771	-	-
EELS, COMMON.	-	-	1,500	215	-	-	700	60	-	-
FLOUNDERS:										
BLACKBACK	-	-	-	-	-	-	2,300	136	-	-
FLUKE	-	-	-	-	-	-	200	16	-	-
HAKE, WHITE	-	-	-	-	-	-	400	15	-	-
HERRING, SEA.	-	-	49,500	700	-	-	-	-	-	-
LAUNCE.	-	-	1,500	45	-	-	-	-	-	-
MACKEREL.	60,400	$5,437	-	-	8,500	$780	-	-	57,100	$4,875
POLLOCK	-	-	-	-	-	-	8,600	389	-	-
SCUP OR PORGY	-	-	-	-	-	-	900	60	-	-
SEA BASS.	-	-	-	-	-	-	6,000	1,200	-	-
SHARKS.	-	-	-	-	-	-	800	48	-	-
SKATES.	-	-	-	-	-	-	200	2	-	-
STRIPED BASS.	-	-	15,300	3,374	-	-	14,000	2,825	4,700	524
WHITE PERCH	-	-	23,900	2,860	-	-	-	-	-	-
UNCLASSIFIED, FOR FOOD. . .	-	-	-	-	-	-	400	29	-	-
TOTAL	60,400	5,437	210,700	8,251	8,500	780	740,100	39,551	61,800	5,399

SPECIES	FLOATING TRAPS		OTTER TRAWLS		POTS		HARPOONS	
	POUNDS	VALUE	POUNDS	VALUE	POUNDS	VALUE	POUNDS	VALUE
ALEWIVES.	14,600	$160	100	$1	-	-	-	-
ANGLERFISH.	-	-	1,800	29	-	-	-	-
BLUEFISH.	25,000	3,362	700	103	-	-	-	-
BUTTERFISH.	275,700	18,735	1,003,700	67,528	-	-	-	-
COD	513,100	25,043	488,600	18,772	-	-	-	-
CREVALLE.	500	16	-	-	-	-	-	-
CUNNER.	-	-	3,500	43	-	-	-	-
DOLPHIN	1,500	146	-	-	-	-	-	-
EELS;								
COMMON.	-	-	-	-	13,900	$2,094	-	-
CONGER.	600	19	4,000	99	-	-	-	-
FLOUNDERS:								
GRAY SOLE	-	-	9,500	820	-	-	-	-
LEMON SOLE.	-	-	66,300	7,827	-	-	-	-
YELLOWTAIL.	-	-	1,138,200	109,475	-	-	-	-
BLACKBACK	5,000	249	1,294,600	68,298	-	-	-	-
DAB	-	-	5,700	86	-	-	-	-
FLUKE	127,800	20,139	341,600	55,003	-	-	-	-
UNCLASSIFIED.	-	-	3,200	367	-	-	-	-
FRIGATE MACKEREL.	43,100	1,888	-	-	-	-	-	-
HADDOCK	-	-	69,600	3,407	-	-	-	-
HAKE:								
RED	-	-	520,700	10,642	-	-	-	-
WHITE	6,300	325	33,100	1,305	-	-	-	-
HALIBUT	-	-	100	27	-	-	-	-
HERRING, SEA.	727,800	12,080	3,479,400	57,927	-	-	-	-
HICKORY SHAD.	400	43	-	-	-	-	-	-
KING WHITING OR "KINGFISH".	900	70	85,100	6,727	-	-	-	-
MACKEREL.	336,900	26,082	39,700	4,330	-	-	-	-
MENHADEN.	38,100	457	-	-	-	-	-	-
POLLOCK	19,700	639	8,600	294	-	-	-	-
SCUP OR PORGY	1,659,900	48,794	746,000	24,643	-	-	-	-
SEA BASS.	177,800	20,431	49,800	5,762	-	-	-	-
SEA ROBIN	8,500	151	-	-	-	-	-	-
SEA TROUT OR WEAKFISH, GRAY	13,900	1,982	1,800	261	-	-	-	-
SHAD.	3,000	122	200	9	-	-	-	-
SHARKS.	5,100	413	5,800	140	-	-	-	-
SKATES.	-	-	200	4	-	-	-	-
SPOT.	300	13	-	-	-	-	-	-
STRIPED BASS.	41,100	8,925	6,100	1,391	-	-	-	-
STURGEON.	1,600	161	1,000	151	-	-	-	-
SWELLFISH	1,900	221	-	-	-	-	-	-
SWORDFISH	-	-	-	-	-	-	66,700	$32,420
TAUTOG.	21,500	963	5,800	189	-	-	-	-
TILEFISH.	-	-	32,700	2,038	-	-	-	-
TUNA AND TUNALIKE FISHES:								
BLUEFIN	11,400	1,178	-	-	-	-	6,500	750
BONITO.	5,200	596	-	-	-	-	-	-
WHITE PERCH	-	-	200	27	-	-	-	-
WHITING	64,400	1,253	595,500	19,599	-	-	-	-
WOLFFISH.	-	-	700	15	-	-	-	-
UNCLASSIFIED:								
FOR FOOD.	1,300	26	13,500	249	-	-	-	-
OTHER	504,200	4,565	11,105,700	79,814	-	-	-	-
CRABS, ROCK	-	-	-	-	108,000	3,250	-	-
LOBSTERS, NORTHERN. . . .	-	-	-	-	354,600	155,859	-	-
PERIWINKLES AND COCKLES . .	-	-	-	-	18,000	3,000	-	-
SQUID	1,422,800	33,590	446,700	13,347	-	-	-	-
TOTAL.	6,090,900	232,837	21,609,500	560,749	494,500	164,203	73,200	33,170

(CONTINUED ON NEXT PAGE)

RHODE ISLAND: CATCH BY GEAR, 1949 - Continued

SPECIES	DREDGES		TON :S		RAKES		HOES	
	POUNDS	VALUE	POUNDS	VALUE	POUNDS	VALUE	POUNDS	VALUE
CLAMS:								
HARD, PUBLIC	255,600	$53,250	1,455,600	$321,712	423,900	$94,381	-	-
OCEAN QUAHOG	62,800	5,232	-	-	-	-	-	-
SOFT, PUBLIC	-	-	-	-	-	-	634,400	$147,138
SURF	-	-	7,300	1,824	-	-	-	-
MUSSELS, SEA	186,000	23,250	-	-	-	-	-	-
OYSTERS, MARKET:								
PUBLIC, SPRING	234,200	116,092	24,500	10,500	-	-	-	-
PUBLIC, FALL	152,100	75,728	-	-	-	-	-	-
PRIVATE, SPRING.	161,100	79,737	-	-	-	-	-	-
PRIVATE, FALL.	107,900	53,605	-	-	-	-	-	-
PERIWINKLES AND COCKLES. . .	70,000	11,600	-	-	-	-	-	-
SCALLOPS, BAY.	303,000	185,490	-	-	-	-	-	-
TOTAL	1,532,700	603,984	1,487,400	334,036	423,900	94,381	634,400	147,138

CONNECTICUT

OPERATING UNITS BY GEAR, 1949

ITEM	HAUL SEINES, COMMON	GILL NETS		LINES, HAND	POUND NETS	STOP NETS	FYKE NETS, FISH
		ANCHOR	DRIFT				
	NUMBER	NUMBER	NUMBER	NUMBER	NUMBER	NUMBER	NUMBER
FISHERMEN:							
ON VESSELS.	-	-	-	2	2	-	-
ON BOATS AND SHORE:							
REGULAR	22	-	9	8	4	-	2
CASUAL.	187	6	162	63	3	15	15
TOTAL	209	6	171	73	9	15	17
VESSELS, MOTOR.	-	-	-	1	1	-	-
NET TONNAGE	-	-	-	7	6	-	-
BOATS:							
MOTOR	59	3	59	41	3	3	6
OTHER	82	-	61	8	1	8	5
APPARATUS:							
NUMBER.	81	3	99	73	5	11	19
LENGTH, YARDS	13,288	-	-	-	-	300	-
SQUARE YARDS.	-	1,100	86,300	-	-	-	-
HOOKS	-	-	-	219	-	-	-

ITEM	DIP NETS, COMMON	OTTER TRAWLS, FISH	POTS		HARPOONS	DREDGES OYSTER, COMMON 1/
			EEL	LOBSTER		
	NUMBER	NUMBER	NUMBER	NUMBER	NUMBER	NUMBER
FISHERMEN:						
ON VESSELS.	2	185	-	22	26	266
ON BOATS AND SHORE:						
REGULAR	10	56	9	55	-	-
CASUAL.	81	69	42	230	-	-
TOTAL	93	310	51	307	26	266
VESSELS:						
MOTOR	1	63	-	11	7	37
NET TONNAGE	6	975	-	73	133	1,112
STEAM	-	-	-	-	-	5
NET TONNAGE	-	-	-	-	-	513
TOTAL VESSELS . .	1	63	-	11	7	42
TOTAL NET TONNAGE	6	975	-	73	133	1,625
BOATS:						
MOTOR	37	71	24	148	-	-
OTHER	39	-	14	52	-	-
ACCESSORY BOATS	-	-	-	-	7	-
APPARATUS:						
NUMBER.	93	134	600	12,609	7	85
YARDS AT MOUTH. . . .	-	1,773	-	-	-	129

SEE FOOTNOTE AT END OF TABLE.   (CONTINUED ON NEXT PAGE)

CONNECTICUT: OPERATING UNITS BY GEAR, 1949 - Continued

ITEM	DREDGES - CONT'D. SCALLOP	TONGS OYSTER	OTHER	RAKES, OTHER THAN FOR OYSTERS	HOES	TOTAL, EXCLUSIVE OF DUPLICATION
	NUMBER	NUMBER	NUMBER	NUMBER	NUMBER	NUMBER
FISHERMEN:						
ON VESSELS	-	-	2	-	2	467
ON BOATS AND SHORE:						
REGULAR	3	9	2	5	4	130
CASUAL	3	35	44	23	40	718
TOTAL	6	44	48	28	46	1,315
VESSELS:						
MOTOR	-	-	1	-	1	108
NET TONNAGE	-	-	6	-	7	2,137
STEAM	-	-	-	-	-	5
NET TONNAGE	-	-	-	-	-	513
TOTAL VESSELS . .	-	-	1	-	1	113
TOTAL NET TONNAGE	-	-	6	-	7	2,650
BOATS:						
MOTOR	3	23	21	15	25	351
OTHER	-	9	20	8	11	247
ACCESSORY BOATS	-	-	-	-	-	7
APPARATUS:						
NUMBER	6	44	48	28	46	-
YARDS AT MOUTH	6	-	-	-	-	-

1/ INCLUDES 1 SUCTION DREDGE, 2 YARDS AT MOUTH.

CONNECTICUT: CATCH BY GEAR, 1949

SPECIES	HAUL SEINES		GILL NETS ANCHOR		DRIFT	
	POUNDS	VALUE	POUNDS	VALUE	POUNDS	VALUE
ALEWIVES	1,138,080	$16,544	-	-	8,000	$155
BLUEFISH	800	206	-	-	-	-
CARP	39,000	3,227	-	-	-	-
CUNNER	-	-	1,000	$20	1,000	15
FLOUNDERS, BLACKBACK	-	-	-	-	1,000	15
GRAYFISH	-	-	-	-	1,000	15
MENHADEN	-	-	6,400	56	1,500	36
MINNOWS	83,700	6,238	-	-	-	-
SCUP OR PORGY	-	-	-	-	1,000	15
SEA ROBIN	-	-	-	-	1,000	15
SHAD	213,200	32,550	-	-	237,600	37,600
SKATES	-	-	-	-	1,000	15
SUCKERS	5,400	283	-	-	-	-
TAUTOG	-	-	-	-	1,000	15
YELLOW PERCH	500	75	-	-	-	-
TOTAL	1,480,600	59,123	7,400	76	254,100	37,896

SPECIES	LINES, HAND		POUND NETS		STOP NETS	
	POUNDS	VALUE	POUNDS	VALUE	POUNDS	VALUE
BLUEFISH	6,700	$1,909	2,100	$840	-	-
BUTTERFISH	-	-	1,500	245	-	-
COD	900	121	-	-	-	-
CUNNER	1,600	75	-	-	-	-
EELS, COMMON	2,300	394	100	20	-	-
FLOUNDERS:						
BLACKBACK	3,000	270	200	9	-	-
DAB	200	9	-	-	-	-
FLUKE	600	106	1,600	239	-	-
UNCLASSIFIED	300	12	-	-	-	-
GRAYFISH	700	14	-	-	-	-
MACKEREL	91,200	11,157	-	-	-	-
MENHADEN	-	-	16,000	116	-	-
POLLOCK	3,900	350	-	-	-	-
SCUP OR PORGY	2,800	215	-	-	-	-
SEA BASS	4,700	754	-	-	-	-
SEA ROBIN	700	14	-	-	-	-
SEA TROUT OR WEAKFISH, GRAY .	100	17	1,400	273	-	-
SHAD	-	-	15,200	2,300	4,600	$725
SHARKS	100	5	-	-	-	-
SKATES	400	16	800	28	-	-

(CONTINUED ON NEXT PAGE) -

CONNECTICUT: CATCH BY GEAR, 1949 - Continued

SPECIES	LINES, HAND		POUND NETS		STOP NETS	
	POUNDS	VALUE	POUNDS	VALUE	POUNDS	VALUE
STRIPED BASS.	8,700	$2,702	-	-	-	-
SWELLFISH	100	5	-	-	-	-
SWORDFISH	300	207	-	-	-	-
TAUTOG	9,100	864	5,300	$625	-	-
TUNA AND TUNALIKE FISHES, BLUEFIN	8,700	730	-	-	-	-
WHITING	500	28	-	-	-	-
SQUID	-	-	3,300	116	-	-
TOTAL.	147,600	19,974	47,500	4,811	4,600	$725

SPECIES	FYKE NETS		DIP NETS		OTTER TRAWLS	
	POUNDS	VALUE	POUNDS	VALUE	POUNDS	VALUE
ANGLERFISH	-	-	-	-	4,000	$140
BLUEFISH	-	-	-	-	400	100
BUTTERFISH . :	-	-	-	-	702,800	71,124
CARP	3,200	$211	-	-	-	-
CATFISH AND BULLHEADS.	7,600	375	200	$20	-	-
COD.	-	-	-	-	589,800	60,000
CUNNER	-	-	-	-	1,100	45
DOLPHIN.	-	-	-	-	600	26
EELS, CONGER	-	-	-	-	6,000	200
FLOUNDERS:						
GRAY SOLE.	-	-	-	-	6,200	545
LEMON SOLE	-	-	-	-	40,000	5,000
YELLOWTAIL	-	-	-	-	550,200	60,060
BLACKBACK.	-	-	-	-	3,905,000	201,600
DAB.	-	-	-	-	22,200	760
FLUKE.	-	-	-	-	369,500	70,056
UNCLASSIFIED	-	-	-	-	4,000	131
GRAYFISH	-	-	-	-	3,600	124
HADDOCK.	-	-	-	-	12,100	1,000
HAKE:						
RED.	-	-	-	-	1,158,800	32,015
WHITE.	-	-	-	-	7,300	450
HERRING,SEA.	-	-	-	-	2,668,600	54,000
KING WHITING OR "KINGFISH" . . .	-	-	-	-	1,000	100
MACKEREL	-	-	-	-	1,000	100
MENHADEN	-	-	-	-	3,200	39
MINNOWS.	11,900	335	4,400	341	-	-
POLLOCK.	-	-	-	-	1,600	241
SCUP OR PORGY.	-	-	-	-	1,758,100	91,287
SEA BASS	-	-	-	-	29,400	5,100
SEA ROBIN.	-	-	-	-	117,800	1,766
SEA TROUT OR WEAKFISH, GRAY. . .	-	-	-	-	1,500	175
SHAD	100	16	-	-	-	-
SHARKS	-	-	-	-	37,300	515
SILVERSIDES.	-	-	-	-	1,500	25
SKATES	-	-	-	-	125,900	1,831
STRIPED BASS	-	-	-	-	100	25
STURGEON	-	-	-	-	500	50
SUCKERS.	4,500	251	-	-	-	-
SUNFISH.	4,700	94	-	-	-	-
SWELLFISH.	-	-	-	-	9,200	260
TAUTOG	-	-	-	-	8,800	705
TILEFISH	-	-	-	-	38,000	3,200
TUNA AND TUNALIKE FISHES:						
BLUEFIN.	-	-	-	-	26,700	3,000
LITTLE	-	-	-	-	200	21
WHITE PERCH.	400	36	-	-	-	-
WHITING.	-	-	-	-	1,019,000	25,227
YELLOW PERCH	9,000	553	-	-	-	-
UNCLASSIFIED:						
FOR FOOD	-	-	-	-	547,500	25,320
OTHER.	-	-	-	-	4,433,800	90,000
CRABS, BLUE, HARD.	-	-	3,400	692	-	-
LOBSTERS, NORTHERN	-	-	-	-	9,800	3,200
CONCHS	-	-	-	-	400	44
SCALLOPS:						
BAY.	-	-	19,700	11,235	-	-
SEA.	-	-	-	-	2,100	1,000
SQUID.	-	-	-	-	304,000	24,094
TOTAL	41,400	1,871	27,700	12,288	18,530,600	834,701

(CONTINUED ON NEXT PAGE)

CONNECTICUT: CATCH BY GEAR, 1949 - Continued

SPECIES	POTS		HARPOONS		DREDGES	
	POUNDS	VALUE	POUNDS	VALUE	POUNDS	VALUE
EELS, COMMON.	18,100	$3,223	-	-	-	-
SWORDFISH	-	-	2,800	$1,350	-	-
LOBSTERS, NORTHERN.	378,500	165,858	-	-	-	-
CONCHS.	41,100	4,335	-	-	-	-
OYSTERS, MARKET:						
PUBLIC, SPRING.	-	-	-	-	4,600	$1,200
PUBLIC, FALL.	-	-	-	-	27,200	10,605
PRIVATE, SPRING	-	-	-	-	1,317,300	357,895
PRIVATE, FALL	-	-	-	-	1,706,200	611,734
SCALLOPS, BAY	-	-	-	-	4,400	2,500
TOTAL.	437,700	173,416	2,800	1,350	3,059,700	983,934

SPECIES	TONGS		RAKES		HOES	
	POUNDS	VALUE	POUNDS	VALUE	POUNDS	VALUE
CLAMS:						
HARD, PUBLIC.	6,100	$2,697	7,200	$3,200	-	-
SOFT, PUBLIC.	-	-	-	-	13,300	$4,093
MUSSELS, SEA.	96,000	6,481	-	-	-	-
OYSTERS, MARKET:						
PUBLIC, SPRING.	8,800	2,493	-	-	-	-
PUBLIC, FALL.	21,500	8,194	-	-	-	-
SANDWORMS	-	-	-	-	200	222
TOTAL.	132,400	19,865	7,200	3,200	13,500	4,315

LANDINGS AT CERTAIN MASSACHUSETTS PORTS, 1942 - 1949

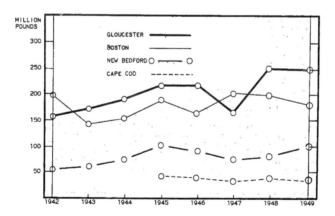

NEW ENGLAND FISHERIES

LANDINGS AT CERTAIN MASSACHUSETTS PORTS [3]

Because of the important role they play in the production of fishery products, detailed daily statistics have been collected and published monthly for the landings at Boston, Gloucester, New Bedford, Provincetown, Massachusetts; and other Cape Cod ports. Landings of fishing craft of all sizes at the ports named are included in the data in the following tables.

It should be noted that these figures represent actual landings which have not been converted to round weight, therefore, the data are not directly comparable to the catch figures shown in the General Review, regional tabulations, or the section entitled ''Review of Certain Major Fisheries.''

During 1949, landings of fishery products at Boston, Gloucester, New Bedford, and Cape Cod ports amounted to 564,825,638 pounds, valued at $34,775,046 to the fishermen. This represented a decrease of 1 percent in volume and a decrease of 18 percent in value compared with 1948. The volume approximated that of the previous year only because of large landings of fish for animal food and reduction into meal and oil. A large portion of the receipts of nearly 40 million pounds of red hake, and nearly 20 million pounds of unclassified species were landed for these purposes. Of the total landings, ocean perch (rosefish) accounted for 32 percent; haddock, 20 percent; hake, 8 percent; and cod, 7 percent. In 1948, ocean perch (rosefish) accounted for 33 percent of the total landings; haddock, 23 percent; cod, 9 percent; and hake, 2 percent. Haddock landings during 1949 were 19.5 million pounds less than the 1948 catch, and receipts of ocean perch (rosefish) decreased 7.6 million pounds compared with the previous year.

Gloucester retained its position as the Massachusetts port with the greatest volume, while Boston led in value. Gloucester receipts accounted for 46 percent of the total poundage landed during the year, but only 30 percent of the total value. Boston was in second place with respect to volume of landings, and New Bedford replaced Gloucester as the number two port with regard to value. Increased landings of the highly valued scallops was responsible for the noticeable monetary gain made by the New Bedford fisheries.

The fishing fleet operating on the fishing banks of the North Atlantic and landing fares at Boston, Gloucester, New Bedford, and Cape Cod ports during 1949, numbered 1,184 craft of all sizes. Of these 342 landed in one or more of the Cape Cod ports. There may be some duplication between the craft operating out of Cape Cod ports and those landing at other ports. The landings listed in the following tables do not represent the entire catch of these vessels, as some of them also landed fares at other New England ports, at New York City, and at more southerly ports in connection with the southern mackerel and the southern trawl fisheries.

Of the total landings, amounting to almost 565 million pounds, 33 percent was taken by large otter trawlers (over 150 gross tons); the same amount was taken by medium otter trawlers (51 to 150 gross tons); 23 percent was caught by small otter trawlers (50 gross tons or under); and the remaining 11 percent was taken by other types of gear.

The following tables contain a detailed summary of information on the landings of fish and shellfish by fishing craft of all sizes in Boston, Gloucester, New Bedford, and Cape Cod ports. Information of the annual landings by ports was previously published in Current Fishery Statistics No. 543, while data on the landings by gear and area appeared in Current Fishery Statistics No. 562. Detailed information on the monthly landings by port and by gear and area of capture also were published in the Current Fishery Statistics series.

---

3 The reader is referred to Section 13 of this document for an account of the years for which surveys of these fisheries have been made.

LANDINGS AT CERTAIN MASSACHUSETTS PORTS

SUMMARY OF LANDINGS, 1949

SPECIES	BOSTON POUNDS	BOSTON VALUE	BOSTON AV. PRICE PER POUND	GLOUCESTER POUNDS	GLOUCESTER VALUE	GLOUCESTER AV. PRICE PER POUND	NEW BEDFORD POUNDS	NEW BEDFORD VALUE	NEW BEDFORD AV. PRICE PER POUND
COD, DRAWN:									
LARGE	13,071,560	$1,025,979	7.85¢	4,196,783	$254,841	6.07¢	656,860	$40,592	6.18¢
MARKET	14,336,423	919,062	6.41	2,452,218	120,872	4.93	2,691,913	192,354	7.14
S RODE	1,236,765	67,483	5.46	327,462	15,737	4.80	731,255	47,596	6.51
CUSK, DRAWN	1,197,454	57,301	4.78	777,498	24,086	3.10	2,600	114	4.38
FLOUNDERS, ROU B:									
GRAY SOLE	1,403,032	147,346	10.50	5,493,925	321,547	5.85	361,855	30,666	8.77
LEMON SOLE	1,562,090	193,657	12.40	4,985	353	7.08	2,911,460	450,274	15.46
YELLOWTAIL	1,701,675	115,687	6.80	567,360	46,575	8.21	19,652,113	1,941,652	9.88
BLACKBACK	2,031,894	189,525	9.33	209,689	15,845	7.56	9,411,095	1,112,566	11.82
DAB	1,408,555	92,850	6.59	1,367,227	62,289	4.55	161,150	11,308	7.02
FLUKE	—	—	—	185	18	9.73	1,430,376	277,600	19.41
HADDOCK, DRAWN:									
LARGE	52,847,974	4,659,317	8.82	6,719,631	454,739	6.77	5,234,438	437,949	8.37
SCROD	37,297,745	2,573,712	6.90	1,796,174	91,933	5.12	4,688,490	289,876	6.18
HAKE:									
RED, ROU B	1,600	99	6.19	17,985	420	2.34	1/39,670,842	1/337,652	0.85
WHITE, DRESSED:									
LARGE	3,244,830	212,924	6.56	1,868,995	77,904	4.17	151,195	5,020	3.32
SMALL	45,600	3,331	7.30	880,667	34,325	3.90	490	14	2.86
HALIBUT, DRAWN	219,364	52,059	23.73	58,306	14,409	24.71	30,672	6,506	21.21
MACKEREL, ROUND	709,365	81,071	11.43	6,876,144	362,098	5.27	342,133	20,484	5.99
POLLOCK, DRAWN	13,177,878	472,115	3.58	6,077,297	154,005	2.53	199,595	5,247	2.63
POLLOCK, ROU B	7,920	224	2.83	69,518	947	1.36	80,130	2,972	3.71
OCEAN PERCH (ROSE-FIS) IN ROUND	12,112,955	497,827	4.11	169,280,942	7,303,940	4.31	—	—	—
SCUP OR PORGY, ROUND	11,935	960	8.04	—	—	—	132,635	5,421	4.09
SWORDFISH, DRESSED	267,020	118,523	44.39	70,146	26,957	38.43	148,850	66,416	44.62
WHITING, DRESSED	12,958,715	526,050	4.06	17,072,991	676,086	3.96	24,270	805	3.32
WHITING, ROUND	35,605	1,195	3.36	2,368,902	41,991	1.77	—	—	—
WOLFFISH, DRAWN	1,332,771	126,391	9.48	148,609	8,437	5.68	96,835	3,974	4.10
SCALLOPS (MEATS)	124,634	45,501	36.51	20,103	6,708	33.37	11,707,165	4,296,883	36.70
OTHER FOR FOOD	124,997	7,128	5.70	7,620,300	183,885	2.41	2,178,607	57,386	2.63
OTHER 2/	—	—	—	14,566,626	155,289	1.07	3,006,530	30,066	1.00
TOTAL, AS LANDED	172,470,300	12,187,317	7.07	250,910,468	10,456,236	4.17	105,693,574	9,670,993	9.15
TOTAL IN 1948, AS LANDED	199,980,363	16,182,503	8.09	251,113,164	11,234,871	4.47	77,571,522	11,772,558	15.18

SEE FOOTNOTES AT END OF TABLE

(CONTINUED ON NEXT PAGE)

LANDINGS AT CERTAIN MASSACHUSETTS PORTS

SUMMARY OF LANDINGS, 1949 - Continued

SPECIES	CAPE COD PORTS			TOTAL 1949			TOTAL 1948		
	POUNDS	VALUE	AV. PRICE PER POUND	POUNDS	VALUE	AV. PRICE PER POUND	POUNDS	VALUE	AV. PRICE PER POUND
COD, DRAWN:									
LARGE	1,338,113	$111,081	8.30¢	19,263,316	$1,432,493	7.44¢	25,076,412	$1,909,667	7.62¢
MARKET	1,243,376	73,982	5.95	20,723,930	1,306,270	6.30	23,189,857	1,704,113	7.35
S RODE	63,244	3,402	5.38	2,359,726	134,218	5.69	3,237,363	211,143	6.52
CUSK, DRAWN	23,641	406	1.72	2,001,193	81,907	4.09	1,945,087	98,601	5.07
FLOU DRWS, ROU B:									
GRAY SOLE	41,845	3,676	8.78	7,290,657	503,435	6.90	2,247,184	201,402	8.96
LEMON SOLE	145,101	17,024	11.73	4,623,656	661,308	14.30	5,252,625	804,895	15.32
YELLOWTAIL	2,337,826	208,660	8.92	24,258,974	2,311,974	9.53	31,427,142	2,925,927	9.31
BLACKBACK	1,384,105	116,274	8.40	13,036,783	1,434,210	11.00	13,737,942	1,595,796	11.62
DAB	35,420	2,254	6.36	2,972,352	168,701	5.68	2,128,871	159,174	7.48
FLUKE	354,952	60,093	16.93	1,785,413	337,711	18.92	2,368,127	489,189	20.66
HADDOCK, DRAWN:									
LARGE	2,035,869	166,100	8.16	66,837,912	5,718,105	8.56	73,545,894	7,118,819	9.68
S RODE	55,207	3,428	6.21	43,837,616	2,958,949	6.75	56,673,534	4,666,811	8.23
HADDOCK, ROUN D, SCROD	—	—	—	—	—	—	1,000	120	12.00
HAKE:									
RED, ROUND	640	13	2.03	39,691,067	338,184	0.85	4,147,947	52,605	1.27
WHITE, DRESSED:									
LARGE	77,379	4,024	5.20	5,342,399	299,872	5.61	5,923,610	354,208	5.98
SMALL	4,486	169	3.77	931,243	37,839	4.06	1,420,211	55,800	3.93
HALIBUT, DRAWN	56,537	20,540	36.33	364,909	93,514	25.63	377,512	98,514	26.10
MACKEREL, ROUND	5,244,225	555,763	10.60	13,171,867	1,019,416	7.74	33,939,911	2,356,753	6.94
POLLOCK, DRAWN	173,551	6,077	3.50	19,628,321	637,444	3.25	27,526,735	1,153,718	4.19
POLLOCK, ROUND	—	—	—	77,438	1,171	1.51	198,640	4,290	2.16
OCEAN PERCH (ROSE-FISH), ROUND	8,105	373	4.60	181,482,132	7,805,112	4.30	189,051,024	7,935,217	4.20
SCUP OR PORGY, ROUN D	304,603	8,729	2.86	449,173	15,110	3.36	1,507,314	43,370	2.88
SWORDFISH, DRESSED	162,380	71,482	44.02	648,400	283,378	43.70	627,133	311,388	49.65
WHITING, DRESSED	4,807,268	162,021	3.37	34,863,244	1,364,962	3.92	28,842,550	1,211,145	4.20
WHITING, ROUND	8,246,898	165,868	2.01	10,651,405	209,054	1.96	13,103,718	264,935	2.02
WOLFFISH, DRAWN	133,133	9,185	6.90	1,711,348	147,987	8.65	1,626,317	135,551	8.33
SCALLOPS (MEATS)	1,327,003	499,200	37.62	13,178,905	4,848,292	36.79	11,638,057	6,098,988	52.40
OTHER FOR FOOD	3,912,851	771,722	4.39	13,836,555	420,121	3.04	12,357,801	560,699	4.54
OTHER 2/	2,233,548	18,954	0.85	19,806,704	204,309	1.03	—	—	-
TOTAL, AS LANDED	35,751,206	2,460,500	6.88	564,825,638	34,775,046	6.16	573,119,518	42,522,838	7.42
TOTAL IN 1948, AS LANDED	44,454,469	3,332,896	7.50	—	—	—	573,119,518	42,522,838	7.42

1/ NEARLY THE ENTIRE CATCH OF RED HAKE LANDED AT NEW BEDFORD WAS USED FOR ANIMAL FOOD OR MANUFACTURE INTO MEAL AND OIL.. AT TIMES SOME TRASH FISH WERE INCLUDED WITH THE LANDINGS OF RED HAKE.

2/ INCLUDES FISH USED FOR REDUCTION AND ANIMAL FOOD.

NOTE---THE WEIGHTS OF FRESH FISH GIVEN IN THESE STATISTICS REPRESENT THE FISH AS LANDED, AND THE VALUES ARE THOSE RECEIVED BY THE FISHERMEN. LARGE COD ARE CLASSIFIED AS THOSE WEIGHING OVER 10 POUNDS; MARKET COD, 2-1/2 TO 10 POUNDS; AND SCROD COD, 1 TO 2-1/2 POUNDS. LARGE HADDOCK ARE THOSE WEIGHING OVER 2-1/2 POUNDS, AND SCROD HADDOCK, 1 TO 2-1/2 POUNDS. LARGE HAKE WEIGHING OVER 6 POUNDS, AND SMALL HAKE, UNDER 6 POUNDS. THE FOLLOWING TERMS INDICATE THE CONDITION IN WHICH FISH WERE CAUGHT: "ROUND" AS CAUGHT; "DRAWN" EVISCERATED; AND "DRESSED", EVISCERATED AND HEADED. IN ADDITION TO THE LANDINGS IN THE ABOVE TABLES, 2,102,400 POUNDS OF FISH LIVERS, VALUED AT $173,739 TO THE FISHERMEN, AND 87,420 POUNDS OF SPAWN, VALUED AT $6,937, WERE LANDED AT THESE PORTS.

LANDINGS AT CERTAIN MASSACHUSETTS PORTS

LANDINGS AT BOSTON, 1949

SPECIES	JANUARY		FEBRUARY		MARCH		APRIL		MAY	
	POUNDS	AV. PRICE PER POUND	POUNDS	AV. PRICE PER POUND	POUNDS	AV. PRICE PER POUND	POUNDS	AV. PRICE PER POUND	POUNDS	AV. PRICE PER POUND
COD, DRAWN:										
LARGE	1,055,544	10.69¢	1,689,200	7.43¢	3,511,528	7.01¢	2,318,775	5.81¢	1,156,749	6.12¢
MARKET	794,550	8.98	720,643	7.06	1,180,860	8.16	1,303,950	5.77	1,189,380	5.01
SCROD	126,360	6.25	123,420	6.71	73,210	6.34	12,785	4.47	48,750	3.53
CUSK, DRAWN	78,660	8.46	93,339	6.91	67,565	7.88	67,370	5.02	73,710	3.62
FLOUNDERS, ROUND:										
GRAY SOLE	164,700	13.15	78,675	12.56	284,603	7.84	74,390	11.37	160,330	7.48
LEMON SOLE	33,775	19.00	26,675	22.04	143,275	14.91	117,250	12.38	303,250	8.29
YELLOWTAIL	83,875	11.02	63,975	10.80	174,275	6.69	325,600	7.40	167,600	5.12
BLACKBACK	114,505	14.76	97,840	11.08	126,307	11.41	57,995	9.93	143,325	6.85
DAB	69,370	10.33	43,765	8.59	97,055	6.84	160,915	6.86	289,985	4.79
HADDOCK, DRAWN:										
LARGE	3,914,040	11.87	5,306,545	8.71	6,021,110	9.72	7,493,075	6.91	6,547,975	6.76
SCROD	2,001,480	9.68	2,672,330	7.37	3,223,250	8.44	4,024,875	5.98	3,513,545	5.59
HAKE:										
RED; ROUND	275	14.91	-	-	825	5.82	-	-	-	-
WHITE, DRESSED:										
LARGE	295,360	9.92	128,540	10.68	157,320	10.78	90,990	6.90	142,135	3.77
SMALL	-	-	33,500	7.80	-	-	100	7.00	20	-
HALIBUT, DRAWN	10,281	23.69	24,372	25.64	26,818	27.66	42,950	26.33	48,644	21.51
MACKEREL, ROUND	2,380	12.44	4,650	10.75	15,900	13.83	72,450	8.39	26,245	14.24
POLLOCK, DRAWN	2,787,000	3.52	1,537,120	3.23	1,358,447	4.20	1,301,605	2.81	665,445	3.20
O FAB PERCH (ROSE-FISH), ROUND	1,599,080	4.31	942,150	4.18	732,525	4.88	772,595	4.84	1,124,695	4.30
SCUP OR PORGY, ROU DW	100	13.00			11,835	8.00	54,985	6.02	1,703,680	4.28
WHITING, DRESSED	17,910	5.92	9,775	9.25	19,355	9.65	2,855	4.03	17,275	1.42
WHITING, ROU DW	50	4.00	275	5.09	7,335	8.34	431,855	7.76	403,660	9.48
WOLFFISH, DRAWN	66,147	11.95	74,635	12.32	149,199	13.17	18,544	37.48	18,720	34.63
SCALLOPS (MEATS)	8,429	40.00	8,801	37.00	70	42.86	5,890	4.89	7,075	5.77
OTHER'FOR FOOD	3,105	2.67	475	6.74	5,635	9.96				
TOTAL, AS LANDED	13,216,976	8.55	13,682,700	7.41	17,388,202	8.22	18,751,939	6.28	17,752,193	5.92
TOTAL IN 1948, AS LA DEB	10,455,298	10.68	13,141,915	10.37	22,029,668	7.42	20,279,371	7.15	18,027,724	7.12

(CONTINUED ON NEXT PAGE)

LANDINGS AT CERTAIN MASSACHUSETTS PORTS

LANDINGS AT BOSTON, 1949 - Continued

SPECIES	JUNE		JULY		AUGUST		SEPTEMBER		OCTOBER	
	POUNDS	AV. PRICE PER POUND	POUNDS	AV. PRICE PER POUND	POUNDS	AV. PRICE PER POUND	POUNDS	AV. PRICE PER POUND	POUNDS	AV. PRICE PER POUND
COD, DRAWN:										
LARGE	754,755	7.51¢	345,120	9.38¢	418,380	10.69¢	396,154	12.32¢	571,420	11.84¢
MARKET	1,805,215	4.82	1,211,795	5.12	1,500,805	5.98	1,390,855	7.53	1,457,535	7.65
SCROD	90,510	3.47	54,530	3.55	95,080	4.94	163,555	6.13	210,210	6.14
CUSK, DRAWN	109,475	3.10	93,850	3.04	157,250	3.46	145,090	3.49	106,885	4.91
FLOUNDERS, ROUND:										
GRAY SOLE	74,029	10.00	79,525	11.01	58,660	12.06	98,265	11.16	74,465	13.22
LEMON SOLE	350,165	9.05	51,640	18.44	146,355	14.37	187,680	12.48	108,155	15.22
YELLOWTAIL	162,515	6.00	62,440	6.93	122,755	6.48	47,850	7.71	76,275	8.28
BLACKBACK	191,610	7.53	35,920	12.37	84,615	11.17	435,855	8.90	224,455	10.05
DAB	164,060	5.78	94,790	4.68	78,360	6.89	97,500	7.06	89,735	7.88
HADDOCK, DRAWN:										
LARGE	4,334,414	7.05	2,600,965	8.32	4,367,795	7.74	4,245,315	9.24	2,787,940	11.56
SCROD	4,224,765	5.36	2,587,885	5.21	4,988,005	6.12	4,353,730	7.38	2,780,500	8.55
HAKE:										
RED, ROUND	-	-	-	-	-	-	-	-	500	2.00
WHITE, DRESSED:										
LARGE	225,880	4.77	251,580	3.87	317,535	4.71	548,745	5.95	465,770	7.09
SMALL	3,190	4.62	1,515	4.03	550	6.00	1,180	5.00	4,445	7.51
HALIBUT, DRAWN	39,295	18.87	5,359	21.80	3,638	27.93	1,828	35.56	4,961	30.94
MACKEREL, ROUND	112,420	7.44	1,320	8.41	25,800	12.03	36,165	14.27	98,890	17.06
POLLOCK, DRAWN	371,335	4.34	343,055	3.88	483,381	3.98	356,325	5.40	906,825	4.96
POLLOCK, &	-	-	385	2.08	7,535	2.87	-	-	-	-
OCEAN PERCH (ROSE-FISH) ROUND	1,125,960	3.41	736,440	3.36	1,493,235	3.57	1,396,430	3.87	1,195,565	4.49
SWORDFISH, DRESSED	21,084	59.14	99,266	42.41	93,507	41.75	53,167	46.87	-	-
WHITING, DRESSED	2,924,311	4.00	2,145,415	4.00	2,326,917	4.00	2,426,284	4.00	1,327,698	4.00
WHITING, ROUND	1,600	1.44	225	-	11,595	8.46	6,785	8.03	2,690	3.05
WOLFFISH, DRAWN	129,945	8.83	19,885	7.30	-	-	31,480	6.71	8,538	8.61
SCALLOPS (MEATS)	25	-	4	-	4,245	35.90	-	-	10,861	36.50
OTHER FOR FOOD	22,520	3.57	7,060	6.00	8,278	5.19	-	-	17,977	7.05
TOTAL, AS LANDED	17,236,073	5.62	10,829,765	6.10	16,794,266	6.34	16,420,238	7.32	12,534,295	8.21
TOTAL IN 1948, AS LANDED	21,102,782	6.92	18,821,807	7.17	17,443,207	8.39	15,942,485	9.53	14,173,606	9.51

(CONTINUED ON NEXT PAGE)

LANDINGS AT CERTAIN MASSACHUSETTS PORTS

LANDINGS AT BOSTON, 1949 - Continued

SPECIES	NOVEMBER POUNDS	NOVEMBER AV. PRICE PER POUND	DECEMBER POUNDS	DECEMBER AV. PRICE PER POUND	TOTAL, 1949 POUNDS	TOTAL, 1949 AV. PRICE PER POUND	TOTAL, 1948 POUNDS	TOTAL, 1948 AV. PRICE PER POUND
COD, DRAWN:								
LARGE	448,239	10.51¢	405,696	9.46¢	13,071,550	7.85¢	16,418,789	8.05¢
MARKET	1,035,550	6.20	745,285	6.20	14,336,423	6.41	16,835,939	7.47
SCROD	167,820	5.16	70,535	4.26	1,236,765	5.46	1,455,590	7.03
CUSK, DRAWN	96,205	4.62	108,055	5.88	1,197,454	4.78	1,075,929	5.80
FLOUNDERS, ROUND:								
GRAY SOLE	122,015	10.07	133,375	12.50	1,403,032	10.50	995,587	11.52
LEMON SOLE	59,075	17.17	32,795	23.26	1,562,090	12.40	2,056,315	13.87
YELLOWTAIL	313,595	5.00	100,032	7.43	1,701,675	6.60	3,258,490	6.68
BLACKBACK	320,435	8.08	199,032	8.14	2,031,894	9.33	1,711,995	11.17
DAB	118,510	6.60	104,510	8.86	1,406,555	6.59	1,129,475	8.73
FLUKE							100	19.00
HADDOCK, DRAWN:								
LARGE	2,565,865	11.25	2,662,935	12.14	52,847,974	8.82	58,129,574	9.96
SCROD	1,733,505	8.58	1,193,875	9.04	37,297,745	6.90	47,177,883	8.43
HADDOCK, ROU DW SCROD							1,000	12.00
HAKE:								
RED, ROUND					1,600	6.19	6,525	6.62
WHITE, DRESSED:								
LARGE	361,470	5.46	259,505	7.82	3,244,830	6.56	3,446,565	7.12
SMALL	3,100	5.45			45,600	7.30	8,945	6.89
HALIBUT, DRAWN	6,841	20.26	4,367	23.04	219,394	23.73	248,226	23.96
MACKEREL, RD	229,100	11.05	85,045	11.11	709,365	11.43	3,472,987	7.39
POLLOCK, DRAWN	1,246,465	3.48	1,820,675	2.91	13,177,878	3.58	17,683,169	4.49
POLLOCK, B.					7,920	2.83	890	4.83
OCEAN PERCH (ROSE-FISH), ROUND	434,135	4.64	570,125	4.24	12,112,955	4.11	11,383,271	4.37
S UP OR PORGY, ROU DW					11,935	8.04		
SWORDFISH, DRESSED					267,024	44.39	303,107	50.46
WHITING, DRESSED	280	2.50	2,205	4.35	12,958,715	4.06	11,373,121	4.40
WHITING, ROUND	50	4.00	1,450	2.62	35,605	3.36	54,655	3.25
WOLFFISH, DRAWN	14,048	8.55	17,389	8.82	1,332,771	9.48	1,168,986	9.27
SCALLOPS (MEATS)	47,772	35.83	7,192	36.00	124,634	36.51	250,252	54.53
OTHER FOR FOOD	9,622	4.60	5,880	4.66	1/ 124,997	5.70	330,998	3.61
TOTAL, AS LANDED	9,332,697	8.17	8,531,046	8.14	172,470,390	7.07	199,980,363	8.09
TOTAL IN 1948, AS LANDED	16,840,913	7.41	11,721,587	8.05			199,980,363	8.09

1/ THE ITEMS UNDER "OTHER FOR FOOD" INCLUDE ANGLERFISH, 495 POUNDS, VALUED AT $14; BUTTERFISH, 26,484 POUNDS, VALUED AT $2,761; CONGER EELS, 650 POUNDS, VALUED AT $15; SEA HERRING, 17,325 POUNDS, VALUED AT $346; RAJAFISH, 24,130 POUNDS, VALUED AT $656; SEA BASS, 1,875 POUNDS, VALUED AT $251; SHAD, 150 POUNDS, VALUED AT $12; SHARKS, 16,213 POUNDS, VALUED AT $1,093; STURGEON, 1,110 POUNDS, VALUED AT $146; TAUTOG, 60 POUNDS, VALUED AT $3; BLUEFIN TUNA, 1,960 POUNDS, VALUED AT $235; MIXED, 32,320 POUNDS, VALUED AT $1,469; PERIWINKLES, 150 POUNDS, VALUED AT $9; AND SQUID, 2,075 POUNDS, VALUED AT $118.

NOTE:--LANDINGS NOT INCLUDED IN THE ABOVE TABLE CONSISTED OF LIVERS, 422,462 POUNDS, VALUED AT $30,799, AND SPAWN, 2,453 POUNDS, VALUED AT $457.

LANDINGS AT CERTAIN MASSACHUSETTS PORTS

LANDINGS AT GLOUCESTER, 1949

SPECIES	JANUARY POUNDS	AV. PRICE PER POUND	FEBRUARY POUNDS	AV. PRICE PER POUND	MARCH POUNDS	AV. PRICE PER POUND	APRIL POUNDS	AV. PRICE PER POUND	MAY POUNDS	AV. PRICE PER POUND
COD, DRAWN:										
LARGE	134,885	6.57¢	269,810	5.39¢	411,105	6.05¢	636,280	5.07¢	960,950	5.02¢
MARKET	91,390	6.79	196,741	5.49	448,263	5.54	361,548	4.44	198,823	3.84
SCROD	7,905	4.90	5,118	4.77	149,549	6.11	60,210	3.74	22,185	3.51
CUSK, DRAWN	22,505	4.88	34,965	4.74	43,615	4.82	100,070	3.69	76,266	2.77
FLOUNDERS, ROUND:										
GRAY SOLE	115,095	7.91	223,460	8.17	3,607,450	5.68	424,691	6.91	264,034	4.92
LEMON SOLE	—	—	—	—	110	21.82	—	—	—	—
YELLOWTAIL	120,216	10.29	66,866	10.51	60,891	9.02	78,645	7.70	34,045	5.51
BLACKBACK	31,685	10.63	34,796	9.34	32,507	9.04	25,479	7.19	12,848	3.93
DAB	47,351	6.84	95,981	6.30	174,185	5.25	209,435	5.00	199,226	3.64
HADDOCK, DRAWN:										
LARGE	92,230	9.21	550,712	7.86	668,095	8.20	1,027,676	5.86	418,269	5.46
SCROD	46,245	7.20	136,860	6.41	228,989	6.71	306,410	5.10	135,175	4.86
HAKE:										
RED, ROUND	975	2.46	—	—	1,115	2.24	3,760	2.26	555	1.98
WHITE, DRESSED:										
LARGE	76,577	5.21	111,005	6.88	73,937	6.01	185,900	2.64	132,821	2.35
SMALL	65,555	5.63	62,945	6.84	77,071	7.27	46,180	3.27	52,120	2.32
HALIBUT, DRAWN	1,584	32.95	875	32.68	2,345	28.27	21,215	25.06	9,942	24.74
MACKEREL, ROUND	—	—	—	—	—	—	—	—	1,212,965	4.75
POLLOCK, DRAWN	122,105	3.20	147,262	2.97	321,393	3.40	746,400	2.33	405,506	2.22
OCEAN PERCH (ROSE- FISH), ROUND	6,650,167	4.34	7,595,108	4.33	8,611,969	5.34	12,722,717	5.09	21,670,388	4.40
WHITING, DRESSED	19,664	5.48	13,562	5.91	2,952	5.96	66,039	4.89	1,619,425	3.60
WHITING, ROUND	29,490	3.83	40,518	4.62	40,690	5.16	50,247	3.84	61,771	2.60
WOLFFISH, ROUND	5,085	5.70	5,396	8.19	19,841	9.38	40,939	5.57	17,618	5.05
SCALLOPS (MEATS)	—	—	—	—	—	—	—	—	2,426	32.48
OTHER FOR FOOD	58,790	3.86	150,065	4.01	64,950	4.56	222,424	3.58	326,642	2.51
OT ® 2/	—	—	—	—	—	—	—	—	9,400	1.16
TOTAL, AS LANDED	7,749,499	4.68	9,744,045	4.81	15,041,022	5.39	17,336,265	5.02	27,843,400	4.33
TOTAL IN 1948, AS LANDED	4,852,972	6.98	9,701,663	6.05	16,486,203	4.95	17,915,185	4.30	30,026,928	3.95

SEE FOOTNOTES AT END OF TABLE

(CONTINUED ON NEXT PAGE)

LANDINGS AT CERTAIN MASSACHUSETTS PORTS

LANDINGS AT GLOUCESTER, 1949 - Continued

SPECIES	JUNE POUNDS	JUNE AV. PRICE PER POUND	JULY POUNDS	JULY AV. PRICE PER POUND	AUGUST POUNDS	AUGUST AV. PRICE PER POUND	SEPTEMBER POUNDS	SEPTEMBER AV. PRICE PER POUND	OCTOBER POUNDS	OCTOBER AV. PRICE PER POUND
COD, DRAWN:										
LARGE	493,643	6.19¢	277,254	6.88¢	181,395	7.13¢	160,047	7.76¢	244,359	8.36¢
MARKET	177,138	3.57	207,861	3.95	95,140	4.44	92,038	5.56	176,358	5.93
60	5,755	3.57	5,390	3.02	215	3.72	320	2.81	7,370	4.45
USKE DRAWN	59,005	2.48	113,035	2.60	84,802	2.62	86,175	2.74	70,235	2.87
FLOUNDERS, ROUND:										
GRAY SOLE	99,625	4.39	83,915	5.13	113,275	5.42	133,364	5.95	151,661	5.88
LEMON SOLE			4,620	6.47			255	11.76		
YELLOWTAIL	50,665	7.10	33,095	8.04	1,520	6.58	14,590	6.59	18,517	6.52
BLACKBACK	3,160	5.51	5,365	5.11	4,415	4.42	3,415	8.64	2,876	7.34
DAB	79,302	3.49	120,728	3.71	101,948	3.87	87,774	4.18	86,930	4.80
HADDOCK, DRAWN:										
LARGE	667,759	5.22	1,079,724	6.03	686,910	5.89	556,328	7.07	428,563	9.12
SCROD	73,695	4.24	492,190	4.00	102,630	4.37	75,175	5.04	83,005	6.04
HAKE:										
RED, ROUND					11,380	2.38	200	2.00		
WHITE, DRESSED:										
LARGE	119,525	2.54	228,670	3.55	172,679	3.31	237,841	4.65	237,235	5.20
SMALL	57,791	2.44	91,875	2.20	73,585	2.30	68,205	2.62	155,785	4.59
HALIBUT, DRAWN	2,645	19.28	2,576	22.48	4,027	24.51	5,197	22.24	6,303	24.18
MACKEREL, ROUND	2,239,167	4.66	1,556,231	4.47	619,311	4.20	230,557	9.50	10,295	9.62
POLLOCK, DRAWN	398,851	2.19	293,197	2.62	394,703	2.53	365,210	3.34	509,865	3.33
POLLOCK, ROUND			7,688	1.30	12,940	1.04	21,075	1.00		
OCEAN PER B (ROSE-FISH), ROUND	21,126,995	3.65	20,103,758	3.72	20,149,653	3.80	15,647,937	4.16	14,053,790	4.84
SWORDFISH, DRESSED			33,881	36.41	30,475	39.29	5,790	51.00		
WHITING, DRESSED	1,236,199	3.87	2,173,943	4.00	3,833,180	4.00	4,628,995	4.00	2,686,906	4.00
WHITING, ROUND	85,625	1.40	255,865	1.50	693,711	1.51	590,098	1.61	413,472	1.56
WOLFFISH, DRAWN	8,040	5.14	20,301	4.69	4,832	3.95	9,070	4.00	6,787	3.71
SCALLOPS (MEATS)									914	40.04
OTHER FOR FOOD	486,161	2.42	963,043	2.72	1,088,535	4.33	2,262,664	1.66	972,138	1.94
OTHER 2/	176,110	0.94	1,173,873	0.99	5,173,104	1.19	2,754,950	1.11	2,841,669	0.94
TOTAL, AS LANDED	27,646,656	3.76	29,328,078	3.77	33,634,365	3.47	28,037,380	3.71	23,365,053	4.19
TOTAL IN 1948, AS LANDED	28,038,433	4.16	31,706,284	3.98	33,661,744	4.16	24,797,953	5.08	22,905,727	4.90

SEE FOOTNOTES AT END OF TABLE

(CONTINUED ON NEXT PAGE)

LANDINGS AT CERTAIN MASSACHUSETTS PORTS

LANDINGS AT GLOUCESTER, 1949 - Continued

SPECIES	NOVEMBER POUNDS	AV. PRICE PER POUND	DECEMBER POUNDS	AV. PRICE PER POUND	TOTAL, 1949 POUNDS	AV. PRICE PER POUND	TOTAL, 1948 POUNDS	AV. PRICE PER POUND
COD, DRAWN:								
LARGE	221,475	8.11¢	205,580	6.20¢	4,196,783	6.07¢	5,528,419	5.99¢
MARK TC	239,910	5.14	167,008	5.18	2,452,218	4.93	2,090,553	5.73
SCROD	30,715	3.64	32,730	3.41	327,462	4.80	77,965	5.02
CUSK, DRAWN	46,915	2.83	39,910	2.82	777,498	3.10	793,568	4.25
FLOUNDERS, ROUND:								
GRAY SOLE	151,345	5.25	126,010	5.68	5,493,925	5.85	1,103,416	6.43
LEMON SOLE	-	-	-	-	4,985	7.08	6,630	7.96
YELLOWTAIL	36,310	5.16	51,900	6.47	567,360	8.21	635,323	8.11
BLACKBACK	17,083	4.99	36,060	5.40	209,689	7.56	146,118	10.29
DAB	110,602	4.34	53,765	4.29	1,367,227	4.56	846,056	5.48
FLUKE	-	-	185	9.73	185	9.73	-	-
HADDOCK, DRAWN:								
LARGE	331,770	8.60	211,575	8.42	6,719,631	6.77	7,537,028	7.66
S ROD	76,715	5.32	39,085	5.31	1,796,174	5.12	3,624,686	6.30
HAKE:								
RED, ROUND	-	-	-	-	17,985	2.34	76,096	2.20
WHITE, DRESSED:								
LARGE	213,935	4.28	78,870	5.57	1,868,995	4.17	1,914,666	4.35
SMALL	86,370	2.95	43,185	3.24	880,667	3.90	1,332,101	404
HALIBUT, DRAWN	833	26.65	764	24.08	58,306	24.71	32,257	24.53
MACKEREL	892,023	8.17	115,595	7.53	6,876,144	5.27	19,866,200	5.22
POLLOCK, DRAWN	1,137,330	2.28	1,235,475	2.17	6,077,297	2.53	9,012,727	3.61
POLLOCK, ROUND	-	-	27,815	1.80	69,518	1.36	192,185	2.14
OCEAN PERCH (ROSE-FISH), ROUND	11,899,109	4.92	9,039,351	5.04	169,280,942	4.31	176,800,876	4.19
SWORDFISH, DRESSED	-	-	-	-	70,146	38.43	42,241	51.30
WHITING, DRESSED	582,176	3.98	7,950	3.99	17,072,992	3.96	12,826,608	4.33
WHITING, ROUND	21,175	2.11	86,240	2.00	2,368,902	1.77	866,363	2.52
WOLFFISH, DRAWN	6,240	4.77	4,460	4.64	148,609	5.68	177,867	5.39
SCALLOPS (AM)	-	-	16,763	33.13	20,103	33.37	66,132	50.69
OTHER FOR FOOD	586,348	1.43	438,340	1.53	1/ 7,620,100	2.41	5,497,083	3.52
OTHER	1,637,850	0.96	799,670	0.95	14,566,625	1.07	-	-
TOTAL, AS LANDED	18,326,229	4.50	12,858,276	4.49	250,910,468	4.17	251,113,164	4.47
TOTAL IN 1948, AS LANDED	19,903,593	4.23	11,112,479	4.33	-	-	251,113,164	4.47

1/ THE ITEMS UNDER "OTHER FOR FOOD" INCLUDE ALEWIVES, 101,516 POUNDS, VALUED AT $1,819; BLUEFISH, 176 POUNDS, VALUED AT $9; BUTTERFISH, 98,872 POUNDS, VALUED AT $2,917; CREVALLE, 208 POUNDS, VALUED AT $4; SEA HERRING, 4,234,586 POUNDS, VALUED AT $59,934; LAUNCE, 3,100 POUNDS, VALUED AT $62; RAJAFISH, 265 POUNDS, VALUED AT $10; SALMON, 309 POUNDS, VALUED AT $10; SHAD, 4,984 POUNDS, VALUED AT $116; SHARKS, 22,546 POUNDS, VALUED AT $183; STRIPED BASS, 1,025 POUNDS, VALUED AT $154; STURGEON, 256 POUNDS, VALUED AT $45; BLUEFIN TUNA, 574,491 POUNDS, VALUED AT $43,203; MIXED, 2,322,633 POUNDS, VALUED AT $70,428; AND SQUID, 255,133 POUNDS, VALUED AT $4,021.

2/ INCLUDES FISH FOR REDUCTION OR ANIMAL FOOD. DATA NOT AVAILABLE BY SPECIES.

NOTE:—LANDINGS NOT INCLUDED IN THE ABOVE TABLE CONSISTED OF LIVERS, 1,673,571 POUNDS, VALUED AT $140,290, AND SPAWN, 75,805 POUNDS, VALUED AT $5,516.

LANDINGS AT CERTAIN MASSACHUSETTS PORTS

LANDINGS AT NEW BEDFORD, 1949

SPECIES	JANUARY		FEBRUARY		MARCH		APRIL		MAY	
	POUNDS	AV. PRICE PER POUND	POUNDS	AV. PRICE PER POUND	POUNDS	AV. PRICE PER POUND	POUNDS	AV. PRICE PER POUND	POUNDS	AV. PRICE PER POUND
COD, DRAWN:										
LARGE	31,005	10.62¢	120,755	5.70¢	172,005	8.12¢	180,045	4.39¢	52,640	4.11¢
MARKET	169,245	10.89	72,870	8.84	148,545	9.40	399,935	6.22	274,465	6.22
S ROD	53,130	9.37	31,275	7.76	174,685	7.36	83,130	4.55	55,910	5.49
USKG DRAWN	560	5.00	785	3.18	720	5.69	–	–	60	3.33
FLOUNDERS, ROUND:										
GRAY SOLE	8,450	9.72	49,525	11.14	173,390	8.23	8,220	7.72	21,630	7.53
LEMON SOLE	220,255	21.95	77,640	22.42	170,570	17.26	250,970	14.34	433,205	10.14
YELLOWTAIL	1,264,845	14.16	1,294,388	13.32	911,915	13.59	357,550	11.98	238,410	9.40
BLACKBACK	503,540	18.13	325,320	17.84	497,165	12.87	705,136	11.54	1,931,548	9.26
DAB	1,025	8.20	4,320	6.90	21,720	9.46	27,270	7.32	67,175	6.14
FLUKE	191,205	19.17	269,550	16.60	191,805	18.88	206,827	17.83	57,202	20.46
HADDOCK, DRAWN:										
LARGE	290,335	12.60	225,170	9.17	378,525	9.96	1,011,315	6.55	974,100	6.61
S ROD	296,685	10.51	149,895	7.78	295,550	8.64	771,785	5.38	996,500	5.15
HAKE:										
RED, ROUND 1/	–	–	–	–	60	3.33	2,098,195	0.76	7,362,543	0.77
WHITE, DRESSED:										
LARGE	6,920	6.04	15,595	6.45	2,840	6.58	50,390	9.37	6,000	4.20
SMALL	55	5.45	–	–	–	–	–	–	–	–
HALIBUT, DRAWN	839	32.06	519	26.78	3,669	21.70	8,045	20.42	10,028	21.82
MACKEREL, ROUND	160	11.25	–	–	5,950	17.41	63,210	8.72	56,475	8.75
POLLOCK, DRAW N	6,460	3.95	16,500	3.05	59,925	2.75	79,715	2.24	17,960	2.59
OCEAN PER B (ROSE-FISH), ROUND	5,630	3.87	10,280	4.80	48,070	3.13	12,130	7.67	12,440	2.61
SCUP OR PORGY, ROUND	5,600	6.39	555	1.00	6,960	3.33	26,900	2.59	14,065	3.68
WHITING, DRESSED	500	–	500	1.00	–	–	26,835	3.41	29,895	4.41
WOLFFISH, DRAWN	325	5.54	3,550	3.92	17,180	5.55	–	–	–	–
SCALLOPS (MEATS)	630,217	40.65	516,082	38.55	596,142	43.78	1,042,797	36.69	1,299,347	32.81
OTHER FOR FOOD	107,020	7.08	118,695	7.45	64,780	10.96	1,485,080	1.29	16,585	6.88
TOTAL, AS LA DED.	3,801,506	18.88	3,303,669	16.85	3,942,181	16.45	8,813,480	8.73	13,928,183	6.42
TOTAL IN 1948, AS LA DEB	3,248,982	19.41	2,916,452	22.81	4,624,951	17.72	6,433,762	15.43	7,998,076	12.96

SEE FOOTNOTES AT END OF TABLE

(CONTINUED ON NEXT PAGE)

NEW ENGLAND FISHERIES

LANDINGS AT CERTAIN MASSACHUSETTS PORTS

LANDINGS AT NEW BEDFORD, 1949 - Continued

SPECIES	JUNE POUNDS	JUNE AV. PRICE PER POUND	JULY POUNDS	JULY AV. PRICE PER POUND	AUGUST POUNDS	AUGUST AV. PRICE PER POUND	SEPTEMBER POUNDS	SEPTEMBER AV. PRICE PER POUND	OCTOBER POUNDS	OCTOBER AV. PRICE PER POUND
COD, DRAWN:										
LARGE	13,195	5.34¢	29,655	5.56¢	2,570	6.46¢	1,240	10.06¢	13,645	8.84¢
MARKET	292,005	5.88	340,785	5.99	100,790	6.56	120,070	8.30	353,770	8.87
SCROD	63,950	5.45	61,590	5.52	20,070	5.86	15,480	7.02	68,420	8.03
CUSK, DRAWN	-	-	100	2.00	-	-	-	-	125	1.60
FLOUNDERS, ROUND:										
GRAY SOLE	52,490	9.00	27,645	9.53	2,455	6.64	-	-	580	7.08
LEMON SOLE	323,890	12.62	143,245	19.26	293,275	13.83	474,005	14.40	176,225	17.73
YELLOWTAIL	675,925	9.44	1,126,155	9.50	3,292,125	8.17	2,921,960	9.30	3,026,225	9.74
BLACKBACK	1,238,915	11.08	605,365	14.96	538,519	12.11	724,720	12.45	754,045	12.13
DAB	28,085	6.97	3,795	8.17	-	-	-	-	1,955	5.52
FLUKE	42,750	22.19	165,141	26.12	83,110	18.13	103,467	23.76	37,595	14.81
HADDOCK, DRAWN:										
LARGE	803,000	6.85	460,308	8.00	88,275	8.65	137,390	9.91	250,605	12.17
SCROD	840,060	5.16	791,010	5.40	160,935	5.84	124,465	8.08	106,285	8.52
HAKE:										
RED, ROUND 1/	7,936,021	0.77	6,905,230	0.97	4,945,200	0.79	2,736,826	0.84	5,491,200	0.96
WHITE, DRESSED:										
LARGE	27,755	3.86	13,945	3.81	3,120	3.40	975	2.46	7,205	4.59
SMALL	195	2.56	-	-	-	-	-	-	-	-
HALIBUT, DRAWN	5,782	19.54	1,130	15.93	-	-	-	-	45	31.11
MACKEREL, ROUND	203,640	3.82	4,303	6.16	805	7.45	205	10.73	4,975	12.02
POLLOCK, DRAWN	2,550	2.39	6,555	2.36	265	4.15	250	4.80	1,675	2.33
OCEAN PERCH (ROSE-FISH), ROUND	-	-	-	-	-	-	-	-	8,605	5.90
SCUP OR PORGY, ROUND	61,685	2.33	4,765	3.42	3,640	3.52	9,310	6.92	2,900	4.00
SWORDFISH, DRESSED	1,676	71.06	76,835	44.13	56,910	43.50	12,565	48.61	718	51.39
WHITING, DRESSED	-	-	4,500	3.24	450	1.56	-	-	305	2.95
WOLFFISH, DRAWN	12,675	3.59	5,285	2.76	-	-	-	-	275	3.64
SCALLOPS (MEATS)	1,489,614	35.28	1,305,461	36.24	1,238,245	34.85	963,412	37.84	826,827	37.99
OTHER FOR FOOD	13,149	7.80	113,940	1.80	85,160	2.46	66,195	6.38	52,530	4.72
TOTAL, AS LANDED	14,129,007	6.93	12,196,743	7.62	10,915,919	8.36	8,412,535	10.56	11,188,735	7.80
TOTAL IN 1948, AS LANDED	8,358,109	13.22	8,853,908	15.38	7,844,141	16.35	7,916,538	16.96	8,460,053	12.78

(CONTINUED ON NEXT PAGE)

SEE FOOTNOTES AT END OF TABLE

LANDINGS AT CERTAIN MASSACHUSETTS PORTS
LANDINGS AT NEW BEDFORD, 1949 - Continued

SPECIES	NOVEMBER POUNDS	NOVEMBER AV. PRICE PER POUND	DECEMBER POUNDS	DECEMBER AV. PRICE PER POUND	TOTAL, 1949 POUNDS	TOTAL, 1949 AV. PRICE PER POUND	TOTAL, 1948 POUNDS	TOTAL, 1948 AV. PRICE PER POUND
COD, DRAWN:								
LARGE	20,425	6.45¢	19,680	6.14¢	656,860	6.18¢	1,492,620	7.48¢
MARKET	344,565	6.28	134,868	6.03	2,691,913	7.14	3,194,040	7.69
S ROD	47,320	5.52	56,295	5.72	731,255	6.51	1,643,305	6.19
USKG, DRAWN	250	5.60	—	—	2,600	4.38	2,630	3.99
FLOUNDERS, RON D:								
GRAY SOLE	1,440	7.71	6,030	5.44	351,655	8.77	91,875	9.50
LEMON SOLE	186,975	17.28	161,225	21.32	2,911,480	15.46	3,071,100	16.36
YELLOWTAIL	2,280,370	8.66	2,260,245	8.68	19,652,313	9.68	25,214,097	9.56
BLACKBACK	957,385	9.33	629,637	11.90	9,452,195	11.82	10,454,574	11.97
DAB	3,230	5.17	2,575	8.08	161,150	7.02	990,715	8.60
FLUKE	43,250	17.28	30,464	14.98	1,430,376	19.41	2,035,792	20.82
HADDOCK, DRAWN:								
LARGE	219,645	10.79	395,770	11.38	5,234,438	9.37	5,630,786	9.72
S ROD	77,050	8.47	78,260	9.50	4,688,490	6.18	5,779,265	7.84
HAKE:								
RED, ROUND 1/	2,195,567	1.00	—	—	39,670,842	0.85	4,063,935	1.24
WHITE, DRESSED:								
LARGE	12,335	4.00	4,115	3.11	151,195	3.32	271,040	3.81
SMALL	95	3.16	145	2.07	490	2.86	9,810	4.25
HALIBUT, DRAWN	—	—	615	23.00	30,612	21.21	34,421	24.84
MACKEREL, ROUND	—	—	2,410	10.25	342,133	5.99	1,683,400	7.60
POLLOCK, DRAWN	4,010	4.86	3,730	3.00	199,595	2.63	374,440	3.97
POLLOCK, ROUND	—	—	—	—	—	—	5,555	2.23
OCEAN PER B (ROSE-								
FISH), ROUND	4,945	5.42	2,600	5.50	80,130	3.71	350,102	4.07
SCUP OR PORGY, ROUND	100	3.00	12,550	7.98	132,635	4.09	873,751	3.06
SWORDFISH, DRESSED	146	56.16	—	—	148,850	44.62	164,561	48.68
WHITING, DRESSED	—	—	—	—	24,270	3.32	800	2.12
WHITI G¾ ROUND	—	—	—	—	—	—	58,761	1.56
WOLFFISH, DRAWN	125	5.60	240	2.08	96,835	4.10	86,115	4.45
SCALLOPS (A1B)	911,262	37.10	887,739	36.57	2/ 11,707,165	36.70	10,081,805	52.37
OTHER FOR FOOD	48,068	2.59	7,405	6.09	2,178,607	2.63	812,217	10.98
OTHER 3/	1,140,715	1.00	1,865,815	1.00	3,006,530	1.00		
TOTAL, AS LANDED	8,499,303	8.90	6,562,313	10.99	105,693,574	9.15	77,571,522	15.18
TOTAL IN 1948, AS LANDED	6,725,846	9.61	4,190,704	15.53	—	—	77,571,522	15.18

1/ NEARLY THE ENTIRE CATCH OF RED HAKE LANDED AT NEW BEDFORD WAS USED FOR ANIMAL FOOD OR MANUFACTURE INTO MEAL AND OIL. AT TIMES SOME TRASH FISH WERE INCLUDED WITH THE LANDINGS OF RED HAKE.

2/ THE ITEMS UNDER "OTHER FOR FOOD" INCLUDE BUTTERFISH, 376,690 POUNDS, VALUED AT $28,733; CONGER EELS, 1,615 POUNDS, VALUED AT $46; OCEAN POUT, 5,175 POUNDS, VALUED AT $71; RAJAFISH, 1,350 POUNDS, VALUED AT $27; SEA BASS, 14,540 POUNDS, VALUED AT $1,437; SHARKS, 152,390 POUNDS, VALUED AT $3,570; STURGEON, 2,677 POUNDS, VALUED AT $309; TAUTOG, 2,405 POUNDS, VALUED AT $125; TILEFISH, 166,305 POUNDS, VALUED AT $12,076; BLUEFIN TUNA, 9,555 POUNDS, VALUED AT $983; MIXED, 1,428,930 POUNDS, VALUED AT $11,729; LOBSTERS, 1,515 POUNDS, VALUED AT $288; AND SQUID, 15,260 POUNDS, VALUED AT $391.

3/ INCLUDES FISH FOR REDUCTION OR ANIMAL FOOD. DATA NOT AVAILABLE BY SPECIES.

NOTE:--LANDINGS NOT INCLUDED IN THE ABOVE TABLE CONSISTED OF LIVERS, 1,249 POUNDS, VALUED AT $756, AND SPAWN, 235 POUNDS, VALUED AT $44.

LANDINGS AT CERTAIN MASSACHUSETTS PORTS

LANDINGS AT CAPE COD PORTS, 1949

SPECIES	JANUARY POUNDS	JANUARY AV. PRICE PER POUND	FEBRUARY POUNDS	FEBRUARY AV. PRICE PER POUND	MARCH POUNDS	MARCH AV. PRICE PER POUND	APRIL POUNDS	APRIL AV. PRICE PER POUND	MAY POUNDS	MAY AV. PRICE PER POUND
COD, DRAWN:										
LARGE	114,691	12.01¢	68,187	9.84¢	103,050	8.57¢	132,682	6.89¢	130,063	5.54¢
MARKET	120,342	9.14	78,817	7.10	83,724	6.87	74,279	5.32	74,291	4.58
SCROD	4,615	7.17	7,355	6.40	4,405	6.31	3,350	4.06	940	4.26
USE5 DRAWN	23	4.35	7,104	6.58	662	4.98	449	2.23	7,136	1.35
FLOUNDERS, ROUND:										
GRAY SOLE	195	10.26	1,395	11.91	7,178	9.08	2,363	8.21	4,665	9.24
LEMON SOLE	2,291	16.66	625	18.56	4,415	14.25	5,731	14.31	4,350	7.06
YELLOWTAIL	146,488	12.85	264,426	11.34	309,306	10.30	139,178	9.42	54,257	7.80
BLACKBACK	23,838	14.88	14,890	11.56	52,562	12.08	180,442	10.92	279,465	5.78
DAB	67	5.97	678	6.93	1,229	8.62	864	3.62	1,596	4.51
FLUKE	16,489	15.04	32,487	15.19	21,984	17.07	25,277	16.26	36,828	18.94
HADDOCK, DRAWN:										
LARGE	72,131	11.18	105,814	9.32	187,233	9.10	69,663	6.68	94,865	7.45
SCROD	430	9.53	—	—	370	8.65	3,220	4.10	1,185	5.49
HAKE, WHITE, DRESSED:										
LARGE	1,440	10.97	2,001	7.30	2,524	8.44	708	5.65	7,538	4.36
SMALL	—	—	250	6.80	15	6.67	896	4.91	1,073	3.36
HALIBUT, DRAWN	334	40.12	474	44.51	7,117	46.09	26,510	34.94	15,934	34.41
MACKEREL, ROUND	—	—	5	20.00	—	—	3,765	12.64	320,127	11.06
POLLOCK, DRAW N	10,283	4.76	2,468	4.26	5,998	4.35	11,081	3.63	28,296	2.88
OCEAN PERCH (ROSE-FISH), ROUND	1,005	3.78	1,140	3.51	1,185	5.40	4,000	5.00	123,755	2.90
S UP OR PORGY, ROUND	1,965	7.02	35	11.42	30	10.00	4	—	109,380	3.34
WHITING, DRESSED	—	—	—	—	—	—	—	—	301,925	2.22
WHITING, ROUND	5,010	2.48	140	2.14	—	—	9,630	4.44	31,941	6.55
WOLFFISH, DRAWN	6,725	7.36	15,058	6.77	31,063	9.68	28,573	6.03	153,491	2.11
SCALLOPS (MEATS)	119,104	40.47	51,096	41.01	49,192	44.45	90,048	36.94	1,280,614	2.17
OTHER FOR FOOD	31,303	4.81	33,339	4.78	43,196	5.16	484,307	3.70	10,375	0.99
OTHER 2/	—	—	—	—	—	—	—	—	—	—
TOTAL, AS LANDED	678,759	16.17	680,794	12.30	916,438	11.59	1,297,020	9.23	3,074,130	5.90
TOTAL IN 1948, AS LANDED	668,099	15.97	877,628	17.22	963,245	14.71	1,986,865	8.73	3,900,288	5.66

SEE FOOTNOTES AT END OF TABLE

(CONTINUED ON NEXT PAGE)

LANDINGS AT CERTAIN MASSACHUSETTS PORTS

LANDINGS AT CAPE COD PORTS, 1949 - Continued

SPECIES	JUNE POUNDS	JUNE AV. PRICE PER POUND	JULY POUNDS	JULY AV. PRICE PER POUND	AUGUST POUNDS	AUGUST AV. PRICE PER POUND	SEPTEMBER POUNDS	SEPTEMBER AV. PRICE PER POUND	OCTOBER POUNDS	OCTOBER AV. PRICE PER LB
COD, DRAWN:										
LARGE	131,778	6.44¢	138,608	7.24¢	125,675	7.49¢	118,994	8.75¢	86,790	9.82¢
MARKET	69,305	4.64	120,699	4.53	120,967	4.50	127,025	5.96	156,880	6.57
SCROD	12,260	4.57	1,990	4.59	480	3.96	35	5.71	4,196	6.74
USK & DRAWN	7,017	1.27	1,158	2.16	1,049	3.81	3,901	1.56	996	1.91
FLOUNDERS, ROUND:										
GRAY SOLE	17,498	7.96	5,971	9.19	245	6.12	1,450	10.14	615	13.01
LEMON SOLE	2,830	10.00	3,783	13.51	12,653	12.71	29,299	11.24	52,136	11.17
YELLOWTAIL	139,935	8.14	209,355	8.50	287,472	6.96	239,539	7.48	144,861	8.76
BLACKBACK	193,415	6.09	50,513	9.17	76,822	8.42	40,677	11.04	75,441	8.66
DAB	12,960	6.25	5,412	5.40	2,237	4.11	5,972	7.74	2,695	8.65
FLUKE, DRAWN:	40,864	16.83	67,779	20.22	48,756	14.43	20,452	17.83	35,926	13.61
HADDOCK, DRAWN:										
LARGE	157,759	6.71	238,509	8.12	430,481	6.50	219,986	8.13	219,735	9.41
SCROD	29,640	5.55	9,500	5.62	987	5.37	1,335	7.86	5,070	8.90
HAKE:										
RED, ROUND	640	2.03	8,818	4.34	10,795	5.26	5,844	5.80	5,491	6.02
WHITE, DRESSED:				-		-				
LARGE	19,462	3.40							140	5.00
SMALL	1,496	2.49								
HALIBUT, DRAWN	2,382	31.02	836	35.53	920	3.56	1,131	39.79	585	39.15
MACKEREL, ROUND	2,291,761	7.94	1,246,846	11.93	1,070,673	13.77	158,970	13.38	106,725	13.21
POLLOCK, DRAWN	77,612	3.66	9,325	4.28	10,104	3.39	9,691	3.92	5,564	4.64
OCEAN PERCH (ROSE-FISH), ROUND	159,212	2.59	13,582	3.37	400	4.00	160	3.75	215	4.19
SCUP OR PORGY, ROUND					2,206	6.80	1,182	8.46	2,602	6.23
SWORDFISH DRESSED	18,747	55.32	87,131	42.70	48,027	42.45	18,475	49.06		
WHITING, DRESSED	1,070,495	3.39	1,190,820	3.44	1,431,993	3.33	829,785	3.34	174,795	3.25
WHITING, ROUND	1,305,705	2.00	1,442,245	1.99	2,036,940	2.00	1,351,354	2.00	1,342,463	2.00
WOLFFISH, DRAWN	10,303	4.71	2,558	4.38	1,279	4.61	2,126	3.20	1,563	3.00
SCALLOPS (MEATS)	84,345	35.42	82,228	35.94	164,171	35.47	144,701	38.13	194,511	40.06
OTH OR FOR FOOD	565,363	2.87	314,571	7.26	344,229	7.58	322,455	7.92	344,976	6.67
OTHER 2/	22,433	1.21	21,670	1.12	25,500	1.08	199,555	0.97	830,190	0.79
TOTAL, AS LANDED	6,374,207	5.64	5,273,807	7.26	6,255,061	6.72	3,844,094	6.11	3,795,193	5.95
TOTAL IN 1948, AS LANDED	10,662,123	5.90	8,746,846	7.65	6,261,623	8.04	4,765,088	6.44	2,969,829	6.96

(CONTINUED ON NEXT PAGE)

SEE FOOTNOTES AT END OF TABLE

LANDINGS AT CERTAIN MASSACHUSETTS PORTS

LANDINGS AT CAPE COD PORTS, 1949 - Continued

SPECIES	NOVEMBER POUNDS	NOVEMBER AV. PRICE PER POUND	DECEMBER POUNDS	DECEMBER AV. PRICE PER POUND	TOTAL, 1949 POUNDS	TOTAL, 1949 AV. PRICE PER POUND	TOTAL, 1948 POUNDS	TOTAL, 1948 AV. PRICE PER POUND
COD, DRAWN:								
LARG E	60,972	8.94¢	126,593	10.34¢	1,338,113	8.30¢	1,636,584	8.90¢
MARKET	90,687	5.13	127,360	5.90	1,243,376	5.95	1,069,325	7.62
S ROCE	4,635	6.26	19,083	4.76	63,244	5.38	60,503	5.30
CUSK, DRAWN	1,113	2.16	33	3.03	23,641	1.72	71,960	3.18
FLOUNDERS, ROUND:								
GRAY SOLE			280	11.07	41,845	8.78	55,306	12.65
LEMON SOLE	18,714	10.13	8,284	16.39	145,101	11.73	116,680	14.11
YELLOWTAIL	179,818	7.37	223,181	7.69	2,337,826	8.92	2,319,232	10.60
BLACKBACK	217,945	8.82	178,095	8.80	1,364,105	8.40	1,425,255	9.68
DABS	850	6.23	860	8.81	35,420	6.36	62,625	10.25
FLUKE	5,825	22.99	2,185	15.88	354,862	16.93	332,235	19.66
HADDOCK, DRAWN:								
LARGE	123,546	9.22	116,147	9.92	2,035,869	8.16	2,248,506	9.18
S ROCE	2,775	10.56	695	11.22	55,207	6.21	91,700	7.51
HAKE:								
RED, ROUND	-	-	-	-	640	2.03	1,391	4.53
WHITE, DRESSED:								
LARGE	10,919	6.21	1,839	6.96	77,379	5.20	291,339	5.14
SMALL	306	4.25	320	4.38	4,486	3.77	69,355	1.33
HALIBUT, DRAWN	158	39.87	156	39.74	56,537	36.33	62,608	35.98
MACKEREL, ROUND	45,353	13.67	-	-	5,244,225	10.60	8,897,324	10.49
POLLOCK, DRAWN	9,870	4.53	53,239	2.88	173,551	3.50	456,399	4.24
OCEAN PERCH (ROSE-FISH), ROUND	-	-	-	-	8,105	4.60	516,775	3.40
S UP OR PORGY, ROUND	15	13.33	15	6.67	304,603	2.86	633,563	2.62
SWORDFISH, DRESSED	-	-	-	-	162,380	44.02	117,224	48.33
WHITING, DRESSED	-	-	-	-	4,807,268	3.37	4,642,021	3.36
WHITING, ROUND	419,824	2.00	31,630	2.64	8,246,896	2.01	12,123,939	1.98
WOLFFISH, DRAWN	842	2.93	1,102	3.63	133,133	6.90	193,349	7.09
SCALLOPS (MEATS)	99,572	38.68	94,544	38.45	1,327,003	37.62	1,239,868	52.38
OTHER FOR FOOD	94,871	4.95	53,627	4.19	1/ 3,912,851	4.39	5,717,503	4.65
OTHER 2/	594,975	0.60	538,850	0.90	2,233,548	0.85		
TOTAL, AS LANDED	1,983,585	6.14	1,578,118	7.24	35,751,206	6.88	44,454,469	7.50
TOTAL IN 1948, AS LANDED	1,734,889	7.40	917,946	10.37	-	-	44,454,469	7.50

1/ THE ITEMS UNDER "OTHER FOR FOOD" INCLUDE AMBERJACK, 113 POUNDS, VALUED AT $9; ANGLERFISH, 240 POUNDS, VALUED AT $7; BLUEFISH, 79 POUNDS, VALUED AT $23; BONITO, 40 POUNDS, VALUED AT $6; BUTTERFISH, 178,709 POUNDS, VALUED AT $15,821; CREVALLE, 915 POUNDS, VALUED AT $27; CUNNER (PERCH), 230 POUNDS, VALUED AT $7; CONGER EELS, 3,495 POUNDS, VALUED AT $157; FRIGATE MACKEREL, 1,257 POUNDS, VALUED AT $55; GRAYFISH, 14 POUNDS; SEA HERRING, 1,352,948 POUNDS, VALUED AT $30,732; KING WHITING, 18 POUNDS, VALUED AT $4; RAJAFISH, 548 POUNDS, VALUED AT $17; SEA BASS, 17,229 POUNDS, VALUED AT $3,575; SEA TROUT OR WEAKFISH, 764 POUNDS, VALUED AT $13; SHAD, 3,774 POUNDS, VALUED AT $367; SHARKS, 5,599 POUNDS, VALUED AT $548; STRIPED BASS, 20,463 POUNDS, VALUED AT $3,351; STURGEON, 1,168 POUNDS, VALUED AT $230; TAUTOG, 9,568 POUNDS, VALUED AT $551; TILEFISH, 34,359 POUNDS, VALUED AT $2,182; BLUEFIN TUNA, 727,360 POUNDS, VALUED AT $74,402; MIXED, 367,603 POUNDS, VALUED AT $12,995; AND SQUID, 1,187,048 POUNDS, VALUED AT $28,563.

2/ INCLUDES FISH FOR REDUCTION OR ANIMAL FOOD. DATA NOT AVAILABLE BY SPECIES.

NOTE:--LANDINGS NOT INCLUDED IN THE ABOVE TABLE CONSISTED OF LIVERS, 5,118 POUNDS, VALUED AT $1,894, AND SPAWN, 8,927 POUNDS, VALUED AT $920.

LANDINGS AT CERTAIN MASSACHUSETTS PORTS

SUMMARY OF FISHERY: BY GEAR AND SUBAREA, 1949

GEAR AND SUBAREA	CRAFT FISHING	TRIPS	DAYS ABSENT	COD, DRAWN LARGE	COD, DRAWN MARKET	COD, DRAWN SCROD	CUSK, DRAWN	FLOUNDERS, ROUND GRAY SOLE	FLOUNDERS, ROUND LEMON SOLE	FLOUNDERS, ROUND YELLOWTAIL
	NUMBER	NUMBER	NUMBER	POUNDS	POUNDS	POUNDS	POUNDS	POUNDS	POUNDS	POUNDS
LINE TRAWLS:										
E. BROWNS AND LA HAVE	2	5.2	55	28,375	51,200	3,500	9,300	-	-	-
SOUTHERN NOVA SCOTIA	2	0.5	4	1,485	3,300	-	2,060	-	-	-
WESTERN BROWNS	2	13.5	155	86,650	100,160	-	55,100	-	-	-
WESTERN NOVA SCOTIA	1	1.3	14	3,175	7,440	-	8,890	-	-	-
WESTERN MAINE	12	323.0	399	398,455	180,605	20,050	208,375	-	-	-
EASTERN MASSACHUSETTS	50	1,770.0	1,801	873,783	696,602	150,960	442,849	900	-	1,995
BR GROUNDS	7	14.3	37	29,260	22,400	225	53,660	-	-	-
WESTERN SIDE SOUTH CHANNEL	5	18.3	79	134,400	255,270	3,315	12,425	-	-	-
EASTERN SIDE SOUTH CHANNEL	2	18.5	17	16,382	29,500	-	16,200	-	-	-
NORTHERN EDGE OF GEORGES	2	10.8	74	273,848	134,250	-	50,250	-	-	-
CENTRAL AND S.E. GEORGES	1	0.1	1	5,985	1,800	-	-	-	-	-
SOUTHWEST GEORGES	1	1.0	16	300	1,300	-	1,900	-	-	-
OFF NO MAN'S LAND	1	11.0	14	-	-	-	-	-	-	-
S. NEW ENGLAND, UNCLASSIFIED	3	0.5	6	3,500	1,750	-	5,250	-	-	-
CAPE COD 1/	49	5,680.0	5,680	1,086,389	852,747	-	22,881	145	105,185	7,260
TOTAL	2/117	7,852.0	8,352	2,941,987	2,338,324	178,050	889,140	1,045	105,185	9,255
HAND LINES:										
EASTERN MASSACHUSETTS	128	1,398.0	1,398	186,016	29,608	75	2,113	-	-	-
CAPE COD 2/	49	582.0	582	46,624	61,946	35	30	-	441	-
TOTAL	2/162	1,980.0	1,980	232,640	91,554	110	2,143	-	441	-
HARPOONS:										
WESTERN BROWNS	4	2.8	55	-	-	-	-	-	-	-
EASTERN MASSACHUSETTS	6	9.0	9	-	-	-	-	-	-	-
EASTERN SIDE SOUTH CHANNEL	1	0.1	2	-	-	-	-	-	-	-
NORTHERN EDGE OF GEORGES	9	11.0	208	-	-	-	-	-	-	-
CENTRAL AND S.E. GEORGES	14	18.1	277	-	-	-	-	-	-	-
SOUTHWEST GEORGES	2	2.0	19	-	-	-	-	-	-	-
NANTUCKET SHOALS & LT'SHIP	1	1.5	3	-	-	-	-	-	-	-
OFF NO MAN'S LAND	15	42.0	225	-	-	-	-	-	-	-
S. NEW ENGLAND, UNCLASSIFIED	10	11.0	38	-	-	-	-	-	-	-
CAPE COD 2/	26	56.0	56	-	-	-	-	-	-	-
TOTAL	2/63	153.0	892	-	-	-	-	-	-	-
OTTER TRAWLS, LARGE:										
NORTHEAST CAPE BRETON	25	63.2	706	83,539	63,260	-	779	110,060	-	-
MIDAINE BANK	20	36.8	400	24,828	19,152	-	7,295	8,692	-	137,250
BANQUEREAU	38	111.0	1,229	572,980	784,301	146,720	6,612	515,253	-	-
CANSO BANK	27	103.8	1,171	257,424	273,668	37,690	11,173	2,052,847	-	-
MIDDLE GROUND	28	24.5	240	64,111	146,133	3,015	580	85,403	150	6,650
N.E. SABLE ISLAND BANK	18	-	-	67,072	140,500	50,470	-	1,350	1,090	198,040
S.E. SABLE ISLAND BANK	4	1.5	12	16,375	29,025	-	785	-	-	2,150
HORSESHOE GROUND	28	32.0	299	105,907	229,926	5,250	3,800	32,390	300	-
S.W. SABLE ISLAND BANK	17	19.7	193	131,725	262,475	13,150	4,725	350	100	57,180
EASTERN NOVA SCOTIA	14	12.9	164	5,555	9,197	-	4,907	12,924	-	29,150
EMERALD BANK	30	17.6	174	64,817	116,140	9,530	-	2,352	160	5,080

(CONTINUED ON NEXT PAGE)

SEE FOOTNOTES AT END OF TABLE

LANDINGS AT CERTAIN MASSACHUSETTS PORTS

SUMMARY OF FISHERY: BY GEAR AND SUBAREA, 1949 - Continued

GEAR AND SUBAREA	CRAFT FISHING (NUMBER)	TRIPS (NUMBER)	DAYS ABSENT (NUMBER)	COD, DRAWN — LARGE (POUNDS)	COD, DRAWN — MARKET (POUNDS)	COD, DRAWN — SCROD (POUNDS)	CUSK, DRAWN (POUNDS)	FLOUNDERS, ROUND — GRAY SOLE (POUNDS)	FLOUNDERS, ROUND — LEMON SOLE (POUNDS)	FLOUNDERS, ROUND — YELLOWTAIL (POUNDS)
OTTER TRAWLS, LARGE – O B INUED:										
CENTRAL NOVA SCOTIA	17	11.1	116	2,006	2,229	40	1,712	3,589		10,200
E. BS AND LA HAVE	59	85.8	821	290,863	455,081	12,225	22,135	26,550	1,495	8,975
SOUTHERN NOVA SCOTIA	47	39.1	349	86,310	175,451	21,900	3,455	17,845	1,200	12,790
WESTERN BNS	40	78.1	626	680,938	577,880	19,250	11,167	4,178	4,475	
WESTERN NOVA SCOTIA	1	1.3	12	2,825				460		
SOUTHERN BAY OF FUNDY	3	0.8	6	330		200				
NOVA SCOTIA, UNCLASSIFICD	4	2.8	33	30,100	18,000	8,400	400	1,819		
EASTERN MAINE	2	1.8	17	2,691	127		2,335	540		
CENTRAL MAINE	1	0.5	6	918	620		944			
WESTERN MAINE	15	15.1	143	26,462	25,508	300	17,318	14,646		
N. NER OF MAINE, UNCL.	1	1.1	7	240	55		100	80		7,500
WESTERN SIDE SOUTH CHANNEL	48	157.6	1,218	492,778	1,258,677	106,435	41,570	92,571	202,410	40,485
EASTERN SIDE SOUTH CHANNEL	51	143.3	1,189	498,116	296,577	9,440	52,599	172,702	137,260	57,210
NORTHERN EDGE OF GEORGES	50	477.6	3,815	2,928,192	4,758,003	410,820	120,285	31,860	373,845	90,670
CENTRAL AND S.E. GEORGES	52	196.3	1,563	4,043,303	1,238,770	37,630	9,500	6,400	313,830	363,210
SOUTHWEST GO B.	26	17.7	142	32,345	41,780		2,256	3,400	35,500	75,115
NANTUCKET SHOALS & LNTSHIP	3	1.1	9	950	12,510	1,000			3,100	200
S. NEW ENGLAND, UNCLASSIFIED	38	70.6	584	271,485	478,305	16,665	6,175	12,345	101,000	69,415
TOTAL	**2/81**	**1,768.0**	**15,736**	**10,758,385**	**11,363,350**	**910,680**	**322,607**	**3,210,105**	**1,176,005**	**1,190,270**
OTTER TRAWLS, MEDIUM:										
NORTHEAST CAPE BRETON	30	56.4	607	76,348	29,905	127,000	800	108,849		4,030
MISAINE BANK	27	38.5	383	37,340	23,565	4,640	3,845	5,758		
BANQUEREAU	30	71.2	781	138,918	112,641	1,336	3,371	236,676		
CANSO BANK	47	122.4	1,260	149,031	75,514	2,671	3,329	1,410,258		
MIDDLE GROUND	38	74.2	750	36,271	22,432		932	30,597		2,700
N.E. SABLE ISLAND BANK	1	0.5	7		1,500	650				
S.E. SABLE ISLAND BANK	1	0.1	7	2,311				3,462		
HORSESHOE GROUND	15	10.1	104	9,345	10,082	650	1,730	602		
S.W. SABLE ISLAND BANK	2	10.6	888	36,290	18,077	378	11,140	34,411		
EASTERN NOVA SCOTIA	38	70.9	234	27,215	9,412		1,801	11,174		
EMERALD BANK	30	25.8	267	9,683	6,473		4,357	7,433		
CENTRAL NOVA SCOTIA	31	27.6	832	46,789	39,310	1,000	20,466	44,336		8,500
E. BROWNS AND LA HAVE	52	84.7	975	150,292	103,368	2,800	16,637	50,916		76,900
SOUTHERN NOVA SCOTIA	60	103.9	119	29,730	67,360	2,500	2,318	9,032		
WESTERN BROWNS	17	14.7	117	9,830	2,494		4,120	3,095	100	
WESTERN NOVA SCOTIA	16	14.1	176	7,377	10,713	300	13,530	10,192		
EASTERN MAINE	23	19.5	48	3,590	1,320		3,205	2,436		
CENTRAL MAINE	7	35.6	955	318,605	204,626	33,308	85,691	277,870	420	3,325
EASTERN MASSACHUSETTS	52	387.0	955	159,678	209,860	36,007	77,177	77,177	125	81,360
BR.	54	770.6	2,860	263,498	118,130	12,740	173,498	165,002	200	1,050
N. GULF OF MAINE, UNCL.	115	503.5	31	13,195	11,475		2,125			
WESTERN SIDE SOUTH CHANNEL	4	734.7	3,652	651,177	1,622,563	166,415	231,157	296,369	342,325	78,805
EASTERN SIDE SOUTH CHANNEL	122	341.2	2,401	379,874	333,706	65,225	73,124	112,362	760,152	556,285
NORTHERN EDGE OF GEORGES	123	45.7	353	155,580	300,510	61,160	7,100	5,833	109,169	58,514
CENTRAL AND S.E. GEORGES	18	256.6	1,736	403,115	277,155	113,195	1,520	760	729,976	5,494,711
SOUTHWEST GEORGES	50	179.9	1,195	59,640	193,320	29,305	150	18,027	366,413	2,087,515

(CONTINUED ON NEXT PAGE)

SEE FOOTNOTES AT END OF TABLE

LANDINGS AT CERTAIN MASSACHUSETTS PORTS

SUMMARY OF FISHERY: BY GEAR AND SUBAREA, 1949 - Continued

GEAR AND SUBAREA	CRAFT FISHING	TRIPS	DAYS ABSENT	COD, DRAWN LARGE	COD, DRAWN MARKET	COD, DRAWN SCROD	CUSK, DRAWN	GRAY SOLE	FLOUNDERS, ROUND LEMON SOLE	YELLOWTAIL
	NUMBER	NUMBER	NUMBER	POUNDS	POUNDS	POUNDS	POUNDS	POUNDS	POUNDS	POUNDS
OTTER TRAWLS, MEDIUM - CONTINUED:										
NANTUCKET SHOALS & LHTSHIP	42	200.1	975	31,645	266,195	89,500	-	50,170	234,940	1,508,505
OFF NO MAN'S LAND	26	82.8	427	535	6,230	870	-	2,385	240	317,000
RHODE ISLAND SHORE	2	3.0	14	80	2,875	1,080	-	-	-	19,325
S. NEW ENGLAND, UNCLASSIFIED	47	117.4	780	111,230	192,120	28,640	2,770	14,850	309,285	397,145
SOUTH	8	7.7	48	-	725	-	-	195	-	29,460
TOTAL	2/192	4,372.0	23,939	3,258,502	4,344,646	781,370	666,163	2,992,442	2,853,345	10,725,130
OTTER TRAWLS, SMALL:										
WESTERN MAINE	44	211.9	542	362,599	170,843	18,980	27,667	194,117	-	24,815
EASTERN MASSACHUSETTS	138	4,971.0	5,442	707,781	645,275	133,537	12,739	530,858	6,165	1,038,608
I MER GROUNDS	14	49.9	245	18,060	11,032	375	18,933	23,156	-	4,800
WESTERN SIDE S UND CHANNEL	112	539.2	1,682	94,236	538,565	143,545	29,404	137,903	44,780	325,995
EASTERN SIDE SOUTH CHANNEL	22	55.2	298	11,835	14,048	3,215	5,502	20,731	113,685	252,025
NORTHERN EDGE OF GEORGES	1	1.6	12	75	1,395	415	-	-	10,875	1,110
CENTRAL AND S.E. GEORGES	26	81.9	461	295	12,415	2,450	-	460	43,885	1,790,785
SOUTHWEST GEORGES	27	89.9	483	6,380	27,275	3,580	-	16,470	42,135	1,103,595
NANTUCKET SHOALS & LHTSHIP	99	605.9	2,469	32,595	285,595	97,655	-	91,575	151,100	2,340,135
OFF NO MAN'S LAND	114	1,528.4	3,017	7,430	131,925	13,000	-	22,265	7,830	2,418,775
SOUTHERN MASSACHUSETTS	36	64.7	206	1,795	16,520	2,275	-	-	3,620	935
RHODE ISLAND SHORE	33	52.7	179	1,425	14,820	1,150	-	85	-	287,685
S. NEW ENGLAND, UNCLASSIFIED	101	498.0	975	4,175	65,863	4,730	-	7,695	15,855	375,543
SOUTH	10	9.7	41	-	1,180	25	-	-	-	32,825
CAPE COD 1/	153	4,367.0	4,367	204,900	325,441	63,209	730	41,700	39,475	2,330,566
TOTAL	2/413	13,127.0	20,422	1,452,581	2,262,182	488,141	94,975	1,087,015	479,405	12,329,197
HAUL SEINES, EASTERN MASSACHUSETTS	1	2.0	2	-	-	-	-	-	-	-
FLOATING TRAPS, EASTERN MASSACHUSETTS	14	912.0	912	80	3,336	-	-	-	-	-
DIP NETS, EASTERN MASSACHUSETTS	14	85.0	85	-	-	-	-	-	-	-
SINK GILL NETS, EASTERN MASSACHUSETTS	13	1,185.0	1,185	617,936	313,176	-	6,165	-	-	242
DRIFT GILL NETS, EASTERN MASSACHUSETTS	36	438.0	439	-	-	-	-	-	-	-
PURSE SEINES:										
CENTRAL MAINE	1	1.0	5	-	-	-	-	-	-	-
WESTERN MAINE	3	3.0	3	-	120	-	-	-	-	-
EASTERN MASSACHUSETTS	39	442.0	456	-	-	-	-	-	-	-
WESTERN SIDE SOUTH CHANNEL	11	-19.0	26	105	-	-	-	-	-	-
OFF NO MAN'S LAND	22	48.0	129	-	-	-	-	-	-	-

SEE FOOTNOTES AT END OF TABLE

(CONTINUED ON NEXT PAGE)

LANDINGS AT CERTAIN MASSACHUSETTS PORTS

SUMMARY OF FISHERY: BY GEAR AND SUBAREA, 1949 - Continued

GEAR AND SUBAREA	CRAFT FISHING (NUMBER)	TRIPS (NUMBER)	DAYS ABSENT (NUMBER)	COD, DRAWN LARGE (POUNDS)	COD, DRAWN MARKET (POUNDS)	COD, DRAWN SCROD (POUNDS)	CUSK, DRAWN (POUNDS)	FLOUNDERS, ROUND GRAY SOLE (POUNDS)	LEMON SOLE (POUNDS)	YELLOWTAIL (POUNDS)
PURSE SEINES - CONTINUED:										
9. NEW ENGLAND, UNCLASSIFIED .	4	4.0	4	-	-	-	-	-	-	-
SOUTH .	4	4.0	8	-	-	-	-	-	-	-
CAPE COD 1/ .	2	6.0	6	-	-	-	-	-	-	-
TOTAL .	2/42	527.0	637	3/105	3/120	-	-	-	-	-
SCALLOP DREDGES:										
EASTERN MASSACHUSETTS .	14	35.5	188	-	-	-	-	-	-	1,120
WESTERN SIDE SOUTH CHANNEL .	70	298.5	2,317	-	-	-	-	-	100	465
EASTERN SIDE SOUTH CHANNEL .	44	63.1	4,433	-	-	-	-	-	830	95
NORTHERN EDGE OF GEORGES .	75	493.0	4,332	-	-	-	-	-	670	-
CENTRAL AND S E. GEORGES .	19	20.2	188	-	-	-	-	-	150	340
SOUTHWEST GEORGES .	47	53.7	461	-	-	-	-	-	-	1,940
NANTUCKET SHOALS & LHTSHIP .	79	467.0	3,504	900	-	-	-	50	-	-
OFF NO MAN'S LAND .	1	7.0	10	-	-	-	-	-	-	-
S. NEW ENGLAND, UNCLASSIFIED .	47	74.0	455	-	4,000	-	-	-	7,525	390
SOUTH .	12	18.0	150	-	-	375	-	-	-	-
CAPE COD 1/ .	93	917.0	917	-	-	-	-	-	-	-
TOTAL .	2/185	2,441.0	12,955	3/900	3/4,000	3/375	-	3/50	3/9,275	3/4,880
POUND NETS:										
CAPE COD 2/ .	19	2,250.0	2,250	200	3,242	-	-	-	-	-
GRAND TOTAL .	2/1,184	37,092.0	89,785	19,263,316	20,723,930	2,358,726	2,001,193	7,290,657	4,623,656	24,258,974

GEAR AND SUBAREA	FLOUNDERS, ROUND - CONTINUED BLACKBACK (POUNDS)	DAB (POUNDS)	FLUKE (POUNDS)	HADDOCK, DRAWN LARGE (POUNDS)	HADDOCK, DRAWN SCROD (POUNDS)	RED, ROUND (POUNDS)	HAKE, WHITE, DRAWN LARGE (POUNDS)	HAKE, WHITE, DRESSED SMALL (POUNDS)	HALIBUT, DRAWN (POUNDS)	MACKEREL, ROUND (POUNDS)
LINE TRAWLS:										
E. BROWNS AND LA HAVE .	-	-	-	72,625	13,600	-	15,730	-	2,672	-
SOUTHERN NOVA SCOTIA .	-	-	-	17,315	4,500	-	4,200	-	180	-
WESTERN BROWNS .	-	-	-	545,740	58,500	-	19,865	-	7,833	-
WESTERN NOVA SCOTIA .	-	-	-	14,380	3,000	-	1,200	-	-	-
WESTERN MAINE .	-	685	-	212,160	6,235	-	-	-	4,516	-
EASTERN MASSACHUSETTS .	4,872	2,985	-	537,540	37,155	1,200	573,240	8,095	13,070	-
I MR GROUNDS .	60	-	-	57,940	2,360	-	860,460	2,805	2,395	-
WESTERN SIDE SOUTH CHANNEL .	-	-	-	426,760	9,660	-	55,225	25	472	-
EASTERN SIDE SOUTH CHANNEL .	-	-	-	53,900	2,700	-	15,600	-	-	-
NORTHERN EDGE OF GEORGES .	-	-	-	184,460	17,900	-	7,700	-	1,647	-
SOUTHWEST GEORGES .	-	-	-	4,700	900	-	250	-	-	-
S. NEW ENGLAND, UNCLASSIFIED .	200	-	-	10,600	2,400	-	3,100	-	447	-
CAPE COD 1/ .	-	599	-	1,761,162	-	-	40,633	-	55,341	-
TOTAL .	5,132	4,169	-	3,897,082	158,910	1,200	1,594,478	10,925	88,573	-

SEE FOOTNOTES AT END OF TABLE

(CONTINUED ON NEXT PAGE)

LANDINGS AT CERTAIN MASSACHUSETTS PORTS

SUMMARY OF FISHERY: BY GEAR AND SUBAREA, 1949 - Continued

GEAR AND SUBAREA	FLOUNDERS, ROUND - CONTINUED			HADDOCK, DRAWN		RED, ROUND	HAKE		HALIBUT, DRAWN	MACKEREL, ROUND
	BLACKBACK	DAB	FLUKE	LARGE	SCROD		WHITE, LARGE	DRESSED, SMALL		
	POUNDS	POUNDS	POUNDS	POUNDS	POUNDS	POUNDS	POUNDS	POUNDS	POUNDS	POUNDS
HAND LINES:										
EASTERN MASSACHUSETTS				490	-	-	392		380	-
CAPE COD 1/	5,628	244	18	24,453	5	-	251	65	15	37
TOTAL	5,628	244	18	24,943	5	-	643	65	395	3/37
OTTER TRAWLS, LARGE:										
NORTHEAST CAPE BRETON	-	9,798	-	127,336	4,651	-	9,553	992	8,281	-
MISAINE BANK	-	6,649	-	205	1,572	-	4,973		1,613	-
BANQUEREAU	-	59,008	-	316,217	255,814	-	32,417	3,894	5,909	-
CANSO BANK	-	71,440	-	49,680	35,573	-	25,760	4,091	2,160	-
MIDDLE GROUND	-	6,540	-	19,664	9,978	-	4,345	993	5,396	-
N.E. ☒ ISLAND BANK	320	200	-	779,660	976,080	-	20,650		5,358	500
B. SABLE ISLAND BANK	-		-			-	16,030			-
HORSESHOE GROUND	-	9,619	-	1,140,658	672,567	-	19,800	4,536	8,554	2,843
S.W. SABLE ISLAND BANK	-	14,720	-	833,910	539,560	-	5,495		4,022	2,300
EASTERN NOVA SCOTIA	80	1,672	-	4,214	1,227	-	14,271	4,808	154	2,317
EMERALD BANK	-	2,711	-	239,187	269,520	-	1,045	580	566	300
CENTRAL NOVA SCOTIA	550	738	-	1,629	1,739	-	52,085	1,701		2, 00
E. BROWNS' AND LA HAVE	560	27,487	-	2,907,908	1,519,152	-	35,679	5,242	14,639	-
WESTERN BROWNS	440	26,304	-	1,733,496	928,077	-	21,410	518	3,247	3, 00
WESTERN NOVA SCOTIA OT1☒	-	44,067	-	4,265,300	2,017,029	-	2,505	199	15,730	25,780
SOUTHERN BAY OF FUNDY	3,450	200	-		1,300	-	1,700			-
NOVA SCOTIA, UNCLASSIFIED	-	1,000	-	1,160	1,100	-	2,175		305	-
EASTERN MAINE	-	331	-	33,000	21,140	-	2,090			-
CENTRAL MAINE	-	287	-	9,479	3,665	-	25,893	3,596		-
INNER GROUNDS	600	3,850	-	4,384	1,473	-	615			-
N. GULF OF MAINE, UNCL.	617,545	215	-	145,424	43,631	-	40	850	939	-
WESTERN SIDE SOUTH CHANNEL	132,825	74,330	-	3,838,520	1,291,262	-	149,926			-
EASTERN SIDE SOUTH CHANNEL	126,752	238,551	-	4,385,394	1,263,140	-	220,428		5,824	4,895
NORTHERN EDGE OF GEORGES	143,938	62,170	-	13,122,965	16,100,530	-	237,780	33,500	14,536	2,550
CENTRAL AND S.E. GEORGES	15,225	26,495	-	6,617,575	5,499,965	-	61,740		43,851	162,770
SOUTHWEST GEORGES	12,730	10,455	-	771,755	367,520	-	3,135		29,219	4,775
NANTUCKET SHOALS & LHTSHIP	73,550	1,500	-	35,930	6,140	-	2,100		3,479	-
S. NEW ENGLAND, UNCLASSIFIED		53,240	-	1,494,815	1,242,675	-	38,505		10,630	3,020
TOTAL	1,128,575	760,612	-	42,812,635	33,175,900	-	1,011,565	65,540	184,412	3/217,150
OTTER TRAWLS, MEDIUM:										
NORTHEAST CAPE BRETON	-	9,357	-	209,480	102,217	-	20,559	135	16,730	250
MISAINE BANK	-	5,925	-	19,425	5,740	-	6,595	4,620	250	-
BANQUEREAU	-	16,439	-	39,966	31,957	-	8,302	774	3,549	-
CANSO BANK	630	37,078	-	36,617	16,049	-	7,603	5,112	52	-
MIDDLE GROUND	-	5,200	-	5,865	2,796	-	2,173	863	983	-
N.E. SABLE ISLAND BANK	-	200	-	6,750	6,850	-	2,250			-
HORSESHOE GROUND	-	1,628	-	38,236	6,045	-	2,218	1,325	90	-
S.W. SABLE ISLAND BANK	-	1,208	-	25,202	4,400	-	473			-
EASTERN NOVA SCOTIA	-	12,205	-	20,104	7,098	-	19,962	10,477	555	-
EMERALD BANK	-	1,155	-	22,387	18,180	-	4,781	1,519	304	-
CENTRAL NOVA SCOTIA	-	7,549	-	17,338	3,855	-	7,936	2,897		249

(CONTINUED ON NEXT PAGE)

SEE FOOTNOTES AT END OF TABLE

LANDINGS AT CERTAIN MASSACHUSETTS PORTS

SUMMARY OF FISHERY: BY GEAR AND SUBAREA, 1949 - Continued

GEAR AND SUBAREA	FLOUNDERS, ROUND - CONTINUED			HADDOCK, DRAWN		RED, ROUND	HAKE, WHITE, LARGE	HAKE, DRESSED SMALL	HALIBUT, DRAWN	MACKEREL, ROUND
	BLACKBACK	DAB	FLUKE	LARGE	SCROD					
	POUNDS	POUNDS	POUNDS	POUNDS	POUNDS	POUNDS	POUNDS	POUNDS	POUNDS	POUNDS
OTTER TRAWLS, MEDIUM - CONTINUED:										
E. BNS AND LA HAVE.	—	17,127	—	277,001	162,113	200	26,675	13,771	1,435	—
SOUTHERN NOVA SCOTIA.	—	44,817	—	724,732	253,951	—	35,432	19,969	350	—
WESTERN BROWNS.	—	3,538	—	350,760	167,357	—	24,922	172	1,022	—
WESTERN NOVA SCOTIA.	—	644	—	31,182	12,674	—	3,120	—	—	—
EASTERN MAINE.	—	4,335	—	40,486	17,015	—	5,807	5,337	—	—
CENTRAL MAINE.	—	2,155	—	11,192	11,079	—	2,610	1,297	—	—
WESTERN MAINE.	14,743	144,535	—	737,490	209,449	—	298,412	116,238	998	—
EASTERN MASSACHUSETTS.	95,603	96,371	185	205,834	52,099	—	52,596	46,285	624	575
INER GROUNDS.	4,937	109,515	—	1,358,918	207,430	400	231,411	132,955	1,705	—
N. GULF OF MAINE, NCL.	—	890	—	18,600	1,210	3,670	3,236	715	—	—
WESTERN SIDE SOUTH CHANNEL	1,248,515	221,532	190	5,533,828	1,704,672	—	664,183	61,015	11,772	3,500
EASTERN SIDE SOUTH CHANNEL	771,490	122,523	245	2,879,239	1,231,409	—	154,720	55,532	12,770	3,870
NORTHERN EDGE OF GEORGES	69,178	8,120	—	721,020	1,153,190	7,005	21,502	—	3,095	—
CENTRAL AND S.E. GEORGES	572,990	26,145	—	1,269,060	1,960,775	60	5,698	—	9,262	—
SOUTHWEST GEORGES. .-.	241,595	34,595	500	2,038,950	1,443,325	—	13,095	—	10,404	3,000
NANTUCKET SHOALS & LHTSHIP	1,349,405	2,665	530	279,500	136,840	—	9,315	—	1,283	1,470
OFF NO MAN'S LAND.	14,440	115	88,435	4,470	45	149,608	8,655	40	—	29,910
RHODE ISLAND SHORE	302,155	33,085	412,115	747,405	774,975	—	19,915	—	—	—
S. NEW E (LB, UNCLASSIFIED	3,970	—	27,110	—	—	99,195	1,785	—	4,696	1,555
SOUTH.	—	—	66,515	—	—	—	—	—	—	—
TOTAL.	4,690,635	971,060	595,925	17,671,017	9,704,995	260,138	1,664,025	484,500	82,016	3/44,519
OTTER TRAWLS, SMALL:										
WESTERN MAINE.	8,405	99,187	—	210,100	86,867	70	171,463	61,395	747	—
EASTERN MASSACHUSETTS.	792,152	979,403	2,485	263,595	113,631	—	165,249	207,889	2,292	12,953
INNER GROUNDS.	2,190	10,032	—	87,230	9,242	7,290	20,072	17,085	293	—
WESTERN SIDE SOUTH CHANNEL	1,576,236	58,204	7,770	681,802	133,507	—	97,589	11,602	1,287	—
EASTERN SIDE SOUTH CHANNEL	862,580	37,351	7,220	131,303	73,035	—	11,230	6,310	322	—
NORTHERN EDGE OF GEORGES	13,235	—	—	3,300	—	150	—	—	345	50
CENTRAL AND S.E. GEORGES	38,905	75	55	29,570	61,450	—	790	—	567	—
SOUTHWEST GEORGES.	56,845	11,400	870	242,910	162,960	—	7,280	100	—	—
NANTUCKET SHOALS & LHTSHIP	1,930,395	1,320	400,609	357,100	53,230	559,575	13,305	95	1,673	—
OFF NO MAN'S LAND.	620,990	—	365,457	16,085	750	30,725,556	6,490	160	—	—
SOUTHERN MASSACHUSETTS	346,180	—	6,690	225	—	—	—	—	—	125
RHODE ISLAND SHORE.	29,120	—	1,73:	225	—	—	170	95	—	628
S. NEW ENGLAND, UNCLASSIFIED	292,112	3,630	25,670	44,138	20,785	8,136,408	49,440	—	235	—
SOUTH.	1,480	—	22,890	—	—	—	—	—	—	—
CAPE COD 1/.	1,375,653	34,577	351,396	250,254	55,202	640	33,863	4,486	1,181	9,659
TOTAL.	7,166,484	1,235,179	1,186,032	2,291,837	777,716	39,429,689	576,940	309,217	9,317	3/23,415
FLOATING TRAPS, EASTERN MASSACHUSETTS.	—	45	—	138,023	90	—	—	—	—	1,312,885
SINK GILL NETS, EASTERN MASSACHUSETTS.	1,934	818	—	—	—	—	492,046	60,995	86	245
DRIFT GILL NETS, EASTERN MASSACHUSETTS.	—	—	—	—	—	—	—	—	—	301,855

SEE FOOTNOTES AT END OF TABLE

(CONTINUED ON NEXT PAGE)

LANDINGS AT CERTAIN MASSACHUSETTS PORTS

SUMMARY OF FISHERY: BY GEAR AND SUBAREA, 1949 - Continued

GEAR AND SUBAREA	FLOUNDERS, ROUND - CONTINUED			HADDOCK, DRAWN		RED, ROUND	HAKE		HALIBUT, DRAWN	MACKEREL, ROUND
	BLACKBACK	DAB	FLUKE	LARGE	SCROD		WHITE, LARGE	DRESSED, SMALL		
	POUNDS	POUNDS	POUNDS	POUNDS	POUNDS	POUNDS	POUNDS	POUNDS	POUNDS	POUNDS
PURSE SEINES:										
CENTRAL MAINE	-	-	-	-	-	-	-	-	-	35,875
WESTERN MAINE	-	-	-	-	-	-	-	-	-	44,550
EASTERN MASSACHUSETTS	-	-	-	-	-	-	-	-	-	3,160,563
WESTERN SIDE SOUTH CHANNEL	-	-	-	-	-	-	-	-	-	394,935
OFF NO MAN'S LAND	-	-	-	-	-	-	-	-	-	2,265,184
S. NEW ENGLAND, UNCLASSIFIED	-	-	-	-	-	-	-	-	-	6,575
SOUTH	-	-	-	-	-	-	-	-	-	129,550
CAPE COD 1/	-	-	-	-	-	-	-	-	-	21,010
TOTAL	-	-	-	-	-	-	-	-	-	6,058,242
SCALLOP DREDGES:										
EASTERN MASSACHUSETTS	260	-	-	-	-	-	-	-	-	-
WESTERN SIDE SOUTH CHANNEL	8,895	-	-	-	-	-	-	-	-	-
EASTERN SIDE SOUTH CHANNEL	7,245	-	-	-	-	-	-	-	-	-
NORTHERN EDGE OF GEORGES	3,912	-	-	-	-	-	-	-	-	-
CENTRAL AND S.E. GEORGES	125	-	-	-	-	-	-	-	-	-
SOUTHWEST GEORGES	410	-	-	-	-	-	-	-	-	-
NANTUCKET SHOALS & LHTSHIP	4,790	-	-	2,375	20,000	40	70	-	110	-
S. NEW ENGLAND, UNCLASSIFIED	10,060	225	-	-	-	-	-	-	-	-
TOTAL	3/35,777	3/225	-	3/2,375	3/20,000	3/40	3/70	-	3/110	-
POUND NETS, CAPE COD 1/	2,614	-	3,438	-	-	-	-	-	-	5,213,519
GRAND TOTAL	13,036,783	2,972,362	1,785,413	66,837,912	43,837,616	39,691,067	5,342,399	931,243	364,909	13,171,867

GEAR AND SUBAREA	POLLOCK		OCEAN PERCH (ROSEFISH), ROUND	SCUP OR PORGY, ROUND	SWORDFISH, DRESSED	WHITING		WOLFFISH, DRAWN	SCALLOPS (MEATS)	OTHER, AS LANDED	TOTAL, AS LANDED
	DRAWN	ROUND				DRESSED	ROUND				
	POUNDS	POUNDS	POUNDS	POUNDS	POUNDS	POUNDS	POUNDS	POUNDS	POUNDS	POUNDS	POUNDS
LINE TRAWLS:											
E. BROWNS AND LA HAVE	2,200	-	-	-	-	-	-	-	-	-	199,202
SOUTHERN NOVA SCOTIA	340	-	-	-	-	-	-	-	-	-	33,380
WESTERN BROWNS	5,910	-	2,000	-	-	-	-	7,600	-	-	889,358
WESTERN NOVA SCOTIA	200	-	-	-	-	-	-	-	-	-	38,285
WESTERN MAINE	116,150	365	-	-	-	-	-	-	-	9,005	1,755,451
EASTERN MASSACHUSETTS	198,901	1,285	4,495	-	-	-	285	18,105	-	14,255	3,213,051
INNER GROUNDS	3,835	-	-	-	-	-	-	76,514	-	650	229,185
WESTERN SIDE SOUTH CHANNEL	2,260	-	-	-	-	390	-	4,575	-	285	855,782
EASTERN SIDE SOUTH CHANNEL	400	-	-	-	-	240	-	-	-	-	132,582
NORTHERN EDGE OF GEORGES	5,100	-	-	-	-	-	-	-	-	-	677,405
CENTRAL AND S.E. GEORGES	-	-	-	-	-	-	-	2,250	-	-	7,785
SOUTHWEST GEORGES	-	-	-	-	-	-	-	225	-	-	9,575
OFF NO MAN'S LAND	-	-	-	-	-	-	-	-	-	99,925	99,925
S. NEW ENGLAND, UNCLASSIFIED	350	-	-	-	-	-	-	-	-	-	27,397
CAPE COD 1/	61,031	-	-	-	-	-	110	60,945	-	1,836	4,056,514
TOTAL	390,727	1,670	6,495	-	-	630	395	170,549	-	125,966	12,925,887

(CONTINUED ON NEXT PAGE)

SEE FOOTNOTES AT END OF TABLE

LANDINGS AT CERTAIN MASSACHUSETTS PORTS

SUMMARY OF FISHERY: BY GEAR AND SUBAREA, 1949 - Continued

GEAR AND SUBAREA	POLLOCK DRAWN	POLLOCK ROUND	OCEAN PERCH (ROSEFISH), ROUND	SCUP OR PORGY, ROUND	SWORDFISH, DRESSED	WHITING DRESSED	WHITING ROUND	WOLFFISH, DRAWN	SCALLOPS (MEATS)	OTHER, AS LANDED	TOTAL, AS LANDED
	POUNDS	POUNDS	POUNDS	POUNDS	POUNDS	POUNDS	POUNDS	POUNDS	POUNDS	POUNDS	POUNDS
HAND LINES:											
EASTERN MASSACHUSETTS	90,358							100		565,429	875,026
CAPE COD 1/	5,752			8,713				95		20,158	174,445
TOTAL	96,110			8,713				195		585,587	1,049,471
HARPOONS:											
NORTHEAST CAPE BRETON (OCC)					190						190
MIDDLE GROUND (OCCASIONAL)					165						165
WESTERN BROWNS					59,274						59,274
EASTERN MASSACHUSETTS (OCC)										5,257	5,257
EASTERN SIDE SOUTH CHANNEL					1,838					1,960	3,798
EASTERN SIDE SOUTH CHANNEL (OCC)					1,000						1,000
NORTHERN EDGE OF GEORGES					99,811						99,811
NORTHERN EDGE OF GEORGES (OCC)					4,035						4,035
CENTRAL AND S.E. GEORGES					215,757						215,757
CENTRAL AND S.E. GEORGES (OCC)					7,550						7,550
SOUTHWEST GEORGES					24,060						24,060
SOUTHWEST GEORGES (OCCASIONAL)					98						98
NANTUCKET SHOALS & LHTSHIP					360						360
NANTUCKET SHOALS & LHTSHIP (OCC)					2,015						2,015
OFF NO MAN'S LAND					49,322						49,322
OFF NO MAN'S LAND (OCCASIONAL)					4,950						4,950
S. NEW ENGLAND, UNCL. (OCC)					14,884					460	15,344
S. NEW ENGLAND, UNCL.					365						365
CAPE COD 1/ (OCCAS. BAL)					137,985					7	137,992
CAPE COD 1/					24,207						24,207
TOTAL					647,866					7,684	655,550
OTTER TRAWLS, LARGE:											
NORTHEAST CAPE BRETON	16,006		10,307,377					644		38,130	10,780,866
MISAINE BANK	2,150		6,725,969					9		15,977	6,811,789
BANQUEREAU	93,033		15,993,964					5,130		91,410	18,120,745
CANSO BANK	28,169		13,509,383					2,571		78,790	16,445,859
MIDDLE GROUND	4,511		6,151,349					1,233		17,849	6,384,898
S.E. SABLE ISLAND BANK	49,890		183,950					660		365	2,835,415
SABLE ISLAND BANK	4,920		755,500					1,150			3,531,414
HORSESHOE GROUND	362,232		709,427					79,810		2,800	2,206,102
S.W. SABLE ISLAND BANK	182,530		33,250					36,260			2,689,673
EASTERN NOVA SCOTIA	19,723		1,595,972					11,084		20,606	2,126,542
EMERALD BANK	135,849		1,266,836					11,521		6,120	1,467,933
CENTRAL NOVA SCOTIA	7,158		1,435,580					548		2,135	9,487,472
E. BROWNS AND LA HAVE	603,432		3,463,437			1,600		60,205		13,186	4,890,602
SOUTHERN NOVA SCOTIA	710,559		1,081,997					47,804		4,415	8,740,501
WESTERN BROWNS	757,141		57,000					223,927		1,870	1,113,690
WESTERN NOVA SCOTIA	8,480		96,820								45,515
SOUTHERN BAY OF FUNDY	19,500		17,900							275	244,505
NOVA SCOTIA, UNCLASSIFIED	20,400		98,000					2,975		10,085	

SEE FOOTNOTES AT END OF TABLE

(CONTINUED ON NEXT PAGE)

LANDINGS AT CERTAIN MASSACHUSETTS PORTS

SUMMARY OF FISHERY: BY GEAR AND SUBAREA, 1949 - Continued

GEAR AND SUBAREA	POLLOCK DRAWN	POLLOCK ROUND	OCEAN PERCH (ROSEFISH), ROUND	SCUP OR PORGY, ROUND	SWORDFISH, DRESSED	WHITING DRESSED	WHITING ROUND	WOLFFISH, DRAWN	SCALLOPS (MEATS)	OTHER, AS LANDED	TOTAL, AS LANDED
	POUNDS	POUNDS	POUNDS	POUNDS	POUNDS	POUNDS	POUNDS	POUNDS	POUNDS	POUNDS	POUNDS
OTTER TRAWLS, LARGE - CONTINUED:											
EASTERN MAINE	21,352		115,657					82			159,913
CENTRAL MAINE	4,760		28,467					28			44,511
WESTERN MAINE			5,100								5,100
INNER GROUNDS	143,565		960,735					1,181		1,160	1,422,608
N. GULF OF MAINE, UNCLASSIFIED	300		4,550	30							6,285
WESTERN SIDE SOUTH CHANNEL	981,333		1,822,977	70				31,620	281	4,216	10,857,535
EASTERN SIDE SOUTH CHANNEL	1,622,472		1,927,988					64,400	230	18,119	11,118,907
NORTHERN EDGE OF GEORGES	3,317,140		80,310				4,500	148,833		17,378	42,143,654
CENTRAL AND S.E. GEORGES	565,245		6,940			2,400	10,000	84,395		25,690	19,134,680
SOUTHWEST GEORGES	85,050		3,250					8,980		850	1,405,661
NANTUCKET SHOALS & LHTSHIP	2,850		400					400	566	65	79,895
S. NEW ENGLAND, UNCLASSIFIED	436,965		95,100					36,120		1,155	4,433,325
TOTAL	10,189,105	-	66,924,585	100	-	4,000	14,500	851,270	3/1,077	372,666	186,645,094
OTTER TRAWLS, MEDIUM:											
NORTHEAST CAPE BRETON	6,945		6,840,665					1,359		32,670	7,587,309
MISAINE BANK	39,415		4,995,671					20		33,530	5,186,339
BANQUEREAU	16,002		9,001,748					2,405		61,131	9,675,215
CA 90 BANK	10,745		12,666,091					1,051		95,819	14,517,650
MIDDLE GROUND	3,590		8,606,780					1,169		23,844	8,743,904
N.E. SABLE ISLAND BANK			3,500								3,500
S. SABLE ISLAND BANK	8,559		838,963							6,850	933,282
HORSESHOE GROUND	560										42,980
S.W. SABLE ISLAND BANK	41,185		5,774,948			1,462	480	1,103		94,720	6,085,252
EASTERN NOVA SCOTIA	13,645		2,516,283					1,190		18,111	2,647,551
CENTRAL BANK	11,087		2,336,661					1,760		42,630	2,467,069
CENTRAL NOVA SCOTIA	100,046		6,296,711					1,135		75,786	7,220,856
E. BROWNS AND LA HAVE	336,648		386,257				120	270		100,447	8,151,326
SOUTHERN NOVA SCOTIA	46,897		780,325			365		10,338		3,375	1,197,709
WESTERN BROWNS	28,720		904,638			1,827		12,136		39,810	920,031
WESTERN NOVA SCOTIA	41,806		238,337			954		23,468		13,380	1,077,798
EASTERN MAINE	8,075							55		1,500	277,950
CENTRAL MAINE	996,424		1,897,496			132,558	56,967	13,887		25,280	5,657,702
WESTERN MAINE	360,990		451,401			3,181,898	535,305	26,785		3,505,477	9,135,552
EASTERN MASSACHUSETTS	842,439		17,840,233			40,691	6,053	4,239	50	714,531	22,232,786
INNER GROUNDS	7,595		123,600			185	400				165,365
W. GULF OF MAINE, UNCLASSIFIED	1,414,952	6,760	12,902,971			237,040	6,835	74,607	422	210,657	27,699,267
WESTERN SIDE SOUTH CHANNEL	645,307		8,210,043			11,470	15,225	39,796	2,419	201,808	16,638,663
EASTERN SIDE SOUTH CHANNEL	159,042		2,375					12,200		270	2,847,858
NORTHERN EDGE OF GEORGES	141,273		20,520	45				10,645	8,981	1,900	11,050,801
CENTRAL AND S.E. GEORGES	26,870			345				11,625	5,406	610	6,585,880
SOUTHWEST GEORGES	6,635		2,000	4,425		3,400		11,295	1,084	16,875	1,212,148
NANTUCKET SHOALS & LHTSHIP										257,925	25,410
OFF NO MAN'S LAND	75									400	
RHODE ISLAND SHORE	63,730									85,650	3,303,449
S. NEW ENGLAND, UNCLASSIFIED	75		49,050	27,720		1,675		8,800	69	33,100	149,810
SOUTH				13,985							
TOTAL	5,390,542	6,760	110,065,442	46,520	-	3,613,525	621,385	274,238	3/18,655	5,698,096	187,545,591

(CONTINUED ON NEXT PAGE)

SEE FOOTNOTES AT END OF TABLE

LANDINGS AT CERTAIN MASSACHUSETTS PORTS

SUMMARY OF FISHERY: BY GEAR AND SUBAREA, 1949 - Continued

GEAR AND SUBAREA	POLLOCK DRAWN (POUNDS)	POLLOCK ROUND (POUNDS)	OCEAN PERCH (ROSEFISH) ROUND (POUNDS)	SCUP OR PORGY, ROUND (POUNDS)	SWORDFISH, DRESSED (POUNDS)	WHITING DRESSED (POUNDS)	WHITING ROUND (POUNDS)	WOLFFISH, DRAWN (POUNDS)	SCALLOPS (MEATS) (POUNDS)	OTHER, AS LANDED (POUNDS)	TOTAL, AS LANDED (POUNDS)
OTTER TRAWLS, SMALL:											
WESTERN MAINE	330,953	-	1,017,886	-	-	290,873	26,967	12,626	-	28,820	3,145,380
EASTERN MASSACHUSETTS	358,633	-	468,433	-	-	24,775,934	1,558,900	247,239	313	7,260,019	40,291,372
INNER GROUNDS	51,690	-	1,383,483	-	-	26,820	1,500	1,770	-	37,720	1,725,483
WESTERN SIDE SOUTH CHANNEL	153,321	-	1,264,403	700	-	1,284,812	12,015	65,292	140	19,250	6,682,097
EASTERN SIDE SOUTH CHANNEL	28,598	-	343,300	-	-	4,080	-	1,734	1,488	7,930	1,125,107
NORTHERN EDGE OF GEORGES	-	-	-	-	-	-	-	-	-	-	37,812
CENTRAL AND S.E. GEORGES	170	-	-	-	-	-	-	250	1,760	85	1,983,745
SOUTHWEST GEORGES	405	-	-	-	-	-	-	-	5,372	590	1,689,754
NANTUCKET SHOALS & LTSHIP	13,010	-	-	-	-	400	-	1,020	2,143	120,367	6,467,887
OFF NO MAN'S LAND	1,060	-	-	3,595	346	4,500	-	12,230	33	2,329,765	6,460,885
SOUTHERN MASSACHUSETTS	-	-	-	18,840	-	100	-	-	-	8,105	455,675
RHODE ISLAND SHORE	345	-	-	69,230	-	-	-	-	50	510	336,385
S. NEW ENGLAND, UNCLASSIFIED	740	-	-	70	-	12,125	-	675	766	2,225,605	11,289,885
SOUTH	175	-	-	2,410	-	-	-	-	-	3,375	65,045
CAPE COD 1/	84,589	-	8,105	3,105	188	4,807,268	7,980,865	72,093	327	2,273,689	20,634,140
TOTAL	1,023,689	-	4,485,610	362,024	3/534	31,206,912	9,580,247	414,929	3/12,392	14,314,929	132,620,592
HAUL SEINES, EASTERN MASSACHUSETTS	-	-	-	-	-	-	-	-	-	3,100	3,100
FLOATING TRAPS, EASTERN MASSACHUSETTS	-	41,193	-	-	-	10,217	101,435	-	-	476,838	1,984,062
DIP NETS, EASTERN MASSACHUSETTS	-	-	-	-	-	-	-	-	-	754,220	754,220
SINK GILL NETS, EASTERN MASSACHUSETTS	2,471,741	27,815	-	-	-	400	300	62	-	21,061	4,153,136
DRIFT GILL NETS, EASTERN MASSACHUSETTS	-	-	-	-	-	27,560	67,220	-	-	3,097	399,732
PURSE SEINES:											
CENTRAL MAINE	100	-	-	-	-	-	-	-	-	-	35,875
WESTERN MAINE	-	-	-	-	-	-	-	-	-	16,350	61,120
EASTERN MASSACHUSETTS	-	-	-	-	-	-	-	-	-	7,243,626	10,404,294
WESTERN SIDE SOUTH CHANNEL	-	-	-	-	-	-	-	-	-	169,180	564,115
OFF NO MAN'S LAND	-	-	-	-	-	-	-	-	-	-	2,265,184
S. NEW ENGLAND, UNCLASSIFIED	-	-	-	-	-	-	-	-	-	-	6,575
SOUTH	-	-	-	-	-	-	-	-	-	-	129,550
CAPE COD 1/	-	-	-	-	-	-	-	-	-	-	21,010
TOTAL	3/100	-	-	-	-	-	-	-	-	7,429,156	13,487,723
SCALLOP DREDGES:											
EASTERN MASSACHUSETTS	-	-	-	-	-	-	-	-	73,697	150	73,957
WESTERN SIDE SOUTH CHANNEL	-	-	-	-	-	-	-	-	2,395,529	-	2,405,884

SEE FOOTNOTES AT END OF TABLE

(CONTINUED ON NEXT PAGE)

LANDINGS AT CERTAIN MASSACHUSETTS PORTS

SUMMARY OF FISHERY: BY GEAR AND SUBAREA, 1949 - Continued

GEAR AND SUBAREA	POLLOCK DRAWN	POLLOCK ROUND	OCEAN PERCH (ROSEFISH), ROUND	SCUP OR PORGY, ROUND	SWORDFISH, DRESSED	WHITING DRESSED	WHITING ROUND	WOLFFISH, DRAWN	SCALLOPS (MEATS)	OTHER, AS LANDED	TOTAL, AS LANDED
	POUNDS	POUNDS	POUNDS	POUNDS	POUNDS	POUNDS	POUNDS	POUNDS	POUNDS	POUNDS	POUNDS
SCALLOP DREDGES - CONTINUED:											
EASTERN SIDE SOUTH CHANNEL	-	-	-	-	-	-	-	-	444,997	-	453,537
NORTHERN EDGE OF GEORGES	-	-	-	-	-	-	-	105	4,133,094	-	4,138,396
CENTRAL AND S.E. GEORGES	-	-	-	-	-	-	-	-	162,908	-	163,183
SOUTHWEST GEORGES	-	-	-	-	-	-	-	-	453,165	-	453,915
NANTUCKET SHOALS & LTSHIP	-	-	-	-	-	-	-	-	3,721,868	-	3,728,748
OFF NO MAN'S LAND	125	-	-	-	-	-	-	-	5,438	-	5,438
S. NEW ENGLAND, UNCLASSIFIED	-	-	-	-	-	-	-	-	295,624	-	341,909
SOUTH 1/	-	-	-	-	-	-	-	-	133,595	-	133,595
CAPE COD 1/	-	-	-	-	-	-	-	-	1,326,676	-	1,326,676
TOTAL	3/125	-	-	-	-	-	-	3/105	13,146,781	150	13,225,238
POUND NETS, CAPE COD 1/	22,129	-	-	11,816	648,400	-	265,923	-	-	3,850,709	9,376,222
GRAND TOTAL	19,628,321	77,438	181,482,132	449,173	648,400	34,863,244	10,651,405	1,711,348	13,178,905	33,643,259	564,825,638

1/ REPRESENTS THE CATCH LANDED AT PROVINCETOWN, WOODS HOLE, CHATHAM, HYANNIS, HARWICH PORT, AND OTHER CAPE COD PORTS EAST OF BUZZARDS BAY. IT IS NOT POSSIBLE TO ALLOCATE THIS CATCH INTO THE SUBAREAS AS DATA ARE NOT COLLECTED ON THE AREA OF CAPTURE FOR THESE PORTS.
2/ EXCLUSIVE OF DUPLICATION, EXCEPT THAT CRAFT LANDING AT CAPE COD PORTS MAY BE DUPLICATED WITH CRAFT FISHING ELSEWHERE.
3/ INCIDENTAL CATCH.

NOTE:--OTTER TRAWLS ARE CLASSIFIED ACCORDING TO THE SIZE OF THE CRAFT. "SMALL" OTTER TRAWL CRAFT ARE THOSE 50 GROSS TONS CAPACITY OR UNDER; "MEDIUM", 51 GROSS TONS TO 150 GROSS TONS; AND "LARGE", 151 GROSS TONS OR GREATER. A SINGLE TRIP IS SHOWN FOR EACH VOYAGE. WHEN A CRAFT OPERATES IN TWO OR MORE SUBAREAS DURING A VOYAGE, A FRACTIONAL PART (IN TENTHS) OF THE TRIP IS ALLOTTED TO THE SUBAREA ON THE BASIS OF THE CATCH TAKEN IN EACH SUBAREA. OCCASIONAL AFTER THE NAME OF A SUBAREA INDICATES THAT THE CRAFT CONTRIBUTING TO THE CATCH AS SHOWN FISHED CHIEFLY WITH ANOTHER TYPE OF GEAR.

OTTER TRAWL IN OPERATION

NEW ENGLAND FISHERIES

LANDINGS AT CERTAIN MASSACHUSETTS PORTS

SUMMARY OF FISHERY: BY AREA AND SUBAREA, 1949

AREA AND SUBAREA	CRAFT FISHING	TRIPS	DAYS ABSENT	COD, DRAWN LARGE	COD, DRAWN MARKET	COD, DRAWN SCROD	CUSK, DRAWN	FLOUNDERS, ROUND GRAY SOLE	FLOUNDERS, ROUND LEMON SOLE	FLOUNDERS, ROUND YELLOWTAIL
	NUMBER	NUMBER	NUMBER	POUNDS	POUNDS	POUNDS	POUNDS	POUNDS	POUNDS	POUNDS
OFF NOVA SCOTIA (XXI):										
NORTHEAST CAPE BRETON	55	119.6	1,313	159,887	93,165	127,000	1,579	218,909	-	4,030
MISAINE BANK	47	75.3	783	62,168	42,717	4,640	3,845	14,450	-	-
BANQUEREAU	68	182.2	2,010	711,898	896,942	148,056	10,666	751,929	150	137,250
CANSO BANK	74	225.7	2,431	416,455	349,182	40,361	9,941	3,463,105	-	-
MIDDLE GROUND	66	118.0	1,241	60,382	68,565	3,015	2,105	116,000	-	-
N.E. SABLE ISLAND BANK	19	25.0	247	69,772	192,400	51,120	580	1,350	1,090	6,650
S.E. SABLE ISLAND BANK	5	1.6	13	16,375	29,025	550	-	-	-	200,740
HORSESHOE GROUND	43	42.1	403	109,218	239,608	5,900	2,515	35,852	300	2,150
S.W. SABLE ISLAND BANK	19	20.3	200	141,070	262,475	13,150	3,800	952	100	57,180
EASTERN NOVA SCOTIA	52	83.8	1,052	41,845	27,274	378	15,865	47,335	-	28,150
EMERALD BANK	60	43.4	408	92,032	125,552	9,530	6,708	13,526	160	-
CENTRAL NOVA SCOTIA	48	38.7	383	11,689	8,702	40	6,069	11,021	-	5,080
E. BROWNS AND LA HAVE	113	175.7	1,708	366,027	545,591	16,725	51,901	70,886	1,495	-
SOUTHERN NOVA SCOTIA	108	140.5	1,328	238,087	282,119	24,700	22,152	68,761	1,200	18,700
WEST RD BROWNS	63	109.1	955	797,318	745,400	21,750	68,585	13,210	4,575	8,975
WESTERN NOVA SCOTIA	20	16.7	143	15,830	9,934	-	13,010	3,555	-	89,690
SOUTHERN BAY OF FUNDY	1	0.8	6	330	-	200	-	-	-	-
NOVA SCOTIA, UNCLASSIFIED	3	2.8	33	30,100	18,000	8,400	400	-	-	-
TOTAL	1/159	1,421.3	14,657	3,340,483	3,936,651	475,515	219,721	4,830,641	9,070	558,595
OFF NEW ENGLAND (XXII):										
EASTERN MAINE	27	21.3	193	10,268	10,840	300	15,865	12,011	-	-
CENTRAL MAINE	10	7.1	59	4,508	1,940	-	4,149	2,976	-	-
WESTERN MAINE	110	925.0	1,900	1,079,059	646,194	72,338	321,733	471,987	420	28,140
EASTERN MASSACHUSETTS	436	12,018.1	12,872	2,495,579	1,888,847	320,579	481,483	608,935	6,290	1,122,205
INNER GROUNDS	150	582.8	3,285	337,270	177,070	13,640	263,409	202,894	200	13,350
NORTHERN 6/ OF MAINE, UNCL.	5	5.0	38	3,435	1,530	-	2,055	2,205	-	-
WESTERN SIDE SOUTH CHANNEL	358	1,767.3	8,974	1,372,591	3,675,075	419,710	314,556	526,843	589,615	446,495
EASTERN SIDE SOUTH CHANNEL	241	605.4	4,340	906,207	673,831	77,880	147,425	305,795	1,011,927	865,985
NORTHERN EDGE OF GEORGES	154	1,039.7	8,794	3,357,695	5,194,158	472,395	177,635	37,193	494,559	150,829
C TRE AND S.E. GEORGES	161	573.2	4,226	4,452,698	5,530,140	153,275	11,020	7,620	1,087,841	7,668,706
SOUTHWEST GEORGES	140	343.2	2,316	69,905	263,300	188,185	4,306	37,897	444,048	3,266,565
NANTUCKET SHOALS & LHTSHIP.	210	1,275.1	6,960	65,590	563,300	13,870	-	141,795	369,140	3,850,780
OFF NO MAN'S LAND	173	1,713.2	3,822	7,965	138,155	2,275	-	24,650	3,620	2,735,775
SOUTHERN MASSACHUSETTS	36	64.7	209	1,795	16,520	2,230	-	-	-	935
RHODE ISLAND SHORE	35	55.7	193	505	17,695	50,410	-	85	-	307
S. NEW ENGLAND, UNCLASSIFIED	242	775.5	2,842	391,290	742,028	63,244	14,195	34,890	433,755	843,493
CAPE COD 2/	333	13,858.0	13,858	1,338,113	1,243,376	2/	23,641	41,845	145,101	2,337,826
TOTAL	1/1,157	35,631.3	74,881	15,922,833	16,785,374	1,883,186	1,781,472	2,459,621	4,614,586	23,638,094
OFF MIDDLE ATLANTIC STATES (XXIII), SOUTH	33	39.4	247	-	1,905	25	-	195	-	62,285
GRAND TOTAL	1/1,184	37,092.0	89,785	19,263,316	20,723,930	2,358,726	2,001,193	7,290,657	4,623,656	24,258,974

(CONTINUED ON NEXT PAGE)

SEE FOOTNOTES AT END OF TABLE

LANDINGS AT CERTAIN MASSACHUSETTS PORTS

SUMMARY OF FISHERY: BY AREA AND SUBAREA, 1949 - Continued

AREA AND SUBAREA	FLOUNDERS, ROUND - CONTINUED			HADDOCK, DRAWN		RED, ROUND	HAKE		HALIBUT, DRAWN	MACKEREL, ROUND
	BLACKBACK	DAB	FLUKE	LARGE	SCROD		WHITE, LARGE	DRESSED SMALL		
	POUNDS	POUNDS	POUNDS	POUNDS	POUNDS	POUNDS	POUNDS	POUNDS	POUNDS	POUNDS
OFF NOVA SCOTIA (XXI):										
NORTHEAST CAPE BRETON	—	19,155	—	336,816	106,868	—	30,122	1,127	25,011	250
MAINE BANK	—	12,574	—	19,630	7,312	—	11,568	4,620	1,863	—
BANQUEREAU	—	75,447	—	355,163	287,771	—	40,719	4,668	9,458	—
CANSO BANK	630	109,518	—	86,297	51,622	—	33,363	9,203	2,212	—
MIDDLE GROUND	—	12,884	—	21,539	12,594	—	6,518	1,856	6,379	—
N.E. SABLE ISLAND BANK	320	6,740	—	786,350	982,930	—	20,900	—	5,358	500
S.E. SABLE ISLAND BANK	—	200	—	—	—	—	—	—	—	—
HORSESHOE GROUND	—	11,247	—	1,178,894	688,612	—	18,248	5,861	8,644	2,843
S.W. SABLE ISLAND BANK	—	15,928	—	859,112	643,960	—	20,273	—	4,022	2,300
EASTERN NOVA SCOTIA	80	13,877	—	24,318	8,325	—	25,457	15,285	709	2,317
EMERALD BANK	—	3,866	—	261,745	287,700	—	19,052	2,099	870	549
CENTRAL NOVA SCOTIA	—	8,287	—	18,967	5,594	—	8,981	4,598	—	2,100
E. BROWNS AND LA HAVE	550	44,614	—	3,257,534	1,694,865	—	94,490	19,013	18,746	3,000
SOUTHERN NOVA SCOTIA	560	71,121	—	2,475,543	1,196,528	200	75,311	20,487	3,777	25,780
WESTERN BROWNS	440	47,605	—	5,161,730	2,242,886	—	66,197	371	24,585	—
WESTERN NOVA SCOTIA	—	644	—	46,162	17,174	—	6,825	3,452	—	—
SOUTHERN BAY OF FUNDY	—	200	—	33,000	21,140	—	1,400	—	—	—
NOVA SCOTIA, UNCLASSIFIED	3,450	1,000	—	—	—	—	700	—	305	—
TOTAL	6,030	453,907	—	14,925,499	8,246,981	200	480,124	92,640	111,939	39,639
OFF NEW ENGLAND (XXII):										
EASTERN MAINE	—	4,666	—	49,965	20,680	—	8,982	5,337	—	—
CENTRAL MAINE	—	2,442	—	15,576	2,552	—	4,700	1,297	—	—
WESTERN MAINE	23,148	244,407	—	1,159,750	302,551	70	1,043,115	185,728	—	35,875
EASTERN MASSACHUSETTS	894,821	1,079,522	2,670	1,145,542	202,975	8,890	1,560,743	318,040	6,251	44,550
INNER GROUNDS	7,607	123,397	—	1,649,312	262,663	3,670	332,681	153,636	16,452	4,789,076
NORTHERN GULF OF MAINE, UNCL.	—	1,105	—	10,498,610	1,210	—	3,845	755	5,333	—
WESTERN SIDE SOUTH CHANNEL	3,451,251	351,056	7,960	7,422,236	3,139,201	7,155	917,972	73,492	19,355	403,380
EASTERN SIDE SOUTH CHANNEL	994,149	398,425	465	14,031,745	2,570,256	60	401,978	61,842	27,681	6,420
NORTHERN EDGE OF GEORGES	213,157	70,290	—	7,916,225	17,278,705	—	266,982	—	48,915	162,770
CENTRAL AND S.E. GEORGES	755,958	52,475	555	3,004,315	7,522,190	—	68,228	33,500	38,826	7,775
SOUTHWEST GEORGES	314,075	56,450	1,400	672,530	1,974,705	—	23,760	100	14,540	1,470
NANTUCKET SHOALS & LTSHIP.	3,297,320	5,485	489,044	20,555	196,210	559,615	23,790	95	2,962	265
OFF NO MAN'S LAND	635,085	115	777,572	225	795	30,875,164	15,145	200	—	2,295,722
SOUTHERN MASSACHUSETTS	346,180	—	6,690	225	—	—	—	—	—	—
RHODE ISLAND SHORE	30,550	—	1,830	—	—	—	170	—	—	—
S. NEW ENGLAND, UNCLASSIFIED	677,887	90,180	52,980	2,289,333	2,060,835	8,235,603	111,020	95	16,118	11,150
CAPE COD 2/	1,384,105	35,420	354,852	2,035,869	55,207	640	77,379	4,486	56,537	5,244,225
TOTAL	13,025,303	2,518,445	1,696,018	51,912,413	35,590,635	39,690,867	4,860,490	838,603	252,970	13,002,678
OFF MIDDLE ATLANTIC STATES (XXIII), SOUTH	5,450	—	89,395	—	—	—	1,785	—	—	129,550
GRAND TOTAL	13,036,783	2,972,352	1,785,413	66,837,912	43,837,616	39,691,067	5,342,399	931,243	364,909	13,171,867

(CONTINUED ON NEXT PAGE)

SEE FOOTNOTES AT END OF TABLE

LANDINGS AT CERTAIN MASSACHUSETTS PORTS

SUMMARY OF FISHERY: BY AREA AND SUBAREA, 1949 - Continued

AREA AND SUBAREA	POLLOCK DRAWN	POLLOCK ROUND	OCEAN PERCH (ROSEFISH), ROUND	SCUP OR PORGY, ROUND	SWORDFISH, DRESSED	WHITING DRESSED	WHITING ROUND	WOLFFISH, DRAWN	SCALLOPS (MEATS)	OTHER, AS LANDED	TOTAL, AS LANDED
	POUNDS	POUNDS	POUNDS	POUNDS	POUNDS	POUNDS	POUNDS	POUNDS	POUNDS	POUNDS	POUNDS
OFF NOVA SCOTIA (xxi):											
NORTHEAST CAPE BRETON	22,951	-	17,148,042	-	190	-	-	2,003	-	70,800	18,367,905
MISAINE BANK	41,555	-	11,721,640	-	-	-	-	29	-	43,507	11,938,126
BANQUEREAU	109,035	-	24,095,712	-	-	-	-	7,535	-	152,541	27,795,260
CANSO BANK	38,914	-	26,175,474	-	-	-	-	3,622	-	174,609	30,963,508
MIDDLE GROUND	8,101	-	14,759,129	-	-	-	-	2,402	-	41,693	15,128,267
N.E. SABLE ISLAND BANK	49,890	-	183,950	-	165	-	-	660	-	365	2,555,015
S.E. SABLE ISLAND BANK	4,920	-	159,000	-	-	-	-	1,150	-	-	213,370
HORSESHOE GROUND	370,801	-	1,638,410	-	-	-	-	80,913	-	9,650	4,464,636
S.W. SABLE ISLAND BANK	183,090	-	33,250	-	-	-	-	37,450	-	-	2,249,042
EASTERN NOVA SC OIA	60,908	-	7,370,920	-	-	1,462	480	2,844	-	115,326	7,774,925
EMERALD BANK	129,694	-	3,783,119	-	-	-	-	12,656	-	20,246	4,774,093
CENTRAL NOVA SCOTIA	27,145	-	3,772,241	-	-	-	-	818	-	48,750	3,935,002
E. BROWNS AND LA HAVE	705,678	-	9,839,402	-	-	-	-	70,543	-	88,972	16,907,532
SOUTHERN NOVA SCOTIA	1,047,547	-	7,380,608	-	-	1,600	120	59,940	-	104,962	13,075,398
WESTERN BROWNS	811,948	-	445,257	-	59,274	-	-	254,995	-	5,245	1,095,641
WESTERN NOVA SCOTIA	37,400	-	877,145	-	-	365	-	-	-	39,810	1,012,206
SOUTHERN BAY OF FUNDY	19,500	-	17,900	-	-	-	-	2,975	-	275	45,515
NOVA S OTIA, UNCLASSIFIED	20,400	-	98,000	-	-	-	-	-	-	10,065	244,505
TOTAL	3,689,487	-	129,498,199	-	59,629	3,427	600	540,535	-	932,736	172,452,448
OFF NEW ENGLAND (xxii):											
EASTERN MAINE	63,158	385	1,020,295	-	-	1,827	-	137	-	13,380	1,237,711
CENTRAL MAINE	12,835	-	266,804	-	-	954	-	28	-	1,500	358,136
WESTERN MAINE	1,443,627	70,293	2,920,472	-	-	423,821	83,934	44,618	-	79,455	10,625,753
EASTERN MASSACHUSETTS	3,518,676	-	924,329	-	-	27,996,249	2,263,445	350,700	74,060	19,854,348	71,994,749
I NER GROUND	1,041,829	-	20,157,350	-	-	67,511	7,400	7,525	-	754,061	25,691,062
NORTHERN OF MAINE, UNCL.	2,975	6,760	-	-	-	-	-	-	-	-	171,650
NORTHERN SIDE SOUTH CHANNEL	2,551,996	-	15,700,351	730	2,838	1,521,852	18,850	176,094	2,296,372	403,778	49,085,680
EA TERN SIDE SOUTH CHANNEL	2,296,777	-	10,490,831	70	103,846	15,550	19,725	105,630	449,134	227,917	29,471,034
NORTHERN EDGE OF GEORGES	3,481,282	-	82,685	-	223,307	-	10,000	163,388	4,133,034	17,648	49,988,971
CENTRAL AND S.E GEORGES	706,688	-	27,460	-	24,158	2,400	-	95,290	173,249	27,675	32,553,101
SOUTHWEST GEORGES	112,325	-	3,250	45	2,375	400	-	24,750	464,509	2,050	10,169,943
NANTUCKET SHOALS & LMTSHIP	22,495	-	2,400	3,940	54,618	7,900	-	23,925	3,725,085	137,327	14,364,623
OFF NO MAN'S LAND	1,135	-	-	23,265	-	100	-	-	5,471	2,686,625	40,327,852
SOUTHERN MASSACHUSETTS	455	-	-	69,230	-	-	-	-	-	8,105	455,675
RHODE ISLAND SHORE	503,910	-	144,150	70	15,249	13,800	-	45,595	297,283	910	361,795
S. NEW ENGLAND, UNCLASSIFIED	173,551	-	8,105	30,130	162,380	-	-	133,133	1,327,003	2,312,810	19,418,249
CAPE COD 2/	-	-	-	304,603	-	4,807,268	8,246,898	-	-	6,146,399	35,751,206
TOTAL	15,938,584	77,438	51,983,933	432,083	588,771	34,859,817	10,650,805	1,170,813	13,045,310	32,674,048	391,895,190
OFF MIDDLE ATLANTIC STATES (xxiii), SOUTH	250	-	-	17,090	-	-	-	-	133,595	36,475	478,000
GRAND TOTAL	19,628,321	77,438	181,482,132	449,173	648,400	34,863,244	10,651,405	1,711,348	13,178,905	33,643,259	564,825,638

1/ EXCLUSIVE OF DUPLICATION, EXCEPT THAT CRAFT LANDING AT CAPE COD PORTS MAY BE DUPLICATED WITH CRAFT FISHING ELSEWHERE.

2/ REPRESENTS THE CATCH LANDED AT PROVINCETOWN, WOODS HOLE, CHATHAM, HYANNIS, HARWICH PORT, AND OTHER CAPE COD PORTS EAST OF BUZZARDS BAY. IT IS NOT POSSIBLE TO ALLOCATE THIS CATCH INTO SUBAREAS AS DATA ARE NOT COLLECTED ON THE AREA OF CAPTURE FOR THESE PORTS.

NOTE:--THE ROMAN NUMERALS APPEARING IN THE ABOVE TABLE REFER TO THE NUMBERS GIVEN THOSE AREAS BY THE NORTH AMERICAN COUNCIL ON FISHERY INVESTIGATIONS.

LANDINGS AT MAINE PORTS

In 1946, the Fish and Wildlife Service, in cooperation with the Maine Department of Sea and Shore Fisheries, began to collect, compile, and publish monthly and annual data on the landings of fish and shellfish in Maine. These data are published in detail in ''Maine Landings'' which is in the Current Fishery Statistics Series of reports issued by the Service. In addition to the individual monthly reports, two annual summaries were published in 1949, one listing the catch by months, (Current Fisheries Statistics, No. 544) and the other listing the catch by gear and county, (Current Fisheries Statistics, No. 548).

The data on Maine landings during 1949 represent the landed weight of fish. Figures on the landings of shellfish and marine products, other than fish, represent the round weight of the catch except for bivalve and univalve mollusks, which are reported in pounds of meats.

Landings of fishery products at Maine ports in 1949 totaled 292,203,570 pounds valued at $14,988,040 to the fishermen. This represented a decrease of 4 percent in quantity of landings and a decrease of 7 percent in value of landings compared with the previous year. Increased landings of ocean perch (rosefish), whiting, menhaden, lobsters, and unclassified fish largely used for reduction, were not sufficient to offset a decline of nearly 33 million pounds in herring receipts. Herring, used principally in canning Maine sardines, accounted for 51 percent of the total poundage and 16 percent of the total value. Although lobsters accounted for only 7 percent of the total catch, they represented 45 percent of the value, making them the most valuable species taken.

During the year, 48,926,666 pounds of fish and shellfish, valued at $1,662,711 were landed in Portland. Prior to 1947, these landings were included in the bulletins entitled ''Landings at Certain New England Ports'', summaries of which appear in annual Statistical Digests. To avoid duplication, beginning in 1947, data on Portland landings were omitted from these bulletins since the data appeared in the monthly and annual Maine reports.

LANDINGS AT MAINE PORTS, BY MONTHS, 1949

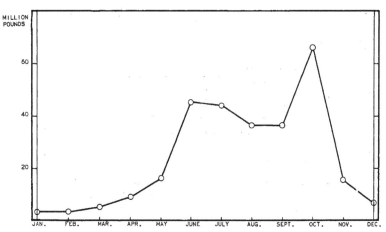

LANDINGS AT MAINE PORTS BY MONTHS, 1949

SPECIES	JANUARY		FEBRUARY		MARCH		APRIL	
FISH	POUNDS	VALUE	POUNDS	VALUE	POUNDS	VALUE	POUNDS	VALUE
COD:								
ROUND:								
LARGE	2,673	$160	3,283	$148	7,000	$331	30,856	$1,070
MARKET.	1,673	50	2,510	83	16,609	652	137,505	4,338
SCROD	359	4	48	1	1,067	21	16,836	259
DRAWN:								
LARGE	63,656	6,046	62,372	4,666	154,811	11,036	254,284	12,123
MARKET.	72,938	3,709	78,753	3,830	183,167	9,341	354,193	13,010
SCROD	4,386	163	3,536	162	8,710	340	66,592	1,923
HADDOCK:								
ROUND:								
LARGE	643	64	79	6	439	40	69,379	3,808
SCROD	-	-	-	-	74	3	12,158	392
DRAWN:								
LARGE	227,019	25,446	137,174	13,664	199,642	19,866	567,284	35,536
SCROD	76,512	4,627	49,360	2,600	62,595	3,611	239,393	9,134
HAKE:								
RED, ROUND.	560	30	485	28	1,690	194	5,300	278
WHITE:								
ROUND	1,287	40	-	-	190	9	931	38
DRAWN	91,179	9,648	94,796	10,336	170,019	19,220	224,529	13,847
POLLOCK:								
ROUND	257	5	-	-	-	-	7,698	97
DRAWN	114,971	4,365	53,866	1,821	218,599	8,505	425,585	9,973
CUSK, DRAWN	50,721	4,575	63,506	4,963	114,263	8,200	164,189	5,899
HALIBUT, DRAWN.	481	184	933	361	1,876	678	5,054	1,470
MACKEREL, ROUND	-	-	-	-	28	3	-	-
FLOUNDERS, ROUND:								
GRAY SOLE	14,853	1,022	21,615	1,455	75,215	3,916	68,198	3,192
LEMON SOLE.	-	-	-	-	565	26	-	-
YELLOWTAIL.	29,260	3,258	13,265	1,455	9,566	1,268	12,389	646
BLACKBACK	107,160	8,368	109,339	6,604	87,641	4,534	58,642	2,756
DAB	19,080	901	24,317	994	56,147	2,128	120,621	3,117
OCEAN PERCH (ROSEFISH),								
ROUND	960,293	36,068	1,443,819	54,276	2,262,562	85,054	3,758,593	150,253
WHITING:								
ROUND	-	-	-	.	2,723	120	-	-
DRESSED	-	-	-	-	-	-	6,594	245
WOLFFISH (CATFISH):								
DRAWN	3,553	154	5,970	248	17,649	728	44,747	1,072
ALEWIVES, ROUND	-	-	-	-	-	.	12,180	348
EELS, ROUND	-	-	2,200	550	-	-	-	-
SHAD, ROUND	25	1	-	-	-	-	-	-
SHARK, DRESSED	130	3	-	-	-	-	-	-
SMELT, ROUND.	33,659	9,490	26,768	9,054	1,286	321	60,080	12,463
STURGEON, DRAWN	-	-	-	-	39	8	-	-
SUCKERS, ROUND.	-	-	9,305	651	-	-	-	-
MISCELLANEOUS	2,500	58	5,180	120	8,655	173	2,449	64
TOTAL	1,879,828	118,439	2,224,479	118,076	3,662,827	180,326	6,736,255	287,351
SHELLFISH, ETC.								
CRABS	16,858	777	13,652	653	49,627	1,303	50,556	1,922
CLAMS:								
SOFT.	746,772	131,812	590,013	107,484	823,494	129,422	1,060,267	124,751
HARD (QUAHOGS).	5,295	721	1,499	225	4,007	673	15,950	3,267
LOBSTERS, MAINE	561,195	239,302	460,951	245,933	509,146	309,447	761,297	348,811
SHRIMP.	-	-	5,500	963	4,200	840	-	-
SCALLOPS, SEA	75,746	29,778	52,123	19,122	59,640	17,981	110	40
MUSSELS, SEA.	91,940	4,961	56,201	2,413	30,485	1,556	15,960	761
PERIWINKLES	468	116	540	180	954	199	306	101
SEA URCHINS (SEA EGGS) . .	8,575	281	2,870	141	1,505	76	-	-
BLOODWORMS.	87	50	907	657	8,848	5,855	25,495	20,355
SANDWORMS	-	-	-	..	-	.	375	150
LIVERS.	59,626	4,785	30,551	2,463	52,075	3,904	89,933	6,340
SPAWN	195	17	310	35	2,302	317	1,467	366
TOTAL.	1,566,757	412,600	1,215,127	380,269	1,546,283	472,573	2,021,716	506,864
GRAND TOTAL.	3,446,595	531,039	3,439,605	498,345	5,209,110	652,899	8,757,971	794,215

(CONTINUED ON NEXT PAGE)

LANDINGS AT MAINE PORTS BY MONTHS, 1949 - Continued

SPECIES	MAY		JUNE		JULY		AUGUST	
FISH	POUNDS	VALUE	POUNDS	VALUE	POUNDS	VALUE	POUNDS	VALUE
COD:								
ROUND:								
LARGE . . .	35,817	$1,074	29,098	$644	6,347	$133	8,426	$208
MARKET. . .	68,223	1,552	28,572	463	28,218	571	3,591	61
SCROD . . .	9,801	102	5,918	60	2,055	22	994	10
DRAWN:								
LARGE . .	405,504	19,894	412,673	24,516	389,285	32,183	279,524	26,155
MARKET . .	263,142	8,646	200,439	5,689	181,740	5,920	158,237	4,720
SCROD . .	33,409	621	13,948	409	7,970	219	10,707	275
HADDOCK:								
ROUND:								
LARGE . . .	13,544	699	3,894	171	9,356	493	2,023	111
SCROD . . .	2,725	76	161	5	798	30	-	-
DRAWN:								
LARGE . . .	260,697	16,594	332,413	18,513	349,770	21,551	507,193	31,134
SCROD . . .	83,707	3,042	105,492	3,545	90,660	3,147	117,319	4,225
HAKE:								
RED, ROUND. .	4,475	67	13,065	408	11,382	399	38,715	2,053
WHITE:								
ROUND . . .	14,480	289	248,504	4,964	470,129	9,395	88,567	1,771
DRAWN . . .	350,751	12,833	538,236	17,809	429,558	12,508	463,826	17,314
POLLOCK:								
ROUND . . .	1,278	21	7,360	75	153,015	1,826	61,814	508
DRAWN . . .	374,194	7,349	412,520	8,791	450,498	9,642	375,866	9,298
CUSK:								
ROUND . .	-	-	-	-	3,977	69	2,699	29
DRAWN . .	155,525	3,748	151,597	4,052	104,780	2,745	109,605	3,160
HALIBUT, DRAWN.	17,166	4,368	6,264	1,720	2,399	582	4,537	1,288
MACKEREL, ROUND	74,248	7,758	484,808	27,010	1,695,068	61,955	501,749	28,500
FLOUNDERS, ROUND								
GRAY SOLE .	74,503	3,082	140,033	5,313	83,030	3,217	106,523	4,432
YELLOWTAIL .	4,000	123	275	8	1,288	53	90	2
BLACKBACK .	19,812	592	20,297	674	18,467	567	43,316	1,313
DAB .	69,088	1,346	74,235	1,535	38,074	818	54,986	1,170
OCEAN PERCH,								
(ROSEFISH),								
ROUND . . .	6,692,634	260,623	9,224,509	302,914	8,343,129	269,148	8,192,472	268,852
WHITING:								
ROUND . . .	486,227	9,393	2,594,604	32,470	4,953,657	50,944	1,994,767	23,669
DRESSED . .	19,291	727	173,458	1,749	2,200	66	-	-
WOLFFISH(CAT-								
FISH),DRAWN. .	34,262	861	22,864	505	11,712	315	3,994	123
ALEWIVES, ROUND	885,857	9,460	2,382,600	21,349	-	-	-	-
BUTTERFISH,ROUND	-	-	-	-	-	-	12	1
EELS, ROUND . .	1,000	160	1,200	192	-	-	-	-
GRAYFISH (DOG-								
FISH),ROUND..	-	-	-	-	-	-	370,000	2,640
HERRING, ROUND.	4,091,964	66,641	24,756,480	369,571	19,729,255	322,221	16,006,960	262,325
MENHADEN, ROUND	-	-	358,780	3,651	2,007,225	18,160	2,661,290	23,228
SALMON,ROUND..	-	-	212	106	740	370	66	31
SHAD,ROUND...	210	4	53	2	235	5	319	13
SHARK,DRESSED .	2,588	84	3,524	111	8,006	277	7,551	238
SMELT,ROUND ..	2,132	257	-	-	212	23	695	120
STURGEON,DRAWN.	5	1	60	10	220	30	-	-
TUNA,ROUND. . .	-	-	4,486	641	101,814	9,481	46,912	4,438
MISCELLANEOUS .	4,980	81	4,765	69	13,460	174	180,160	1,306
TOTAL. . .	14,557,249	442,168	42,757,477	859,714	39,699,729	839,259	32,405,506	724,731
SHELLFISH, ETC.:								
CRABS	138,297	3,515	100,554	3,241	44,941	1,974	78,769	1,566
CLAMS:								
SOFT. . . .	1,299,602	197,391	942,631	165,723	764,835	154,609	475,399	83,695
HARD(QUAHOGS)	69,949	12,724	89,364	20,315	41,866	7,377	254,339	34,680
LOBSTERS,MAINE.	1,007,920	379,461	807,192	346,191	1,949,145	678,584	3,383,442	1,123,435
SHRIMP.	-	-	153	3	-	-	-	-
SCALLOPS, SEA .	-	-	9,907	3,517	18,108	6,405	16,230	5,468
MUSSELS, SEA. .	49,385	1,073	-	-	-	-	-	-
PERIWINKLES . .	594	209	1,377	705	927	307	936	311
SQUID	-	-	10,110	179	5,620	120	-	-
BLOODWORMS . .	33,873	25,254	46,121	33,008	51,696	35,959	49,966	37,004
SANDWORMS . . .	2,628	1,447	4,144	2,850	3,163	1,453	1,968	1,042
SEA MOSS. . . .	140,000	2,800	450,000	9,000	120,000	1,440	255,000	3,060
LIVERS.	115,350	8,021	165,820	11,325	229,057	16,295	222,308	15,584
SPAWN	116	11	10	1	-	-	-	-
TOTAL. . .	2,857,714	631,906	2,627,383	596,068	3,229,358	904,522	4,738,357	1,305,835
GRAND TOTAL .	17,414,963	1,074,074	45,384,860	1,455,782	42,929,097	1,743,781	37,143,863	2,030,566

(CONTINUED ON NEXT PAGE)

SPECIES	SEPTEMBER		OCTOBER		NOVEMBER		DECEMBER	
FISH	POUNDS	VALUE	POUNDS	VALUE	POUNDS	VALUE	POUNDS	VALUE
COD:								
ROUND:								
LARGE.	805	$ 24	6,162	$185	7,637	$230	6,604	$198
MARKET	362	5	5,618	84	6,832	103	4,915	74
SCROD.	133	2	3,675	36	422	4	3,704	37
DRAWN:								
LARGE.	197,280	17,268	131,683	9,879	127,658	7,091	94,910	5,516
MARKET	147,780	5,262	206,955	8,668	104,602	3,599	74,613	2,953
SCROD.	5,347	167	6,344	242	6,901	160	2,160	87
HADDOCK:								
ROUND:								
LARGE.	237	14	405	24	-	-	-	-
DRAWN:								
LARGE.	556,777	38,432	769,967	59,532	542,875	40,359	394,943	38,064
SCROD.	152,524	4,999	215,642	10,103	87,463	4,454	74,465	4,049
HAKE:								
RED, ROUND	55,335	3,028	49,570	3,018	4,760	196	875	53
WHITE:								
ROUND.	8,262	151	24,150	483	18,309	366	5,881	118
DRAWN.	450,803	20,546	357,259	17,518	289,044	11,932	146,042	9,475
POLLOCK:								
ROUND.	172	2	826	12	424,573	4,691	118	2
DRAWN.	410,294	13,542	826,807	23,109	735,272	16,563	662,123	14,247
CUSK:								
ROUND.	307	6	1,963	29	1,610	25	2,071	30
DRAWN.	88,102	3,494	92,452	4,231	44,030	2,378	51,153	3,263
HALIBUT, DRAWN	1,927	569	1,759	485	1,171	339	873	241
MACKEREL, ROUND. . . .	277,666	15,994	312,259	15,805	5,943	544	-	-
FLOUNDERS, ROUND .								
GRAY SOLE.	71,616	3,725	55,110	2,817	25,503	1,334	24,782	1,343
LEMON SOLE	-	-	-	-	445	42	125	5
YELLOWTAIL	7,277	223	25,617	1,127	5,948	177	10,750	403
BLACKBACK.	70,710	2,867	146,615	5,865	47,710	1,916	93,172	3,718
DAB.	53,345	1,550	37,163	1,073	19,066	580	19,468	565
OCEAN PERCH (ROSEFISH) .								
ROUND	5,757,429	203,830	3,677,909	156,935	2,895,842	127,035	2,293,419	99,033
WHITING:								
ROUND.	2,045,111	25,337	86,263	1,152	32,452	325	10,162	153
DRESSED.	-	-	13,409	469	7,909	277	2,674	94
WOLFFISH (CATFISH),								
DRAWN	2,957	105	1,398	52	7,553	77	1,788	55
BUTTERFISH, ROUND. . . .	-	-	415	9	-	-	-	-
EELS, ROUND.	14,500	3,190	22,900	4,580	-	-	-	-
GRAYFISH (DOGFISH),								
ROUND	-	-	132,000	1,312	52,000	520	33,000	330
HERRING, ROUND	21,473,220	349,683	54,588,660	890,452	8,489,660	136,216	757,690	11,274
MENHADEN, ROUND.	50	1	-	-	-	-	-	-
SHAD, ROUND.	1,095	42	2,300	111	480	22	190	6
SHARK, DRESSED	19,056	718	12,906	512	3,439	135	2,248	95
SMELT, ROUND	942	188	13,438	3,203	12,440	3,136	7,123	1,748
STURGEON, DRAWN.	85	20	6,317	569	-	-	-	-
TUNA ROUND	75	5	1,048,555	7,556	565,081	5,485	152,023	1,271
MISCELLANEOUS	393,600	3,000						
TOTAL.	32,265,183	718,039	62,884,271	1,231,237	14,575,029	370,312	4,934,064	198,500
SHELLFISH, ETC.								
CRABS.	135,012	2,606	40,017	785	42,081	1,143	24,035	732
CLAMS:								
SOFT	421,209	75,532	463,323	76,466	461,788	80,528	573,539	92,288
HARD (QUAHOGS) . . .	41,052	7,389	37,213	5,367	20,878	3,778	8,382	1,967
LOBSTERS, MAINE.	3,696,569	1,126,665	3,072,161	963,448	1,807,205	538,706	1,256,272	396,978
SCALLOPS, SEA.	9,893	3,648	8,477	3,035	148,191	52,300	110,491	38,551
MUSSELS, SEA	-	-	5,325	355	30,330	1,269	106,695	2,957
PERIWINKLES.	1,872	597	123	42	531	42	1,660	377
SQUID.	470	10	3,875	86	-	-	-	-
SEA URCHINS (SEA EGGS). .	32,940	782	290	8	6,680	173	26,630	830
BLOODWORMS	47,105	40,490	33,224	28,425	59,163	41,747	35,231	27,218
SANDWORMS.	3,031	2,188	2,219	1,206	5,950	2,905	10,333	5,659
SEA MOSS	160,000	2,404	-	-	-	-	-	-
LIVERS.	218,102	13,894	208,458	14,562	229,832	16,330	158,225	10,434
SPAWN	-	-	1,520	113	22,680	1,279	18,696	957
TOTAL.	4,767,255	1,276,205	3,876,225	1,093,898	2,845,309	740,200	2,330,189	578,948
GRAND TOTAL.	37,032,438	1,994,244	66,760,496	2,325,135	17,420,338	1,110,512	7,264,253	777,448

(CONTINUED ON NEXT PAGE)

LANDINGS AT MAINE PORTS BY MONTHS, 1949 - Continued

SPECIES	1949			1948		
FISH	POUNDS	VALUE	AV. PRICE PER POUND	POUNDS	VALUE	AV. PRICE PER POUND
COD:						
ROUND:						
LARGE.	144,708	$4,405	3.04¢	218,430	$7,272	3.33¢
MARKET	304,629	8,036	2.64	302,621	8,734	2.89
SCROD.	45,012	558	1.24	45,620	513	1.12
DRAWN:						
LARGE.	2,573,640	176,373	6.85	3,797,836	262,408	6.91
MARKET	2,026,559	75,347	3.72	1,804,213	75,396	4.18
SCROD.	170,010	4,768	2.80	217,700	6,052	2.78
HADDOCK:						
ROUND:						
LARGE.	99,999	5,430	5.43	102,548	7,103	6.93
SCROD.	15,916	506	3.18	11,993	386	3.22
DRAWN:						
LARGE.	4,845,754	358,691	7.40	4,338,459	354,866	8.18
SCROD.	1,355,132	57,536	4.25	1,598,299	79,636	4.98
HAKE:						
RED, ROUND	186,212	9,762	5.24	60,005	2,394	3.99
WHITE:						
ROUND.	880,770	17,624	2.00	1,140,646	19,995	1.75
DRAWN.	3,606,042	172,996	4.80	4,433,077	211,387	4.77
POLLOCK:						
ROUND.	657,111	7,239	1.10	116,961	2,430	2.08
DRAWN.	5,070,595	127,205	2.51	6,183,591	206,702	3.34
CUSK:						
ROUND.	12,627	188	1.49	-	-	-
DRAWN	1,189,923	50,708	4.26	1,014,369	45,834	4.52
HALIBUT, DRAWN	44,440	12,285	27.64	42,757	12,598	29.46
MACKEREL, ROUND.	3,351,769	157,569	4.70	4,091,530	191,917	4.69
FLOUNDERS, ROUND:						
GRAY SOLE.	760,981	34,848	4.58	753,385	45,724	6.07
LEMON SOLE.	1,135	73	6.43	8,366	630	7.53
YELLOWTAIL.	119,725	8,743	7.30	117,718	7,345	6.24
BLACKBACK.	832,881	39,774	4.78	870,194	53,123	6.10
DAB.	585,591	15,777	2.69	563,869	18,931	3.36
OTHER.	-	-	-	990	20	2.02
OCEAN PERCH (ROSEFISH),						
ROUND	55,502,605	2,014,071	3.63	49,041,410	1,711,769	3.49
WHITING:						
ROUND.	12,205,966	143,564	1.18	8,412,173	105,708	1.26
DRESSED	225,534	3,627	1.61	242,381	7,910	3.26
WOLFFISH (CATFISH):						
ROUND.	-	-	-	3,236	127	3.92
DRAWN.	158,847	4,295	2.70	213,406	8,575	4.02
ALEWIVES, ROUND.	3,280,647	31,157	.95	1,867,820	11,370	.61
BUTTERFISH, ROUND.	227	10	4.41	-	-	-
EELS, ROUND.	41,800	8,672	20.75	20,231	3,534	17.47
GRAYFISH (DOGFISH),						
ROUND	587,000	4,802	.82	-	-	-
HERRING, ROUND	149,893,689	2,408,383	1.61	182,460,955	3,486,455	1.91
MENHADEN, ROUND.	5,027,345	45,040	.90	24,109	227	.94
SALMON, ROUND.	1,018	507	49.80	-	-	-
SHAD, ROUND.	4,908	206	4.20	2,552	86	3.37
SHARK, DRESSED	59,448	2,173	3.66	49,419	1,621	3.28
SKATE WINGS.	-	-	-	695	35	5.04
SMELT, ROUND	160,776	40,003	24.88	542,236	137,291	25.32
STURGEON, DRAWN.	409	69	16.87	228	39	17.10
SUCKERS, ROUND	9,305	651	7.00	4,143	544	13.13
SWORDFISH, DRAWN	-	-	-	461	258	55.96
TUNA, ROUND.	159,604	15,134	9.48	229,138	19,095	8.33
MISCELLANEOUS.	2,381,408	19,357	.81	98,377	3,123	3.17
TOTAL	258,581,897	6,088,152	2.35	275,048,146	7,119,163	2.59

(CONTINUED ON NEXT PAGE)

LANDINGS AT MAINE PORTS BY MONTHS, 1949 - Continued

SPECIES	1949			1948		
	POUNDS	VALUE	AV. PRICE PER POUND	POUNDS	VALUE	AV. PRICE PER POUND
SHELLFISH, ETC.						
CRABS.	734,399	$20,217	2.75	340,086	$19,878	5.84
CLAMS:						
SOFT	8,622,872	1,419,691	16.46	8,969,362	1,801,207	20.08
HARD (QUAHOGS)	589,794	98,483	16.70	288,677	60,348	20.90
LOBSTERS, MAINE.	19,272,495	6,696,961	34.75	15,923,053	6,439,474	40.44
SHRIMP	9,853	1,806	18.33	27,325	3,122	11.42
SCALLOPS, SEA.	508,016	179,845	35.34	453,685	217,662	47.98
MUSSELS, SEA	386,321	15,345	3.97	124,129	13,365	10.77
PERIWINKLES.	10,288	3,186	30.97	19,773	6,213	31.42
SQUID.	20,075	395	1.97	-	-	-
SEA URCHINS (SEA EGGS) . .	79,490	2,291	2.88	180,085	4,448	2.47
BLOODWORMS	401,716	297,021	73.94	567,987	305,044	53.71
SANDWORMS.	33,811	18,910	55.93	77,871	57,307	73.59
SEA MOSS	1,125,000	18,704	1.66	1,483,721	29,675	2.00
LIVERS	1,779,347	123,937	6.96	1,509,274	104,993	6.96
SPAWN.	47,296	3,096	6.55	24,342	1,697	6.97
TOTAL	33,621,673	8,899,888	26.47	29,989,371	9,064,433	30.22
GRAND TOTAL	292,203,570	14,988,040	5.13	305,037,517	16,183,596	5.30

NOTE:--THE FACTORS USED IN THE ABOVE TABLES TO CONVERT NUMBERS OR BUSHELS OF SHELLFISH, ETC., TO POUNDS
ARE AS FOLLOWS: CRABS, 3 TO A POUND; CLAMS, SOFT, PUBLIC, 15 POUNDS OF MEATS PER BUSHEL; CLAMS, HARD
(QUAHOGS), 11 POUNDS OF MEATS PER BUSHEL; BLOODWORMS, 44 WORMS PER POUND; SANDWORMS, 40 WORMS PER POUND,
HERRING, 70 POUNDS PER BUSHEL; AND PERIWINKLES, 18 POUNDS OF MEATS PER BUSHEL.

MAINE LANDINGS, 1949

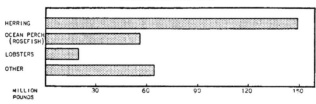

VALUE OF MAINE LANDINGS, 1949

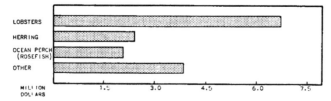

SECTION 3.- MIDDLE ATLANTIC FISHERIES

(Area XXIII)[4]

The 1949 catch of fish and shellfish in the coastal areas of the Middle Atlantic States (New York, New Jersey, and Delaware) totaled 520,976,400 pounds valued at $27,117,133 to the fishermen. This represented an increase of 4 percent in quantity but a decrease of 5 percent in value compared with the previous year. Menhaden accounted for 75 percent of the total 1949 landings in the Middle Atlantic States, and 16 percent of the total value.

The fisheries of the Middle Atlantic Area remained in a fairly healthy condition during 1949 with most of the major fisheries either holding their own or making slight gains in production. However, the continued failure of the pound net fishery was noticeable in New York and New Jersey. There were two factors which helped save many of the pound net operators from complete financial collapse during the year. These were successful summer retail markets, and prolonged winter operations. The pound net fisheries being located in the center of the popular resort areas, found a ready retail market for their fish during the summer months while production was at its peak. The profits recognized from direct retail sales coupled with the elimination of additional shipping and icing charges greatly aided the hard-pressed pound net operators. Prior to 1949 it had been customary to take the pound nets from the water in the early fall before the beginning of the autumnal storms, however with a non-productive season behind them and good fishing weather at hand, many operators left their equipment in the water. Migratory species continued to make their appearance in the nets throughout the winter. Out-of-season prices were received for these fish and, although some gear was lost because of storms, a new phase of seasonal operations was inaugurated.

The New England mackerel fleet made its appearance in the Middle Atlantic Area in early April and recorded an exceptionally successful season. During 1949, the purse seine operators caught almost 17 million pounds of mackerel. The 1948 mackerel purse seine season in the Middle Atlantic area had been unusually unsuccessful with slightly over one half million pounds being taken. The 1949 fall mackerel season was not so successful for hand line operators and gill netters as the spring season had been for the purse seine fleet. In the fall, the mackerel failed to school or to respond favorable to chumming operations. These two factors were mainly responsible for the failure of the fall season.

The menhaden catch in the Middle Atlantic area was only 3.2 million pounds above the amount taken the previous year. The prices paid for oil dropped greatly during 1949, but meal prices showed a marked increase and in part compensated for the fish oil problem.

The 1949 production of oysters in New York and New Jersey recorded a noticeable gain compared with the previous year. Increased plantings and a good demand for fresh stock again made this fishery the most valuable single item in the Middle Atlantic Area.

The failure of the soft clam production during 1949 was due mainly to the depletion of the famed Shrewsbury River clam beds in northern New Jersey. In 1949, because of pollution and intensive digging, these once-productive beds reached a point where constructive measures had to be taken if they are ever again to become the fertile grounds they were in the past. During the year, the state began studies to determine what measures should be adopted to preserve and build up these valuable grounds.

---

[4] *This number was assigned to this area by the North American Council on Fishery Investigations. It should be explained that there are included in this area craft whose principal fishing ports are in the area but at times fish elsewhere. A notable example is the southern trawl fishery which extends into Area XXIV.*

The last complete survey of the fishery transporting, wholesaling, and manufacturing industries was made for 1940. In that year, 215 men were employed in the operation of 72 vessels and boats engaged in the transporting trade, and 5,880 persons were employed in wholesale and manufacturing establishments. The latter employees received $6,736,554 in salaries and wages during 1940. Detailed statistics on these branches of the industry for that year can be found in ''Fishery Statistics of the United States, 1944'', (Statistical Digest No. 16).

Condensed summary data on the operating units and catch by states of the Middle Atlantic fisheries, appearing on the following pages, have previously been published in Current Fishery Statistics No. 693.

MIDDLE ATLANTIC CATCH, 1949

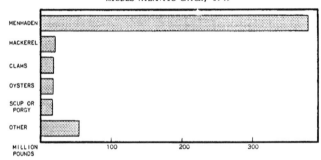

VALUE OF MIDDLE ATLANTIC CATCH, 1949

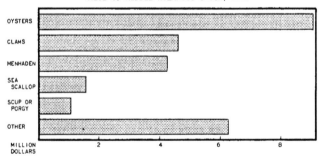

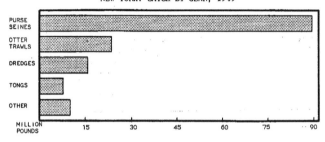

NEW YORK: CATCH BY GEAR, 1949

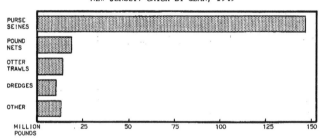

NEW JERSEY: CATCH BY GEAR, 1949

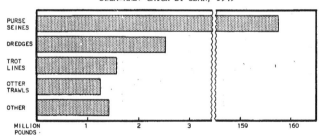

DELAWARE: CATCH BY GEAR, 1949

MIDDLE ATLANTIC FISHERIES
SECTIONAL SUMMARIES
SUMMARY OF CATCH, 1949

PRODUCT	NEW YORK		NEW JERSEY	
	POUNDS	VALUE	POUNDS	VALUE
FISH	120,048,800	$4,453,553	191,492,100	$4,536,262
SHELLFISH, ETC..	25,456,200	9,911,247	17,505,400	5,208,298
TOTAL.	145,505,000	14,364,800	208,997,500	9,744,560

PRODUCT	DELAWARE		TOTAL	
	POUNDS	VALUE	POUNDS	VALUE
FISH	161,733,200	$1,839,801	473,274,100	$10,829,616
SHELLFISH, ETC..	4,740,700	1,167,972	47,702,300	16,287,517
TOTAL.	166,473,900	3,007,773	520,976,400	27,117,133

SUMMARY OF OPERATING UNITS, 1949

ITEM	NEW YORK	NEW JERSEY	DELAWARE	TOTAL
	NUMBER	NUMBER	NUMBER	NUMBER
FISHERMEN:				
ON VESSELS	916	1,832	685	3,433
ON BOATS AND SHORE:				
REGULAR.	2,884	1,810	159	4,853
CASUAL	4,353	2,325	207	6,885
TOTAL.	8,153	5,967	1,051	15,171
VESSELS, MOTOR	211	333	46	590
NET TONNAGE.	4,776	6,874	2,459	14,109
BOATS:				
MOTOR.	3,320	2,227	155	5,702
OTHER.	349	946	69	1,364
ACCESSORY BOATS.	42	72	69	183
APPARATUS:				
PURSE SEINES:				
MACKEREL	-	4	-	4
LENGTH, YARDS.	-	1,550	-	1,550
MENHADEN	8	18	23	49
LENGTH, YARDS.	3,200	5,710	6,900	15,810
OTHER.	-	2	-	2
LENGTH, YARDS.	-	800	-	800
HAUL SEINES, COMMON.	136	23	58	217
LENGTH, YARDS.	80,818	6,900	17,400	105,118
GILL NETS:				
DRIFT.	205	1,329	44	1,578
SQUARE YARDS	631,500	647,938	87,168	1,366,606
RUNAROUND.	-	17	5	22
SQUARE YARDS	-	68,000	20,000	88,000
STAKE.	102	551	18	671
SQUARE YARDS	57,125	951,731	26,902	1,035,758
LINES:				
HAND	649	254	-	903
HOOKS.	1,300	470	-	1,770
TRAWL OR TROT WITH HOOKS	191	339	85	615
HOOKS.	71,500	102,600	51,000	225,100
TROLL.	-	21	-	21
HOOKS.	-	42	-	42
TROT WITH BAITS OR SNOODS.	-	62	-	62
BAITS OR SNOODS.	-	43,000	-	43,000
POUND NETS	153	77	-	230
WEIRS.	-	30	-	30
STOP NETS.	-	18	-	18
LENGTH, YARDS.	-	9,000	-	9,000
FYKE NETS, FISH.	543	239	81	863
DIP NETS, COMMON	-	20	30	50
OTTER TRAWLS, FISH	158	106	8	272
YARDS AT MOUTH	2,453	2,224	158	4,835
BEAM TRAWLS, SHRIMP.	-	21	-	21
YARDS AT MOUTH	-	35	-	35
POTS:				
CONCH.	1,605	-	-	1,605
CRAB	-	55	900	955
EEL.	721	1,114	450	2,285
FISH	680	15,185	-	15,865
LOBSTER.	2,836	6,950	-	9,786
HARPOONS	5	-	-	5

(CONTINUED ON NEXT PAGE)

SUMMARY OF OPERATING UNITS, 1949 - Continued

ITEM	NEW YORK	NEW JERSEY	DELAWARE	TOTAL
	NUMBER	NUMBER	NUMBER	NUMBER
APPARATUS - CONTINUED:				
DREDGES:				
CLAM.	53	76	-	129
YARDS AT MOUTH.	36	70	-	106
CRAB.	-	38	-	38
YARDS AT MOUTH.	-	72	-	72
OYSTER, COMMON.	70	272	34	376
YARDS AT MOUTH.	96	272	34	402
SCALLOP	92	34	-	126
YARDS AT MOUTH.	267	112	-	379
TONGS:				
OYSTER.	874	207	65	1,146
OTHER	5,767	475	-	6,242
RAKES, OTHER THAN FOR OYSTERS	372	669	47	1,088
HOES.	-	185	-	185

CATCH BY STATES, 1949

SPECIES	NEW YORK		NEW JERSEY	
FISH	POUNDS	VALUE	POUNDS	VALUE
ALEWIVES.	99,000	$2,991	19,900	$597
ANGLERFISH.	48,400	2,510	9,100	273
BLUEFISH.	251,200	39,522	1,055,400	121,347
BUTTERFISH.	1,520,400	221,363	1,499,700	97,983
CARP.	56,600	4,488	65,000	3,330
CATFISH AND BULLHEADS	38,500	4,244	111,600	5,742
COD	2,356,800	229,073	1,386,600	135,786
CROAKER			85,200	5,142
CUNNER.	2,600	104	500	9
DOLPHIN	100	4	100	10
DRUM, BLACK	-	-	800	44
EELS:				
COMMON.	228,800	39,848	128,200	25,640
CONGER.	8,600	260	43,600	1,309
FLOUNDERS:				
GRAY SOLE	10,800	909	13,600	816
LEMON SOLE.	376,600	60,040	11,600	649
YELLOWTAIL.	1,461,900	122,989	57,000	2,850
BLACKBACK	1,911,000	195,190	111,600	5,517
DAB	46,300	2,742	-	-
FLUKE	3,560,000	641,628	3,024,500	446,622
UNCLASSIFIED.	28,300	1,516	2,700	187
FRIGATE MACKEREL.	25,800	1,000	64,900	1,967
GRAYFISH.	53,700	2,109	1,800	54
GROUPER	-	-	2,100	210
HADDOCK	1,197,300	78,768	8,500	722
HAKE:				
RED	589,100	22,614	354,700	10,698
WHITE	59,000	3,355	57,200	1,716
HALIBUT	3,700	700	-	-
HERRING, SEA.	219,500	6,245	1,961,700	25,748
HICKORY SHAD.	-	-	3,100	93
KING MACKEREL	-	-	25,000	1,968
KING WHITING OR "KINGFISH".	33,800	4,950	-	-
LAUNCE.	22,500	2,000	-	-
MACKEREL.	1,886,300	290,572	19,066,500	412,966
MENHADEN.	89,488,700	939,631	143,173,600	1,639,207
MULLET.	-	-	1,200	104
PILOTFISH	-	-	17,400	850
POLLOCK	41,300	1,500	900	63
SCUP OR PORGY	7,285,000	644,989	9,363,900	459,921
SEA BASS.	1,299,200	230,672	3,756,500	454,139
SEA ROBIN	16,900	515	23,900	602
SEA TROUT OR WEAKFISH, GRAY	405,700	81,489	2,567,800	301,891
SHAD.	899,500	141,457	1,406,600	252,180
SHARKS.	24,100	1,206	19,100	708
SILVERSIDES	220,300	13,185	-	-
SKATES.	47,800	2,362	12,800	384
SPOT.	10,000	500	12,300	1,469
STRIPED BASS.	626,000	156,455	21,200	4,820
STURGEON.	11,300	3,975	3,600	1,080
SUCKERS	5,700	555	2,000	342
SUNFISH	1,700	174	-	-
SWELLFISH	822,800	56,704	57,800	3,043
SWORDFISH	21,900	10,900	100	75
TAUTOG.	5,000	400	65,900	1,992
TILEFISH.	914,300	66,162	49,400	2,964

(CONTINUED ON NEXT PAGE)

CATCH BY STATES, 1949 - Continued

SPECIES	NEW YORK		NEW JERSEY	
FISH - CONTINUED	POUNDS	VALUE	POUNDS	VALUE
TUNA AND TUNALIKE FISHES:				
BLUEFIN	33,500	$6,697	30,700	$4,455
BONITO	-	-	16,900	2,532
LITTLE	99,000	8,769	606,100	42,018
TOTAL TUNA	132,500	15,466	653,700	49,005
WHITE BAIT	28,000	4,204	-	-
WHITE PERCH	51,900	6,693	33,000	1,640
WHITING	998,700	56,945	579,200	17,376
WOLFFISH	7,500	200	-	-
YELLOW PERCH	3,700	543	-	-
UNCLASSIFIED:				
FOR FOOD	527,900	34,399	498,000	32,412
OTHER	53,800	538	-	-
TOTAL	120,048,800	4,453,553	191,492,100	4,536,262
SHELLFISH, ETC.				
CRABS, BLUE:				
HARD	-	-	1,994,200	185,304
SOFT AND PEELERS	-	-	12,700	4,064
TOTAL CRABS	-	-	2,006,900	189,368
HORSESHOE CRABS	-	-	630,000	2,563
LOBSTERS, NORTHERN	344,100	160,835	315,200	148,165
SHRIMP	-	-	90,000	45,000
CLAMS:				
HARD, PUBLIC	7,023,700	2,351,200	3,995,300	1,438,141
HARD, PRIVATE	270,000	90,000	49,900	11,583
SOFT, PUBLIC	74,300	27,834	937,500	164,062
SURF	4,903,700	470,433	407,700	39,219
TOTAL CLAMS	12,271,700	2,939,467	5,390,400	1,653,005
CONCHS	101,500	26,580	30,000	4,500
MUSSELS, SEA	126,600	25,330	-	-
OYSTERS, MARKET:				
PUBLIC, SPRING	226,900	151,175	28,700	11,275
PUBLIC, FALL	226,900	151,175	57,100	22,436
PRIVATE, SPRING	3,682,700	2,455,115	2,815,200	1,104,320
PRIVATE, FALL	3,999,200	2,666,095	4,184,700	1,645,593
TOTAL OYSTERS	8,135,700	5,423,560	7,085,700	2,783,624
SCALLOPS:				
BAY	23,100	27,834	-	-
SEA	3,309,200	1,243,707	998,600	349,370
SQUID	1,144,300	63,934	939,900	28,198
TERRAPIN, DIAMOND-BACK	-	-	4,400	220
TURTLES, SNAPPER	-	-	14,300	4,285
TOTAL	25,456,200	9,911,247	17,505,400	5,208,298
GRAND TOTAL	145,505,000	14,364,800	208,997,500	9,744,560

SPECIES	DELAWARE		TOTAL	
FISH	POUNDS	VALUE	POUNDS	VALUE
ALEWIVES	25,700	$771	144,600	$4,359
ANGLERFISH	-	-	57,500	2,783
BLUEFISH	62,700	6,897	1,369,300	167,766
BUTTERFISH	67,500	3,380	3,087,700	322,726
CARP	-	-	121,600	7,818
CATFISH AND BULLHEADS	3,000	180	153,100	10,166
COD	400	40	3,743,800	364,899
CROAKER	88,000	11,400	173,200	16,542
CUNNER	-	-	3,100	113
DOLPHIN	-	-	200	14
DRUM, BLACK	12,500	625	13,300	669
EELS:				
COMMON	57,400	8,780	414,400	74,268
CONGER	-	-	52,200	1,569
FLOUNDERS:				
GRAY SOLE	-	-	24,400	1,725
LEMON SOLE	-	-	388,200	60,689
YELLOWTAIL	-	-	1,518,900	125,839
BLACKBACK	12,000	540	2,034,600	201,247
DAB	-	-	46,300	2,742
FLUKE	8,300	1,245	6,592,800	1,089,495
UNCLASSIFIED	7,800	1,170	38,800	2,873
FRIGATE MACKEREL	-	-	90,700	2,967
GRAYFISH	-	-	55,500	2,163
GROUPER	-	-	2,100	210

(CONTINUED ON NEXT PAGE)

CATCH BY STATES, 1949 - Continued

SPECIES	DELAWARE		TOTAL	
FISH - CONTINUED	POUNDS	VALUE	POUNDS	VALUE
HADDOCK	-	-	1,205,800	$79,490
HAKE:				
RED	-	-	943,800	33,312
WHITE	-	-	116,200	5,071
HALIBUT	-	-	3,700	700
HERRING, SEA.	-	-	2,181,200	31,993
HICKORY SHAD.	-	-	3,100	93
KING MACKEREL	9,400	$752	34,400	2,720
KING WHITING OR "KINGFISH".	-	-	33,800	4,950
LAUNCE.	-	-	22,500	2,000
MACKEREL.	-	-	20,952,800	703,538
MENHADEN.	159,748,100	1,677,355	392,410,400	4,256,193
MULLET.	29,500	2,360	30,700	2,464
PILOTFISH	-	-	17,400	850
POLLOCK	-	-	42,200	1,563
SCUP OR PORGY	155,800	7,790	16,804,700	1,112,700
SEA BASS.	5,100	612	5,060,800	685,423
SEA ROBIN	-	-	40,800	1,117
SEA TROUT OR WEAKFISH, GRAY	1,038,000	29,835	4,012,500	413,215
SHAD.	57,500	8,625	2,363,600	402,262
SHARKS.	-	-	43,200	1,914
SILVERSIDES	-	-	220,300	13,185
SKATES.	-	-	60,600	2,746
SPOT.	26,200	2,882	48,500	4,851
STRIPED BASS.	255,000	67,930	902,200	229,205
STURGEON.	9,600	3,780	24,500	8,835
SUCKERS	-	-	7,700	897
SUNFISH	-	-	1,700	174
SWELLFISH	-	-	880,600	59,747
SWORDFISH	-	-	22,000	10,975
TAUTOG.	-	-	70,900	2,392
TILEFISH.	-	-	963,700	69,126
TUNA AND TUNALIKE FISHES:				
BLUEFIN	-	-	64,200	11,152
BONITO.	-	-	16,900	2,532
LITTLE.	-	-	705,100	50,787
TOTAL TUNA.	-	-	786,200	64,471
WHITE BAIT.	-	-	28,000	4,204
WHITE PERCH	47,200	2,360	132,100	10,693
WHITING	-	-	1,577,900	74,321
WOLFFISH.	-	-	7,500	200
YELLOW PERCH.	1,000	60	4,700	603
UNCLASSIFIED:				
FOR FOOD.	5,400	432	1,031,300	67,243
OTHER	-	-	53,800	538
TOTAL	161,733,200	1,839,801	473,274,100	10,829,616
SHELLFISH, ETC.				
CRABS, BLUE:				
HARD.	2,233,000	207,350	4,227,200	392,654
SOFT AND PEELERS.	57,600	18,912	70,300	22,976
TOTAL CRABS	2,290,600	226,262	4,297,500	415,630
HORSESHOE CRABS	-	-	630,000	2,563
LOBSTERS, NORTHERN.	300	75	659,600	309,075
SHRIMP.	100	40	90,100	45,040
CLAMS:				
HARD, PUBLIC.	59,800	18,268	11,078,800	3,807,609
HARD, PRIVATE	189,000	57,750	508,900	159,333
SOFT, PUBLIC.	-	-	1,011,800	191,896
SURF.	-	-	5,311,400	509,652
TOTAL CLAMS	248,800	76,018	17,910,900	4,668,490
CONCHS.	-	-	131,500	31,080
MUSSELS, SEA.	-	-	126,600	25,330
OYSTERS, MARKET:				
PUBLIC, SPRING.	-	-	255,600	162,450
PUBLIC, FALL.	-	-	284,000	173,611
PRIVATE, SPRING	915,800	361,450	7,413,700	3,920,885
PRIVATE, FALL	1,274,200	503,800	9,458,100	4,815,488
TOTAL OYSTERS	2,190,000	865,250	17,411,400	9,072,434
SCALLOPS:				
BAY	-	-	23,100	27,834
SEA	-	-	4,307,800	1,593,077
SQUID	10,900	327	2,095,100	92,459
TERRAPIN, DIAMOND-BACK.	-	-	4,400	220
TURTLES, SNAPPER.	-	-	14,300	4,285
TOTAL	4,740,700	1,167,972	47,702,300	16,287,517
GRAND TOTAL	166,473,900	3,007,773	520,976,400	27,117,133

SUPPLEMENTARY REVIEW OF THE CATCH OF CERTAIN SHELLFISH, 1949

ITEM		NEW YORK		NEW JERSEY	
		QUANTITY	VALUE	QUANTITY	VALUE
CRABS, BLUE:					
HARD	NUMBER	-	-	5,982,600	$185,304
SOFT AND PEELERS	DO	-	-	50,800	4,064
HORSESHOE CRABS.	POUNDS PER CRAB	-	-	210,000	2,563
CLAMS:					
HARD, PUBLIC	U.S. STANDARD BUSHEL	585,308	$2,351,200	443,922	1,438,141
HARD, PRIVATE.	DO	22,500	90,000	5,544	11,583
SOFT, PUBLIC	DO	4,644	27,834	46,875	164,062
SURF	DO	408,642	470,433	33,975	39,219
CONCHS	DO	6,767	26,580	2,143	4,500
MUSSELS, SEA	DO	12,660	25,330	-	-
OYSTERS, MARKET:					
PUBLIC, SPRING	DO	30,253	151,175	4,100	11,275
PUBLIC, FALL	DO	30,253	151,175	8,157	22,436
PRIVATE, SPRING.	DO	491,027	2,455,115	402,171	1,104,320
PRIVATE, FALL.	DO	533,227	2,666,095	597,814	1,645,593
SCALLOPS:					
BAY.	DO	4,620	27,834	-	-
SEA.	DO	551,533	1,243,707	166,433	349,370

ITEM		DELAWARE		TOTAL	
		QUANTITY	VALUE	QUANTITY	VALUE
CRABS, BLUE:					
HARD	NUMBER	6,699,000	$207,350	12,681,600	$392,654
SOFT AND PEELERS	DO	230,400	18,912	281,200	22,976
HORSESHOE CRABS.	POUNDS PER CRAB	-	-	210,000	2,563
CLAMS:					
HARD, PUBLIC	U.S. STANDARD BUSHEL	6,644	18,268	1,035,874	3,807,609
HARD, PRIVATE.	DO	21,000	57,750	49,044	159,333
SOFT, PUBLIC	DO	-	-	51,519	191,896
SURF	DO	-	-	442,617	509,652
CONCHS	DO	-	-	8,910	31,080
MUSSELS, SEA	DO	-	-	12,660	25,330
OYSTERS, MARKET:					
PUBLIC, SPRING	DO	-	-	34,353	162,450
PUBLIC, FALL	DO	-	-	38,410	173,611
PRIVATE, SPRING.	DO	152,633	361,450	1,045,831	3,920,885
PRIVATE, FALL.	DO	212,367	503,800	1,343,408	4,815,488
SCALLOPS:					
BAY.	DO	-	-	4,620	27,834
SEA.	DO	-	-	717,966	1,593,077

NOTE:--BUSHELS REPRESENT U.S. STANDARD BUSHEL OF 2,150.4 CUBIC INCHES CAPACITY.

AVERAGE WEIGHTS OF CERTAIN SHELLFISH, 1949

ITEM		NEW YORK	NEW JERSEY	DELAWARE
		QUANTITY	QUANTITY	QUANTITY
CRABS, BLUE:				
HARD	NUMBER PER POUND	-	3.00	3.00
SOFT AND PEELERS	DO	-	4.00	4.00
HORSESHOE CRABS.	POUNDS PER CRAB	-	3.00	-
CLAMS:				
HARD, PUBLIC	LBS. MEATS PER U.S. BUSHEL	12.00	9.00	9.00
HARD, PRIVATE.	DO	12.00	9.00	9.00
SOFT, PUBLIC	DO	16.00	20.00	-
SURF	DO	12.00	12.00	-
CONCHS	DO	15.00	14.00	-
MUSSELS, SEA	DO	10.00	-	-
OYSTERS, MARKET:				
PUBLIC, SPRING	DO	7.50	7.00	-
PUBLIC, FALL	DO	7.50	7.00	-
PRIVATE, SPRING.	DO	7.50	7.00	6.00
PRIVATE, FALL.	DO	7.50	7.00	6.00
SCALLOPS:				
BAY.	DO	5.00	-	-
SEA.	DO	6.00	6.00	-

NOTE:--BUSHELS REPRESENT U.S. STANDARD BUSHEL OF 2,150.4 CUBIC INCHES CAPACITY.

MANUFACTURED FISHERY PRODUCTS, VARIOUS YEARS 1/

ITEM	YEAR	UNIT	NEW YORK QUANTITY	NEW YORK VALUE	NEW JERSEY PENNSYLVANIA & DELAWARE QUANTITY	NEW JERSEY PENNSYLVANIA & DELAWARE VALUE
BY MANUFACTURING ESTABLISHMENTS:						
BUFFALOFISH, SMOKED	1940	POUNDS	315,000	$68,700	-	-
BUTTERFISH, SMOKED.	1940	DO	290,700	56,740	80,850	$27,447
CARP, SMOKED.	1940	DO	40,000	12,900	60,500	24,650
CHUB, CISCO AND TULLIBEE, SMOKED. .	1940	DO	1,710,000	477,000	508,000	217,600
COD:						
FRESH AND FROZEN FILLETS.	1949	DO	2,394,320	694,719	401,785	126,036
SALTED FILLETS.	1940	DO	-	-	685,200	205,560
SMOKED FILLETS.	1940	DO	64,600	12,920	-	-
EELS, COMMON , SMOKED.	1940	DO	100,000	28,100	4,100	1,360
FLOUNDERS, FRESH AND FROZEN FILLETS	1949	DO	3,739,113	1,500,198	207,537	87,080
HADDOCK:						
FRESH AND FROZEN FILLETS.	1949	DO	1,701,320	527,989	507,094	167,209
SMOKED:						
FILLETS	1940	DO	113,100	17,274	57,140	13,461
FINNAN HADDIE	1940	DO	115,000	14,950	34,900	5,595
WHOLE	1940	DO	-	-	28,700	5,740
HAKE, FRESH FILLETS	1949	DO	98,000	19,800	(2)	(2)
HERRING, SEA:						
BLOATERS, SMOKED HARD	1940	DO	-	-	490,500	73,055
KIPPERED.	1940	DO	63,000	11,600	2,500	375
SPICED.	1940	DO	-	-	35,000	2,500
LAKE TROUT, SMOKED.	1940	DO	67,000	19,700	72,000	31,200
LINGCOD, SMOKED	1940	DO	800	100	-	-
MACKEREL, SMOKED, WHOLE	1940	DO	49,000	9,250	10,100	2,520
MENHADEN:						
DRY SCRAP AND MEAL.	1949	TONS	(2)	(2)	3/33,206	3/4,918,546
OIL	1949	GALLONS	(2)	(2)	3,201,065	1,464,605
PADDLEFISH, SMOKED.	1940	POUNDS	125,000	53,850	-	-
SABLEFISH, SMOKED	1940	DO	-	-	95,000	42,750
SALMON:						
KIPPERED.	1940	DO	430,000	167,900	355,000	159,250
SMOKED, WHOLE.	1940	DO	5,120,000	1,697,500	1,081,000	426,400
SHAD, SMOKED.	1940	DO	70,000	9,000	45,000	13,250
STURGEON, SMOKED.	1940	DO	417,000	322,250	88,000	67,000
TUNA, SMOKED.	1940	DO	-	-	700	175
WHITEFISH, SMOKED	1940	DO	1,750,000	618,500	320,000	112,300
WHITING, SMOKED	1940	DO	-	-	131,500	19,725
CLAMS:						
CANNED:						
WHOLE AND MINCED (HARD AND SURF)	1949	STANDARD CASES	74,027	684,798	-	-
CHOWDER, JUICE AND BROTH (HARD)	1949	DO	14,775	45,190	(2)	(2)
FRESH-SHUCKED (HARD AND SURF) . .	1940	GALLONS	-	-	16,215	26,205
MUSSEL-SHELL AND MARINE PEARL-SHELL						
BUTTONS.	1949	GROSS	922,562	1,713,355	1,664,378	2,423,224
OYSTERS, FRESH-SHUCKED (EASTERN). .	1940	GALLONS	249,450	523,625	788,737	1,398,319
OYSTER-SHELL PRODUCTS:						
GRIT.	1949	TONS	-	-	5,266	80,894
LIME, UNBURNED.	1949	DO	-	-	1,846	6,565
UNCLASSIFIED PRODUCTS:						
PACKAGED FISH	1949	POUNDS	4/21,000	4/9,800	5/43,088	5/12,386
CANNED.	1949	STANDARD CASES	6/72,948	6/643,151	(7)	(7)
MISCELLANEOUS PRODUCTS.	1949	-	-	8/2,368,135	-	9/5,055,291
TOTAL.			-	12,528,995	-	17,218,273

1/ DATA ON THE PRODUCTION OF THE DIFFERENT PRODUCTS ARE FOR THE YEARS INDICATED.
2/ THIS ITEM HAS BEEN INCLUDED UNDER "UNCLASSIFIED PRODUCTS".
3/ INCLUDES A SMALL QUANTITY OF ACID SCRAP PRODUCED IN DELAWARE.
4/ INCLUDES FRESH FILLETS OF BLUEFISH, POLLOCK, AND STRIPED BASS.
5/ INCLUDES FRESH AND FROZEN FILLETS OF HAKE, MACKEREL, POLLOCK, RED DRUM, AND MISCELLANEOUS SPECIES.
6/ INCLUDES CANNED ANIMAL FOOD; SALMON, STURGEON AND WHITEFISH CAVIAR; HERRING AND SALMON SALAD SPREAD; FISH
   CAKES; CONCHS; CRAB MEAT CREOLE, NEWBURG, AND IN CURRY SAUCE; FROG LEGS NEWBURG; LOBSTER BISQUE, NEWBURG,
   SOUP, AND STEW; OYSTER BISQUE; SCALLOPS IN MUSHROOM SOUP; SHRIMP NEWBURG; SHRIMP CURRIED; TERRAPIN AND
   TURTLE MEAT, SOUP, AND STEW; BOUILLABAISSE; AND SEAFOOD NEWBURG.
7/ THIS ITEM HAS BEEN INCLUDED UNDER "MISCELLANEOUS PRODUCTS".
8/ INCLUDES SHARK, WHALE, AND MISCELLANEOUS LIVER OILS; MENHADEN DRY SCRAP AND MEAL, OIL AND FISH SOLUBLES;
   AND MISCELLANEOUS MEAL.
9/ INCLUDES CANNED CLAM CHOWDER; COD, SHARK, AND MISCELLANEOUS LIVER OILS; HORSESHOE CRAB AND MISCELLANEOUS
   DRY SCRAP; AND MENHADEN FISH SOLUBLES.
NOTE:--SOME OF THE ABOVE PRODUCTS MAY HAVE BEEN MANUFACTURED FROM PRODUCTS IMPORTED FROM ANOTHER STATE OR A
   FOREIGN COUNTRY; THEREFORE THEY CANNOT BE CORRELATED DIRECTLY WITH THE CATCH WITHIN THE STATE.

SUMMARY OF MANUFACTURED FISHERY PRODUCTS, VARIOUS YEARS

SUMMARY OF STATES STATE	SUMMARY OF STATES VALUE	SUMMARY OF PRODUCTS ITEM	YEAR	UNIT	QUANTITY	VALUE
NEW YORK . .	$12,528,995	PACKAGED FISH	1949	POUNDS	9,113,257	$3,145,217
NEW JERSEY .	11,258,101	CANNED FISH AND SHELLFISH .	1949	STANDARD CASES	802,458	5,793,832
PENNSYLVANIA	2,602,217	FISHERY BYPRODUCTS.	1949		-	13,809,923
DELAWARE . .	3,357,955	PACKAGED SHELLFISH.	1940	POUNDS	9,226,018	1,948,149
TOTAL . .	29,747,268	SALTED, DRIED AND PICKLED .	1940	DO	720,200	208,060
		SMOKED AND KIPPERED	1940	DO	14,305,690	4,842,087
		TOTAL.	-	-	-	29,747,268

MIDDLE ATLANTIC FISHERIES

NEW YORK

OPERATING UNITS BY GEAR, 1949

ITEM	PURSE SEINES, MENHADEN	HAUL SEINES, COMMON	GILL NETS		LINES		POUND NETS
			DRIFT	STAKE	HAND	TRAWL OR TROT WITH HOOKS	
	NUMBER	NUMBER	NUMBER	NUMBER	NUMBER	NUMBER	NUMBER
FISHERMEN:							
ON VESSELS	165	16	3	-	6	16	8
ON BOATS AND SHORE:							
REGULAR	-	187	40	15	128	36	55
CASUAL	-	170	387	204	516	53	67
TOTAL	165	373	430	219	650	105	130
VESSELS, MOTOR	8	5	1	-	2	2	3
NET TONNAGE	732	30	7	-	57	39	28
BOATS:							
MOTOR	-	131	198	102	286	48	47
OTHER	-	-	2	-	39	3	-
ACCESSORY BOATS	24	5	-	-	-	8	-
APPARATUS:							
NUMBER	8	136	205	102	649	191	153
LENGTH, YARDS	3,200	80,818	-	-	-	-	-
SQUARE YARDS	-	-	631,500	57,125	-	-	-
HOOKS	-	-	-	-	1,300	71,500	-

ITEM	FYKE NETS, FISH	OTTER TRAWLS, FISH	POTS				HARPOONS
			CONCH	EEL	FISH	LOBSTER	
	NUMBER	NUMBER	NUMBER	NUMBER	NUMBER	NUMBER	NUMBER
FISHERMEN:							
ON VESSELS	-	359	-	-	-	2	15
ON BOATS AND SHORE:							
REGULAR	19	80	8	10	7	65	-
CASUAL	47	51	18	31	2	215	-
TOTAL	66	490	26	41	9	282	15
VESSELS, MOTOR	-	98	-	-	-	1	5
NET TONNAGE	-	2,090	-	-	-	7	84
BOATS:							
MOTOR	33	60	13	10	5	140	-
OTHER	18	-	-	13	-	19	-
ACCESSORY BOATS	-	-	-	-	-	-	5
APPARATUS:							
NUMBER	543	158	1,605	721	680	2,836	5
YARDS AT MOUTH	-	2,453	-	-	-	-	-

ITEM	DREDGES			TONGS		RAKES, OTHER THAN FOR OYSTERS	TOTAL, EXCLUSIVE OF DUPLICATION
	CLAM	OYSTER, COMMON	SCALLOP	OYSTER	OTHER		
	NUMBER	NUMBER	NUMBER	NUMBER	NUMBER	NUMBER	NUMBER
FISHERMEN:							
ON VESSELS	73	156	224	-	22	-	916
ON BOATS AND SHORE:							
REGULAR	30	-	18	477	2,667	212	2,884
CASUAL	14	-	4	397	3,078	160	4,353
TOTAL	117	156	246	874	5,767	372	8,153
VESSELS, MOTOR	33	35	35	-	14	-	211
NET TONNAGE	382	790	1,265	-	95	-	4,776
BOATS:							
MOTOR	20	-	11	676	2,673	115	3,320
OTHER	-	-	-	18	287	68	349
ACCESSORY BOATS	-	-	-	-	-	-	42
APPARATUS:							
NUMBER	53	70	92	874	5,767	372	-
YARDS AT MOUTH	36	96	267	-	-	-	-

(CONTINUED ON NEXT PAGE)

NEW YORK: CATCH BY GEAR, 1949

SPECIES	PURSE SEINES		HAUL SEINES		GILL NETS			
					DRIFT		SET	
	POUNDS	VALUE	POUNDS	VALUE	POUNDS	VALUE	POUNDS	VALUE
ALEWIVES	-	-	98,900	$2,989	100	$2	-	-
BLUEFISH	-	-	2,700	450	21,200	3,350	-	-
BUTTERFISH	-	-	-	-	400	50	-	-
CARP	-	-	53,800	4,144	700	98	200	$16
CATFISH AND BULLHEADS	-	-	1,300	164	400	40	-	-
COD	-	-	300	32	7,000	746	-	-
FLOUNDERS:								
BLACKBACK	-	-	1,100	115	-	-	-	-
FLUKE	-	-	900	175	-	-	-	-
GRAYFISH	-	-	600	25	-	-	-	-
KING WHITING OR "KINGFISH"	-	-	3,500	505	-	-	-	-
LAUNCE	-	-	22,500	2,000	-	-	-	-
MACKEREL	160,200	$20,000	8,600	1,317	28,000	4,629	-	-
MENHADEN	89,488,700	939,631	178,300	16,081	-	-	-	-
SCUP OR PORGY	-	-	-	-	-	-	-	-
SEA TROUT OR WEAKFISH, GRAY	-	-	225,500	45,848	44,400	8,286	-	-
SHAD	-	-	43,900	5,637	452,300	68,158	264,000	39,600
SPOT	-	-	-	-	10,000	500	-	-
STRIPED BASS	-	-	592,100	147,977	1,700	372	600	130
STURGEON	-	-	-	-	3,200	1,005	700	254
SUCKERS	-	-	1,400	110	600	61	-	-
SUNFISH	-	-	300	30	-	-	-	-
SWELLFISH	-	-	9,100	630	-	-	-	-
WHITE BAIT	-	-	28,000	4,204	-	-	-	-
WHITE PERCH	-	-	39,900	5,474	3,700	526	4,100	300
YELLOW PERCH	-	-	-	-	100	18	-	-
UNCLASSIFIED, FOR FOOD	-	-	51,900	3,422	5,300	316	-	-
TOTAL	89,648,900	959,631	1,364,000	241,329	579,100	88,157	269,600	40,300

SPECIES	LINES				POUND NETS		FYKE NETS	
	HAND		TRAWL OR TROT WITH HOOKS					
	POUNDS	VALUE	POUNDS	VALUE	POUNDS	VALUE	POUNDS	VALUE
BLUEFISH	1,500	$231	-	-	213,000	$33,080	-	-
BUTTERFISH	-	-	-	-	306,900	58,814	-	-
CARP	-	-	200	$16	-	-	1,700	$214
CATFISH AND BULLHEADS	-	-	19,600	1,916	-	-	17,200	2,124
COD	6,000	675	793,700	86,662	2,400	250	-	-
CUNNER	-	-	-	-	2,500	100	-	-
EELS, COMMON	-	-	800	150	29,200	4,811	3,300	556
FLOUNDERS:								
BLACKBACK	-	-	-	-	16,500	1,711	192,000	19,097
FLUKE	-	-	-	-	18,500	3,549	-	-
FRIGATE MACKEREL	-	-	-	-	25,800	1,000	-	-
GRAYFISH	-	-	-	-	8,500	331	-	-
HAKE, RED	-	-	-	-	42,100	1,651	-	-
HERRING, SEA	-	-	-	-	117,200	3,365	-	-
KING WHITING OR "KINGFISH"	-	-	-	-	15,700	2,309	-	-
MACKEREL	1,464,500	223,260	-	-	171,800	32,884	-	-
POLLOCK	5,500	400	-	-	-	-	-	-
SCUP OR PORGY	4,800	417	-	-	71,000	6,325	-	-
SEA BASS	44,300	8,759	-	-	3,600	700	-	-
SEA TROUT OR WEAKFISH, GRAY	1,000	225	-	-	112,400	22,533	-	-
SHAD	-	-	-	-	139,200	27,922	-	-
SHARKS	-	-	-	-	600	32	-	-
SILVERSIDES	-	-	-	-	220,300	13,185	-	-
SKATES	-	-	-	-	1,900	97	-	-
STRIPED BASS	17,500	4,400	-	-	4,300	1,100	-	-
SUCKERS	-	-	-	-	-	-	3,700	384
SUNFISH	-	-	-	-	-	-	1,400	144
SWELLFISH	-	-	-	-	755,700	52,004	-	-
TILEFISH	-	-	592,800	41,344	-	-	-	-
TUNA:								
BLUEFIN	9,500	1,900	-	-	24,000	4,797	-	-
LITTLE	-	-	-	-	99,000	8,769	-	-
WHITE PERCH	-	-	100	8	-	-	4,100	385
WHITING	-	-	-	-	111,800	5,636	-	-
YELLOW PERCH	-	-	-	-	-	-	3,600	525
UNCLASSIFIED, FOR FOOD	11,700	682	-	-	91,500	5,933	500	35
SQUID	-	-	-	-	242,600	12,550	-	-
TOTAL	1,556,300	240,949	1,407,200	130,096	2,848,000	305,440	227,500	23,464

(CONTINUED ON NEXT PAGE)

NEW YORK: CATCH BY GEAR, 1949 - Continued

SPECIES	OTTER TRAWLS		POTS		HARPOONS	
	POUNDS	VALUE	POUNDS	VALUE	POUNDS	VALUE
ANGLERFISH.	48,400	$2,510	-	-	-	-
BLUEFISH.	12,800	2,411	-	-	-	-
BUTTERFISH.	1,213,100	162,499	-	-	-	-
COD	1,547,400	140,708	-	-	-	-
CUNNER.	100	4	-	-	-	-
DOLPHIN	100	4	-	-	-	-
EELS:						
COMMON.	-	-	195,500	$34,331	-	-
CONGER.	8,600	260	-	-	-	-
FLOUNDERS:						
GRAY SOLE	10,800	909	-	-	-	-
LEMON SOLE.	376,600	60,040	-	-	-	-
YELLOWTAIL.	1,461,900	122,989	-	-	-	-
BLACKBACK	1,701,400	174,267	-	-	-	-
DAB	46,300	2,742	-	-	-	-
FLUKE	3,540,600	637,904	-	-	-	-
UNCLASSIFIED.	28,300	1,516	-	-	-	-
GRAYFISH.	44,600	1,753	-	-	-	-
HADDOCK	1,197,300	78,768	-	-	-	-
HAKE:						
RED	547,000	20,963	-	-	-	-
WHITE	59,000	3,355	-	-	-	-
HALIBUT	3,700	700	-	-	-	-
HERRING, SEA.	102,300	2,880	-	-	-	-
KING WHITING OR "KINGFISH".	14,600	2,136	-	-	-	-
MACKEREL.	53,200	8,482	-	-	-	-
POLLOCK	35,800	1,100	-	-	-	-
SCUP OR PORGY	7,030,400	622,141	500	25	-	-
SEA BASS. . . . . . : . . .	1,200,300	211,066	51,000	10,147	-	-
SEA ROBIN	16,900	515	-	-	-	-
SEA TROUT OR WEAKFISH, GRAY	23,400	4,597	-	-	-	-
SHAD. . . . . . . :	700	140	-	-	-	-
SHARKS. . . . . . . : . . .	23,500	1,174	-	-	-	-
SKATES.	45,900	2,265	-	-	-	-
STRIPED BASS.	9,800	2,476	-	-	-	-
STURGEON.	7,400	2,716	-	-	-	-
SWELLFISH	58,000	4,070	-	-	-	-
SWORDFISH	-	-	-	-	21,900	$10,900
TAUTOG.	5,000	400	-	-	-	-
TILEFISH.	321,500	24,818	-	-	-	-
WHITING	886,900	51,307	-	-	-	-
WOLFFISH. . . . . . : . . .	7,500	200	-	-	-	-
UNCLASSIFIED:						
FOR FOOD.	367,000	24,011	-	-	-	-
OTHER	53,800	538	-	-	-	-
LOBSTERS, NORTHERN.	68,600	16,385	275,500	144,450	-	-
CONCHS.	-	-	101,500	26,580	-	-
SCALLOPS, SEA	62,600	22,535	-	-	-	-
SQUID	901,700	51,384	-	-	-	-
TOTAL.	23,144,800	2,471,638	624,000	215,533	21,900	10,900

SPECIES	DREDGES		TONGS		RAKES	
	POUNDS	VALUE	POUNDS	VALUE	POUNDS	VALUE
CLAMS:						
HARD, PUBLIC	-	-	7,023,700	$2,351,200	-	-
HARD, PRIVATE.	-	-	270,000	90,000	-	-
SOFT, PUBLIC	-	-	-	-	74,300	$27,834
SURF	4,878,700	$468,037	25,000	2,396	-	-
MUSSELS, SEA	40,800	8,160	85,800	17,170	-	-
OYSTERS, MARKET:						
PUBLIC, SPRING	-	-	226,900	151,175	-	-
PUBLIC, FALL	-	-	226,900	151,175	-	-
PRIVATE, SPRING.	3,682,700	2,455,115	-	-	-	-
PRIVATE, FALL.	3,999,200	2,666,095	-	-	-	-
SCALLOPS:						
BAY	23,100	27,834	-	-	-	-
SEA	3,246,600	1,221,172	-	-	-	-
TOTAL	15,871,100	6,846,413	7,858,300	2,753,116	74,300	27,834

NEW JERSEY

OPERATING UNITS BY GEAR, 1949.

ITEM	PURSE SEINES			HAUL SEINES, COMMON	GILL NETS			LINES
	MACKEREL	MENHADEN	OTHER		DRIFT	RUNAROUND	STAKE	HAND
	NUMBER	NUMBER	NUMBER	NUMBER	NUMBER	NUMBER	NUMBER	NUMBER
FISHERMEN:								
ON VESSELS	54	411	24	-	42	2	14	54
ON BOATS AND SHORE:								
REGULAR	-	-	-	2	84	25	109	76
CASUAL	-	-	-	70	59	7	217	124
TOTAL	54	411	24	72	185	34	340	254
VESSELS, MOTOR	4	18	2	-	20	1	7	24
NET TONNAGE	194	896	54	-	230	5	74	310
BOATS:								
MOTOR	-	-	-	18	67	16	107	99
OTHER	-	-	-	14	15	-	133	-
ACCESSORY BOATS	12	54	6	-	-	-	-	-
APPARATUS:								
NUMBER	4	18	2	23	1,329	17	551	254
LENGTH, YARDS	1,550	5,710	800	6,900	-	-	-	-
SQUARE YARDS	-	-	-	-	647,938	68,000	951,731	-
HOOKS, BAITS, OR SNOODS	-	-	-	-	-	-	-	470

ITEM	LINES – CONTINUED			POUND NETS	WEIRS	STOP NETS	FYKE NETS, FISH	DIP NETS, COMMON
	TRAWL OR TROT WITH HOOKS	TROLL	TROT WITH BAITS OR SNOODS					
	NUMBER	NUMBER	NUMBER	NUMBER	NUMBER	NUMBER	NUMBER	NUMBER
FISHERMEN:								
ON VESSELS	32	-	-	101	-	-	-	-
ON BOATS AND SHORE:								
REGULAR	72	-	35	45	-	-	1	-
CASUAL	14	21	27	30	16	36	13	20
TOTAL	118	21	62	176	16	36	14	20
VESSELS, MOTOR	16	-	-	14	-	-	-	-
NET TONNAGE	174	-	-	95	-	-	-	-
BOATS:								
MOTOR	42	14	62	13	2	7	6	7
OTHER	-	-	-	-	5	6	8	13
APPARATUS:								
NUMBER	339	21	62	77	30	18	239	20
LENGTH, YARDS	-	-	-	-	-	9,000	-	-
HOOKS, BAITS, OR SNOODS	102,600	42	43,000	-	-	-	-	-

ITEM	OTTER TRAWLS, FISH	BEAM TRAWLS, SHRIMP	POTS				DREDGES	
			CRAB	EEL	FISH	LOBSTER	CLAM	CRAB
	NUMBER	NUMBER	NUMBER	NUMBER	NUMBER	NUMBER	NUMBER	NUMBER
FISHERMEN:								
ON VESSELS	312	-	-	-	14	2	81	32
ON BOATS AND SHORE:								
REGULAR	15	15	-	8	47	54	22	6
CASUAL	-	6	2	48	-	-	3	-
TOTAL	327	21	2	56	61	56	106	38
VESSELS, MOTOR	99	-	-	-	7	1	40	16
NET TONNAGE	2,125	-	-	-	53	9	425	125
BOATS:								
MOTOR	7	21	1	35	24	27	13	3
OTHER	-	-	1	16	-	-	-	-
APPARATUS:								
NUMBER	106	21	55	1,114	15,185	6,950	76	38
YARDS AT MOUTH	2,224	35	-	-	-	-	70	-

ITEM	DREDGES CONT'D		TONGS		RAKES, OTHER THAN FOR OYSTERS	HOES	BY HAND, OTHER THAN FOR OYSTERS	TOTAL, EXCLUSIVE OR DUPLICATION
	OYSTER, COMMON	SCALLOP	OYSTER	OTHER				
	NUMBER	NUMBER	NUMBER	NUMBER	NUMBER	NUMBER	NUMBER	NUMBER
FISHERMEN:								
ON VESSELS	797	93	-	-	-	-	-	1,832
ON BOATS AND SHORE:								
REGULAR	-	-	112	145	228	50	30	1,810
CASUAL	-	-	95	330	441	135	171	2,325
TOTAL	797	93	207	475	669	185	201	5,967
VESSELS, MOTOR	136	17	-	-	-	-	-	333
NET TONNAGE	2,917	480	-	-	-	-	-	6,874
BOATS:								
MOTOR	-	-	147	295	430	60	90	2,227
OTHER	-	-	35	80	124	95	73	946
ACCESSORY BOATS	-	-	-	-	-	-	-	72
APPARATUS:								
NUMBER	272	34	207	475	669	185	-	-
YARDS AT MOUTH	272	112	-	-	-	-	-	-

(CONTINUED ON NEXT PAGE)

MIDDLE ATLANTIC FISHERIES

NEW JERSEY: CATCH BY GEAR, 1949

SPECIES	PURSE SEINES		HAUL SEINES		GILL NETS DRIFT		RUNAROUND	
	POUNDS	VALUE	POUNDS	VALUE	POUNDS	VALUE	POUNDS	VALUE
ALEWIVES	-	-	4,100	$123	3,000	$90	-	-
BLUEFISH	11,600	$935	-	-	253,000	32,166	22,400	$2,624
BUTTERFISH	-	-	-	-	9,800	886	-	-
CARP	-	-	11,500	575	-	-	-	-
CATFISH AND BULLHEADS . . .	-	-	10,400	545	-	-	-	-
COD	-	-	-	-	200	20	-	-
CROAKER	-	-	-	-	600	36	3,000	210
FLOUNDERS:								
YELLOWTAIL	-	-	-	-	100	5	-	-
BLACKBACK	-	-	500	25	500	25	-	-
FRIGATE MACKEREL	-	-	-	-	100	6	-	-
HERRING, SEA	-	-	-	-	7,000	80	-	-
MACKEREL	16,830,400	233,477	-	-	454,700	36,483	11,800	944
MENHADEN	129,822,000	1,453,999	-	-	-	-	-	-
MULLET	-	-	800	68	-	-	-	-
POLLOCK	-	-	-	-	100	4	-	-
SCUP OR PORGY	1,350,500	57,118	-	-	200	24	-	-
SEA BASS	-	-	-	-	200	24	-	-
SEA TROUT OR WEAKFISH, GRAY	141,700	10,817	200	24	36,700	4,440	126,000	15,122
SHAD	-	-	10,700	1,679	133,900	25,184	-	-
SHARKS	400	12	-	-	7,200	351	-	-
STRIPED BASS	-	-	2,000	400	4,300	860	-	-
WHITE PERCH	-	-	10,300	414	10,700	601	-	-
CRABS, BLUE, HARD	-	-	12,200	1,137	-	-	-	-
TOTAL	148,156,600	1,756,358	62,700	4,990	922,100	101,261	163,200	18,900

SPECIES	GILL NETS - CONT'D. STAKE		LINES HAND		TRAWL OR TROT WITH HOOKS		TROLL	
	POUNDS	VALUE	POUNDS	VALUE	POUNDS	VALUE	POUNDS	VALUE
ALEWIVES	6,800	$204	-	-	-	-	-	-
ANGLERFISH	-	-	-	-	100	$3	-	-
BLUEFISH	100	11	350,200	$40,981	-	-	6,000	$720
BUTTERFISH	300	21	-	-	-	-	-	-
CATFISH AND BULLHEADS . . .	2,700	162	-	-	-	-	-	-
COD	-	-	12,700	878	1,177,300	113,280	-	-
DOLPHIN	-	-	100	10	-	-	-	-
EELS, CONGER	-	-	-	-	800	24	-	-
FLOUNDERS:								
BLACKBACK	6,000	250	-	-	-	-	-	-
FLUKE	100	15	700	108	-	-	-	-
FRIGATE MACKEREL	-	-	100	5	-	-	-	-
HAKE, RED	-	-	100	3	-	-	-	-
KING MACKEREL	-	-	100	9	-	-	-	-
MACKEREL	21,600	1,782	1,069,800	86,024	-	-	-	-
MULLET	200	20	-	-	-	-	-	-
SCUP OR PORGY	-	-	13,700	717	-	-	-	-
SEA BASS	900	18	4,600	886	-	-	-	-
SEA TROUT OR WEAKFISH, GRAY	700	84	10,700	1,188	-	-	-	-
SHAD	953,800	169,996	300	47	-	-	-	-
SHARKS	-	-	1,100	33	-	-	-	-
SKATES	-	-	-	-	1,800	54	-	-
STRIPED BASS	1,700	408	200	40	-	-	-	-
TAUTOG	-	-	100	3	-	-	-	-
TUNA AND TUNALIKE FISHES:								
BLUEFIN	-	-	9,500	1,300	-	-	-	-
BONITO	-	-	200	30	-	-	100	12
LITTLE	-	-	100	6	-	-	-	-
WHITE PERCH	7,800	415	-	-	-	-	-	-
TOTAL	1,002,700	173,386	1,474,300	132,268	1,180,000	113,361	6,100	732

SPECIES	LINES - CONT'D. TROT WITH BAITS OR SNOODS		POUND NETS		WEIRS		STOP NETS	
	POUNDS	VALUE	POUNDS	VALUE	POUNDS	VALUE	POUNDS	VALUE
BLUEFISH	-	-	342,200	$37,642	-	-	-	-
BUTTERFISH	-	-	986,100	66,866	-	-	-	-
CARP	-	-	-	-	-	-	53,500	$2,755
CATFISH AND BULLHEADS . . .	-	-	-	-	-	-	26,500	1,435
COD	-	-	130,200	14,322	-	-	-	-
CROAKER	-	-	4,600	276	-	-	-	-
CUNNER	-	-	500	9	-	-	-	-
DRUM, BLACK	-	-	800	44	-	-	-	-
EELS:								
COMMON	-	-	-	-	15,000	$3,000	-	-
CONGER	-	-	500	15	-	-	-	-

(CONTINUED ON NEXT PAGE)

NEW JERSEY: CATCH BY GEAR, 1949 - Continued

SPECIES	LINES - CONT'D. TROT WITH BAITS OR SNOODS		POUND NETS		WEIRS		STOP NETS	
	POUNDS	VALUE	POUNDS	VALUE	POUNDS	VALUE	POUNDS	VALUE
FLOUNDERS:								
YELLOWTAIL	-	-	3,000	$150	-	-	-	-
BLACKBACK	-	-	-	-	40,000	$2,400	-	-
FLUKE	-	-	47,600	7,140	-	-	-	-
FRIGATE MACKEREL	-	-	64,200	1,926	-	-	-	-
GRAYFISH	-	-	1,800	54	-	-	-	-
HAKE, RED	-	-	194,500	5,835	-	-	-	-
HERRING, SEA	-	-	1,898,600	25,082	-	-	-	-
HICKORY SHAD	-	-	3,100	93	-	-	-	-
KING MACKEREL	-	-	2,600	182	-	-	-	-
MACKEREL	-	-	605,000	48,400	-	-	-	-
MENHADEN	-	-	13,351,600	185,208	-	-	-	-
MULLET	-	-	200	16	-	-	-	-
PILOTFISH	-	-	17,300	845	-	-	-	-
SCUP OR PORGY	-	-	1,037,600	53,981	-	-	-	-
SEA BASS	-	-	21,700	2,604	-	-	-	-
SEA ROBIN	-	-	12,700	378	-	-	-	-
SEA TROUT OR WEAKFISH, GRAY	-	-	984,400	118,128	-	-	-	-
SHAD	-	-	300,700	54,126	5,000	750	-	-
SHARKS	-	-	1,700	51	-	-	-	-
SKATES	-	-	5,600	168	-	-	-	-
SPOT	-	-	12,200	1,464	-	-	-	-
STRIPED BASS	-	-	200	40	-	-	-	-
STURGEON	-	-	1,300	390	-	-	-	-
SUCKERS	-	-	-	-	-	-	1,800	$332
SWELLFISH	-	-	47,000	2,719	-	-	-	-
TAUTOG	-	-	800	24	-	-	-	-
TUNA AND TUNALIKE FISHES:								
BLUEFIN	-	-	20,300	3,045	-	-	-	-
BONITO	-	-	16,500	2,475	-	-	-	-
LITTLE	-	-	606,000	42,012	-	-	-	-
WHITING	-	-	354,600	10,638	-	-	-	-
UNCLASSIFIED, FOR FOOD	-	-	486,200	31,470	-	-	-	-
CRABS, BLUE, HARD	1,080,800	$100,480	-	-	-	-	-	-
HORSESHOE, CRABS	-	-	-	-	630,000	2,563	-	-
SQUID	-	-	424,700	12,742	-	-	-	-
TERRAPIN, DIAMOND-BACK	-	-	4,400	220	-	-	-	-
TOTAL	1,080,800	100,480	21,993,000	730,780	690,000	8,713	81,800	4,522

SPECIES	FYKE NETS		DIP NETS		OTTER TRAWLS		BEAM TRAWLS	
	POUNDS	VALUE	POUNDS	VALUE	POUNDS	VALUE	POUNDS	VALUE
ALEWIVES	5,900	$177	-	-	-	-	-	-
ANGLERFISH	-	-	-	-	9,000	$270	-	-
BLUEFISH	-	-	-	-	69,900	6,268	-	-
BUTTERFISH	-	-	-	-	503,500	30,210	-	-
CATFISH AND BULLHEADS	72,000	3,600	-	-	-	-	-	-
COD	-	-	-	-	66,200	7,286	-	-
CROAKER	-	-	-	-	77,000	4,620	-	-
EELS, CONGER	-	-	-	-	39,400	1,182	-	-
FLOUNDERS:								
GRAY SOLE	-	-	-	-	13,600	816	-	-
LEMON SOLE	-	-	-	-	11,600	649	-	-
YELLOWTAIL	-	-	-	-	53,900	2,695	-	-
BLACKBACK	22,600	945	-	-	42,000	1,872	-	-
FLUKE	-	-	-	-	2,976,100	439,359	-	-
UNCLASSIFIED	-	-	-	-	2,700	187	-	-
FRIGATE MACKEREL	-	-	-	-	500	30	-	-
GROUPERS	-	-	-	-	2,100	210	-	-
HADDOCK	-	-	-	-	8,500	722	-	-
HAKE:								
RED	-	-	-	-	147,800	4,434	-	-
WHITE	-	-	-	-	57,200	1,716	-	-
HERRING, SEA	-	-	-	-	56,100	586	-	-
KING MACKEREL	-	-	-	-	22,300	1,777	-	-
MACKEREL	-	-	-	-	73,200	5,856	-	-
PILOTFISH	-	-	-	-	100	5	-	-
POLLOCK	-	-	-	-	800	59	-	-
SCUP OR PORGY	-	-	-	-	6,962,100	348,105	-	-
SEA BASS	-	-	-	-	2,239,900	270,545	-	-
SEA ROBIN	-	-	-	-	11,200	224	-	-
SEA TROUT OR WEAKFISH, GRAY	-	-	-	-	1,267,400	152,088	-	-
SHAD	-	-	-	-	2,200	398	-	-
SHARKS	-	-	-	-	8,700	261	-	-
SKATES	-	-	-	-	5,400	162	-	-
SPOT	-	-	-	-	100	5	-	-
STRIPED BASS	-	-	-	-	12,800	3,072	-	-
STURGEON	-	-	-	-	2,300	690	-	-

(CONTINUED ON NEXT PAGE)

NEW JERSEY: CATCH BY GEAR, 1949 - Continued

SPECIES	FYKE NETS		DIP NETS		OTTER TRAWLS		BEAM TRAWLS	
	POUNDS	VALUE	POUNDS	VALUE	POUNDS	VALUE	POUNDS	VALUE
SWELLFISH	-	-	-	-	10,800	$324	-	-
SWORDFISH	-	-	-	-	100	75	-	-
TAUTOG	-	-	-	-	21,000	630	-	-
TILEFISH	-	-	-	-	49,400	2,964	-	-
TUNA AND TUNALIKE FISHES:								
BLUEFIN	-	-	-	-	900	110	-	-
BONITO	-	-	-	-	100	15	-	-
WHITE PERCH	4,100	$205	-	-	100	5	-	-
WHITING	-	-	-	-	224,600	6,738	-	-
UNCLASSIFIED, FOR FOOD	-	-	-	-	11,800	942	-	-
CRABS, BLUE:								
HARD	-	-	14,000	$1,300	-	-	-	-
SOFT AND PEELERS	-	-	12,200	3,904	-	-	-	-
LOBSTERS, NORTHERN	-	-	-	-	37,800	9,450	-	-
SHRIMP	-	-	-	-	-	-	90,000	$45,000
CONCHS	-	-	-	-	30,000	4,500	-	-
SCALLOPS, SEA	-	-	-	-	3,600	1,120	-	-
SQUID	-	-	-	-	515,200	15,456	-	-
TOTAL	104,600	4,927	26,200	5,204	15,651,000	1,328,688	90,000	45,000

SPECIES	POTS		DREDGES		TONGS	
	POUNDS	VALUE	POUNDS	VALUE	POUNDS	VALUE
ALEWIVES	100	$3	-	-	-	-
EELS:						
COMMON	113,200	22,640	-	-	-	-
CONGER	2,900	88	-	-	-	-
HAKE, RED	12,300	426	-	-	-	-
SEA BASS	1,489,200	180,062	-	-	-	-
SUCKERS	200	10	-	-	-	-
TAUTOG	44,000	1,335	-	-	-	-
CRABS, BLUE:						
HARD	12,200	1,137	875,000	$81,250	-	-
SOFT AND PEELERS	500	160	-	-	-	-
LOBSTERS, NORTHERN	277,400	138,715	-	-	-	-
CLAMS:						
HARD, PUBLIC	-	-	569,000	205,497	1,901,900	$682,190
HARD, PRIVATE	-	-	39,500	7,875	-	-
SURF	-	-	407,700	39,219	-	-
OYSTERS, MARKET:						
PUBLIC, SPRING	-	-	-	-	28,700	11,275
PUBLIC, FALL	-	-	-	-	57,100	22,436
PRIVATE, SPRING	-	-	2,778,900	1,090,078	36,300	14,242
PRIVATE, FALL	-	-	4,168,400	1,639,239	16,300	6,354
SCALLOPS, SEA	-	-	995,000	348,250	-	-
TOTAL	1,952,000	344,576	9,833,500	3,411,408	2,040,300	736,497

SPECIES	RAKES		HOES		BY HAND	
	POUNDS	VALUE	POUNDS	VALUE	POUNDS	VALUE
CLAMS:						
HARD, PUBLIC	1,220,700	$440,778	-	-	303,700	$109,676
HARD, PRIVATE	10,400	3,708	-	-	-	-
SOFT, PUBLIC	-	-	937,500	$164,062	-	-
TURTLE, SNAPPER	-	-	-	-	14,300	4,285
TOTAL	1,231,100	444,486	937,500	164,062	318,000	113,961

OYSTER DREDGER

DELAWARE

OPERATING UNITS BY GEAR, 1949

ITEM	PURSE SEINES, MENHADEN	HAUL SEINES, COMMON	GILL NETS DRIFT	GILL NETS RUNAROUND	GILL NETS STAKE
	NUMBER	NUMBER	NUMBER	NUMBER	NUMBER
FISHERMEN:					
ON VESSELS	575	-	-	-	-
ON BOATS AND SHORE:					
REGULAR.	-	53	10	10	4
CASUAL	-	126	36	-	14
TOTAL.	575	179	46	10	18
VESSELS, MOTOR	23	-	-	-	-
NET TONNAGE.	2,019	-	-	-	-
BOATS:					
MOTOR.	-	30	19	3	11
OTHER.	-	26	9	2	-
ACCESSORY BOATS.	69	-	-	-	-
APPARATUS:					
NUMBER	23	58	44	5	18
LENGTH, YARDS.	6,900	17,400	-	-	-
SQUARE YARDS	-	-	87,168	20,000	26,902

ITEM	LINES, TROT WITH BAITS OR SNOODS	FYKE NETS, FISH	DIP NETS, COMMON	OTTER TRAWLS, FISH	POTS CRAB
	NUMBER	NUMBER	NUMBER	NUMBER	NUMBER
FISHERMEN:					
ON VESSELS	-	-	-	20	-
ON BOATS AND SHORE:					
REGULAR.	27	-	-	-	9
CASUAL	58	18	30	-	12
TOTAL.	85	18	30	20	21
VESSELS, MOTOR	-	-	-	8	-
NET TONNAGE.	-	-	-	137	-
BOATS:					
MOTOR.	61	10	16	-	9
OTHER.	24	8	14	-	-
APPARATUS:					
NUMBER	85	81	30	8	900
HOOKS, BAITS, OR SNOODS.	51,000	-	-	-	-
YARDS AT MOUTH	-	-	-	158	-

ITEM	POTS - CONT'D. EEL	DREDGES OYSTER, COMMON	TONGS, OYSTER	RAKES, OTHER THAN FOR OYSTERS	TOTAL, EXCLUSIVE OF DUPLICATION
	NUMBER	NUMBER	NUMBER	NUMBER	NUMBER
FISHERMEN:					
ON VESSELS	-	90	-	-	685
ON BOATS AND SHORE:					
REGULAR.	-	8	45	30	159
CASUAL	5	-	20	17	207
TOTAL.	5	98	65	47	1,051
VESSELS, MOTOR	-	15	-	-	46
NET TONNAGE.	-	303	-	-	2,459
BOATS:					
MOTOR.	2	2	40	20	155
OTHER.	3	-	20	17	69
ACCESSORY BOATS.	-	-	-	-	69
APPARATUS:					
NUMBER	450	34	65	47	-
YARDS AT MOUTH	-	34	-	-	-

DELAWARE: CATCH BY GEAR, 1949

SPECIES	PURSE SEINES POUNDS	PURSE SEINES VALUE	HAUL SEINES POUNDS	HAUL SEINES VALUE	GILL NETS DRIFT POUNDS	GILL NETS DRIFT VALUE
ALEWIVES	-	-	7,000	$210	-	-
BLUEFISH	-	-	5,600	616	-	-
CATFISH AND BULLHEADS. . .	-	-	3,000	180	-	-
CROAKER.	-	-	9,000	1,350	-	-
FLOUNDERS, BLACKBACK . . .	-	-	6,500	320	-	-
KING MACKEREL.	-	-	4,300	344	-	-
MENHADEN	159,748,100	$1,677,355	-	-	-	-

(CONTINUED ON NEXT PAGE)

MIDDLE ATLANTIC FISHERIES

DELAWARE: CATCH BY GEAR, 1949 - Continued

SPECIES	PURSE SEINES		HAUL SEINES		GILL NETS — DRIFT	
	POUNDS	VALUE	POUNDS	VALUE	POUNDS	VALUE
MULLET.	-	-	28,000	$2,240	-	-
SEA TROUT OR WEAKFISH, GRAY .	-	-	91,500	9,235	5,500	$550
SHAD.	-	-	-	-	25,500	3,825
SPOT.	-	-	-	-	8,500	935
STRIPED BASS.	-	-	199,500	53,245	4,500	1,215
STURGEON.	-	-	100	30	9,000	3,600
WHITE PERCH	-	-	18,800	940	100	5
YELLOW PERCH.	-	-	1,000	60	-	-
TOTAL	159,748,100	$1,677,355	374,300	68,770	53,100	10,130

SPECIES	GILL NETS CONT'D. — RUNAROUND		STAKE		LINES, TROT WITH BAITS OR SNOODS	
	POUNDS	VALUE	POUNDS	VALUE	POUNDS	VALUE
ALEWIVES.	1,500	$45	-	-	-	-
BLUEFISH.	55,000	6,050	-	-	-	-
CROAKER	60,000	7,200	-	-	-	-
SEA TROUT OR WEAKFISH, GRAY .	55,000	6,600	11,500	$1,150	-	-
SHAD.	-	-	31,000	4,650	-	-
SPOT.	11,500	1,265	1,000	110	-	-
STRIPED BASS.	4,500	1,215	2,500	675	-	-
WHITE PERCH	-	-	3,500	175	-	-
CRABS, BLUE, HARD	-	-	-	-	1,582,000	$146,900
TOTAL	187,500	22,375	49,500	6,760	1,582,000	146,900

SPECIES	FYKE NETS		DIP NETS		OTTER TRAWLS	
	POUNDS	VALUE	POUNDS	VALUE	POUNDS	VALUE
ALEWIVES.	3,000	$90	-	-	14,200	$426
BLUEFISH.	-	-	-	-	2,100	231
BUTTERFISH.	-	-	-	-	67,600	3,380
COD	-	-	-	-	400	40
CROAKER	1,500	225	-	-	17,500	2,625
DRUM, BLACK	-	-	-	-	12,500	625
EELS, COMMON.	3,400	680	-	-	-	-
FLOUNDERS:						
BLACKBACK	5,500	220	-	-	8,300	1,245
FLUKE	-	-	-	-	7,800	1,170
UNCLASSIFIED.	-	-	-	-	5,100	408
KING MACKEREL . . . . . . 1 .	-	-	-	-	-	-
MULLET.	1,500	120	-	-	155,800	7,790
SCUP OR PORGY	-	-	-	-	5,100	612
SEA BASS.	-	-	-	-	867,000	11,550
SEA TROUT OR WEAKFISH, GRAY .	7,500	750	-	-	1,000	150
SHAD.	-	-	-	-	1,700	187
SPOT.	3,500	385	-	-	25,000	6,750
STRIPED BASS.	19,000	4,830	-	-	500	150
STURGEON.	-	-	-	-	17,800	890
WHITE PERCH	7,000	350	-	-	5,400	432
UNCLASSIFIED, FOR FOOD. . . .	-	-	-	-	-	-
CRABS, BLUE, SOFT AND PEELERS	-	-	57,600	$18,912	-	-
LOBSTERS, NORTHERN.	-	-	-	-	300	75
SHRIMP.	-	-	-	-	100	40
SQUID	-	-	-	-	10,900	327
TOTAL	51,900	7,650	57,600	18,912	1,226,100	39,103

SPECIES	POTS		DREDGES		TONGS		RAKES	
	POUNDS	VALUE	POUNDS	VALUE	POUNDS	VALUE	POUNDS	VALUE
EELS, COMMON.	54,000	$8,100	-	-	-	-	-	-
CRABS, BLUE, HARD	504,000	46,800	147,000	$13,650	-	-	-	-
CLAMS, HARD:								
PUBLIC.	-	-	-	-	-	-	59,800	$18,268
PRIVATE	-	-	189,000	57,750	-	-	-	-
OYSTERS, MARKET:								
PRIVATE, SPRING	-	-	911,000	360,250	4,800	$1,200	-	-
PRIVATE, FALL	-	-	1,267,000	500,500	7,200	3,300	-	-
TOTAL	558,000	54,900	2,514,000	932,150	12,000	4,500	59,800	18,268

HUDSON RIVER SHAD FISHERY

During 1949, the shad fishery in the Hudson River gave employment to 845 fishermen, who marketed 1,727,370 pounds of shad with a value of $286,515 to the fishermen. This represented a decrease of 27 percent in quantity and a decrease of 14 percent in value compared with the previous year. There was a decline of 114 fishermen employed in the Hudson River shad fishery during 1949 compared with 1948. The average price per pound received by fishermen in 1949 was 16.6 cents compared with 14.1 cents in 1948.

Stake gill nets accounted for 69 percent of the production by weight; drift gill nets, 29 percent; and haul seines, the remaining 2 percent.

In 1949, the shad taken averaged 3.49 pounds per fish -- slightly larger than the average of 3.31 pounds in the previous year.

Statistics of the operating units and catch of shad in the Hudson River for 1949 by New York and New Jersey fishermen are also included in the operating unit and catch data for the two states.

SUMMARY OF OPERATING UNITS AND CATCH, 1949

ITEM	NEW YORK			NEW JERSEY			TOTAL		
OPERATING UNITS	NUMBER			NUMBER			NUMBER		
FISHERMEN: ON BOATS AND SHORE:									
REGULAR.	32			77			109		
CASUAL .	590			146			736		
TOTAL	622			223			845		
BOATS:									
MOTOR.	277			49			326		
OTHER.	2			135			137		
APPARATUS:									
HAUL SEINES.	43			-			43		
LENGTH, YARDS. . . .	6,930						6,930		
GILL NETS:									
DRIFT.	191			14			205		
SQUARE YARDS . . .	621,000			32,500			653,500		
STAKE.	102			161			263		
SQUARE YARDS . . .	57,125			368,561			425,686		
	NUMBER	POUNDS	VALUE	NUMBER	POUNDS	VALUE	NUMBER	POUNDS	VALUE
SHAD CAUGHT:									
HAUL SEINES.	13,030	43,300	$5,637	-	-	-	13,030	43,300	$5,637
DRIFT GILL NETS. . . .	135,694	441,500	68,158	16,865	51,156	$8,408	152,559	492,656	76,566
STAKE GILL NETS. . . .	71,835	264,000	39,600	257,678	927,414	164,712	329,513	1,191,414	204,312
TOTAL	220,559	748,800	113,395	274,543	978,570	173,120	495,102	1,727,370	286,515

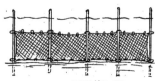

STAKE GILL NET

MIDDLE ATLANTIC FISHERIES
LANDINGS AT NEW YORK CITY

Landings of fishery products at Fulton Market, New York City, during 1949, by fishing craft of all sizes amounted to 14,973,000 pounds. This was an increase of nearly 975,000 pounds or 7 percent compared with the landings of the previous year.

Of the 1949 landings, 81 percent consisted of fish, with shellfish making up the remaining 19 percent. Receipts of shellfish registered a decrease of 417,000 pounds or 13 percent compared with the landings made in 1948, while finfish recorded a gain of 1,392,000 pounds or 13 percent compared with the landings of the previous year.

The more important species landed at the Fulton Market in New York City during 1949 were scup or porgy, 4,731,000 pounds; sea scallops, 2,522,000 pounds; fluke, 1,497,000 pounds; yellowtail, 1,128,000 pounds; haddock, 1,077,000 pounds; and tilefish, 874,000 pounds. The landings of these six species comprised 79 percent of the total.

LANDINGS AT NEW YORK CITY: BY MONTHS, 1949

SPECIES	JANUARY	FEBRUARY	MARCH	APRIL	MAY	JUNE	JULY
FISH	POUNDS	POUNDS	POUNDS	POUNDS	POUNDS	POUNDS	POUNDS
ANGLERFISH	445	-	-	-	-	-	-
BLUEFISH	520	30	118	959	160	-	-
BUTTERFISH	205,195	37,615	99,130	100,140	14,355	9,805	-
COD:							
LARGE	6,140	780	22,750	27,050	9,670	2,980	415
MARKET	42,825	19,980	6,280	6,160	12,730	92,195	65,180
CUNNER	140	-	-	-	-	-	-
EELS, CONGER . . . ! . . .	1,120	1,735	4,091	535	300	-	-
FLOUNDERS:							
BLACKBACK	33,000	3,270	2,550	-	1,155	32,640	54,100
DAB, SEA	-	-	/50	4,425	20,935	8,620	3,700
FLUKE.	224,667	389,913	409,890	260,186	59,540	1,895	-
GRAY SOLE! !	485	585	-	345	2,200	4,885	-
LEMON SOLE . !	7,885	-	11,875	28,145	28,745	29,180	-
YELLOWTAIL (DABS). . . .	32,520	24,015	6,300	19,930	5,250	22,730	98,465
HADDOCK.	41,325	-	83,960	241,564	275,150	282,280	22,045
HAKE, WHITE.	3,525	7,525	7,575	5,045	10,915	3,405	·1,110
HALIBUT.	110	-	70	567	1,315	1,295	314
HERRING, SEA	800	-	-	-	-	-	-
MACKEREL	-	185	-	134,770	38,600	80	-
POLLOCK.	525	14	9,270	19,940	5,320	280	365
RAJAFISH	2,605	240	1,460	-	-	-	-
SCUP OR PORGY.	904,390	894,780	1,086,225	709,200	304,275	88,330	7,500
SEA BASS	146,625	171,215	163,890	118,330	27,100	8,180	-
SEA ROBIN	300	2,190	-	-	400	-	-
SEA TROUT OR WEAKFISH,							
GRAY	175	355	613	545	200	15	-
SHAD	-	90	-	-	-	-	-
SHARKS	-	45	-	268	95 ·	-	-
STURGEON	-	-	-	-	190	-	-
TILEFISH	126,365	133,540	202,723	45,670	101,990	61,500	17,131
WHITING.	-	995	-	27,550	1,300	-	-
WOLFFISH	40	-	-	1,250	3,940	1,930	340
UNCLASSIFIED	6,714	12,135	13,373	26,293	6,000	960	-
TOTAL	1,788,541	1,701,132	2,132,893	1,777,867	931,830	653,185	270,665
SHELLFISH							
LOBSTERS, NORTHERN	190	770	1,040	2,394	8,450	-	-
SCALLOPS, SEA (MEATS). . .	47,160	107,883	81,900	246,897	242,172	72,324	209,223
SQUID.	21,000	34,058	87,521	95,580	11,000	-	-
TOTAL	68,340	142,711	170,461	344,871	261,622	72,324	209,223
GRAND TOTAL	1,856,881	1,843,843	2,303,354	2,122,738	1,193,452	725,509	479,888

FULTON MARKET, NEW YORK CITY

LANDINGS AT NEW YORK CITY: BY MONTHS, 1949 - Continued

SPECIES	AUGUST	SEPTEMBER	OCTOBER	NOVEMBER	DECEMBER	TOTAL
FISH	POUNDS	POUNDS	POUNDS	POUNDS	POUNDS	POUNDS
ANGLERFISH	-	-	-	-	-	445
BLUEFISH	60	-	-	2,375	1,580	5,802
BUTTERFISH	-	10,900	-	7,610	93,330	578,080
COD:						
LARGE	1,265	-	785	4,640	5,160	81,635
MARKET.	57,840	2,085	26,530	50,680	16,415	398,900
CUNNER	-	-	-	-	-	140
DOLPHIN.	75	-	-	-	-	75
EELS, CONGER	-	-	-	180	140	8,101
FLOUNDERS:						
BLACKBACK	41,480	4,260	16,460	31,715	45,790	266,420
DAB, SEA	550	-	750	525	70	40,325
FLUKE	-	5,380	10,385	17,715	117,899	1,497,370
GRAY SOLE	-	-	-	-	50	8,550
LEMON SOLE.	85,650	85,890	63,220	31,900	4,085	376,575
YELLOWTAIL (DABS)	227,255	48,960	257,055	266,559	119,440	1,128,479
HADDOCK.	34,190	23,220	28,955	14,150	29,925	1,076,764
HAKE, WHITE.	2,200	-	635	5,648	1,000	48,683
HALIBUT.	42	-	-	-	35	3,748
HERRING, SEA	-	-	-	-	-	800
MACKEREL	-	-	560	-	-	174,195
POLLOCK.	-	-	-	140	200	35,054
RAJAFISH	-	-	-	750	-	5,055
SCUP OR PORGY.	1,800	35,640	10,620	257,410	430,350	4,730,520
SEA BASS	-	320	1,400	12,455	11,829	661,344
SEA ROBIN.	-	-	100	-	-	2,990
SEA TROUT OR WEAKFISH, GRAY	-	-	-	70	25	1,998
SHAD	-	-	-	-	-	90
SHARKS	-	-	-	-	-	408
STURGEON	-	-	-	-	-	190
SWORDFISH	-	-	-	-	48	48
TILEFISH	13,700	8,600	-	53,375	109,520	874,114
TUNA ,BLUEFIN	-	-	1,970	-	-	1,970
WHITING.	-	-	-	190	250	30,285
WOLFFISH	-	-	-	-	-	7,500
UNCLASSIFIED	215	50,000	-	1,000	6,305	122,995
TOTAL	466,322	275,255	419,425	759,087	993,446	12,169,648
SHELLFISH						
LOBSTERS, NORTHERN	-	-	-	3,260	4,315	20,409
SCALLOPS, SEA (MEATS). . . .	439,308	316,314	434,988	162,576	161,118	2,521,863
SQUID.	-	-	-	6,860	5,240	261,259
TOTAL	439,308	316,314	434,988	172,696	170,673	2,803,531
GRAND TOTAL	905,630	591,569	854,413	931,783	1,164,119	14,973,179

LANDINGS AT NEW YORK CITY, 1938 - 1949

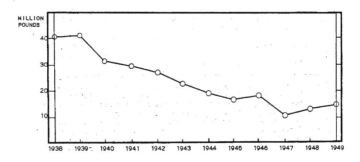

SECTION 4.- CHESAPEAKE FISHERIES

(Area XXIII)[5]

Luring 1949 the fisheries of the Chesapeake States (Maryland and Virginia) totaled 334,656,500 pounds, valued at $25,182,313 to the fishermen. This represents a decrease of 29.7 million pounds or 8 percent in quantity and 2.4 million dollars or 9 percent in value compared with the previous year. The number of fishermen operating in the Chesapeake States during 1949 amounted to 18,346 compared with 19,990 in 1948, while the number of fishing vessels of 5 net tons and over increased from 466 in 1948 to 504 in 1949.

Because of the importance of the Chesapeake oyster industry, this phase of the fisheries will be mentioned first. Although the annual oyster production figure in the Chesapeake Bay and tributaries registered only a slight decrease compared with the previons year, regional shortages appeared in some areas. Local production failed at Annapolis; in the Potomac, particularly on the Virginia side; and in the Rappahannock. Annapolis suffered because of a decrease in bay dredging; the Potomac because increased enforcement discouraged widespread illegal oystering practices; and the Rappahannock because of an unidentified mortality which decimated many beds and brought about a color condition in the surviving oysters making them difficult to market. Leased oyster-planting ground in Virginia climbed steadily to reach 100,000 acres as against Maryland's figure of 8,000 acres. Unionization of oyster shuckers in the Chesapeake area slowly gained ground while a similar movement for oyster tongers failed.

The menhaden fishery suffered a severe drop in the price of oil when the value fell from the 1948 high of $1.40 a gallon to 40¢ and stayed there. This was partly compensated by a rise in the value of scrap which gained approximately $50 a ton above its 1948 price of $105. During 1949, scouting planes were used to help locate the schools of menhaden which appeared in the bay in greater numbers than in previous years. Two versions of a floating trawl were developed independently by menhaden operators, but these operations were suspended at the close of the season in view of rather negative results. Equipment for the salvaging of fish solubles was installed in a number of the plants in the Chesapeake area during 1949. A state agency regulating waterways pollution had discouraged the discharge of stickwater into adjacent creeks, and it was probable that additional plants would install equipment for the processing of the stickwater.

The croaker fishery continued to decline during 1949. Even though the catch was still above 14 million pounds, the sharp decline from its position among the volume leaders has been noteworthy. Because of this scarcity, croakers brought the highest prices on record. Scientific investigations into the croaker ecology began, with progress reports due the following year.

The shad runs on the whole were not plentiful, but the market opened at a high of 52¢ per pound for roe shad at the dockside. A vast majority of the shad were small first spawners, seldom exceeding 3.5 pounds. Three small shad-hatching operations were conducted by Virginia while Maryland hatched shad in cooperation with the Fish and Wildlife Service at Fort Belvoir, Virginia, and released numbers of fry in the bay tributaries.

Alewives or river herring were present in Virginia waters in the greatest numbers since 1943. Canning, salting and pickling plants worked at capacity, however the demand for the canned product was weak. Canned roe moved more satisfactorily. Increased alewife catches caused several pearl-essence processing plants to reopen; these were closed during the periods of alewife scarcity.

The appearance of mackerel off Wachapreague and Willis Wharf, Virginia, early in the year gave employment and profit to many who would otherwise have been made idle by the scarcity of other fish during this period.

---

[5] *This number has been assigned to this area by the North American Council of Fishery Investigations. It should be explained that there may be included under this area, craft whose principal fishing ports are in this area but at times fish elsewhere. Data on the operating units and catch of the fisheries of Maryland have been taken largely from statistics collected by the Maryland Department of Tidewater Fisheries. A portion of the data on the fisheries of Virginia have likewise been obtained from the Virginia Commission of Fisheries. Supplementary surveys, compilations, and analyses, have been made by agents of this Service in order that the figures may be presented in a manner comparable with those of other sections.*

CHESAPEAKE FISHERIES

Crabs, both hard and soft, were plentiful enough to reach the glut stage more than once, and toward the close of the year, winter dredgers were forced to limit their catches. This oversupply was accompanied by a price drop for the raw product.

The growth of filleting and freezing fish remained slow, and in some cases of short supply, as in croakers, ground was lost. The production of frozen oysters and clams increased moderately.

Fisheries investigation continued and the Virginia Fisheries Laboratory pursued 'five main projects. They were: crab conservation, seed-oyster propagation, shad spawning and survival, fishery publicity and education, and water testing for phosphates. The Maryland Laboratory continued its program of investigations with nearly fifty projects, ranging from a survey of the diatom flora of the bay to an inquiry into unlicensed, or non-commercial, fishing activities. Both states added boats and men to their enforcement fleets and restored airplane patrols which had temporarily been discontinued because of disasters.

The last complete survey of the transporting, wholesaling, and manufacturing indus- tries was for 1940. In that year, 1,023 men were employed in the operation of 544 vessels engaged in the transporting trade and 12,331 persons were employed in whole- sale and manufacturing establishments. The latter employees received $3,552,827 in salaries and wages during 1940. Detailed statistics on these branches of the industry for 1940 can be found in 'Fishery Statistics of the United States, 1944' (Statistical Digest No. 16).

Condensed summary data of the catch by states of the Chesapeake Fisheries, appearing on the following pages, have previously been published in Current Fishery Statistics No. 683.

CHESAPEAKE STATES CATCH, 1949

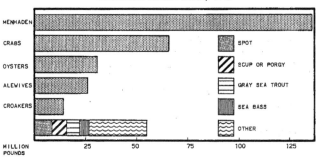

VALUE OF THE CHESAPEAKE STATES CATCH, 1949

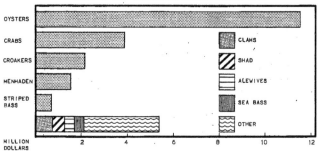

CHESAPEAKE FISHERIES

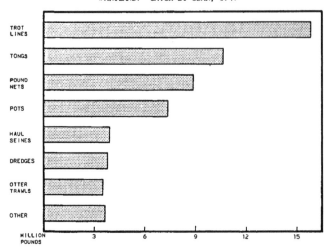

MARYLAND: CATCH BY GEAR, 1949

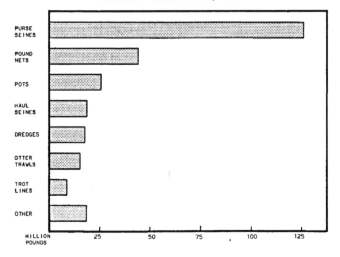

VIRGINIA: CATCH BY GEAR, 1949

SECTIONAL SUMMARIES

SUMMARY OF CATCH, 1949

PRODUCT	MARYLAND		VIRGINIA		TOTAL	
	POUNDS	VALUE	POUNDS	VALUE	POUNDS	VALUE
FISH	20,144,300	$1,766,136	212,637,100	$7,270,685	232,781,400	$9,036,821
SHELLFISH, ETC	38,837,400	6,817,696	63,037,700	9,327,796	101,875,100	16,145,492
TOTAL.	58,981,700	8,583,832	275,674,800	16,598,481	334,656,500	25,182,313

SUMMARY OF OPERATING UNITS, 1949

ITEM	MARYLAND	VIRGINIA	TOTAL
	NUMBER	NUMBER	NUMBER
FISHERMEN:			
ON VESSELS	532	1,618	2,150
ON BOATS AND SHORE:			
REGULAR.	5,082	4,191	9,273
CASUAL	2,996	3,927	6,923
TOTAL.	8,610	9,736	18,346
VESSELS:			
MOTOR.	24	369	393
NET TONNAGE.	340	5,045	5,385
SAIL	111	-	111
NET TONNAGE.	1,227	-	1,227
TOTAL VESSELS.	135	369	504
TOTAL NET TONNAGE.	1,567	5,045	6,612
BOATS:			
MOTOR.	4,281	3,841	8,122
OTHER.	1,749	2,118	3,867
ACCESSORY BOATS.	-	73	73
APPARATUS:			
PURSE SEINES, MENHADEN	-	18	18
LENGTH, YARDS.	-	6,750	6,750
HAUL SEINES, COMMON.	272	318	590
LENGTH, YARDS.	85,200	202,480	287,680
GILL NETS:			
ANCHOR	133	56	189
SQUARE YARDS	232,600	25,000	257,600
DRIFT.	307	617	924
SQUARE YARDS	997,100	1,093,580	2,090,680
STAKE.	428	612	1,040
SQUARE YARDS	944,400	477,800	1,422,200
LINES:			
HAND	264	555	819
HOOKS.	500	690	1,190
TRAWL OR TROT WITH HOOKS . .	12	10	22
HOOKS.	3,500	3,900	7,400
TROT WITH BAITS OR SNOODS. .	1,137	634	1,771
BAITS OR SNOODS.	732,300	389,450	1,121,750
POUND NETS	585	1,293	1,878
STOP NETS.	-	6	6
LENGTH, YARDS.	-	4,400	4,400
FYKE NETS:			
CRAB		1,051	1,051
FISH	375	776	1,151
DIP NETS, COMMON	757	419	1,176
OTTER TRAWLS, FISH	12	52	64
YARDS AT MOUTH	270	1,125	1,395
SLAT TRAPS	-	4	4
POTS:			
CRAB	19,100	51,400	70,500
EEL.	21,268	2,786	24,054
FISH	786	1,628	2,414
TURTLE	461	374	835
SCRAPES.	354	163	517
YARDS AT MOUTH	442	185	627
DREDGES:			
CRAB	30	339	369
YARDS AT MOUTH	26	485	511
OYSTER, COMMON	312	524	836
YARDS AT MOUTH	404	591	995
OTHER.	7	-	7
YARDS AT MOUTH	16	-	16
TONGS:			
OYSTER	4,033	2,420	6,453
OTHER.	49	504	553
RAKES:			
OYSTER	-	66	66
OTHER.	84	598	682

CATCH BY STATES, 1949

SPECIES	MARYLAND		VIRGINIA		TOTAL	
FISH	POUNDS	VALUE	POUNDS	VALUE	POUNDS	VALUE
ALEWIVES	4,905,600	$114,748	22,002,900	$389,524	26,968,500	$504,272
BLUEFISH	86,700	9,336	305,100	41,164	391,800	50,500
BOWFIN	200	10	-	-	200	10
BUTTERFISH	104,000	5,477	993,300	67,590	1,097,300	73,067
CARP	360,800	21,460	921,600	50,577	1,282,400	72,037
CATFISH AND BULLHEADS.	571,500	37,057	1,446,500	99,593	2,018,000	136,650
COD.	33,800	1,352	3,200	157	37,000	1,509
CRAPPIE.	2,400	150	-	-	2,400	150
CROAKER.	2,352,000	272,024	12,380,700	1,836,524	14,732,700	2,108,548
DOLPHIN.	200	12	-	-	200	12
DRUM:						
BLACK.	10,100	563	58,500	2,318	68,600	2,881
RED OR REDFISH	1,100	88	76,400	5,640	77,500	5,728
EELS:						
COMMON	819,200	110,756	498,600	48,327	1,317,800	159,083
CONGER	4,200	126	25,100	753	29,300	879
FLOUNDERS.	782,700	106,693	2,361,300	315,102	3,144,000	421,795
GIZZARD SHAD	13,100	557	190,800	3,836	203,900	4,393
HAKE:						
RED.	1,600	48	-	-	1,600	48
WHITE.	800	32	16,900	676	17,700	708
HALIBUT.	500	75	-	-	500	75
HARVESTFISH OR "STARFISH". . . .	28,900	1,445	572,100	31,895	601,000	33,340
HERRING, SEA	4,200	98	81,400	1,927	85,600	2,025
HICKORY SHAD	37,100	2,270	209,600	8,384	246,700	10,654
HOGCHOKER.	3,300	132	-	-	3,300	132
KING WHITING OR "KINGFISH" . . .	5,000	450	189,100	17,483	194,100	17,933
MACKEREL	363,200	32,688	2,838,000	296,001	3,201,200	328,689
MENHADEN	1,680,300	13,679	136,131,800	1,538,597	137,812,100	1,552,276
MULLET	-	-	59,800	3,729	59,800	3,729
PIGFISH.	-	-	12,200	518	12,200	518
PIKE OR PICKEREL	22,400	4,534	-	-	22,400	4,534
POLLOCK.	-	-	400	16	400	16
POMPANO.	-	-	100	24	100	24
SAND PERCH	11,000	524	19,000	647	30,000	1,171
SCUP OR PORGY.	1,524,400	66,683	5,984,400	411,092	7,508,800	477,775
SEA BASS	435,600	34,848	4,244,800	430,807	4,680,400	465,655
SEA ROBIN.	-	-	15,300	608	15,300	608
SEA TROUT OR WEAKFISH:						
GRAY	614,100	68,647	6,061,700	394,687	6,675,800	463,334
SPOTTED.	-	-	108,900	15,546	108,900	15,546
SHAD	1,083,300	173,894	2,800,300	416,885	3,883,600	590,779
SHARKS	29,200	584	441,500	13,172	470,700	13,756
SKATES	800	8	-	-	800	8
SPANISH MACKEREL	-	-	15,900	2,104	15,900	2,104
SPOT	248,700	23,670	8,410,600	529,498	8,659,300	353,168
STRIPED BASS	2,629,000	540,281	1,913,000	233,728	4,542,000	774,009
STURGEON	4,600	1,162	11,700	2,930	16,300	4,092
SUCKERS.	11,400	544	1,800	92	13,200	636
SUNFISH.	1,200	57	-	-	1,200	57
SWELLFISH.	800	24	422,700	12,499	423,500	12,523
TAUTOG	5,600	397	11,700	700	17,300	1,097
TILEFISH	100	8	3,300	198	3,400	206
TUNA AND TUNALIKE FISHES:						
BONITO	-	-	60,900	6,892	60,900	6,892
LITTLE	700	28	24,200	967	24,900	995
TOTAL TUNA AND TUNALIKE FISHES	700	28	85,100	7,859	85,800	7,887
WHITE PERCH.	1,101,100	91,247	699,500	36,615	1,800,600	127,862
WHITING.	3,400	68	2,900	87	6,300	155
YELLOW PERCH	182,200	27,486	7,600	576	189,800	28,062
YELLOW PIKE.	100	17	-	-	100	17
UNCLASSIFIED, FOR FOOD	2,100	99	-	-	2,100	99
TOTAL.	20,144,300	1,766,136	212,637,100	7,270,685	232,781,400	9,036,821

(CONTINUED ON NEXT PAGE)

EEL POT

CATCH BY STATES, 1949 - Continued

SPECIES	MARYLAND		VIRGINIA		TOTAL	
SHELLFISH, ETC.	POUNDS	VALUE	POUNDS	VALUE	POUNDS	VALUE
CRABS, BLUE:						
HARD	22,132,200	$883,446	40,652,800	$2,249,695	62,785,000	$3,133,141
SOFT AND PEELERS	2,331,100	393,447	2,509,700	423,598	4,840,800	817,045
TOTAL CRABS	24,463,300	1,276,893	43,162,500	2,673,293	67,625,800	3,950,186
LOBSTERS, NORTHERN	1,100	235	900	265	2,000	500
SHRIMP	300	90	-	-	300	90
CLAMS:						
HARD, PUBLIC	137,600	55,040	880,300	373,013	1,017,900	428,053
HARD, PRIVATE.	98,500	39,400	616,400	268,342	714,900	307,742
SOFT, PUBLIC	1,600	225	-	-	1,600	225
TOTAL CLAMS	237,700	94,665	1,496,700	641,355	1,734,400	736,020
CONCHS	80,600	4,163	77,900	6,352	158,500	10,515
OYSTERS, MARKET:						
PUBLIC, SPRING	6,211,700	2,424,260	2,476,200	830,430	8,687,900	3,254,690
PUBLIC, FALL	6,310,500	2,461,440	1,915,300	627,510	8,225,800	3,088,950
PRIVATE, SPRING.	619,700	258,535	7,067,100	2,342,905	7,686,800	2,601,440
PRIVATE, FALL.	575,800	242,570	6,600,400	2,187,410	7,176,200	2,429,980
TOTAL OYSTERS	13,717,700	5,386,805	18,059,000	5,988,255	31,776,700	11,375,060
SCALLOPS, SEA.	300	90	8,200	3,280	8,500	3,370
SQUID.	47,700	3,339	146,000	6,078	193,700	9,417
TERRAPIN, DIAMOND-BACK . . .	236,000	47,200	16,900	3,380	252,900	50,500
TURTLES:						
LOGGERHEAD	-	-	600	18	600	18
SNAPPER.	52,700	4,216	69,000	5,520	121,700	9,736
TOTAL	38,837,400	6,817,696	63,037,700	9,327,796	101,875,100	16,145,492
GRAND TOTAL	58,981,700	8,583,832	275,674,800	16,598,481	334,656,500	25,182,313

SUPPLEMENTARY REVIEW OF THE CATCH OF CERTAIN SHELLFISH, 1949

PRODUCT		MARYLAND		VIRGINIA		TOTAL	
		QUANTITY	VALUE	QUANTITY	VALUE	QUANTITY	VALUE
CRABS, BLUE:							
HARD.	NUMBER	62,698,100	$883,446	119,397,600	$2,249,695	182,095,700	$3,133,141
SOFT AND PEELERS	DO	9,248,000	393,447	10,011,000	423,598	19,259,000	817,045
CLAMS:							
HARD:							
PUBLIC. . . .	U.S.STANDARD BUSHEL	19,657	55,040	125,757	373,013	145,414	428,053
PRIVATE . . .	DO	14,071	39,400	88,057	268,342	102,128	307,742
SOFT, PUBLIC. .	DO	133	225	-	-	133	225
CONCHS	DO	4,030	4,163	3,895	6,352	7,925	10,515
OYSTERS, MARKET:							
PUBLIC, SPRING.	DO	1,270,524	2,424,260	540,420	830,430	1,810,944	3,254,690
PUBLIC, FALL. .	DO	1,401,529	2,461,440	457,315	627,510	1,868,844	3,088,950
PRIVATE, SPRING	DO	125,201	258,535	1,573,455	2,342,905	1,698,656	2,601,440
PRIVATE, FALL .	DO	126,669	242,570	1,573,469	2,187,410	1,700,138	2,429,980
SCALLOPS, SEA . .	DO	50	90	1,367	3,280	1,417	3,370

NOTE:--BUSHELS REPRESENT U.S. STANDARD BUSHEL OF 2,150.4 CUBIC INCHES CAPACITY.

AVERAGE WEIGHTS OF CERTAIN SHELLFISH, 1949

PRODUCT		MARYLAND	VIRGINIA
		QUANTITY	QUANTITY
CRABS, BLUE:			
HARD	NUMBER PER POUND	2.83	2.94
SOFT AND PEELERS . . .	DO	3.97	3.99
CLAMS:			
HARD:			
PUBLIC	LBS. MEATS PER U.S. BUSHEL	7.00	7.00
PRIVATE.	DO	7.00	7.00
SOFT, PUBLIC	DO	12.00	-
CONCHS	DO	20.00	20.00
OYSTERS, MARKET:			
PUBLIC, SPRING	DO	4.89	4.58
PUBLIC, FALL	DO	4.50	4.10
PRIVATE, SPRING. . . .	DO	4.95	4.49
PRIVATE, FALL.	DO	4.55	4.19
SCALLOPS, SEA.	DO	6.00	6.00

NOTE:--BUSHELS REPRESENT U.S. STANDARD BUSHEL OF 2,150.4 CUBIC INCHES CAPACITY.

CHESAPEAKE FISHERIES

MANUFACTURED FISHERY PRODUCTS, VARIOUS YEARS 1/

ITEM	YEAR	UNIT	MARYLAND QUANTITY	MARYLAND VALUE	VIRGINIA QUANTITY	VIRGINIA VALUE
BY MANUFACTURING ESTABLISHMENTS:						
ALEWIVES:						
CANNED.	1949	STANDARD CASES	67,828	$295,021	44,166	$174,377
ROE, CANNED.	1949	DO	10,404	154,791	28,759	506,040
SALTED:						
CORNED.	1940	POUNDS	30,000	800	2,179,300	53,196
PICKLED 2/.	1940	DO	2,406,150	84,371	2,445,350	92,448
TIGHT-PACK CUT.	1940	DO	-	-	280,100	12,698
WITH ROE.	1940	DO	-	-	62,700	3,874
SMOKED.	1940	DO	5,000	500	-	-
BUTTERFISH, SMOKED.	1940	DO	79,000	19,750	-	-
CARP, SMOKED.	1940	DO	2,800	800	-	-
CHUB, CISCO AND TULLIBEE, SMOKED ·	1940	DO	186,000	58,100	-	-
EELS, SMOKED.	1940	DO	23,000	6,625	-	-
FLOUNDERS:						
FRESH FILLETS	1949	DO	-	-	59,100	18,020
FROZEN FILLETS.	1949	DO	-	-	21,100	6,878
HERRING, SEA, SMOKED.	1940	DO	48,000	5,600	-	-
LAKE TROUT, SMOKED.	1940	DO	9,000	3,150	-	-
MACKEREL, CANNED.	1949	STANDARD CASES	18,954	139,470	-	-
MENHADEN:						
MEAL AND DRY SCRAP.	1949	TONS	-	-	15,100	2,417,735
OIL	1949	GALLONS	-	-	739,442	292,971
SABLEFISH, SMOKED	1940	POUNDS	30,000	8,000	-	-
SALMON, SMOKED.	1940	DO	195,000	67,350	-	-
SEA BASS, FRESH & FROZEN FILLETS						
AND SPLIT "BUTTERFLY"	1949	DO	-	-	105,600	28,045
SEA TROUT:						
FRESH FILLETS	1949	DO	-	-	64,000	16,540
FROZEN FILLETS. . . . . "	1949	DO	-	-	39,258	11,852
FRESH SPLIT "BUTTERFLY"	1949	DO	-	-	37,000	10,480
FROZEN SPLIT "BUTTERFLY". . . .	1949	DO	-	-	11,000	3,180
STURGEON, SMOKED.	1940	DO	8,000	6,600	-	-
WHITEFISH, SMOKED	1940	DO	33,500	11,725	-	-
CLAMS, HARD, FRESH-SHUCKED. . . .	1940	GALLONS	-	-	4,450	8,170
CRABS, HARD:						
MEAT, FRESH-COOKED.	1940	POUNDS	2,050,280	726,339	1,891,237	690,600
MEAL AND SCRAP.	1949	TONS	3,450	227,564	2,731	153,290
MUSSELS, SEA, STEAMED AND SHUCKED	1940	POUNDS	-	-	901,978	187,354
OYSTERS, FRESH-SHUCKED.	1940	GALLONS	2,439,138	2,741,365	2,191,988	2,666,544
UNCLASSIFIED PRODUCTS:						
PACKAGED FISH	1949	POUNDS	-	-	3/114,100	3/27,335
CANNED.	1949	STANDARD CASES	4/49,917	4/520,205	(5)	(5)
MISCELLANEOUS PRODUCTS.	1949	-	-	6/1,668,856	-	7/462,751
TOTAL.		-	-	6,746,982	-	7,844,378

1/ DATA ON THE PRODUCTION OF THE DIFFERENT PRODUCTS ARE FOR THE YEARS INDICATED.
2/ THIS ITEM IS USUALLY AN INTERMEDIATE PRODUCT AND ALTHOUGH INCLUDED IN THE TOTAL MAY BE SHOWN IN ITS FINAL
STAGE OF PROCESSING IN THIS OR ANOTHER STATE.
3/ INCLUDES FRESH AND FROZEN CROAKER AND PORGY FILLETS AND FRESH SPLIT "BUTTERFLIED" SEA ROBIN.
4/ INCLUDES CANNED ANCHOVY PASTE, MACKEREL ROE, MENHADEN, SHAD, SHAD ROE, SWELLFISH, TUNA, CLAM CHOWDER, CRAB
MEAT, AND ANIMAL FOOD.
5/ THIS ITEM IS INCLUDED WITH MISCELLANEOUS PRODUCTS.
6/ INCLUDES MARINE PEARL-SHELL BUTTONS , OYSTER-SHELL GRIT AND UNBURNED LIME, AND MISCELLANEOUS MEAL AND OIL.
7/ INCLUDES CANNED FISH CAKES AND ANIMAL FOOD; MENHADEN FISH SOLUBLES; OYSTER-SHELL GRIT, BURNED, AND UNBURNED.
LIME;PEARL ESSENCE; AND MISCELLANEOUS MEAL, SCRAP, AND OIL.
NOTE:--SOME OF THE ABOVE PRODUCTS MAY HAVE BEEN MANUFACTURED FROM PRODUCTS IMPORTED FROM ANOTHER STATE OR A
FOREIGN COUNTRY; THEREFORE THEY CANNOT BE CORRELATED DIRECTLY WITH THE CATCH WITHIN THE STATE.

SUMMARY OF MANUFACTURED FISHERY PRODUCTS, VARIOUS YEARS

SUMMARY OF PRODUCTS ITEM	YEAR	UNIT	QUANTITY	VALUE
PACKAGED FISH.	1949	POUNDS	451,158	$122,330
CANNED FISH AND SHELLFISH. . . .	1949	STANDARD CASES	228,273	1,816,065
FISHERY BYPRODUCTS	1949	-	-	5,197,006
PACKAGED SHELLFISH	1940	POUNDS	45,404,785	7,020,372
SALTED, DRIED AND PICKLED. . . .	1940	POUNDS	7,403,600	247,387
SMOKED AND KIPPERED	1940	POUNDS	619,300	188,200
TOTAL.	-	-	-	14,591,360

MARYLAND

OPERATING UNITS BY GEAR, 1949

ITEM	HAUL SEINES, COMMON	GILL NETS		
		ANCHOR	DRIFT	STAKE
	NUMBER	NUMBER	NUMBER	NUMBER
FISHERMEN:				
ON VESSELS	-	-	39	-
ON BOATS AND SHORE:				
REGULAR.	483	119	351	479
CASUAL	709	136	212	216
TOTAL..	1,192	255	602	695
VESSELS, MOTOR	-	-	13	-
NET TONNAGE.	-	-	168	-
BOATS:				
MOTOR.	272	133	286	394
OTHER.	339	8	8	50
APPARATUS:				
NUMBER	272	133	307	428
LENGTH, YARDS.	85,200	-	-	-
SQUARE YARDS	-	232,600	997,100	944,400

ITEM	LINES			POUND NETS
	HAND	TRAWL OR TROT WITH HOOKS	TROT WITH BAITS OR SNOODS	
	NUMBER	NUMBER	NUMBER	NUMBER
FISHERMEN:				
ON VESSELS	-	3	-	-
ON BOATS AND SHORE:				
REGULAR	69	4	864	364
CASUAL	97	6	273	273
TOTAL	166	13	1,137	637
VESSELS, MOTOR	-	1	-	-
NET TONNAGE.	-	7	-	-
BOATS:				
MOTOR.	71	8	1,043	220
OTHER.	-	1	84	185
APPARATUS:				
NUMBER	264	12	1,137	585
HOOKS, BAITS OR SNOODS	500	3,500	732,300	-

ITEM	FYKE NETS, FISH	DIP NETS, COMMON	OTTER TRAWLS, FISH	POTS
				CRAB
	NUMBER	NUMBER	NUMBER	NUMBER
FISHERMEN:				
ON VESSELS	-	-	62	-
ON BOATS AND SHORE:				
REGULAR.	91	123	-	320
CASUAL	66	634	-	116
TOTAL	157	757	62	436
VESSELS, MOTOR	-	-	12	-
NET TONNAGE.	-	-	217	-
BOATS:				
MOTOR.	106	108	-	391
OTHER.	19	649	-	-
APPARATUS:				
NUMBER	375	757	12	19,100
YARDS AT MOUTH	-	-	270	-

(CONTINUED ON NEXT PAGE)

CHESAPEAKE FISHERIES

MARYLAND: OPERATING UNITS BY GEAR, 1949 – Continued

ITEM	POTS - CONTINUED			SCRAPES
	EEL	FISH	TURTLE	
	NUMBER	NUMBER	NUMBER	NUMBER
FISHERMEN:				
ON BOATS AND SHORE:				
REGULAR	223	61	32	296
CASUAL	261	46	12	48
TOTAL	484	107	44	344
BOATS:				
MOTOR	290	64	27	275
OTHER	91	12	9	-
APPARATUS:				
NUMBER	21,268	786	461	354
YARDS AT MOUTH	-	-	-	442

ITEM	DREDGES			TONGS
	CRAB	OYSTER COMMON	OTHER	OYSTER
	NUMBER	NUMBER	NUMBER	NUMBER
FISHERMEN:				
ON VESSELS	6	458	-	-
ON BOATS AND SHORE:				
REGULAR	18	96	11	3,482
CASUAL	3	-	-	551
TOTAL	27	554	11	4,033
VESSELS:				
MOTOR	2	8	-	-
NET TONNAGE	24	72	-	-
SAIL	-	111	-	-
NET TONNAGE	-	1,227	-	-
TOTAL VESSELS.	2	119	-	-
TOTAL NET TONNAGE.	24	1,299	-	-
BOATS:				
MOTOR	15	48	7	2,802
OTHER	-	-	-	159
APPARATUS:				
NUMBER	30	312	7	4,033
YARDS AT MOUTH	26	404	16	-

ITEM	TONGS, CONT'D OTHER	RAKES, OTHER THAN FOR OYSTERS	BY HAND, OTHER THAN FOR OYSTERS	TOTAL, EXCLUSIVE OF DUPLICATION
	NUMBER	NUMBER	NUMBER	NUMBER
FISHERMEN:				
ON VESSELS	-	-	-	532
ON BOATS AND SHORE:				
REGULAR	30	70	194	5,082
CASUAL	19	14	173	2,996
TOTAL	49	84	367	8,610
VESSELS:				
MOTOR	-	-	-	24
NET TONNAGE	-	-	-	340
SAIL	-	-	-	111
NET TONNAGE	-	-	-	1,227
TOTAL VESSELS.	-	-	-	135
TOTAL NET TONNAGE.	-	-	-	1,567
BOATS:				
MOTOR	16	20	79	4,281
OTHER	24	43	120	1,749
APPARATUS:				
NUMBER	49	84	-	-

CHESAPEAKE FISHERIES

MARYLAND: CATCH BY GEAR, 1949

SPECIES	HAUL SEINES		GILL NETS					
			ANCHOR		DRIFT		STAKE	
	POUNDS	VALUE	POUNDS	VALUE	POUNDS	VALUE	POUNDS	VALUE
ALEWIVES	101,100	$3,176	18,800	$423	38,500	$963	125,700	$2,806
BLUEFISH	7,400	566	-	-	2,900	425	300	19
BOWFIN	200	10	-	-	-	-	-	-
BUTTERFISH	-	-	-	-	1,400	70	-	-
CARP	278,300	16,992	500	26	1,400	81	7,400	336
CATFISH AND BULLHEADS	110,300	6,763	4,000	229	8,500	622	30,700	2,103
CRAPPIE	300	17	-	-	-	-	-	-
CROAKER	1,775,400	194,283	100	14	2,200	311	8,900	1,236
EELS, COMMON	3,300	482	1,100	90	1,900	227	11,200	1,671
FLOUNDERS	1,100	117	200	15	-	-	600	58
GIZZARD SHAD	2,800	96	400	23	-	-	2,900	143
HERRING, SEA	-	-	-	-	4,200	98	-	-
HICKORY SHAD	8,600	434	1,500	103	3,000	196	11,800	845
MACKEREL	-	-	-	-	357,600	32,184	-	-
MENHADEN	119,400	1,198	1,800	18	2,000	20	5,000	50
PIKE OR PICKEREL	3,400	771	1,100	186	-	-	4,500	789
SAND PERCH	7,900	387	100	2	-	-	-	-
SEA TROUT OR WEAKFISH, GRAY	33,900	5,100	300	53	700	105	400	72
SHAD	8,000	1,133	125,600	18,090	134,000	20,175	270,600	45,888
SHARKS	-	-	-	-	18,500	370	-	-
SPOT	183,800	16,831	-	-	300	30	500	52
STRIPED BASS	745,700	150,046	123,600	27,601	374,100	80,111	624,200	132,714
SUCKERS	8,900	405	100	7	-	-	300	14
SUNFISH	300	14	-	-	-	-	800	41
WHITE PERCH	316,400	25,939	29,000	2,673	96,100	8,477	116,900	10,811
YELLOW PERCH	40,200	5,982	4,000	594	3,900	512	18,500	3,079
YELLOW PIKE	100	17	-	-	-	-	-	-
UNCLASSIFIED, FOR FOOD	100	3	-	-	200	10	200	13
TOTAL	3,756,900	430,762	312,200	50,147	1,051,400	144,987	1,241,400	202,740

SPECIES	LINES						POUND NETS	
	HAND		TRAWL OR TROT WITH HOOKS		TROT WITH BAITS OR SNOODS			
	POUNDS	VALUE	POUNDS	VALUE	POUNDS	VALUE	POUNDS	VALUE
ALEWIVES	-	-	-	-	-	-	4,645,300	$106,399
BLUEFISH	17,000	$2,500	-	-	-	-	46,100	3,946
BUTTERFISH	-	-	-	-	-	-	5,800	567
CARP	-	-	-	-	-	-	36,500	1,876
CATFISH AND BULLHEADS	-	-	10,800	$756	-	-	109,500	6,744
COD	-	-	32,600	1,304	-	-	-	-
CRAPPIE	-	-	-	-	-	-	400	25
CROAKER	1,900	259	-	-	-	-	337,900	46,012
DRUM, BLACK	-	-	-	-	-	-	4,600	233
EELS, COMMON	-	-	-	-	-	-	13,300	1,489
FLOUNDERS	2,400	288	-	-	-	-	52,600	4,845
GIZZARD SHAD	-	-	-	-	-	-	6,500	268
HICKORY SHAD	-	-	-	-	-	-	11,300	644
MENHADEN	-	-	-	-	-	-	1,551,900	12,389
PIKE OR PICKEREL	-	-	-	-	-	-	7,800	1,487
SAND PERCH	-	-	-	-	-	-	1,800	86
SEA BASS	2,300	184	-	-	-	-	-	-
SEA TROUT OR WEAKFISH, GRAY	7,100	568	-	-	-	-	307,100	41,521
SHAD	-	-	-	-	-	-	544,600	68,548
SHARKS	1,100	22	-	-	-	-	-	-
SPOT	1,000	80	-	-	-	-	33,100	3,681
STRIPED BASS	22,300	3,540	-	-	-	-	722,200	143,105
STURGEON	-	-	-	-	-	-	200	62
SUCKERS	-	-	-	-	-	-	1,000	52
TAUTOG	400	28	-	-	-	-	100	12
WHITE PERCH	-	-	-	-	-	-	476,300	37,209
YELLOW PERCH	-	-	-	-	-	-	11,200	1,671
UNCLASSIFIED, FOR FOOD	-	-	-	-	-	-	1,600	73
CRABS, BLUE:								
HARD	-	-	-	-	15,465,100	$604,354	-	-
SOFT AND PEELERS	-	-	-	-	158,600	27,382	-	-
TURTLES, SNAPPER	2,000	160	-	-	-	-	-	-
TOTAL	57,500	7,629	43,400	2,060	15,623,700	631,736	8,928,700	502,946

(CONTINUED ON NEXT PAGE)

CHESAPEAKE FISHERIES

MARYLAND: CATCH BY GEAR, 1949 — Continued

SPECIES	FYKE NETS		DIP NETS		OTTER TRAWLS	
	POUNDS	VALUE	POUNDS	VALUE	POUNDS	VALUE
ALEWIVES	36,200	$981	-	-	-	-
BLUEFISH	-	-	-	-	13,000	$1,880
BUTTERFISH	-	-	-	-	96,800	4,840
CARP	36,700	2,149	-	-	-	-
CATFISH AND BULLHEADS	95,900	5,714	-	-	-	-
COD	-	-	-	-	1,200	48
CRAPPIE	1,700	108	-	-	-	-
CROAKER	200	29	-	-	225,400	29,880
DOLPHIN	-	-	-	-	200	12
DRUM:						
BLACK	-	-	-	-	5,500	330
RED OR REDFISH	-	-	-	-	1,100	88
EELS:						
COMMON	4,000	548	-	-	4,200	126
CONGER	-	-	-	-	724,500	101,200
FLOUNDERS	1,300	169	-	-		
GIZZARD SHAD	500	27	-	-	-	-
HAKE:						
RED	-	-	-	-	1,600	48
WHITE	-	-	-	-	800	32
HALIBUT	-	-	-	-	500	75
HARVESTFISH OR "STARFISH"	-	-	-	-	28,900	1,445
HICKORY SHAD	900	48	-	-	-	-
KING WHITING OR "KINGFISH"	-	-	-	-	5,000	450
MACKEREL	-	-	-	-	5,600	504
MENHADEN	200	4	-	-	-	-
PIKE OR PICKEREL	5,600	1,301	-	-	-	-
SAND PERCH	600	31	-	-	600	18
SCUP OR PORGY	-	-	-	-	1,524,400	66,683
SEA BASS	-	-	-	-	433,300	34,664
SEA TROUT OR WEAKFISH, GRAY	1,000	140	-	-	263,600	21,088
SHAD	200	30	-	-	300	30
SHARKS	-	-	-	-	9,600	192
SKATES	-	-	-	-	800	8
SPOT	200	16	-	-	29,800	2,980
STRIPED BASS	10,000	2,119	-	-	6,900	1,044
STURGEON	-	-	-	-	4,400	1,100
SUCKERS	1,100	66	-	-	-	-
SUNFISH	100	2	-	-	-	-
SWELLFISH	-	-	-	-	800	24
TAUTOG	-	-	-	-	5,100	357
TILEFISH	-	-	-	-	100	8
TUNA, LITTLE	-	-	-	-	700	28
WHITE PERCH	65,200	6,102	-	-	1,200	36
WHITING	-	-	-	-	3,400	68
YELLOW PERCH	104,400	15,648	-	-	-	-
CRABS, BLUE:						
HARD	-	-	11,300	$562	-	-
SOFT AND PEELERS	-	-	153,800	28,410	-	-
LOBSTERS, NORTHERN	-	-	-	-	1,100	235
SHRIMP	-	-	-	-	300	90
CONCHS	-	-	-	-	80,600	4,163
SCALLOPS, SEA	-	-	-	-	300	90
SQUID	-	-	-	-	47,700	3,339
TOTAL	366,000	35,232	165,100	28,972	3,529,300	277,203

SPECIES	POTS		SCRAPES		DREDGES	
	POUNDS	VALUE	POUNDS	VALUE	POUNDS	VALUE
CATFISH AND BULLHEADS	201,800	$14,126	-	-	-	-
EELS, COMMON	784,400	106,249	-	-	-	-
HOGCHOKER	-	-	-	-	3,300	$132
CRABS, BLUE:						
HARD	6,276,400	256,560	86,000	$2,870	293,400	19,100
SOFT AND PEELERS	77,900	13,655	1,940,800	324,000	-	-
CLAMS:						
HARD:						
PUBLIC	-	-	-	-	1,400	560
PRIVATE	-	-	-	-	900	360
SOFT, PUBLIC	-	-	-	-	1,600	225

(CONTINUED ON NEXT PAGE)

MARYLAND: CATCH BY GEAR, 1949 – Continued

SPECIES	POTS		SCRAPES		DREDGES	
	POUNDS	VALUE	POUNDS	VALUE	POUNDS	VALUE
OYSTERS, MARKET:						
PUBLIC, SPRING	-	-	-	-	1,436,500	$574,600
PUBLIC, FALL	-	-	-	-	1,479,000	591,640
PRIVATE, SPRING.	-	-	-	-	233,000	100,140
PRIVATE, FALL.	-	-	-	-	237,000	100,930
TERRAPIN, DIAMOND-BACK . . .	-	-	-	-	48,500	9,700
TURTLES, SNAPPER	50,700	$4,056	-	-	-	-
TOTAL	7,391,200	394,646	2,026,800	$326,870	3,734,600	1,397,387

SPECIES	TONGS		RAKES		BY HAND	
	POUNDS	VALUE	POUNDS	VALUE	POUNDS	VALUE
CLAMS, HARD.						
PUBLIC.	26,200	$10,480	61,000	$24,400	49,000	$19,600
PRIVATE	45,000	18,000	52,600	21,040	-	-
OYSTERS, MARKET:						
PUBLIC, SPRING	4,775,200	1,849,660	-	-	-	-
PUBLIC, FALL.	4,831,500	1,869,800	-	-	-	-
PRIVATE, SPRING	386,700	158,395	-	-	-	-
PRIVATE, FALL	338,800	141,640	-	-	-	-
TERRAPIN, DIAMOND-BACK. . .	-	-	-	-	187,500	37,500
TOTAL.	10,403,400	4,047,975	113,600	45,440	236,500	57,100

VIRGINIA

OPERATING UNITS BY GEAR, 1949

ITEM	PURSE SEINES, MENHADEN	HAUL SEINES, COMMON	GILL NETS		
			ANCHOR	DRIFT	STAKE
	NUMBER	NUMBER	NUMBER	NUMBER	NUMBER
FISHERMEN:					
ON VESSELS.	484	95	-	75	-
ON BOATS AND SHORE:					
REGULAR	-	629	68	334	478
CASUAL.	-	683	38	737	351
TOTAL.	484	1,407	106	1,146	829
VESSELS, MOTOR.	18	19	-	25	-
NET TONNAGE	1,090	124	-	230	-
BOATS:					
MOTOR	-	299	50	507	447
OTHER	-	336	6	82	59
ACCESSORY BOATS	54	19	-	-	-
APPARATUS:					
NUMBER.	18	318	56	617	512
LENGTH, YARDS	6,750	202,480	-	-	-
SQUARE YARDS.	-	-	25,000	1,093,580	477,800

ITEM	LINES			POUND NETS	STOP NETS
	HAND	TRAWL OR TROT WITH HOOKS	TROT WITH BAITS OR SNOODS		
	NUMBER	NUMBER	NUMBER	NUMBER	NUMBER
FISHERMEN:					
ON VESSELS.	-	-	4	-	-
ON BOATS AND SHORE:					
REGULAR	65	5	500	910	12
CASUAL.	98	5	149	685	-
TOTAL	163	10	653	1,595	12

(CONTINUED ON NEXT PAGE)

VIRGINIA: OPERATING UNITS 1949 – Continued

ITEM	LINES			POUNDS NETS	STOP NETS
	HAND	TRAWL OR TROT WITH HOOKS	TROT WITH BAITS OR SNOODS		
	NUMBER	NUMBER	NUMBER	NUMBER	NUMBER
VESSELS, MOTOR	-	-	2	-	-
NET TONNAGE	-	-	10	-	-
BOATS:					
MOTOR	82	9	607	465	5
OTHER	11	1	25	407	1
APPARATUS:					
NUMBER	555	10	634	1,293	6
LENGTH, YARDS	-		-	-	4,400
HOOKS, BAITS OR SNOODS	690	3,900	389,450	-	-

ITEM	FYKE NETS		DIP NETS, COMMON	OTTER TRAWLS, FISH	SLAT TRAPS
	CRAB	FISH			
	NUMBER	NUMBER	NUMBER	NUMBER	NUMBER
FISHERMEN:					
ON VESSELS	-	-	-	261	-
ON BOATS AND SHORE:					
REGULAR	169	152	252	6	-
CASUAL	55	81	167	-	4
TOTAL	224	233	419	267	4
VESSELS, MOTOR	-	-	-	50	-
NET TONNAGE	-	-	-	1,220	-
BOATS:					
MOTOR	171	157	156	2	-
OTHER	21	12	263	-	4
APPARATUS:					
NUMBER	1,051	776	419	52	4
YARDS AT MOUTH	-	-	-	1,125	-

ITEM	POTS				SCRAPES
	CRAB	EEL	FISH	TURTLE	
	NUMBER	NUMBER	NUMBER	NUMBER	NUMBER
FISHERMEN:					
ON BOATS AND SHORE:					
REGULAR	839	135	88	20	140
CASUAL	352	57	37	14	43
TOTAL	1,191	192	125	34	183
BOATS:					
MOTOR	1,028	151	73	21	112
OTHER	-	6	5	14	-
APPARATUS:					
NUMBER	51,400	2,786	1,628	374	163
YARDS AT MOUTH	-	-	-	-	185

ITEM	DREDGES		TONGS		RAKES
	CRABS	OYSTER, COMMON	OYSTER	OTHER	OYSTER
	NUMBER	NUMBER	NUMBER	NUMBER	NUMBER
FISHERMEN:					
ON VESSELS	277	318	186	4	-
ON BOATS AND SHORE:					
REGULAR	134	507	1,572	304	26
CASUAL	-	13	662	199	40
TOTAL	411	838	2,420	507	66
VESSELS, MOTOR	95	115	78	2	-
NET TONNAGE	1,008	1,159	451	12	-
BOATS:					
MOTOR	82	246	1,580	269	16
OTHER	-	37	190	137	45
APPARATUS:					
NUMBER	339	524	2,420	504	66
YARDS AT MOUTH	485	591	-	-	-

(CONTINUED ON NEXT PAGE)

VIRGINIA: OPERATING UNITS 1949 – Continued

ITEM	RAKES – CONT'D.	BY HAND		TOTAL EXCULUSIVE OF DUPLICATION
	OTHER	OYSTER	OTHER	
FISHERMEN:	NUMBER	NUMBER	NUMBER	NUMBER
ON VESSELS	-	-	-	1,618
ON BOATS AND SHORE:				
REGULAR	339	389	303	4,191
CASUAL.	259	83	114	3,927
TOTAL.	598	472	417	9,736
VESSELS, MOTOR	-	-	-	369
NET TONNAGE.	-	-	-	5,045
BOATS:				
MOTOR.	124	90	63	3,841
OTHER.	358	307	258	2,118
ACCESSORY BOATS	-	-	-	73
APPARATUS:				
NUMBER	598	-	-	-

VIRGINIA: CATCH BY GEAR, 1949

GILL NETS

	VALUE
ALEWIVES	$660
BLUEFISH	224
BUTTERFISH	188
CARP	175
CATFISH AND BULLHEADS. . . .	196
CROAKER.	-
DRUM:	
BLACK.	
RED OR REDFISH	
EELS, COMMON	-
FLOUNDERS.	-
GIZZARD SHAD	20
HARVESTFISH OR STARFISH. .	-
HERRING, SEA	192
HICKORY SHAD	156
KING WHITING OR "KINGFISH"	-
MACKEREL	238,430
MENHADEN	53
MULLET	385
PIGFISH.	-
POMPANO.	
SAND PERCH	
SEA BASS	
SEA TROUT OR WEAKFISH:	
GRAY	-
SPOTTED.	-
SHAD	108,852
SHARKS	9,135
SPANISH MACKEREL	-
SPOT	-
STRIPED BASS	1,234
STURGEON	-
SUCKERS.	-
SWELLFISH	
TAUTOG . . . . :	
TUNA AND TUNALIKE FISHES:	
BONITO	-
LITTLE	-
WHITE PERCH.	349
CRABS, BLUE, HARD.	-
TERRAPIN, DIAMOND-BACK . .	-
TURTLES, SNAPPER	-
TOTAL.	

	VALUE
ALEWIVES	-
BLUEFISH	-
CARP	
CATFISH AND BULLHEADS. .	
CROAKER.	
DRUM:	

CHESAPEAKE FISHERIES

VIRGINIA: CATCH BY GEAR, 1949 - Continued

SPECIES	GILL NETS-CONT'D. STAKE		LINES HAND		LINES TRAWL OR TROT WITH HOOKS		LINES TROT WITH BAITS OR SNOODS	
	POUNDS	VALUE	POUNDS	VALUE	POUNDS	VALUE	POUNDS	VALUE
FLOUNDERS	-	-	27,100	$4,060	-	-	-	-
GIZZARD SHAD	1,200	$24	-	-	-	-	-	-
HICKORY SHAD	11,700	468	-	-	-	-	-	-
KING WHITING OR "KINGFISH"	-	-	300	26	-	-	-	-
MENHADEN	41,000	303	-	-	-	-	-	-
MULLET	5,300	318	-	-	-	-	-	-
SCUP OR PORGY	-	-	16,800	1,749	-	-	-	-
SEA BASS	-	-	33,700	3,370	-	-	-	-
SEA TROUT OR WEAKFISH:								
GRAY	900	54	7,900	649	-	-	-	-
SPOTTED	-	-	600	96	-	-	-	-
SHAD	595,300	87,303	-	-	-	-	-	-
SHARKS	-	-	3,500	105	-	-	-	-
SPOT	140,700	6,134	8,900	890	-	-	-	-
STRIPED BASS	175,000	20,404	-	-	-	-	-	-
TUNA AND TUNALIKE FISHES,								
BONITO	-	-	100	11	-	-	-	-
WHITE PERCH	48,300	2,745	-	-	-	-	-	-
CRABS, BLUE:								
HARD	-	-	-	-	98,300	$33,100	8,896,800	$607,061
SOFT AND PEELERS	800	128	-	-	1,600	270	78,700	13,275
TURTLES, SNAPPER	-	-	21,000	1,680	-	-	-	-
TOTAL	1,101,300	120,407	191,400	19,832	117,100	34,573	8,975,500	620,336

SPECIES	POUND NETS		STOP NETS		FYKE NETS		DIP NETS	
	POUNDS	VALUE	POUNDS	VALUE	POUNDS	VALUE	POUNDS	VALUE
ALEWIVES	20,591,300	$361,330	-	-	601,800	$12,036	-	-
BLUEFISH	200,400	27,493	-	-	-	-	-	-
BUTTERFISH	765,200	43,738	-	-	-	-	-	-
CARP	34,500	1,098	71,000	$3,580	72,100	2,840	-	-
CATFISH AND BULLHEADS	224,700	15,728	-	-	380,000	26,425	-	-
CROAKER	4,103,800	514,071	-	-	8,300	1,118	-	-
DRUM:								
BLACK	50,800	1,998	-	-	-	-	-	-
RED OR REDFISH	14,400	1,009	-	-	-	-	-	-
EELS, COMMON	86,200	10,498	-	-	22,600	2,173	-	-
FLOUNDERS	447,400	60,361	-	-	15,400	2,045	-	-
GIZZARD SHAD	21,700	434	-	-	56,700	1,134	-	-
HARVESTFISH OR "STARFISH"	525,300	29,393	-	-	-	-	-	-
HERRING, SEA	19,800	396	-	-	-	-	-	-
HICKORY SHAD	173,900	6,956	-	-	3,800	152	-	-
KING WHITING OR "KINGFISH"	40,900	3,815	-	-	-	-	-	-
MACKEREL	104,300	17,203	-	-	-	-	-	-
MENHADEN	7,330,800	54,005	-	-	10,300	81	-	-
MULLET	11,900	750	-	-	5,500	323	-	-
PIGFISH	7,600	312	-	-	-	-	-	-
SAND PERCH	3,300	132	-	-	-	-	-	-
SCUP OR PORGY	12,200	982	-	-	-	-	-	-
SEA BASS	14,400	1,483	-	-	-	-	-	-
SEA TROUT OR WEAKFISH:								
GRAY	4,501,000	282,497	-	-	17,800	1,188	-	-
SPOTTED	48,400	7,001	-	-	-	-	-	-
SHAD	1,220,600	183,229	-	-	131,000	18,991	-	-
SHARKS	32,300	967	-	-	-	-	-	-
SPANISH MACKEREL	15,300	2,014	-	-	-	-	-	-
SPOT	3,246,900	278,552	-	-	5,500	362	-	-
STRIPED BASS	481,200	59,762	-	-	167,700	24,002	-	-
STURGEON	3,100	775	-	-	100	30	-	-
SUCKERS	-	-	-	-	1,000	56	-	-
SWELLFISH	307,400	9,217	-	-	-	-	-	-
TAUTOG	8,500	537	-	-	-	-	-	-
TUNA AND TUNALIKE FISHES:								
BONITO	56,600	6,401	-	-	-	-	-	-
LITTLE	19,300	772	-	-	-	-	-	-
WHITE PERCH	139,800	7,482	-	-	246,200	13,108	-	-
YELLOW PERCH	1,000	70	-	-	6,600	506	-	-
CRAB, BLUE:								
HARD	15,700	527	-	-	30,700	1,029	3,800	$133
SOFT AND PEELERS	-	-	-	-	908,600	154,043	115,500	19,540
SQUID	6,100	300	-	-	-	-	-	-
TERRAPIN, DIAMOND-BACK	-	-	-	-	1,400	280	-	-
TURTLES, LOGGERHEAD	600	18	-	-	-	-	-	-
TOTAL	44,888,600	2,093,306	71,000	3,580	2,693,100	261,922	119,300	19,673

(CONTINUED ON NEXT PAGE)

VIRGINIA: CATCH BY GEAR, 1949 - Continued

SPECIES	OTTER TRAWLS		SLAT TRAPS		POTS		SCRAPES	
	POUNDS	VALUE	POUNDS	VALUE	POUNDS	VALUE	POUNDS	VALUE
ALEWIVES	-	-	13,600	$272	-	-	-	-
BLUEFISH	20,500	$2,165	-	-	-	-	-	-
BUTTERFISH	181,000	12,876	-	-	-	-	-	-
CATFISH AND BULLHEADS. .	-	-	-	-	632,600	$42,910	-	-
COD.	3,200	157	-	-	-	-	-	-
CROAKER.	1,623,800	233,054	-	-	-	-	-	-
DRUM:								
BLACK	2,400	153	-	-	-	-	-	-
RED OR REDFISH	400	28	-	-	-	-	-	-
EELS:								
COMMON	-	-	-	-	373,200	34,154	-	-
CONGER	25,100	753	-	-	-	-	-	-
FLOUNDERS.	1,641,800	215,950	-	-	-	-	-	-
HAKE, WHITE. . . . . , .	16,900	676	-	-	-	-	-	-
HARVESTFISH OR "STARFISH".	35,500	1,830	-	-	-	-	-	-
HERRING, SEA	52,000	1,339	-	-	-	-	-	-
KING WHITING OR "KINGFISH"	123,100	11,370	-	-	-	-	-	-
MACKEREL	393,400	40,280	-	-	-	-	-	-
PIGFISH.	3,600	158	-	-	-	-	-	-
POLLOCK.	400	16	-	-	-	-	-	-
SAND PERCH	15,300	503	-	-	-	-	-	-
SCUP OR PORGY.	5,955,400	408,361	-	-	-	-	-	-
SEA BASS	4,195,600	425,822	-	-	-	-	-	-
SEA ROBIN	15,300	608	-	-	-	-	-	-
SEA TROUT OR WEAKFISH,								
GRAY	933,000	72,907	-	-	-	-	-	-
SHAD	300	38	-	-	-	-	-	-
SHARKS	79,100	2,302	-	-	-	-	-	-
SPOT	13,000	1,144	-	-	-	-	-	-
STRIPED BASS	7,300	932	-	-	-	-	-	-
STURGEON	7,800	1,950	-	-	-	-	-	-
SWELLFISH.	51,100	1,356	-	-	-	-	-	-
TAUTOG	2,000	90	-	-	-	-	-	-
TILEFISH	3,300	198	-	-	-	-	-	-
TUNA,								
LITTLE	100	3	-	-	-	-	-	-
WHITE PERCH.	6,800	204	-	-	-	-	-	-
WHITING.	2,900	87	-	-	-	-	-	-
CRABS, BLUE:								
HARD.	-	-	-	-	25,177,600	1,119,847	13,000	$425
SOFT AND PEELERS. . . .	-	-	-	-	256,600	42,992	886,500	149,770
LOBSTERS, NORTHERN . . .	900	265	-	-	-	-	-	-
CONCHS	28,500	2,280	-	-	-	-	-	-
SCALLOPS, SEA.	8,200	3,280	-	-	-	-	-	-
SQUID.	139,900	5,778	-	-	-	-	-	-
TERRAPIN, DIAMOND-BACK .	-	-	-	-	-	-	5,900	1,180
TURTLES, SNAPPER	-	-	-	-	46,900	3,752	-	-
TOTAL	15,588,900	1,448,913	13,600	272	26,486,900	1,243,655	905,400	151,375

SPECIES	DREDGES		TONGS		RAKES		BY HAND	
	POUNDS	VALUE	POUNDS	VALUE	POUNDS	VALUE	POUNDS	VALUE
CRABS, BLUE:								
HARD	6,407,400	$487,424	-	-	-	-	-	-
SOFT AND PEELERS . . .	-	-	-	-	-	-	261,400	$43,580
CLAMS, HARD:								
PUBLIC	70,400	28,080	333,800	$138,162	368,700	$161,871	107,400	44,880
PRIVATE.	56,900	22,848	162,600	70,144	389,900	172,350	7,000	3,000
CONCHS	48,200	3,976	-	-	-	-	1,200	96
OYSTERS, MARKET:								
PUBLIC, SPRING	129,300	43,600	2,344,700	786,240	-	-	2,200	590
PUBLIC, FALL	145,500	48,730	1,765,600	577,680	-	-	4,200	1,100
PRIVATE, SPRING. . . .	5,597,300	1,866,440	1,021,200	338,425	61,800	20,540	386,800	117,500
PRIVATE, FALL.	5,481,600	1,820,980	876,700	289,620	37,800	12,510	204,300	64,300
TERRAPIN, DIAMOND-BACK .	-	-	-	-	-	-	8,000	1,600
TOTAL	17,936,600	4,322,078	6,504,600	2,200,291	858,200	367,271	982,500	276,646

POTOMAC RIVER SHAD AND ALEWIFE FISHERY

The catch of shad in the Potomac River during 1949 amounted to 327,255 fish weighing 909,600 pounds, and valued at $136,360 to the fishermen. The catch of alewives in the Potomac for the same year was 22,471,100 fish weighing 11,390,400 pounds, valued at $185,097.

Compared with 1948, the catch of shad showed an increase of 26 percent in poundage and 20 percent in value. Alewives registered an increase of 19 percent in quantity but a decrease of 6 percent in value compared with the previous year.

A total of 754 fishermen were employed in this fishery, 236 more than during the previous year.

Statistics on the yield and operating units of shad and alewives in the Potomac River are also included in the catch and operating unit data for Maryland and Virginia.

SUMMARY OF CATCH AND OPERATING UNITS, 1949

ITEM	MARYLAND			VIRGINIA			TOTAL		
OPERATING UNITS	NUMBER			NUMBER			NUMBER		
FISHERMEN, ON BOATS ON SHORE:									
REGULAR.	90			274			364		
CASUAL	122			268			390		
TOTAL . . .	212			542			754		
BOATS:									
MOTOR.	81			214			295		
OTHER.	35			123			158		
APPARATUS:									
HAUL SEINES.	12			28			40		
LENGTH, YARDS. . .	4,800			14,100			18,900		
GILL NETS:									
DRIFT.	16			37			53		
SQUARE YARDS . .	35,100			90,400			155,500		
STAKE	62			123			185		
SQUARE YARDS . .	107,700			92,000			199,700		
POUND NETS	62			290			352		
FYKE NETS	-			62			62		
CATCH.	NUMBER	POUNDS	VALUE	NUMBER	POUNDS	VALUE	NUMBER	POUNDS	VALUE
SHAD CATCH:									
HAUL SEINES.	570	1,400	$177	11,800	32,400	$4,773	12,370	33,800	$4,950
DRIFT GILL NETS. . .	5,530	14,600	2,300	84,600	228,200	35,000	90,130	242,800	37,300
STAKE GILL NETS. . .	36,700	95,800	12,660	52,200	150,100	22,711	88,900	245,900	35,371
POUND NETS	10,000	27,000	4,411	124,540	356,400	53,780	134,540	383,400	58,191
FYKE NETS.	-	-	-	1,315	3,700	548	1,315	3,700	548
TOTAL	52,800	138,800	19,548	274,455	770,800	116,812	327,255	909,600	136,360
ALEWIVES CAUGHT:									
HAUL SEINES.	11,300	5,200	140	155,300	75,800	1,474	166,600	81,000	1,614
DRIFT GILL NETS. . .	7,900	3,700	101	6,200	3,000	60	14,100	6,700	161
STAKE GILL NETS. . .	19,700	9,200	256	-	-	-	19,700	9,200	256
POUND NETS	537,000	255,500	5,270	21,681,700	11,012,800	177,292	22,218,700	11,268,300	182,562
FYKE NETS.	-	-	-	52,000	25,200	504	52,000	25,200	504
TOTAL	575,900	273,600	5,767	21,895,200	11,116,800	179,330	22,471,100	11,390,400	185,097

SECTION 5.- SOUTH ATLANTIC FISHERIES

(Area XXIV)[6]

During 1949, due to budgetary limitations, no general canvass was conducted in the South Atlantic States (North Carolina, South Carolina, Georgia, and the East Coast of Florida). The catch and operating unit figures used in the following tables for this area are for 1945, with the exception of the East Coast of Florida. The catch figures for the East Coast of Florida are for 1945 while the operating units are for 1940.

The total quantity of menhaden used for reduction purposes in the South Atlantic area during 1949 was collected in connection with the annual canned fish and byproducts survey. Since nearly the entire catch of menhaden is used in the manufacture of oil and meal, the poundage used for reduction may be considered the total landings of these fish. During 1949, landings of menhaden in this region totaled 262,446,370 pounds, valued at $2,349,704. This represented an increase of 5 percent in quantity but a decrease of 6 percent in value compared with the previous year.

The total production of canned fishery products and byproducts in the South Atlantic States during 1949 was valued at $7,525,117. North Carolina ranked first with products totaling $4,294,042 to the processor; South Carolina was second with $1,547,864; followed by the East Coast of Florida with $1,281,811; and Georgia, with $401,400. A total of 41 plants was engaged in canning and processing fishery products and byproducts in the South Atlantic area during 1949.

The last complete survey of the fishery transporting, wholesaling and manufacturing industries was made in 1940. In that year, 264 men were employed in the operation of 124 vessels and boats engaged in the transporting trade and 6,897 persons were employed in wholesale and manufacturing establishments. The latter employees received a total of $1,801,129 in salaries and wages in 1940. (Data on the transporting, wholesaling, and manufacturing industries for both coasts of Florida have been included in this section). Detailed statistics on these branches of the industry for 1940 can be found in ''Fishery Statistics of the United States, 1944'' (Statistical Digest No. 16).

Detailed statistics covering the fisheries of the South Atlantic States during 1945 can be found in ''Fishery Statistics of the United States, 1945'' (Statistical Digest No. 18). Condensed summary data of these figures appear in the following tables.

---

[6] These numbers were assigned to these areas by the North Atlantic Council on Fishery Investigations. The catch of fishery products in Lake Okeechobee is included in the Florida catch tables.

SHRIMP TRAWLER

SOUTH ATLANTIC FISHERIES

SECTIONAL SUMMARIES

SUMMARY OF CATCH, 1945

PRODUCT	NORTH CAROLINA		SOUTH CAROLINA		GEORGIA	
	POUNDS	VALUE	POUNDS	VALUE	POUNDS	VALUE
FISH	179,177,300	$3,732,650	3,029,100	$300,680	1,176,900	$129,571
SHELLFISH, ETC.	18,991,500	1,762,602	7,826,500	598,709	20,220,800	1,219,965
TOTAL.	198,168,800	5,495,252	10,855,600	899,389	21,397,700	1,349,536

PRODUCT	FLORIDA, EAST COAST 1/		TOTAL	
	POUNDS	VALUE	POUNDS	VALUE
FISH	156,193,500	$5,351,170	339,576,800	$9,514,071
SHELLFISH, ETC.	18,330,500	2,037,003	65,369,300	5,618,279
TOTAL.	174,524,000	7,389,173	404,946,100	15,132,350

1/ INCLUDES DATA ON THE CATCH IN LAKE OKEECHOBEE.

SUMMARY OF OPERATING UNITS

ITEM	NORTH CAROLINA, 1945	SOUTH CAROLINA, 1945	GEORGIA, 1945	FLORIDA, EAST COAST 1/, 1940	TOTAL, VARIOUS YEARS
	NUMBER	NUMBER	NUMBER	NUMBER	NUMBER
FISHERMEN:					
ON VESSELS	1,372	190	341	552	2,455
ON BOATS AND SHORE:					
REGULAR.	4,771	746	351	1,646	7,514
CASUAL	1,313	553	434	603	2,900
TOTAL.	7,456	1,489	1,126	2,798	12,869
VESSELS:					
MOTOR.	286	83	148	97	614
NET TONNAGE.	3,352	885	1,362	1,361	6,960
SAIL	45	-	-	-	45
NET TONNAGE.	595	-	-	-	595
TOTAL VESSELS.	331	83	148	97	659
TOTAL NET TONNAGE. . . .	3,947	885	1,362	1,361	7,555
BOATS:					
MOTOR.	1,918	138	163	877	3,096
OTHER.	1,018	561	400	881	2,860
ACCESSORY BOATS.	206	-	-	30	236
APPARATUS:					
PURSE SEINES, MENHADEN . . .	30	-	-	15	45
LENGTH, YARDS.	7,950	-	-	4,290	12,240
HAUL SEINES:					
COMMON	214	24	-	100	338
LENGTH, YARDS.	31,240	5,725	-	84,890	121,855
LONG	163	-	-	13	176
LENGTH, YARDS.	139,100	-	-	11,600	150,700
GILL NETS:					
ANCHOR	620	43	16	9	688
SQUARE YARDS	419,350	16,550	1,600	9,000	446,500
DRIFT.	139	28	96	37	300
SQUARE YARDS	88,760	22,400	39,921	72,700	223,781
RUNAROUND.	323	70	43	431	867
SQUARE YARDS	232,760	20,999	33,000	486,620	773,379
STAKE. . . . .●.	1,936	22	122	5	2,085
SQUARE YARDS	165,875	13,600	19,470	5,000	203,945
TRAMMEL NETS	-	-	-	8	8
SQUARE YARDS	-	-	-	8,000	8,000
LINES:					
HAND	200	34	-	501	735
HOOKS.	200	34	-	551	785
TRAWL OR TROT WITH HOOKS .	-	-	20	195	215
HOOKS.	-	-	2,300	70,600	72,900
TROLL.	11	-	-	424	435
HOOKS.	11	-	-	424	435
TROT WITH BAITS OR SNOODS.	914	266	175	113	1,468
BAITS OR SNOODS.	535,900	133,000	81,300	42,300	792,500
POUND NETS	2,520	-	-	-	2,520
FYKE NETS, FISH.	308	-	-	45	353
DIP NETS, COMMON	237	1	1	28	267
CAST NETS.	-	4	-	38	42
OTTER TRAWLS:					
FISH	9	-	-	-	9
YARDS AT MOUTH	196	-	-	-	196
SHRIMP	521	194	272	123	1,110
YARDS AT MOUTH	9,356	4,550	6,900	2,811	23,617

SEE FOOTNOTE AT END OF TABLE   (CONTINUED ON NEXT PAGE)

SUMMARY OF OPERATING UNITS - Continued

ITEM	NORTH CAROLINA, 1945	SOUTH CAROLINA, 1945	GEORGIA, 1945	FLORIDA, EAST COAST 1/, 1940	TOTAL, VARIOUS YEARS
	NUMBER	NUMBER	NUMBER	NUMBER	NUMBER
APPARATUS - CONTINUED:					
POTS:					
SPINY LOBSTER.	-	-	-	5,900	5,900
CRAB	-	-	1,540	5,790	7,330
EEL.	535	-	-	-	535
FISH	250	100	210	9,960	10,520
SPEARS	270	51	-	49	370
DREDGES, OYSTER, COMMON. . . .	346	-	-	3	349
YARDS AT MOUTH	346	-	-	5	351
TONGS, OYSTER.	69	50	18	22	159
RAKES, OTHER THAN FOR OYSTERS	262	14	-	4	280
GRABS.	-	160	48	-	208
HOOKS, LOBSTER . . . . . 1 . .	-	-	-	16	16

1/ INCLUDES DATA ON THE NUMBER OF FISHERMEN AND FISHING CRAFT, AND THE QUANTITY OF GEAR OPERATED IN LAKE OKEECHOBEE.

CATCH BY STATES, 1945

SPECIES	NORTH CAROLINA		SOUTH CAROLINA		GEORGIA	
FISH	POUNDS	VALUE	POUNDS	VALUE	POUNDS	VALUE
ALEWIVES	8,022,100	$176,783	-	-	-	-
AMBERJACK.	400	20	-	-	-	-
BLUEFISH	627,000	75,600	11,000	$1,650	-	-
BUTTERFISH	30,000	1,800	-	-	-	-
CARP	882,100	26,463	-	-	-	-
CATFISH AND BULLHEADS.	1,171,500	75,786	25,000	2,240	93,000	$7,440
CROAKER.	4,214,600	337,208	102,000	14,620	10,000	800
DRUM:						
BLACK.	141,700	4,332	25,500	3,810	10,000	1,000
RED OR REDFISH	223,900	13,434	50,000	6,440	10,000	1,000
EELS, COMMON	116,000	5,581	-	-	5,000	400
FLOUNDERS.	1,203,600	141,232	230,000	31,120	307,200	18,432
GIZZARD SHAD	8,000	160	-	-	-	-
HAKE, WHITE.	3,900	390	-	-	-	-
HARVEST FISH OR "STAR ISH." . .	811,700	48,902	-	-	-	-
HICKORY SHAD	854,400	68,224	11,800	1,770	17,500	1,400
KING WHITING OR "KINGISH" . . .	1,157,500	57,925	157,000	12,560	460,700	27,644
MENHADEN	141,533,000	974,631	-	-	-	-
MULLET	3,240,900	259,296	889,000	61,510	15,500	1,240
PIGFISH.	480,700	33,649	-	-	-	-
PINFISH.	3,100	99	-	-	-	-
POMPANO.	23,300	5,825	-	-	-	-
SCUP OR PORGY.	113,200	9,056	-	-	-	-
SEA BASS	190,600	28,590	163,000	23,190	-	-
SEA CATFISH.	-	-	6,500	780	-	-
SHAD	912,000	198,613	89,000	31,150	221,500	66,450
SHARKS	1,200	72	-	-	-	-
SHEEPSHEAD, SALT-WATER	11,200	672	-	-	2,000	240
SNAPPER, RED	4,100	410	-	-	-	-
SPANISH MACKEREL	506,700	60,804	-	-	-	-
SPOT	6,264,700	314,235	1,084,000	72,280	-	-
SEA TROUT OR WEAKFISH:						
GRAY	4,736,800	525,422	-	-	-	-
SPOTTED.	500,100	99,651	148,000	23,320	20,000	2,400
STRIPED BASS	608,500	121,156	1,100	220	-	-
STURGEON	900	225	36,200	14,020	4,500	1,125
SUCKERS.	7,000	210	-	-	-	-
SWELLFISH.	200	6	-	-	-	-
TUNA AND TUNALIKE FISHES, BONITO	60,100	4,808	-	-	-	-
WHITE PERCH.	501,100	60,240	-	-	-	-
YELLOW PERCH	9,500	1,140	-	-	-	-
TOTAL.	179,177,300	3,732,650	3,029,100	300,680	1,176,900	129,571
SHELLFISH, ETC.						
CRABS:						
BLUE:						
HARD	5,696,400	284,820	2,364,100	72,125	3,566,100	96,630
SOFT AND PEELERS	184,300	55,290	-	-	-	-
SHRIMP	10,614,300	849,160	4,695,500	403,562	16,392,100	1,067,684
CLAMS, HARD, PUBLIC.	502,200	151,447	1,300	375	-	-
MUSSELS, SEA	-	-	43,000	5,375	-	-
OYSTERS, MARKET:						
PUBLIC, SPRING	1,079,200	256,840	80,200	11,262	-	-
PUBLIC, FALL	603,100	138,170	41,800	6,578	-	-
PRIVATE, SPRING.	14,200	2,980	347,000	61,224	139,000	27,321
PRIVATE, FALL	10,600	2,220	253,100	38,083	116,100	22,705
TOTAL OYSTERS.	1,707,100	400,210	722,100	117,147	255,100	50,026

(CONTINUED ON NEXT PAGE)

CATCH BY STATES, 1945 - Continued

SPECIES	NORTH CAROLINA		SOUTH CAROLINA		GEORGIA	
SHELLFISH, ETC. - CONTINUED	POUNDS	VALUE	POUNDS	VALUE	POUNDS	VALUE
SCALLOPS, BAY.	22,200	$7,770	-	-	-	-
SQUID.	2,300	230	-	-	-	-
TERRAPIN, DIAMOND-BACK	2,700	675	500	$125	7,500	$5,625
ROCKWEED	260,000	13,000	-	-	-	-
TOTAL.	18,991,500	1,762,602	7,826,500	598,709	20,220,800	1,219,965
GRAND TOTAL.	198,168,800	5,495,252	10,855,600	899,389	21,397,700	1,349,536

SPECIES	FLORIDA, EAST COAST 1/		TOTAL	
FISH	POUNDS	VALUE	POUNDS	VALUE
ALEWIVES	428,200	$8,562	8,450,300	$185,345
AMBERJACK.	107,500	2,541	107,900	2,561
BARRACUDA.	40,700	2,342	40,700	2,342
BLUEFISH	1,273,600	227,085	1,911,600	304,335
BLUE RUNNER OR HARDTAIL. . . .	91,300	5,857	91,300	5,857
BUTTERFISH	27,200	2,054	57,200	3,854
CABIO OR CRAB EATER.	32,800	2,090	32,800	2,090
CARP	-	-	882,100	26,463
CATFISH AND BULLHEADS.	9,600,300	1,055,952	10,889,800	1,141,418
CRAPPIE.	932,900	204,748	932,900	204,748
CREVALLE	122,100	6,105	122,100	6,105
CROAKER.	145,300	13,114	4,471,900	365,742
DOLPHIN.	79,800	7,980	79,800	7,980
DRUM:				
BLACK.	501,600	40,318	678,800	49,460
RED OR REDFISH	758,800	95,875	1,042,700	116,749
EELS, COMMON	59,800	2,392	180,800	8,373
FLOUNDERS.	345,700	51,855	2,086,500	242,639
GIZZARD SHAD	550,000	11,000	558,000	11,160
GROUPERS	1,416,800	138,179	1,416,800	138,179
GRUNTS	75,600	5,338	75,600	5,338
HAKE, WHITE.	-	-	3,900	390
HARVEST FISH OR "STARFISH" . .	-	-	811,700	48,902
HICKORY SHAD	84,900	3,900	969,600	75,294
HOGFISH.	15,300	1,224	15,300	1,224
JEWFISH.	216,300	29,750	216,300	29,750
KING MACKEREL.	2,781,500	395,800	2,781,500	395,800
KING WHITING OR "KINGFISH" . .	1,511,700	46,439	3,286,900	144,568
MENHADEN	114,745,900	739,517	256,278,900	1,714,148
MULLET	7,812,300	640,239	11,957,700	962,285
MUTTONFISH	207,900	37,028	207,900	37,028
PERMIT	600	45	600	45
PIGFISH.	41,800	3,344	522,500	36,993
PINFISH.	9,800	490	12,900	589
POMPANO.	332,700	130,651	356,000	136,476
SCUP OR PORGY.	-	-	113,200	9,056
SEA BASS	100,800	14,682	454,400	66,462
SEA CATFISH.	4,500	180	11,000	960
SHAD	842,400	126,365	2,064,900	422,578
SHARKS	2,027,700	32,200	2,028,900	32,272
SHEEPSHEAD:				
FRESH-WATER.	161,800	13,239	161,800	13,239
SALT-WATER	-	-	13,200	912
SNAPPERS:				
MANGROVE	112,700	14,406	112,700	14,406
RED.	246,300	54,440	250,400	54,850
SNOOK OR SERGEANTFISH.	205,400	26,796	205,400	26,796
SPANISH MACKEREL	5,471,800	659,619	5,978,500	730,423
SPOT	161,500	12,740	7,510,200	399,255
SEA TROUT OR WEAKFISH:				
GRAY	33,400	3,476	4,770,200	528,898
SPOTTED.	912,300	181,560	1,580,400	306,931
STRIPED BASS	-	-	609,600	121,376
STURGEON	200	50	41,800	15,420
SUCKERS.	-	-	7,000	210
SUNFISH.	1,255,100	238,416	1,255,100	238,416
SWELLFISH.	-	-	200	6
TRIPLETAIL	41,100	3,007	41,100	3,007
TUNA AND TUNALIKE FISHES,				
BONITO	-	-	60,100	4,808
WHITE PERCH.	-	-	501,100	60,240
YELLOW PERCH	-	-	9,500	1,140
YELLOWTAIL	265,800	58,180	265,800	58,180
TOTAL.	156,193,500	5,351,170	339,576,800	9,514,071

SEE FOOTNOTE AT END OF TABLE
(CONTINUED ON NEXT PAGE)

CATCH BY STATES, 1945 - Continued

SPECIES	FLORIDA, EAST COAST 1/		TOTAL	
SHELLFISH, ETC.	POUNDS	VALUE	POUNDS	VALUE
CRABS:				
BLUE:				
HARD	5,391,200	$134,910	17,017,800	$598,485
SOFT AND PEELERS	2,000	480	186,300	55,770
STONE.	80,500	20,935	80,500	20,935
LOBSTERS, SPINY.	572,100	116,427	572,100	116,427
SHRIMP	11,879,200	1,663,088	43,581,100	3,983,494
CLAMS, HARD, PUBLIC.	3,000	1,500	506,500	153,322
CONCHS	3,900	390	3,900	390
MUSSELS, SEA	-	-	43,000	5,375
OYSTERS, MARKET:				
PUBLIC, SPRING	9,000	5,040	1,168,400	273,142
PUBLIC, FALL	9,000	5,040	653,900	149,788
PRIVATE, SPRING.	68,000	38,080	568,200	129,605
PRIVATE, FALL.	51,500	28,840	431,300	91,848
TOTAL OYSTERS.	137,500	77,000	2,821,800	644,383
SCALLOPS, BAY.	-	-	22,200	7,770
SQUID.	-	-	2,300	230
TERRAPIN, DIAMOND-BACK	5,400	1,350	16,100	7,775
TURTLES:				
GREEN.	1,100	110	1,100	110
LOGGERHEAD	15,000	1,645	15,000	1,645
SNAPPER.	44,600	3,568	44,600	3,568
SOFT-SHELL	195,000	15,600	195,000	15,600
ROCKWEED	-	-	260,000	13,000
TOTAL.	18,330,500	2,037,003	65,369,300	5,618,279
GRAND TOTAL.	174,524,000	7,389,173	404,946,100	15,132,350

1/ INCLUDES DATA ON THE CATCH IN LAKE OKEECHOBEE.

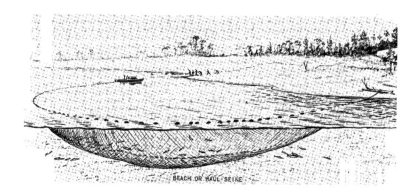

BEACH OR HAUL SEINE

993093 O - 52 - 11

SOUTH ATLANTIC FISHERIES

MANUFACTURED FISHERY PRODUCTS, VARIOUS YEARS 1/

ITEM			NORTH AND SOUTH CAROLINA		GEORGIA AND FLORIDA	
BY MANUFACTURING ESTABLISHMENTS:	YEAR	UNIT	QUANTITY	VALUE	QUANTITY	VALUE
ALEWIVES:						
ROE, CANNED.	1949	STANDARD CASES	4,943	$89,162	-	-
CORNED, SALTED	1940	POUNDS	3,220,150	69,291	-	-
BLUE RUNNER, SALTED.	1940	DO	-	-	250,000	$10,000
GROUPER:						
FRESH FILLETS.	1949	DO	-	-	365,767	156,337
FROZEN FILLETS AND STEAKS. .	1949	DO	-	-	245,652	82,424
KING MACKEREL, SMOKED.	1940	DO	-	-	3,500	525
MENHADEN:						
ROE, SALTED.	1940	DO	1,000	250	-	-
MEAL AND DRY SCRAP	1949	TONS	2/23,502	3,503,489	6,070	1,006,765
OIL.	1949	GALLONS	751,687	259,901	259,834	93,262
MULLET, SALTED	1940	POUNDS	277,800	23,100	976,500	58,100
MULLET ROE, SALTED	1940	DO	-	-	60,000	14,825
SEA BASS STEAKS, FRESH . . .	1949	DO	-	-	10,000	2,880
SEA TROUT FILLETS, FRESH . .	1949	DO	-	-	12,000	7,520
SNAPPER, RED:						
FRESH AND FROZEN FILLETS . .	1949	DO	-	-	20,700	13,155
FRESH AND FROZEN STEAKS. . .	1949	DO	-	-	19,000	9,570
SNOOK FILLETS, FRESH	1949	DO	-	-	9,000	5,280
SPANISH MACKEREL FILLETS,						
FRESH AND FROZEN	1949	DO	-	-	86,500	30,940
SPOT, SALTED	1940	DO	159,400	9,580	-	-
CLAMS, HARD, FRESH-SHUCKED . .	1940	GALLONS	2,100	3,040	100	200
CRAB MEAT, BLUE, FRESH-COOKED .	1940	POUNDS	604,336	228,954	883,106	328,922
LOBSTERS, SPINY, FRESH-COOKED .	1940	DO	-	-	49,000	16,400
OYSTERS:						
CANNED	1949	STANDARD CASES	67,186	873,123	(3)	(3)
FRESH-SHUCKED.	1940	GALLONS	102,234	99,841	92,996	118,978
SCALLOPS, BAY, FRESH-SHUCKED .	1940	DO	2,868	5,449	12,960	36,490
SHRIMP FROZEN, PACKAGED. . . .	1940	POUNDS	-	-	155,300	30,756
UNCLASSIFIED PRODUCTS:						
CANNED	1949	STANDARD CASES	4/43,171	4/836,838	5/24,816	5/397,908
MISCELLANEOUS.	1949	-	-	6/299,613	-	7/795,045
TOTAL		-	-	6,301,631	-	3,216,282

1/ DATA ON THE PRODUCTION OF THE DIFFERENT PRODUCTS ARE FOR THE YEARS INDICATED.
2/ INCLUDES A SMALL QUANTITY OF ACID SCRAP PRODUCED IN NORTH CAROLINA.
3/ THIS ITEM HAS BEEN INCLUDED UNDER "UNCLASSIFIED PRODUCTS".
4/ INCLUDES CANNED RED DRUM, MENHADEN AND SHAD ROE, CRAB MEAT, DEVILED CRAB, SHRIMP, BARBECUED SHRIMP, AND SHRIMP PASTE.
5/ INCLUDES CANNED CRAB MEAT, OYSTERS, SHRIMP, TERRAPIN SOUP AND MEAT, AND GREEN TURTLE SOUP AND MEAT.
6/ INCLUDES FRESH PACKAGED FILLETS OF CROAKER, FLOUNDER, RED DRUM, SEA BASS, SEA TROUT, SPANISH MACKEREL, AND STRIPED BASS; AGAR-AGAR; CRAB SHELLS (FOR TABLE USE); CRAB, SHRIMP AND MISCELLANEOUS DRY SCRAP AND MEAL; MISCELLANEOUS OIL; AND FISH SOLUBLES.
7/ INCLUDES FROZEN TRIGGERFISH FILLETS, SHARK LIVER OIL, FISH SOLUBLES, CRAB MEAL, AND OYSTER SHELL GRIT AND LIME.
NOTE:--SOME OF THE ABOVE PRODUCTS MAY HAVE BEEN MANUFACTURED FROM PRODUCTS IMPORTED FROM ANOTHER STATE OR A FOREIGN COUNTRY; THEREFORE THEY CANNOT BE CORRELATED DIRECTLY WITH THE CATCH WITHIN THE STATE.

SUMMARY OF MANUFACTURED FISHERY PRODUCTS, VARIOUS YEARS

SUMMARY OF STATES STATE	VALUE
NORTH CAROLINA.	$4,687,027
SOUTH CAROLINA.	1,614,604
GEORGIA	481,542
FLORIDA	2,734,740
TOTAL.	9,517,913

SUMMARY OF PRODUCTS ITEM	YEAR	UNIT	QUANTITY	VALUE
PACKAGED FISH.	1949	POUNDS	823,744	$329,101
CANNED FISH AND SHELLFISH.	1949	STANDARD CASES	140,116	2,197,031
FISHERY BYPRODUCTS	1949	-	-	5,937,080
PACKAGED SHELLFISH	1940	POUNDS	3,538,499	869,030
SALTED, DRIED AND PICKLED	1940	DO	4,944,850	185,146
SMOKED AND KIPPERED.	1940	DO	3,500	525
TOTAL			-	9,517,913

SECTION 6:- GULF FISHERIES

(Area XXV)[7]

During 1949, the fisheries of the Gulf Area (West Coast of Florida, Alabama, Mississippi, Louisiana and Texas), amounted to 524,588,200 pounds, valued at $49,705,775 to the fishermen. The number of fishermen operating in the Gulf during 1949 totaled 22,861, while the number of fishing vessels of 5 net tons and over, rose to a new high of 2,244. This was the first complete general canvass which has been conducted in the Gulf States since 1940. A survey of the fisheries of Alabama, Mississippi, Louisiana, and Texas was made for 1948, and a canvass of the Gulf, except for the operating units in Florida, was made for 1945.

The year 1949 was marked with several important developments in the field of commercial fisheries in the Gulf of Mexico. The menhaden industry continued its rapid growth with the completion of another new reduction plant in Louisiana. The menhaden catch in the Gulf was far above the figure of the previous year, but most plant operators felt that they expended more effort to obtain the fish during this season than they did in 1948. With a narrowing margin of profits resulting from a depressed fats and oil market, more attention was directed toward the utilization of menhaden stickwater in the production of condensed fish solubles.

The most important development in the Gulf shrimp fishery during the year was the exploitation of the grooved shrimp fishery at Brownsville, Texas, early in April. Fishermen had been taking grooved shrimp in varying quantities for many years, but the pace quickened during 1948, and in April, 1949, the real strike occurred. Craft operating a few hours out of Brownsville, Texas, in 18 to 27 fathoms of water began taking large quantities of the grooved shrimp, and shrimp vessels from as far as North Carolina moved into the area to initiate this new fishery. The exploitation of these new shrimp grounds was apparently the result of two main trends; first, the heavy construction of more modern trawlers of the larger type, capable of going to sea and remaining longer than their less seaworthy predecessors; and second, the movement toward the Mexican Coast in search of migrating schools of the common shrimp, bound for the grounds off Carmen, Mexico. Elsewhere along the coast the grooved shrimp was taken with varying degrees of success. Mississippi fishermen reported a substantial part of their 1949 catch to be the grooved shrimp taken during the summer months. Largest grooved shrimp catches were made at night which necessitated changing the usual method of shrimping in this area.

With shrimp production at a high level during the summer months, the freezers filled to capacity in record time, and by the beginning of the fall shrimping season, most freezers were blocked and the dealers were forced to sell considerable quantities of shrimp on the fresh market. This created a glut, and dealers were caught in a squeeze between wholesale prices in distant cities and a price agreement with fishermen. In many areas the fishermen were forced to take a lower price for their product. The fishermen generally accepted the reduced prices and continued to fish rather than tie up the fleets with strikes.

Imports of shrimp, principally from Mexico, continued to increase. In 1947, these imports totaled 13,275,000 pounds; in 1948, 21,563,000 pounds; and in 1949, 29,673,000 pounds. Many producers became alarmed by this trend and a considerable amount of speculation regarding the ultimate size of these growing imports was indulged in.

During 1949, there was a greater demand by the trade for shrimp of a uniform size and this brought about a trend toward mechanical grading. The same grader which was used by canning plants for grading cooked shrimp meats was put into operation. This type of mechanical grader when used for the grading of uncooked headless shrimp was probably as efficient as hand grading, but the limited capacity of the machine was the outstanding objection to its use. A machine designed to peel raw shrimp was also introduced to the shrimp industry during 1949.

---

[7] These numbers were assigned to these areas by the North Atlantic Council on Fishery Investigations. The catch of the Mississippi River and tributaries does not appear in this section.

Landings of crabs in 1949 declined generally throughout the Gulf Area. This was due, at least partially, to economic considerations. Fishermen in the Gulf were not willing to fish for crabs at a price that would allow competition with Chesapeake Bay crab meat. Consequently the demand for crabs was poor during the summer months when production is normally high.

The last complete survey of the fishery transporting, wholesaling, and manufacturing industries in Alabama, Mississippi, Louisiana and Texas was made in 1940. In that year 413 men were employed in the operation of 209 vessels engaged in the transporting trade and 12,029 persons were employed in wholesale and manufacturing establishments. The latter employees received a total of $2,013,213 in salaries and wages in 1940. (Data on the transporting, wholesaling and manufacturing industries for the west coast of Florida, which are also for 1940, have been included in Section 5, under the heading ''South Atlantic Fisheries''). Detailed statistics on these branches of the industry for 1940 can be found in ''Fishery Statistics of the United States, 1944'' (Statistical Digest No. 16).

The following tables contain summarized and detailed information on the catch and operating units for the West Coast of Florida, Alabama, Mississippi, Louisiana and Texas for 1949. Condensed summary data of the operating units and catch for these states appearing on the following pages, have been previously published in Current Fishery Statistics. No. 682.

GULF CATCH, 1949

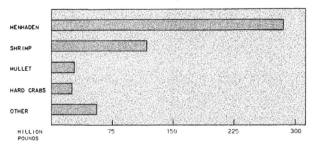

VALUE OF GULF CATCH, 1949

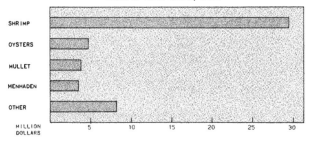

FLORIDA, WEST COAST: CATCH BY GEAR, 1949

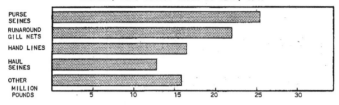

ALABAMA: CATCH BY GEAR, 1949

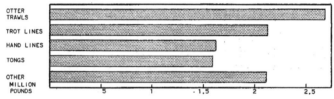

MISSISSIPPI: CATCH BY GEAR, 1949

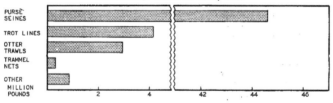

LOUISIANA: CATCH BY GEAR, 1949

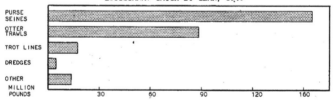

TEXAS: CATCH BY GEAR, 1949

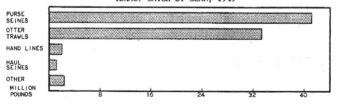

GULF FISHERIES
SECTIONAL SUMMARIES

SUMMARY OF CATCH, 1949

PRODUCT	FLORIDA, WEST COAST		ALABAMA		MISSISSIPPI	
	POUNDS	VALUE	POUNDS	VALUE	POUNDS	VALUE
FISH	86,788,600	$7,893,002	3,777,400	$596,589	45,428,600	$603,847
SHELLFISH, ETC . .	6,631,500	1,705,613	6,377,700	1,377,162	7,466,400	1,021,425
TOTAL.	93,420,100	9,578,615	10,155,100	1,973,751	52,895,000	1,625,272

PRODUCT	LOUISIANA		TEXAS		TOTAL	
	POUNDS	VALUE	POUNDS	VALUE	POUNDS	VALUE
FISH	174,769,300	$3,442,836	45,184,800	$1,150,072	355,948,700	$13,686,346
SHELLFISH, ETC . .	113,817,900	23,960,801	34,346,000	7,974,428	168,639,500	36,019,429
TOTAL.	288,587,200	27,403,637	79,530,800	9,124,500	524,588,200	49,705,775

SUMMARY OF OPERATING UNITS, 1949

ITEM	FLORIDA, WEST COAST	ALABAMA	MISSISSIPPI	LOUISIANA	TEXAS	TOTAL
	NUMBER	NUMBER	NUMBER	NUMBER	NUMBER	NUMBER
FISHERMAN:						
ON VESSELS	1,653	247	1,175	2,590	1,731	7,396
ON BOATS AND SHORE:						
REGULAR.	4,361	1,070	1,418	4,630	1,848	13,277
CASUAL	1,397	254	96	266	175	2,188
TOTAL.	7,411	1,521	2,689	7,486	3,754	22,861
VESSELS:						
MOTOR.	317	70	307	910	640	2,244
NET TONNAGE.	4,225	828	4,787	12,741	12,099	34,680
BOATS:						
MOTOR.	1,840	549	805	2,250	1,030	6,474
OTHER.	2,983	326	109	1,284	192	4,894
ACCESSORY BOATS.	126	3	42	90	15	276
APPARATUS:						
PURSE SEINES, MENHADEN . . .	6	-	14	28	5	53
LENGTH, YARDS.	2,250	-	5,150	10,425	2,000	20,125
HAUL SEINES, COMMON.	222	7	1	44	21	295
LENGTH, YARDS.	126,100	2,425	60	7,105	11,320	147,010
GILL NETS:						
DRIFT.	2	-	-	-	-	2
SQUARE YARDS	310	-	-	-	-	310
RUNAROUND.	1,921	25	-	-	-	1,946
SQUARE YARDS	2,669,803	10,500	-	-	-	2,680,303
STAKE.	-	-	-	2	14	16
SQUARE YARDS	-	-	-	330	3,525	3,855
TRAMMEL NETS	790	67	53	127	52	1,089
SQUARE YARDS	604,721	28,780	12,850	33,002	25,663	705,016
LINES:						
HAND	3,093	178	100	130	401	3,902
HOOKS.	4,845	300	114	167	575	6,001
TRAWL OR TROT WITH HOOKS .	23	28	-	444	344	839
HOOKS.	12,550	10,270	-	89,620	44,720	157,160
TROLL.	399	-	-	-	3	402
HOOKS.	399	-	-	-	3	402
TROT WITH BAITS OR SNOODS.	119	151	261	856	43	1,430
BAITS OR SNOODS.	95,200	70,100	120,700	377,600	11,075	674,675
POUND NETS	1	-	-	-	-	1
STOP NETS.	4	-	-	-	-	4
LENGTH, YARDS.	2,000	-	-	-	-	2,000
FYKE NETS, FISH.	-	129	-	913	23	1,065
DIP NETS:						
COMMON	30	-	-	94	-	124
DROP	-	-	-	6,800	-	6,800
CAST NETS.	38	-	52	-	-	90
OTTER TRAWLS, SHRIMP . . .	157	401	876	2,623	1,426	5,483
YARDS AT MOUTH	2,449	6,137	16,231	48,211	30,849	103,877
TRAPS, BRUSH	-	-	-	88,500	-	88,500
POTS:						
SPINY LOBSTER.	11,840	-	-	-	-	11,840
CRAB	2,530	-	-	150	1,340	4,020
FISH	-	235	-	-	-	235
SPEARS	55	34	-	-	43	132
DREDGES:						
CLAM	3	-	-	-	-	3
YARDS AT MOUTH	3	-	-	-	-	3
OYSTER, COMMON	-	-	246	122	25	393
YARDS AT MOUTH	-	-	260	146	29	435
SCALLOP.	36	-	-	-	-	36
YARDS AT MOUTH	36	-	-	-	-	36

(CONTINUED ON NEXT PAGE)

SUMMARY OF OPERATING UNITS, 1949 — Continued

ITEM	FLORIDA, WEST COAST	ALABAMA	MISSISSIPPI	LOUISIANA	TEXAS	TOTAL
	NUMBER	NUMBER	NUMBER	NUMBER	NUMBER	NUMBER
APPARATUS:- CONTINUED:						
TONGS, OYSTER.	358	577	254	856	105	2,150
RAKES, OTHER THAN FOR OYSTERS	16	-	-	-	-	16
GRABS, FROG.	-	-	-	27	-	27
COQUINA SCOOPS	2	-	-	-	-	2
HOOKS, SPONGE.	29	-	-	-	-	29
DIVING OUTFIT.	40	-	-	-	-	40

CATCH BY STATES, 1949

SPECIES	FLORIDA, WEST COAST		ALABAMA		MISSISSIPPI	
FISH	POUNDS	VALUE	POUNDS	VALUE	POUNDS	VALUE
AMBERJACK.	102,800	$5,614	-	-	-	-
BARRACUDA.	43,100	2,236	-	-	-	-
BLUEFISH	564,000	75,229	5,300	$741	2,100	$256
BLUERUNNER OR HARDTAIL . . .	1,092,100	32,375	41,600	1,664	800	40
BUFFALOFISH.	-	-	68,400	4,788	-	-
CABIO OR CRAB EATER.	19,900	1,179	1,500	210	1,300	173
CATFISH AND BULLHEADS. . . .	26,200	5,230	99,900	21,978	-	-
CERO	2,300	210	-	-	-	-
CIGARFISH.	4,000	124	-	-	-	-
CREVALLE	418,500	14,003	2,900	116	-	-
CROAKER.	120,400	7,569	23,800	1,428	9,300	465
DOLPHIN.	100	7	-	-	-	-
DRUM:						
BLACK.	186,000	12,640	60,600	4,187	30,700	2,455
RED OR REDFISH	1,670,000	221,210	111,700	22,435	76,100	15,981
EELS, COMMON	200	10	-	-	-	-
FLOUNDERS.	289,800	50,957	89,300	16,770	40,900	7,775
GROUPERS	8,052,900	794,810	180,000	19,800	29,200	4,060
GRUNTS	84,600	6,936	-	-	-	-
HOGFISH.	14,700	1,488	-	-	-	-
JEWFISH.	177,900	9,340	3,600	396	-	-
KING MACKEREL.	1,415,200	185,364	1,600	160	-	-
KING WHITING OR "KINGFISH" .	137,700	11,635	49,200	2,953	75,400	3,770
MENHADEN	24,879,400	269,470	-	-	44,578,500	485,906
MOJARRA.	514,500	30,820	-	-	-	-
MOONFISH	31,800	1,590	-	-	-	-
MULLET	29,749,400	3,113,332	950,600	75,740	200,300	16,024
MUTTONFISH	45,100	7,229	4,500	675	-	-
PADDLEFISH OR SPOONBILL CAT.	-	-	-	-	-	-
PERMIT	20,700	1,116	-	-	-	-
PIGFISH.	49,600	3,327	-	-	-	-
PINFISH.	10,200	408	-	-	-	-
POMPANO.	644,900	336,570	1,100	528	-	-
SEA CATFISH	1,020,300	40,902	31,800	1,908	24,700	1,235
SEA TROUT OR WEAKFISH:						
SPOTTED.	4,278,600	836,920	143,000	31,502	102,900	24,633
WHITE.	279,500	24,623	74,900	5,185	93,900	4,695
SHEEPSHEAD:						
FRESH-WATER.	9,100	637	3,500	175	-	-
SALT-WATER	218,300	18,236	45,400	4,511	17,800	1,749
SNAPPER:						
MANGROVE	162,200	18,929	-	-	-	-
RED.	5,184,500	1,210,564	1,343,200	335,800	135,900	33,975
WHITE.	31,100	3,370	-	-	-	-
SNOOK OR SERGEANTFISH. . . .	681,400	88,180	-	-	-	-
SPADEFISH.	200	10	-	-	-	-
SPANISH MACKEREL	3,445,000	376,204	422,500	41,778	1,200	114
SPOT	235,500	14,939	5,800	344	4,900	245
STURGEON	4,000	480	900	145	-	-
TENPOUNDER	679,700	21,434	8,400	336	300	12
TRIGGERFISH.	14,300	710	-	-	-	-
TRIPLETAIL	2,700	210	2,400	336	2,400	284
YELLOWTAIL	174,200	34,626	-	-	-	-
TOTAL.	86,788,600	7,893,002	3,777,400	596,589	45,428,600	603,847

(CONTINUED ON NEXT PAGE)

GULF FISHERIES

CATCH BY STATES, 1949 - Continued

SPECIES	FLORIDA, WEST COAST		ALABAMA		MISSISSIPPI	
SHELLFISH, ETC.	POUNDS	VALUE	POUNDS	VALUE	POUNDS	VALUE
CRABS:						
BLUE:						
HARD	2,055,700	$90,790	2,128,000	$106,400	4,163,000	$208,150
STONE.	53,100	26,555	-	-	-	-
TOTAL CRABS.	2,108,800	117,345	2,128,000	106,400	4,163,000	208,150
LOBSTER, SPINY	1,481,800	188,704	-	-	-	-
SHRIMP	1,634,000	372,272	2,663,900	608,485	2,841,500	674,650
CLAMS:						
COQUINA.	100	30	-	-	-	-
HARD, PUBLIC	84,900	29,420	-	-	-	-
TOTAL CLAMS.	85,000	29,450	-	-	-	-
CONCHS	500	40	-	-	-	-
OYSTERS, MARKET:						
PUBLIC, SPRING	570,200	237,519	1,198,200	503,244	456,400	136,424
PUBLIC, FALL	399,500	160,313	369,000	151,290	5,500	2,201
PRIVATE, SPRING.	115,300	47,473	11,700	4,914	-	-
PRIVATE, FALL.	1,400	588	6,900	2,829	-	-
TOTAL OYSTERS	1,086,400	445,893	1,585,800	662,277	461,900	138,625
SCALLOPS, BAY.	135,900	58,504	-	-	-	-
TERRAPIN, DIAMOND-BACK	15,400	632	-	-	-	-
TURTLES:						
GREEN.	11,000	1,110	-	-	-	-
LOGGERHEAD	2,000	200	-	-	-	-
FROGS.	2,000	660	-	-	-	-
SPONGES:						
GRASS.	6,500	6,530	-	-	-	-
SHEEPSHEAD	57,700	435,176	-	-	-	-
YELLOW	4,500	9,097	-	-	-	-
TOTAL	6,631,500	1,685,613	6,377,700	1,377,162	7,466,400	1,021,425
GRAND TOTAL	93,420,100	9,578,615	10,155,100	1,973,751	52,895,000	1,625,272

SPECIES	LOUISIANA		TEXAS		TOTAL	
FISH	POUNDS	VALUE	POUNDS	VALUE	POUNDS	VALUE
AMBERJACK.	-	-	-	-	102,800	$5,614
BARRACUDA.	-	-	-	-	43,100	2,236
BLUEFISH	5,100	$765	1,600	$214	578,100	77,205
BLUE RUNNER OR HARDTAIL. . . .	1,100	44	-	-	1,135,600	34,123
BUFFALOFISH.	716,000	58,054	10,000	693	794,400	63,535
CABIO OR CRAB EATER.	2,200	278	2,500	177	27,400	2,017
CARP	24,000	1,440	-	-	24,000	1,440
CATFISH AND BULLHEADS.	3,691,700	785,692	18,400	4,228	3,836,200	817,118
CERO	-	-	-	-	2,300	210
CIGARFISH.	-	-	-	-	4,000	124
.REVALLE	100	4	-	-	421,500	14,123
CROAKER.	63,000	4,557	14,800	869	231,300	14,888
DOLPHIN.	-	-	-	-	100	7
DRUM:						
BLACK.	206,500	16,498	747,000	68,377	1,230,800	104,157
RED OR REDFISH	479,900	100,582	519,900	10?,116	2,857,600	464,324
EELS, COMMON	-	-	-	-	200	10
FLOUNDERS.	180,900	3?,673	219,900	50,001	820,800	160,176
GARFISH.	181,800	10,299	-	-	181,800	10,299
GROUPERS	5,200	728	130,000	15,593	8,397,300	834,991
GRUNTS	-	-	-	-	84,600	6,936
HOGFISH.	-	-	-	-	14,700	1,488
JEWFISH.	-	-	5,300	?98	186,800	10,234
KING MACKEREL.	1,400	98	800	50	1,?19,000	185,672
KING WHITING OR "KINGFISH" . .	273,600	19,745	99,700	5,718	635,600	43,821
MENHADEN	165,913,400	2,018,307	41,135,300	473,757	276,506,600	3,247,440
MOJARRA.	-	-	-	-	51,500	30,820
MOONFISH	-	-	-	-	31,800	1,590
MULLET	571,400	45,551	421,700	31,136	31,892,900	3,281,783
MUTTONFISH	-	-	-	-	45,100	7,229
PADDLEFISH OR SPOONBILL CAT. .	43,200	8,175	-	-	47,700	8,850
PERMIT	-	-	-	-	20,700	1,116
PIGFISH.	-	-	-	-	49,600	3,337
PINFISH.	-	-	-	-	10,200	408
POMPANO.	-	-	100	48	646,100	337,?0
SAFISH	3,900	1,390	-	-	34,900	1,396
SEA CATFISH.	163,800	10,518	1?1,400	7,912	1,372,000	62,?75
SEA TROUT OR WEAKFISH:						
SPOTTED.	69?,600	172,?07	614,400	1?1,387	5,831,500	,1,206,649
WHITE.	193,700	15,737	15,100	79?	657,100	51,032

(CONTINUED ON NEXT PAGE)

CATCH BY STATES, 1949 – Continued

SPECIES	LOUISIANA		TEXAS		TOTAL	
FISH – CONTINUED	POUNDS	VALUE	POUNDS	VALUE	POUNDS	VALUE
SHARKS	42,900	$1,716	25,000	$250	67,900	$1,966
SHEEPSHEAD:						
FRESH-WATER.	889,400	69,784	-	-	902,000	70,596
SALT-WATER	170,700	19,337	13,900	1,362	466,100	45,195
SNAPPER:						
MANGROVE	-	-	-	-	162,200	18,929
RED.	169,900	41,523	1,054,400	242,506	7,887,900	1,864,368
WHITE.	-	-	-	-	31,100	3,370
SNOOK OR SERGEANTFISH.	-	-	400	28	681,800	88,208
SPADEFISH.	-	-	-	-	200	10
SPANISH MACKEREL	5,300	599	2,200	270	3,876,200	418,965
SPOT	18,100	2,030	1,300	71	265,600	17,629
STURGEON	100	10	-	-	5,000	635
TENPOUNDER	12,400	496	-	-	700,800	22,278
TRIGGERFISH.	-	-	-	-	14,300	710
TRIPLETAIL	15,000	2,003	100	9	22,600	2,842
TUNA, LITTLE	-	-	100	10	100	10
YELLOWTAIL	-	-	-	-	174,200	34,626
TOTAL.	174,769,300	3,442,836	45,184,800	1,150,072	355,948,700	13,686,346
SHELLFISH. ETC.						
CRABS:						
BLUE:						
HARD	17,873,700	554,601	374,100	22,422	26,594,500	982,363
SOFT AND PEELERS	455,300	192,282	-	-	455,300	192,282
STONE.	-	-	-	-	53,100	26,555
TOTAL CRABS.	18,329,000	746,883	374,100	22,422	27,102,900	1,201,200
CRAYFISH, FRESH-WATER.	39,900	666	-	-	39,900	666
LOBSTER, SPINY	-	-	-	-	1,481,800	188,704
SHRIMP . . . . . . ✱	85,706,900	19,732,728	33,668,000	7,819,074	126,514,300	29,207,209
CLAMS:						
COGUINA.	-	-	-	-	100	30
HARD, PUBLIC	-	-	-	-	84,900	29,420
TOTAL CLAMS.	-	-	-	-	85,000	29,450
CONCHS	-	-	-	-	500	40
OYSTER, MARKET:						
PUBLIC, SPRING	3,240,200	756,165	247,300	110,118	5,712,300	1,743,470
PUBLIC, FALL	19,000	5,909	52,000	22,584	845,000	342,297
PRIVATE, SPRING.	4,999,600	2,105,649	-	-	5,126,600	2,158,036
PRIVATE, FALL.	1,428,700	591,618	-	-	1,437,000	595,035
TOTAL OYSTERS.	9,687,500	3,459,341	299,300	132,702	13,120,900	4,838,838
SCALLOPS, BAY.	-	-	-	-	135,900	58,504
SQUID.	4,000	160	4,600	230	8,600	390
TERRAPIN, DIAMOND-BACK	-	-	-	-	15,00	632
TURTLES:						
GREEN.	5,300	590	-	-	16,300	1,700
LOGGERHEAD	500	40	-	-	2,500	240
SNAPPER.	3,200	280	-	-	3,200	280
FROGS.	41,600	20,113	-	-	43,600	20,773
SPONGES:						
GRASS.	-	-	-	-	6,500	6,530
SHEEPSHEAD	-	-	-	-	57,700	455,176
YELLOW	-	-	-	-	4,500	9,097
TOTAL.	113,817,900	23,960,801	34,3 6,000	7,974,428	168,639,500	36,019,429
GRAND TOTAL.	288,587,200	27,403,637	79,530,800	9,124,500	524,588,200	49,705,775

NOTE:--A TOTAL OF 8,652,600 POUNDS OF SHRIMP AND 1,790,800 POUNDS OF OYSTERS LISTED FOR LOUISIANA WERE TAKEN BY MISSISSIPPI CRAFT IN LOUISIANA WATERS AND LANDED IN MISSISSIPPI.

AVERAGE WEIGHTS OF CERTAIN SHELLFISH, 1949

		QUANTITY
CRABS:		
BLUE:		
HARD	NUMBER PER POUND	1.74
SOFT AND PEELERS	DO	-
STONE.	DO	
CLAMS:		
COQUINA.	LBS. MEATS PER U.S. BUSHEL	
HARD, PUBLIC . . .	DO	
CONCHS	DO	-
OYSTERS, MARKET:		
PUBLIC, SPRING . .	DO	4.28
PUBLIC, FALL . . .	DO	4.00
PRIVATE, SPRING. .	LO	-
PRIVATE, FALL. . .	DO	
SCALLOPS. BAY. . . .	DO	

SUPPLEMENTARY REVIEW OF THE CATCH OF CERTAIN SHELLFISH, 1949

ITEM		FLORIDA, WEST COAST		ALABAMA		MISSISSIPPI	
		QUANTITY	VALUE	QUANTITY	VALUE	QUANTITY	VALUE
CRABS:							
BLUE, HARD	NUMBER	4,264,428	$90,790	5,102,880	$106,400	8,325,996	$208,150
SOFT	DO	53,100	26,555	-	-	-	-
CLAMS:							
COQUINA.	U.S. STANDARD BUSHEL	12	30	-	-	-	-
HARD, PUBLIC . . .	DO	10,547	29,420	-	-	-	-
CONCHS	DO	33	40	-	-	-	-
OYSTERS, MARKET:							
PUBLIC, SPRING . . .	DO	137,775	237,519	230,423	503,244	127,522	136,424
PUBLIC, FALL	DO	100,156	160,313	82,000	151,290	1,410	2,201
PRIVATE, SPRING. .	DO	27,452	47,473	2,250	4,914	-	-
PRIVATE, FALL. . .	DO	333	588	1,533	2,829	-	-
SCALLOPS, BAY	DO	76,858	58,504	-	-	-	-

ITEM		LOUISIANA		TEXAS		TOTAL	
		QUANTITY	VALUE	QUANTITY	VALUE	QUANTITY	VALUE
CRABS:							
BLUE:							
HARD	NUMBER	37,376,256	$554,601	651,108	$22,422	55,720,668	$982,363
SOFT A D PEELERS	DO	1,336,584	192,282	-	-	1,336,584	192,282
STONE.	DO	-	-	-	-	53,100	26,555
CLAMS:							
COQUINA.	U.S. STANDARD BUSHEL	-	-	-	-	12	30
HARD, PUBLIC . . .	DO	-	-	-	-	10,547	29,420
CONCHS	DO	-	-	-	-	33	40
OYSTERS, MARKET:							
PUBLIC, SPRING . .	DO	935,843	756,165	57,755	110,118	1,489,317	1,743,470
PUBLIC, FALL . . .	DO	4,833	5,909	13,000	22,584	201,399	342,297
PRIVATE, SPRING. .	DO	1,184,133	2,105,649	-	-	1,213,835	2,158,036
PRIVATE, FALL. . .	DO	365,147	591,618	-	-	367,013	595,035
SCALLOPS, BAY. . . .	DO	-	-	-	-	26,858	58,504

NOTE:--BUSHELS REPRESENT U.S. STANDARD BUSHEL OF 2,150.4 CUBIC INCHES CAPACITY.

CAST NET

TROT LINE

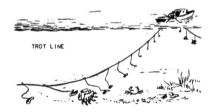

MANUFACTURED FISHERY PRODUCTS, VARIOUS YEARS 1/

ITEM	YEAR	UNIT	MISSISSIPPI AND ALABAMA		LOUISIANA AND TEXAS	
			QUANTITY	VALUE	QUANTITY	VALUE
BY MANUFACTURING ESTABLISHMENTS:						
MENHADEN:						
MEAL AND DRY SCRAP.	1949	TONS	(2)	(2)	22,038	$3,786,428
OIL	1949	GALLONS	(2)	(2)	2,244,269	828,505
SEA TROUT, SALTED	1940	POUNDS	-	-	3,000	649
CRABS, HARD, BLUE:						
CANNED.	1949	STANDARD CASES	8,887	$153,442	10,857	217,241
MEAT, FRESH-COOKED.	1940	POUNDS	286,051	88,357	1,482,681	393,646
OYSTERS:						
CANNED.	1949	STANDARD CASES	92,865	1,371,009	177,357	2,491,455
FRESH-SHUCKED	1940	GALLONS	84,284	136,305	294,924	446,331
LIME AND GRIT	1949	TONS	-	-	243,308	1,473,343
SHRIMP:						
CANNED.	1949	STANDARD CASES	134,174	2,264,705	495,800	8,371,199
SPECIALTIES, CANNED	1949	DO	(2)	(2)	3,192	86,527
COOKED,PEELED	1940	POUNDS	211,425	58,530	863,895	237,586
FROZEN, PACKAGED.	1940	DO	1,986,119	263,034	12,403,660	1,713,015
SUN DRIED	1940	DO	-	-	1,930,400	326,416
MEAL OR BRAN.	1949	TONS	-	-	1,208	109,292
TURTLE SOUP, CANNED.	1949	STANDARD CASES	-	-	1,313	32,428
UNCLASSIFIED PRODUCTS:						
BY PRODUCTS	1949	-	-	3/1,078,888	-	(4)
MISCELLANEOUS PRODUCTS. . . .	1949	-	-	5/ 45,310	-	6/98,939
TOTAL.		-	-	5,459,581	-	20,613,000

1/ DATA ON THE PRODUCTION OF THE DIFFERENT PRODUCTS ARE FOR THE YEARS INDICATED.
2/ THIS ITEM HAS BEEN INCLUDED UNDER "UNCLASSIFIED PRODUCTS."
3/ INCLUDES MENHADEN MEAL, DRY SCRAP, AND OIL; MISCELLANEOUS MEAL; AND FISH SOLUBLES.
4/ THIS ITEM HAS BEEN INCLUDED WITH MISCELLANEOUS PRODUCTS.
5/ INCLUDES CANNED SPECIALTY PACKS OF CRAB, OYSTER, AND SHRIMP;FRESH GROUPER FILLETS; FRESH STEAKS OF GROUPER, RED SNAPPER, AND SEA BASS; AND FROZEN STEAKS OF GROUPER AND RED SNAPPER.
6/ INCLUDES SPECIALTY PACKS OF CANNED GRAYFISH BISQUE; SOFT SHELL CRABS, LOBSTER BISQUE, SMOKED OYSTERS, DEVILED OYSTERS, OYSTER SOUP, BOUILLABAISSE, AND GUMBO; AND MENHADEN FISH SOLUBLES.
NOTE:--SOME OF THE ABOVE PRODUCTS MAY HAVE BEEN MANUFACTURED FROM PRODUCTS IMPORTED FROM ANOTHER STATE OR A FOREIGN COUNTRY; THEREFORE THEY CANNOT BE CORRELATED DIRECTLY WITH THE CATCH WITHIN THE STATE.

SUMMARY OF MANUFACTURED FISHERY PRODUCTS, VARIOUS YEARS

SUMMARY OF STATES STATE	VALUE
MISSISSIPPI.	$4,570,966
ALABAMA.	888,615
LOUISIANA.	18,143,176
TEXAS.	2,469,824
TOTAL	26,072,581

SUMMARY OF PRODUCTS ITEM	YEAR	UNIT	QUANTITY	VALUE
CANNED FISH AND SHELLFISH.	1949	STANDARD CASES	927,179	$15,072,804
PACKAGED FISH AND BYPRODUCTS . . .	1949	-	-	7,335,907
PACKAGED SHELLFISH	1940	POUNDS	22,481,426	3,663,221
SALTED, DRIED AND PICKLED.	1940	DO	3,000	649
TOTAL			-	26,072,581

GULF FISHERIES
FLORIDA (WEST COAST)

OPERATING UNITS BY GEAR, 1949

ITEM	PURSE SEINES, MENHADEN	HAUL SEINES, COMMON	GILL NETS DRIFT	GILL NETS RUNAROUND	TRAMMEL NETS
	NUMBER	NUMBER	NUMBER	NUMBER	NUMBER
FISHERMEN:					
ON VESSELS.	120	132	-	113	38
ON BOATS AND SHORE:					
REGULAR	-	532	4	2,475	961
CASUAL.	-	136	-	59	-
TOTAL	120	800	4	2,647	999
VESSELS, MOTOR.	6	26	-	34	13
NET TONNAGE	249	235	-	276	107
BOATS:					
MOTOR	-	90	2	882	357
OTHER	-	93	-	1,505	562
ACCESSORY BOATS	18	36	-	67	21
APPARATUS:					
NUMBER.	6	222	2	1,921	790
LENGTH, YARDS	2,250	126,100	-	-	-
SQUARE YARDS.	-	-	310	2,669,803	604,721

ITEM	LINES HAND	LINES TRAWL OR TROT WITH HOOKS	LINES TROLL	LINES TROT WITH BAITS OR SNOODS	POUND NETS
	NUMBER	NUMBER	NUMBER	NUMBER	NUMBER
FISHERMEN:					
ON VESSELS.	1,099	3	8	-	-
ON BOATS AND SHORE:					
REGULAR	1,011	9	102	82	4
CASUAL	1,012	12	93	29	-
TOTAL	3,122	24	203	111	4
VESSELS, MOTOR.	195	1	6	-	-
NET TONNAGE	2,965	9	34	-	-
BOATS:					
MOTOR	509	-	153	24	2
OTHER	1,123	21	-	82	-
APPARATUS:					
NUMBER.	3,093	23	399	119	1
HOOKS, BAITS, OR SNOODS. .	4,845	12,550	399	95,200	-

ITEM	STOP NETS	DIP NETS, COMMON	CAST NETS	OTTER TRAWLS, SHRIMP	POTS CRAB	POTS SPINY LOBSTER
	NUMBER	NUMBER	NUMBER	NUMBER	NUMBER	NUMBER
FISHERMEN:						
ON VESSELS.	-	-	-	86	-	-
ON BOATS AND SHORE:						
REGULAR	12	25	21	208	27	96
CASUAL.	-	5	17	18	3	15
TOTAL	12	30	38	312	30	111
VESSELS, MOTOR.	-	-	-	41	-	-
NET TONNAGE	-	-	-	373	-	-
BOATS:						
MOTOR	4	-	-	113	23	107
OTHER	-	27	12	-	3	-
APPARATUS:						
NUMBER.	4	30	38	157	2,530	11,840
LENGTH, YARDS	2,000	-	-	-	-	-
YARDS AT MOUTH.	-	-	-	2,449	-	-

(CONTINUED ON NEXT PAGE)

SHRIMP TRAWLER

FLORIDA (WEST COAST): OPERATING UNITS BY GEAR, 1949 - Continued

ITEM	SPEARS	DREDGES		TONGS, OYSTER	RAKES, OTHER THAN FOR OYSTERS	SCOOPS
		CLAM	SCALLOP			
	NUMBER	NUMBER	NUMBER	NUMBER	NUMBER	NUMBER
FISHERMEN:						
ON VESSELS.	-	-	-	8	-	-
ON BOATS AND SHORE:						
REGULAR	36	5	39	298	16	-
CASUAL.	19	-	-	56	-	3
TOTAL	55	5	39	362	16	3
VESSELS, MOTOR.	-	-	-	4	-	-
NET TONNAGE	-	-	-	20	-	-
BOATS:						
MOTOR	-	2	36	38	-	-
OTHER	-	-	-	276	16	3
ACCESSORY BOATS	-	-	-	3	-	-
APPARATUS:						
NUMBER.	55	3	36	358	16	3
YARDS AT MOUTH.	-	3	36	-	-	-

ITEM	HOOKS, SPONGE	DIVING OUTFIT	BY HAND		TOTAL, EXCLUSIVE OF DUPLICATION
			OYSTER	OTHER	
	NUMBER	NUMBER	NUMBER	NUMBER	NUMBER
FISHERMEN:					
ON VESSELS.	7	171	-	-	1,653
ON BOATS AND SHORE:					
REGULAR	50	52	10	47	4,351
CASUAL.	-	-	-	-	1,397
TOTAL	57	223	10	47	7,411
VESSELS, MOTOR.	3	28	-	-	317
NET TONNAGE	35	245	-	-	4,225
BOATS:					
MOTOR	-	12	-	-	1,840
OTHER	25	-	-	10	2,983
ACCESORY BOATS.	-	-	-	-	126
APPARATUS:					
NUMBER.	29	40	10	-	-

FLORIDA (WEST COAST): CATCH BY GEAR, 1949

SPECIES	PURSE SEINES		HAUL SEINES		GILL NETS			
					DRIFT		RUNAROUND	
	POUNDS	VALUE	POUNDS	VALUE	POUNDS	VALUE	POUNDS	VALUE
AMBERJACK.	-	-	7,800	$390	-	-	13,500	$789
BLUEFISH	-	-	158,100	20,362	-	-	365,800	49,408
BLUE RUNNER OR HARDTAIL. . .	-	-	797,400	22,856	-	-	79,200	3,532
CABIO OR CRAB EATER.	-	-	600	48	-	-	500	39
CIGARFISH.	-	-	4,000	124	-	-	-	-
CREVALLE	-	-	142,400	4,935	-	-	176,600	5,832
CROAKER.	-	-	64,300	4,178	-	-	34,800	2,220
DRUM:								
BLACK.	-	-	51,200	3,292	-	-	46,300	2,890
RED OR REDFISH.	-	-	394,600	51,454	-	-	402,200	54,599
EELS, COMMON	-	-	200	10	-	-	-	-
FLOUNDERS.	-	-	42,600	6,532	-	-	70,800	10,288
GRUNTS	-	-	2,900	202	-	-	9,900	1,296
HOGFISH.	-	-	500	45	-	-	6,700	397
JEWFISH.	-	-	-	-	-	-	900	30
KING MACKEREL.	-	-	2,100	210	-	-	549,800	71,602
KING WHITING OR "KINGFISH"	-	-	44,400	4,043	-	-	37,500	3,179
MENHADEN	24,859,700	$268,485	17,700	885	-	-	1,000	50
MOJARRA.	-	-	284,800	16,353	-	-	170,000	11,351
MOONFISH	-	-	30,200	1,510	-	-	500	25
MULLET	-	-	8,970,500	965,490	-	-	15,363,600	1,599,233
PERMIT	-	-	3,000	300	-	-	2,100	108
PIGFISH.	-	-	9,400	682	-	-	7,800	432
PINFISH.	-	-	5,300	178	-	-	4,900	230
POMPANO.	-	-	65,400	35,200	-	-	114,400	62,710
SEA CATFISH.	-	-	340,800	13,426	-	-	398,200	15,826
SHEEPSHEAD:								
FRESH-WATER.	-	-	-	-	-	-	100	7
SALT-WATER	-	-	55,400	4,980	-	-	53,900	5,276

(CONTINUED ON NEXT PAGE)

FLORIDA (WEST COAST): CATCH BY GEAR, 1949 - Continued

SPECIES	PURSE SEINES		HAUL SEINES		GILL NETS DRIFT		RUNAROUND	
	POUNDS	VALUE	POUNDS	VALUE	POUNDS	VALUE	POUNDS	VALUE
SNAPPER:								
MANGROVE.	-	-	45,100	$5,08	-	-	12,000	$1,415
RED	-	-	-	-	-	-	100	10
SNOOK OR SERGEANTFISH . .	-	-	106,200	12,636	-	-	38,500	7,882
SPADEFISH	-	-	200	10	-	-	-	-
SPANISH MACKEREL.	-	-	255,900	36,322	-	-	2,669,900	282,941
SPOT.	-	-	137,900	8,558	-	-	46,700	3,050
SEA TROUT OR WEAKFISH:								
SPOTTED	-	-	622,900	121,656	-	-	1,283,500	256,093
WHITE	-	-	94,700	7,342	-	-	107,300	11,033
STURGEON.	-	-	-	-	4,000	$480	-	-
TENPOUNDER.	-	-	511,700	16,196	-	-	146,900	4,405
TRIPLETAIL.	-	-	1,000	80	-	-	1,000	70
YELLOWTAIL.	-	-	700	42	-	-	-	-
TURTLES:								
GREEN	-	-	-	-	-	-	500	60
LOGGERHEAD.	-	-	-	-	-	-	2,000	200
TOTAL	24,859,700	$268,485	13,271,900	1,365,608	4,000	480	22,219,400	2,468,408

| SPECIES | TRAMMEL NETS | | LINES | | | | | |
			HAND		TRAWL OR TROT WITH HOOKS		TROLL	
	POUNDS	VALUE	POUNDS	VALUE	POUNDS	VALUE	POUNDS	VALUE
AMBERJACK.	100	$5	15,000	$590	-	-	66,400	$3,840
BARRACUDA.	-	-	38,700	1,940	-	-	4,400	296
BLUEFISH	27,200	3,600	4,800	765	-	-	5,200	744
BLUE RUNNER OR HAROTAIL. . .	73,500	2,942	139,700	2,790	-	-	2,300	255
CABIO OR CRAB EATER.	500	40	18,300	1,052	-	-	-	-
CATFISH AND BULLHEADS. . . .	-	-	4,500	900	21,700	$4,330	-	-
CERO	-	-	2,300	210	-	-	-	-
CREVALLE	19,200	637	60,200	2,022	-	-	20,100	577
CROAKER.	7,300	468	5,500	443	-	-	-	-
DOLPHIN.	-	-	100	7	-	-	-	-
DRUM:								
BLACK.	69,400	5,093	14,000	855	-	-	-	-
RED OR REDFISH	396,800	52,223	453,200	59,684	-	-	-	-
FLOUNDERS.	58,200	9,650	12,500	1,961	-	-	-	-
GROUPERS	82,000	8,200	7,970,900	786,610	-	-	-	-
GRUNTS	2,500	200	69,300	5,238	-	-	-	-
HOGFISH.	200	18	7,300	1,028	-	-	-	-
JEWFISH.	-	-	177,000	9,310	-	-	-	-
KING MACKEREL.	5,400	864	5,100	1,055	-	-	852,800	111,633
KING WHITING OR "KINGFISH" .	24,200	2,305	1,600	128	-	-	-	-
MENHADEN	1,000	50	-	-	-	-	-	-
MOJARRA.	37,400	1,987	22,300	1,129	-	-	-	-
MOONFISH	500	25	600	30	-	-	-	-
MULLET	4,638,000	465,816	239,100	19,130	-	-	-	-
MUTTONFISH	-	-	45,100	7,229	-	-	-	-
PERMIT	15,400	698	200	10	-	-	-	-
PIGFISH.	5,500	345	26,900	1,868	-	-	-	-
POMPANO.	448,700	228,950	1,800	970	-	-	-	-
SEA CATFISH.	72,800	2,921	206,700	8,659	-	-	-	-
SHEEPSHEAD:								
FRESH-WATER.	9,000	630	-	-	-	-	-	-
SALT-WATER	94,200	6,745	14,800	1,235	-	-	-	-
SNAPPER:								
MANGROVE	15,600	1,820	89,500	10,613	-	-	-	-
RED.	400	50	5,184,000	1,210,504	-	-	-	-
WHITE.	-	-	31,100	3,370	-	-	-	-
SNOOK OR SERGEANTFISH. . . .	6,400	764	529,800	66,838	-	-	500	60
SPANISH MACKEREL	293,600	34,239	131,600	13,762	-	-	91,900	8,810
SPOT	32,600	2,134	4,200	210	-	-	-	-
SEA TROUT OR WEAKFISH:								
SPOTTED.	773,600	152,380	1,385,300	257,801	-	-	2,000	400
WHITE.	33,100	2,776	8,600	840	-	-	-	-
TENPOUNDER	1,100	33	20,000	800	-	-	-	-
TRIGGERFISH.	-	-	14,300	710	-	-	-	-
TRIPLETAIL	500	40	200	20	-	-	-	-
YELLOWTAIL	600	40	172,900	34,544	-	-	-	-
TURTLES, GREEN	0,500	1,050	-	-	-	-	-	-
TOTAL.	7,257,000	989,738	17,129,000	2,516,860	21,700	4,330	1,045,600	126,615

(CONTINUED ON NEXT PAGE)

FLORIDA (WEST COAST): CATCH BY GEAR, 1949 - Continued

SPECIES	LINES - LONY'D. TROT WITH BAITS OR SNOODS POUNDS	VALUE	POUND NETS POUNDS	VALUE	STOP NETS POUNDS	VALUE	DIP NETS POUNDS	VALUE
BLUEFISH	-	-	-	-	2,900	$350	-	-
CROAKER	-	-	6,600	$200	1,900	60	-	-
DRUM:								
BLACK	-	-	5,100	510	-	-	-	-
RED OR REDFISH	-	-	23,200	3,250	-	-	-	-
FLOUNDERS	-	-	6,900	800	-	-	-	-
KING WHITING OR "KINGFISH"	-	-	-	-	3,000	340	-	-
MULLET	-	-	-	-	445,900	53,510	-	-
POMPANO	-	-	14,600	8,740	-	-	-	-
SEA CATFISH	-	-	-	-	1,300	50	-	-
SPANISH MACKEREL	-	-	-	-	2,100	230	-	-
SPOT	-	-	14,100	987	-	-	-	-
SEA TROUT OR WEAKFISH:								
SPOTTED	-	-	30,600	7,040	180,700	41,550	-	-
WHITE	-	-	2,600	260	7,500	750	-	-
CRABS, BLUE, HARD	1,963,800	$86,205	-	-	-	-	3,300	$155
SCALLOPS, BAY	-	-	-	-	-	-	49,700	20,874
TOTAL	1,963,800	86,205	102,900	21,787	645,300	96,840	53,000	21,029

SPECIES	CAST NETS POUNDS	VALUE	OTTER TRAWLS POUNDS	VALUE	POTS POUNDS	VALUE	SPEARS POUNDS	VALUE
FLOUNDERS	-	-	20,400	$2,264	-	-	79,200	$19,462
KING WHITING OR "KINGFISH"	-	-	27,000	1,640	-	-	-	-
MULLET	92,300	$10,153	-	-	-	-	-	-
SEA CATFISH	-	-	500	20	-	-	-	-
SEA TROUT OR WEAKFISH, WHITE	-	-	25,700	1,622	-	-	-	-
CRABS:								
BLUE, HARD	-	-	-	-	88,600	$4,430	-	-
STONE	-	-	-	-	49,700	24,855	-	-
LOBSTER, SPINY	-	-	-	-	1,481,800	188,704	-	-
SHRIMP	5,400	1,285	1,628,600	370,987	-	-	-	-
FROGS	-	-	-	-	-	-	900	297
TOTAL	97,700	11,438	1,702,200	376,533	1,620,100	217,989	80,100	19,759

SPECIES	DREDGES POUNDS	VALUE	TONGS POUNDS	VALUE	RAKES POUNDS	VALUE	COQUINA SCOOPS POUNDS	VALUE
CLAMS:								
COQUINA	-	-	-	-	-	-	100	$30
HARD, PUBLIC	7,700	$2,400	-	-	-	-	-	-
OYSTERS, MARKET:								
PUBLIC, SPRING	-	-	561,800	$233,981	-	-	-	-
PUBLIC, FALL	-	-	394,500	158,313	-	-	-	-
PRIVATE, SPRING	-	-	115,300	47,473	-	-	-	-
PRIVATE, FALL	-	-	1,400	588	-	-	-	-
SCALLOPS, BAY	30,900	14,290	-	-	45,600	$19,152	-	-
TOTAL	38,600	16,690	1,073,000	440,355	45,600	19,152	100	30

SPECIES	HOOKS, SPONGE POUNDS	VALUE	DIVING OUTFITS POUNDS	VALUE	BY HAND POUNDS	VALUE
CRABS, STONE	-	-	-	-	3,400	$1,700
CLAMS, HARD, PUBLIC	-	-	-	-	77,200	27,020
CONCHS	-	-	-	-	500	40
OYSTERS, MARKET:						
PUBLIC, SPRING	-	-	-	-	8,400	3,538
PUBLIC, FALL	-	-	-	-	5,000	2,000
SCALLOPS, BAY	-	-	-	-	9,700	4,188
TERRAPIN, DIAMOND-BACK	-	-	-	-	15,400	632
FROGS	-	-	-	-	1,100	363
SPONGES:						
GRASS	4,000	$4,030	2,500	$2,500	-	-
SHEEPSWOOL	5,400	52,466	52,300	402,710	-	-
YELLOW	1,000	2,027	3,500	7,070	-	-
TOTAL	10,400	58,523	58,300	412,280	120,700	39,481

GULF FISHERIES
ALABAMA

OPERATING UNITS BY GEAR, 1949

ITEM	HAUL SEINES, COMMON	GILL NETS, RUNAROUND	TRAMMEL NETS	LINES		
				HAND	TRAWL OR TROT WITH HOOKS	TROT WITH BAITS OR SNOODS
	NUMBER	NUMBER	NUMBER	NUMBER	NUMBER	NUMBER
FISHERMEN:						
ON VESSELS	18	-	-	122	-	-
ON BOATS AND SHORE:						
REGULAR.	12	75	61	26	19	129
CASUAL	-	-	6	30	9	22
TOTAL.	30	75	67	178	28	151
VESSELS, MOTOR	3	-	-	14	-	-
NET TONNAGE.	23	-	-	258	-	-
BOATS:						
MOTOR.	3	25	31	26	7	121
OTHER.	3	25	36	30	21	30
ACCESSORY BOATS.	3	-	-	-	-	-
APPARATUS:						
NUMBER	7	25	67	178	28	151
LENGTH, YARDS.	2,425	-	-	-	-	-
SQUARE YARDS	-	10,500	28,780	-	-	-
HOOKS, BAITS OR SNOODS .	-	-	-	300	10,270	70,100

ITEM	FYKE NETS, FISH	OTTER TRAWLS, SHRIMP	POTS, FISH	SPEARS	TONGS, OYSTER	TOTAL, EXCLUSIVE OF DUPLICATION
	NUMBER	NUMBER	NUMBER	NUMBER	NUMBER	NUMBER
FISHERMEN:						
ON VESSELS	-	115	-	-	-	247
ON BOATS AND SHORE:						
REGULAR.	9	658	11	28	423	1,020
CASUAL	2	-	10	6	209	254
TOTAL.	11	773	21	34	632	1,521
VESSELS, MOTOR	-	57	-	-	-	70
NET TONNAGE.	-	614	-	-	-	828
BOATS:						
MOTOR.	5	344	6	-	347	549
OTHER.	6	-	15	-	216	326
ACCESSORY BOATS.	-	-	-	-	-	3
APPARATUS:						
NUMBER	129	401	235	34	577	-
YARDS AT MOUTH	-	6,137	-	-	-	-

ALABAMA: CATCH BY GEAR, 1949

SPECIES	HAUL SEINES		GILL NETS, RUNAROUND		TRAMMEL NETS		LINES HAND	
	POUNDS	VALUE	POUNDS	VALUE	POUNDS	VALUE	POUNDS	VALUE
BLUEFISH	300	$42	1,900	$266	3,100	$433	-	-
BLUE RUNNER OR HARDTAIL. .	4,100	164	25,600	1,024	11,900	476	-	-
CABIO OR CRAB EATER. . . .	-	-	700	98	800	112	-	-
CREVALLE	-	-	1,600	64	1,300	52	-	-
CROAKER.	3,600	216	700	42	17,600	1,056	1,900	$114
DRUM:								
BLACK.	12,600	812	-	-	40,600	2,842	7,400	533
RED OR REDFISH	12,900	2,580	700	140	68,300	13,660	29,800	6,055
FLOUNDERS.	6,700	1,270	2,500	475	26,000	4,914	1,600	301
GROUPERS	-	-	-	-	-	-	180,000	19,800
JEWFISH.	-	-	-	-	-	-	3,600	396
KING MACKEREL.	-	-	1,600	160	-	-	-	-
KING WHITING OR "KINGFISH"	5,900	354	3,500	210	27,800	1,669	3,300	198
MULLET	111,100	8,888	18,600	1,488	820,900	65,364	-	-
POMPANO.	-	-	500	240	600	288	-	-
SEA CATFISH.	10,200	612	1,900	114	15,300	918	4,400	264
SEA TROUT OR WEAKFISH:								
SPOTTED.	22,300	4,906	5,100	1,122	82,900	18,238	32,700	7,236
WHITE.	22,400	1,565	900	60	27,600	1,890	12,600	872
SHEEPSHEAD, SALT-WATER . .	7,900	770	700	65	33,800	3,368	3,000	308
SNAPPER, RED	-	-	-	-	-	-	1,343,200	335,800
SPANISH MACKEREL	-	-	415,500	41,090	7,000	688	-	-
SPOT	400	24	-	-	5,400	320	-	-
STURGEON	-	-	-	-	900	145	-	-
TENPOUNDER	800	32	5,000	200	2,600	104	-	-
TRIPLETAIL	-	-	1,600	224	800	112	-	-
TOTAL	221,200	22,235	488,600	47,082	1,195,200	116,649	1,623,500	371,877

(CONTINUED ON NEXT PAGE)

ALABAMA: CATCH BY GEAR, 1949 - Continued

LINES - CONTINUED

SPECIES	TRAWL OR TROT WITH HOOKS		TROT WITH BAITS OR SNOODS		FYKE NETS	
	POUNDS	VALUE	POUNDS	VALUE	POUNDS	VALUE
BUFFALOFISH.	-	-	-	-	68,400	$4,788
CATFISH AND BULLHEADS. . .	57,500	$12,650	-	-	300	66
PADDLEFISH OR SPOONBILL CAT	-	-	-	-	4,500	675
SHEEPSHEAD, FRESH-WATER. .	800	40	-	-	2,700	135
CRABS, BLUE, HARD.	-	-	2,128,000	$106,400	-	-
TOTAL	58,300	12,690	2,128,000	106,400	75,900	5,664

SPECIES	OTTER TRAWLS		POTS		SPEARS		TONGS	
	POUNDS	VALUE	POUNDS	VALUE	POUNDS	VALUE	POUNDS	VALUE
CATFISH AND BULLHEADS. . .	-	-	42,100	$9,262	-	-	-	-
FLOUNDERS	14,300	$2,574	-	-	38,200	$7,236	-	-
KING WHITING OR "KINGFISH"	8,700	522	-	-	-	-	-	-
SEA TROUT OR WEAKFISH, WHITE.	11,400	798	-	-	-	-	-	-
SHRIMP	2,663,900	608,485	-	-	-	-	-	-
OYSTERS, MARKET:								
PUBLIC, SPRING	-	-	-	-	-	-	1,198,200	$503,244
PUBLIC, FALL	-	-	-	-	-	-	369,000	151,290
PRIVATE, SPRING.	-	-	-	-	-	-	11,700	4,914
PRIVATE, FALL.	-	-	-	-	-	-	6,900	2,829
TOTAL	2,698,300	612,379	42,100	9,262	38,200	7,236	1,585,800	662,277

MISSISSIPPI

OPERATING UNITS BY GEAR, 1949

ITEM	PURSE SEINES, MENHADEN	HAUL SEINES, COMMON	TRAMMEL NETS	LINES	
				HAND	TROT WITH BAITS OR SNOODS
	NUMBER	NUMBER	NUMBER	NUMBER	NUMBER
FISHERMEN:					
ON VESSELS	284	-	-	6	-
ON BOATS AND SHORE:					
REGULAR.	-	3	63	46	219
CASUAL	-	-	13	48	42
TOTAL.	284	3	76	100	261
VESSELS, MOTOR	14	-	-	1	-
NET TONNAGE.	770	-	-	11	-
BOATS:					
MOTOR.	-	1	28	46	234
OTHER.	-	1	35	44	27
ACCESSORY BOATS.	42	-	-	-	-
APPARATUS:					
NUMBER	14	1	53	100	261
LENGTH, YARDS.	5,450	60	-	-	-
SQUARE YARDS.	-	-	12,850	-	-
HOOKS, BAITS OR SNOODS	-	-	-	114	120,700

ITEM	CAST NETS	OTTER TRAWLS, SHRIMP	DREDGES, OYSTER, COMMON	TONGS, OYSTER	TOTAL EXCLUSIVE OF DUPLICATION
	NUMBER	NUMBER	NUMBER	NUMBER	NUMBER
FISHERMEN:					
ON VESSELS	-	640	490	-	1,175
ON BOATS AND SHORE:					
REGULAR.	41	1,177	23	191	1,418
CASUAL	11	-	-	63	96
TOTAL.	52	1,817	513	254	2,689
VESSELS, MOTOR	-	287	117	-	307
NET TONNAGE.	-	3,963	1,551	-	4,787
BOATS:					
MOTOR.	-	589	6	196	805
OTHER.	-	-	-	57	109
ACCESSORY BOATS.	-	-	-	-	42
APPARATUS:					
NUMBER	52	876	246	254	-
YARDS AT MOUTH	-	16,231	260	-	-

993093 O - 52 - 12

MISSISSIPPI: CATCH BY GEAR, 1949

SPECIES	PURSE SEINES		HAUL SEINES		TRAMMEL NETS	
	POUNDS	VALUE	POUNDS	VALUE	POUNDS	VALUE
BLUEFISH	-	-	-	-	2,100	$256
BLUE RUNNER OR HARDTAIL	-	-	-	-	800	40
CABIO OR CRAB EATER	-	-	-	-	1,000	131
CROAKER	-	-	1,100	$55	5,500	275
DRUM:						
BLACK	-	-	1,600	128	18,400	1,472
RED OR REDFISH	-	-	2,800	588	49,200	10,332
FLOUNDERS	-	-	800	156	8,600	1,634
KING WHITING OR "KINGFISH"	-	-	1,300	65	22,500	1,125
MENHADEN	44,578,500	$485,906	-	-	-	-
MULLET	-	-	-	-	135,400	10,832
SEA CATFISH	-	-	2,000	100	8,700	435
SEA TROUT OR WEAKFISH:						
SPOTTED	-	-	3,400	816	62,900	15,033
WHITE	-	-	1,900	95	36,000	1,800
SHEEPSHEAD, SALT-WATER	-	-	3,300	325	10,300	1,010
SPANISH MACKEREL	-	-	-	-	1,200	114
SPOT	-	-	-	-	4,900	245
TENPOUNDER	-	-	-	-	300	12
TRIPLETAIL	-	-	-	-	2,300	272
TOTAL	44,578,500	485,906	18,200	2,328	370,100	45,018

SPECIES	LINES				CAST NETS	
	HAND		TROT WITH BAITS OR SNOODS			
	POUNDS	VALUE	POUNDS	VALUE	POUNDS	VALUE
CABIO OR CRAB EATER	300	$42	-	-	-	-
CROAKER	2,700	135	-	-	-	-
DRUM:						
BLACK	10,700	855	-	-	-	-
RED OR REDFISH	24,100	5,061	-	-	-	-
FLOUNDERS	2,700	513	-	-	-	-
GROUPERS	29,200	4,060	-	-	-	-
KING WHITING OR "KINGFISH"	6,400	320	-	-	-	-
MULLET	-	-	-	-	64,900	$5,192
SEA CATFISH	14,000	700	-	-	-	-
SEA TROUT OR WEAKFISH:						
SPOTTED	36,600	8,784	-	-	-	-
WHITE	21,900	1,095	-	-	-	-
SHEEPSHEAD, SALT-WATER	4,200	414	-	-	-	-
SNAPPER, RED	135,900	33,975	-	-	-	-
TRIPLETAIL	100	12	-	-	-	-
CRABS, BLUE, HARD	-	-	4,163,000	$208,150	-	-
TOTAL	288,800	55,966	4,163,000	208,150	64,900	5,192

SPECIES	OTTER TRAWLS		DREDGES		TONGS	
	POUNDS	VALUE	POUNDS	VALUE	POUNDS	VALUE
FLOUNDERS	28,800	$5,472	-	-	-	-
KING WHITING OR "KINGFISH"	45,200	2,260	-	-	-	-
SEA TROUT OR WEAKFISH,						
WHITE	34,100	1,705	-	-	-	-
SHRIMP	2,841,500	674,650	-	-	-	-
OYSTERS, MARKET:						
PUBLIC, SPRING	-	-	336,600	$93,581	119,800	$42,843
PUBLIC, FALL	-	-	-	-	5,500	2,201
TOTAL	2,949,600	684,087	336,600	93,581	125,300	45,044

NOTE:--THE PRODUCTION OF FISHERY PRODUCTS BY MISSISSIPPI CRAFT IN LOUISIANA WATERS HAS BEEN INCLUDED WITH THE CATCH FOR LOUISIANA. THESE CATCHES WERE AS FOLLOWS: BY OYSTER DREDGES, PUBLIC SPRING OYSTERS, 1,774,900 POUNDS OF MEATS, VALUED AT $425,880; AND PUBLIC FALL OYSTERS, 12,900 POUNDS OF MEATS, VALUED AT $3,225; BY OYSTER TONGS, PUBLIC SPRING OYSTERS, 3,000 POUNDS OF MEATS, VALUED AT $720; AND BY SHRIMP TRAWLS, SHRIMP, 8,652,600 POUNDS, VALUED AT $2,069,091.

FYKE NETTING

LOUISIANA

OPERATING UNITS BY GEAR, 1949

ITEM	PURSE SEINES, MENHADEN	HAUL SEINES, COMMON	GILL NETS, STAKE	TRAMMEL NETS	LINES	
					HAND	TRAWL OR TROT WITH HOOKS
	NUMBER	NUMBER	NUMBER	NUMBER	NUMBER	NUMBER
FISHERMEN:						
ON VESSELS	557	-	-	16	28	-
ON BOATS AND SHORE:						
REGULAR.	-	108	2	271	80	312
CASUAL	-	7	2	10	22	132
TOTAL.	557	115	4	297	130	444
VESSELS, MOTOR	28	-	-	3	6	-
NET TONNAGE.	2,028	-	-	28	102	-
BOATS:						
MOTOR.	-	27	2	62	69	220
OTHER.	-	54	2	157	13	214
ACCESSORY BOATS.	84	-	-	6	-	-
APPARATUS:						
NUMBER	28	44	2	127	130	444
LENGTH, YARDS.	10,425	7,105	-	-	-	-
SQUARE YARDS	-	-	330	33,002	-	-
HOOKS, BAITS OR SNOODS .	-	-	-	-	167	89,620

ITEM	LINES - CONT'D. TROT WITH BAITS OR SNOODS	FYKE NETS, FISH	DIP NETS		OTTER TRAWLS, SHRIMP	BRUSH TRAPS
			COMMON	DROP		
	NUMBER	NUMBER	NUMBER	NUMBER	NUMBER	NUMBER
FISHERMEN:						
ON VESSELS	-	-	-	-	1,891	-
ON BOATS AND SHORE:						
REGULAR.	731	71	84	90	3,430	125
CASUAL	125	10	15	32	-	-
TOTAL.	856	81	99	122	5,321	125
VESSELS, MOTOR	-	-	-	-	866	-
NET TONNAGE.	-	-	-	-	10,532	-
BOATS:						
MOTOR.	592	62	-	88	1,757	91
OTHER.	264	18	69	30	-	34
APPARATUS:						
NUMBER	856	913	94	6,800	2,623	88,500
HOOKS, BAITS OR SNOODS .	377,600	-	-	-	-	-
YARDS AT MOUTH	-	-	-	-	48,211	-

ITEM	POTS, CRAB	DREDGES, OYSTER, COMMON	TONGS, OYSTER	GRABS, FROG	BY HAND, OTHER THAN FOR OYSTER	TOTAL, EXCLUSIVE OF DUPLICATION
	NUMBER	NUMBER	NUMBER	NUMBER	NUMBER	NUMBER
FISHERMEN:						
ON VESSELS	-	169	-	-	-	2,590
ON BOATS AND SHORE:						
REGULAR.	3	80	856	54	11	4,630
CASUAL	-	-	-	-	-	266
TOTAL.	3	249	856	54	11	7,486
VESSELS, MOTOR	-	41	-	-	-	910
NET TONNAGE.	-	506	-	-	-	12,741
BOATS:						
MOTOR.	1	20	60	-	-	2,250
OTHER.	-	-	722	27	-	1,284
ACCESSORY BOATS.	-	-	-	-	-	90
APPARATUS:						
NUMBER	150	122	856	27	-	-
YARDS AT MOUTH	-	146	-	-	-	-

LOUISIANA: CATCH BY GEAR, 1949

SPECIES	PURSE SEINES		HAUL SEINES		GILL NETS, STAKE		TRAMMEL NETS	
	POUNDS	VALUE	POUNDS	VALUE	POUNDS	VALUE	POUNDS	VALUE
BLUEFISH	-	-	-	-	-	-	5,100	$765
BLUE RUNNER OR HARDTAIL	-	-	-	-	-	-	1,100	44
BUFFALOFISH	-	-	171,900	$14,634	5,400	$432	-	-
CABIO OR CRAB EATER	-	-	300	38	-	-	1,700	212
CARP	-	-	13,000	780	-	-	-	-
CATFISH AND BULLHEADS	-	-	156,700	32,835	1,400	294	-	-
CREVALLE	-	-	-	-	-	-	100	4
CROAKER	-	-	30,300	2,130	-	-	30,100	2,219
DRUM:								
BLACK	-	-	52,500	4,194	-	-	140,300	11,208
RED OR REDFISH	-	-	114,500	24,033	-	-	344,500	72,146
FLOUNDERS	-	-	17,600	3,337	-	-	26,300	5,032
GARFISH	-	-	160,200	9,003	2,500	150	5,700	342
KING MACKEREL	-	-	-	-	-	-	1,100	77
KING WHITING OR "KINGFISH"	-	-	66,100	5,360	-	-	49,600	3,905
MENHADEN	165,913,400	$2,018,307	-	-	-	-	-	-
MULLET	-	-	125,200	9,953	-	-	446,200	35,598
PADDLEFISH OR SPOONBILL CAT	-	-	42,100	7,999	1,100	176	-	-
SEA CATFISH	-	-	83,800	5,384	-	-	72,000	4,578
SEA TROUT OR WEAKFISH:								
SPOTTED	-	-	166,000	40,728	-	-	481,500	120,231
WHITE	-	-	50,900	4,720	-	-	96,300	7,859
SHARKS	-	-	12,900	516	-	-	14,300	572
SHEEPSHEAD:								
FRESH-WATER	-	-	270,300	19,532	1,500	90	-	-
SALT-WATER	-	-	35,400	4,012	-	-	131,200	14,838
SPANISH MACKEREL	-	-	400	42	-	-	4,900	557
SPOT	-	-	7,800	547	-	-	10,300	1,483
STURGEON	-	-	-	-	-	-	100	10
TENPOUNDER	-	-	9,000	360	-	-	3,400	136
TRIPLETAIL	-	-	5,500	737	-	-	9,400	1,252
CRABS, BLUE:								
HARD	-	-	11,200	346	-	-	-	-
SOFT AND PEELERS	-	-	82,300	34,590	-	-	-	-
SHRIMP	-	-	8,400	1,877	-	-	-	-
FROGS	-	-	1,200	600	-	-	-	-
TOTAL	165,913,400	2,018,307	1,695,500	228,287	11,900	1,142	1,875,200	283,068

SPECIES	LINES						FYKE NETS	
	HAND		TRAWL OR TROT WITH HOOKS		TROT WITH BAITS OR SNOODS			
	POUNDS	VALUE	POUNDS	VALUE	POUNDS	VALUE	POUNDS	VALUE
BUFFALOFISH	-	-	-	-	-	-	538,700	$42,988
CABIO OR CRAB EATER	200	$28	-	-	-	-	-	-
CARP	-	-	-	-	-	-	11,000	660
CATFISH AND BULLHEADS	4,500	945	3,388,000	$721,319	-	-	40,000	8,501
CROAKER	2,600	208	-	-	-	-	-	-
DRUM:								
BLACK	13,700	1,096	-	-	-	-	-	-
RED OR REDFISH	20,900	4,403	-	-	-	-	-	-
FLOUNDERS	2,300	442	-	-	-	-	-	-
GARFISH	1,100	66	8,400	504	-	-	3,900	234
GROUPERS	5,200	728	-	-	-	-	-	-
KING MACKEREL	300	21	-	-	-	-	-	-
KING WHITING OR "KINGFISH"	3,100	279	-	-	-	-	-	-
SEA CATFISH	8,000	556	-	-	-	-	-	-
SEA TROUT OR WEAKFISH:								
SPOTTED	45,100	11,248	-	-	-	-	-	-
WHITE	9,800	872	-	-	-	-	-	-
SHEEPSHEAD:								
FRESH-WATER	-	-	179,700	15,460	-	-	437,900	34,702
SALT-WATER	4,100	487	-	-	-	-	-	-
SNAPPER, RED	169,500	41,425	-	-	-	-	-	-
TRIPLETAIL	100	14	-	-	-	-	-	-
CRABS, BLUE, HARD	-	-	-	-	17,274,400	$535,324	-	-
TURTLE, SNAPPER	-	-	2,200	180	-	-	1,000	100
TOTAL	290,500	62,818	3,578,300	737,463	17,274,400	535,324	1,032,500	87,185

(CONTINUED ON NEXT PAGE)

LOUISIANA: CATCH BY GEAR, 1949 - Continued

SPECIES	DIP NETS		OTTER TRAWLS		BRUSH NETS		POTS	
	POUNDS	VALUE	POUNDS	VALUE	POUNDS	VALUE	POUNDS	VALUE
CATFISH AND BULLHEADS . .	101,100	$21,788	-	-	-	-	-	-
FLOUNDERS	-	-	134,700	$25,862	-	-	-	-
KING WHITING OR "KINGFISH"	-	-	154,800	10,201	-	-	-	-
SAWFISH	-	-	34,900	1,396	-	-	-	-
SEA TROUT OR WEAKFISH,								
WHITE	-	-	36,700	2,286	-	-	-	-
SHARKS.	-	-	15,700	628	-	-	-	-
SNAPPER, RED.	-	-	400	98	-	-	-	-
CRABS, BLUE:								
HARD.	466,200	14,320	36,500	1,195	-	-	85,400	$3,416
SOFT AND PEELERS. . . .	160,400	67,368	-	-	212,600	$90,324	-	-
CRAYFISH.	39,900	666	-	-	-	-	-	-
SHRIMP.	-	-	85,698,500	19,730,851	-	-	-	-
SQUID	-	-	4,000	160	-	-	-	-
TURTLE:								
GREEN	-	-	5,300	590	-	-	-	-
LOGGERHEAD.	-	-	500	40	-	-	-	-
TOTAL.	767,600	104,142	86,122,000	19,773,307	212,600	90,324	85,400	3,416

SPECIES	DREDGES		TONGS		GRABS, FROG		BY HAND	
	POUNDS	VALUE	POUNDS	VALUE	POUNDS	VALUE	POUNDS	VALUE
OYSTERS, MARKET:								
PUBLIC, SPRING	3,232,700	$753,465	7,500	$2,700	-	-	-	-
PUBLIC, FALL	12,900	3,225	6,100	2,684	-	-	-	-
PRIVATE, SPRING.	1,650,800	694,017	3,348,800	1,411,632	-	-	-	-
PRIVATE, FALL.	408,800	167,625	1,019,900	423,993	-	-	-	-
FROGS.	-	-	-	-	36,700	$17,744	3,700	$1,769
TOTAL	5,305,200	1,618,332	4,382,300	1,841,009	36,700	17,744	3,700	1,769

NOTE:--THE PRODUCTION OF FISHERY PRODUCTS BY MISSISSIPPI CRAFT IN LOUISIANA WATERS HAS BEEN INCLUDED WITH THE
CATCH FOR LOUISIANA. THESE CATCHES WERE AS FOLLOWS: BY OYSTER DREDGES, PUBLIC SPRING OYSTERS, 1,774,900
POUNDS OF MEATS, VALUED AT $425,880; AND PUBLIC FALL OYSTERS, 12,900 POUNDS OF MEATS, VALUED AT $3,225; BY
OYSTER TONGS, PUBLIC SPRING OYSTERS, 3,000 POUNDS OF MEATS, VALUED AT $720; AND BY SHRIMP TRAWLS, SHRIMP,
8,652,600 POUNDS, VALUED AT $2,069,091.

TEXAS

OPERATING UNITS BY GEAR, 1949

ITEM	PURSE SEINES, MENHADEN	HAUL SEINES, COMMON	GILL NETS, STAKE	TRAMMEL NETS	LINES			
					HAND	TRAWL OR TROT WITH HOOKS	TROLL	TROT WITH BAITS OR SNOODS
	NUMBER	NUMBER	NUMBER	NUMBER	NUMBER	NUMBER	NUMBER	NUMBER
FISHERMEN:								
ON VESSELS.	96	-	-	-	150	-	-	-
ON BOATS AND SHORE:								
REGULAR	-	47	22	89	150	184	-	30
CASUAL.	-	32	2	15	101	40	3	13
TOTAL	96	79	24	104	401	224	3	43
VESSELS, MOTOR.	5	-	-	-	25	-	-	-
NET TONNAGE	238	-	-	-	442	-	-	-
BOATS:								
MOTOR	-	6	10	30	154	163	3	31
BOATS	-	42	8	36	64	58	-	12
ACCESSORY BOATS	15	-	-	-	-	-	-	-
APPARATUS:								
NUMBER.	5	21	14	52	401	344	3	43
LENGTH, YARDS	2,000	11,320	-	-	-	-	-	-
SQUARE YARDS.	-	-	3,525	25,663	-	-	-	-
HOOKS, BAITS OR SNOODS.	-	-	-	-	575	44,720	3	11,075

(CONTINUED ON NEXT PAGE)

TEXAS: OPERATING UNITS BY GEAR, 1949 – Continued

ITEM	FYKE NETS, FISH	OTTER TRAWLS, SHRIMP	POTS, CRABS	SPEARS	DREDGES, OYSTER, COMMON	TONGS, OYSTER	BY HAND, OYSTER	TOTAL, EXCLUSIVE OF DUPLICATION
	NUMBER	NUMBER	NUMBER	NUMBER	NUMBER	NUMBER	NUMBER	NUMBER
FISHERMEN:								
ON VESSELS	-	1,518	-	-	20	-	-	1,731
ON BOATS AND SHORE:								
REGULAR	4	1,578	29	15	52	92	12	1,848
CASUAL	-	-	11	28	-	13	-	175
TOTAL	4	3,096	40	43	72	105	12	3,754
VESSELS, MOTOR	-	627	-	-	5	-	-	640
NET TONNAGE	-	11,678	-	-	23	-	-	12,099
BOATS:								
MOTOR	-	799	34	-	17	65	-	1,030
BOATS	4	-	5	-	-	14	-	192
ACCESSORY BOATS	-	-	-	-	-	-	-	15
APPARATUS:								
NUMBER	23	1,426	1,340	43	25	105	-	-
YARDS AT MOUTH	-	30,849	-	-	29	-	-	-

TEXAS: CATCH BY GEAR, 1949

SPECIES	PURSE SEINES		HAUL SEINES		GILL NETS, STAKE		TRAMMEL NETS	
	POUNDS	VALUE	POUNDS	VALUE	POUNDS	VALUE	POUNDS	VALUE
BLUEFISH	-	-	1,600	$214	-	-	-	-
BUFFALOFISH	-	-	-	-	-	-	700	$42
CABIO OR CRAB EATER . . .	-	-	-	-	-	-	200	14
CROAKER	-	-	600	34	-	-	4,800	275
DRUM:								
BLACK	-	-	86,500	8,591	6,100	$588	60,500	5,518
RED OR REDFISH	-	-	111,300	23,269	19,400	2,751	143,200	28,910
FLOUNDERS	-	-	22,500	5,120	3,200	728	21,600	4,961
JEWFISH	-	-	600	60	-	-	100	10
KING WHITING OR "KINGFISH"	-	-	-	-	200	11	5,400	296
MENHADEN	41,135,300	$473,757	-	-	-	-	-	-
MULLET	-	-	317,200	23,838	-	-	103,900	7,290
POMPANO	-	-	100	48	-	-	-	-
SEA CATFISH	-	-	1,000	54	15,200	885	68,300	4,056
SEA TROUT OR WEAKFISH:								
SPOTTED	-	-	128,000	29,440	25,500	5,865	181,500	41,794
WHITE	-	-	-	-	1,000	60	5,500	302
SHEEPSHEAD, SALT-WATER . .	-	-	1,400	139	1,700	168	3,800	366
SNAPPER, RED	-	-	1,700	391	-	-	-	-
SNOOK OR SERGEANT FISH . .	-	-	400	28	-	-	-	-
SPANISH MACKEREL	-	-	1,600	202	-	-	100	10
SPOT	-	-	400	20	-	-	600	33
TRIPLETAIL	-	-	-	-	-	-	100	9
TOTAL	41,135,300	473,757	674,900	91,448	72,300	11,056	600,300	93,886

SPECIES	LINES							
	HAND		TRAWL OR TROT WITH HOOKS		TROLL		TROT WITH BAITS OR SNOODS	
	POUNDS	VALUE	POUNDS	VALUE	POUNDS	VALUE	POUNDS	VALUE
CABIO OR CRAB EATER . . .	2,100	$149	-	-	-	-	-	-
CATFISH AND BULLHEADS . .	5,400	1,134	13,000	$3,094	-	-	-	-
CROAKER	400	20	-	-	-	-	-	-
DRUM:								
BLACK	193,800	17,522	400,100	36,158	-	-	-	-
REC OR REDFISH	93,400	18,566	152,600	30,620	-	-	-	-
FLOUNDERS	37,400	8,541	4,900	1,120	-	-	-	-
GROUPERS	129,900	15,581	-	-	-	-	-	-
JEWFISH	3,600	338	-	-	-	-	-	-
KING MACKEREL	-	-	-	-	700	$40	-	-
KING WHITING OR "KINGFISH"	2,200	115	-	-	-	-	-	-
SEA CATFISH	34,700	2,181	11,200	685	-	-	-	-
SEA TROUT OR WEAKFISH,								
SPOTTED	218,400	50,236	61,000	14,052	-	-	-	-
SHARKS	-	-	25,000	250	-	-	-	-
SHEEPSHEAD, SALT-WATER . .	5,400	534	1,600	155	-	-	-	-
SNAPPER, RED	1,051,700	241,885	-	-	-	-	-	-
SPANISH MACKEREL	400	46	-	-	-	-	-	-
TUNA, LITTLE	100	10	-	-	-	-	-	-
CRABS, BLUE, HARD	100	8	-	-	-	-	137,800	$8,407
TOTAL	1,779,000	356,866	669,400	86,134	700	40	137,800	8,407

(CONTINUED ON NEXT PAGE)

TEXAS: CATCH BY GEAR, 1949 - Continued

SPECIES	FYKE NETS POUNDS	VALUE	OTTER TRAWLS POUNDS	VALUE	POTS POUNDS	VALUE	SPEARS POUNDS	VALUE
BUFFALOFISH	9,300	$651	-	-	-	-	-	-
CABIO OR CRAB EATER	-	-	200	$14	-	-	-	-
CROAKER	-	-	9,000	540	-	-	-	-
FLOUNDERS	-	-	88,000	20,102	-	-	42,300	$9,429
GROUPERS.	-	-	100	12	-	-	-	-
JEWFISH	-	-	1,000	90	-	-	-	-
KING MACKEREL	-	-	100	10	-	-	-	-
KING WHITING OR "KINGFISH".	-	-	91,900	5,296	-	-	-	-
MULLET.	-	-	100	8	-	-	-	-
SEA CATFISH	-	-	1,000	51	-	-	-	-
SEA TROUT OR WEAKFISH, WHITE	-	-	8,600	430	-	-	-	-
SNAPPER, RED.	-	-	1,000	230	-	-	-	-
SPANISH MACKEREL.	-	-	100	12	-	-	-	-
SPOT.	-	-	300	18	-	-	-	-
CRABS, BLUE, HARD	-	-	7,900	545	228,300	$13,462	-	-
SHRIMP.	-	-	33,668,000	7,819,074	-	-	-	-
SQUID	-	-	4,600	230	-	-	-	-
TOTAL.	9,300	651	33,881,900	7,846,662	228,300	13,462	42,300	9,429

SPECIES	DREDGES POUNDS	VALUE	TONGS POUNDS	VALUE	BY HAND POUNDS	VALUE
OYSTERS, MARKET: PUBLIC, SPRING	90,800	$40,860	117,600	$52,920	38,900	$16,338
PUBLIC, FALL	9,700	4,293	42,300	18,291	-	-
TOTAL	100,500	45,153	159,900	71,211	38,900	16,338

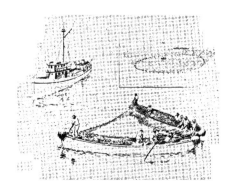

MENHADEN PURSE-SEINING OPERATIONS

TARPON SPRINGS SPONGE FISHERY

During 1949, a total of 83,947 pounds of sponges, valued at $470,804 was sold on the Exchange at Tarpon Springs, Florida. This was an increase of 9,483 pounds or 13 percent in volume, and of $4,867 or 1 percent in value compared with the transactions of the previous year.

Sales of sponges on the Exchange during 1949 were as follows:

	Bunches	Pounds	Value
Large Wool	740	8,140	$101,411
Small Wool	487	3,409	40,527
Wool Rags	9,655	63,366	313,238
Yellow	1,244	5,287	9,097
Grass	899	3,745	6,531

In addition to the sponges shown above, sponges having an estimated value of $48,000 were sold outside the Exchange.

The 1949 total poundage was the second lowest recorded in the 36 years for which data are available. The lowest year was reached in 1948 when 74,464 pounds of sponges were sold at the Exchange.

Domestic production of sponges has declined markedly since 1938. This is attributed to three reasons: first, lack of scientific management and control of the sponge beds; second, a fungus blight which began in 1939 and has seriously damaged the beds; and third, increased commercial production of artificial sponges.

Sponges are sold by "the bunch", which consists of a string of sponges (strung) on a cord 60 inches long. As the weight of these bunches varies considerably, an estimated average weight per bunch for each classification is used in calculating the weight landed. These conversion factors may be found in Section 13 under the heading "Conversion Factors."

SPONGE DIVER

SECTION 7.- PACIFIC COAST STATES FISHERIES[8]

During 1949, the production of fish and shellfish in the Pacific Coast States (Washington, Oregon, and California) totaled 1,364,518,500 pounds, valued at $100,373,114 to the fishermen. This represents an increase of 20 percent in volume, but a decrease of 12 percent in value compared with the landings of the previous year.

Receipts of tuna and tunalike fishes again broke all records in 1949 when over 332 million pounds were landed. These record landings were made even though the clipper fleet suffered a large decline in production as the result of two tie-ups. The first, of about five-weeks duration, occurred in the spring while prices were being negotiated, and the second for 60 to 90 days, was imposed by canners in the fall to prevent piling up of excessive stocks. The fleet of smaller clippers and trollers was exceptionally successful in taking albacore and skipjack. The purse-seine fleet had a good season in the spring fishing for yellowfin and skipjack. With the exception of albacore, the same prices which were paid for raw tuna during 1948 remained in effect until early June, 1949; at that date the fishermen were forced to accept sharp price cuts. The lowered prices per ton were as follows: yellowfin, $340 to $310; bluefin, $330 to $300; skipjack, $320 to $290; bonito, $235 to $195; and yellowtail, $225 to $185. Albacore prices in 1948 ranged from $750 down to almost $500 per ton. Dockside prices for albacore in 1949 were reduced to approximately $400 per ton from the start of the season in June, and some were reduced to less than $350 per ton in the latter part of the season.

The 1949 catch of Pacific salmon rose more than 30 million pounds above the take of the previous year. Although 1949 was a cycle year for the pink salmon in Puget Sound, the receipts of this species were still more than 7.5 million pounds below the almost 52 million pound catch of pinks made in 1947. Early runs of chinook or king salmon off Cape Flattery and other Washington Coastal waters were disappointing, but the main migratory run was late, and off-shore catches materially improved during the summer season. The outstanding factor for the noticeable decrease in the catch of chum salmon was caused by a fleet tie-up at the start of the fall fishing, and extending over a period of several weeks. By the time an agreement was reached, the major chum migrations had passed on into the spawning areas. Subsequent fishing failed to produce adequate catches to recoup what would have been taken if fishing had been carried out during the entire season. During this period, great amounts of Canadian and Alaskan-caught fish were imported to satisfy the demands of the fresh markets and canneries. The sockeye run was actually much greater than the catch indicated, since the opening of the season was delayed until July 17 by the International Sockeye Commission to allow the early run to escape and was further delayed until July 25 by a price disagreement.

The pilchard fishery of the Pacific Coast recorded a gain of over 260 million pounds compared with the previous year. Although the legal season for pilchard in California began on August 1 at Monterey and San Francisco, fishing was delayed three weeks pending negotiation of a contract which called for a $40 per-ton price. At the end of

---

[8] Data on the operating units and catch of the fisheries of the Pacific Coast States have been taken largely from statistics collected by the various State agencies. Supplementary surveys, compilations, and analyses, have been made by agents of this Service in order that the figures may be presented in a manner comparable with those of other sections. While statistics on the fisheries of California are for the calendar year, those for Oregon and Washington are for the fiscal year ending March 31, 1950, except that statistics of the halibut fishery for Washington are for the calendar year.

August, fishing was again suspended until September 12 at Monterey and 10 days later at San Francisco, when a new price of $35 per ton was agreed upon. The open season in southern California began on October 1, but a price renegotiation delayed fishing in that area for all but a few small craft until October 9, when a new price of $32.50 per ton was agreed upon at all ports in the state. Starting on November 9, a disagreement over deviations from the contract price again idled the major portion of the southern fleet for about five weeks. These periods of idleness, occurring at times when fishing conditions appeared very favorable, tended to reduce greatly the potential production of the area.

The 1949 halibut season which extended from May 1 through July 12, was 73 days, compared with 72 days in 1948 and 109 days in 1947. The use of stainless steel ground lines by halibut fishing vessels became more common during the season, and by the end of the year several fishing equipment manufacturers had developed gurdies and other equipment for operating this type of gear.

The mackerel catch in California was another fishery which suffered from price disagreements. Although mackerel production recorded an increase of 26 percent above the previous year, jack mackerel recorded a 30 percent decrease. The seiners caught fewer fish during 1949 while renegotiating sardine price contracts, whereas the small craft, fishing with scoop nets for mackerel only had a much better season than they had experienced in several years. Prices of $60 and $50 per ton paid for mackerel and jack mackerel respectively, in the early part of 1949 were changed to $50 and $40 per ton in the early fall. The prices remained at the latter level for the remainder of the year.

Razor clam production from the Washington Coastal beaches was limited during 1949 since the state had reduced the quota to 700,000 pounds because of a decline in clam populations of the beaches. A quota of 1,200,000 pounds was allowed the previous year.

Extreme winter weather curtailed crab fishing in many areas of the northwest. Great damage was also done during the winter when productive oyster beds were frozen solid.

The last complete survey of the fishery transporting, wholesaling, and manufacturing industries was made for 1940. In that year 141 men were employed on 58 vessels operating in the transporting trade and 19,109 persons were employed in wholesale and manufacturing establishments. The latter employees received $11,440,359 in salaries and wages during 1940. Detailed statistics on these branches of the industry for 1940 can be found in 'Fishery Statistics of the United States, 1944' (Statistical Digest No. 16).

Condensed summary data of the operating units and catch by states of the Pacific Coast States Fisheries, appearing on the following pages, have been previously published in Current Fishery Statistics No. 653.

PACIFIC COAST STATES CATCH, 1949

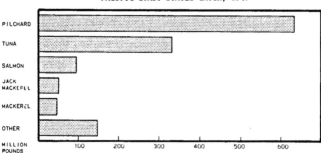

WASHINGTON: CATCH BY GEAR, 1949

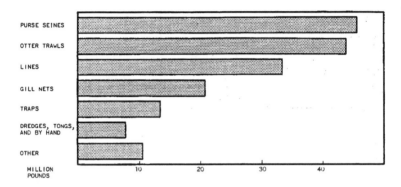

OREGON: CATCH BY GEAR, 1949

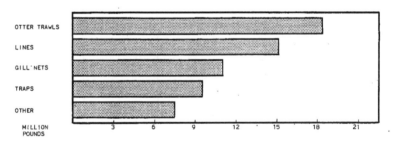

CALIFORNIA: CATCH BY DISTRICTS, 1949

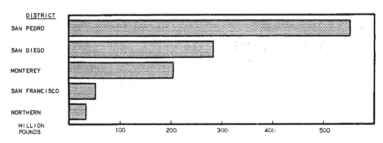

SECTIONAL SUMMARIES

SUMMARY OF CATCH, 1949

PRODUCT	WASHINGTON		OREGON	
	POUNDS	VALUE	POUNDS	VALUE
FISH	152,372,100	$17,114,920	51,093,900	$6,076,768
SHELLFISH, ETC	21,788,700	3,688,028	10,002,500	988,679
TOTAL	174,160,800	20,802,948	61,096,400	7,065,447

PRODUCT	CALIFORNIA		TOTAL	
	POUNDS	VALUE	POUNDS	VALUE
FISH	1,108,012,700	$70,183,149	1,311,478,700	$93,374,837
SHELLFISH, ETC.	20,458,500	2,253,595	52,249,700	6,930,302
WHALE PRODUCTS	790,100	67,975	790,100	67,975
TOTAL	1,129,261,300	72,504,719	1,364,518,500	100,373,114

SUMMARY OF OPERATING UNITS, 1949

ITEM	WASHINGTON			
	PUGET SOUND DISTRICT	COASTAL DISTRICT	COLUMBIA RIVER DISTRICT	TOTAL
	NUMBER	NUMBER	NUMBER	NUMBER
FISHERMEN:				
ON VESSELS	4,672	830	54	5,556
ON BOATS AND SHORE	2,742	3,566	1,089	7,397
TOTAL	7,414	4,396	1,143	12,953
VESSELS, MOTOR	956	337	27	1,320
NET TONNAGE	20,085	4,322	243	24,650
BOATS:				
MOTOR	1,266	558	707	2,531
OTHER	394	246	32	672
ACCESSORY BOATS	296	-	-	296
APPARATUS:				
PURSE SEINES AND LAMPARA NETS:				
PILCHARD	-	-	-	-
LENGTH, YARDS	-	-	-	-
SALMON	296	-	-	296
LENGTH, YARDS	185,000	-	-	185,000
HAUL SEINES	135	4	4	143
LENGTH, YARDS	12,800	400	400	13,600
GILL NETS:				
SALMON	696	504	490	1,690
SQUARE YARDS	1,134,750	560,500	1,568,000	3,263,250
SHARK	1,535	110	-	1,645
SQUARE YARDS	1,262,250	90,000	-	1,352,250
SMELT	-	-	5	5
SQUARE YARDS	-	-	1,875	1,875
LINES :				
TRAWL, SET OR HAND	31,618	40	273	31,931
HOOKS	639,652	800	27,300	667,752
TROLL:				
SALMON	3,564	2,138	490	6,192
HOOKS	17,820	10,512	2,450	30,782
TUNA	2/ 605	2/ 264	2/ 6	2/ 875
HOOKS	605	264	6	875
POUND NETS	3/ 7	-	-	3/ 7
BRUSH WEIRS	1	-	-	1
DIP NETS	38	54	400	492
REEF NETS	137	-	-	137
BEAM TRAWLS	6	-	-	6
YARDS AT MOUTH	55	-	-	55
OTTER TRAWLS	162	8	-	170
YARDS AT MOUTH	2,400	120	-	2,520
TRAPS:				
CRAB	18,300	19,550	1,100	38,950
CRAWFISH	-	-	60	60
OCTOPUS	350	-	-	350
SHRIMP	250	-	-	250
DREDGES, TONGS AND BY HAND	41	122	-	163
SHOVELS	375	2,750	-	3,125

SEE FOOTNOTES AT END OF TABLE

(CONTINUED ON NEXT PAGE)

SUMMARY OF OPERATING UNITS, 1949 - Continued

ITEM	OREGON COLUMBIA RIVER DISTRICT	OREGON COASTAL DISTRICT	OREGON TOTAL	CALIFORNIA TOTAL	GRAND TOTAL (EXCLUSIVE OF DUPLICATION)
	NUMBER	NUMBER	NUMBER	NUMBER	NUMBER
FISHERMEN:					
ON VESSELS	1,409	459	1,868	10,401	15,579
ON BOATS AND SHORE	1,730	1,689	3,419	5,399	16,215
TOTAL.	3,139	2,148	5,287	15,800	31,794
VESSELS, MOTOR	414	187	601	1,893	3,232
NET TONNAGE.	8,658	2,368	11,026	61,428	84,178
BOATS:					
MOTOR.	829	782	1,611	2,940	7,082
OTHER.	72	68	140	12	824
ACCESSORY BOATS.	2	-	2	895	1,193
APPARATUS:					
PURSE SEINES AND LAMPARA NETS:					
PILCHARD	-	-	-	311	311
LENGTH, YARDS.	-	-	-	147,275	147,275
SALMON	-	-	-	-	296
LENGTH, YARDS.	-	-	-	-	185,000
TUNA	1/ 2	-	1/ 2	149	151
LENGTH, YARDS.	1,300	-	1,300	100,575	101,875
OTHER.	-	-	-	126	126
LENGTH, YARDS.	-	-	-	32,723	32,723
HAUL SEINES.	23	12	35	9	187
LENGTH, YARDS.	13,800	2,000	15,800	1,350	30,750
GILL NETS:					
BARRACUDA.	-	-	-	34	34
SQUARE YARDS	-	-	-	264,350	264,350
"CALIFORNIA HALIBUT". . .	-	-	-	13	13
SQUARE YARDS	-	-	-	48,750	48,750
SALMON	781	856	1,637	229	3,556
SQUARE YARDS	2,055,500	715,000	2,770,500	978,975	7,012,725
SEA BASS	-	-	-	78	78
SQUARE YARDS	-	-	-	463,398	463,398
SHAD	-	-	-	106	106
SQUARE YARDS	-	-	-	493,218	493,218
SHARK.	1,215	390	1,605	132	2,840
SQUARE YARDS	1,037,150	342,000	1,379,150	1,083,179	3,241,929
SMELT.	70	-	70	-	75
SQUARE YARDS	26,000	-	26,000	-	27,875
CRAB	-	-	-	10	10
SQUARE YARDS	-	-	-	28,880	28,880
OTHER.	-	-	-	133	133
SQUARE YARDS	-	-	-	137,522	137,522
TRAMMEL NETS	-	-	-	54	54
SQUARE YARDS	-	-	-	313,470	313,470
LINES:					
TRAWL, SET OR HAND . . .	1,287	350	1,637	11,014	43,732
HOOKS.	28,700	7,000	35,700	421,094	1,102,746
TROLL:					
SALMON	1,454	1,812	3,266	5,608	14,209
HOOKS.	6,760	8,150	14,910	25,628	67,288
TUNA	2/1,298	2/245	2/1,543	2/15,998	16,174
HOOKS.	1,298	245	1,543	15,998	16,174
OTHER.	-	-	-	722	722
HOOKS.	-	-	-	722	722
POUND NETS	3/35	-	3/35	-	42
BRUSH WEIRS.	-	-	-	-	1
FYKE NETS.	-	-	-	1,600	1,600
DIP NETS	487	-	487	66	1,045
BRAIL OR SCOOP NETS. . . .	-	-	-	1,454	1,454
BAG NETS, SHRIMP	-	-	-	1	1
LENGTH, YARDS.	-	-	-	720	720
REEF NETS.	-	-	-	-	137
BEAM TRAWLS.	-	-	-	19	25
YARDS AT MOUTH	-	-	-	127	182
OTTER TRAWLS	64	19	83	96	326
YARDS AT MOUTH	960	285	1,245	1,398	4,818
TRAPS:					
CRAB	8,700	16,400	25,100	15,418	77,743
CRAWFISH	1,100	-	1,100	-	1,160
OCTOPUS.	-	-	-	25	375
LOBSTER.	-	-	-	6,348	6,348
SHRIMP	-	-	-	-	250
HARPOONS:					
SWORDFISH.	-	-	-	118	118
WHALE.	-	-	-	2	2

SEE FOOTNOTES AT END OF TABLE   (CONTINUED ON NEXT PAGE)

PACIFIC COAST STATES FISHERIES

SUMMARY OF OPERATING UNITS, 1949 - Continued

ITEM	OREGON			CALIFORNIA	GRAND TOTAL (EXCLUSIVE OF DUPLICATION)
	COLUMBIA RIVER DISTRICT	COASTAL DISTRICT	TOTAL	TOTAL	
	NUMBER	NUMBER	NUMBER	NUMBER	NUMBER
APPARATUS - CONTINUED:					
RAKES:					
OYSTERS.	-	-	-	8	8
MUSSELS.	-	-	-	12	12
DREDGES AND TONGS.	-	26	26	23	212
SHOVELS.	-	744	744	93	3,962

1/ USED ONLY IN THE TUNA FISHERY OFF CENTRAL AMERICA.
2/ USED ONLY BY VESSELS THAT TROLLED OR FISHED EXCLUSIVELY FOR TUNA AND DID NOT TROLL FOR SALMON. DOES NOT INCLUDE TUNA GEAR USED BY VESSELS THAT ALSO TROLLED FOR SALMON.
3/ FISHED ONLY ON INDIAN RESERVATIONS.

NOTE:--STATISTICS ON THE OPERATION OF VESSELS ARE FOR CRAFT MAKING THEIR HOME PORT IN ONE OF THE DISTRICTS OF WASHINGTON, OREGON, OR CALIFORNIA. VESSELS AS WELL AS ALL TYPES OF GEAR OPERATED, HAVE BEEN INCLUDED IN EACH STATE IN WHICH EACH VESSEL OPERATED, EXCEPT THAT VESSELS OPERATING IN ALASKA ARE NOT INCLUDED ABOVE. THE TOTAL EXCLUSIVE OF DUPLICATION REPRESENTS THE TOTAL OPERATING UNITS IN THE PACIFIC COAST STATES, EXCLUSIVE OF THOSE IN ALASKA.

CATCH BY STATES, 1949

SPECIES	WASHINGTON		OREGON 1/	
FISH	POUNDS	VALUE	POUNDS	VALUE
ANCHOVIES.	402,000	$6,100	-	
CARP	-	-	600	$17
COD.	6,245,300	231,078	5,400	188
FLOUNDERS:				
"SOLE"	9,822,800	594,776	9,261,900	462,397
OTHER	564,900	22,465	392,700	9,541
CRAYFISH	10,645,200	450,621	3,422,700	288,271
HAKE	64,200	239	77,400	471
HALIBUT.	13,465,500	2,423,598	609,600	99,048
HERRING, SEA	839,800	41,987	69,400	2,776
LAMPREY.	-	-	369,900	9,248
LINGCOD.	5,416,600	512,917	938,900	98,427
PERCH.	150,600	17,289	7,700	769
PILCHARD	56,400	3,104	9,000	234
RATFISH.	1,471,600	13,344	-	-
ROCKFISHES	13,246,000	591,538	4,774,000	174,625
SABLEFISH.	3,784,300	377,148	554,500	44,455
SALMON:				
CHINOOK OR KING.	9,589,200	2,107,488	9,493,400	1,668,880
CHUM OR KETA	5,212,800	656,098	726,800	58,145
PINK	44,214,800	4,421,459	-	-
RED OR SOCKEYE	7,045,600	1,500,464	12,800	2,571
SILVER OR COHO	10,529,000	1,764,763	2,604,500	343,918
TOTAL SALMON	76,591,400	10,450,272	12,837,500	2,073,514
SHAD	71,900	4,837	1,392,000	94,294
SHARKS	617,200	309,553	551,000	300,439
SKATES	1,005,000	14,969	-	-
SMELT:				
EULACHON	2,444,600	136,399	833,900	65,244
SURF OR SILVER	651,700	65,168	-	-
STEELHEAD TROUT.	198,300	27,320	852,100	119,331
STRIPED BASS	-	-	24,800	1,705
STURGEON	182,900	30,817	269,000	50,450
TUNA AND TUNALIKE FISHES:				
ALBACORE	4,433,900	789,381	6,327,000	1,104,142
SKIPJACK OR STRIPED.	-	-	1,941,800	269,227
YELLOWFIN.	-	-	5,571,100	807,868
TOTAL TUNA	4,433,900	789,381	13,839,900	2,181,237
TOTAL.	152,372,100	17,114,920	51,093,900	6,076,768

(CONTINUED ON NEXT PAGE)

CATCH BY STATES, 1949 - Continued

SPECIES	WASHINGTON		OREGON 1/	
SHELLFISH	POUNDS	VALUE	POUNDS	VALUE
CRABS, DUNGENESS	13,142,500	$1,331,859	9,346,500	$836,325
CRAWFISH, FRESH-WATER.	600	121	45,400	9,847
SHRIMP	67,100	16,774	-	-
CLAMS:				
HARD	373,800	114,156	-	-
RAZOR.	302,700	193,121	77,200	48,922
MIXED.	-	-	32,300	7,681
TOTAL CLAMS.	676,500	307,277	109,500	56,603
OCTOPUS.	47,300	2,362	-	-
OYSTERS, MARKET:				
PACIFIC.	7,634,600	1,741,207	501,100	85,904
WESTERN OR NATIVE.	203,000	278,400	-	-
TOTAL OYSTERS.	7,837,600	2,0 9,607	501,100	85,904
SCALLOPS, BAY.	16,500	9,986	-	-
SQUID.	600	42	-	-
TOTAL.	21,788,700	3,688,028	10,002,500	988,679
GRAND TO AL.	174, 60,800	20,802,948	61,096,400	7,065,447

SPECIES	CALIFORNIA 1/		TOTAL	
FISH - CONTINUED	POUNDS	VALUE	POUNDS	VALUE
ANCHOVIES.	3,322,300	$56,104	3,724,300	$62,204
BARRACUDA.	2,457,700	365,594	2,457,700	365,594
CABEZONE	16,000	530	16,000	530
CABRILLA	210,100	27,792	210,100	27,792
CARP	405,500	12,946	406,100	12,963
CATFISH.	201,700	38,566	201,700	38,566
COD.	-	-	6,250,700	231,266
FLOUNDERS:				
"CALIFORNIA HALIBUT"	1,256,400	236,997	1,256,400	236,997
"SOLE"	19,692,800	917,769	38,777,500	1,974,942
OTHER.	1,173,900	58,229	2,131,500	90,235
FLYINGFISH	34,300	2,652	34,300	2,652
GRAYFISH	(2)	(2)	14,067,900	738,892
GROUPERS	290,600	49,282	290,600	49,282
HAKE	-	-	141,600	710
HALIBUT.	167,300	33,457	14,242,400	2,556,103
HARDHEAD	17,400	4,904	17,400	4,904
HERRING, SEA	379,300	7,210	1,288,500	51,973
JACK MACKEREL.	51,250,100	1,111,123	51,250,100	1,111,123
KINGFISH	764,400	40,125	764,400	40,125
LAMPREY.	-	-	369,900	9,248
LINGCOD.	1,654,000	125,448	8,009,500	736,792
MACKEREL	49,771,300	1,285,892	49,771,300	1,285,892
MULLET	72,000	5,410	72,000	5,410
PERCH.	326,600	48,558	484,900	66,616
PILCHARD	633,475,000	10,756,897	633,540,400	10,760,235
POMPANO.	89,300	25,899	89,300	25,899
RATFISH.	-	-	1,471,600	13,344
ROCK BASS.	192,300	25,790	192,300	25,790
ROCKFISHES	5,937,600	331,101	23,957,600	1,097,264
SABLEFISH.	1,737,400	131,747	6,076,200	553,350
SALMON:				
CHINOOK OR KING.	6,429,700	1,509,303	25,512,300	5,285,671
CHUM OR KETA	-	-	5,939,600	714,243
PINK	-	-	44,214,800	4,421,459
RED OR SOCKEYE	-	-	7,050,400	1,503,035
SILVER OR COHO	-	-	13,133,500	2,108,681
TOTAL SALMON.	6,429,700	1,509,303	95,858,600	14,033,089
SCULPIN.	148,400	26,930	148,400	26,930
SEA BASS:				
BLACK.	114,400	16,160	114,400	16,160
WHITE.	1,409,600	290,864	1,409,600	290,864
SHAD	735,800	46,983	2,199,700	146,114
SHARKS	2/ 1,551,000	2/ 833,347	2,719,200	1,443,339
SHEEPSHEAD	61,600	4,389	61,600	4,389
SKATES	123,400	2,953	1,128,400	17,922
SMELT:				
EULACHON	-	-	3,278,500	201,643
SURF OR SILVER	712,000	51,681	1,363,700	116,849
SPANISH MACKEREL	3,700	308	3,700	308
STEELHEAD TROUT.	-	-	1,050,400	146,651
STRIPED BASS	-	-	24,800	1,786
STURGEON	-	-	451,900	81,273
SWORDFISH.	198,400	87,506	198,400	87,506

SEE FOOTNOTES AT END OF TABLE   (CONTINUED ON NEXT PAGE)

PACIFIC COAST STATES FISHERIES

CATCH BY STATES, 1949 - Continued

SPECIES	CALIFORNIA 1/		TOTAL	
FISH - CONTINUED	POUNDS	VALUE	POUNDS	VALUE
TUNA AND TUNALIKE FISHES:				
ALBACORE	44,033,500	$8,144,993	54,794,400	$10,038,516
BLUEFIN.	4,389,400	712,702	4,389,400	712,702
BONITO	1,829,500	178,181	1,829,500	178,181
SKIPJACK OR STRIPED.	78,570,400	11,653,994	80,512,200	11,923,221
YELLOWFIN.	184,972,300	30,191,412	190,543,400	30,999,280
TOTAL TUNA	313,795,100	50,881,282	332,068,900	53,851,900
WHITEBAIT.	241,800	23,690	241,800	23,690
WHITEFISH.	31,200	2,523	31,200	2,523
YELLOWTAIL	7,319,500	686,000	7,319,500	686,000
UNCLASSIFIED	241,800	19,208	241,800	19,208
TOTAL.	1,108,012,700	70,183,149	1,311,478,700	93,374,837
SHELLFISH				
CRABS:				
DUNGENESS.	3/11,116,300	3/ 1,294,239	33,605,300	3,462,423
ROCK	3/ 600	3/ 117	600	117
CRAWFISH, FRESH-WATER.	-	-	46,000	9,968
LOBSTERS, SPINY.	834,300	283,325	834,300	283,325
SHRIMP	804,400	49,127	871,500	65,901
ABALONE.	713,600	398,259	713,600	398,259
CLAMS:				
HARD	4/ 20,400	4/ 11,984	394,200	126,140
RAZOR.	-	-	379,900	242,043
MIXED.	-	-	32,300	7,681
TOTAL CLAMS.	20,400	11,984	806,400	375,864
OCTOPUS.	75,100	5,973	122,400	8,335
OYSTERS, MARKET:				
EASTERN.	6,500	4,654	6,500	4,654
PACIFIC.	28,200	21,744	8,163,900	1,848,855
WESTERN OR NATIVE.	-	-	203,000	278,400
TOTAL OYSTERS.	34,700	26,398	8,373,400	2,131,909
SCALLOPS, BAY.	-	-	16,500	9,986
SQUID.	6,859,100	184,173	6,859,700	184,215
TOTAL.	20,458,500	2,253,595	52,249,700	6,930,302
WHALE PRODUCTS				
LIVER.	28,000	8,000	28,000	8,000
MEAL:				
BONE	100,000	2,500	100,000	2,500
MEAT	100,000	5,000	100,000	5,000
OIL:				
WHALE.	209,600	13,975	209,600	13,975
SPERM.	352,500	38,500	352,500	38,500
TOTAL.	790,100	67,975	790,100	67,975
GRAND TOTAL.	1,129,261,300	72,504,719	1,364,518,500	100,373,114

1/ INCLUDES THE CATCH TAKEN OFF LATIN AMERICA.
2/ CATCH OF GRAYFISH IN CALIFORNIA IS INCLUDED WITH SHARKS.
3/ ROCK CRABS IN SAN PEDRO DISTRICT ARE INCLUDED WITH DUNGENESS CRABS.
4/ INCLUDES A SMALL QUANTITY OF MUSSELS.

NOTE:--PRIOR TO 1941, THE POUNDAGE OF HALIBUT, SABLEFISH, LINGCOD, AND ROCKFISHES REPORTED FOR WASHINGTON AND
OREGON REPRESENTED THE DRESSED WEIGHT OF THE FISH LANDED. BEGINNING WITH THE DATA FOR 1941, ALL CATCH
STATISTICS ARE SHOWN IN ROUND WEIGHTS. THE LANDED WEIGHT OF LINGCOD, SABLEFISH, AND ROCKFISHES (EXCEPT IN THE
OTTER TRAWL FISHERIES IN WHICH THE FISH ARE LANDED ROUND) WAS CONVERTED TO ROUND WEIGHT BY MULTIPLYING THE
DRESSED WEIGHT BY THE FACTOR 1.43. THE FACTOR USED TO CONVERT HALIBUT FROM MARKETED WEIGHT WAS 1.33. THE
POUNDAGE AND VALUE OF THE CATCH SHOWN FOR WASHINGTON AND OREGON INCLUDE 3,053,827 POUNDS OF FISH LIVERS AND
VISCERA, VALUED AT $2,064,806 TO THE FISHERMEN, COMPRISING THIS TOTAL WERE: COD LIVERS, 58,589 POUNDS,
$3,808; GRAYFISH LIVERS, 1,688,158 POUNDS, $718,165; HAKE LIVERS, 4,466 POUNDS, $670; HALIBUT LIVERS, 188,354
POUNDS, $231,368; LINGCOD LIVERS, 115,009 POUNDS, $237,633; RATFISH LIVERS, 78,581 POUNDS, $3,929; ROCKFISH
LIVERS, 11,997 POUNDS, $10,418; SABLEFISH LIVERS, 108,187 POUNDS, $124,337; SKATE LIVERS, 29,609 POUNDS,
$2,962; SOUPFIN SHARK LIVERS, 133,191 POUNDS, $608,907; OTHER SHARK LIVERS, 6,996 POUNDS, $944; AND HALIBUT,
LINGCOD, AND SABLEFISH VISCERA, 630,690 POUNDS, $121,665. SIMILAR DATA FOR CALIFORNIA ARE NOT AVAILABLE.
MOST OF THE CARCASSES OF DOGFISH AND SOUPFIN SHARK WERE NOT LANDED, BUT WERE DISCARDED AT SEA AFTER REMOVAL
OF THE LIVERS. A PORTION OF THE TUNA CATCH TAKEN OFF LATIN AMERICA BY UNITED STATES FISHERMEN, WHICH IS
INCLUDED IN THIS TABLE, MAY ALSO BE INCLUDED IN U. S. IMPORT STATISTICS.

MANUFACTURED FISHERY PRODUCTS, VARIOUS YEARS 1/

ITEM	YEAR	UNIT	WASHINGTON		OREGON		CALIFORNIA	
			QUANTITY	VALUE	QUANTITY	VALUE	QUANTITY	VALUE
BY MANUFACTURING ESTABLISHMENTS:								
ANCHOVIES, CANNED...	1949	STD. CASES	(2)	(2)	-	-	3,612	$30,184
BARRACUDA:								
SALTED, DRY.....	1940	POUNDS	-	-	-	-	19,465	2,433
SMOKED......	1940	DO	-	-	-	-	1,000	200
CHUB, SMOKED.....	1940	DO	-	-	-	-	40,000	18,000
COD:								
FRESH FILLETS....	1949	DO	1,285,942	$183,761	(2)	(2)	-	-
FROZEN FILLETS...	1949	DO	449,029	84,294	(2)	(2)	-	-
SALTED:								
DRY.......	1940	DO	2,163,507	168,444	-	-	357,010	50,764
BONELESS AND ABSOLUTELY BONELESS	1940	DO	655,518	106,215	-	-	318,018	65,489
FLOUNDERS:								
FRESH FILLETS....	1949	DO	2,635,727	649,282	103,596	$24,681	575,429	140,516
FROZEN FILLETS...	1949	DO	1,188,759	328,477	1,927,300	514,956	1,752,315	479,438
HALIBUT:								
FRESH FILLETS....	1949	DO	11,865	4,709	-	-	-	-
FROZEN FILLETS...	1949	DO	157,862	64,258	(2)	(2)	(2)	(2)
FROZEN STEAKS....	1949	DO	3,393,148	1,275,077	(2)	(2)	(2)	(2)
HERRING:								
SPICED.......	1940	DO	18,890	2,614	-	-	-	-
SMOKED BLOATERS...	1940	DO	66,000	5,359	-	-	4,406	660
JEWFISH FILLETS,								
DRY SALTED.....	1940	DO	-	-	-	-	8,857	1,107
LINGCOD:								
FRESH FILLETS....	1949	DO	553,106	93,835	5,016	796	(2)	(2)
FROZEN FILLETS...	1949	DO	465,678	90,256	74,621	15,928	(2)	(2)
FROZEN STEAKS....	1949	DO	253,450	44,427	10,164	1,220	-	-
MACKEREL:								
CANNED.......	1949	STD. CASES	-	-	-	-	916,810	5,766,415
SALTED, DRY.....	1940	POUNDS	-	-	-	-	8,548	598
PILCHARDS:								
CANNED.......	1949	STD. CASES	-	-	-	-	3,768,212	21,334,825
SALTED, DRY.....	1940	POUNDS	-	-	-	-	9,683	968
MEAL........	1949	TONS	-	-	-	-	39,278	6,219,717
OIL.........	1949	GALLONS	-	-	-	-	6,123,140	2,872,532
ROCKFISHES:								
FRESH FILLETS....	1949	POUNDS	2,854,100	400,986	172,642	23,054	(2)	(2)
FROZEN FILLETS...	1949	DO	936,789	148,280	737,282	130,210	(2)	(2)
SABLEFISH:								
FROZEN FILLETS AND STEAKS.......	1949	DO	61,381	15,730	(2)	(2)	(2)	(2)
SALTED.......	1940	DO	58,090	3,281	-	-	-	-
KIPPERED......	1940	DO	223,373	37,855	-	-	390,496	80,116
SALMON:								
FROZEN STEAKS....	1949	DO	1,374,641	573,255	(2)	(2)	(2)	(2)
CANNED:								
CHINOOK OR KING..	1949	STD. CASES	33,890	752,595	122,858	3,763,967	1,113	21,240
CHUM OR KETA...	1949	DO	208,855	3,023,655	10,797	167,791	-	-
PINK......	1949	DO	553,967	8,832,216	-	-	-	-
RED OR SOCKEYE...	1949	DO	107,460	3,407,135	341	12,166	-	-
SILVER OR COHO..	1949	DO	69,548	1,465,681	15,595	477,791	-	-
STEEL HEADTROUT..	1949	DO	-	-	8,881	243,575	-	-
TOTAL CANNED SALMON....	-	DO	973,740	17,481,282	158,472	4,665,290	1,113	21,240
EGGS FOR BAIT, CANNED......	1949	DO	10,719	275,744	-	-	-	-
SALTED:								
MILD CURED....	1940	POUNDS	3,414,675	707,633	27,225	5,296	848,610	173,412
HARD SALTED....	1940	DO	-	-	-	-	28,000	4,200
BELLIES......	1940	DO	7,600	520	-	-	-	-
EGGS FOR CAVIAR..	1940	DO	291,518	26,856	-	-	-	-
SMOKED......	1940	DO	400,249	66,464	41,012	12,853	362,039	148,386
KIPPERED......	1940	DO	1,118,013	224,380	62,270	7,771	2,000	560
OIL:								
EDIBLE......	1949	GALLONS	-	-	14,652	25,716	-	-
INDUSTRIAL....	1949	DO	85,800	36,116	-	-	-	-
SEA BASS, DRY SALTED.	1940	POUNDS	-	-	-	-	11,531	1,441
SHAD:								
CANNED......	1949	STD. CASES	(2)	(2)	12,159	91,667	(2)	(2)
SHAD ROE......	1949	DO	(2)	(2)	3,049	208,684	(2)	(2)
SHARK-LIVER OIL....	1949	GALLONS	226,840	2,100,472	(2)	(2)	117,071	1,889,890

SEE FOOTNOTES AT END OF TABLE   (CONTINUED ON NEXT PAGE)

PACIFIC COAST STATES FISHERIES

MANUFACTURED FISHERY PRODUCTS, VARIOUS YEARS 1/ - Continued

ITEM	YEAR	UNIT	WASHINGTON QUANTITY	WASHINGTON VALUE	OREGON QUANTITY	OREGON VALUE	CALIFORNIA QUANTITY	CALIFORNIA VALUE
BY MANUFACTURING ESTABLISHMENTS - CONTINUED:								
STURGEON:								
CANNED, SMOKED AND KIPPERED.	1949	STD. CASES	118	$9,236	245	$11,083	-	-
KIPPERED	1940	POUNDS	-	-	1,588	349	-	-
ROE, SALTED.	1940	DO	60	120	-	-	-	-
TUNA AND TUNALIKE FISHES:								
CANNED, SOLID, FLAKES, AND GRATED:								
TUNA:								
ALBACORE	1949	STD. CASES	3/107,754	3/1,414,288	3/539,964	3/7,788,229	1,022,957	$15,471,412
YELLOWFIN. . . .	1949	DO	-	-	(3)	(3)	3,753,906	49,273,930
BLUEFIN.	1949	DO	-	-	-	-	76,877	999,642
SKIPJACK	1949	DO	(3)	(3)	(3)	(3)	4/1,384,019	4/17,708,064
TONNC.	1949	DO	-	-	-	-	168,642	2,579,943
TOTAL TUNA . .	1949	DO	107,754	1,414,288	539,964	7,788,229	6,406,401	86,032,991
TUNALIKE FISHES:								
BONITO	1949	DO	-	-	-	-	33,734	365,444
YELLOWTAIL . . .	1949	DO	-	-	-	-	126,133	1,305,084
TOTAL TUNALIKE FISHES. . . .	1949	DO	-	-	-	-	159,867	1,670,528
TOTAL TUNA AND TUNALIKE FISHES	1949	DO	107,754	1,414,288	539,964	7,788,229	6,566,268	87,703,519
DRY SALTED	1940	POUNDS	-	-	-	-	140,828	17,513
KIPPERED	1940	DO	-	-	818	164	-	-
WHITEFISH, SMOKED. . .	1940	POUNDS	-	-	-	-	7,000	3,150
ABALONE STEAKS	1940	DO	-	-	-	-	333,991	126,716
CLAMS:								
RAZOR, MINCED, CANNED	1949	STD. CASES	3,704	72,075	(2)	(2)	-	-
HARD, CANNED:								
WHOLE AND MINCED .	1949	DO	22,668	276,835	-	-	(2)	(2)
NECTAR	1949	DO	4,088	15,753	-	-	-	-
HARD, FRESH-SHUCKED.	1940	GALLONS	2,406	3,580	-	-	-	-
CRABS, DUNGENESS:								
CANNED:								
NATURAL.	1949	STD. CASES	55,004	1,434,938	36,419	829,318	(2)	(2)
COCKTAILS.	1949	DO	221	6,632	323	9,685	-	-
MEAT, FRESH-COOKED .	1940	POUNDS	337,351	119,320	939,695	254,170	103,272	38,947
OYSTERS:								
CANNED:								
NATURAL.	1949	STD. CASES	109,141	1,709,096	(2)	(2)	-	-
SMOKED	1949	DO	1,977	176,396	-	-	-	-
COCKTAILS.	1949	DO	46	1,336	-	-	-	-
STEW AND SPREAD. .	1949	DO	2,603	46,150	-	-	-	-
FRESH-SHUCKED:								
EASTERN.	1940	GALLONS	-	-	154	385	-	-
PACIFIC.	1940	DO	344,755	430,408	114,970	138,669	18,677	30,584
WESTERN OR NATIVE.	1940	DO	14,667	109,264	9,322	68,920	4,178	37,602
SCALLOPS, BAY, FRESH-SHUCKED	1940	GALLONS	1,860	5,580	-	-	-	-
SHRIMP COCKTAILS, CANNED.	1949	STD. CASES	110	3,190	295	8,872	-	-
SQUID, CANNED.	1949	STD. CASES	-	-	-	-	85,999	341,232
WHALE:								
SPERM OIL.	1949	GALLONS	-	-	-	-	47,000	38,500
OTHER OIL.	1949	DO	-	-	-	-	27,950	13,975
MEAL		TONS	-	-	-	-	117	16,088
ANIMAL FOOD.	1949	DO	(2)	(2)	-	-	896,489	4,222,300
FISH SOLUBLES.	1949	DO	-	-	-	-	45,012,840	2,248,071
UNCLASSIFIED PRODUCTS:								
PACKAGED FISH. . . .	1949	POUNDS	-	-	5/88,060	5/33,600	6/727,919	6/141,982
CANNED FISH. . . .	1949	STD. CASES	7/19,379	7/86,280	9/5,257	9/70,689	9/6,503	9/77,750,
BYPRODUCTS:								
MEAL	1949	TONS	10/2,538	10/333,466	11/1,862	11/226,390	12/20,991	12/3,273,909
OIL AND LIVER OIL.	1949	GALLONS	13/162,259	13/3,691,732	(14)	(14)	15/665,474	15/913,636
MISCELLANEOUS PRODUCTS.	1949	-	-	16/56,650	-	17/104,215	-	18/4,226,792
TOTAL.		-	-	35,202,187	-	15,272,860	-	142,775,359

SEE FOOTNOTES ON NEXT PAGE

(CONTINUED ON NEXT PAGE)

MANUFACTURED FISHERY PRODUCTS, VARIOUS YEARS 1/ - Continued

1/ DATA ON THE PRODUCTION OF THE DIFFERENT PRODUCTS ARE FOR THE YEARS INDICATED.
2/ THIS ITEM HAS BEEN INCLUDED UNDER "UNCLASSIFIED PRODUCTS".
3/ THE PRODUCTION OF YELLOWFIN HAS BEEN INCLUDED WITH THE ALBACORE PRODUCTION IN WASHINGTON AND THE PRODUCTION OF YELLOWFIN AND SKIPJACK IN THE ALBACORE PRODUCTION OF OREGON.
4/ INCLUDES A SMALL PRODUCTION OF LITTLE TUNA.
5/ INCLUDES FRESH OR FROZEN COD, HALIBUT, ROCKFISH, SABLEFISH, AND UNCLASSIFIED FILLETS; AND HALIBUT AND SABLEFISH STEAKS.
6/ INCLUDES FRESH OR FROZEN HALIBUT, LINGCOD, ROCKFISH, SABLEFISH AND SMELT FILLETS; AND HALIBUT AND SABLEFISH STEAKS.
7/ INCLUDES CANNED ANCHOVIES, SMOKED SALMON, SHAD, SMOKED SHAD, SHAD ROE, SMOKED CRAB MEAT, AND ANIMAL FOOD.
8/ INCLUDES CANNED KIPPERED SALMON, SMOKED STEELHEAD, KIPPERED SHAD, RAZOR CLAMS, AND OYSTERS.
9/ INCLUDES CANNED MULLET, SHAD, SHAD ROE, FISH CAKES, PISMO CLAMS, AND CRAB MEAT.
10/ INCLUDES SALMON, CRAB, AND UNCLASSIFIED MEAL.
11/ INCLUDES TUNA, CRAB AND UNCLASSIFIED MEAL.
12/ INCLUDES ANCHOVY, SHARK, TUNA AND MACKEREL, CRAB, SQUID, AND UNCLASSIFIED MEAL.
13/ INCLUDES TUNA AND UNCLASSIFIED BODY OIL; TUNA AND MISCELLANEOUS LIVER OIL, AND VISCERA OIL.
14/ THIS ITEM HAS BEEN INCLUDED WITH MISCELLANEOUS PRODUCTS.
15/ INCLUDES ANCHOVY, TUNA, MACKEREL AND UNCLASSIFIED BODY OIL; AND TUNA, WHALE AND UNCLASSIFIED LIVER OIL.
16/ INCLUDES CLAM AND OYSTER-SHELL GRIT AND OYSTER-SHELL LIME.
17/ INCLUDES TUNA, AND UNCLASSIFIED BODY OIL; LINGCOD, ROCKFISH, SOLE, AND SHARK LIVER OIL; VISCERA OIL; AND OYSTER-SHELL GRIT AND LIME.
18/ INCLUDES OYSTER-SHELL LIME AND GRIT, AGAR AGAR, GLUE, AND KELP PRODUCTS.

NOTE:--SOME OF THE ABOVE PRODUCTS MAY HAVE BEEN IMPORTED FROM ANOTHER STATE OR A FOREIGN COUNTRY; THEREFORE THEY CANNOT BE CORRELATED DIRECTLY WITH THE CATCH WITHIN THE STATE.

SUMMARY OF MANUFACTURED FISHERY PRODUCTS, VARIOUS YEARS

ITEM	YEAR	UNIT	QUANTITY	VALUE
PACKAGED FISH	1949	POUNDS	21,795,821	$5,463,008
CANNED FISH AND SHELLFISH . . .	1949	STANDARD CASES	14,322,461	156,190,213
FISHERY BYPRODUCTS.	1949	-	-	28,287,867
PACKAGED SHELLFISH.	1940	POUNDS	5,185,463	1,364,145
SALTED, DRIED AND PICKLED FISH.	1940	DO	8,378,743	1,336,290
SMOKED AND KIPPERED FISH. . . .	1940	DO	2,739,154	608,883
TOTAL	-	-	-	193,250,406

WASHINGTON

CATCH BY DISTRICTS, 1949

SPECIES	PUGET SOUND DISTRICT		COASTAL DISTRICT		COLUMBIA RIVER DISTRICT	
FISH	POUNDS	VALUE	POUNDS	VALUE	POUNDS	VALUE
ANCHOVIES.	-	-	402,000	$6,100	-	-
COD.	6,243,400	$231,007	1,900	71	-	-
FLOUNDERS:						
"SOLE"	9,776,800	592,473	29,300	1,467	16,700	$836
OTHER.	557,100	22,284	2,900	81	4,900	100
GRAYFISH 1/.	10,587,000	447,828	58,200	2,793	-	-
HAKE	64,200	239	-	-	-	-
HALIBUT.	13,455,600	2,422,020	8,900	1,396	1,000	182
HERRING, SEA	838,600	41,926	1,200	61	-	-
LINGCOD.	5,091,100	480,579	298,800	29,338	26,700	3,000
PERCH.	145,300	16,707	5,300	582	-	-
PILCHARD	56,400	3,104	-	-	-	-
RATFISH.	1,471,600	13,344	-	-	-	-
ROCKFISHES	13,014,100	583,136	136,600	4,591	95,300	3,811
SABLEFISH.	3,778,300	376,529	-	-	6,000	619
SALMON:						
CHINOOK OR KING.	4,107,900	997,546	2,000,000	496,030	3,481,300	613,912
CHUM OR KETA	4,290,800	562,996	658,800	52,046	263,200	21,056
PINK	44,196,700	4,419,659	17,500	1,744	600	56
RED OR SOCKEYE	6,164,600	1,232,930	869,900	265,311	11,100	2,223
SILVER OR COHO	6,886,400	1,121,257	2,879,500	543,404	763,100	100,102
SHAD	2,600	194	-	-	69,300	4,643
SHARKS:						
SOUPFIN.	569,900	307,783	1,800	950	-	-
OTHER.	45,500	820	-	-	-	-
SKATE.	1,005,000	14,969	-	-	-	-
SMELT:						
EULACHON	-	-	-	-	2,444,600	136,399
SURF OR SILVER	115,500	11,554	536,200	53,614	-	-
STEELHEAD TROUT.	22,400	3,070	133,700	18,310	42,200	5,940
STURGEON	13,400	1,894	22,600	3,164	146,900	25,759
TUNA, ALBACORE	943,800	167,998	3,343,400	595,128	146,700	26,255
TOTAL	133,444,000	14,093,846	11,408,500	2,076,181	7,519,600	944,893
SHELLFISH						
CRABS.	1,355,100	162,618	10,837,400	1,083,740	950,000	85,501
CRAWFISH	-	-	-	-	600	121
SHRIMP	67,100	16,774	-	-	-	-
CLAMS:						
HARD:						
BUTTER	68,000	16,308	-	-	-	-
LITTLE NECK.	305,400	97,731	400	117	-	-
RAZOR.	-	-	302,700	193,121	-	-
OCTOPUS.	47,300	2,362	-	-	-	-
OYSTERS, MARKET:						
PACIFIC.	2,286,900	521,405	5,347,700	1,219,802	-	-
WESTERN OR NATIVE.	203,000	278,400	-	-	-	-
SCALLOPS, BAY.	16,500	9,986	-	-	-	-
SQUID.	600	42	-	-	-	-
TOTAL	4,349,900	1,105,626	16,488,200	2,496,780	950,600	85,622
GRAND TOTAL	137,793,900	15,199,472	27,896,700	4,572,961	8,470,200	1,030,515

1/ CAUGHT ALMOST ENTIRELY FOR UTILIZATION OF THE LIVERS IN THE EXTRACTION OF VITAMIN OILS. MOST OF THE CARCASSES WERE DISCARDED.

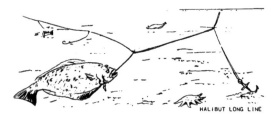

HALIBUT LONG LINE

PUGET SOUND DISTRICT OF WASHINGTON: OPERATING UNITS, 1949 [1]

ITEM	PURSE SEINES, SALMON	HAUL SEINES	GILL NETS — SALMON DRIFT	GILL NETS — SALMON SET [2]	GILL NETS — SHARK	LINES — TRAWL, SET AND HAND	LINES — TROLL SALMON
	NUMBER	NUMBER	NUMBER	NUMBER	NUMBER	NUMBER	NUMBER
FISHERMEN:							
ON VESSELS.	2,321	-	89	-	221	1,260	702
ON BOATS AND SHORE. . .	68	342	671	55	135	133	460
TOTAL.	2,389	342	760	55	356	1,393	1,162
VESSELS, MOTOR.	283	-	57	-	62	198	364
NET TONNAGE	6,904	-	472	-	1,538	6,062	3,988
BOATS:							
MOTOR	13	103	540	37	110	96	345
OTHER	-	32	44	18	4	12	-
ACCESSORY BOATS	296	-	-	-	-	-	-
APPARATUS:							
NUMBER.	296	135	641	55	1,535	31,618	3,564
LENGTH, YARDS	185,000	12,800	-	-	-	-	-
SQUARE YARDS.	-	-	1,121,750	13,000	1,262,250	-	-
HOOKS	-	-	-	-	-	639,652	17,820

ITEM	LINES—CONT'D TROLL—CONT'D TUNA [3]	POUND NETS [2]	BRUSH WEIRS	DIP NETS	REEF NETS	BEAM TRAWLS	OTTER TRAWLS
	NUMBER	NUMBER	NUMBER	NUMBER	NUMBER	NUMBER	NUMBER
FISHERMEN:							
ON VESSELS.	410	-	-	-	-	6	704
ON BOATS AND SHORE. . .	-	24	4	38	548	8	-
TOTAL.	410	24	4	38	548	14	704
VESSELS, MOTOR.	99	-	-	-	-	2	162
NET TONNAGE	3,402	-	-	-	-	18	5,140
BOATS:							
MOTOR	-	7	1	13	-	4	-
OTHER	-	-	-	6	274	-	-
APPARATUS:							
NUMBER.	605	7	1	38	137	6	162
YARDS AT MOUTH.	-	-	-	-	-	55	2,400
HOOKS	605	-	-	-	-	-	-

ITEM	TRAPS — CRAB	TRAPS — OCTOPUS	TRAPS — SHRIMP	DREDGES, OYSTER	TONGS AND BY HAND, OYSTER	SHOVELS	TOTAL, EXCLUSIVE OF DUPLICATION
	NUMBER	NUMBER	NUMBER	NUMBER	NUMBER	NUMBER	NUMBER
FISHERMEN:							
ON VESSELS.	43	2	-	6	-	-	4,672
ON BOATS AND SHORE. . .	160	6	8	2	125	375	2,742
TOTAL.	203	8	8	8	125	375	7,414
VESSELS, MOTOR.	18	1	-	2	-	-	956
NET TONNAGE	247	13	-	45	-	-	20,085
BOATS:							
MOTOR	148	4	8	1	26	-	1,266
OTHER	8	1	-	-	10	-	394
ACCESSORY BOATS	-	-	-	-	-	-	308
APPARATUS:							
NUMBER.	18,300	350	250	6	35	375	-
YARDS AT MOUTH.	-	-	-	12	-	-	-

1/ STATISTICS IN THIS TABLE INCLUDE ALL CRAFT OPERATING IN THE STATE MAKING THEIR HOME PORT IN THIS DISTRICT, AND ALL CRAFT OPERATING IN THE STATE WHOSE HOME PORT IS NOT WITHIN THE STATE BUT WHO LANDED THE MAJOR PORTION OF THEIR WASHINGTON CATCH IN THIS DISTRICT.
2/ FISHED ONLY ON INDIAN RESERVATIONS.
3/ INCLUDES ONLY VESSELS THAT TROLLED OR FISHED EXCLUSIVELY FOR TUNA AND DID NOT TROLL FOR SALMON. MANY OF THE SALMON TROLLERS ALSO TROLLED FOR TUNA.

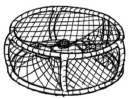

PACIFIC COAST CRAB POT

PUGET SOUND DISTRICT OF WASHINGTON: CATCH BY GEAR, 1949

SPECIES	PURSE SEINES POUNDS	VALUE	HAUL SEINES 1/ POUNDS	VALUE	GILL NETS SALMON DRIFT POUNDS	VALUE	GILL NETS SALMON SET 3/ POUNDS	VALUE
FISH								
COD	-	-	100	$3	-	-	-	-
FLOUNDERS:								
"SOLE"	100	$6	200	12	-	-	-	-
OTHER	1,000	39	800	34	100	$4	-	-
GRAYFISH 2/	1,500	62	1,600	68	74,600	3,157	7,400	$24
HAKE	-	-	-	-	-	-	-	-
HERRING, SEA	5,000	252	647,800	32,390	-	-	-	-
LINGCOD	200	10	-	-	300	14	-	-
PERCH	500	56	140,900	16,201	-	-	-	-
PILCHARD	-	-	56,400	3,104	-	-	-	-
ROCKFISHES	-	-	4,500	196	-	-	-	-
SALMON:								
CHINOOK OR KING	540,100	67,515	18,900	2,364	439,100	96,163	20,600	2,576
CHUM OR KETA	3,078,700	421,782	40,600	5,405	710,800	94,533	267,200	35,542
PINK	33,328,700	3,332,867	521,000	52,095	6,804,200	680,420	-	-
RED OR SOCKEYE	4,886,500	977,306	-	-	790,300	158,065	-	-
SILVER OR COHO	3,422,600	431,243	9,300	1,171	1,217,400	254,438	61,500	7,746
SMELT, SURF OR SILVER	3,400	340	112,100	11,214	-	-	-	-
STEELHEAD TROUT 3/	-	-	-	-	-	-	22,400	3,070
TOTAL	45,268,300	5,231,478	1,554,200	124,257	10,036,800	1,286,794	379,100	48,958
SHELLFISH								
SQUID	-	-	600	42	-	-	-	-
OCTOPUS	-	-	1,200	61	-	-	-	-
TOTAL	-	-	1,800	103	-	-	-	-
GRAND TOTAL	45,268,300	5,231,478	1,556,000	124,360	10,036,800	1,286,794	379,100	48,958

SPECIES	GILL NETS – CONT'D SHARK POUNDS	VALUE	LINES TRAWL, SET AND HAND POUNDS	VALUE	LINES TROLL POUNDS	VALUE	POUND NETS 3/ POUNDS	VALUE
FISH								
COD	1,600	$60	7,800	$290	3,900	$144	-	-
FLOUNDERS, "SOLE"	800	49	7,800	474	3,900	234	-	-
GRAYFISH 2/	2,042,700	86,405	754,400	31,912	6,200	260	-	-
HALIBUT	-	-	13,379,000	2,408,229	76,600	13,791	-	-
LINGCOD	76,700	9,349	822,500	100,348	670,700	81,822	-	-
RATFISH	23,900	179	1,500	12	-	-	-	-
ROCKFISHES	12,900	861	431,400	28,905	50,100	2,507	-	-
SABLEFISH	400	45	3,092,100	327,763	31,400	3,324	-	-
SALMON:								
CHINOOK OR KING	-	-	-	-	2,894,000	804,533	65,400	$8,176
CHUM OR KETA	-	-	-	-	-	-	12,400	1,650
PINK	-	-	-	-	80,200	8,018	279,500	27,950
RED OR SOCKEYE	-	-	-	-	-	-	12,500	2,492
SILVER OR COHO	-	-	-	-	1,860,300	386,941	64,800	8,159
SHARKS:								
SOUPFIN 2/	530,300	286,376	22,000	11,907	-	-	-	-
OTHER 2/	12,500	225	22,600	407	1,600	29	-	-
SKATE	1,200	47	1,700	71	-	-	-	-
STURGEON	-	-	600	84	-	-	-	-
TUNA, ALBACORE	-	-	-	-	943,800	167,998	-	-
TOTAL	2,703,000	383,596	18,543,400	2,910,402	6,622,700	1,469,601	434,600	48,427
SHELLFISH								
OCTOPUS	400	20	1,300	64	300	13	-	-
TOTAL	400	20	1,300	64	300	13	-	-
GRAND TOTAL	2,703,400	383,616	18,544,700	2,910,466	6,623,000	1,469,614	434,600	48,427

SPECIES	BRUSH WEIRS POUNDS	VALUE	DIP NETS POUNDS	VALUE	REEF NETS POUNDS	VALUE	BEAM TRAWLS POUNDS	VALUE	OTTER TRAWLS POUNDS	VALUE
FISH										
COD	-	-	-	-	-	-	-	-	6,230,000	$230,510
FLOUNDERS:										
"SOLE"	-	-	-	-	-	-	-	-	9,764,000	591,698
OTHER	-	-	-	-	-	-	-	-	555,200	22,207
GRAYFISH 2/	-	-	-	-	-	-	-	-	7,706,000	325,964
HAKE	-	-	-	-	-	-	-	-	56,800	215
HERRING, SEA	173,800	$8,688	11,800	$588	-	-	-	-	200	8
LINGCOD	-	-	-	-	-	-	-	-	3,520,600	289,031
PERCH	-	-	-	-	-	-	-	-	3,900	450
RATFISH	-	-	-	-	-	-	-	-	1,446,200	13,153
ROCKFISHES	-	-	-	-	-	-	-	-	12,515,200	550,667

SEE FOOTNOTES AT END OF TABLE   (CONTINUED ON NEXT PAGE)

PUGET SOUND DISTRICT OF WASHINGTON: CATCH BY GEAR, 1949 - Continued

SPECIES	BRUSH WEIRS		DIP NETS		REEF NETS		BEAM TRAWLS		OTTER TRAWLS	
	POUNDS	VALUE	POUNDS	VALUE	POUNDS	VALUE	POUNDS	VALUE	POUNDS	VALUE
FISH - CONTINUED										
SABLEFISH	-	-	-	-	-	-	-	-	654,400	$45,397
SALMON:										
CHINOOK OR KING . . .	-	-	-	-	129,800	$16,219	-	-	-	-
CHUM OR KETA.	-	-	-	-	181,100	24,084	-	-	-	-
PINK.	-	-	-	-	3,183,100	318,309	-	-	-	-
RED OR SOCKEYE. . . .	-	-	-	-	475,300	95,067	-	-	-	-
SILVER OR COHO. . . .	-	-	-	-	250,500	31,559	-	-	-	-
SHAD.	-	-	-	-	-	-	-	-	2,600	194
SHARKS:										
SOUPFIN 2/.	-	-	-	-	-	-	-	-	17,600	9,500
OTHER 2/.	-	-	-	-	-	-	-	-	8,800	159
SKATE	-	-	-	-	-	-	-	-	1,002,100	14,851
STURGEON.	-	-	-	-	-	-	-	-	12,800	1,810
TOTAL	173,800	$8,688	11,800	$588	4,219,800	485,238	-	-	43,496,400	2,095,814
SHELLFISH										
SHRIMP.	-	-	-	-	-	-	23,500	$5,866	-	-
OCTOPUS	-	-	-	-	-	-	-	-	18,800	939
SCALLOPS 7/	-	-	-	-	-	-	16,500	9,986	-	-
TOTAL	-	-	-	-	-	-	40,000	15,852	18,800	939
GRAND TOTAL . . .	173,800	8,688	11,800	588	4,219,800	485,238	40,000	15,852	43,515,200	2,096,753

SPECIES	TRAPS						DREDGES, TONGS, AND BY HAND		SHOVELS	
	CRAB		OCTOPUS		SHRIMP					
	POUNDS	VALUE	POUNDS	VALUE	POUNDS	VALUE	POUNDS	VALUE	POUNDS	VALUE
FISH										
LINGCOD	100	$5	-	-	-	-	-	-	-	-
TOTAL	100	5	-	-	-	-	-	-	-	-
SHELLFISH										
CRABS 4/.	1,355,100	162,618	-	-	-	-	-	-	-	-
SHRIMP.	-	-	-	-	43,600	$10,908	-	-	-	-
CLAMS, HARD: 5/										
BUTTER.	-	-	-	-	-	-	-	-	68,000	$16,308
LITTLE NECK	-	-	-	-	-	-	-	-	305,400	97,731
OCTOPUS	-	-	25,300	$1,265	-	-	-	-	-	-
OYSTERS, MARKET 6/:										
PACIFIC	-	-	-	-	-	-	2,286,900	$521,405	-	-
WESTERN	-	-	-	-	-	-	203,000	278,400	-	-
TOTAL	1,355,100	162,618	25,300	1,265	43,600	10,908	2,489,900	799,805	373,400	114,039
GRAND TOTAL . . .	1,355,200	162,623	25,300	1,265	43,600	10,908	2,489,900	799,805	373,400	114,039

1/ THE SALMON CAUGHT BY HAUL SEINES WERE TAKEN ONLY BY INDIANS ON RESERVATIONS.
2/ CAUGHT ALMOST ENTIRELY FOR THE UTILIZATION OF THE LIVERS IN THE EXTRACTION OF VITAMIN OILS. MOST OF THE CARCASSES WERE DISCARDED.
3/ FISHED ONLY ON INDIAN RESERVATIONS.
4/ THE WEIGHT OF CRABS SHOWN IS BASED ON AN AVERAGE OF 22 POUNDS PER DOZEN.
5/ THE STATISTICS ON HARD CLAMS ARE BASED ON YIELDS OF 25 PERCENT OF EDIBLE MEAT.
6/ THE STATISTICS ON OYSTERS ARE BASED ON 18 PERCENT EDIBLE MEATS FOR NATIVE OYSTERS AND 10 PERCENT FOR PACIFIC OYSTERS.
7/ THE WEIGHTS OF BAY SCALLOPS ARE BASED ON 8.5 POUNDS PER GALLON WHEN SHUCKED.
NOTE:--THE QUANTITIES SHOWN REPRESENT THE ROUND WEIGHT OF THE CATCH OF FISH AND SHELLFISH EXCEPT FOR BIVALVE MOLLUSKS, WHICH ARE REPORTED IN POUNDS OF MEATS. THE POUNDAGE AND VALUE OF THE CATCH SHOWN ABOVE INCLUDES THE FOLLOWING ITEMS OF LIVERS AND VISCERA: COD LIVERS, 58,534 POUNDS, VALUE $3,805; GRAYFISH LIVERS, 1,270,434 POUNDS, VALUE $444,652; HAKE LIVERS, 1,988 POUNDS, VALUE $199; HALIBUT LIVERS, 180,083 POUNDS, VALUE $225,104; LINGCOD LIVERS 92,203 POUNDS, VALUE $184,406; RATFISH LIVERS, 78,581 POUNDS, VALUE $3,929; ROCKFISH LIVERS 9,347 POUNDS, VALUE $9,347; SABLEFISH LIVERS, 93,714 POUNDS, VALUE $112,457; SKATE LIVERS, 29,609 POUNDS, VALUE $2,962; SOUPFIN SHARK LIVERS 68,396 POUNDS, VALUE $307,783; OTHER SHARK LIVERS, 5,460 POUNDS, VALUE $820, AND, HALIBUT, LINGCOD AND SABLEFISH VISCERA 570,886 POUNDS, VALUE $113,439.

COASTAL DISTRICT OF WASHINGTON: OPERATING UNITS, 1949 1/

ITEM	HAUL SEINES	GILL NETS		SHARK	TRAWL OR SET	LINES	
		SALMON				TROLL	
		DRIFT	SET 2/			SALMON	TUNA 3/
	NUMBER	NUMBER	NUMBER	NUMBER	NUMBER	NUMBER	NUMBER
FISHERMEN:							
ON VESSELS	-	7	-	8	4	494	112
ON BOATS AND SHORE . . .	12	308	200	2	-	253	7
TOTAL	12	315	200	10	4	747	119
VESSELS, MOTOR	-	5	-	3	1	241	41
NET TONNAGE	-	46	-	75	8	2,556	828
BOATS:							
MOTOR	2	284	65	1	-	172	3
OTHER	2	15	118	-	-	-	-
APPARATUS:							
NUMBER	4	304	200	110	40	2,138	264
LENGTH, YARDS	400	-	-	-	-	-	-
SQUARE YARDS	-	516,500	44,000	90,000	-	-	-
HOOKS	-	-	-	-	800	10,512	264

ITEM	DIP NETS	OTTER TRAWLS	TRAPS, CRAB	TONGS, AND BY HAND, OYSTER	DREDGES, OYSTER 4/	SHOVELS	TOTAL, EXCLUSIVE OF DUPLICATION
	NUMBER	NUMBER	NUMBER	NUMBER	NUMBER	NUMBER	NUMBER
FISHERMEN:							
ON VESSELS	-	32	229	-	54	-	830
ON BOATS AND SHORE . . .	54	-	35	180	15	2,750	3,566
TOTAL	54	32	264	180	69	2,750	4,396
VESSELS, MOTOR	-	8	82	-	18	-	337
NET TONNAGE	-	208	1,083	-	320	-	4,322
BOATS:							
MOTOR	15	-	23	56	6	-	558
OTHER	8	-	-	107	-	-	246
APPARATUS:							
NUMBER	54	8	19,550	75	47	2,750	-
YARDS AT MOUTH . . .	-	120	-	-	94	-	-

1/ STATISTICS IN THIS TABLE INCLUDE ALL CRAFT OPERATING IN THE STATE MAKING THEIR HOME PORT IN THIS DISTRICT, AND ALL CRAFT OPERATING IN THE STATE WHOSE HOME PORT IS NOT WITHIN THE STATE BUT WHO LANDED THE MAJOR PORTION OF THEIR WASHINGTON CATCH IN THIS DISTRICT.
2/ FISHED ONLY ON INDIAN RESERVATIONS.
3/ INCLUDES ONLY VESSELS THAT TROLLED OR FISHED EXCLUSIVELY FOR TUNA AND DID NOT TROLL FOR SALMON. MANY OF THE SALMON TROLLERS ALSO TROLLED FOR TUNA.
4/ INCLUDES ONE SUCTION DREDGE.

COASTAL DISTRICT OF WASHINGTON: CATCH BY GEAR, 1949

SPECIES	HAUL SEINES		GILL NETS				SHARK	
			SALMON					
			DRIFT		SET 2/			
	POUNDS	VALUE	POUNDS	VALUE	POUNDS	VALUE	POUNDS	VALUE
FISH								
ANCHOVIES	402,000	$6,100	-	-	-	-	-	-
FLOUNDERS, "SOLE" . . .	-	-	-	-	-	-	1,400	$70
GRAYFISH 1/	-	-	9,400	$452	-	-	5,600	271
HERRING, SEA	1,200	61	-	-	-	-	-	-
LINGCOD	-	-	-	-	-	-	5,200	524
PERCH	5,100	556	-	-	-	-	-	-
ROCKFISHES	-	-	-	-	-	-	3,100	108
SALMON:								
CHINOOK OR KING . . .	-	-	319,000	49,442	168,600	$26,131	-	-
CHUM OR KETA	-	-	567,600	44,842	91,200	7,204	-	-
PINK	-	-	100	8	-	-	-	-
RED OR SOCKEYE . . .	-	-	-	-	869,900	265,311	-	-
SILVER OR COHO . . .	-	-	587,300	89,859	423,200	64,745	-	-
SMELT, SURF OR SILVER .	367,800	36,777	-	-	-	-	-	-
SHARK, SOUPFIN 1/ . .	-	-	-	-	-	-	1,000	549
STEELHEAD TROUT 2/ . .	-	-	-	-	133,700	18,310	-	-
STURGEON	-	-	22,100	3,091	100	14	200	28
TOTAL	776,100	43,494	1,505,500	187,694	1,686,700	381,715	16,500	1,550
GRAND TOTAL . . .	776,100	43,494	1,505,500	187,694	1,686,700	381,715	16,500	1,550

SEE FOOTNOTES AT END OF TABLE   (CONTINUED ON NEXT PAGE)

COASTAL DISTRICT OF WASHINGTON: CATCH BY GEAR, 1949 - Continued

SPECIES	LINES				DIP NETS		OTTER TRAWLS	
	TRAWL OR SET		TROLL					
FISH	POUNDS	VALUE	POUNDS	VALUE	POUNDS	VALUE	POUNDS	VALUE
COD	-	-	1,300	$49	-	-	600	$22
FLOUNDERS:								
"SOLE"	-	-	-	-	-	-	27,900	1,397
OTHER	-	-	-	-	-	-	2,900	81
GRAYFISH 1/	3,200	$153	100	4	-	-	39,900	1,913
HALIBUT	400	67	8,500	1,329	-	-	-	-
LINGCOD	-	-	275,900	27,587	-	-	13,100	996
PERCH	-	-	-	-	200	$26	-	-
ROCKFISHES	-	-	95,700	3,350	-	-	37,700	1,131
SALMON:								
CHINOOK OR KING . . .	-	-	1,512,400	420,457	-	-	-	-
PINK	-	-	17,400	1,736	-	-	-	-
SILVER OR COHO . . .	-	-	1,869,000	388,800	-	-	-	-
SMELT, SURF OR SILVER .	-	-	-	-	168,400	16,837	-	-
SHARK, SOUPFIN 1/ . . .	600	297	200	104	-	-	-	-
STURGEON	-	-	200	31	-	-	-	-
TUNA, ALBACORE	-	-	3,343,400	595,128	-	-	-	-
TOTAL	4,200	517	7,124,100	1,438,575	168,600	16,863	122,100	5,540
GRAND TOTAL . . .	4,200	517	7,124,100	1,438,575	168,600	16,863	122,100	5,540

SPECIES	TRAPS, CRAB		DREDGES, TONGS, AND BY HAND		SHOVELS	
FISH	POUNDS	VALUE	POUNDS	VALUE	POUNDS	VALUE
LINGCOD	4,600	$231	-	-	-	-
ROCKFISHES	100	2	-	-	-	-
TOTAL	4,700	233	-	-	-	-
SHELLFISH						
CRABS 3/	10,837,400	1,083,740	-	-	-	-
CLAMS:						
HARDSHELL	-	-	-	-	400	$117
RAZOR 4/	-	-	-	-	302,700	193,121
OYSTERS, MARKET,						
PACIFIC 5/	-	-	5,347,700	$1,219,802	-	-
TOTAL	10,837,400	1,083,740	5,347,700	1,219,802	303,100	193,238
GRAND TOTAL . . .	10,842,100	1,083,973	5,347,700	1,219,802	303,100	193,238

1/ CAUGHT ALMOST ENTIRELY FOR THE UTILIZATION OF THE LIVERS IN THE EXTRACTION OF VITAMIN OILS. MOST OF THE CARCASSES WERE DISCARDED.
2/ FISHED ONLY ON INDIAN RESERVATIONS.
3/ THE WEIGHT OF CRABS SHOWN ABOVE IS BASED ON A WEIGHT OF 24 POUNDS PER DOZEN.
4/ THE WEIGHT OF RAZOR CLAMS IS BASED ON A YIELD OF 42 PERCENT OF EDIBLE MEAT.
5/ THE STATISTICS ON OYSTERS USED IN THIS TABLE ARE BASED ON YIELDS OF 12 PERCENT EDIBLE MEATS.

NOTE:--THE QUANTITIES SHOWN REPRESENT THE ROUND WEIGHT OF THE CATCH OF FISH AND SHELLFISH EXCEPT FOR BIVALVE MOLLUSKS, WHICH ARE REPORTED IN POUNDS OF MEATS. THE POUNDAGE AND VALUE OF THE CATCH SHOWN ABOVE INCLUDES THE FOLLOWING ITEMS OF LIVERS AND VISCERA: GRAYFISH LIVERS, 6,980 POUNDS, VALUE $2,793; HALIBUT LIVERS, 113 POUNDS, VALUE $145; LINGCOD LIVERS, 2,021 POUNDS, VALUE $4,042; ROCKFISH LIVERS, 100 POUNDS, VALUE $51; SOUPFIN SHARK LIVERS, 211 POUNDS, VALUE $950; AND HALIBUT AND LINGCOD VISCERA, 2,701 POUNDS, VALUE $790.

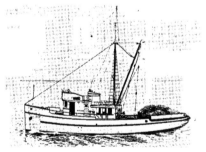

. WEST COAST PURSE SEINER

COLUMBIA RIVER DISTRICT OF WASHINGTON: OPERATING UNITS, 1949 [1]

ITEM	HAUL SEINES [2]	GILL NETS SALMON	GILL NETS SMELT	LINES TRAWL OR SET	LINES TROLL SALMON	LINES TROLL TUNA [3]	DIP NETS	TRAPS CRAB	TRAPS CRAWFISH	TOTAL EXCLUSIVE OF DUPLICATION
FISHERMEN:	NUMBER	NUMBER	NUMBER	NUMBER	NUMBER	NUMBER	NUMBER	NUMBER	NUMBER	NUMBER
ON VESSELS	-	2	-	-	51	-	-	7	-	54
ON BOATS AND SHORE	12	566	-	52	138	2	400	14	2	1,089
TOTAL	12	568	5	52	189	2	400	21	2	1,143
VESSELS, MOTOR	-	1	-	-	27	-	-	6	-	27
NET TONNAGE	-	10	-	-	243	-	-	62	-	243
BOATS:										
MOTOR	4	475	5	42	82	1	168	4	2	707
OTHER	4	15	-	10	-	-	9	-	-	32
APPARATUS:										
NUMBER	4	490	5	273	490	6	400	1,100	60	-
LENGTH, YARDS	400	-	-	-	-	-	-	-	-	-
SQUARE YARDS	-	1,568,000	1,875	-	-	-	-	-	-	-
HOOKS	-	-	-	27,300	2,450	6	-	-	-	-

[1] STATISTICS IN THIS TABLE INCLUDE ALL CRAFT OPERATING IN THE STATE MAKING THEIR HOME PORT IN THIS DISTRICT, AND ALL CRAFT OPERATING IN THE STATE WHOSE HOME PORT IS NOT WITHIN THE STATE BUT WHO LANDED THE MAJOR PORTION OF THEIR WASHINGTON CATCH IN THIS DISTRICT.
[2] CATCH SOLD IN OREGON.
[3] INCLUDES ONLY VESSELS THAT TROLLED OR FISHED EXCLUSIVELY FOR TUNA AND DID NOT TROLL FOR SALMON. MANY OF THE SALMON TROLLERS ALSO TROLLED FOR TUNA.

COLUMBIA RIVER DISTRICT OF WASHINGTON: CATCH BY GEAR, 1949 [1]

SPECIES	GILL NETS SALMON, DRIFT POUNDS	VALUE	GILL NETS SMELT POUNDS	VALUE	LINES TRAWL OR SET POUNDS	VALUE	LINES TROLL POUNDS	VALUE
FISH								
FLOUNDERS, OTHER	3,100	$46	-	-	-	-	-	-
HALIBUT	-	-	-	-	1,000	$182	-	-
LINGCOD	100	4	-	-	-	-	22,300	$2,679
ROCKFISHES	-	-	-	-	1,000	42	36,600	1,463
SABLEFISH	-	-	-	-	6,000	619	-	-
SALMON:								
CHINOOK OR KING	2,752,600	459,687	-	-	-	-	500,600	116,128
CHUM OR KETA	261,400	20,914	-	-	-	-	-	-
PINK	6,700	1,335	-	-	-	-	600	56
RED OR SOCKEYE	-	-	-	-	-	-	-	-
SILVER OR COHO	224,800	30,129	-	-	-	-	538,300	69,973
SHAD	62,600	4,195	-	-	-	-	-	-
SMELT, EULACHON	-	-	479,900	$47,987	-	-	-	-
STEELHEAD TROUT	40,900	5,760	-	-	-	-	-	-
STURGEON	128,100	22,287	-	-	9,200	1,793	-	-
TUNA, ALBACORE	-	-	-	-	-	-	146,700	26,255
TOTAL	3,480,300	544,357	479,900	47,987	17,200	2,636	1,245,400	216,611
GRAND TOTAL	3,480,300	544,357	479,900	47,987	17,200	2,636	1,245,400	216,611

SPECIES	DIP NETS POUNDS	VALUE	OTTER TRAWLS POUNDS	VALUE	TRAPS CRAB POUNDS	VALUE	TRAPS CRAWFISH POUNDS	VALUE
FISH								
FLOUNDERS:								
"SOLE"	-	-	16,700	$836	-	-	-	-
OTHER	-	-	1,800	54	-	-	-	-
LINGCOD	-	-	3,600	288	700	$29	-	-
ROCKFISHES	-	-	57,700	2,306	-	-	-	-
SALMON:								
CHINOOK OR KING	228,100	$38,097	-	-	-	-	-	-
CHUM OR KETA	1,800	142	-	-	-	-	-	-
RED OR SOCKEYE	4,400	888	-	-	-	-	-	-
SHAD	6,700	448	-	-	-	-	-	-
SMELT, EULACHON	1,964,700	88,412	-	-	-	-	-	-
STEELHEAD TROUT	1,300	180	-	-	-	-	-	-
STURGEON	9,300	1,622	-	-	-	-	-	-
TOTAL	2,216,300	129,789	79,800	3,484	700	29	-	-
SHELLFISH								
CRABS [2]	-	-	-	-	950,000	85,501	-	-
CRAWFISH	-	-	-	-	-	-	600	$121
TOTAL	-	-	-	-	950,000	85,501	600	121
GRAND TOTAL	2,216,300	129,789	79,800	3,484	950,700	85,530	600	121

[1] THE FOLLOWING SPECIES LANDED IN THE COLUMBIA RIVER DISTRICT WERE CAUGHT OFF THE COAST: SOLE, HALIBUT, LINGCOD, ROCKFISHES, SABLEFISH, ALBACORE TUNA, CRABS, AND MOST OF THE TROLL CAUGHT SALMON.
[2] THE WEIGHT OF CRABS SHOWN IS BASED ON A WEIGHT OF 24 POUNDS PER DOZEN.
NOTE:--THE QUANTITIES SHOWN REPRESENT THE ROUND WEIGHT OF THE CATCH OF FISH AND SHELLFISH. THE POUNDAGE AND VALUE OF THE CATCH SHOWN ABOVE INCLUDES THE FOLLOWING ITEMS OF LIVERS: LINGCOD LIVERS, 240 POUNDS, VALUE $288, AND SABLEFISH LIVERS, 820 POUNDS, VALUE $1,640.

OREGON

CATCH BY DISTRICTS, 1949

SPECIES	COLUMBIA RIVER DISTRICT		COASTAL DISTRICT	
FISH	POUNDS	VALUE	POUNDS	VALUE
CARP.	600	$17	-	-
COD	5,400	188	-	-
FLOUNDERS:				
"SOLE".	7,750,200	388,343	1,511,700	$74,054
OTHER	375,100	9,099	17,600	442
GRAYFISH 1/	3,270,800	276,232	151,900	12,039
HAKE.	-	-	77,400	471
HALIBUT	352,000	55,257	257,600	43,791
HERRING, SEA.	-	-	69,400	2,776
LAMPREY	369,900	9,248	-	-
LINGCOD	505,200	48,528	433,700	49,899
PERCH	-	-	7,700	769
PILCHARD.	-	-	9,000	234
ROCKFISHES.	3,075,500	119,992	1,698,500	54,633
SABLEFISH	203,000	16,350	351,500	28,105
SALMON:				
CHINOOK OR KING	8,017,900	1,361,810	1,475,500	307,070
CHUM OR KETA.	281,800	22,545	445,000	35,600
RED OR SOCKEYE.	12,600	2,571	-	-
SILVER OR COHO.	838,300	115,107	1,766,200	228,811
SHAD.	367,400	24,625	1,024,600	69,669
SHARKS:				
SOUPFIN	432,200	241,213	105,900	59,102
OTHER	11,500	110	1,400	14
SMELT, EULACHON	833,900	65,244	-	-
STEELHEAD TROUT	771,700	108,805	80,400	10,526
STRIPED BASS.	-	-	24,800	1,786
STURGEON.	267,700	50,326	1,300	130
TUNA:				
ALBACORE.	4,553,200	815,019	1,773,800	289,123
SKIPJACK 2/	1,941,800	269,227	-	-
YELLOWFIN 2/.	5,571,100	807,868	-	-
TOTAL. . . . . :	39,809,000	4,807,724	11,284,900	1,269,044
SHELLFISH				
CRABS	4,484,100	403,569	4,862,400	432,756
CRAWFISH, FRESH-WATER . . . . . : . . .	45,400	9,847	-	-
CLAMS:				
RAZOR	-	-	77,200	48,922
MIXED	-	-	32,300	7,681
OYSTERS, MARKET, PACIFIC. . . . . . :	-	-	501,100	85,904
TOTAL.	4,529,500	413,416	5,473,000	575,263
GRAND TOTAL.	44,338,500	5,221,140	16,757,900	1,844,307

1/ CAUGHT ALMOST ENTIRELY FOR THE UTILIZATION OF THE LIVERS IN THE EXTRACTION OF VITAMIN OILS. MOST OF THE
   CARCASSES WERE DISCARDED.
2/ THE CATCH OF SKIPJACK AND YELLOWFIN WAS TAKEN BY PURSE SEINES AND LINES SOUTH OF THE INTERNATIONAL BOUNDARY.
   ALL OR PART OF THIS CATCH MAY BE DUPLICATED IN IMPORT STATISTICS.

COLUMBIA RIVER DISTRICT OF OREGON: OPERATING UNITS, 1949 1/

ITEM	PURSE SEINES, TUNA 2/	HAUL SEINES	GILL NETS				LINES	
			SALMON		SHARK	SMELT	TRAWL AND SET	TROLL SALMON
			DRIFT	SET				
FISHERMEN:	NUMBER	NUMBER	NUMBER	NUMBER	NUMBER	NUMBER	NUMBER	NUMBER
ON VESSELS.	23	-	2	-	160	-	263	361
ON BOATS AND SHORE. .	-	201	703	73	-	70	24	179
TOTAL.	23	201	705	73	160	70	287	540
VESSELS, MOTOR.	2	-	1	-	41	-	66	139
NET TONNAGE	114	-	11	-	654	-	902	2,263
BOATS:								
MOTOR	-	14	628	53	-	70	18	107
OTHER	-	23	-	10	-	-	3	-
ACCESSORY BOATS	2	-	-	-	-	-	-	-
APPARATUS:								
NUMBER.	2	23	629	152	1,215	70	1,287	1,454
LENGTH, YARDS	1,300	13,800	-	-	-	-	-	-
SQUARE YARDS.	-	-	2,013,000	42,500	1,037,150	26,000	-	-
HOOKS	-	-	-	-	-	-	28,700	6,760

SEE FOOTNOTES AT END OF TABLE   (CONTINUED ON NEXT PAGE)

COLUMBIA RIVER DISTRICT OF OREGON: OPERATING UNITS, 1949[1] - Continued

ITEM	LINES - CONT'D. TROLL - CONT'D. TUNA [3]	POUND NETS	DIP NETS	OTTER TRAWLS	TRAPS CRAB	TRAPS CRAWFISH	TOTAL, EXCLUS:VE OF DUPLICATION
	NUMBER	NUMBER	NUMBER	NUMBER	NUMBER	NUMBER	NUMBER
FISHERMEN:							
ON VESSELS.	556	-	-	250	102	-	1,409
ON BOATS AND SHORE.	7	65	487	-	24	22	1,730
TOTAL.	563	65	487	250	126	22	3,139
VESSELS, MOTOR. . . .	152	--	-	64	36	-	414
NET TONNAGE	4,033	-	-	1,866	514	-	8,658
BO∼TS:							
MOTOR	3	24	-	-	12	10	829
OTHER	-	31	-	-	-	8	72
ACCESSORY BOATS . . .	-	-	-	-	-	-	3
APPARATUS:							
NUMBER.	1,298	35	487	64	8,700	1,100	-
YARDS AT MOUTH. . .	-	-	-	960	-	-	-
HOOKS	1,298	-	-	-	-	-	-

1/ SIAIISTICS IN THIS TABLE INCLUDE ALL CRAFT OPERATING IN THE STATE MAKING THEIR HOME PORT IN THIS DISTRICT,
AND ALL CRAFT OPERATING IN THE STATE WHOSE HOME PORT IS NOT WITHIN THE STATE BUT WHO LANDED THE MAJOR PORTION
OF THEIR OREGON CATCH IN THIS DISTRICT.
2/ TUNA PURSE SEINES WERE OPERATED ONLY IN WATERS OFF CENTRAL AMERICA.
3/ INCLUDES ONLY VESSELS THAT TROLLED OR FISHED EXCLUSIVELY FOR TUNA AND DID NOT TROLL FOR SALMON. MANY OF THE
SALMON TROLLERS ALSO TROLLED FOR TUNA.

COLUMBIA RIVER DISTRICT OF OREGON: CATCH BY GEAR, 1949[1]

SPECIES	PURSE SEINES		HAUL SEINES		GILL NETS SALMON DRIFT		GILL NETS SALMON SET	
FISH	POUNDS	VALUE	POUNDS	VALUE	POUNDS	VALUE	POUNDS	VALUE
CARP.	-	-	600	$17	-	-	-	-
FLOUNDERS, OTHER.	-	-	-	-	94,400	$1,510	-	-
LINGCOD	-	-	-	-	100	4	-	-
SALMON:								
CHINOOK OR KING	-	-	948,500	158,396	5,610,200	936,897	46,700	$7,795
CHUM OR KETA. .	-	-	29,900	2,389	233,500	18,680	1,100	90
RED OR SOCKEYE.	-	-	900	187	1,900	372	1,000	207
SILVER OR COHO.	-	-	112,400	15,067	451,600	60,512	4,500	600
SHAD.	-	-	33,300	2,233	333,600	22,354	-	-
STEELHEAD TROUT .	-	-	202,800	28,595	225,600	31,814	6,600	926
STURGEON.	-	-	1,300	250	206,700	38,844	16,300	3,191
TUNA:								
SKIPJACK [3]. .	565,000	$62,709	-	-	-	-	-	-
YELLOWFIN [3]. .	2,409,300	283,007	-	-	-	-	-	-
TOTAL . . .	2,974,300	345,716	1,329,700	207,134	7,157,600	1,110,987	76,200	12,809
GRAND TOTAL	2,974,300	345,716	1,329,700	207,134	7,157,600	1,110,987	76,200	12,809

SPECIES	GILL NETS - CONTINUED SHARK		SMELT		LINES TRAWL, SET AND HAND		TROLL	
FISH	POUNDS	VALUE	POUNDS	VALUE	POUNDS	VALUE	POUNDS	VALUE
COD	-	-	-	-	300	$7	-	-
FLOUNDERS, "SOLE"	300	$23	-	-	2,600	179	-	-
GRAYFISH [2] . . .	6,500	515	-	-	16,800	1,334	-	-
HALIBUT	-	-	-	-	351,700	55,216	300	$41
LINGCOD	2,700	342	-	-	135,900	17,265	17,000	1,885
ROCKFISHES. . . .	3,100	129	-	-	34,500	1,413	11,800	431
SABLEFISH	-	-	-	-	138,100	12,287	-	-
SALMON:								
CHINOOK OR KING	-	-	-	-	-	-	223,900	60,229
SILVER OR COHO.	-	-	-	-	-	-	163,400	24,673
SHARKS:								
SOUPFIN [2]. .	429,600	239,740	-	-	800	465	400	232
OTHER [2]. . .	10,900	104	-	-	-	-	-	-
SMELT, EULACHON .	-	-	531,400	$53,143	-	-	-	-
STEELHEAD TROUT .	-	-	-	-	-	-	100	14
STURGEON.	100	5	-	-	17,400	3,350	-	-
TUNA:								
ALBACORE. . . .	-	-	-	-	-	-	4,553,200	815,019
SKIPJACK [3]. .	-	-	-	-	1,376,800	206,518	-	-
YELLOWFIN [3]. .	-	-	-	-	3,161,800	524,861	-	-
TOTAL . . .	453,200	240,858	531,400	53,143	5,236,700	822,895	4,970,100	902,524
GRAND TOTAL	453,200	240,858	531,400	53,143	5,236,700	822,895	4,970,100	902,524

SEE FOOTNOTES AT END OF TABLE   (CONTINUED ON NEXT PAGE)

COLUMBIA RIVER DISTRICT OF OREGON: CATCH BY GEAR, 1949[1] - Continued

SPECIES	POUND NETS		DIP NETS		OTTER TRAWLS		TRAPS CRAB		TRAPS CRAWFISH	
FISH	POUNDS	VALUE	POUNDS	VALUE	POUNDS	VALUE	POUNDS	VALUE	POUNDS	VALUE
COD	-	-	-	-	5,100	$181	-	-	-	-
FLOUNDERS:										
"SOLE".	-	-	-	-	7,747,300	388,141	-	-	-	-
OTHER	22,500	$361	-	-	258,200	7,228	-	-	-	-
GRAYFISH 2/ . . .	-	-	-	-	3,247,500	274,383	-	-	-	-
LAMPREY	-	-	369,900	$9,248	-	-	-	-	-	-
LINGCOD	100	4	-	-	345,000	28,807	4,400	$221	-	-
ROCKFISHES. . . .	-	-	-	-	3,026,100	118,019	-	-	-	-
SABLEFISH	-	-	-	-	64,900	4,063	-	-	-	-
SALMON:										
CHINOOK OR KING	398,500	66,543	790,100	131,950	-	-	-	-	-	-
CHUM OR KETA. .	17,300	1,386	-	-	-	-	-	-	-	-
RED OR SOCKEYE.	900	177	8,100	1,628	-	-	-	-	-	-
SILVER OR COHO.	104,800	14,046	1,600	209	-	-	-	-	-	-
SHAD.	300	23	200	15	-	-	-	-	-	-
SHARKS:										
SOUPFIN 2/. . .	-	-	- . .	-	1,400	776	-	-	-	-
OTHER 2/. . . .	-	-	-	-	600	6	-	-	-	-
SMELT, EULACHON.	-	-	302,500	12,101	-	-	-	-	-	-
STEELHEAD TROUT .	126,300	17,806	210,300	29,650	-	-	-	-	-	-
STURGEON.	2,700	518	19,900	3,905	3,300	263	-	-	-	-
TOTAL.	673,400	100,864	1,702,600	188,706	14,699,400	821,867	4,400	221	-	-
SHELLFISH										
CRABS 4/.	-	-	-	-	-	-	4,484,100	403,569	-	-
CRAWFISH, FRESH-WATER. . .	-	-	-	-	-	-	-	-	45,400	$9,847
TOTAL. . . .	-	-	-	-	-	-	4,484,100	403,569	45,400	9,847
GRAND TOTAL.	673,400	100,864	1,702,600	188,705	14,699,400	821,867	4,488,500	403,790	45,400	9,847

1/ THE FOLLOWING SPECIES ARE TAKEN OFF THE OREGON AND WASHINGTON COASTS BUT LANDED IN THE COLUMBIA RIVER DISTRICT: COD, SOLE, GRAYFISH, HALIBUT, LINGCOD, ROCKFISHES, SABLEFISH, SHARK, TUNA, CRABS AND SOME OF THE STURGEON, AND MOST OF THE FLOUNDERS AND TROLL CAUGHT SALMON.
2/ CAUGHT ALMOST ENTIRELY FOR THE UTILIZATION OF THE LIVERS IN THE EXTRACTION OF VITAMIN OILS. MOST OF THE CARCASSES WERE DISCARDED.
3/ CAUGHT IN WATERS OFF CENTRAL AMERICA, BUT SHIPPED TO OREGON AS PRODUCTS OF AMERICAN FISHERIES.
4/ THE WEIGHT OF CRABS SHOWN IS BASED ON AN AVERAGE OF 25 POUNDS PER DOZEN.
NOTE:—THE QUANTITIES SHOWN REPRESENT THE ROUND WEIGHT OF THE CATCH OF FISH AND SHELLFISH. THE POUNDAGE AND VALUE OF THE CATCH SHOWN ABOVE INCLUDES THE FOLLOWING ITEMS OF LIVERS AND VISCERA: COD LIVERS, 55 POUNDS, VALUE $3; GRAYFISH LIVERS, 392,503 POUNDS, VALUE $259,051; HALIBUT LIVERS, 4,710 POUNDS, VALUE $3,533; LINGCOD LIVERS, 8,886 POUNDS, VALUE $21,149; ROCKFISH LIVERS, 935 POUNDS, VALUE $374; SABLEFISH LIVERS, 4,448 POUNDS, VALUE $3,336; SOUPFIN SHARK LIVERS, 51,874 POUNDS, VALUE $241,213; OTHER SHARK LIVERS, 1,376 POUNDS, VALUE $110; AND HALIBUT, LINGCOD AND SABLEFISH VISCERA, 25,132 POUNDS, VALUE $3,493.

COASTAL DISTRICT OF OREGON: OPERATING UNITS, 1949[1]

ITEM	HAUL SEINES	GILL NETS			LINES		
		SALMON		SHARK	TRAWL AND SET	TROLL	
		DRIFT	SET			SALMON	TUNA 2/
FISHERMEN:	NUMBER	NUMBER	NUMBER	NUMBER	NUMBER	NUMBER	NUMBER
ON VESSELS.	-	-	-	56	15	304	115
ON BOATS AND SHORE. . .	36	420	143	8	14	331	6
TOTAL.	36	420	143	64	29	635	121
VESSELS, MOTOR.	-	-	-	15	5	132	36
NET TONNAGE	-	-	-	262	64	1,192	749
BOATS:							
MOTOR . . . . :	12	401	104	4	7	255	3
OTHER	12	10	37	-	-	-	-
APPARATUS:							
NUMBER.	12	411	445	390	350	1,812	245
LENGTH, YARDS	2,000	-	-	-	-	-	-
SQUARE YARDS.	-	586,000	129,000	342,000	-	-	-
HOOKS	-	-	-	-	7,000	8,150	245

SEE FOOTNOTES AT END OF TABLE   (CONTINUED ON NEXT PAGE)

COASTAL DISTRICT OF OREGON: OPERATING UNITS, 1949[1]- Continued

ITEM	OTTER TRAWLS	TRAPS, CRAB	DREDGES, OYSTER	TONGS AND BY HAND, OYSTER	SHOVELS	TOTAL, EXCLUSIVE OF DUPLICATION
	NUMBER	NUMBER	NUMBER	NUMBER	NUMBER	NUMBER
FISHERMEN:						
ON VESSELS.	64	119	3	-	-	459
ON BOATS AND SHORE. . .	5	155	6	47	744	1,689
TOTAL.	69	274	9	47	744	2,148
VESSELS, MOTOR.	17	43	1	-	-	187
NET TONNAGE	507	487	15	-	-	2,368
BOATS:						
MOTOR	2	126	2	6	-	782
OTHER	-	-	-	12	-	68
APPARATUS:						
NUMBER.	19	16,400	6	20	744	-
YARDS AT MOUTH. . . .	285	-	12	-	-	-

1/ STATISTICS IN THIS TABLE INCLUDE ALL CRAFT OPERATING IN THE STATE MAKING THEIR HOME PORT IN THIS DISTRICT, AND ALL CRAFT OPERATING IN THE STATE WHOSE HOME PORT IS NOT WITHIN THE STATE BUT WHO LANDED THE MAJOR PORTION OF THEIR OREGON CATCH IN THIS DISTRICT.
2/ INCLUDES ONLY VESSELS THAT TROLLED OR FISHED EXCLUSIVELY FOR TUNA AND DID NOT TROLL FOR SALMON. MANY OF THE SALMON TROLLERS ALSO TROLLED FOR TUNA.

COASTAL DISTRICT OF OREGON: CATCH BY GEAR, 1949

SPECIES	HAUL SEINES		GILL NETS				LINES	
			SALMON		SHARK		TRAWL OR SET	
FISH	POUNDS	VALUE	POUNDS	VALUE	POUNDS	VALUE	POUNDS	VALUE
FLOUNDERS:								
"SOLE".	5,000	$225	-	-	1,900	$93	3,100	$156
OTHER	3,800	96	2,800	$69	-	-	1,000	25
GRAYFISH 1/	-	-	-	-	3,100	248	1,600	127
HALIBUT	-	-	-	-	-	-	249,700	42,440
HERRING, SEA. . . .	69,400	2,776	-	-	-	-	-	-
LINGCOD	-	-	-	-	6,900	838	78,800	9,615
PERCH	6,700	669	1,000	100	-	-	-	-
PILCHARD	9,000	234	-	-	-	-	-	-
ROCKFISHES. . . .	74,900	2,772	-	-	2,100	76	-	-
SABLEFISH	-	-	-	-	100	8	315,200	25,848
SALMON:								
CHINOOK OR KING .	-	-	338,600	62,643	-	-	-	-
CHUM OR KETA. . .	-	-	445,000	35,600	-	-	-	-
SILVER OR COHO. .	-	-	639,500	83,133	-	-	-	-
SHAD.	-	-	1,023,800	69,618	-	-	-	-
SHARKS:								
SOUPFIN	-	-	-	-	103,200	57,614	800	465
OTHER	-	-	-	-	-	-	600	6
STEELHEAD TROUT . .	-	-	80,400	10,526	-	-	-	-
STRIPED BASS. . . .	-	-	24,800	1,786	-	-	-	-
STURGEON.	-	-	1,000	114	-	-	-	-
TOTAL	168,800	6,772	2,556,900	263,569	117,300	58,877	650,800	78,682
GRAND TOTAL . .	168,800	6,772	2,556,900	263,569	117,300	58,877	650,800	78,682

SPECIES	LINES - CONT'D. TROLL·		OTTER TRAWLS		TRAPS, CRAB		DREDGES, TONGS, AND BY HAND		SHOVELS	
FISH	POUNDS	VALUE	POUNDS	VALUE	POUNDS	VALUE	POUNDS	VALUE	POUNDS	VALUE
FLOUNDERS:										
"SOLE".	100	$4	1,501,600	$73,576	-	-	-	-	-	-
OTHER	200	5	9,700	244	100	$3	-	-	-	-
GRAYFISH 1/	400	33	146,800	11,631	-	-	-	-	-	-
HAKE.	-	-	77,400	471	-	-	-	-	-	-
HALIBUT	7,900	1,351	-	-	-	-	-	-	-	-
LINGCOD	191,200	20,361	156,200	19,061	600	24	-	-	-	-
ROCKFISHES. . . .	51,600	1,547	1,569,900	50,238	-	-	-	-	-	-
SABLEFISH	-	-	36,200	2,249	-	-	-	-	-	-
SALMON:										
CHINOOK OR KING .	1,136,900	244,427	-	-	-	-	-	-	-	-
SILVER OR COHO. .	1,126,700	145,678	-	-	-	-	-	-	-	-
SHAD.	-	-	800	51	-	-	-	-	-	-
SHARKS:										
SOUPFIN	200	93	1,700	930	-	-	-	-	-	-
OTHER	500	5	300	3	-	-	-	-	-	-

SEE FOOTNOTES AT END OF TABLE   (CONTINUED ON NEXT PAGE)

COASTAL DISTRICT OF OREGON: CATCH BY GEAR, 1949 - Continued

SPECIES	LINES – CONT'D. TROLL		O TER TRAWLS		TRAPS, CRAB		DREDGES, TONGS, AND BY HAND		SHOVELS	
	POUNDS	VALUE	POUNDS	VALUE	POUNDS	VALUE	POUNDS	VALUE	POUNDS	VALUE
FISH - CONT'D										
STURGEON. . . .	-	-	300	$16	-	-	-	-	-	-
TUNA, ALBACORE.	1,773,800	$289,123	- -	-	-	-	-	-	-	-
TOTAL . .	4,289,500	702,627	3,500,900	158,470	700	$27	-	-	-	-
SHELLFISH										
CRABS 2/. . . .	-	-	-	-	4,862,400	432,756	-	-	-	-
CLAMS:										
RAZOR 3/. . .	-	-	-	-	-	-	-	-	77,200	$48,922
MIXED 4/. . .	-	-	-	-	-	-	-	-	32,300	7,681
OYSTERS, MARKET,										
PACIFIC 5/. .	-	-	-	-	-	-	501,100	$85,904	-	-
TOTAL. . .	-	-	-	-	4,862,400	432,756	501,100	85,904	109,500	56,603
GRAND TOTAL	4,289,500	702,627	3,500,900	158,470	4,863,100	432,783	501,100	85,904	109,500	56,603

1/ CAUGHT ALMOST ENTIRELY FOR THE UTILIZATION OF THE LIVERS IN THE EXTRACTION OF VITAMIN OILS. MOST OF THE
CARCASSES WERE DISCARDED.
2/ THE WEIGHT OF CRABS SHOWN IS BASED ON AN AVERAGE OF 25 POUNDS PER DOZEN.
3/ THE WEIGHT OF RAZOR CLAMS IS THAT OF EDIBLE MEATS, BASED ON A YIELD OF 42 PERCENT OF THE ROUND WEIGHT.
4/ MIXED CLAMS CONSIST PRINCIPALLY OF EASTERN SOFT SHELL CLAMS. THE WEIGHT SHOWN IS THAT OF EDIBLE MEATS,
BASED ON A YIELD OF 21 PERCENT OF THE ROUND WEIGHT.
5/ THE STATISTICS ON OYSTERS USED IN THIS TABLE ARE BASED ON A YIELD OF 12 PERCENT OF EDIBLE MEATS.

NOTE:--THE QUANTITIES SHOWN REPRESENT THE ROUND WEIGHT OF THE CATCH OF FISH AND SHELLFISH, EXCEPT FOR BIVALVE
MOLLUSKS, WHICH ARE REPORTED IN POUNDS OF MEATS. THE POUNDAGE AND VALUE OF THE CATCH SHOWN ABOVE INCLUDES
THE FOLLOWING ITEMS OF LIVERS AND VISCERA: GRAYFISH LIVERS, 18,241 POUNDS, VALUE $11,669; HAKE LIVERS, 2,478
POUNDS, VALUE $471; HALIBUT LIVERS, 3,448 POUNDS, VALUE $2,586; LINGCOD LIVERS, 11,659 POUNDS, VALUE $27,748;
ROCKFISH LIVERS, 1,615 POUNDS, VALUE $646; SABLEFISH LIVERS, 9,205 POUNDS, VALUE $6,904; SOUPFIN SHARK LIVERS,
12,710 POUNDS, VALUE $58,961; OTHER SHARK LIVERS, 160 POUNDS, VALUE $14, AND HALIBUT, LINGCOD AND SABLEFISH
VISCERA, 31,971 POUNDS, VALUE $3,943.

VALUE OF PACIFIC COAST STATES CATCH, 1949

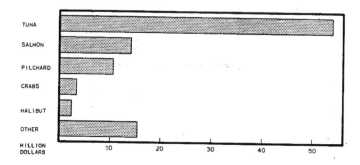

PACIFIC COAST STATES FISHERIES
CALIFORNIA
CATCH BY DISTRICTS, 1949

SPECIES	NORTHERN DISTRICT		SAN FRANCISCO DISTRICT		MONTEREY DISTRICT	
FISH	POUNDS	VALUE	POUNDS	VALUE	POUNDS	VALUE
ANCHOVIES	-	-	216,500	$4,091	1,482,700	$17,496
CABEZONE	100	$15	4,600	113	10,400	272
CARP	92,200	922	241,200	9,735	-	-
CATFISH	-	-	201,700	38,566	-	-
FLOUNDERS:						
"CALIFORNIA HALIBUT"	-	-	9,000	1,531	97,800	19,310
"SOLE"	13,830,700	578,123	4,504,100	258,984	720,600	43,454
OTHER	332,000	14,673	671,500	31,824	135,400	8,474
HALIBUT	86,100	19,679	81,200	13,778	-	
HARDHEAD	-	-	17,400	4,904		
HERRING, SEA	2,700	68	274,600	6,334	100,100	761
JACK MACKEREL	-	-	-	-	4,179,500	92,785
KINGFISH	-	-	2,300	147	210,600	11,919
LINGCOD	1,130,400	84,210	382,600	28,504	95,200	8,084
MACKEREL	-	-	3,000	49	233,800	4,115
PERCH	77,700	8,799	100,900	14,574	33,000	3,291
PILCHARD	14,800	522	33,879,200	577,467	262,375,400	4,565,331
POMPANO	-	-	-	-	62,800	20,813
ROCK BASS	-	-	-	-	2,600	312
ROCKFISHES	3,267,000	118,269	521,100	34,756	1,347,500	101,876
SABLEFISH	1,277,200	109,312	50,800	1,876	329,300	11,424
SALMON	2,601,400	617,574	3,354,600	772,596	468,700	117,612
SEA BASS, WHITE	700	173	8,700	1,993	53,100	9,020
SHAD	-	-	735,800	46,983	-	-
SHARKS, INCLUDING GRAYFISH	147,700	193,712	1/178,900	1/512,415	608,300	11,496
SKATES	1,600	17	77,200	1,158	23,400	549
SMELT	26,400	1,855	436,700	32,971	116,700	6,479
SWORDFISH	-	-	300	90	300	86
TUNA AND TUNALIKE FISHES:						
ALBACORE	2,817,500	427,697	1,505,100	231,032	5,125,400	804,687
BLUEFIN	-	-	2/222,700	2/36,746	2/ 7,800	2/1,714
WHITEBAIT	211,400	19,579	29,900	4,043	500	68
UNCLASSIFIED	42,100	1,730	43,300	1,439	2,200	60
TOTAL	25,959,200	2,196,929	47,754,900	2,668,699	277,823,100	5,861,488
SHELLFISH						
CRABS, DUNGENESS	7,255,200	806,055	3,790,300	479,082	24,300	4,008
SHRIMP	-	-	800,400	47,546	4,000	1,581
ABALONE	-	-	4,300	3,040	15,100	9,060
CLAMS, HARD	1,600	568	-	-	4/1,900	4/708
OCTOPUS	20,500	1,025	24,200	1,476	25,600	3,037
OYSTERS, MARKET:						
EASTERN	-	-	6,500	4,654		-
PACIFIC	-	-	13,400	13,053	-	-
SQUID	-	-	-	-	6,816,000	181,987
TOTAL	7,277,300	807,648	4,639,100	548,851	6,886,900	200,381
WHALE PRODUCTS						
LIVER	28,000	8,000	-	-	-	-
MEAL:						
BONE	100,000	2,500	-	-	-	-
MEAT	100,000	5,000	-	-	-	-
OIL:						
WHALE	209,600	13,975	-	-	-	-
SPERM	352,500	38,500	-	-	-	-
TOTAL	790,100	67,975	-	-	-	-
GRAND TOTAL	34,026,600	3,072,552	52,394,000	3,217,550	284,710,000	6,061,869

SPECIES	SAN PEDRO DISTRICT					
	OFF CALIFORNIA		OFF LATIN AMERICA		TOTAL	
FISH	POUNDS	VALUE	POUNDS	VALUE	POUNDS	VALUE
ANCHOVIES	1,614,900	$34,259	-	-	1,614,900	$34,259
BARRACUDA	612,900	93,946	1,243,800	$189,306	1,856,700	283,252
CABEZONE	900	130	-	-	900	130
CABRILLA	-	-	192,600	25,967	192,600	25,967
CARP	71,300	2,209	-	-	71,300	2,209
FLOUNDERS:						
"CALIFORNIA HALIBUT"	843,900	161,023	58,200	11,439	902,100	172,462
"SOLE"	635,600	36,948	100	5	635,700	36,953
OTHER	35,000	3,258	-	-	35,000	3,258

(CONTINUED ON NEXT PAGE)

CALIFORNIA: CATCH BY DISTRICTS, 1949 - Continued

SPECIES	SAN PEDRO DISTRICT - CONTINUED					
	OFF CALIFORNIA		OFF LATIN AMERICA		TOTAL	
FISH CONTINUED	POUNDS	VALUE	POUNDS	VALUE	POUNDS	VALUE
FLYINGFISH.	34,300	$2,652	-	-	34,300	$2,652
GROUPERS	-	-	249,400	$44,163	249,400	44,163
JACK MACKEREL	47,044,600	1,017,961	-	-	47,044,600	1,017,961
KINGFISH. . .	533,600	26,582	-	-	533,600	26,582
LINGCOD	36,900	3,736	300	26	37,200	3,762
MACKEREL.	49,084.300	1,260,749	-	-	49,084,300	1,260,749
MULLET.	36,200	3,083	-	-	36,200	3,083
PERCH	115,000	21,894	-	-	115,000	21,894
PILCHARD.	331,502,300	5,554,263	-	-	331,502,300	5,554,263
POMPANO	26,500	5,086	-	-	26,500	5,086
ROCK BASS	.109,900	15,368	39,100	5,733	149,000	21,101
ROCKFISHES.	707,100	67,877	1,100	99	708,200	67,976
SABLEFISH	80,000	9,126	-	-	80,000	9,126
SALMON. . . . . ▾ . .	5,000	1,521	-	-	5,000	1,521
SCULPIN	124,800	23,702	1,100	215	125,900	23,917
SEA BASS:						
BLACK	7,800	1,157	74,000	10,403	81,800	11,560
WHITE	745,400	161,154	256,200	57,089	1,001,600	218,243
SHARKS, INCLUDING GRAYFISH. . .	502,500	105,933	8,500	1,742	511,000	107,675
SHEEPSHEAD.	41,400	2,942	7,600	556	49,000	3,498
SKATES.	20,900	1,203	-	-	20,900	1,203
SMELT	119,600	9,371	-	-	119,600	9,371
SPANISH MACKEREL.	-	-	900	86	900	86
SWORDFISH	124,600	55,232	9,500	4,247	134,100	59,479
TUNA AND TUNALIKE FISHES:						
ALBACORE.	4,023,900	729,881	5,712,000	1,061,286	9,735,900	1,791,167
BLUEFIN	2,238,500	363,529	1,826,700	296,654	4,065,200	660,183
BONITO.	84,200	8,184	1,590,900	154,475	1,675,100	162,659
SKIPJACK OR STRIPED	15,300	2,232	23,910,800	3,493,368	23,926,100	3,495,600
YELLOWFIN	4,500	728	70,049,800	11,390,100	70,054,300	11,390,828
WHITEFISH . . . :	10,600	914	1,800	160	12,400	1,074
YELLOWTAIL.	9,400	869	5,276,600	490,725	5,286,000	491,594
UNCLASSIFIED.	58,900	6,581	1,700	201	60,600	6,782
TOTAL.	441,262,500	9,795,283	110,512,700	17,238,045	551,775,200	27,033,328
SHELLFISH						
CRABS, DUNGENESS.	3/46,500	3/5,094	-	-	3/46,500	3/ 5,094
LOBSTERS, SPINY	692,400	222,626	-	-	692,400	222,626
ABALONE	672,900	376,561	-	-	672,900	376,561
CLAMS, .HARD.	300	59	-	-	300	59
OCTOPUS.	4,700	424	-	-	4,700	424
OYSTERS, MARKET, PACIFIC. . . .	14,800	8,691	-	-	14,800	8,691
SQUID	43,100	2,186	-	-	43,100	2,186
TOTAL.	1,474,700	615,641	-	-	1,474,700	615,641
GRAND TOTAL.	442,737,200	10,410,924	110,512,700	17,238,045	553,249,900	27,648,969

SPECIES	SAN DIEGO DISTRICT					
	OFF CALIFORNIA		OFF LATIN AMERICA		TOTAL	
FISH	POUNDS	VALUE	POUNDS	VALUE	POUNDS	VALUE
ANCHOVIES	8,200	$258	-	-	8,200	$258
BARRACUDA	290,700	39,829	310,300	$42,513	601,000	82,342
CABRILLA	-	-	17,500	1,825	17,500	1,825
CARP	800	80	-	-	800	80
FLOUNDERS:						
"CALIFORNIA HALIBUT".	128,800	22,739	118,700	20,955	247,500	43,694
"SOLE".	1,700	255	-	-	1,700	255
GROUPERS.	-	-	41,200	5,119	41,200	5,119
HERRING, SEA.	1,900	47	-	-	1,900	47
JACK MACKEREL	26,000	377	-	-	26,000	377
KINGFISH.	17,900	1,477	-	-	17,900	1,477
LINGCOD	·8,300	853	300	35	8,600	888
MACKEREL.	450,200	20,979	-	-	450,200	20,979
MULLET.	35,800	2,327	-	-	35,800	2,327
PILCHARD.	5,703,300	59,314	-	-	5,703,300	59,314
ROCK BASS	25,600	2,752	15,100	1,625	40,700	4,377
ROCKFISHES.	80,800	7,084	13,000	1,140	93,800	8,224
SABLEFISH	100	9	-	-	100	9

(CONTINUED ON NEXT PAGE)

PACIFIC COAST STATES FISHERIES

CALIFORNIA: CATCH BY DISTRICTS, 1949 - Continued

SPECIES	SAN DIEGO DISTRICT - CONTINUED					
	OFF CALIFORNIA		OFF LATIN AMERICA		TOTAL	
FISH - CONTINUED	POUNDS	VALUE	POUNDS	VALUE	POUNDS	VALUE
SCULPIN	22,300	$2,992	200	$21	22,500	$3,013
SEA BASS:						
BLACK	9,400	1,330	23,200	3,270	32,600	4,600
WHITE	137,600	24,476	207,900	36,959	345,500	61,435
SHARKS, INCLUDING GRAYFISH.	97,500	7,432	8,100	617	105,600	8,049
SHEEPSHEAD.	7,100	501	5,500	390	12,600	891
SKATES.	200	16	100	10	300	26
SMELT	12,600	1,005	-	-	12,600	1,005
SPANISH MACKEREL.	-	-	2,800	222	2,800	222
SWORDFISH	16,600	7,279	47,100	20,572	63,700	27,851
TUNA AND TUNALIKE FISHES:						
ALBACORE.	6,984,700	1,374,587	17,864,900	3,515,823	24,849,600	4,890,410
BLUEFIN	27,700	4,151	66,000	9,908	93,700	14,059
BONITO.	15,000	1,511	139,400	14,011	154,400	15,522
SKIPJACK OR STRIPED . . .	11,400	1,710	54,632,900	8,156,684	54,644,300	8,158,394
YELLOWFIN	5,400	885	114,912,600	18,799,699	114,918,000	18,800,584
WHITEFISH	2,100	160	16,700	1,289	18,800	1,449
YELLOWTAIL.	8,300	796	2,025,200	193,610	2,033,500	194,406
UNCLASSIFIED.	88,600	8,701	5,000	496	93,600	9,197
TOTAL	14,226,600	1,595,912	190,473,700	30,826,793	204,700,300	32,422,705
SHELLFISH						
CRABS, ROCK	600	117	-	-	600	117
LOBSTERS, SPINY	141,900	60,699	-	-	141,900	60,699
ABALONE	21,300	9,598	-	-	21,300	9,598
CLAMS, HARD	4/16,600	4/10,649	-	-	4/16,600	4/10,649
OCTOPUS	100	11	-	-	100	11
TOTAL.	180,500	81,074	-	-	180,500	81,074
GRAND TOTAL	14,407,100	1,676,986	190,473,700	30,826,793	204,880,800	32,503,779

1/ INCLUDES 12,200 POUNDS, VALUED AT $34,899, TAKEN OFF LATIN AMERICA.
2/ TAKEN OFF LATIN AMERICA.
3/ INCLUDES ROCK CRABS.
4/ INCLUDES A SMALL AMOUNT OF MUSSELS.

CALIFORNIA: CATCH BY WATERS, 1949

SPECIES	OFF CALIFORNIA		OFF LATIN AMERICA	
FISH	POUNDS	VALUE	POUNDS	VALUE
ANCHOVIES	3,322,300	$56,104	-	-
BARRACUDA	903,600	133,775	1,554,100	$231,819
CABEZONE.	16,000	530	-	-
CABRILLA.	-	-	210,100	27,792
CARP.	405,500	12,946	-	-
CATFISH	201,700	38,566	-	-
FLOUNDERS:				
"CALIFORNIA HALIBUT".	1,079,500	204,603	176,900	32,394
"SOLE".	19,692,700	917,764	100	5
OTHER	1,173,900	58,229	-	-
FLYINGFISH.	34,300	2,652	-	-
GROUPERS.	-	-	290,600	49,282
HALIBUT	167,300	33,457	-	-
HARDHEAD.	17,400	4,904	-	-
HERRING, SEA.	379,300	7,210	-	-
JACK MACKEREL	51,250,100	1,111,123	-	-
KINGFISH.	764,400	40,125	-	-
LINGCOD	1,653,400	125,387	600	61
MACKEREL.	49,771,300	1,285,892	-	-
MULLET.	72,000	5,410	-	-
PERCH	326,500	48,558	-	-
PILCHARD.	633,475,000	10,756,897	-	-
POMPANO	89,300	25,899	-	-
ROCK BASS	138,100	18,432	54,200	7,358
ROCKFISHES.	5,923,500	329,862	14,100	1,239
SABLEFISH	1,737,400	131,747	-	-
SALMON.	6,429,700	1,509,303	-	-
SCULPIN	147,100	26,694	1,300	236
SEA BASS:				
BLACK	17,200	2,487	97,200	13,673
	(CONTINUED ON NEXT PAGE)			

CALIFORNIA: CATCH BY WATERS, 1949 - Continued

SPECIES	OFF CALIFORNIA		OFF LATIN AMERICA	
	POUNDS	VALUE	POUNDS	VALUE
FISH - CONTINUED				
SEA BASS, CONTINUED:				
WHITE.	945,500	$196,816	464,100	$94,048
SHAD	735,800	46,983	-	-
SHARKS, INCLUDING GRAYFISH	1,522,200	796,089	28,800	37,258
SHEEPSHEAD	48,500	3,443	13,100	946
SKATES	123,300	2,943	100	10
SMELT.	712,000	51,681	-	-
SPANISH MACKEREL	-	-	3,700	308
SWORDFISH.	141,800	62,687	56,600	24,819
TUNA AND TUNALIKE FISHES:				
ALBACORE	20,456,600	3,567,884	23,576,900	4,577,109
BLUEFIN.	2,266,200	367,680	2,123,200	345,022
BONITO	99,200	9,695	1,730,300	168,486
SKIPJACK OR STRIPED.	26,700	3,942	78,543,700	11,650,052
YELLOWFIN.	9,900	1,613	184,962,400	30,189,799
WHITEBAIT.	241,800	23,690	-	-
WHITEFISH.	12,700	1,074	18,500	1,449
YELLOWTAIL	17,700	1,665	7,301,800	684,335
UNCLASSIFIED	235,100	18,511	6,700	697
TOTAL	806,783,600	22,044,952	301,229,100	48,138,197
SHELLFISH				
CRABS, DUNGENESS AND ROCK	11,116,900	1,294,356	-	-
LOBSTERS, SPINY.	834,300	283,325	-	-
SHRIMP	804,400	49,127	-	-
ABALONE.	713,600	398,259	-	-
CLAMS, HARD 1/	20,400	11,984	-	-
OCTOPUS.	75,100	5,973	-	-
OYSTERS, MARKET:				
EASTERN.	6,500	4,654	-	-
PACIFIC.	28,200	21,744	-	-
SQUID.	6,859,100	184,173	-	-
TOTAL	20,458,500	2,253,595	-	-
WHALE PRODUCTS				
LIVER.	28,000	8,000	-	-
MEAL:				
BONE	100,000	2,500	-	-
MEAT	100,000	5,000	-	-
OIL:				
WHALE.	209,600	13,975	-	-
SPERM.	352,500	38,500	-	-
TOTAL	790,100	67,975	-	-
GRAND TOTAL	828,032,200	24,366,522	301,229,100	48,138,197

1/ INCLUDES A SMALL QUANTITY OF MUSSELS.

NOTE:--COMPLETE DATA ON THE GEAR WERE NOT OBTAINED FOR 1949. INFORMATION ON THE CATCH OF CERTAIN SPECIES
BY GEAR CAN BE FOUND IN SECTION 12. THE CATCH BY DISTRICT AND GEAR IS TABULATED IN THAT SECTION FOR
PACIFIC MACKEREL, PILCHARD, SALMON, TUNA, AND WHALES.

GILL NET DRYING

LANDINGS BY HALIBUT FLEET AT SEATTLE, WASH.

During 1949, landings of halibut, lingcod, rockfishes, and sablefish at Seattle, Washington, by the United States halibut fleet amounted to 11,623,000 pounds, valued at $2,157,000 to the fishermen. In addition, a total of 762,841 pounds of assorted fish livers and viscera, valued at $432,634 was landed by these vessels. The combined landings were 4 percent larger than in 1948. However, the value was 1 percent less than in the previous year.

A summary of the 1949 landings at Seattle by the United States halibut fleet is contained below. The landings represent the dressed weight of the catch, and are not directly comparable with data contained in the sectional and State catch tables. For additional information on the Pacific Coast halibut fishery, the reader is referred to Section 12 of this Digest entitled ''Peview of Certain Major Fisheries''.

LANDINGS BY HALIBUT FLEET AT SEATTLE BY FISHING GROUNDS, 1949[1]/

FISHING GROUNDS	TRIPS	HALIBUT					LINGCOD	
		NO. 1		NO. 2			
	NUMBER	POUNDS	VALUE	POUNDS	VALUE	POUNDS	VALUE
WEST OF CAPE SPENCER.	154	3,574,995	$784,443	3,252,136	$637,739	83	$4
SOUTH OF CAPE SPENCER	330	1,378,131	334,964	913,933	162,146	497,111	47,550
TOTAL,1949.	484	4,953,126	1,119,407	4,166,069	799,885	497,194	47,554
TOTAL,1948.	461	4,977,632	1,132,984	4,102,106	746,601	491,683	53,744

FISHING GROUNDS	ROCKFISHES		SABLEFISH		TOTAL	
	POUNDS	VALUE	POUNDS	VALUE	POUNDS	VALUE
WEST OF CAPE SPENCER.	265	$13	12,145	$802	6,839,624	$1,423,001
SOUTH OF CAPE SPENCER	196,836	13,111	1,797,707	176,609	4,783,718	734,380
TOTAL,1949.	197,101	13,124	1,809,852	177,411	11,623,342	2,157,391
TOTAL,1948.	229,699	14,387	1,372,309	227,947	11,173,428	2,175,663

1/ IN ADDITION, VESSELS OF THE SEATTLE HALIBUT FLEET LANDED THE FOLLOWING QUANTITIES OF FISH LIVERS AND VISCERA: - GRAYFISH (DOGFISH) LIVERS, 55,300 POUNDS, VALUED AT $11,060; HALIBUT LIVERS AND VISCERA 472,375 POUNDS, VALUED AT $264,912; LINGCOD LIVERS AND VISCERA, 45,741 POUNDS, VALUED AT $49,222; SABLEFISH LIVERS AND VISCERA, 162,887 POUNDS, VALUED AT $95,922; ROCKFISH LIVERS, 7,644 POUNDS, VALUED AT $7,644; SOUPFIN SHARK LIVERS, 239 POUNDS, VALUED AT $1,076; AND MISCELLANEOUS LIVERS AND VISCERA, 18,655 POUNDS, VALUED AT $2,798 TO FISHERMEN.

LANDINGS BY HALIBUT FLEET AT SEATTLE BY MONTHS, 1949[1]/

MONTH	TRIPS	HALIBUT					LINGCOD	
		NO. 1		NO. 2			
	NUMBER	POUNDS	VALUE	POUNDS	VALUE	POUNDS	VALUE
JANUARY.	16	-	-	-	--	132,837	$12,476
FEBRUARY	7	-	-	-	-	53,910	5,978
MARCH.	13	-	-	-	-	65,489	7,784
APRIL.	9	-	-	-	--	48,947	5,429
MAY.	83	1,773,115	$378,726	1,045,653	$197,637	26,926	1,512
JUNE	92	1,462,982	362,600	1,275,145	256,956	11,462	540
JULY	97	1,524,883	320,566	1,820,231	337,792	658	33
AUGUST	31	38,245	11,474	2,758	816	1,312	67
SEPTEMBER.	48	78,448	23,571	19,918	5,975	5,568	328
OCTOBER.	50	53,188	15,790	2,354	709	31,733	2,389
NOVEMBER	27	22,265	6,680	-	-	37,880	2,899
DECEMBER	11	-	--	-	-	79,472	8,121
TOTAL,1949	484	4,953,126	1,119,407	4,166,069	799,835	497,194	47,554
TOTAL,1948	461	4,977,632	1,132,934	4,102,105	746,601	491,693	53,744
1949 COMPARED WITH 1948	+5%	-1%	-1%	+2%	+7%	+1%	-12%

(CONTINUED ON NEXT PAGE)

LANDINGS BY HALIBUT FLEET AT SEATTLE BY MONTHS, 1949[1]/ Continued

MONTH	ROCKFISHES		SABLEFISH		TOTAL	
	POUNDS	VALUE	POUNDS	VALUE	POUNDS	VALUE
JANUARY.	18,831	$1,777	–	–	151,668	$14,253
FEBRUARY	9,732	964	–	–	63,642	6,942
MARCH.	14,804	1,605	1,614	$202	81,907	9,591
APRIL.	3,196	302	–	–	52,143	5,731
MAY.	4,118	204	2,229	191	2,852,041	578,270
JUNE	9,114	462	3,635	365	2,762,338	620,923
JULY	1,586	80	94,613	10,417	3,441,971	668,888
AUGUST	23,213	1,155	401,336	41,661	466,864	55,173
SEPTEMBER.	53,669	2,683	544,763	53,763	703,366	86,320
OCTOBER.	38,134	1,845	508,831	49,151	634,250	68,883
NOVEMBER	15,722	1,796	246,647	21,963	322,514	33,337
DECEMBER	4,982	251	6,184	698	90,638	9,070
TOTAL, 1949	197,101	13,124	1,809,852	177,411	11,623,342	2,157,381
TOTAL, 1948	229,698	14,387	1,372,309	227,947	11,173,428	2,175,663
1949 COMPARED WITH 1948	-14%	-9%	+32%	-22%	+4%	-1%

[1]/ IN ADDITION, VESSELS OF THE SEATTLE HALIBUT FLEET LANDED THE FOLLOWING QUANTITIES OF FISH LIVERS AND
VISCERA: - GRAYFISH (DOGFISH) LIVERS, 55,300 POUNDS, VALUED AT $11,060; HALIBUT LIVERS AND VISCERA 472,375
POUNDS, VALUED AT $264,912; LINGCOD LIVERS AND VISCERA, 45,741 POUNDS, VALUED AT $49,222; SABLEFISH LIVERS
AND VISCERA, 162,887 POUNDS, VALUED AT $95,922; ROCKFISH LIVERS, 7,644 POUNDS, VALUED AT $7,644; SOUPFIN
SHARK LIVERS, 239 POUNDS, VALUED AT $1,076; AND MISCELLANEOUS LIVERS AND VISCERA, 18,655 POUNDS, VALUED AT
$2,798 TO THE FISHERMEN.

NOTE: THE 1949 HALIBUT FISHING SEASON OPENED ON MAY 1. GROUNDS SOUTH OF CAPE SPENCER (AREA 2) CLOSED ON
JUNE 3, AND GROUNDS WEST OF CAPE SPENCER (AREA 3) CLOSED ON JULY 12, A TOTAL OF 73 FISHING DAYS. IN 1948,
THE FISHING SEASON LASTED 72 DAYS AND IN 1947, 109 DAYS.

HALIBUT SCHOONER

RECEIPTS BY SEATTLE WHOLESALE DEALERS

The total quantity of fresh and frozen fish, shellfish, livers, and viscera received by Seattle wholesale dealers during 1949 from all sources totaled 88,520,910 pounds. This represented an increase of 7 percent compared with the amount received during the previous year.

The waters of Washington and Oregon were again the principal sources of supply, contributing 57 percent of the total receipts. Alaska was second, supplying 26 percent; and British Columbia third, with 16 percent. Other sources supplied the remaining 1 percent.

The following table contains information on the receipts by species, origin, and condition of the various species for 1949. More detailed information on these receipts can be obtained from the daily and monthly reports issued by the Service's Seattle Market News Office.

FISHERY PRODUCTS RECEIVED BY SEATTLE WHOLESALE DEALERS, 1949

ITEM			POUNDS	VALUE
FISH				
CARP, LOCAL	OTHER	ROUND	27,685	$1,938
COD, TRUE, LOCAL	EX-VESSEL	DRESSED	629,487	35,251
COD, TRUE, LOCAL	EX-VESSEL	ROUND	1,252,650	42,590
COD, TRUE, LOCAL	OTHER		43,815	1,972
COD, TRUE, ALASKA, FROZEN	DO		3,050	153
TOTAL, COD, TRUE			1,929,002	79,966
DOLLY VARDEN TROUT, ALASKA, FROZEN	DO		15,235	3,199
FLOUNDER, LOCAL	EX-VESSEL	ROUND	102,817	4,113
FLOUNDER, LOCAL	OTHER		17,013	681
TOTAL FLOUNDER			119,830	4,794
HALIBUT, LOCAL, NO. 1	EX-VESSEL	DRESSED	4,953,126	1,119,407
HALIBUT, LOCAL, NO. 2	DO	DO	4,156,069	799,885
HALIBUT, LOCAL, UNCLASSIFIED	OTHER		413,696	86,462
HALIBUT, ALASKA	DO		13,692	2,161
HALIBUT, ALASKA, FROZEN	DO		12,528,461	1,976,991
HALIBUT, BRITISH COLUMBIA	DO		615,301	97,095
HALIBUT, BRITISH COLUMBIA, FROZEN	DO		1,151,193	181,658
TOTAL HALIBUT			23,841,538	4,263,659
HERRING, LOCAL	DO	ROUND	26,835	1,342
HERRING, ALASKA, FROZEN	DO		83,100	3,324
HERRING, BRITISH COLUMBIA, FROZEN	DO		82,914	3,317
TOTAL HERRING			192,949	7,983
LINGCOD, LOCAL	EX-VESSEL	DRESSED	1,775,023	134,902
LINGCOD, LOCAL	DO	ROUND	489,579	24,479
LINGCOD, LOCAL	OTHER		444,562	28,007
LINGCOD, ALASKA, FROZEN	DO		82,256	4,113
LINGCOD, BRITISH COLUMBIA	DO		147,441	11,795
LINGCOD, BRITISH COLUMBIA, FROZEN	DO		52,213	4,177
TOTAL LINGCOD			2,991,074	207,473
PERCH, LOCAL	DO	ROUND	116,784	13,430
PERCH, BRITISH COLUMBIA	DO		8,777	1,009
TOTAL PERCH			125,561	14,439
PILCHARD, LOCAL	DO	DO	49,275	2,710
ROCKFISHES, LOCAL	EX-VESSEL	DRESSED	194,544	10,700
ROCKFISHES, LOCAL	DO	ROUND	7,989,124	351,522
ROCKFISHES, LOCAL	OTHER		151,772	8,008
ROCKFISHES, ALASKA, FROZEN	DO		4,076	163
ROCKFISHES, BRITISH COLUMBIA	DO		16,020	641
ROCKFISHES, BRITISH COLUMBIA, FROZEN	DO		900	36
TOTAL ROCKFISHES			8,366,436	371,070
SABLEFISH, LOCAL	EX-VESSEL	DRESSED	1,884,611	186,577
SABLEFISH, LOCAL	DO	ROUND	178,591	8,930
SABLEFISH, LOCAL	OTHER		245,557	13,369
SABLEFISH, ALASKA, FROZEN	DO		1,373,242	92,395
SABLEFISH, BRITISH COLUMBIA	DO		13,925	836
TOTAL SABLEFISH			3,696,926	297,107

(CONTINUED ON NEXT PAGE)

FISHERY PRODUCTS RECEIVED BY SEATTLE WHOLESALE DEALERS, 1949 - Continued

ITEM			POUNDS	VALUE
FISH - CONTINUED				
SALMON:				
CHINOOK, LOCAL, LARGE.	EX-VESSEL	DRAWN	345,335	$130,191
CHINOOK, LOCAL, SMALL. . . . . . :	DO	DO	278,832	85,880
CHINOOK, LOCAL, WHITE.	DO	DO	190,774	46,930
CHINOOK, UNCLASSIFIED.	DO	ROUND	57,981	7,364
CHINOOK, UNCLASSIFIED.	OTHER		3,153,543	834,112
CHINOOK, CALIFORNIA.	DO		7,908	1,509
CHINOOK, COLUMBIA RIVER.	DO		270,329	51,362
CHINOOK, ALASKA. . . . . . . :	DO		244,812	59,979
CHINOOK, ALASKA, FROZEN.	DO		1,439,465	352,669
CHINOOK, BRITISH COLUMBIA.	DO		4,127,331	994,687
CHINOOK, BRITISH COLUMBIA, FROZEN.	DO		313,548	75,565
TOTAL CHINOOK SALMON			10,429,857	2,640,248
CHUM, LOCAL.	EX-VESSEL	ROUND	492,877	71,467
CHUM, LOCAL.	OTHER		906,631	131,462
CHUM, ALASKA, FROZEN	DO		847,720	93,249
CHUM, BRITISH COLUMBIA	DO		1,997,987	219,779
CHUM, BRITISH COLUMBIA, FROZEN	DO		3,567,437	392,418
TOTAL CHUM SALMON.			7,812,652	908,375
PINK, LOCAL.	EX-VESSEL	ROUND	433,095	43,310
PINK, LOCAL.	OTHER		983,609	98,361
PINK, ALASKA, FROZEN	DO		372,331	29,787
PINK, BRITISH COLUMBIA	DO		184,482	14,759
PINK, BRITISH COLUMBIA, FROZEN	DO		29,896	2,392
TOTAL PINK SALMON.			2,003,413	188,609
SILVER, LOCAL.	EX-VESSEL	DRAWN	294,402	70,951
SILVER, LOCAL.	DO	ROUND	162,311	32,787
SILVER, LOCAL.	OTHER		3,110,496	688,975
SILVER, LOCAL, FROZEN.	DO		45,378	10,051
SILVER, ALASKA	DO		245	49
SILVER, ALASKA, FROZEN	DO		2,628,504	525,701
SILVER, BRITISH COLUMBIA	DO		15,080	3,016
SILVER, BRITISH COLUMBIA, FROZEN	DO		52,978	10,596
TOTAL SILVER SALMON.			6,309,394	1,342,126
SOCKEYE, LOCAL	DO	ROUND	248,399	49,680
SOCKEYE, ALASKA, FROZEN.	DO		565,895	113,179
TOTAL SOCKEYE SALMON			814,294	162,859
UNCLASSIFIED, ALASKA, FROZEN	DO		2,575	412
UNCLASSIFIED, BRITISH COLUMBIA , FROZEN. . .	DO		33,486	5,358
TOTAL UNCLASSIFIED SALMON.			36,061	5,770
TOTAL ALL SALMON			27,405,671	5,247,987
SHAD, CALIFORNIA	DO		8,929	1,473
SMELT, EULACHON, LOCAL	DO	DO	191,087	18,459
SMELT, EULACHON, BRITISH COLUMBIA.	DO		12,840	1,240
SMELT, EULACHON, BRITISH COLUMBIA, FROZEN. .	DO		20,800	2,009
SMELT, SILVER, LOCAL	DO	DO	576,432	57,643
TOTAL SMELT.			801,159	79,351
SOLE, ENGLISH, LOCAL	EX-VESSEL	ROUND	2,597,024	129,851
SOLE, ENGLISH, LOCAL	OTHER		74,895	3,745
SOLE, PETRALE, LOCAL	EX-VESSEL	DO	2,984,131	208,869
SOLE, PETRALE, LOCAL	OTHER		27,558	1,929
SOLE, UNCLASSIFIED, LOCAL.	EX-VESSEL	DO	60,165	3,008
SOLE, UNCLASSIFIED, BRITISH COLUMBIA	OTHER		27,009	1,621
TOTAL SOLE			5,770,782	349,043
SWORDFISH, JAPAN, FROZEN	DO		56,081	11,216
TUNA, ALBACORE, LOCAL.	EX-VESSEL	ROUND	404,056	71,922

(CONTINUED ON NEXT PAGE)

PACIFIC COAST STATES FISHERIES

FISHERY PRODUCTS RECEIVED BY SEATTLE WHOLESALE DEALERS, 1949 - Continued

ITEM			POUNDS	VALUE
FISH - CONTINUED				
TUNA, ALBACORE, LOCAL.	OTHER	ROUND	169,804	$30,225
TUNA, ALBACORE, BRITISH COLUMBIA	DO		111,903	18,285
TUNA, ALBACORE, BRITISH COLUMBIA, FROZEN . . .	DO		174,127	28,452
TUNA, ALBACORE, JAPAN, FROZEN.	DO		438,452	64,891
TUNA, BLUEFIN, CALIFORNIA, FROZEN.	DO		7,783	1,129
TOTAL TUNA			1,306,125	214,904
FILLETS, SOLE, LOCAL	DO		65,361	16,340
FILLETS, SOLE, LOCAL, FROZEN	DO		39,288	9,822
FILLETS, SOLE, BRITISH COLUMBIA.	DO		5,557	1,279
FILLETS, SOLE, BRITISH COLUMBIA, FROZEN. . . .	DO		351,952	80,949
FILLETS, SOLE, OTHER, LOCAL.	DO		64,672	12,934
FILLETS, SOLE, OTHER, LOCAL, FROZEN.	DO		11,487	2,297
FILLETS, SOLE, OTHER, ALASKA , FROZEN.	DO		520	104
FILLETS, SOLE, OTHER, BRITISH COLUMBIA	DO		13,850	2,770
FILLETS, SOLE, OTHER, BRITISH COLUMBIA,FROZEN.	DO		108,964	21,793
TOTAL FILLETS.			661,651	143,287
UNCLASSIFIED, LOCAL.	EX-VESSEL		4,189	419
UNCLASSIFIED, LOCAL, OTHER	OTHER		47,455	3,796
UNCLASSIFIED, LOCAL, OTHER, FROZEN	DO		5,415	1,218
UNCLASSIFIED, ALASKA, FROZEN	DO		3,412	171
TOTAL UNCLASSIFIED			60,471	5,604
ALL FISH				
FRESH, LOCAL	EX-VESSEL		31,920,793	3,621,325
FRESH, LOCAL, OTHER.	OTHER		11,167,936	2,110,580
FRESH, ALASKA.	DO		258,749	62,199
FRESH, BRITISH COLUMBIA.	DO		7,297,503	1,368,811
FRESH, OTHER SOURCES	DO		287,165	54,341
TOTAL FRESH.			50,932,146	7,217,249
FROZEN, LOCAL.	DO		101,568	23,388
FROZEN, ALASKA	DO		19,949,842	3,185,610
FROZEN, BRITISH COLUMBIA	DO		5,940,408	808,720
FROZEN, OTHER SOURCES.	DO		502,316	77,236
TOTAL FROZEN			26,494,134	4,094,954
TOTAL FRESH AND FROZEN FISH.			77,426,280	11,312,203
SHELLFISH (MEATS)				
CLAMS, BUTTER, LOCAL			27,094	7,559
CLAMS, LITTLE NECK, LOCAL.			120,465	38,308
CLAMS, RAZOR, LOCAL.			1,151	459
CLAMS, UNCLASSIFIED, ALASKA, FROZEN.			6,797	1,733
CLAMS, UNCLASSIFIED, BRITISH COLUMBIA.			203,891	51,990
TOTAL CLAMS.			359,388	100,049
CLAM MEAT, LOCAL			234	60
CLAM MEAT, ALASKA, FROZEN.			16,524	4,247
CLAM MEAT, BRITISH COLUMBIA.			38,947	10,009
CLAM MEAT, JAPAN, FROZEN			4,000	800
TOTAL CLAM MEAT.			59,705	15,116
CRABS, DUNGENESS, LOCAL, IN SHELL.			1,126,271	132,900
CRABS, BRITISH COLUMBIA.			15,190	1,823
TOTAL CRABS.			1,141,461	134,723
CRAB MEAT, LOCAL			120,368	99,905
CRAB MEAT, ALASKA, FROZEN.			337,533	280,152
TOTAL CRAB MEAT.			457,901	380,057
LOBSTER, CALIFORNIA.			17,741	9,758
LOBSTER, MEXICO.			54,351	29,893
LOBSTER, BRITISH COLUMBIA.			7,275	4,001
TOTAL LOBSTER.			79,367	43,652

(CONTINUED ON NEXT PAGE)

FISHERY PRODUCTS RECEIVED BY SEATTLE WHOLESALE DEALERS, 1949 - Continued

ITEMS	POUNDS	VALUE
SHELLFISH (MEATS) - CONTINUED		
OCTOPUS, LOCAL	14,030	$551
OYSTERS, EASTERN SHUCKED	4,261	3,528
OYSTERS, OLYMPIA, LOCAL, SHUCKED	13,750	31,350
OYSTERS, PACIFIC, LOCAL, SHUCKED	1,681,318	781,813
TOTAL OYSTERS.	1,699,329	816,691
SCALLOPS, BAY, LOCAL, SHUCKED.	7,825	4,742
SCALLOPS, BAY, JAPAN, FROZEN	5,886	2,943
SCALLOPS, BAY, NOVIA SCOTIA, FROZEN.	40,016	22,009
TOTAL SCALLOPS	53,727	29,694
SHRIMP, LOCAL.	935	234
SHRIMP, MEXICO	21,990	10,995
SHRIMP, GULF	200	100
SHRIMP, GULF, FROZEN	4,900	2,450
SHRIMP, ALASKA, FROZEN	22,500	11,250
TOTAL SHRIMP	50,525	25,029
SHRIMP MEAT, GULF, FROZEN.	15,364	11,523
SHRIMP MEAT, ALASKA, FROZEN.	492,972	369,729
TOTAL SHRIMP MEAT.	508,336	381,252
SQUID, LOCAL	615	42
SQUID, CALIFORNIA.	71,335	5,707
TOTAL SQUID.	71,950	5,749
ALL SHELLFISH		
FRESH, LOCAL	3,114,056	1,097,933
FRESH, BRITISH COLUMBIA.	265,293	67,823
FRESH, OTHER	159,878	59,981
TOTAL FRESH.	3,549,227	1,225,737
FROZEN, ALASKA	876,326	667,111
FROZEN, OTHER.	70,156	39,725
TOTAL FROZEN	946,492	706,836
TOTAL FRESH AND FROZEN SHELLFISH	4,495,719	1,932,573
ALL FISH AND SHELLFISH		
FRESH.	54,481,373	8,442,986
FROZEN	27,440,626	4,801,790
TOTAL FRESH AND FROZEN FISH AND SHELLFISH.	81,921,999	13,244,776
LIVERS AND VISCERA		
GRAYFISH (DOGFISH), LOCAL. . . . . . :	1,625,391	
GRAYFISH (DOGFISH), ALASKA, FROZEN	105,958	
HALIBUT AND VISCERA, ALASKA, FROZEN.	1,055,212	
LINGCOD, LOCAL	196,254	
SABLEFISH AND VISCERA, ALASKA, FROZEN.	254,062	
SOUPFIN SHARK, LOCAL	238,189	
UNCLASSIFIED, LOCAL.	2,543,697	
UNCLASSIFIED, ALASKA, FROZEN	362,100	
UNCLASSIFIED, BRITISH COLUMBIA, FROZEN	107,721	
UNCLASSIFIED, JAPAN, FROZEN.	96,382	
UNCLASSIFIED, IMPORTS, OTHER 1/.	22,945	
TOTAL LIVERS AND VISCERA	5,598,911	
GRAND TOTAL ALL FISH, SHELLFISH, LIVERS AND VISCERA.	88,520,910	

1/ FROM ARGENTINA, PORTUGAL AND GUATEMALA.

SECTION 8.- LAKE FISHERIES [9]

During 1949, the commercial catch of fish and shellfish in the Great Lakes and the International Lakes of Northern Minnesota amounted to 85,692,600 pounds, valued at $11,458,418 to the fishermen. This represented an increase of 2 percent in quantity but a decrease of 10 percent in value compared with the previous year. In addition, the Canadian catch in these lakes amounted to 29,204,324 pounds. Lake Erie was the leading producer, with United States fishermen taking 34,249,300 pounds and Canadian fishermen, 18,652,500 pounds. Lake Michigan was second in production with 25,573,200 pounds, the entire amount being taken by United States fishermen.

The total 1949 fisheries production in the Great Lakes area was maintained at a normal level and prices for some species held up exceptionally well. However, a marked decrease in demand was reflected in the catch of certain other species. Yellow pike production recorded a substantial increase over the previous year, with good prices prevailing at various periods. Whitefish production was down over 3 million pounds compared with 1948, and the prices paid for this species during the year ranged widely but averaged approximately 34 cents per pound. Herring prices ranged from 2 to 12 cents per pound and maintained an average of approximately 3-1/2 cents per pound. The November and December runs of herring in Lake Michigan and Lake Superior were the most productive, with large quantities of this catch going to fur ranches for animal food. Sucker "mullet" production held up well and prices averaging 4 cents per pound were received during 1949. Large quantities of this species were shipped to the nearby metropolitan areas during certain religious holidays. The catch of lake trout continued to decrease and the 1949 take of this species (3,308,800 pounds) was the smallest since 1913 when continuous records first became available. The consistent decrease in lake trout production is believed to have been at least partially caused by the sea lamprey in the Great Lakes. Extensive studies and practices on methods of lamprey control were carried out by the United States Fish and Wildlife Service in the Great Lakes during 1949.

The most recent data available on operating units employed in the fisheries of the Great Lakes and the International Lakes of Northern Minnesota are for 1940. In that year, 5,142 United States fishermen were employed. If the lakes fisheries have followed the same trend as the fisheries of other areas, it may be assumed that the number of fishermen employed was considerably greater for 1949.

The last complete survey of the fishery transporting, wholesaling, and manufacturing industries was made for 1940. In that year, 33 men were employed on 11 vessels operating in the transporting trade, and 3,030 persons were employed in the wholesale and manufacturing establishments. The latter employees received $2,842,680 in salaries and wages in 1940. Detailed statistics on these branches of the industry for 1940 can be found in "Fishery Statistics of the United States, 1944" (Statistical Digest No. 16), and in the Digests for the years from 1940 to 1943 inclusive.

---

9   The statistics of the catch were obtained principally from records of the various state agencies and from the Dominion Bureau of Statistics, Ottawa, Canada. In all cases, the statistics collected are for the calendar year. The season opens on May 15 on Rainy and Namakan Lakes and on Lake of the Woods the season opens on June 1. Since 1941, on Lake of the Woods, and since 1947 on Rainy and Namakan Lakes, there has been but one season which ends on December 31. Actually the season ends with the freeze-up, and few, if any, fishermen fish under the ice.

The following tables contain a summary of the United States and Canadian catch in the Great Lakes and International Lakes of Northern Minnesota as well as detailed data on the catch by gear. Condensed summary data on the catch by states of the Lake Fisheries have been previously published in Current Fishery Statistics No. 662. Historical data on the fisheries of the Great Lakes can be found in the Report of the International Board of Inquiry for the Great Lakes, which can be purchased from the Superintendent of Documents, Washington 25, D. C.

UNITED STATES AND CANADA: LAKES CATCH, 1949

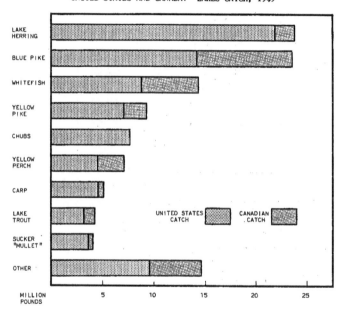

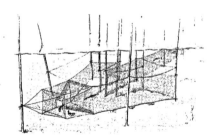

GREAT LAKES TRAP NET

LAKE FISHERIES

SUMMARY OF UNITED STATES AND CANADIAN CATCH, 1949

SPECIES	LAKE ONTARIO			LAKE ERIE		
	UNITED STATES	CANADA	TOTAL	UNITED STATES	CANADA	TOTAL
	POUNDS	POUNDS	POUNDS	POUNDS	POUNDS	POUNDS
BLUE PIKE.	85,700	46,300	132,000	13,999,500	9,471,100	23,470,600
BOWFIN	(2)	(1)	-	12,600	(1)	12,600
BUFFALOFISH.	-	(1)	-	5,400	(1)	5,400
BULLHEADS.	87,200	(1)	87,200	124,600	(1)	124,600
BURBOT	300	400	700	304,700	189,800	494,500
CARP	20,500	136,900	157,400	2,234,000	264,000	2,498,000
CATFISH.	500	582,600	583,100	867,200	155,500	1,022,700
CHUBS.	-	(1)	-	-	(1)	-
CISCO.	45,900	(1)	45,900	88,400	(1)	88,400
EELS	19,500	36,900	56,400	-	(1)	-
GARFISH.	(2)	(1)	-	30,000	(1)	30,000
GIZZARD SHAD	-	(1)	-	170,500	(1)	170,500
GOLDFISH	-	167,600	167,600	-	259,800	259,800
LAKE HERRING	(2)	16,900	16,900	(2)	1,000	1,000
LAKE TROUT	(2)	(1)	-	7,400	(1)	7,400
MOONEYE.	-	(1)	-	10,500	(1)	10,500
PIKE OR PICKEREL (JACKS)	5,400	20,000	25,400	-	(1)	-
QUILLBACK.	-	(1)	-	-	(1)	-
ROCK BASS.	20,100	(1)	20,100	7,600	(1)	7,600
SAUGER	-	800	800	390,100	284,700	674,800
SHEEPSHEAD	-	(1)	-	3,084,700	(1)	3,084,700
SMELT.	4,100	202,900	207,000	-	14,400	14,400
STURGEON	2,500	3,100	5,600	19,200	11,000	30,200
SUCKER "MULLET".	27,400	48,900	76,300	634,100	72,100	706,200
SUNFISH.	8,800	(1)	8,800	-	(1)	-
TULLIBEE	-	87,800	87,800	-	400	400
WHITE BASS	100	700	800	807,200	980,600	1,787,800
WHITEFISH:						
COMMON	2,400	195,200	197,600	3,478,600	3,468,500	6,947,100
MENOMINEE.	-	(1)	-	-	(1)	-
YELLOW PERCH	18,700	121,100	139,800	2,659,200	2,126,700	4,785,900
YELLOW PIKE.	1,900	33,300	35,200	5,313,800	828,700	6,142,500
CRAWFISH	-	(1)	-	-	(1)	-
UNCLASSIFIED	-	240,700	240,700	-	524,200	524,200
TOTAL	351,000	1,942,100	2,293,100	34,249,300	18,652,500	52,901,800

SPECIES	LAKE HURON			LAKE MICHIGAN	LAKE SUPERIOR		
	UNITED STATES	CANADA	TOTAL	UNITED STATES	UNITED STATES	CANADA	TOTAL
	POUNDS	POUNDS	POUNDS	POUNDS	POUNDS	POUNDS	POUNDS
BLUE PIKE.	-	(1)	-	1,000	-	(1)	-
BOWFIN	8,300	(1)	8,300	200	-	(1)	-
BUFFALOFISH.	18,400	(1)	18,400	94,700	-	(1)	-
BULLHEADS	600	85,600	86,200	27,900	6,100	23,500	29,600
BURBOT	952,400	58,700	1,011,100	1,361,200	(1)	100	100
CARP	166,700	21,100	187,800	27,400	-	(1)	-
CATFISH.	147,900	(1)	147,900	7,421,200	162,600	(1)	162,600
CHUBS.	-	(1)	-	-	-	(1)	-
CISCO.	-	(1)	-	(1)	-	(1)	-
EELS	-	(1)	-	-	-	(1)	-
GARFISH.	1,600	(1)	1,600	-	-	(1)	-
GIZZARD SHAD	-	(1)	-	-	-	(1)	-
GOLDFISH	1,951,900	158,000	2,109,900	6,778,300	13,204,100	1,270,700	14,474,800
LAKE HERRING	900	328,400	329,300	342,100	2,965,800	1,184,900	4,150,700
LAKE TROUT	100	(1)	100	-	-	(1)	-
MOONEYE.	13,500	43,900	57,400	29,700	700	3,900	4,600
PIKE OR PICKEREL (JACKS)	-	(1)	-	-	-	(1)	-
QUILLBACK.	12,100	(1)	12,100	800	(1)	(1)	-
ROCK BASS.	300	3,000	3,300	100	200	15,200	15,400
SAUGER	1,900	(1)	1,900	41,200	-	(1)	-
SHEEPSHEAD	11,600	1,000	12,600	1,539,900	1,000	(1)	1,000
SMELT.	-	12,900	12,900	-	-	500	500
STURGEON	1,022,300	208,700	1,231,000	1,810,300	63,600	62,000	125,600
SUCKER "MULLET".	-	345,200	345,200	-	-	(1)	-
SUNFISH.	400	14,700	15,100	-	-	74,200	74,200
TULLIBEE	-			-	-	200	200
WHITE BASS							
WHITEFISH:							
COMMON	530,200	1,268,300	1,798,500	3,491,900	1,283,700	251,600	1,535,300
MENOMINEE.	21,800	(1)	21,800	106,200	15,800	(1)	15,800
YELLOW PERCH	517,600	202,500	720,100	1,377,500	300	400	700
YELLOW PIKE.	200,000	466,900	666,900	1,119,900	26,400	130,700	157,100
CRAWFISH	-	(1)	-	1,700	-	(1)	-
UNCLASSIFIED	-	16,300	16,300	-	-	2,200	2,200
TOTAL.	5,580,500	3,235,200	8,815,700	25,573,200	17,730,300	3,020,100	20,750,400

SEE FOOTNOTES AT END OF TABLE (CONTINUED ON NEXT PAGE)

SUMMARY OF UNITED STATES AND CANADIAN CATCH, 1949 - Continued

SPECIES	NAMAKAN LAKE			RAINY LAKE		
	UNITED STATES	CANADA	TOTAL	UNITED STATES	CANADA	TOTAL
	POUNDS	POUNDS	POUNDS	POUNDS	POUNDS	POUNDS
BLUE PIKE	-	(1)	-	-	(1)	-
BOWFIN	-	(1)	-	-	(1)	-
BUFFALOFISH	-	(1)	-	-	(1)	-
BULLHEADS	-	(1)	-	-	(1)	-
BURBOT	5,100	(1)	5,100	37,200	(1)	37,200
CARP	-	(1)	-	-	(1)	-
CATFISH	-	(1)	-	-	(1)	-
CHUBS	-	(1)	-	-	(1)	-
CISCO	-	(1)	-	-	(1)	-
EELS	-	(1)	-	-	(1)	-
GARFISH	-	(1)	-	-	(1)	-
GIZZARD SHAD	-	(1)	-	-	(1)	-
GOLDFISH	-	(1)	-	-	(1)	-
LAKE HERRING	-	(1)	-	-	(1)	-
LAKE TROUT	-	(1)	-	-	(1)	-
MOONEYE	-	(1)	-	-	(1)	-
PIKE OR PICKEREL (JACKS)	-	2,988	2,988	19,200	128,695	147,895
QUILLBACK	-	(1)	-	(1)	(1)	-
ROCK BASS	-	(1)	-	-	(1)	-
SAUGER	-	(1)	-	-	(1)	-
SHEEPSHEAD	-	(1)	-	-	(1)	-
SMELT	-	(1)	-	-	(1)	-
STURGEON	-	504	504	-	684	684
SUCKER "MULLET"	5,200	(1)	5,200	41,300	(1)	41,300
SUNFISH	-	(1)	-	-	(1)	-
TULLIBEE	12,900	5,200	18,100	25,100	71,624	96,724
WHITE BASS	-	-	-	-	(1)	-
WHITEFISH:						
COMMON	7,600	2,251	9,851	40,300	73,849	114,149
MENOMINEE	-	(1)	-	-	(1)	-
YELLOW PERCH	-	(1)	-	200	2,670	2,870
YELLOW PIKE	-	1,490	1,490	34,500	160,414	194,914
CRAWFISH	-	(1)	-	-	(1)	-
UNCLASSIFIED	-	5,000	5,000	-	176,377	176,377
TOTAL	30,800	17,433	48,233	197,800	614,313	812,113

SPECIES	LAKE OF THE WOODS			TOTAL, ALL LAKES		
	UNITED STATES	CANADA	TOTAL	UNITED STATES	CANADA	TOTAL
	POUNDS	POUNDS	POUNDS	POUNDS	POUNDS	POUNDS
BLUE PIKE	-	(1)	-	14,085,200	9,517,400	23,602,600
BOWFIN	-	(1)	-	21,900	(1)	21,900
BUFFALOFISH	-	(1)	-	5,600	(1)	5,600
BULLHEADS	28,900	(1)	28,900	353,800	(1)	353,800
BURBOT	458,800	(1)	458,800	840,700	299,300	1,140,000
CARP	-	88	88	4,568,100	459,788	5,027,888
CATFISH	-	31,577	31,577	1,061,800	790,777	1,852,577
CHUBS	-	(1)	-	7,731,700	(1)	7,731,700
CISCO	-	(1)	-	134,300	(1)	134,300
EELS	-	(1)	-	19,500	36,900	56,400
GARFISH	-	(1)	-	(2)	(1)	-
GIZZARD SHAD	-	(1)	-	31,600	(1)	31,600
GOLDFISH	-	(1)	-	170,500	(1)	170,500
LAKE HERRING	-	(1)	-	21,934,300	1,856,100	23,790,400
LAKE TROUT	-	2,228	2,228	3,308,800	1,533,428	4,842,228
MOONEYE	-	(1)	-	7,500	(1)	7,500
PIKE OR PICKEREL (JACKS)	86,700	387,300	474,000	165,700	586,783	752,483
QUILLBACK	2,100	(1)	2,100	2,100	(1)	2,100
ROCK BASS	-	(1)	-	40,600	(1)	40,600
SAUGER	116,900	(1)	116,900	507,600	303,700	811,300
SHEEPSHEAD	-	(1)	-	3,127,800	(1)	3,127,800
SMELT	-	(1)	-	1,556,600	(1)	1,556,600
STURGEON	-	(1)	-	21,700	28,688	50,388
SUCKER "MULLET"	71,400	(1)	71,400	3,675,600	391,700	4,067,300
SUNFISH	-	(1)	-	8,800	(1)	8,800
TULLIBEE	771,600	17,767	789,367	809,600	602,191	1,411,791
WHITE BASS	-	(1)	-	807,700	996,200	1,803,900
WHITEFISH:						
COMMON	2,400	218,670	221,070	8,837,100	5,478,370	14,315,470
MENOMINEE	-	(1)	-	143,800	(1)	143,800
YELLOW PERCH	21,700	12,557	34,257	4,595,200	2,465,927	7,061,127
YELLOW PIKE	419,200	751,769	1,170,969	7,115,700	2,373,273	9,488,973
CRAWFISH	-	(1)	-	1,700	(1)	1,700
UNCLASSIFIED	-	300,722	300,722	-	1,265,499	1,265,499
TOTAL	1,979,700	1,722,678	3,702,378	85,692,600	29,204,324	114,896,924

1/ WHERE THERE IS A CANADIAN CATCH OF THESE SPECIES, IT IS SHOWN UNDER "UNCLASSIFIED".
2/ LESS THAN 50 POUNDS.

UNITED STATES: CATCH BY STATES, 1949

SPECIES	NEW YORK		PENNSYLVANIA		OHIO	
	POUNDS	VALUE	POUNDS	VALUE	POUNDS	VALUE
BLUE PIKE.	990,300	$94,536	2,479,100	$210,258	10,615,800	$1,263,190
BOWFIN	(1)	1	-	-	4,400	133
BUFFALOFISH.	-	-	-	-	5,400	856
BULLHEADS.	87,200	16,241	-	-	84,800	10,175
BURBOT	4,700	106	1,400	73	298,800	17,611
CARP	20,500	414	900	19	1,677,700	50,675
CATFISH.	1,300	134	100	6	839,100	150,693
CISCO.	49,400	9,406	27,600	8,258	57,300	19,079
EELS	19,500	1,731	-	-	-	-
GARFISH.	(1)	1	-	-	-	-
GIZZARD SHAD	-	-	-	-	30,000	900
GOLDFISH	-	-	-	-	170,500	8,526
LAKE TROUT	(1)	5	-	-	(1)	4
MOONEYE	-	-	-	-	7,300	362
PIKE OR PICKEREL (JACKS)	5,400	523	-	-	3,800	489
ROCK BASS.	20,100	986	-	-	378,800	48,563
SAUGER	-	-	9,100	1,700	3,010,800	120,433
SHEEPSHEAD	-	-	-	-	-	-
SMELT.	4,100	606	-	-	-	-
STURGEON	2,500	2,147	(1)	18	19,200	19,517
SUCKER "MULLET".	33,500	1,913	5,600	165	585,200	11,781
SUNFISH.	8,800	663	-	-	-	-
WHITE BASS	4,800	422	49,500	4,201	723,900	93,597
WHITEFISH, COMMON.	1,015,200	268,444	1,728,400	472,642	737,400	253,595
YELLOW PERCH	29,900	3,142	108,300	11,082	2,507,600	362,829
YELLOW PIKE.	7,500	1,502	26,000	4,111	4,924,300	1,030,806
TOTAL.	2,304,700	402,923	4,436,000	712,532	26,682,100	3,464,034

SPECIES	MICHIGAN		INDIANA		ILLINOIS	
	POUNDS	VALUE	POUNDS	VALUE	POUNDS	VALUE
BOWFIN	16,500	$529	-	-	-	-
BUFFALOFISH	-	-	200	$33	-	-
BULLHEADS	71,500	7,079	-	-	-	-
BURBOT.	5,000	276	-	-	-	-
CARP.	1,545,600	47,701	2,000	56	-	-
CATFISH	195,100	44,255	-	-	-	-
CHUBS	2,575,500	470,762	-	-	1,299,300	$246,870
GIZZARD SHAD.	1,600	30	-	-	-	-
LAKE HERRING.	8,470,900	299,184	19,200	713	25,100	1,760
LAKE TROUT.	2,405,300	949,647	-	-	3,700	1,394
MOONEYE	200	8	-	-	-	-
PIKE OR PICKEREL (JACKS). . . .	38,100	4,592	200	21	-	-
ROCK BASS	20,500	2,415	-	-	-	-
SAUGER.	11,900	1,781	-	-	-	-
SHEEPSHEAD.	74,900	2,112	-	-	-	-
SMELT	1,062,900	99,272	600	55	-	-
SUCKER "MULLET"	2,273,500	106,918	1,500	69	-	-
WHITE BASS.	29,500	3,342	-	-	-	-
WHITEFISH:						
COMMON.	4,040,700	1,503,550	400	158	200	68
MENOMINEE	130,500	24,476	-	-	-	-
YELLOW PERCH.	928,500	134,261	6,300	954	168,300	35,844
YELLOW PIKE	1,635,700	414,109	-	-	-	-
TOTAL	25,533,900	4,116,399	30,400	2,059	1,495,600	285,936

SPECIES	WISCONSIN		MINNESOTA		TOTAL	
	POUNDS	VALUE	POUNDS	VALUE	POUNDS	VALUE
BLUE PIKE	-	-	-	-	14,085,200	$1,567,984
BOWFIN	1,000	$35	-	-	21,900	698
BUFFALOFISH	-	-	-	-	5,600	889
BULLHEADS	81,400	11,393	28,900	$4,630	353,800	49,518
BURBOT.	27,600	551	503,200	5,810	840,700	24,647
CARP.	1,321,400	52,856	-	-	4,568,100	151,720
CATFISH	26,200	5,765	-	-	1,061,800	200,853
CHUBS	3,803,200	565,834	53,700	10,730	7,731,700	1,294,196
CISCO	-	-	-	-	134,300	36,743
EELS.	-	-	-	-	19,500	1,731
GARFISH	(1)	(1)	-	-	(1)	1
GIZZARD SHAD.	-	-	-	-	31,600	930

SEE FOOTNOTE AT END OF TABLE   (CONTINUED ON NEXT PAGE)

UNITED STATES: CATCH BY STATES, 1949 - Continued

SPECIES	WISCONSIN POUNDS	WISCONSIN VALUE	MINNESOTA POUNDS	MINNESOTA VALUE	TOTAL POUNDS	TOTAL VALUE
GOLDFISH	-	-	-	-	170,500	$8,526
LAKE HERRING	9,365,200	$324,326	4,053,900	$162,160	21,934,300	788,143
LAKE TROUT	629,400	304,967	270,400	98,663	3,308,800	1,354,680
MOONEYE	-	-	-	-	7,500	370
PIKE OR PICKEREL (JACKS)	12,300	1,231	105,900	7,990	165,700	14,946
QUILLBACK	-	-	2,100	40	2,100	40
ROCK BASS	-	-	-	-	40,600	3,401
SAUGER	-	-	116,900	9,350	507,600	59,694
SHEEPSHEAD	33,000	3,301	-	-	3,127,800	127,546
SMELT	489,000	48,899	-	-	1,556,600	148,832
STURGEON	-	-	-	-	21,700	21,682
SUCKER "MULLET"	657,900	32,895	118,400	2,417	3,675,600	156,158
SUNFISH	-	-	-	-	8,800	663
TULLIBEE	-	-	809,600	47,440	809,600	47,440
WHITE BASS	-	-	-	-	807,700	101,562
WHITEFISH:						
COMMON	1,251,200	524,440	63,600	16,700	8,837,100	3,039,597
MENOMINEE	12,400	1,242	900	170	143,800	25,888
YELLOW PERCH	824,400	123,667	21,900	2,850	4,595,200	674,629
YELLOW PIKE	68,500	17,123	453,700	86,540	7,115,700	1,554,191
CRAWFISH	1,700	520	-	-	1,700	520
TOTAL	18,605,800	2,019,045	6,603,100	455,490	85,692,600	11,458,418

1/ LESS THAN 50 POUNDS OR 50 CENTS.

UNITED STATES: CATCH BY LAKES, 1949

SPECIES	LAKE ONTARIO NEW YORK POUNDS	VALUE	LAKE ERIE NEW YORK POUNDS	VALUE	PENNSYLVANIA POUNDS	VALUE
BLUE PIKE	85,700	$16,351	904,600	$78,185	2,479,100	$210,258
BOWFIN	(1)	1	-	-	-	-
BULLHEADS	87,200	16,241	-	-	-	-
BURBOT	300	5	4,400	101	1,400	73
CARP	20,500	414	(1)	(1)	900	18
CATFISH	500	49	800	85	100	6
CISCO	45,900	8,351	3,500	1,055	27,600	8,258
EELS	19,500	1,731	-	-	-	-
GARFISH	(1)	1	-	-	-	-
LAKE TROUT	(1)	5	-	-	-	-
PIKE OR PICKEREL (JACKS)	5,400	523	-	-	-	-
ROCK BASS	20,100	986	-	-	-	-
SHEEPSHEAD	-	-	-	-	9,100	1,700
SMELT	4,100	606	-	-	-	-
STURGEON	2,500	2,109	(1)	38	(1)	18
SUCKER "MULLET"	27,400	1,738	6,100	175	5,600	165
SUNFISH	8,900	663	-	-	-	-
WHITE BASS	100	5	4,700	417	49,500	4,201
WHITEFISH, COMMON	2,400	1,133	1,012,800	267,311	1,728,400	472,642
YELLOW PERCH	18,700	1,894	11,200	1,248	108,300	11,082
YELLOW PIKE	1,900	462	5,600	1,040	26,000	4,111
TOTAL	351,000	53,268	1,953,700	349,655	4,436,000	712,532

SPECIES	LAKE ERIE - CONTINUED OHIO POUNDS	VALUE	MICHIGAN POUNDS	VALUE	TOTAL POUNDS	VALUE
BLUE PIKE	10,615,800	$1,263,190	-	-	13,999,500	$1,551,633
BOWFIN	4,400	133	8,200	$284	12,600	417
BUFFALOFISH	5,400	856	-	-	5,400	856
BULLHEADS	84,800	10,175	39,800	4,247	124,600	14,422
BURBOT	298,800	17,831	100	3	304,700	18,008
CARP	1,677,700	50,675	555,400	17,226	2,234,000	67,919
CATFISH	839,100	150,693	27,200	4,274	867,200	155,058
CISCO	57,300	19,079	-	-	88,400	28,392
GIZZARD SHAD	30,000	900	-	-	30,000	900
GOLDFISH	170,500	8,526	-	-	170,500	8,526
LAKE TROUT	(1)	4	-	-	(1)	4
MOONEYE	7,300	362	100	7	7,400	369

SEE FOOTNOTE AT END OF TABLE   (CONTINUED ON NEXT PAGE)

UNITED STATES: CATCH BY LAKES, 1949 - Continued

SPECIES	LAKE ERIE - CONTINUED					
	OHIO		MICHIGAN		TOTAL	
	POUNDS	VALUE	POUNDS	VALUE	POUNDS	VALUE
PIKE OR PICKEREL (JACKS). . . .	3,800	$489	6,700	$889	10,500	$1,378
ROCK BASS	-	-	7,600	966	7,600	966
SAUGER.	378,800	48,563	11,300	1,689	390,100	50,252
SHEEPSHEAD.	3,010,800	120,433	64,800	1,464	3,084,700	123,597
STURGEON.	19,200	19,517	-	-	19,200	19,573
SUCKER "MULLET".	585,200	11,781	37,200	984	634,100	13,105
WHITE BASS.	723,900	93,597	29,100	3,265	807,200	101,480
WHITEFISH, COMMON	737,400	253,595	-	-	3,478,600	993,548
YELLOW PERCH.	2,507,600	362,829	32,100	5,701	2,659,200	380,860
YELLOW PIKE	4,924,300	1,030,806	357,900	50,886	5,313,800	1,086,843
TOTAL.	26,682,100	3,464,034	1,177,500	91,885	34,249,300	4,618,106

SPECIES	LAKE HURON		LAKE MICHIGAN			
	MICHIGAN		MICHIGAN		INDIANA	
	POUNDS	VALUE	POUNDS	VALUE	POUNDS	VALUE
BOWFIN	8,300	$245	(1)	(1)	-	-
BUFFALOFISH	-	-	-	-	200	$33
BULLHEADS.	18,400	1,936	13,300	$896	-	-
BURBOT	600	21	2,900	193	-	-
CARP	952,400	29,348	37,800	1,127	2,000	56
CATFISH.	166,700	39,764	1,200	217	-	-
CHUBS.	147,900	34,219	2,410,800	434,674	-	-
GIZZARD SHAD	1,600	30	-	-	-	-
LAKE HERRING	1,951,900	86,520	2,397,000	88,539	19,200	713
LAKE TROUT	900	393	223,200	96,408	-	-
MOONEYE.	100	1	-	-	-	-
PIKE OR PICKEREL (JACKS) . . .	13,500	1,690	17,500	2,076	200	21
ROCK BASS.	12,100	1,377	800	72	-	-
SAUGER	300	47	100	16	-	-
SHEEPSHEAD	1,900	104	8,200	544	-	-
SMELT.	11,600	461	1,051,300	98,811	600	55
SUCKER "MULLET".	1,022,300	54,142	1,180,000	50,717	1,500	69
WHITE BASS	400	77	-	-	-	-
WHITEFISH:						
COMMON	530,200	217,085	3,006,700	1,100,459	400	158
MENOMINEE.	21,800	4,422	95,800	18,372	-	-
YELLOW PERCH	517,600	70,620	378,500	57,910	6,300	954
YELLOW PIKE.	200,000	52,360	1,075,200	310,059	-	-
TOTAL	5,580,500	594,862	11,900,300	2,261,090	30,400	2,059

SPECIES	LAKE MICHIGAN - CONTINUED					
	ILLINOIS		WISCONSIN		TOTAL	
	POUNDS	VALUE	POUNDS	VALUE	POUNDS	VALUE
BOWFIN	-	-	1,000	$35	1,000	$35
BUFFALOFISH.	-	-	-	-	200	33
BULLHEADS.	-	-	81,400	11,393	94,700	12,289
BURBOT	-	-	25,000	500	27,900	693
CARP	-	-	1,321,400	52,855	1,361,200	54,038
CATFISH.	-	-	26,200	5,765	27,400	5,982
CHUBS.	1,299,300	$246,870	3,711,100	552,040	7,421,200	1,233,584
GARFISH.	-	-	(1)	(1)	(1)	(1)
LAKE HERRING	25,100	1,760	4,337,000	173,480	6,778,300	264,492
LAKE TROUT	3,700	1,394	115,200	53,005	342,100	150,807
PIKE OR PICKEREL (JACKS) . . .	-	-	12,000	1,198	29,700	3,295
ROCK BASS.	-	-	-	-	800	72
SAUGER	-	-	-	-	100	16
SHEEPSHEAD	-	-	33,000	3,301	41,200	3,845
SMELT.	-	-	488,000	48,797	1,539,900	147,663
SUCKER "MULLET".	-	-	628,800	31,439	1,810,300	82,225
WHITEFISH:						
COMMON	200	68	484,600	203,419	3,491,900	1,304,104
MENOMINEE.	-	-	10,400	1,040	106,200	19,412
YELLOW PERCH	168,300	35,844	824,400	123,667	1,377,500	218,375
YELLOW PIKE.	-	-	44,700	11,180	1,119,900	321,239
CRAWFISH	-	-	1,700	520	1,700	520
TOTAL	1,496,600	285,936	12,145,900	1,273,634	25,573,200	3,822,719

SEE FOOTNOTE AT END OF TABLE   (CONTINUED ON NEXT PAGE)

UNITED STATES: CATCH BY LAKES, 1949 - Continued

SPECIES	LAKE SUPERIOR					
	MICHIGAN		WISCONSIN		MINNESOTA	
	POUNDS	VALUE	POUNDS	VALUE	POUNDS	VALUE
BURBOT.	1,400	$59	2,600	$51	2,100	$20
CARP.	(1)	(1)	(1)	1	-	-
CHUBS	16,800	1,869	92,100	13,794	53,700	10,730
LAKE HERRING.	4,122,000	124,125	5,028,200	150,846	4,053,900	162,160
LAKE TROUT.	2,181,200	852,845	514,200	251,962	270,400	98,663
PIKE OR PICKEREL (JACKS).	400	37	300	33	-	-
SAUGER.	200	29	-	-	-	-
SMELT	-	-	1,000	102	-	-
SUCKER "MULLET"	34,000	1,075	29,100	1,456	500	5
WHITEFISH:						
COMMON.	503,800	186,006	766,600	321,021	13,300	4,390
MENOMINEE	12,900	1,682	2,000	202	900	170
YELLOW PERCH.	300	30	(1)	(1)	-	-
YELLOW PIKE	2,600	804	23,800	5,943	-	-
TOTAL.	6,875,600	1,168,562	6,459,900	745,411	4,394,800	276,138

SPECIES	LAKE SUPERIOR - CONT'D.		LAKE OF THE WOODS, RAINY LAKE, AND NAMAKAN LAKE		TOTAL, ALL LAKES	
	TOTAL					
	POUNDS	VALUE	POUNDS	VALUE	POUNDS	VALUE
BLUE PIKE.	-	-	-	-	14,085,200	$1,567,984
BOWFIN	-	-	-	-	21,900	698
BUFFALOFISH.	-	-	-	-	5,600	889
BULLHEADS.	-	-	28,900	$4,630	353,800	49,518
BURBOT	6,100	$130	501,100	5,790	840,700	24,647
CARP	(1)	1	-	-	4,568,100	151,720
CATFISH.	-	-	-	-	1,061,800	200,853
CHUBS.	162,600	26,393	-	-	7,731,700	1,294,196
CISCO.	-	-	-	-	134,300	36,743
EELS	-	-	-	-	19,500	1,731
GARFISH.	-	-	-	-	(1)	1
GIZZARD SHAD	-	-	-	-	31,600	930
GOLDFISH	-	-	-	-	170,500	8,526
LAKE HERRING	13,204,100	437,131	-	-	21,934,300	788,143
LAKE TROUT	2,965,800	1,203,471	-	-	3,308,800	1,354,680
MOONEYE.	-	-	-	-	7,500	370
PIKE OR PICKEREL (JACKS)	700	70	105,900	7,990	165,700	14,946
QUILLBACK.	-	-	2,100	40	2,100	40
ROCK BASS.	(1)	(1)	-	-	40,600	3,401
SAUGER	200	29	116,900	9,350	507,600	59,694
SHEEPSHEAD	-	-	-	-	3,127,800	127,546
SMELT.	1,000	102	-	-	1,556,600	148,832
STURGEON	-	-	-	-	21,700	21,662
SUCKER "MULLET".	63,600	2,536	117,900	2,412	3,675,600	156,158
SUNFISH.	-	-	-	-	8,800	663
TULLIBEE	-	-	809,600	47,440	809,600	47,440
WHITE BASS	-	-	-	-	807,700	101,562
WHITEFISH:						
COMMON	1,283,700	511,417	50,300	12,310	8,837,100	3,039,597
MENOMINEE.	15,800	2,054	-	-	143,800	25,888
YELLOW PERCH	300	30	21,900	2,850	4,595,200	674,629
YELLOW PIKE	26,400	6,747	453,700	86,540	7,115,700	1,554,191
CRAWFISH	-	-	-	-	1,700	520
TOTAL	17,730,300	2,190,111	2,208,300	179,352	85,692,600	11,458,418

1/ LESS THAN 50 POUNDS OR 50 CENTS.

UNITED STATES: CATCH BY LAKES, 1949

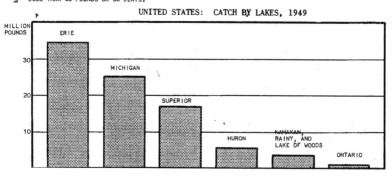

UNITED STATES : CATCH BY LAKE, STATE, AND GEAR, 1949

SPECIES	LAKE ONTARIO					
	NEW YORK					
	GILL NETS		TRAP NETS		FYKE AND HOOP NETS	
	POUNDS	VALUE	POUNDS	VALUE	POUNDS	VALUE
BLUE PIKE	77,200	$14,492	8,500	$1,859	-	-
BOWFIN	-	-	(1)	1	-	-
BULLHEADS	3,500	944	49,600	8,724	34,100	$5,573
BURBOT	-	-	300	5	-	-
CARP	1,000	30	16,700	343	2,800	41
CATFISH	-	-	500	49	-	-
CISCO	45,700	8,317	200	34	-	-
EELS	-	-	19,100	1,695	400	36
GARFISH	-	-	(1)	1	-	-
LAKE TROUT	(1)	5	-	-	-	-
PIKE OR PICKEREL (JACKS)	-	-	4,100	379	1,300	144
ROCK BASS	200	48	19,900	938	-	-
SMELT	4,100	606	-	-	-	-
STURGEON	2,500	2,109	-	-	-	-
SUCKER "MULLET"	6,700	1,028	18,000	610	2,700	100
SUNFISH	100	9	8,300	604	400	50
WHITE BASS	-	-	100	5	-	-
WHITEFISH, COMMON	1,100	367	1,300	766	-	-
YELLOW PERCH	7,500	1,044	10,300	773	900	77
YELLOW PIKE	200	50	1,700	412	-	-
TOTAL	149,800	29,049	158,600	17,198	42,600	7,021

SPECIES	LAKE ONTARIO - CONTINUED		LAKE ERIE			
	NEW YORK - CONTINUED		NEW YORK			
	TOTAL		GILL NETS		TRAP NETS	
	POUNDS	VALUE	POUNDS	VALUE	POUNDS	VALUE
BLUE PIKE	85,700	$16,351	851,600	$73,786	53,000	$4,399
BOWFIN	(1)	1	-	-	-	-
BULLHEADS	87,200	16,241	-	-	-	-
BURBOT	300	5	4,400	101	-	-
CARP	20,500	414	(1)	(1)	-	-
CATFISH	500	49	100	4	700	81
CISCO	45,900	8,351	3,500	1,055	-	-
EELS	19,500	1,731	-	-	-	-
GARFISH	(1)	1	-	-	-	-
LAKE TROUT	(1)	5	-	-	-	-
PIKE OR PICKEREL (JACKS)	5,400	523	-	-	-	-
ROCK BASS	20,100	986	-	-	-	-
SMELT	4,100	606	-	-	-	-
STURGEON	2,500	2,109	(1)	38	-	-
SUCKER "MULLET"	27,400	1,738	700	20	5,400	155
SUNFISH	8,800	663	-	-	-	-
WHITE BASS	100	5	4,100	376	600	41
WHITEFISH, COMMON	2,400	1,133	1,012,800	267,311	-	-
YELLOW PERCH	18,700	1,894	8,400	877	2,800	371
YELLOW PIKE	1,900	462	1,800	312	3,800	728
TOTAL	351,000	53,268	1,887,400	343,880	66,300	5,775

SPECIES	LAKE ERIE - CONTINUED					
	NEW YORK - CONTINUED		PENNSYLVANIA			
	TOTAL		GILL NETS		POUNDS NETS	
	POUNDS	VALUE	POUNDS	VALUE	POUNDS	VALUE
BLUE PIKE	904,600	$78,185	2,447,000	$207,693	32,100	$2,565
BURBOT	4,400	101	1,400	73	-	-
CARP	(1)	(1)	-	-	900	18
CATFISH	800	85	-	-	100	6
CISCO	3,500	1,055	27,300	8,190	300	68
SHEEPSHEAD	-	-	700	27	8,400	1,673
STURGEON	(1)	38	-	-	(1)	18
SUCKER "MULLET"	6,100	175	5,000	153	600	12
WHITE BASS	4,700	417	27,300	2,200	22,200	2,001
WHITEFISH, COMMON	1,012,800	267,311	1,690,000	460,358	38,400	12,284
YELLOW PERCH	11,200	1,248	87,300	8,872	21,000	2,210
YELLOW PIKE	5,600	1,040	14,200	2,524	11,800	1,587
TOTAL	1,953,700	349,655	4,300,700	690,090	135,800	22,442

SEE FOOTNOTE AT END OF TABLE   (CONTINUED ON NEXT PAGE)

UNITED STATES: CATCH BY LAKE, STATE, AND GEAR, 1949 - Continued

SPECIES	PENNSYLVANIA - CONTINUED		OHIO			
	TOTAL		GILL NETS		TRAP NETS	
	POUNDS	VALUE	POUNDS	VALUE	POUNDS	VALUE
BLUE PIKE	2,479,100	$210,258	356,700	$32,102	10,258,700	$1,231,040
BOWFIN	-	-	-	-	(1)	1
BUFFALOFISH	-	-	-	-	200	27
BULLHEADS	-	-	400	54	34,600	4,150
BURBOT	1,400	73	4,800	190	280,500	16,830
CARP	900	18	34,400	1,376	255,600	7,666
CATFISH	100	6	5,700	681	323,500	58,236
CISCO	27,600	8,258	48,600	16,049	8,500	2,958
GOLDFISH	-	-	100	6	16,500	826
LAKE TROUT	-	-	(1)	2	-	-
MOONEYE	-	-	(1)	(1)	1,800	89
PIKE OR PICKEREL (JACKS)	-	-	-	-	(1)	3
SAUGER	-	-	148,800	16,369	216,500	30,315
SHEEPSHEAD	9,100	1,700	5,600	226	2,013,800	80,551
STURGEON	(1)	18	17,800	17,769	1,400	1,717
SUCKER "MULLET"	5,600	165	7,600	228	557,200	11,144
WHITE BASS	49,500	4,201	12,800	1,157	558,800	72,645
WHITEFISH, COMMON	1,728,400	472,642	395,700	130,577	341,400	122,913
YELLOW PERCH	108,300	11,082	443,700	53,249	2,053,900	308,089
YELLOW PIKE	26,000	4,111	110,000	19,807	4,610,600	968,226
TOTAL	4,436,000	712,532	1,592,700	289,842	21,533,500	2,917,426

LAKE ERIE - CONTINUED

SPECIES	OHIO - CONTINUED					
	FYKE AND HOOP NETS		HAUL SEINES		TOTAL	
	POUNDS	VALUE	POUNDS	VALUE	POUNDS	VALUE
BLUE PIKE	100	$12	300	$36	10,615,800	$1,263,190
BOWFIN	-	-	4,400	132	4,400	133
BUFFALOFISH	-	-	5,200	829	5,400	856
BULLHEADS	6,500	780	43,300	5,191	84,800	10,175
BURBOT	(1)	(1)	13,500	811	298,800	17,831
CARP	28,500	856	1,359,200	40,777	1,677,700	50,675
CATFISH	6,800	1,227	503,100	90,549	839,100	150,693
CISCO	-	-	200	72	57,300	19,079
GIZZARD SHAD	-	-	30,000	900	30,000	900
GOLDFISH	100	2	153,800	7,692	170,500	8,526
LAKE TROUT	-	-	(1)	2	(1)	4
MOONEYE	(1)	1	5,500	272	7,300	362
PIKE OR PICKEREL (JACKS)	300	30	3,500	456	3,800	489
SAUGER	3,500	482	10,000	1,397	378,800	48,563
SHEEPSHEAD	26,900	1,076	964,500	38,580	3,010,800	120,433
STURGEON	(1)	31	-	-	19,200	19,517
SUCKER "MULLET"	11,200	224	9,200	185	585,200	11,781
WHITE BASS	41,400	5,382	110,900	14,413	723,900	93,597
WHITEFISH, COMMON	200	74	100	31	737,400	253,595
YELLOW PERCH	7,200	1,075	2,800	416	2,507,600	362,829
YELLOW PIKE	137,400	28,848	66,300	13,925	4,924,300	1,030,806
TOTAL	270,100	40,100	3,285,800	216,666	26,682,100	3,464,034

LAKE ERIE - CONTINUED

SPECIES	MICHIGAN					
	GILL NETS		TRAP NETS		FYKE AND HOOP NETS	
	POUNDS	VALUE	POUNDS	VALUE	POUNDS	VALUE
BOWFIN	-	-	2,300	$80	5,900	$204
BULLHEADS	-	-	13,200	1,412	20,200	2,152
BURBOT	-	-	-	-	100	3
CARP	-	-	129,100	4,004	63,100	1,957
CATFISH	-	-	16,400	2,585	5,400	853
MOONEYE	-	-	100	7	-	-
PIKE OR PICKEREL (JACKS)	-	-	3,000	394	2,400	319
ROCK BASS	-	-	5,800	732	1,300	171
SAUGER	-	-	10,300	1,545	1,000	144
SHEEPSHEAD	-	-	54,500	1,232	6,100	138
SUCKER "MULLET"	-	-	32,700	864	4,500	120
WHITE BASS	-	-	23,100	2,596	5,500	612
YELLOW PERCH	-	-	24,200	4,310	7,900	1,387
YELLOW PIKE	400	$63	322,800	45,880	31,500	4,477
TOTAL	400	63	637,500	65,641	154,900	12,537

SEE FOOTNOTE AT END OF TABLE

(CONTINUED ON NEXT PAGE)

UNITED STATES: CATCH BY LAKE, STATE, AND GEAR, 1949 - Continued

SPECIES	LAKE ERIE - CONTINUED					
	MICHIGAN - CONTINUED					
	HAUL SEINES		SET LINES		TOTAL	
	POUNDS	VALUE	POUNDS	VALUE	POUNDS	VALUE
BOWFIN.	-	-	-	-	8,200	$284
BULLHEADS	5,900	$629	500	$54	39,800	4,247
BURBOT.	-	-	-	-	100	3
CARP.	363,100	11,261	100	4	555,400	17,226
CATFISH	2,900	448	2,500	388	27,200	4,274
MOONEYE	-	-	-	-	100	7
PIKE OR PICKEREL (JACKS).	1,300	176	-	-	6,700	889
ROCK BASS	500	63	-	-	7,600	966
SAUGER.	-	-	-	-	11,300	1,689
SHEEPSHEAD.	3,000	68	1,200	26	64,800	1,464
SUCKER "MULLET".	(1)	(1)	-	-	37,200	984
WHITE BASS.	500	57	-	-	29,100	3,265
YELLOW PERCH.	(1)	2	(1)	2	32,100	5,701
YELLOW PIKE	3,200	461	(1)	5	357,900	50,886
TOTAL.	380,400	13,165	4,300	479	1,177,500	91,885

SPECIES	LAKE HURON					
	MICHIGAN					
	GILL NETS		POUNDS NETS		TRAP NETS	
	POUNDS	VALUE	POUNDS	VALUE	POUNDS	VALUE
BOWFIN.	-	-	-	-	7,300	$215
BULLHEADS	-	-	-	-	9,300	977
BURBOT.	-	-	-	-	600	21
CARP.	3,800	$116	200	$6	212,100	6,536
CATFISH	700	181	(1)	9	113,200	26,996
CHUBS	147,900	34,215	(1)	4	1,600	30
GIZZARD SHAD.	-	-	-	-	1,600	30
LAKE HERRING.	53,900	2,389	163,900	7,264	1,734,000	76,864
LAKE TROUT.	400	154	(1)	1	500	238
MOONEYE	-	-	-	-	100	1
PIKE OR PICKEREL (JACKS).	100	6	(1)	(1)	10,300	1,296
ROCK BASS	-	-	-	-	8,800	1,002
SAUGER.	(1)	(1)	-	-	300	47
SHEEPSHEAD.	-	-	-	-	1,900	104
SMELT	-	-	-	-	200	7
SUCKER "MULLET"	6,800	361	10,800	571	827,700	43,857
WHITE BASS.	-	-	-	-	400	77
WHITEFISH:						
COMMON.	37,600	15,380	10,700	4,391	481,900	197,314
MENOMINEE	21,300	4,315	100	11	400	96
YELLOW PERCH.	31,100	4,236	5,200	711	409,500	55,873
YELLOW PIKE	200	56	100	23	195,700	51,242
TOTAL.	303,800	61,409	191,000	12,991	4,015,800	462,793

SPECIES	LAKE HURON - CONTINUED					
	MICHIGAN - CONTINUED					
	FYKE AND HOOP NETS		HAUL SEINES		SET LINES	
	POUNDS	VALUE	POUNDS	VALUE	POUNDS	VALUE
BOWFIN.	1,000	$29	(1)	$1	-	-
BULLHEADS	7,500	792	1,600	167	-	-
BURBOT.	-	-	(1)	(1)	-	-
CARP.	25,600	790	710,300	21,888	400	$12
CATFISH	1,000	237	44,500	10,607	7,300	1,734
LAKE HERRING.	-	-	100	3	-	-
PIKE OR PICKEREL (JACKS).	2,400	299	700	89	-	-
ROCK BASS	3,100	350	200	25	-	-
SMELT	-	-	11,400	454	-	-
SUCKER "MULLET"	116,400	6,167	60,600	3,186	-	-
YELLOW PERCH.	67,000	9,146	4,600	632	200	22
YELLOW PIKE	200	43	3,800	996	-	-
TOTAL.	224,200	17,853	837,800	38,048	7,900	1,768

SEE FOOTNOTE AT END OF TABLE　　　　　(CONTINUED ON NEXT PAGE)

SPECIES	LAKE HURON - CONTINUED MICHIGAN - CONTINUED TOTAL		LAKE MICHIGAN MICHIGAN			
			FYKE AND HOOP NETS		HAUL SEINES	
	POUNDS	VALUE	POUNDS	VALUE	POUNDS	VALUE
BOWFIN	8,300	$245	-	-	-	-
BULLHEADS.	18,400	1,936	1,800	$119	-	-
BURBOT	600	21	-	-	-	-
CARP	952,400	29,348	200	6	3,700	$109
CATFISH.	165,700	39,764	100	10	-	-
CHUBS.	147,900	34,219	-	-	-	-
GIZZARD SHAD	1,600	30	-	-	-	-
LAKE HERRING	1,951,900	86,520	2,000	73	(1)	(1)
LAKE TROUT	900	393	-	-	-	-
MOONEYE.	100	1	-	-	-	-
PIKE OR PICKEREL (JACKS).	13,500	1,690	5,300	633	-	-
ROCK BASS.	12,100	1,377	300	25	-	-
SAUGER	300	47	-	-	-	-
SHEEPSHEAD	1,900	104	600	41	-	-
SMELT.	11,600	461	-	-	-	-
SUCKER "MULLET".	1,022,300	54,142	32,000	1,376	(1)	2
WHITE BASS	400	77	-	-	-	-
WHITEFISH:						
COMMON	530,200	217,085	(1)	15	-	-
MENOMINEE.	21,800	4,422	-	-	-	-
YELLOW PERCH	517,600	73,620	4,200	634	-	-
YELLOW PIKE.	200,000	52,360	33,400	9,619	-	-
TOTAL	5,580,500	594,862	79,900	12,551	3,700	111

SPECIES	LAKE MICHIGAN - CONTINUED MICHIGAN - CONTINUED					
	SET LINES		GILL NETS		POUNDS NETS	
	POUNDS	VALUE	POUNDS	VALUE	POUNDS	VALUE
BULLHEADS.	-	-	100	$9	100	$5
BURBOT.	-	-	1,700	111	-	-
CARP.	-	-	2,800	83	600	18
CATFISH	-	-	(1)	2	100	23
CHUBS	-	-	2,410,800	434,674	-	-
LAKE HERRING.	-	-	1,546,700	57,131	756,300	27,936
LAKE TROUT.	-	-	219,400	94,759	3,500	1,519
PIKE OR PICKEREL (JACKS).	-	-	1,000	118	400	50
ROCK BASS	-	-	(1)	1	(1)	(1)
SAUGER.	-	-	100	16	-	-
SHEEPSHEAD.	-	-	-	-	200	14
SMELT	-	-	140,800	13,237	910,200	85,545
SUCKER "MULLET"	-	-	446,300	19,176	77,200	3,319
WHITEFISH:						
COMMON.	-	-	1,931,100	706,795	1,007,200	368,629
MENOMINEE	-	-	94,500	18,120	500	94
YELLOW PERCH.	(1)	$1	342,000	52,329	4,200	645
YELLOW PIKE.	-	-	437,000	126,030	160,700	46,347
TOTAL.	(1)	1	7,574,300	1,522,591	2,921,200	534,144

SPECIES	LAKE MICHIGAN - CONTINUED MICHIGAN - CONTINUED					
	TRAP NETS		HAND LINES AND TROLL LINES		TOTAL	
	POUNDS	VALUE	POUNDS	VALUE	POUNDS	VALUE
BOWFIN	(1)	(1)	-	-	(1)	(1)
BULLHEADS.	11,300	$763	(1)	(1)	13,300	$896
BURBOT	1,200	82	-	-	2,900	193
CARP	30,500	911	-	-	37,800	1,127
CATFISH.	1,000	182	-	-	1,200	217
CHUBS.	-	-	-	-	2,410,800	434,674
LAKE HERRING	92,000	3,399	-	-	2,397,000	86,539
LAKE TROUT	300	130	-	-	223,200	96,408
PIKE OR PICKEREL (JACKS)	10,800	1,275	-	-	17,500	2,076
ROCK BASS.	500	46	-	-	800	72
SAUGER	-	-	-	-	100	16
SHEEPSHEAD	7,400	489	-	-	8,200	544
SMELT.	300	29	-	-	1,051,300	98,811
SUCKER "MULLET".	624,500	26,844	(1)	(1)	1,180,000	50,717
WHITEFISH:						
COMMON.	68,400	25,020	-	-	3,006,700	1,100,459
MENOMINEE.	800	158	-	-	95,800	18,372
YELLOW PERCH	27,800	4,257	300	$44	378,500	57,910
YELLOW PIKE.	432,200	124,641	11,900	3,422	1,075,200	310,059
TOTAL	1,309,000	188,226	12,200	3,466	11,900,300	2,261,090

SEE FOOTNOTE AT END OF TABLE

(CONTINUED ON NEXT PAGE)

LAKE FISHERIES

UNITED STATES: CATCH BY LAKE, STATE, AND GEAR, 1949 - Continued

LAKE MICHIGAN - CONTINUED

INDIANA

SPECIES	GILL NETS		POUNDS NETS		FYKE AND HOOP NETS	
	POUNDS	VALUE	POUNDS	VALUE	POUNDS	VALUE
BUFFALOFISH.	-	-	200	$33	-	-
CARP	1,000	$30	800	23	100	$1
LAKE HERRING	15,700	580	3,400	127	(1)	1
PIKE OR PICKEREL (JACKS) .	-	-	200	21	(1)	3
SMELT.	-	-	-	-	-	-
SUCKER "MULLET".	1,100	51	400	17	-	-
WHITEFISH, COMMON.	-	-	400	158	-	-
YELLOW PERCH	5,100	787	600	86	300	42
TOTAL	22,900	1,448	6,000	465	400	47

LAKE MICHIGAN - CONTINUED

SPECIES	INDIANA - CONTINUED				ILLINOIS	
	DIP NETS		TOTAL		GILL NETS	
	POUNDS	VALUE	POUNDS	VALUE	POUNDS	VALUE
BUFFALOFISH.	-	-	200	$33	-	-
CARP	100	$2	2,000	56	1,299,300	$246,870
CHUBS.	-	-	-	-	25,100	1,760
LAKE HERRING	100	5	19,200	713	3,700	1,394
LAKE TROUT	-	-	-	-	-	-
PIKE OR PICKEREL (JACKS) .	-	-	200	21	-	-
SMELT.	600	52	600	55	-	-
SUCKER "MULLET".	(1)	1	1,500	69	200	68
WHITEFISH, COMMON.	-	-	400	158	168,300	35,844
YELLOW PERCH	300	39	6,300	954	-	-
TOTAL	1,100	99	30,400	2,059	1,496,600	285,936

LAKE MICHIGAN - CONTINUED

WISCONSIN

SPECIES	GILL NETS		POUND NETS		TRAP NETS	
	POUNDS	VALUE	POUNDS	VALUE	POUNDS	VALUE
BULLHEADS.	1,700	$234	1,300	$177	-	-
BURBOT	3,300	66	17,300	345	-	-
CARP	1,900	75	5,000	200	-	-
CATFISH.	100	32	100	18	-	-
CHUBS.	3,592,500	535,267	118,600	16,771	-	-
LAKE HERRING	1,617,600	64,703	2,667,800	106,713	-	-
LAKE TROUT	72,000	31,864	43,100	21,119	-	-
PIKE OR PICKEREL (JACKS) .	3,500	349	1,800	177	-	-
SHEEPSHEAD	200	18	3,300	333	-	-
SMELT.	339,300	33,927	144,800	14,475	-	-
SUCKER "MULLET".	339,500	16,973	24,400	1,219	-	-
WHITEFISH:						
COMMON	221,500	93,033	262,200	109,992	-	-
MENOMINEE.	9,500	946	900	94	-	-
YELLOW PERCH	397,900	59,679	34,600	5,198	-	-
YELLOW PIKE.	3,200	796	12,600	3,149	-	-
CRAWFISH	-	-	-	-	1,000	$297
TOTAL	6,603,700	837,962	3,337,800	279,980	1,000	297

LAKE MICHIGAN - CONTINUED

WISCONSIN - CONTINUED

SPECIES	FYKE AND HOOP NETS		HAUL SEINES		SET LINES	
	POUNDS	VALUE	POUNDS	VALUE	POUNDS	VALUE
BOWFIN.	(1)	(1)	1,000	$35	-	-
BULLHEADS	78,400	$10,982	-	-	-	-
BURBOT.	4,000	80	-	-	400	$9
CARP.	118,000	4,720	1,196,500	47,860	-	-
CATFISH	2,100	452	23,900	5,263	-	-
CHUBS	-	-	(1)	2	-	-
GARFISH	-	-	(1)	(1)	-	-
LAKE HERRING.	51,500	2,061	100	3	-	-
LAKE TROUT.	100	22	-	-	-	-
PIKE OR PICKEREL (JACKS)	6,600	664	100	8	-	-
SHEEPSHEAD.	14,600	1,456	14,900	1,494	-	-
SMELT	3,600	362	300	33	-	-

SEE FOOTNOTE AT END OF TABLE

(CONTINUED ON NEXT PAGE)

UNITED STATE: CATCH BY LAKE, STATE, AND GEAR, 1949 – Continued

SPECIES	LAKE MICHIGAN – CONTINUED WISCONSIN – CONTINUED FYKE AND HOOP NETS		HAUL SEINES		SET LINES	
	POUNDS	VALUE	POUNDS	VALUE	POUNDS	VALUE
SUCKER "MULLET"	259,500	$12,977	5,400	$270	-	-
WHITEFISH, COMMON	(1)	10	900	384	-	-
YELLOW PERCH	391,500	58,733	(1)	1	400	$56
YELLOW PIKE	25,900	6,489	3,000	746	-	-
CRAWFISH	(1)	1	700	222	-	-
TOTAL	955,800	99,009	1,246,800	56,321	800	65

SPECIES	LAKE MICHIGAN – CONTINUED WISCONSIN – CONTINUED TOTAL		LAKE SUPERIOR MICHIGAN FYKE AND HOOP NETS		HAUL SEINES	
	POUNDS	VALUE	POUNDS	VALUE	POUNDS	VALUE
BOWFIN	1,000	$35	-	-	-	-
BULLHEADS.	81,400	11,393	-	-	-	-
BURBOT	25,000	500	200	$6	-	-
CARP	1,321,400	52,855	-	-	-	-
CATFISH.	26,200	5,765	-	-	-	-
CHUBS	3,711,100	552,040	-	-	-	-
GARFISH	(1)	(1)	-	-	-	-
LAKE HERRING	4,337,000	173,480	-	-	15,900	$479
LAKE TROUT	115,200	53,005	-	-	-	-
PIKE OR PICKEREL (JACKS) .	12,000	1,198	(1)	(1)	-	-
ROCK BASS	-	-	(1)	(1)	-	-
SHEEPHEAD	33,000	3,301	-	-	-	-
SMELT.	488,000	48,797	-	-	-	-
SUCKER "MULLET".	628,800	31,439	2,900	93	500	14
WHITEFISH:						
COMMON.	484,600	203,419	(1)	1	-	-
MENOMINEE.	10,400	1,040	-	-	900	119
YELLOW PERCH	824,400	123,667	(1)	(1)	-	-
YELLOW PIKE.	44,700	11,180	200	59	-	-
CRAWFISH	1,700	520	-	-	-	-
TOTAL	12,145,900	1,273,634	3,300	159	17,300	612

SPECIES	LAKE SUPERIOR – CONTINUED MICHIGAN – CONTINUED SET LINES		GILL NETS		POUND NETS	
	POUNDS	VALUE	POUNDS	VALUE	POUNDS	VALUE
BURBOT	1,000	$45	200	$8	(1)	(1)
CHUBS	-	-	16,800	1,867	(1)	$2
LAKE HERRING	-	-	4,091,100	123,194	14,800	445
LAKE TROUT	402,100	157,222	1,670,800	653,262	28,100	10,968
PIKE OR PICKEREL (JACKS)	-	-	100	11	-	-
SAUGER	-	-	200	29	-	-
SUCKER "MULLET". . . .	-	-	21,000	665	1,200	38
WHITEFISH:						
COMMON.	-	-	186,300	68,781	180,300	66,573
MENOMINEE.	-	-	12,000	1,560	(1)	3
YELLOW PERCH	-	-	300	30	(1)	(1)
YELLOW PIKE.	(1)	2	200	66	1,500	455
TOTAL	403,100	157,269	5,999,000	849,473	225,900	78,485

SEE FOOTNOTE AT END OF TABLE   (CONTINUED ON NEXT PAGE)

UNITED STATES: CATCH BY LAKE, STATE, AND GEAR, 1949 - Continued

SPECIES	LAKE SUPERIOR - CONTINUED					
	MICHIGAN - CONTINUED					
	TRAP NETS		HAND LINES AND TROLL LINES		TOTAL	
	POUNDS	VALUE	POUNDS	VALUE	POUNDS	VALUE
BURBOT	(1)	(1)	-	-	1,400	$59
CARP	(1)	(1)	-	-	(1)	(1)
CHUBS	-	-	-	-	16,800	1,869
LAKE HERRING	200	$6	-	-	4,122,000	124,125
LAKE TROUT	5,000	1,971	75,200	$29,423	2,181,200	852,846
PIKE OR PICKEREL (JACKS)	300	26	-	-	400	37
ROCK BASS	(1)	(1)	-	-	(1)	(1)
SAUGER	-	-	-	-	200	29
SUCKER "MULLET"	8,400	265	-	-	34,000	1,075
WHITEFISH:						
COMMON	137,200	50,651	-	-	503,800	186,006
MENOMINEE	(1)	(1)	-	-	12,900	1,682
YELLOW PERCH	-	-	-	-	300	30
YELLOW PIKE	700	222	-	-	2,600	804
TOTAL	151,800	53,141	75,200	29,423	6,875,600	1,168,562

SPECIES	LAKE SUPERIOR - CONTINUED					
	WISCONSIN					
	GILL NETS		POUNDS NETS		HAUL SEINES	
	POUNDS	VALUE	POUNDS	VALUE	POUNDS	VALUE
BURBOT	600	$11	2,000	$40	-	-
CARP	-	-	(1)	1	-	-
CHUBS	92,100	13,794	(1)	(1)	-	-
LAKE HERRING	4,937,500	148,125	90,700	2,721	-	-
LAKE TROUT	431,900	211,607	60,300	29,569	-	-
PIKE OR PICKEREL (JACKS)	(1)	(1)	300	27	-	-
SMELT	200	22	(1)	(1)	800	$80
SUCKER "MULLET"	6,800	340	22,300	1,116	-	-
WHITEFISH:						
COMMON	204,800	85,987	561,700	234,996	-	-
MENOMINEE	1,900	188	100	14	-	-
YELLOW PERCH	-	-	(1)	(1)	-	-
YELLOW PIKE	600	139	23,200	5,804	-	-
TOTAL	5,676,400	460,219	760,600	274,288	800	80

SPECIES	LAKE SUPERIOR - CONTINUED					
	WISCONSIN - CONTINUED				MINNESOTA	
	SET LINES		TOTAL		GILL NETS	
	POUNDS	VALUE	POUNDS	VALUE	POUNDS	VALUE
BURBOT	-	-	2,600	$51	2,100	$20
CARP	-	-	(1)	-	-	-
CHUBS	-	-	92,100	13,794	53,700	10,730
LAKE HERRING	-	-	5,028,200	150,846	4,053,900	162,160
LAKE TROUT	22,000	$10,786	514,200	251,962	205,200	74,875
PIKE OR PICKEREL (JACKS)	-	-	300	33	-	-
SMELT	-	-	1,000	102	-	-
SUCKER "MULLET"	-	-	29,100	1,456	500	5
WHITEFISH:						
COMMON	100	38	766,600	321,021	13,300	4,390
MENOMINEE	-	-	2,000	202	900	170
YELLOW PERCH	-	-	(1)	(1)	-	-
YELLOW PIKE	-	-	23,800	5,943	-	-
TOTAL	22,100	10,824	6,459,900	745,411	4,329,600	252,350

SEE FOOTNOTE AT END OF TABLE.   (CONTINUED ON NEXT PAGE)

SPECIES	LAKE SUPERIOR - CONTINUED				LAKE OF THE WOODS	
	MINNESOTA - CONTINUED				MINNESOTA	
	SET LINES		TOTAL		GILL NETS	
	POUNDS	VALUE	POUNDS	VALUE	POUNDS	VALUE
BULLHEADS	-	-	-	-	1,700	$267
BURBOT	-	-	2,100	$20	48,900	490
CHUBS	-	-	53,700	10,730	-	-
LAKE HERRING.	-	-	4,053,900	162,160	-	-
LAKE TROUT.	65,200	$23,788	270,400	98,663	-	-
PIKE OR PICKEREL (JACKS). .	-	-	-	-	59,400	4,157
QUILLBACK	-	-	-	-	100	2
SAUGER.	-	-	-	-	85,600	6,845
SUCKER "MULLET"	-	-	500	5	43,300	867
TULLIBEE	-	-	-	-	321,800	19,308
WHITEFISH:						
COMMON	-	-	13,300	4,390	700	108
MENOMINEE	-	-	900	170	-	-
YELLOW PERCH.	-	-	-	-	16,600	2,155
YELLOW PIKE	-	-	-	-	303,600	57,684
TOTAL	65,200	23,788	4,394,800	276,138	881,700	91,883

SPECIES	LAKE OF THE WOODS - CONTINUED					
	MINNESOTA - CONTINUED					
	POUND NETS		TRAP NETS		FYKE AND HOOP NETS	
	POUNDS	VALUE	POUNDS	VALUE	POUNDS	VALUE
BULLHEADS	300	$46	900	$154	26,000	$4,163
BURBOT.	345,600	3,457	63,500	635	800	8
PIKE OR PICKEREL (JACKS).	14,100	987	6,800	477	6,400	449
QUILLBACK	300	6	1,700	32	-	-
SAUGER	14,300	1,118	14,800	1,182	2,500	205
SUCKER "MULLET"	14,900	298	7,800	157	5,400	108
TULLIBEE.	266,500	15,995	183,300	10,997	-	-
WHITEFISH, COMMON	1,400	208	300	44	-	-
YELLOW PERCH.	700	98	2,000	264	2,400	311
YELLOW PIKE	63,800	12,117	45,900	8,720	5,900	1,119
TOTAL	721,600	34,322	327,000	22,662	49,400	6,363

SPECIES	LAKE OF THE WOODS- CONTINUED		NAMAKIN LAKE		RAINY LAKE	
	MINNESOTA - CONTINUED		MINNESOTA		MINNESOTA	
	TOTAL		GILL NETS		GILL NETS	
	POUNDS	VALUE	POUNDS	VALUE	POUNDS	VALUE
BULLHEADS	28,900	$4,630	-	-	-	-
BURBOT.	458,800	4,590	5,100	$100	32,800	$970
PIKE OR PICKEREL (JACKS)	86,700	6,070	-	-	16,800	1,684
QUILLBACK	2,100	40	-	-	-	-
SAUGER.	116,900	9,350	-	-	-	-
SUCKER "MULLET"	71,100	1,430	5,200	150	36,000	726
TULLIBEE.	771,600	46,300	12,900	390	24,100	719
WHITEFISH, COMMON	2,400	360	7,600	1,890	36,900	9,209
YELLOW PERCH.	21,700	2,820	-	-	200	30
YELLOW PIKE	419,200	79,640	-	-	30,600	6,110
TOTAL.	1,979,700	155,230	30,800	2,530	177,400	19,447

SPECIES	RAINY LAKE - CONTINUED			
	MINNESOTA - CONTINUED			
	POUND NETS		TOTAL	
	POUNDS	VALUE	POUNDS	VALUE
BURBOT	4,400	$130	37,200	$1,100
PIKE OR PICKEREL (JACKS)	2,400	236	19,200	1,920
QUILLBACK.	-	-	(1)	(1)
SUCKER " MULLET"	5,300	106	41,300	832
TULLIBEE	1,000	31	25,100	750
WHITEFISH, COMMON.	3,400	852	40,300	10,060
YELLOW PERCH	(1)	(1)	200	30
YELLOW PIKE.	3,900	790	34,500	6,900
TOTAL	20,400	2,145	197,800	21,592

1/ LESS THAN 50 POUNDS OR 50 CENTS.

LAKE FISHERIES

MANUFACTURED FISHERY PRODUCTS, VARIOUS YEARS 1/

ITEM	YEAR	UNIT	NEW YORK AND PENNSYLVANIA		OHIO		MICHIGAN	
			QUANTITY	VALUE	QUANTITY	VALUE	QUANTITY	VALUE
BY MANUFACTURING ESTABLISHMENTS:								
ALEWIVES, SPICED.	1940	POUNDS	405,000	$40,500	75,000	$7,500	5,000	$700
BLUE PIKE, FRESH AND FROZEN FILLETS	1949	DO	1,077,566	462,102	1,160,987	467,982	162,705	92,162
BUFFALOFISH, SMOKED	1940	DO	-	-	-	-	19,000	5,700
BUTTERFISH, SMOKED.	1940	DO	-	-	1,000	200	2,300	5,750
CARP, SMOKED.	1940	DO	-	-	-	-	-	-
CHUB, CISCO, AND TULLIBEE, SMOKED .	1940	DO	75,000	23,140	42,000	8,600	225,000	74,330
EELS, SMOKED.	1940	DO	19,500	4,890	-	-	-	-
HERRING, LAKE:								
FRESH FILLETS	1949	DO	(2)	(2)	-	-	201,200	7,172
FROZEN FILLETS	1949	DO	-	-	-	-	76,268	11,803
SALTED.	1940	DO	-	-	-	-	1,624,574	47,788
SMOKED.	1940	DO	22,000	6,200	-	-	130,542	19,840
HERRING, SEA:								
SPICED.	1940	DO	200,000	20,000	-	-	10,000	1,000
SMOKED.	1940	DO	24,000	1,680	-	-	-	-
LAKE TROUT:								
FRESH AND FROZEN FILLETS.	1949	DO	6,900	3,475	(2)	(2)	(2)	(2)
SMOKED.	1940	DO	-	-	-	-	143,000	43,440
MACKEREL, SMOKED.	1940	DO	-	-	-	-	5,200	1,300
MOONEYE, SMOKED	1940	DO	-	-	5,000	600	-	-
SABLEFISH, SMOKED	1940	DO	-	-	46,000	11,500	222,000	51,710
SALMON:								
SMOKED.	1940	DO	20,000	6,000	73,000	25,550	97,000	32,400
KIPPERED.	1940	DO	39,000	11,340	-	-	245,000	61,450
SAUGER, FRESH AND FROZEN FILLETS.	1949	DO	276,274	130,508	19,350	8,990	(2)	(2)
SHAD SMOKED	1940	DO	-	-	-	-	-	-
SHEEPSHEAD, SMOKED.	1940	DO	-	-	8,000	1,000	-	-
STURGEON, SMOKED.	1940	DO	1,000	900	-	-	-	-
WHITEFISH, COMMON:								
FRESH AND FROZEN FILLETS.	1949	DO	27,555	13,756	59,000	29,420	7,700	4,500
SMOKED.	1940	DO	34,578	9,758	10,000	3,000	109,500	30,670
WHITEFISH, MENOMINEE, SMOKED.	1940	DO	-	-	-	-	10,000	2,500
YELLOW PERCH, FRESH AND FROZEN FILLETS	1949	DO	23,851	11,028	133,286	59,585	23,872	13,345
YELLOW PIKE, FRESH AND FROZEN FILLETS	1949	DO	121,398	64,452	101,552	45,249	20,048	11,746
UNCLASSIFIED PRODUCTS:								
PACKAGED FISH	1949	DO	3/7,100	3/2,795	4/26,759	4/10,118	5/155,764	5/33,829
MISCELLANEOUS PRODUCTS.	1949	DO	-	-	-	-	-	-
TOTAL.			-	812,524	-	679,294	-	553,135

ITEM	YEAR	UNIT	ILLINOIS AND INDIANA		WISCONSIN		MINNESOTA	
			QUANTITY	VALUE	QUANTITY	VALUE	QUANTITY	VALUE
BY MANUFACTURING ESTABLISHMENTS:								
ALEWIVES, SPICED.	1940	POUNDS	3,012,349	$301,750	241,150	$23,160	40,000	$5,500
BLUE PIKE, FRESH AND FROZEN FILLETS	1949	DO	381,915	148,143	132,500	49,520	-	-
BUFFALOFISH, SMOKED	1940	DO	10,000	2,500	-	-	-	-
BUTTERFISH, SMOKED.	1940	DO	5,000	1,500	-	-	-	-
CARP, SMOKED.	1940	DO	30,000	4,000	10,000	900	-	-
CHUB, CISCO, AND TULLIBEE, SMOKED .	1940	DO	1,789,647	552,796	273,307	80,580	99,718	22,373
EELS, SMOKED.	1940	DO	30,455	7,626	-	-	-	-
HERRING, LAKE:								
FRESH FILLETS	1949	DO	(2)	(2)	(2)	(2)	-	-
FROZEN FILLETS.	1949	DO	-	-	51,500	7,700	-	-
SALTED.	1940	DO	-	-	1,264,000	42,800	110,000	4,000
SMOKED.	1940	DO	246,515	33,700	597,400	66,170	81,740	8,552
HERRING, SEA:								
SPICED.	1940	DO	962,229	111,397	271,750	21,740	140,000	14,000
SMOKED.	1940	DO	62,400	15,240	-	-	-	-
LAKE TROUT:								
FRESH AND FROZEN FILLETS.	1940	DO	(2)	(?)	76,900	45,470	-	-
SMOKED.	1940	DO	194,755	61,458	291,096	81,262	17,920	3,632
MACKEREL, SMOKED.	1940	DO	-	-	-	-	-	-
MOONEYE, SMOKED	1940	DO	-	-	-	-	-	-
SABLEFISH, SMOKED	1940	DO	32,495	9,054	106,500	24,900	-	-
SALMON:								
SMOKED.	1940	DO	607,886	252,669	20,000	5,000	18,000	3,240
KIPPERED.	1940	DO	195,415	66,740	86,406	19,407	10,000	2,250
SAUGER, FRESH AND FROZEN FILLETS.	1949	DO	248,283	104,103	357,000	143,600	-	-
SHAD, SMOKED.	1940	DO	12,000	3,000	-	-	-	-
SHEEPSHEAD, SMOKED.	1940	DO	-	-	-	-	-	-
STURGEON, SMOKED.	1940	DO	15,000	13,500	-	-	-	-
WHITEFISH, COMMON:								
FRESH AND FROZEN FILLETS.	1949	DO	33,000	15,100	56,800	25,160	-	-
SMOKED.	1940	DO	17,091	4,784	19,000	4,750	2,000	600
WHITEFISH, MENOMINEE, SMOKED.	1940	DO	-	-	-	-	-	-
YELLOW PERCH, FRESH AND FROZEN FILLETS	1949	DO	29,707	17,566	207,400	104,044	-	-
YELLOW PIKE, FRESH AND FROZEN FILLETS	1949	DO	348,126	168,626	101,500	55,800	-	-
UNCLASSIFIED PRODUCTS:								
PACKAGED FISH	1949	DO	6/662,400	6/283,450	(7)	(7)	-	-
MISCELLANEOUS PRODUCTS.	1949	-				8/61,311		9/7,402
TOTAL.			-	2,178,702	-	863,274	-	71,549

SEE FOOTNOTES ON NEXT PAGE (CONTINUED ON NEXT PAGE)

MANUFACTURED FISHERY PRODUCTS, VARIOUS YEARS 1/- Continued

1/ DATA ON THE PRODUCTION OF THE VARIOUS PRODUCTS ARE FOR THE YEARS INDICATED.
2/ THIS ITEM HAS BEEN INCLUDED WITH UNCLASSIFIED PRODUCTS.
3/ INCLUDES FRESH FILLETS OF LAKE HERRING AND WHITE BASS.
4/ INCLUDES FRESH AND FROZEN FILLETS OF LAKE TROUT, SHEEPSHEAD, WHITE BASS, AND UNCLASSIFIED SPECIES; AND
    FROZEN SALMON STEAKS.
5/ INCLUDES FRESH AND FROZEN FILLETS OF LAKE TROUT, SAUGER, SMELT, STURGEON, AND PICKEREL; AND FROZEN SALMON
    STEAKS.
6/ INCLUDES FRESH FILLETS OF LAKE HERRING AND LAKE TROUT, FRESH AND FROZEN FILLETS OF SALMON AND UNCLASSIFIED
    STEAKS.
7/ THIS ITEM IS INCLUDED WITH MISCELLANEOUS PRODUCTS.
8/ INCLUDES FRESH FILLETS OF LAKE HERRING AND SMELT, AND CANNED WHITEFISH CAVIAR.
9/ INCLUDES UNCLASSIFIED FISH MEAL.

NOTE:--SOME OF THE ABOVE PRODUCTS MAY HAVE BEEN IMPORTED FROM ANOTHER STATE OR A FOREIGN COUNTRY; THEREFORE
       THEY CANNOT BE CORRELATED DIRECTLY WITH THE CATCH WITHIN THE STATE.

SUMMARY OF MANUFACTURED FISHERY PRODUCTS, VARIOUS YEARS

STATES	SUMMARY OF STATES	VALUE
NEW YORK.		$724,917
PENNSYLVANIA.		87,607
OHIO.		679,294
MICHIGAN.		553,135
ILLINOIS.		2,166,702
INDIANA		12,000
WISCONSIN		863,274
MINNESOTA		71,549
TOTAL		5,158,478

SUMMARY OF PRODUCTS ITEM	YEAR	UNIT	QUANTITY	VALUE
FRESH AND FROZEN PACKAGED FISH.	1949	POUNDS	6,438,168	$2,658,349
CANNED AND BYPRODUCTS	1949	"	"	62,663
SALTED, DRIED AND PICKLED	1940	POUNDS	8,361,052	641,835
SMOKED AND KIPPERED	1940	DO	6,526,266	1,795,631
TOTAL.	"	"	"	5,158,478

SECTION 9.- MISSISSIPPI RIVER FISHERIES

The most recent complete catch statistics of the fisheries of the Mississippi River and its tributaries are those collected for the year 1931. The yield of fishery products in that year amounted to 82,382,523 pounds, valued at $2,897,357, which was a decrease of 22 percent in quantity and 36 percent in value compared with the quantity and value of the catch of 1922, when the most recent preceding survey was made. Data for 1931 are presented in the General Review Section as complete data are not available for any year since.

Shown below are two supplementary tables which were supplied by the Upper Mississippi River Conservation Commission, which list the commercial catch statistics of the five upper Mississippi River states (Illinois, Iowa, Minnesota, Missouri, and Wisconsin) for the year 1949. In 1931, the five states recorded 15,427,389 pounds of finfish; in 1949, the catch in these states was reported as 8,890,771 pounds. The production of shellfish in this area in 1931 amounted to 13,684,254 pounds. The catch of shellfish was not reported in 1949.

Detailed statistics on the fisheries of the Mississippi River and its Tributaries for 1931 were published in Appendix III, to Report of Commissioner of Fisheries for the fiscal year 1933 entitled ''Fishery Industries, of the United States, 1932.''

A summary of these fisheries in 1931 was published in the Bureau of Fisheries annual reports entitled ''Fishery Industries of the United States,'' for the years 1933 to 1939, inclusive and in Statistical Bulletin No. 994. Information regarding the production of cured fishery products in the Mississippi River area in 1931, and byproducts in 1949 is shown.

CATCH BY SPECIES, UPPER MISSISSIPPI RIVER, 1949

SPECIES	MISSOURI	ILLINOIS	IOWA.	WISCONSIN	MINNESOTA	TOTAL	VALUE
	POUNDS	POUNDS	POUNDS	POUNDS	POUNDS	POUNDS	
CARP.	155,586	863,366	373,390	2,778,650	591,251	4,762,443	$214,310
BUFFALO	74,427	828,422	171,020	556,937	124,565	1,755,371	228,198
SHEEPSHEAD. . . .	39,534	211,008	77,268	437,211	67,991	833,012	66,641
CATFISH	49,142	307,396	117,666	605,132	53,354	1,132,690	249,192
BULLHEAD.	645	5,498	8,664	1,275	591	16,673	2,384
STURGEON.	6,941	2,539	106	2,609	-	12,195	1,707
PADDLEFISH. . . .	7,233	24,491	-	-	-	31,724	4,759
SUCKERS	2,094	6,348	4,994	59,027	4,239	76,702	3,452
QUILLBACK	7,921	25,251	4,623	68,331	5,891	112,017	5,041
NORTHERN PIKE . .	-	-	8,367	-	-	8,367	1,673
MOONEYE	-	2,630	7,778	6,294	441	17,143	669
EEL	513	740	160	9	-	1,422	171
DOGFISH	724	4,142	1,024	7,392	4,046	17,328	450
GAR	10,200	73,140	3,571	9,406	1,610	97,927	3,232
TURTLE.	-	-	1,271	3,446	-	4,717	236
OTHER	-	-	1,131	9,909	-	11,040	430
TOTAL. . . .	·354,960	2,354,971	781,033	4,545,828	853,979	8,890,771	782,545

NOTE:--THESE FIGURES WERE FURNISHED BY THE UPPER MISSISSIPPI RIVER CONSERVATION COMMISSION. SPECIES NAMES ARE THOSE USED BY THE COMMISSION IN ITS REPORT.

CATCH BY GEAR, UPPER MISSISSIPPI RIVER, 1949

SPECIES	MISSOURI	ILLINOIS	IOWA	WISCONSIN	MINNESOTA
	PERCENT	PERCENT	PERCENT	PERCENT	PERCENT
SET LINES.	9.5	1.4	-	10.4	8.9
SEINES	8.8	20.2	-	63.7	46.8
GILL NETS	-	-	-	22.4	43.8
TRAMMEL NETS	27.8	15.2	-	-	-
HOOP NETS	53.9	57.0	-	1.3	-
BASKET TRAPS	-	6.2	-	2.2	-
UNKNOWN.	-	-	100.0	-	0.5
TOTAL.	100.0	100.0	100.0	100.0	100.0

NOTE:--THESE FIGURES WERE FURNISHED BY THE UPPER MISSISSIPPI RIVER CONSERVATION COMMISSION.

MANUFACTURED FISHERY PRODUCTS, VARIOUS YEARS 1/

ITEM	STATES OF MANUFACTURE	YEAR	UNIT	QUANTITY	VALUE
BY MANUFACTURING ESTABLISHMENTS:					
SMOKED FISH:					
BUFFALOFISH	IOWA AND PENNSYLVANIA	1931	POUNDS	25,700	$3,245
CARP	PENNSYLVANIA	1931	DO	700	245
BUTTERFISH	PENNSYLVANIA	1931	DO	2,400	800
CHUBS	OHIO, TENNESSEE, PENNSYLVANIA	1931	DO	106,600	26,650
EELS	NEBRASKA	1931	DO	31,300	8,138
LAKE TROUT	PENNSYLVANIA	1931	DO	2,100	315
PADDLEFISH	TENNESSEE	1931	DO	20,000	5,000
SABLEFISH	OHIO	1931	DO	30,000	10,500
SALMON	IOWA, MINNESOTA, OHIO, PENNSYLVANIA	1931	DO	312,400	71,730
STURGEON	IOWA, NEBRASKA	1931	DO	183,300	46,595
TULLIBEE	IOWA, OHIO, PENNSYLVANIA	1931	DO	108,600	21,360
WHITEFISH	MINNESOTA, NEBRASKA, TENNESSEE	1931	DO	275,000	52,200
MUSSELL-SHELL PRODUCTS:					
BUTTONS	ARKANSAS, IOWA, MISSOURI	1949	GROSS	4,354,016	3,251,823
LIME, GRIT AND CUTSHELLS . . .	IOWA	1949	TONS	4,155	71,251
MISCELLANEOUS 2/	IOWA AND OHIO	1949	-	-	171,680
TOTAL			-	-	3,741,332

1/ DATA FOR MUSSELL-SHELL PRODUCTS, MARINE PEARL-SHELL BUTTONS AND CANNED TURTLE SOUP ARE FOR 1949. ALL OTHER DATA ARE FOR 1931.
2/ INCLUDES THE VALUES OF MARINE PEARL-SHELL BUTTONS IN IOWA AND CANNED TURTLE SOUP IN OHIO.

NOTE:--SOME OF THE ABOVE PRODUCTS MAY HAVE BEEN MANUFACTURED FROM PRODUCTS IMPORTED FROM ANOTHER STATE OR A FOREIGN COUNTRY; THEREFORE, THEY CANNOT BE CORRELATED DIRECTLY WITH THE CATCH FROM WITHIN THE STATE.

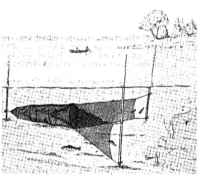

FYKE NET WITH WINGS

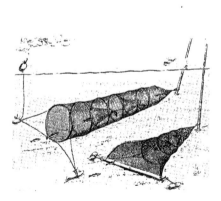

FYKE OR HOOPS NETS

SECTION 10.- ALASKA FISHERIES [10]

During 1949, the commercial catch of fishery products in Alaska totaled 472,889,281 pounds, valued at $39,299,005 to the fishermen. This represented a decrease of 17 percent in quantity but an increase of 25 percent in value compared with the previous year.

The 1949 season in Alaska produced 388,345,000 pounds of salmon with a value of $32,662,000. This was an increase of 49,975,000 pounds or 15 percent in quantity and $9,519,000 or 41 percent in value compared with the salmon receipts during 1948. The noticeable increase in the salmon catch during 1949 was caused by the unusually heavy run of pink salmon in southeastern Alaska. The 175,683,000 pound catch of pinks in this area was the largest yearly production since 1941 when 240,245,000 pounds were landed.

During 1949, there were 125 plants canning fish and shellfish in Alaska, 6 less than in 1948. Employment in the Alaskan fisheries during 1949, was given to 28,603 persons, as compared with 30,767 in 1948. The majority of these employees were engaged in the salmon canning industry, while others worked in the canned shellfish, fresh, frozen, cured, and byproducts industries. These industries have become so interrelated in recent years that a detailed employment segragation by industries would be most difficult.

The total pack of canned salmon was 4,391,601 cases, valued at $81,263,171. This was an increase of 9 percent in quantity and a decrease of 16 percent in value compared with the production in 1948 when 4,014,891 cases, valued at $96,528,730 were packed.

There was a noticeable increase in the marketing of fresh salmon in Alaska during 1949. Pink and chum salmon, normally used almost exclusively for canning, comprised more than 40 percent of the total output. This resulted mainly from the sale of these two species to British Columbia canneries during the peak of the southeastern Alaska season when catches far exceeded the capacity of the Alaska canneries.

During 1949, the herring quota was reduced in the Kodiak area from 390,000 to 250,000 barrels; the Prince William Sound area from 180,000 to 150,000 barrels; and the southeastern Alaska area from 400,000 to 200,000 barrels. A barrel of herring weighs 250 pounds. The catch of herring in Alaska during 1949 totaled 33,061,172 pounds. This represents a decrease of 141,388,082 pounds compared with the 1948 season.

Because of a price disagreement between fishermen and plant operators, only 4 herring reduction plants operated in Alaska during 1949, compared with 17 plants the previous year. This caused the herring catch to fall far short of the lowered quotas.

There were 833 seines used in the Alaska fisheries during 1949. Of this amount, 701 were purse seines and 132 were haul seines. The number of gill nets used was 4,924. In addition to the above, there were 353 traps of which, 116 were driven or pile traps and 237 floating traps. These figures are exclusive of duplication which occurred when purse seines and beach seines were used in more than one field.

Since the success of the Alaska salmon fisheries depends to a great degree upon the success of the parent spawning run, a determined effort was carried out in that area during 1949 to provide new grounds and to improve the accessible spawning areas then in use. The removal of such obstructions as log jams and beaver dams was only a part of the program to increase and improve spawning conditions. Other projects included the operation of 15 weirs for counting the escapement of salmon enroute to the spawning grounds. These were used to determine the proportion of the total runs being taken for commercial purposes and to ascertain the time of arrival and duration of the runs.

---

10 *Statistics on the fisheries of Alaska are collected and compiled by the Alaska Branch of the Service.*

Continued exploratory fishing operations were carried out in the Bering Sea during
1949, by the Branch of Commercial Fisheries of the Fish and Wildlife Service. The
activities of the chartered research vessel Deep Sea were directed primarily toward the
location of king crabs and bottom fish in the Bering Sea. During the summer, trawl
drags were made in the vicinity of Nome, St. Lawrence Island, St. Matthew Island, and
Nunivak Island. The Alaskan and the purple species of king crab were taken, but they
were of small size and widely scattered. These trawls also yielded five species of
shrimp, however the gear in use was not particularly well suited to the shrimping
operations. Cod and flatfish catches of numerical significance were made in the vicinity
of Nunivak Island. Other exploratory operations were carried out by the Fish and Wildlife Service research vessel Oregon which operated in Alaskan waters as far north as
Sitka in search of the pelagic albacore. Scattered albacore were located off southeastern Alaska, but this species was not found in quantities of commercial importance.

ALASKA CATCH, 1949

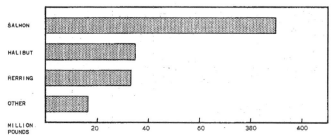

VALUE OF ALASKA CATCH, 1949

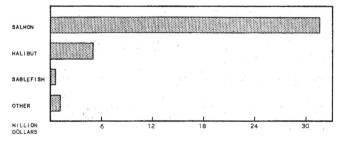

ALASKA FISHERIES

SUMMARY OF DISTRICT, 1949

ITEM	SOUTHEAST ALASKA	CENTRAL ALASKA	WESTERN ALASKA	TOTAL 1/
PERSONS ENGAGED	NUMBER	NUMBER	NUMBER	NUMBER
IN FISHING	5,261	3,276	2,220	10,757
IN TRANSPORTING.	829	819	546	2,194
IN WHOLESALE AND MANUFACTURING INDUSTRIES.	7,104	4,938	3,616	15,659
TOTAL 1/	13,185	9,033	6,382	28,603
CRAFT EMPLOYED				
VESSELS FISHING.	1,281	342	14	1,601
BOATS FISHING.	1,135	1,077	1,390	3,473
VESSELS TRANSPORTING	167	193	142	502
BOATS TRANSPORTING	120	90	44	254
BOATS USED OTHER THAN IN FISHING OR TRANSPORTING . .	13	12	13	38
SCOWS, HOUSEBOATS, PILE DRIVERS, ETC.	159	186	139	484
TOTAL 1/	2,872	1,900	1,742	6,349
WHOLESALE AND MANUFACTURING ESTABLISHMENTS	91	97	39	227

ITEM	SOUTHEAST ALASKA		CENTRAL ALASKA		WESTERN ALASKA		TOTAL	
CATCH	POUNDS	VALUE	POUNDS	VALUE	POUNDS	VALUE	POUNDS	VALUE
FISH:								
SALMON. . .	231,896,520	$22,561,784	111,652,375	$7,723,397	44,796,264	$2,377,316	388,345,160	$32,662,497
OTHER . . .	69,842,119	5,319,672	5,888,198	722,250	2,185,547	54,639	77,915,864	6,096,561
SHELLFISH . .	2,710,063	208,132	2,711,249	259,398	1,206,945	72,417	6,628,257	539,947
TOTAL .	304,448,702	28,089,588	120,251,823	8,705,045	48,188,756	2,504,372	472,889,281	39,299,005
PRODUCTS AS PREPARED FOR MARKET								
SALMON. . . .	139,236,778	45,029,966	63,463,276	25,801,425	29,916,304	15,281,275	232,616,358	86,112,666
HERRING . . .	14,758,370	935,908	323,042	8,198	-	-	15,091,412	944,106
HALIBUT . . .	23,306,839	4,670,960	4,206,405	754,794	-	-	27,513,244	5,425,754
COD	-	-	-	-	660,664	74,680	660,664	74,680
TROUT	13,056	3,254	1,193	227	-	-	14,249	3,481
SABLEFISH . .	4,265,033	527,920	16,738	2,015	-	-	4,281,771	529,935
ROCKFISHES. .	10,167	2,584	-	-	-	-	10,167	2,584
LINGCOD . . .	130,000	12,354	-	-	-	-	130,000	12,354
SHARK LIVERS AND OIL (CHIEFLY DOGFISH) . .	143,581	40,889	2,201	330	-	-	145,782	41,219
SKATE LIVERS.	7,995	800	-	-	-	-	7,995	800
UNCL. LIVERS AND OIL	21,814	4,168	1,523	228	-	-	23,337	4,396
CLAMS	-	-	621,828	683,960	-	-	621,828	683,960
CRABS	114,537	101,546	264,871	249,897	495,621	271,155	875,029	622,598
SHRIMP. . . .	521,703	473,790	-	-	-	-	521,703	473,790
OYSTERS . . .	1,584	934	-	-	-	-	1,584	934
FUR-SEAL BYPRODUCTS .	-	-	-	-	1,062,750	76,219	1,062,750	76,219
TOTAL .	182,531,457	51,805,073	68,901,077	27,501,074	32,135,339	15,703,329	283,567,873	95,009,476

1/ EXCLUSIVE OF DUPLICATION.
NOTE:--DATA ON CATCHES AND PRODUCTS AS PREPARED FOR MARKET INCLUDE FARES OF VESSELS OF U. S. REGISTRY LANDED AT ALASKAN AND BRITISH COLUMBIA PORTS, AND FARES OF COD AND KING CRAB FISHING VESSELS OPERATING ON THE HIGH SEAS OFF THE ALASKAN COAST AND LANDED IN PACIFIC COAST PORTS.

SUMMARY OF OPERATING UNITS, 1949

ITEM	SOUTHEAST ALASKA	CENTRAL ALASKA	WESTERN ALASKA	TOTAL 1/	ITEM - CONTINUED	SOUTHEAST ALASKA	CENTRAL ALASKA	WESTERN ALASKA	TOTAL 1/
	NUMBER	NUMBER	NUMBER	NUMBER	APPARATUS-CONTINUED:	NUMBER	NUMBER	NUMBER	NUMBER
FISHERMEN. . . .	5,261	3,276	2,220	10,757	GILL NETS.	399	3,106	1,419	4,924
VESSELS FISHING:					YARDS.	107,124	432,850	303,350	843,324
MOTOR.	1,281	342	14	1,597	BEAM TRAWLS. . . .	7	-	-	7
NET TONNAGE.	15,168	4,326	996	19,861	LINES:				
BOATS FISHING:					HAND LINES (COD)	2	-	50	52
MOTOR.	1,021	892	3	1,790	SKATES OF LINES	6,628	-	-	6,628
OTHER.	114	185	1,387	1,683	(HALIBUT)				
APPARATUS:					HOOKS (SABLEFISH,				
TRAPS. . . .	216	137	-	353	ETC.	22,761	-	-	22,761
PURSE SEINES .	266	447	9	701	TROLL (SALMON) .	26,004	18	-	26,022
YARDS. . .	106,076	126,218	3,420	220,156	CRAB POTS.	340	997	-	1,337
HAUL SEINES. .	12	119	4	132	CLAM SHOVELS . . .	-	289	-	289
YARDS. . . .	1,980	27,226	600	29,206	OTTER TRAWLS				
GILL NETS.					(BOTTOMFISH) . .	1	-	-	1
(DOGFISH). .	10	-	-	10	(KING CRAB) . .	-	1	3	3
YARDS. . . .	3,400	-	-	3,400					

1/ EXCLUSIVE OF DUPLICATION.

SUMMARY OF CATCH, 1949 1/

ITEM	SOUTHEAST ALASKA		CENTRAL ALASKA		WESTERN ALASKA		TOTAL	
FISH	POUNDS	VALUE	POUNDS	VALUE	POUNDS	VALUE	POUNDS	VALUE
SALMON:								
CHINOOK OR KING.	9,601,260	$1,786,799	2,581,960	$290,470	1,892,480	$141,936	14,075,700	$2,219,205
CHUM OR KETA . .	23,154,752	1,591,889	20,256,680	759,625	3,322,568	132,903	46,734,000	2,484,417
PINK	175,682,704	16,470,253	53,266,700	3,062,835	200	5	228,949,604	19,533,093
RED OR SOCKEYE .	2,938,794	391,839	28,888,098	3,129,544	39,102,000	2,085,440	70,928,892	5,606,823
SILVER OR COHO .	20,519,010	2,321,004	6,658,939	480,923	479,016	17,032	27,656,964	2,818,959
HERRING.	32,738,130	409,227	323,042	4,845	-	-	33,061,172	414,072
HALIBUT.	29,676,538	4,442,741	5,519,805	715,161	-	-	35,196,343	5,157,902
COD.	-	-	-	-	2,185,547	54,639	2,185,547	54,639
TROUT:								
DOLLY VARDEN . .	13,730	1,030	1,591	119	-	-	15,321	1,149
STEELHEAD. . . .	4,275	415	-	-	-	-	4,275	415
SABLEFISH. . . .	5,728,306	425,807	25,418	1,567	-	-	5,753,724	427,374
ROCKFISHES . . .	13,353	2,302	-	-	-	-	13,353	2,302
LINGCOD.	178,804	9,979	-	-	-	-	178,804	9,979
SHARK.	1,289,108	23,203	18,342	330	-	-	1,307,450	23,533
SKATE.	199,875	800	-	-	-	-	199,875	800
UNCL. LIVERS AND								
VISCERA 2/. . . .	-	4,168	-	228	-	-	-	4,396
TOTAL. . . .	301,738,639	27,881,456	117,540,574	8,445,647	46,981,811	2,431,955	466,261,024	38,759,058
SHELLFISH								
CLAMS:								
BUTTER	-	-	5,652	339	-	-	5,652	339
COCKLES.	-	-	8,316	499	-	-	8,316	499
RAZOR.	-	-	1,699,695	203,693	-	-	1,699,695	203,693
CRABS:								
DUNGENESS. . . .	430,815	25,849	997,586	54,867	-	-	1,428,401	80,716
KING	-	-	-	-	1,206,945	72,417	1,206,945	72,417
SHRIMP	2,267,934	181,434	-	-	-	-	2,267,934	181,434
OYSTERS.	11,314	849	-	-	-	-	11,314	849
TOTAL. . . .	2,710,063	208,132	2,711,249	259,398	1,206,945	72,417	6,628,257	539,947
GRAND TOTAL.	304,448,702	28,089,588	120,251,823	8,705,045	48,188,756	2,504,372	472,889,281	39,299,005

1/ INCLUDES CATCHES OF HALIBUT, SABLEFISH, LINGCOD, AND ROCKFISHES LANDED BY VESSELS OF U. S. REGISTRY IN.
BRITISH COLUMBIA PORTS. ROUND WEIGHTS OF FISH TAKEN BY HALIBUT VESSELS WERE OBTAINED BY MULTIPLYING REPORTED
WEIGHTS, REPRESENTING POUNDAGE OF FISH EVISCERATED AND WITH HEADS OFF, BY THE FOLLOWING FACTORS: HALIBUT,
1.33; AND SABLEFISH, LINGCOD, AND ROCKFISHES, 1.43. VALUES INCLUDE PAYMENTS RECEIVED FOR LIVERS AND VISCERA
AS FOLLOWS: HALIBUT, $797,259; SABLEFISH, $165,701 LINGCOD, $6,839 AND ROCKFISHES, $700.
2/ UNCLASSIFIED LIVERS AND VISCERA ARE LISTED FOR VALUE ONLY AS IT IS ASSUMED THAT ROUND WEIGHTS OF THE
FISH ARE REPORTED ELSEWHERE.

TRANSPORTING, WHOLESALE AND MANUFACTURING, 1949

ITEM	SOUTHEAST ALASKA	CENTRAL ALASKA	WESTERN ALASKA	TOTAL 1/
	NUMBER	NUMBER	NUMBER	NUMBER
TRANSPORTING:				
PERSONS ENGAGED.	829	819	546	2,194
CRAFT TRANSPORTING:				
VESSELS, MOTOR	167	193	142	502
NET TONNAGE.	6,708	9,026	6,592	22,326
BOATS, MOTOR	30	17	25	72
BOATS, OTHER	90	73	19	182
LIGHTERS, AND SCOWS.	113	141	104	358
WHOLESALE AND MANUFACTURING,				
PERSONS ENGAGED	7,104	4,938	3,616	15,658
ESTABLISHMENTS:				
HANDLING FRESH AND FROZEN FISH AND SHELLFISH	52	23	8	80
CURING FISH.	26	11	10	47
CANNING FISH AND SHELLFISH	37	68	23	125
MANUFACTURING BYPRODUCTS	6	4	1	11
TOTAL 1/.	91	97	39	227

1/ EXCLUSIVE OF DUPLICATION.

NOTE:--IN ADDITION 38 BOATS AND 126 SCOWS, HOUSEBOATS, PILE DRIVERS, AND PULLERS WERE USED FOR PURPOSES OTHER THAN
FISHING AND TRANSPORTING.

MANUFACTURED FISHERY PRODUCTS, 1949

ITEM	SOUTHEAST ALASKA		CENTRAL ALASKA		WESTERN ALASKA		TOTAL	
FRESH	POUNDS	VALUE	POUNDS	VALUE	POUNDS	VALUE	POUNDS	VALUE
SALMON:								
FOOD	2,625,298	$499,639	33,589	$5,226	-	-	2,658,887	$504,865
BAIT	4,650	46	-	-	-	-	4,650	46
ANIMAL FOOD. . . .	-	-	14,900	1,158	-	-	14,900	1,158
HERRING FOR BAIT . .	1,537,000	19,055	108,042	1,923	-	-	1,645,042	20,978
HALIBUT 1/	4,698,177	870,307	12,148	2,648	-	-	4,710,325	872,955
HALIBUT LIVERS 1/. .	428,240	544,108	19,418	26,187	-	-	447,658	570,295
HALIBUT VISCERA 1/ .	767,776	201,518	36,758	10,084	-	-	804,534	211,602
LINGCOD.	10,570	317	-	-	-	-	10,570	317
LINGCOD LIVERS . . .	4,885	7,690	-	-	-	-	4,885	7,690
LINGCOD VISCERA. . .	77	23	-	-	-	-	77	23
ROCKFISHES:								
LIVERS	488	490	-	-	-	-	488	490
VISCERA.	9	3	-	-	-	-	9	3
SABLEFISH 1/	36,020	2,787	-	-	-	-	36,020	2,787
SABLEFISH LIVERS 1/.	109,473	161,143	34	53	-	-	109,507	161,196
SABLEFISH VISCERA 1/	174,851	40,930	-	-	-	-	174,851	40,930
SHARK LIVERS (CHIEFLY								
DOGFISH) 1/	122,945	35,421	2,201	330	-	-	125,146	35,751
SKATE LIVERS	7,995	800	-	-	-	-	7,995	800
UNCLASSIFIED FISH								
LIVERS.	16,005	2,663	1,523	228	-	-	17,528	2,891
CRABS:								
DUNGENESS, COLD-								
PACKED.	52,938	46,332	1,005	1,005	-	-	53,943	47,337
KING, COLD-PACKED.	-	-	-	-	34,500	$37,950	34,500	37,950
SHRIMP MEAT:								
COLD-PACKED. . . .	491,327	461,225	-	-	-	-	491,327	461,225
IN BULK.	4,118	3,322	-	-	-	-	4,118	3,322
OYSTERS, SHUCKED . .	1,584	934	-	-	-	-	1,584	934
TOTAL.	11,094,426	2,898,753	229,618	48,842	34,500	37,950	11,358,544	2,985,545
FROZEN								
SALMON:								
FOOD.	10,255,785	2,149,063	655,079	111,436	1,241,705	280,052	12,152,569	2,540,551
BAIT.	51,800	2,515	-	-	-	-	51,800	2,515
HERRING FOR BAIT. .	4,217,300	74,422	215,000	6,275	-	-	4,432,300	80,697
HALIBUT	17,261,301	2,943,064	4,073,441	699,384	-	-	21,334,742	3,642,448
HALIBUT FILLETS								
AND STEAKS	138,396	34,599	64,640	16,491	-	-	203,036	51,090
HALIBUT CHEEKS . .	1,070	246	-	-	-	-	1,070	246
LINGCOD	114,468	4,324	-	-	-	-	114,468	4,324
ROCKFISHES.	9,338	391	-	-	-	-	9,338	391
SABLEFISH	3,873,790	301,796	14,018	1,562	-	-	3,887,808	303,358
TROUT:								
DOLLY VARDEN. . .	10,300	2,480	1,193	227	-	-	11,493	2,707
STEELHEAD	206	27	-	-	-	-	206	27
CLAMS:								
BUTTER, MEAT. . . .	-	-	2,016	504	-	-	2,016	504
RAZOR:								
MEAT.	-	-	300	150	-	-	300	150
IN SHELL. . . .	-	-	45,687	10,692	-	-	45,687	10,692
CRABS:								
DUNGENESS:								
MEAT.	-	-	39,510	19,755	-	-	39,510	19,755
IN SHELL. . . .	9,111	1,556	15,966	2,895	-	-	25,077	4,451
KING:								
MEAT.	-	-	-	-	129,708	117,520	129,708	117,520
IN SHELL. . . .	-	-	-	-	3,363	868	3,363	868
LEGS AND CLAWS.	-	-	3,500	1,750	328,050	114,817	331,550	116,567
SHRIMP:								
MEAT	1,328	1,660	-	-	-	-	1,328	1,660
IN SHELL.	24,930	7,583	-	-	-	-	24,930	7,583
TOTAL.	35,969,123	5,523,726	5,130,350	871,121	1,702,826	513,257	42,802,299	6,908,104
CURED								
SALMON:								
MILD CURED. . . .	3,493,794	1,400,361	23,925	6,115	157,575	62,975	3,675,294	1,469,451
PICKLED	-	-	91,925	21,340	186,800	67,242	278,725	88,582
SMOKED.	8,803	2,755	7,443	6,289	-	-	16,246	9,044
KIPPERED.	-	-	11,511	9,108	-	-	11,511	9,108
COD:								
DRY-SALTED. . . .	-	-	-	-	655,664	72,680	655,664	72,680
TONGUES, SALTED .	-	-	-	-	5,000	2,000	5,000	2,000
SABLEFISH:								
SALTED.	63,181	8,730	2,686	400	-	-	65,867	9,130
SMOKED.	5,458	1,364	-	-	-	-	5,458	1,364
TROUT, STEELHEAD,								
SMOKED	150	47	-	-	-	-	150	47
TOTAL.	3,571,386	1,413,257	137,490	43,252	1,005,039	204,897	4,713,915	1,661,406

MANUFACTURED FISHERY PRODUCTS, 1949 - Continued

ITEM	SOUTHEAST ALASKA		CENTRAL ALASKA		WESTERN ALASKA		TOTAL	
CANNED	POUNDS	VALUE	POUNDS	VALUE	POUNDS	VALUE	POUNDS	VALUE
SALMON:								
CHINOOK OR KING	48,720	$23,740	1,680,960	$849,809	670,752	$385,064	2,400,432	$1,258,613
CHUM OR KETA.	11,687,184	3,594,161	10,547,712	3,414,396	1,742,352	572,829	23,977,248	7,581,386
PINK.	100,991,136	33,493,760	27,760,704	9,427,948	-	-	128,751,840	42,921,708
RED OR SOCKEYE.	1,898,496	1,080,210	18,850,512	10,605,060	25,698,000	13,820,804	46,447,008	25,506,074
SILVER OR COHO.	5,996,112	2,627,716	3,018,048	1,285,347	219,120	92,309	9,233,280	4,005,372
SCRAPS FOR DOG FOOD	-	-	3,600	450	-	-	3,600	450
TROUT, STEELHEAD.	2,400	700	-	-	-	-	2,400	700
CLAMS:								
BUTTER.	-	-	540	415	-	-	540	415
BUTTER, JUICE.	-	-	3,360	300	-	-	3,360	300
COCKLES	-	-	2,772	2,570	-	-	2,772	2,570
RAZOR	-	-	567,153	669,329	-	-	567,153	669,329
CRABS, DUNGENESS.	52,488	53,658	204,890	224,492	-	-	257,378	278,150
TOTAL	120,676,536	40,873,945	62,640,251	26,480,116	28,330,224	14,871,006	211,647,011	82,225,067
BYPRODUCTS								
OIL:								
SALMON.	375,000	30,000	123,930	7,596	-	-	498,930	37,596
HERRING.	4,506,765	332,723	-	-	-	-	4,506,765	332,723
HALIBUT:								
LIVER	6,326	52,028	-	-	-	-	6,326	52,028
VISCERA	5,553	25,090	-	-	-	-	5,553	25,090
ROCKFISH LIVER.	332	1,700	-	-	-	-	332	1,700
SABLEFISH:								
LIVER	1,688	8,570	-	-	-	-	1,688	8,570
VISCERA	572	2,600	-	-	-	-	572	2,600
SHARK LIVER (CHIEFLY DOGFISH)	20,636	5,468	-	-	-	-	20,636	5,468
UNCL. FISH LIVER	5,809	1,505	-	-	-	-	5,809	1,505
FUR-SEAL.	-	-	-	-	369,400	20,592	369,400	20,592
MEAL:								
SALMON.	1,800,000	126,000	639,438	50,147	-	-	2,439,438	176,147
HERRING.	4,497,305	509,708	-	-	-	-	4,497,305	509,708
FUR-SEAL.	-	-	-	-	693,350	55,627	693,350	55,627
TOTAL	11,219,986	1,095,392	763,368	57,743	1,062,750	76,219	13,046,104	1,229,354
GRAND TOTAL.	182,531,457	51,805,073	68,901,077	27,501,074	32,135,339	15,703,329	283,567,873	95,009,476

1/ INCLUDES LANDINGS OF ALASKA FLEET IN BRITISH COLUMBIA PORTS.

REVIEW OF THE PRODUCTION OF CANNED FISHERY PRODUCTS, 1949 [1]

ITEM	SOUTHEAST ALASKA [2]		CENTRAL ALASKA [3]		WESTERN ALASKA		TOTAL	
FISH	CASES	VALUE	CASES	VALUE	CASES	VALUE	CASES	VALUE
SALMON:								
CHINOOK OR KING.	1,015	$23,740	35,020	$849,809	13,974	$385,064	50,009	$1,258,613
CHUM OR KETA.	243,483	3,594,161	219,744	3,414,396	36,299	572,829	499,526	7,581,386
PINK.	2,103,982	33,493,760	578,348	9,427,948	-	-	2,682,330	42,921,708
RED OR SOCKEYE.	39,552	1,080,210	392,719	10,605,060	535,375	13,820,804	967,646	25,506,074
SILVER OR COHO.	124,919	2,627,716	62,876	1,285,347	4,565	92,309	192,360	4,005,372
SCRAPS (DOG FOOD)	-	-	75	450	-	-	75	450
TROUT, STEELHEAD.	50	700	-	-	-	-	50	700
TOTAL	2,513,001	40,820,287	1,288,782	25,583,010	590,213	14,871,006	4,391,996	81,274,303
SHELLFISH								
CLAMS:								
BUTTER.	-	-	36	415	-	-	36	415
BUTTER, JUICE.	-	-	140	300	-	-	140	300
COCKLES	-	-	185	2,570	-	-	185	2,570
RAZOR.	-	-	37,846	669,329	-	-	37,846	669,329
CRABS, DUNGENESS.	2,692	53,658	10,507	224,492	-	-	13,199	278,150
TOTAL	2,692	53,658	48,714	897,106	-	-	51,406	950,764
GRAND TOTAL.	2,515,693	40,873,945	1,337,496	26,480,116	590,213	14,871,006	4,443,402	82,225,067

1/ THE PACKS OF SALMON AND TROUT HAVE BEEN CONVERTED TO "STANDARD CASES" OF 48 ONE-POUND CANS; CLAMS TO "STANDARD CASES" OF 48 10-OUNCE CANS CONTAINING 5 OUNCES OF MEAT PER CAN AND CRABS TO THE EQUIVALENT OF 48 1/2-POUND CANS TO THE CASE, EACH CAN CONTAINING 6 1/2 OUNCES OF MEAT.
2/ INCLUDES 300 CASES OF BARBECUED CHUM SALMON, VALUED AT $9,000.
3/ INCLUDES THE FOLLOWING SMOKED SALMON: 8 CASES COHO, VALUED AT $428; 2 CASES KING, VALUED AT $150; AND 20 CASES RED, VALUED AT $1,107.

SUPPLEMENTARY REVIEW OF THE PRODUCTION OF FISHERY BYPRODUCTS, 1949

ITEM		SOUTHEAST ALASKA		CENTRAL ALASKA		WESTERN ALASKA		TOTAL	
		QUANTITY	VALUE	QUANTITY	VALUE	QUANTITY	VALUE	QUANTITY	VALUE
MEAL:									
SALMON.	TONS	900	$126,000	320	$50,147	-	-	1,220	$176,147
HERRING	DO	2,249	509,708	-	-	-	-	2,249	509,708
FUR-SEAL.	DO	-	-	-	-	347	$55,627	347	55,627
OIL:									
SALMON.	GALLONS	50,000	30,000	16,524	7,596	-	-	66,524	37,596
HERRING	DO	600,902	332,723	-	-	-	-	600,902	332,723
HALIBUT LIVER . .	DO	844	52,028	-	-	-	-	844	52,028
HALIBUT VISCERA .	DO	740	25,090	-	-	-	-	740	25,090
SABLEFISH LIVER .	DO	225	8,570	-	-	-	-	225	8,570
SABLEFISH VISCERA	DO	76	2,600	-	-	-	-	76	2,600
ROCKFISH LIVER. .	DO	44	1,700	-	-	-	-	44	1,700
SHARK (DOGFISH) .	DO	2,751	5,468	-	-	-	-	2,751	5,468
UNCL. FISH LIVER.	DO	774	1,505	-	-	-	-	774	1,505
FUR-SEAL.	DO	-	-	-	-	49,253	20,592	49,253	20,592
TOTAL.		-	1,095,392	-	57,743	-	76,219	-	1,229,354

SUPPLEMENTARY REVIEW OF THE CATCH OF SALMON, 1949

SPECIES	SOUTHEAST ALASKA		CENTRAL ALASKA		WESTERN ALASKA		TOTAL	
	NUMBER	VALUE	NUMBER	VALUE	NUMBER	VALUE	NUMBER	VALUE
CHINOOK OR KING	480,063	$1,786,799	129,098	$290,470	94,624	$141,936	703,785	$2,219,205
CHUM OR KETA .	2,894,344	1,591,889	2,532,085	759,625	415,321	132,903	5,841,750	2,484,417
PINK	43,920,676	16,470,253	13,316,675	3,062,835	50	5	57,237,401	19,533,093
RED OR SOCKEYE	489,799	391,839	4,814,683	3,129,544	6,517,000	2,085,440	11,821,482	5,606,823
SILVER OR COHO	2,279,890	2,321,004	739,882	480,923	53,224	17,032	3,072,996	2,818,959
TOTAL . .	50,064,772	22,561,784	21,532,423	7,723,397	7,080,219	2,377,316	78,677,414	32,662,497

NOTE:-THE SALMON CATCH IS REPORTED HERE IN NUMBERS OF FISH; ESTIMATED ROUND WEIGHTS ARE SHOWN IN THE CATCH TABLE.

SUMMARY OF CATCH, 1930 - 1949

(EXPRESSED IN THOUSANDS OF POUNDS AND THOUSANDS OF DOLLARS)

YEAR	SALMON		HERRING		SHELLFISH		OTHER FISH		WHALE PRODUCTS		TOTAL	
	QUANTITY	VALUE	QUANTITY	VALUE	QUANTITY	VALUE	QUANTITY	VALUE	QUANTITY	VALUE	QUANTITY	VALUE
1930	426,442	8,041	145,672	1,093	1,980	108	37,192	3,044	9,415	470	620,702	12,756
1931	467,664	7,758	103,567	777	2,170	120	24,724	1,388	-	-	598,125	10,043
1932	452,536	5,766	127,578	548	2,913	156	15,829	501	7,664	91	606,520	7,062
1933	467,349	7,498	140,580	703	2,709	147	16,757	741	3,378	69	630,773	9,158
1934	624,652	9,831	165,637	828	2,732	166	16,894	832	9,354	251	819,269	11,958
1935	434,004	6,970	189,287	946	2,542	147	12,503	640	10,374	390	648,710	9,093
1936	726,853	11,857	172,829	864	2,550	152	21,297	1,019	8,814	334	932,343	14,226
1937	593,384	11,877	206,446	1,032	3,058	219	22,895	1,110	9,036	479	834,819	14,717
1938	589,706	9,943	179,735	899	2,526	159	21,982	1,039	4,874	180	798,823	12,220
1939	452,166	9,256	185,462	927	2,241	129	22,673	1,009	3,855	137	666,397	11,458
1940	439,182	8,420	94,158	471	2,547	154	27,801	1,567	-	-	563,688	10,612
1941	543,024	12,609	163,467	535	2,988	148	26,790	1,747	-	-	736,269	15,039
1942	430,867	13,398	43,833	328	2,500	107	44,979	4,101	-	-	522,179	17,934
1943	457,307	14,588	90,549	530	3,222	166	43,567	5,222	-	-	594,645	20,506
1944	393,318	14,527	113,279	1,142	3,965	185	50,637	4,560	-	-	561,199	20,414
1945	402,635	15,564	139,760	1,356	5,578	216	48,070	5,152	-	-	596,052	22,288
1946	391,689	17,089	198,231	1,982	6,955	390	54,571	9,415	-	-	651,446	28,876
1947	381,808	19,571	187,889	2,077	4,444	377	39,668	6,665	-	-	613,809	28,690
1948	338,369	23,144	174,449	1,853	7,436	516	46,645	5,981	-	-	566,899	31,494
1949	388,345	32,662	33,061	414	6,628	540	44,855	5,683	-	-	472,889	39,299

FUR SEALS

SECTION 11.- HAWAII

The following tabulation of the catch of fish and shellfish in the Territory of Hawaii has been compiled from monthly reports submitted by the Board of Commissioners of Agriculture and Forestry of the Territory of Hawaii, Division of Fish and Game. The catch listed has not been included in the tabulations of the catch of the United States and Alaska listed in the sections entitled ''General Review'' or ''Review of Certain Major Fisheries''.

The commercial catch of fishery products in the Hawaiian Islands during 1949 totaled 15,042,755 pounds valued at $3,718,474. This represents an increase of 3 percent in quantity but a decrease of 10 percent in value compared with the landings of the previous year.

HAWAII: CATCH BY MONTHS, 1949.

SPECIES		JANUARY		FEBRUARY		MARCH		APRIL	
ENGLISH	HAWAIIAN	POUNDS	VALUE	POUNDS	VALUE	POUNDS	VALUE	POUNDS	VALUE
OCEAN CATCH:									
AMBERJACK. . .	KAHALA. . .	17,808	$7,937	24,767	$7,293	26,719	$9,534	30,686	$10,492
BIG-EYED SCAD.	AKULE . . .	36,352	25,761	26,803	16,504	28,400	20,146	32,024	23,260
BLUE CREVALLE.	OMILU . . .	3,104	2,048	4,563	2,361	4,083	2,013	3,569	1,759
BONE FISH OR									
LADYFISH . .	OIO	9,940	3,786	6,505	2,824	4,086	1,589	2,444	997
CONVICT TANG .	MANINI. . .	1,850	1,101	2,053	1,233	1,769	1,032	3,230	1,720
DOLPHIN. . . .	MAHAMAHI. .	2,914	1,340	7,549	3,214	16,899	6,161	24,177	8,036
GOATFISH (M.									
AURIFLAMMA)	WEKE-ULA. .	1,932	1,459	1,336	1,154	1,633	1,273	1,883	1,482
GOATFISH (M.									
SAMOENSIS)	WEKE. . . .	2,565	1,822	3,781	2,692	4,096	2,630	7,536	4,989
GOATFISH (P.									
FRATERCULUS)	MOANO . . .	1,486	1,333	2,099	1,845	2,593	2,158	2,827	2,415
GOATFISH (P.									
PORPHYREUS)	KUMU. . . .	1,137	1,418	1,865	2,139	1,425	1,572	1,401	1,690
JACK CREVALLE	ULUA. . . .	9,463	5,001	17,669	7,313	16,455	7,446	15,915	6,943
LOBSTER, SPINY	ULA	2,330	1,766	2,192	1,526	3,078	2,220	4,170	3,026
MACKEREL . . .	OPELU . . .	37,990	13,602	28,965	11,127	24,749	11,249	19,058	9,317
MILKFISH . . .	AWA	1,656	564	1,045	303	1,636	410	3,212	1,088
MULLET	AMAAMA. . .	-	-	-	-	9,071	6,453	2,866	2,392
OCTOPUS. . . .	HEE	2,913	1,711	1,325	773	523	336	757	494
SEA BASS . . .	HAPUUPUU. .	3,280	1,733	5,888	2,200	4,904	2,295	4,636	2,132
SNAPPER:									
GRAY	UKU	3,201	1,884	4,540	2,176	3,525	1,794	2,920	1,401
PINK	KALEKALE. .	1,794	991	2,089	1,345	3,205	2,185	3,561	2,326
PINK	OPAKAPAKA .	17,760	10,231	19,192	9,139	21,748	11,217	13,142	6,686
RED.	EHU	2,024	1,632	3,028	2,519	5,547	4,186	4,462	3,954
RED.	ULAULA. . .	3,710	3,047	11,877	8,497	15,156	9,733	11,532	8,455
SQUIRREL OR									
BIG-EYED FISH	UU.	2,255	1,754	3,871	2,713	4,938	3,113	3,417	2,523
SWORDFISH. . .	A'U	55,491	24,726	141,503	44,824	109,415	43,813	108,725	44,702
THREADFISH . .	MOI	519	379	1,808	1,879	478	402	1,257	1,017
TUNA:									
ALBACORE · ·	AHIPALAHA .	}							
BIG-EYED · ·		} 109,226	55,464	173,554	70,860	124,633	64,571	125,259	60,661
BLUEFIN · ·	AHI · · ·	}							
YELLOWFIN· ·		}							
SKIPJACK · ·	AKU	64,870	20,525	104,877	27,331	109,422	33,637	215,977	65,562
BONITO · ·	KAWAKAWA. .	2,062	865	8,181	2,296	8,903	2,711	6,302	1,912
TOTAL TUNA · · · · ·		176,158	76,854	286,612	100,487	242,958	100,919	347,538	128,135
WAHOO.	ONO	1,614	650	3,184	1,071	1,998	720	3,759	1,302
UNCLASSIFIED .	. . . . . .	17,185	6,341	36,184	11,344	24,648	6,979	23,344	6,810
TOTAL OCEAN CATCH		418,431	200,871	652,293	250,495	585,745	263,578	684,248	289,543
POND CATCH: 1/									
BARRACUDA. . .	KAKU. . . .	59	55	36	31	-	-	53	52
BONEFISH OR									
LADYFISH . .	OIO	530	344	448	198	44	29	808	525
CLAM (V.									
PHILIPPINARUM)	OLEPE . . .	971	311	1,210	390	1,015	325	1,115	357
CRABS:	PAPAI . . .								
WHITE. . . .	KUAHONU . .	139	63	60	18	-	-	119	53
SAMOAN . . .	. . . . . .	602	238	513	234	544	234	367	163
RED.	MOALA . . .	10	5	110	39	-	-	-	-
JACK CREVALLE.	ULUA. . . .	-	-	2	2	-	-	29	17
MILKFISH . . .	AWA	632	323	718	447	936	410	1,508	622
MOUNTAIN BASS									
OR SESELE. .	AHOLEHOLE .	16	10	462	387	539	451	286	228
MULLET	AMAAMA. . .	3,245	3,180	2,632	2,583	866	798	959	928
TEN POUNDER. .	AWAAWA. . .	355	224	20	12	46	35	68	50
UNCLASSIFIED .	. . . . . .	29	25	-	-	83	15	33	10
TOTAL POND CATCH.		6,588	4,778	6,211	4,341	4,073	2,337	5,345	3,005
GRAND TOTAL		425,019	205,649	658,504	254,836	589,818	265,915	689,593	292,548

HAWAIIAN FISHERIES

HAWAII: CATCH BY MONTHS, 1949 - Continued

SPECIES (ENGLISH)	HAWAIIAN	MAY POUNDS	MAY VALUE	JUNE POUNDS	JUNE VALUE	JULY POUNDS	JULY VALUE	AUGUST POUNDS	AUGUST VALUE
OCEAN CATCH:									
AMBERJACK	KAHALA	12,735	$3,352	12,555	$2,960	9,618	$2,236	6,965	$2,503
BIG-EYED SCAD	AKULE	68,850	42,557	41,644	23,100	41,984	26,800	40,281	24,553
BLUE CREVALLE	OMILU	2,668	990	1,676	700	9,551	3,257	8,949	3,867
BONEFISH OR LADYFISH	OIO	6,635	2,779	5,543	1,921	6,429	2,513	4,658	2,061
CONVICT TANG	MANINI	1,355	665	2,121	389	1,541	707	1,139	623
DOLPHIN	MAHAMAHI	27,994	7,770	23,102	5,954	17,435	5,171	6,894	2,871
GOATFISH (M. AURIFLAMMA)	WEKE-ULA	1,155	786	1,045	706	1,325	921	1,258	863
GOATFISH (M. SAMOENSIS)	WEKE	7,549	4,230	4,077	2,049	3,874	2,193	5,738	3,996
GOATFISH (P. FRATERCULUS)	MOANO	3,536	2,511	3,164	2,393	2,659	2,044	3,416	2,680
GOATFISH (P. PORPHYREUS)	KUMU	1,745	1,960	1,203	1,210	1,313	1,388	1,032	1,019
JACK CREVALLE	ULUA	20,884	7,637	14,104	5,084	19,538	7,009	17,467	7,451
LOBSTER, SPINY	ULA	10,312	6,057	1,559	1,099	223	189	196	130
MACKEREL	OPELU	10,356	4,557	4,381	2,261	4,789	2,958	21,241	10,267
MILKFISH	AWA	2,690	917	2,711	679	3,555	760	1,240	251
MULLET	AMAAMA	2,952	2,003	3,834	2,876	6,646	4,737	2,765	2,270
OCTOPUS	HEE	554	328	704	377	606	344	1,206	714
SEA BASS	HAPJUPUU	8,991	2,472	6,060	2,142	2,442	1,011	4,295	1,732
SNAPPER:									
GRAY	UKU	3,850	1,404	12,794	5,031	17,172	6,425	6,972	3,034
PINK	KALEKALE	2,247	1,103	2,085	1,179	1,542	925	2,594	1,376
PINK	OPAKAPAKA	15,420	5,647	15,156	4,847	15,136	5,697	10,034	4,686
RED	EHU	6,720	4,162	6,985	4,509	5,733	4,190	5,070	3,723
RED	ULAULA	18,272	9,809	8,676	3,867	8,980	4,527	5,538	3,456
SQUIRREL OR BIG-EYED FISH	UU	5,579	4,102	6,441	5,049	9,498	7,183	10,000	7,211
SWORDFISH	A'U	108,278	30,493	90,009	23,221	79,758	29,662	103,621	39,172
THREADFISH	MOI	1,530	972	2,593	1,709	8,560	6,015	3,352	2,444
TUNA: ALBACORE / BIG-EYED / BLUEFIN / YELLOWFIN	AHIPALAHA / AHI	142,824	50,345	168,177	53,421	151,555	48,798	126,384	44,662
SKIPJACK	AKU	928,626	138,758	2,152,251	258,019	1,504,119	186,199	2,187,272	264,088
BONITO	KAWAKAWA	4,725	1,050	3,307	892	4,690	1,247	5,455	1,423
TOTAL TUNA		1,076,175	190,153	2,333,735	312,332	1,660,364	236,244	2,319,111	310,173
WAHOO	ONO	6,524	1,880	5,757	1,574	6,263	1,943	6,078	2,065
UNCLASSIFIED		31,612	8,387	31,250	7,519	30,859	7,406	26,943	7,703
TOTAL OCEAN CATCH		1,467,158	349,683	2,645,064	427,237	1,977,393	374,455	2,628,043	452,894
POND CATCH: 1/									
BARRACUDA	KAKU	44	38	182	149	61	50	201	147
BONEFISH OR LADYFISH	OIO	40	26	24	16	96	56	124	58
CLAM (v. PHILIPPINARUM)	OLEPE	989	316	982	314	-	-	3,461	1,105
CRABS:	PAPAI								
WHITE	KUAHONU	218	98	349	145	136	61	240	92
SAMOAN		365	162	303	134	121	52	101	31
RED	MOALA	-	-	61	45	-	-	90	41
JACK CREVALLE	ULUA	267	149	-	-	-	-		
MILKFISH	AWA	502	214	1,482	572	1,274	493	1,319	521
MOUNTAIN BASS OR SESSELE	AHOLEHOLE	190	107	128	64	4	2	12	10
MULLET	AMAAMA	99	106	22	23	226	192	461	404
SHRIMP	OPAE	-	-	-	-	50	57	62	62
TENPOUNDER	AWAAWA	38	31	-	-	241	152	277	130
UNCLASSIFIED		-	-	13	3	-	-	56	56
TOTAL POND CATCH		2,752	1,247	3,546	1,465	2,209	1,135	6,404	2,627
GRAND TOTAL		1,469,920	350,930	2,648,610	428,702	1,979,602	375,590	2,634,447	455,521

SEE FOOTNOTE AT END OF TABLE   (CONTINUED ON NEXT PAGE)

HAWAII: CATCH BY MONTHS, 1949 - Continued

SPECIES		SEPTEMBER		OCTOBER		NOVEMBER	
ENGLISH	HAWAIIAN	POUNDS	VALUE	POUNDS	VALUE	POUNDS	VALUE
OCEAN CATCH:							
AMBERJACK.	KAHALA. . .	7,664	$2,795	7,259	$2,323	11,904	$3,498
BIG-EYED SCAD . .	AKULE . . .	57,234	31,938	32,441	20,782	61,381	34,674
BLUE CREVALLE. . .	OMILU . . .	4,713	1,703	4,862	1,756	3,403	1,473
BONEFISH OR							
LADYFISH . . .	OIO	9,912	4,009	9,044	3,626	10,033	3,542
CONVICT TANG . . .	MANINI. . .	1,678	832	2,362	1,032	1,734	840
DOLPHIN.	MAHAMAHI. .	9,423	4,173	14,679	5,901	11,444	4,089
GOATFISH (M.							
AURIFLAMMA). . .	WEKE-ULA. .	1,883	1,507	975	682	3,134	2,067
GOATFISH (M.							
SAMOENSIS) . . .	WEKE. . . .	6,223	3,602	5,696	3,294	3,724	2,187
GOATFISH (P.							
FRATERCULUS) . .	MOANO . . .	3,834	2,774	2,659	1,854	1,832	1,334
GOATFISH (P.							
PORPHYREUS). . .	KUMU. . . .	1,069	1,142	987	1,100	1,048	1,169
JACK CREVALLE. . .	ULUA. . . .	17,987	7,332	15,545	6,099	12,052	4,562
LOBSTER, SPINY . .	ULA	7,015	3,791	3,891	2,377	1,983	1,079
MACKEREL	OPELU . . .	23,735	9,064	15,942	6,736	23,976	11,070
MILKFISH	AWA	2,805	590	1,166	272	1,590	711
MULLET	AMAAMA. . .	4,220	3,192	3,703	2,841	3,902	2,708
OCTOPUS.	HEE	2,795	1,687	3,489	1,911	1,915	977
SEA BASS	HAPUUPUU. .	3,948	1,586	6,479	2,071	5,307	1,873
SNAPPER:							
GRAY	UKU	4,855	2,209	4,810	2,108	2,835	1,231
PINK	KALEKALE. .	1,881	1,047	2,651	1,387	2,445	1,310
PINK	OPAKAPAKA .	20,875	8,960	16,390	6,655	24,987	9,035
RED.	EHU	4,748	3,354	4,177	2,600	4,131	2,374
RED.	ULAULA. . .	5,002	3,519	8,797	5,551	7,543	4,765
SQUIRREL OR							
BIG-EYED FISH .	UU.	15,781	10,543	4,532	3,312	5,140	3,284
SWORDFISH.	A'U	66,597	30,733	91,045	39,503	66,836	22,562
THREADFISH	MOI	2,166	1,491	1,366	871	524	431
TUNA:							
ALBACORE	AHIPALAHA .						
BIG-EYED							
BLUEFIN	AHI	110,534	46,783	199,070	63,098	219,865	60,650
YELLOWFIN . . .							
SKIPJACK	AKU	963,083	125,257	458,235	69,717	215,891	39,541
BONITO	KAWAKAWA. .	5,898	1,326	3,089	556	2,244	477
TOTAL TUNA.		1,079,515	173,366	660,394	132,371	438,000	100,668
WAHOO.	ONO	5,805	2,269	4,475	1,381	1,546	486
UNCLASSIFIED . . .	. . . . . .	29,379	8,250	25,569	6,713	16,463	4,747
TOTAL OCEAN CATCH		1,402,743	327,452	955,385	267,109	730,912	228,766
POND CATCH: 1/							
BARRACUDA	KAKU. . . .	17	14	164	164	9	4
BONEFISH OR							
LADYFISH. . . .	OIO	290	150	585	319	320	192
CLAM (V.							
PHILLPPINARUM)	OLEPE . . .	727	232	369	130	515	169
CRABS:	PAPAI . . .						
WHITE	KUAHONU . .	64	29	34	15	-	-
SAMOAN. . . .		207	78	159	64	52	17
JACK CREVALLE .	ULUA. . . .	-	-	230	161	-	-
MILKFISH . . .	AWA	786	286	1,188	471	424	172
MULLET. . . . : .	AMAAMA. . .	213	195	437	388	1,426	1,285
SHRIMP.	OPAE. . . .	55	55	37	37	20	20
TENPOUNDER. . . .	AWAAWA. . .	60	9	18	9	79	40
UNCLASSIFIED. . .	. . . . . .			20	20	-	-
TOTAL POND CATCH		2,419	1,048	3,241	1,778	2,845	1,899
GRAND TOTAL		1,405,162	328,500	958,626	268,887	733,757	230,665

SEE FOOTNOTE AT END OF TABLE

(CONTINUED ON NEXT PAGE)

HAWAII: CATCH BY MONTHS, 1949 - Continued

SPECIES		DECEMBER		TOTAL	
ENGLISH	HAWAIIAN	POUNDS	VALUE	POUNDS	VALUE
OCEAN CATCH:					
AMBERJACK	KAHALA	21,365	$5,412	190,335	$60,335
BIG-EYED SCAD	AKULE	33,697	19,646	501,091	309,721
BLUE CREVALLE	OMILU	1,725	570	52,866	22,497
BONEFISH OR LADYFISH	OIO	9,344	3,474	84,573	33,115
CONVICT TANG	MANINI	1,718	876	22,550	11,550
DOLPHIN	MAHAMAHI	8,227	3,612	170,737	58,292
GOATFISH (M. AURIFLAMMA)	WEKE-ULA	3,336	2,346	20,895	15,246
GOATFISH (M. SAMOENSIS)	WEKE	6,879	3,914	61,738	37,598
GOATFISH (P. FRATERCULUS)	MOANO	2,836	2,034	32,941	25,375
GOATFISH (P. PORPHYREUS)	KUMU	1,895	1,832	16,121	17,639
JACK CREVALLE	ULUA	15,510	5,568	193,589	77,445
LOBSTER, SPINY	ULA	6,195	3,009	42,134	26,269
MACKEREL	OPELU	29,276	10,028	244,459	102,235
MILKFISH	AWA	222	52	23,528	6,597
MULLET	AMAAMA	-	-	39,959	29,472
OCTOPUS	HEE	2,094	1,151	18,881	10,813
SEA BASS	HAPUUPUU	7,604	2,424	63,834	23,671
SNAPPER:					
GRAY	UKU	4,152	1,878	71,626	30,575
PINK	KALEKALE	3,647	1,831	29,741	17,005
PINK	OPAKAPAKA	35,738	13,398	225,578	96,198
RED	EHU	6,109	4,083	58,734	41,285
RED	ULAULA	13,340	8,435	118,433	73,661
SQUIRREL OR BIG-EYED FISH	UU	5,914	4,095	77,366	54,882
SWORDFISH	AU	80,338	23,928	1,101,616	397,359
THREADFISH	MOI	473	334	24,726	17,944
TUNA:					
ALBACORE	AHIPALAHA				
BIG-EYED					
BLUEFIN	AHI	362,011	95,787	2,013,092	715,100
YELLOWFIN					
SKIPJACK	AKU	151,705	27,007	9,066,328	1,254,641
BONITO	KAWAKAWA	2,903	681	57,759	15,436
TOTAL TUNA		516,619	123,475	11,137,179	1,985,177
WAHOO	ONO	1,954	641	48,957	15,282
UNCLASSIFIED		22,519	7,030	315,954	89,229
TOTAL OCEAN CATCH		842,716	256,086	14,990,141	3,687,169
POND CATCH: 1/					
BARRACUDA	KAKU	69	69	895	783
BONEFISH OR LADYFISH	OIO	787	441	4,095	2,354
CLAM (V. PHILIPPINARUM)	OLEPE	-	-	11,354	3,649
CRABS:	PAPAI	-	-	1,359	574
WHITE	KUAHONU	60	18	3,394	1,425
SAMOAN	MOALA	-	-	271	130
RED		-	-	-	-
JACK CREVALLE	ULUA	102	41	630	370
MILKFISH	AWA	756	319	11,525	4,850
MOUNTAIN BASS OR SESSELE	AHOLEHOLE	86	64	1,723	1,323
MULLET	AMAAMA	4,619	4,432	15,205	14,514
SHRIMP	OPAE	50	50	274	281
TENPOUNDER	AWAWA	322	177	1,524	849
UNCLASSIFIED		130	34	364	203
TOTAL POND CATCH		6,981	5,645	52,614	31,305
GRAND TOTAL		849,697	260,731	15,042,755	3,718,474

1/ SALT-WATER

SECTION 12.- REVIEW OF CERTAIN MAJOR FISHERIES

There are presented in this section of the Digest complete data on the catch of certain of the major species of fish and shellfish taken commercially in the United States and Alaska. Although these data are included in the detailed catch tables for the various states, they have been republished in individual fishery tables in this portion of the report to provide readers with a single source of catch data for cod, haddock, halibut, mackerel, menhaden, ocean perch (rosefish), pilchard, salmon, tuna, and whales. Statistics on the oyster and shrimp fisheries are being omitted this year since data were not collected in the South Atlantic States for 1949, and a substantial portion of the catch of these items comes from that area. Most of the above species are taken by fishermen operating in several states or districts, and a number are taken by several types of fishing gear. Because of this, the casual reader of the Digest often experiences difficulty in locating complete data on the catch of the species in individual state catch tables. The information contained in this section includes the volume and value of the catch by individual types of gear and by states and districts.

PRINCIPAL UNITED STATES AND ALASKA FISHERIES

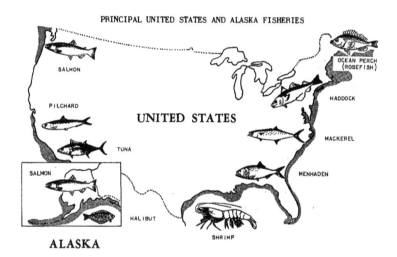

UNITED STATES AND ALASKA COD FISHERY

During 1949, the fishermen of the United States and Alaska caught 71,011,847 pounds of cod valued at $4,029,563 to the fishermen. This was a decrease of 11 percent in quantity and 21 percent in value compared with the previous year.

Otter trawls accounted for 75 percent of the cod catch; lines, 20 percent; and gill nets, 4 percent. Other types of gear, principally floating traps and pound nets made up the remaining 1 percent.

Massachusetts, with a catch of 50.4 million pounds of cod, led in the production of this species, followed by Washington, (6.2 million pounds), and Maine, (6.1 million pounds).

In all areas, except Alaska, the major portion of the catch was taken with otter trawls. Lines accounted for the entire Alaska catch.

SUMMARY OF COD CATCH, 1949

STATE	OTTER TRAWLS		LINES		GILL NETS		FLOATING TRAPS	
	POUNDS	VALUE	POUNDS	VALUE	POUNDS	VALUE	POUNDS	VALUE
NEW ENGLAND:								
MAINE	2,324,900	$104,042	2,151,700	$87,160	1,598,800	$124,716	-	-
NEW HAMPSHIRE .	-	-	2,700	784	-	-	-	-
MASSACHUSETTS .	42,230,700	2,399,548	6,883,300	431,599	1,276,600	89,502	8,000	$396
RHODE ISLAND. .	488,600	18,772	705,600	34,771	-	-	513,100	25,043
CONNECTICUT . .	589,800	60,000	900	121	-	-	-	-
TOTAL. . .	45,634,000	2,582,362	9,744,200	554,435	2,875,400	214,218	521,100	25,439
MIDDLE ATLANTIC:								
NEW YORK. . . .	1,547,400	140,708	799,700	87,337	7,000	746	-	-
NEW JERSEY. . .	66,200	7,286	1,190,000	114,158	200	20	-	-
DELAWARE. . . .	400	40	-	-	-	-	-	-
TOTAL	1,614,000	148,034	1,989,700	201,495	7,200	766	-	-
CHESAPEAKE:								
MARYLAND. . . .	1,200	48	32,600	1,304	-	-	-	-
VIRGINIA. . . .	3,200	157	-	-	-	-	-	-
TOTAL. . .	4,400	205	32,600	1,304	-	-	-	-
PACIFIC COAST:								
WASHINGTON. . .	6,230,600	230,532	13,000	483	1,600	60	-	-
OREGON.	5,100	181	300	7	-	-	-	-
TOTAL. . .	6,235,700	230,713	13,300	490	1,600	60	-	-
ALASKA.	-	-	2,185,547	54,639	-	-	-	-
GRAND TOTAL	53,488,100	2,961,314	13,965,347	812,363	2,884,200	215,044	521,100	25,439

STATE	DREDGES		POUND NETS		PURSE SEINES		HAUL SEINES		TOTAL	
	POUNDS	VALUE	POUNDS	VALUE –	POUNDS	VALUE	POUNDS	VALUE	POUNDS	VALUE
NEW ENGLAND:										
MAINE	-	-	-	-	-	-	-	-	6,075,400	$315,918
NEW HAMPSHIRE .	-	-	-	-	-	-	-	-	2,700	784
MASSACHUSETTS .	6,200	$273	13,700	$511	200	$12	-	-	50,418,700	2,921,841
RHODE ISLAND. .	-	-	-	-	-	-	-	-	1,707,300	78,586
CONNECTICUT . .	-	-	-	-	-	-	-	-	590,700	60,121
TOTAL. . .	6,200	273	13,700	511	200	12	-	-	58,794,800	3,377,250
MIDDLE ATLANTIC:										
NEW YORK. . . .	-	-	2,400	250	-	-	300	$32	2,356,800	229,073
NEW JERSEY. . .	-	-	130,200	14,322	-	-	-	-	1,386,600	135,786
DELAWARE. . . .	-	-	-	-	-	-	-	-	400	40
TOTAL. . .	-	-	132,600	14,572	-	-	300	32	3,743,800	364,899
CHESAPEAKE:										
MARYLAND. . . .	-	-	-	-	-	-	-	-	33,800	1,352
VIRGINIA. . . .	-	-	-	-	-	-	-	-	3,200	157
TOTAL. . .	-	-	-	-	-	-	-	-	37,000	1,509
PACIFIC COAST:										
WASHINGTON. . .	-	-	-	-	-	-	100	3	6,245,300	231,078
OREGON.	-	-	-	-	-	-	-	-	5,400	188
TOTAL. . .	-	-	-	-	-	-	100	3	6,250,700	231,266
ALASKA.	-	-	-	-	-	-	-	-	2,185,547	54,639
GRAND TOTAL	6,200	273	146,300	15,083	200	12	400	35	71,011,847	4,029,563

DORY

ATLANTIC COAST HADDOCK FISHERY

The production of haddock in the United States during 1949 amounted to 134,970,400 pounds, valued at $9,250,400 to the fishermen. This was a decrease of 14 percent in quantity and 26 percent in value compared with the previous year. Scrod haddock accounted for nearly 40 percent of the total haddock catch.

Otter trawls accounted for 96 percent of the total production. The remaining 4 percent was taken with hand and trawl lines, gill nets and dredges.

Of the total catch, 99 percent was landed in the New England States. The remaining 1 percent was taken in New York and New Jersey. Massachusetts accounted for 94 percent of the total landings.

SUMMARY OF HADDOCK CATCH, 1949

STATE	LINES, HAND AND TRAWL		OTTER TRAWLS		GILL NETS		DREDGES		TOTAL	
	POUNDS	VALUE	POUNDS	VALUE	POUNDS	VALUE	POUNDS	VALUE	POUNDS	VALUE
NEW ENGLAND:										
MAINE	524,100	$36,125	6,474,300	$416,563	186,400	$16,077	-	-	7,184,800	$468,765
NEW HAMPSHIRE	1,400	142	-	-	-	-	-	-	1,400	142
MASSACHUSETTS	4,652,200	355,840	121,661,500	8,326,949	157,500	13,557	25,500	$1,250	126,496,700	8,697,596
RHODE ISLAND.	-	-	69,600	3,407	-	-	-	-	69,600	3,407
CONNECTICUT .	-	-	12,100	1,000	-	-	-	-	12,100	1,000
TOTAL. . .	5,177,700	392,107	128,217,500	8,747,919	343,900	29,634	25,500	1,250	133,764,600	9,170,910
MIDDLE ATLANTIC:										
NEW YORK. . .	-	-	1,197,300	78,768	-	-	-	-	1,197,300	78,768
NEW JERSEY. .	-	-	8,500	722	-	-	-	-	8,500	722
TOTAL. . .	-	-	1,205,800	79,490	-	-	-	-	1,205,800	79,490
GRAND TOTAL	5,177,700	392,107	129,423,300	8,827,409	343,900	29,634	25,500	1,250	134,970,400	9,250,400

PACIFIC COAST HALIBUT FISHERY

The total North Pacific halibut catch by both United States and Canadian craft during 1949 totaled 53,622,000 pounds, a decrease of a half million pounds compared with the previous year.

The 1949 halibut season which extended from May 1 through July 12, was 73 days, compared with 72 days in 1948 and 109 days in 1947.

Landings of halibut in Alaska ports, which has steadily risen from 7 million pounds in 1939 to a record high of almost 24 million pounds in 1948, declined to 22.3 million pounds in 1949. This decrease in Alaska landings of halibut was reflected in a marked increase in the landings of United States fishing craft at British Columbia ports. It is believed that the diversion to Canadian ports was in protest against new licenses imposed on fishermen during the year by the Alaska Territorial Legislature.

Data on landings of halibut listed in the following tables represent the dressed weight of the fish, which is the weight upon which the quota is based, while those in the various state and sectional tables represent the round weight of the catch. In the sectional tables, halibut landed in Canada by vessels of United States registry is credited to Alaska. The dressed weight can be converted to round weight by multiplying by 1.33.

REVIEW OF CERTAIN MAJOR FISHERIES

SUMMARY OF UNITED STATES HALIBUT FLEET OPERATING UNITS, 1949

ITEM	WASHINGTON FLEET	ALASKA FLEET	TOTAL
	NUMBER	NUMBER	NUMBER
REGULAR HALIBUT VESSELS:			
NUMBER.	185	296	481
NET TONNAGE	6,024	4,089	10,113
CREW.	1,265	1,174	2,439
SKATES OF LINES	5,692	5,283	10,975
REGULAR HALIBUT BOATS:			
NUMBER.	1	45	46
CREW.	2	92	94
SKATES OF LINES	7	345	352
BOATS PRIMARILY IN OTHER FISHERIES BUT LANDING SMALL FARES OF HALIBUT 1/:			
NUMBER.	–	125	125
CREW.	–	250	250
SKATES OF LINES	–	1,000	1,000

1/ DOES NOT INCLUDE TROLLERS OR OTHER BOATS CATCHING HALIBUT INCIDENTAL TO OTHER FISHING OPERATIONS.
NOTE:--THE FLEET CLASSIFICATION IS THAT OF THE INTERNATIONAL FISHERIES COMMISSION, UNDER WHICH CRAFT LISTED BY THE COMMISSION AS HAVING THEIR HOME PORT IN ALASKA ARE INCLUDED IN THE "ALASKA FLEET" AND ALL OTHER CRAFT OF UNITED STATES REGISTRY ARE INCLUDED IN THE "WASHINGTON FLEET" IF THEY LAND HALIBUT IN SEATTLE, BRITISH COLUMBIA, OR ALASKA.

SUMMARY OF UNITED STATES AND CANADIAN HALIBUT CATCH, 1949
(EXPRESSED IN THOUSANDS OF POUNDS AND THOUSANDS OF DOLLARS)

FLEET CLASSIFICATION	LANDED IN						TOTAL	
	SEATTLE, WASHINGTON		BRITISH COLUMBIA		ALASKA			
	QUANTITY	VALUE	QUANTITY	VALUE	QUANTITY	VALUE	QUANTITY	VALUE
UNITED STATES AND ALASKA FLEET.	9,119	1,918	4,208	785	21,628	3,474	34,955	6,177
BRITISH COLUMBIA FLEET.	42	8	17,997	3,090	628	102	18,667	3,200
TOTAL.	9,161	1,926	22,205	3,875	22,256	3,576	53,622	9,377

NOTE:--STATISTICS IN THE ABOVE TABLES ARE COMPILED FROM DATA COLLECTED BY THE INTERNATIONAL FISHERIES COMMISSION FOR WASHINGTON AND BRITISH COLUMBIA, AND BY THE FISH AND WILDLIFE SERVICE FOR ALASKA. THIS TABULATION DOES NOT INCLUDE LANDINGS AT PORTS SOUTH OF SEATTLE, WASHINGTON, WHICH AVERAGE LESS THAN 3 PERCENT OF THE ANNUAL PACIFIC COAST CATCH.

CATCH BY UNITED STATES HALIBUT FLEET, 1949

ITEM	LANDED IN						TOTAL	
	SEATTLE, WASHINGTON		BRITISH COLUMBIA		ALASKA			
	POUNDS	VALUE	POUNDS	VALUE	POUNDS	VALUE	POUNDS	VALUE
ALL VESSELS AND BOATS:								
HALIBUT.	9,119,195	$1,917,745	4,207,907	$785,056	21,627,525	$3,473,770	34,954,627	$6,176,571
SABLEFISH.	1,819,613	178,398	36,020	2,787	3,929,783	280,414	5,785,416	461,599
LINGCOD.	497,674	47,578	–	–	2,415	72	500,089	47,650
ROCKFISHES	197,526	13,145	–	–	33,499	1,228	231,025	14,373
TOTAL	11,634,008	2,156,866	4,243,927	787,843	25,593,222	3,755,484	41,471,157	6,700,193

NOTE:-- IN ADDITION TO THE ABOVE, THERE WERE 1,149,567 POUNDS OF HALIBUT, SABLEFISH, LINGCOD, ROCKFISHES, GRAYFISH (DOGFISH), SOUPFIN SHARK AND MISCELLANEOUS FISH LIVERS VALUED AT $1,255,823 LANDED BY THE UNITED STATES HALIBUT FLEET AT PACIFIC COAST PORTS DURING 1949. THESE VESSELS ALSO LANDED 1,502,632 POUNDS OF HALIBUT, SABLEFISH, LINGCOD AND ROCKFISH VISCERA VALUED AT $428,871. VESSELS OF THE CANADIAN HALIBUT FLEET LANDED A TOTAL OF 18,666,765 POUNDS OF HALIBUT VALUED AT $3,199,923 DURING 1949, OF WHICH 41,795 POUNDS VALUED AT $8,346 WERE LANDED AT SEATTLE, AND 627,984 POUNDS VALUED AT $101,807 WERE LANDED IN ALASKA.
STATISTICS IN THE ABOVE TABLES ARE COMPILED FROM DATA COLLECTED BY THE INTERNATIONAL FISHERIES COMMISSION FOR WASHINGTON AND BRITISH COLUMBIA, AND BY THE FISH AND WILDLIFE SERVICE FOR ALASKA. THIS TABULATION DOES NOT INCLUDE LANDINGS AT PORTS SOUTH OF SEATTLE, WASHINGTON, WHICH AVERAGE LESS THAN 3 PERCENT OF THE ANNUAL PACIFIC COAST CATCH.

ATLANTIC COAST MACKEREL FISHERY

During 1949, the mackerel catch on the Atlantic Coast amounted to 42,070,100 pounds, valued at $2,308,037 to the fishermen. This represented a decrease of 18 percent in quantity and 38 percent in value compared with the previous year. The largest decrease occurred in purse seine landings in Massachusetts which totaled only 6.2 million pounds, a decline of 17.6 million pounds compared with the mackerel landings by purse seines in that area in 1948. The pound net catch, taken principally in Massachusetts, decreased 29 percent compared with 1948.

New Jersey accounted for 45 percent of the 1949 mackerel catch, while Massachusetts and Maine recorded 33 and 8 percent respectively. Landings in Rhode Island, Connecticut, New York, Maryland and Virginia yielded the remaining 14 percent.

SUMMARY OF ATLANTIC MACKEREL CATCH, 1949

STATE	PURSE SEINES		HAUL SEINES		STOP SEINES		GILL NETS ANCHOR	
	POUNDS	VALUE	POUNDS	VALUE	POUNDS	VALUE	POUNDS	VALUE
NEW ENGLAND:								
MAINE.	2,051,700	$96,284	-	-	61,900	$3,097	-	-
MASSACHUSETTS. . .	6,165,800	338,382	-	-	-	-	100	$29
RHODE ISLAND . . .	60,400	5,437	-	-	-	-	-	-
TOTAL.	8,277,900	440,103	-	-	61,900	3,097	100	29
MIDDLE ATLANTIC:								
NEW YORK	160,200	20,000	8,600	$1,317	-	-	-	-
NEW JERSEY	16,830,400	233,477	-	-	-	-	-	-
TOTAL	16,990,600	253,477	8,600	1,317	-	-	-	-
CHESAPEAKE,								
VIRGINIA	-	-	2,100	88	-	-	-	-
TOTAL.	-	-	2,100	88	-	-	-	-
GRAND TOTAL. .	25,268,500	693,580	10,700	1,405	61,900	3,097	100	29

STATE	GILL NETS - CONTINUED						LINES HAND	
	DRIFT		RUNAROUND		STAKE			
	POUNDS	VALUE	POUNDS	VALUE	POUNDS	VALUE	POUNDS	VALUE
NEW ENGLAND:								
MAINE.	352,200	$25,055	-	-	-	-	6,900	$517
MASSACHUSETTS. . .	303,200	26,256	-	-	-	-	-	-
RHODE ISLAND . . .	8,500	780	-	-	-	-	-	-
CONNECTICUT. . . .	-	-	-	-	-	-	91,200	11,157
TOTAL.	663,900	52,091	-	-	-	-	98,100	11,674
MIDDLE ATLANTIC:								
NEW YORK	28,000	4,629	-	-	-	-	1,464,500	223,260
NEW JERSEY	454,700	36,483	11,800	$944	21,600	$1,782	1,069,800	86,024
TOTAL.	482,700	41,112	11,800	944	21,600	1,782	2,534,300	309,284
CHESAPEAKE:								
MARYLAND	357,600	32,184	-	-	-	-	-	-
VIRGINIA	2,338,200	238,430	-	-	-	-	-	-
TOTAL.	2,695,800	270,614	-	-	-	-	-	-
GRAND TOTAL. .	3,842,400	363,817	11,800	944	21,600	1,782	2,632,400	320,958

STATE	LINES - CONTINUED TROLL		POUND NETS		FLOATING TRAPS	
	POUNDS	VALUE	POUNDS	VALUE	POUNDS	VALUE
NEW ENGLAND:						
MAINE.	-	-	-	-	334,500	$16,427
MASSACHUSETTS. . .	-	-	5,674,400	$580,957	1,540,800	80,756
RHODE ISLAND . . .	57,100	$4,875	-	-	336,900	26,082
TOTAL.	57,100	4,875	5,674,400	580,957	2,212,200	123,265
MIDDLE ATLANTIC:						
NEW YORK	-	-	171,800	32,884	-	-
NEW JERSEY	-	-	605,000	48,400	-	-
TOTAL.	-	-	776,800	81,284	-	-
CHESAPEAKE,						
VIRGINIA	-	-	104,300	17,203	-	-
TOTAL.	-	-	104,300	17,203	-	-
GRAND TOTAL. .	57,100	4,875	6,555,500	679,444	2,212,200	123,265

(CONTINUED ON NEXT PAGE)

SUMMARY OF ATLANTIC MACKEREL CATCH, 1949 - Continued

STATE	WEIRS		OTTER TRAWLS		TOTAL	
	POUNDS	VALUE	POUNDS	VALUE	POUNDS	VALUE
NEW ENGLAND:						
MAINE.	544,700	$16,189	-	-	3,351,900	$157,569
MASSACHUSETTS. . .	-	-	285,100	$39,100	13,969,400	1,065,480
RHODE ISLAND . . .	-	-	39,700	4,330	502,600	41,504
CONNECTICUT. . . .	-	-	1,000	100	92,200	11,257
TOTAL.	544,700	16,189	325,800	43,530	17,916,100	1,275,810
MIDDLE ATLANTIC:						
NEW YORK	-	-	53,200	8,482	1,886,300	290,572
NEW JERSEY	-	-	73,200	5,856	19,066,500	412,966
TOTAL.	-	-	126,400	14,338	20,952,800	703,538
CHESAPEAKE:						
MARYLAND	-	-	5,600	504	363,200	32,688
VIRGINIA	-	-	393,400	40,280	2,838,000	296,001
TOTAL.	-	-	399,000	40,784	3,201,200	328,689
GRAND TOTAL. .	544,700	16,189	851,200	98,652	42,070,100	2,308,037

PACIFIC COAST MACKEREL FISHERY

The catch of Pacific mackerel during 1949 amounted to 49,771,300 pounds, valued at $1,285,892 to the fishermen. This represented an increase of 26 percent in quantity but a decrease of 7 percent in value compared with the previous year.

The entire Pacific mackerel catch was taken in California. The San Pedro District accounted for 99 percent of the 1949 catch with the San Diego, Monterey, and San Francisco Districts contributing the remaining 1 percent.

Mackerel taken by brail or scoop nets accounted for 56 percent of the 1949 catch while purse seines caught 43 percent. The remaining 1 percent was taken with lines and gill and trammel nets.

SUMMARY OF PACIFIC MACKEREL CATCH, 1949

DISTRICT	PURSE SEINES		GILL AND TRAMMEL NETS		LINES	
	POUNDS	VALUE	POUNDS	VALUE	POUNDS	VALUE
CALIFORNIA:						
SAN FRANCISCO. . . .	3,000	$49	-	-	-	-
MONTEREY	233,600	4,112	200	$3	-	-
SAN PEDRO.	21,114,200	541,930	9,800	250	249,900	$6,411
SAN DIEGO.	98,000	4,566	9,200	427	340,000	15,843
TOTAL	21,448,800	550,657	19,200	680	589,900	22,254

DISTRICT	BRAIL OR SCOOP NETS		TOTAL	
	POUNDS.	VALUE	POUNDS	VALUE
CALIFORNIA:				
SAN FRANCISCO. . . .	-	-	3,000	$49
MONTEREY	-	-	233,800	4,115
SAN PEDRO.	27,710,400	$712,158	49,084,300	1,260,749
SAN DIEGO.	3,000	143	450,200	20,979
TOTAL.	27,713,400	712,301	49,771,300	1,285,892

ATLANTIC AND GULF COAST MENHADEN FISHERY

The catch of menhaden in 1949 established a new record of 1,081,741,400 pounds, valued at $11,540,313 to the fishermen. The catch was far larger than that of any other species taken by United States and Alaska fishermen. Practically the entire 1949 menhaden production was used in the manufacture of oil and meal, with only small quantities being used for bait.

No survey was made of the fisheries of the South Atlantic States (North Carolina, South Carolina, Georgia, and the East Coast of Florida) for 1949. However, in conducting the canned fish and byproducts survey for that year, information was obtained on the total quantity of menhaden used for reduction purposes in these states. Since nearly the entire catch is used for the manufacture of oil and meal, the poundage utilized for reduction has been listed as the landings in those states which were not canvassed for 1949 data.

SUMMARY OF MENHADEN CATCH, 1949

STATE	PURSE SEINES		HAUL SEINES		GILL NETS	
	POUNDS	VALUE	POUNDS	VALUE	POUNDS	VALUE
NEW ENGLAND:						
MAINE.	5,019,000	$44,942	-	-	-	-
MASSACHUSETTS.	6,961,800	83,424	-	-	-	-
CONNECTICUT.	-	-	-	-	7,900	$92
TOTAL	11,980,800	128,366	-	-	7,900	92
MIDDLE ATLANTIC:						
NEW YORK	89,488,700	939,631	-	-	-	-
NEW JERSEY	129,822,000	1,453,999	-	-	-	-
DELAWARE	159,748,100	1,677,355	-	-	-	-
TOTAL	379,058,800	4,070,985	-	-	-	-
CHESAPEAKE:						
MARYLAND	-	-	119,400	$1,198	8,800	88
VIRGINIA	126,430,300	1,466,592	2,312,500	17,563	47,900	356
TOTAL	126,430,300	1,466,592	2,431,900	18,761	56,700	444
SOUTH ATLANTIC:						
NORTH CAROLINA	227,679,400	1,980,811	-	-	-	-
SOUTH CAROLINA	4,706,750	44,243	-	-	-	-
EAST COAST OF FLORIDA. .	30,060,220	324,650	-	-	-	-
TOTAL	262,446,370	2,349,704	-	-	-	-
GULF:						
WEST COAST OF FLORIDA. .	24,959,680	268,485	17,700	885	1,000	50
MISSISSIPPI.	44,578,500	485,906	-	-	-	-
LOUISIANA.	165,913,400	2,018,307	-	-	-	-
TEXAS.	41,135,300	473,757	-	-	-	-
TOTAL	276,486,880	3,246,455	17,700	885	1,000	50
GRAND TOTAL	1,056,403,150	11,262,102	2,449,600	19,646	65,600	586

STATE	POUNDS NETS		FLOATING TRAPS		FYKE NETS	
	POUNDS	VALUE	POUNDS	VALUE	POUNDS	VALUE
NEW ENGLAND:						
MAINE.	-	-	6,500	$65	-	-
MASSACHUSETTS.	458,400	$4,977	34,100	324	-	-
RHODE ISLAND	-	-	38,100	457	-	-
CONNECTICUT.	16,000	116	-	-	-	-
TOTAL	474,400	5,093	78,700	864	-	-
MIDDLE ATLANTIC:						
NEW JERSEY	13,351,600	185,208	-	-	-	-
TOTAL	13,351,600	185,208	-	-	-	-
CHESAPEAKE:						
MARYLAND	1,551,900	12,389	-	-	200	$4
VIRGINIA	7,330,800	54,005	-	-	10,300	81
TOTAL	8,882,700	66,394	-	-	10,500	85
GRAND TOTAL	22,708,700	256,695	78,700	864	10,500	85

(CONTINUED ON NEXT PAGE)

SUMMARY OF MENHADEN CATCH, 1949 - Continued

STATE	OTTER TRAWLS		WEIRS		TRAMMEL NETS		TOTAL	
	POUNDS	VALUE	POUNDS	VALUE	POUNDS	VALUE	POUNDS	VALUE
NEW ENGLAND:								
MAINE.	-	-	1,800	$33	-	-	5,027,300	$45,040
MASSACHUSETTS. . . .	19,200	$231	-	-	-	-	7,473,500	88,956
RHODE ISLAND	-	-	-	-	-	-	38,100	457
CONNECTIUCT.	3,200	39	-	-	-	-	27,100	247
TOTAL	22,400	270	1,800	33	-	-	12,566,000	134,700
MIDDLE ATLANITC:								
NEW YORK	-	-	-	-	-	-	89,488,700	939,631
NEW JERSEY	-	-	-	-	-	-	143,173,600	1,639,207
DELAWARE	-	-	-	-	-	-	159,748,100	1,677,355
TOTAL	-	-	-	-	-	-	392,410,400	4,256,193
CHESAPEAKE:								
MARYLAND	-	-	-	-	-	-	1,680,300	13,679
VIRGINIA	-	-	-	-	-	-	136,131,800	1,538,597
TOTAL	-	-	-	-	-	-	137,812,100	1,552,276
SOUTH ATLANTIC:								
NORTH CAROLINA . . .	-	-	-	-	-	-	227,679,400	1,980,811
SOUTH CAROLINA . . .	-	-	-	-	-	-	4,706,750	44,243
EAST COAST OF FLORIDA	-	-	-	-	-	-	30,060,220	324,650
TOTAL	-	-	-	-	-	-	262,446,370	2,349,704
GULF:								
WEST COAST OF FLORIDA	-	-	-	-	1,000	$50	24,879,380	269,470
MISSISSIPPI.	-	-	-	-	-	-	44,578,500	485,906
LOUISIANA.	-	-	-	-	-	-	165,913,400	2,018,307
TEXAS.	-	-	-	-	-	-	41,135,300	473,757
TOTAL.	-	-	-	-	1,000	50	276,506,580	3,247,440
GRAND TOTAL . .	22,400	$270	1,800	33	1,000	50	1,081,741,450	11,540,313

NOTE:--TO CONVERT WEIGHT IN POUNDS TO NUMBER OF FISH DIVIDE BY 0.67.

TROLLER

OCEAN PERCH FISHERY

The 1949 catch of ocean perch (rosefish) totaled 236,986,700 pounds, valued at $9,819,266 to the fishermen. This represents a decrease of less than 1 percent in quantity but an increase of 2 percent in value compared with the previous year. Seventy-seven percent of the 1949 catch was landed at Massachusetts ports, and the remaining 23 percent was landed in Maine, principally Rockland and Portland. Gloucester accounted for over 93 percent of the poundage landed in Massachusetts.

The entire ocean perch (rosefish) catch is used for producing fillets, most of which are frozen. Waste from filleting is used in the manufacture of rosefish meal and oil.

SUMMARY OF OCEAN PERCH (ROSEFISH) CATCH, 1949

STATE	LINES, TRAWL OR TROT WITH HOOKS		OTTER TRAWLS		GILL NETS		TOTAL	
	POUNDS	VALUE	POUNDS	VALUE	POUNDS	VALUE	POUNDS	VALUE
NEW ENGLAND:								
MAINE.	400	$11	55,502,100	$2,014,058	100	$2	55,502,600	$2,014,071
MASSACHUSETTS.	6,500	487	181,477,600	7,804,708	-	-	181,484,100	7,805,195
TOTAL . . .	6,900	498	236,979,700	9,818,766	100	2	236,986,700	9,819,266

PACIFIC COAST PILCHARD FISHERY

During 1949, the catch of pilchards amounted to 633,540,400 pounds, valued at $10,760,235 to the fishermen. This represented an increase of 70 percent in quantity but a decrease of 2 percent in value compared with the previous year.

The price paid to fishermen at the beginning of the 1949 season was $40 per ton compared with $67.50 per ton the previous season. The prices dropped to $32.50 per ton by the end of the season, compared to $50 per ton at the close of the 1948 season. Price disagreements, occurring at times when fishing conditions appeared exceptionally good, reduced the potential production of the area.

SUMMARY OF PILCHARD CATCH, 1949

STATE AND DISTRICT	HAUL SEINES		PURSE SEINES, LAMPARA AND RING NETS		GILL NETS		OTTER TRAWLS		TOTAL	
	POUNDS	VALUE	POUNDS	VALUE	POUNDS	VALUE	POUNDS	VALUE	POUNDS	VALUE
WASHINGTON:										
PUGET SOUND DISTRICT.	56,400	$3,104	-	-	-	-	-	-	56,400	$3,104
OREGON:										
COASTAL DISTRICT. . .	9,000	234	-	-	-	-	-	-	9,000	234
CALIFORNIA:										
NORTHERN DISTRICT . .	-	-	-	-	14,800	$522	-	-	14,800	522
SAN FRANCISCO DISTRICT	-	-	33,848,400	$576,941	800	16	30,000	$510	33,879,200	577,467
MONTEREY DISTRICT . .	-	-	262,370,900	4,565,241	2,900	58	1,600	32	262,375,400	4,565,331
SAN PEDRO DISTRICT. .	-	-	331,502,300	5,554,263	-	-	-	-	331,502,300	5,554,263
SAN DIEGO DISTRICT. .	-	-	5,703,300	59,314	-	-	-	-	5,703,300	59,314
TOTAL CALIFORNIA . .	-	-	633,424,900	10,755,759	18,500	596	31,600	542	633,475,000	10,756,897
GRAND TOTAL. . . .	65,400	3,338	633,424,900	10,755,759	18,500	596	31,600	542	633,540,400	10,760,235

993093 O - 52 - 17

PACIFIC COAST SALMON FISHERY

The 1949 salmon catch in the Pacific Coast States and Alaska totaled 484,203,800 pounds -- over 80 million pounds more than in 1948. Landings in the Pacific Coast States increased over 30 million pounds compared with the previous year, while those in Alaska increased almost 50 million pounds. In the Puget Sound District of Washington, where pink salmon are taken in quantity only in the odd-numbered years, the catch of this species amounted to 65.6 million pounds. The catch of pink salmon in this area during 1948 was only 1,600 pounds. Landings of this species in Alaska rose from 113.4 million pounds in 1948 to 228.9 million pounds in 1949. The largest gain came in southeastern Alaska.

The most important types of gear used in taking salmon in 1949 were purse seines, 173 million pounds; pound nets (including floating traps), 170 million pounds; and gill nets, 93 million pounds. Smaller quantities were also taken by lines, reef nets, haul seines and dip nets.

SALMON CATCH BY DISTRICTS AND GEAR, 1949

GEAR AND SPECIES	ALASKA			
	SOUTHEASTERN	CENTRAL	WESTERN	TOTAL
	POUNDS	POUNDS	POUNDS	POUNDS
PURSE SEINES:				
CHINOOK OR KING	9,840	67,640	3,960	81,440
CHUM OR KETA	9,645,888	13,486,904	493,520	23,626,312
PINK	61,975,320	32,228,640	68	94,204,028
RED OR SOCKEYE	445,662	6,348,060	522,684	7,316,406
SILVER OR COHO	1,266,399	837,036	12,987	2,116,422
TOTAL	73,343,109	52,968,280	1,033,219	127,344,608
GILL NETS:				
CHINOOK OR KING	147,980	1,864,500	1,888,520	3,901,000
CHUM OR KETA	285,960	1,911,688	2,829,048	5,026,696
PINK	330,900	1,339,500	132	1,670,532
RED OR SOCKEYE	1,601,550	12,139,680	38,579,316	52,320,546
SILVER OR COHO	818,478	3,581,478	466,029	4,865,985
TOTAL	3,184,868	20,836,846	43,763,045	67,784,759
LINES:				
CHINOOK OR KING	9,443,180	-	-	9,443,180
CHUM OR KETA	646,544	-	-	646,544
PINK	546,592	-	-	546,592
RED OR SOCKEYE	11,352	-	-	11,352
SILVER OR COHO	13,308,246	-	-	13,308,246
TOTAL	23,955,914	-	-	23,955,914
POUND NETS:				
CHINOOK OR KING	260	649,820	-	650,080
CHUM OR KETA	12,576,360	4,858,088	-	17,434,448
PINK	112,829,892	19,698,560	-	132,528,452
RED OR SOCKEYE	880,230	10,400,358	-	11,280,588
SILVER OR COHO	5,125,887	2,240,424	-	7,366,311
TOTAL	131,412,629	37,847,250	-	169,259,879
GRAND TOTAL	231,896,520	111,652,376	44,796,264	388,345,160

GEAR AND SPECIES	WASHINGTON							
	PUGET SOUND		WASHINGTON COAST		COLUMBIA RIVER		TOTAL	
	POUNDS	VALUE	POUNDS	VALUE	POUNDS	VALUE	POUNDS	VALUE
PURSE SEINES:								
CHINOOK OR KING	540,100	$67,515	-	-	-	-	540,100	$67,515
CHUM OR KETA	3,078,700	421,782	-	-	-	-	3,078,700	421,782
PINK	33,328,700	3,332,867	-	-	-	-	33,328,700	3,332,867
RED OR SOCKEYE	4,886,500	977,306	-	-	-	-	4,886,500	977,306
SILVER OR COHO	3,422,600	431,243	-	-	-	-	3,422,600	431,243
TOTAL	45,256,600	5,230,713	-	-	-	-	45,256,600	5,230,713
HAUL SEINES:								
CHINOOK OR KING	18,900	2,364	-	-	-	-	18,900	2,364
CHUM OR KETA	40,600	5,405	-	-	-	-	40,600	5,405
PINK	521,000	52,095	-	-	-	-	521,000	52,095
SILVER OR COHO	9,300	1,171	-	-	-	-	9,300	1,171
TOTAL	589,800	61,035	-	-	-	-	589,800	61,035

(CONTINUED ON NEXT PAGE)

SALMON CATCH BY DISTRICTS AND GEAR, 1949 - Continued

GEAR AND SPECIES	WASHINGTON - CONTINUED							
	PUGET SOUND		WASHINGTON COAST		COLUMBIA RIVER		TOTAL	
	POUNDS	VALUE	POUNDS	VALUE	POUNDS	VALUE	POUNDS	VALUE
GILL NETS:								
CHINOOK OR KING	459,700	$98,739	487,600	$75,573	2,752,600	$459,687	3,699,900	$633,999
CHUM OR KETA	978,000	130,075	658,800	52,046	261,400	20,914	1,898,200	203,035
PINK	6,804,200	680,420	100	8	-	-	6,804,300	680,428
RED OR SOCKEYE	790,300	158,065	869,900	265,311	6,700	1,335	1,666,900	424,711
SILVER OR COHO	1,278,900	262,184	1,010,500	154,604	224,800	30,129	2,514,200	446,917
TOTAL	10,311,100	1,329,483	3,026,900	547,542	3,245,500	512,065	16,583,500	2,389,090
LINES:								
CHINOOK OR KING	2,894,000	804,533	1,512,400	420,457	500,600	116,128	4,907,000	1,341,118
PINK	80,200	8,018	17,400	1,736	600	56	98,200	9,810
SILVER OR COHO	1,860,300	386,941	1,869,000	388,800	538,300	69,973	4,267,600	845,714
TOTAL	4,834,500	1,199,492	3,398,800	810,993	1,039,500	186,157	9,272,800	2,196,642
POUND NETS:								
CHINOOK OR KING	65,400	8,176	-	-	-	-	65,400	8,176
CHUM OR KETA	12,400	1,650	-	-	-	-	12,400	1,650
PINK	279,500	27,950	-	-	-	-	279,500	27,950
RED OR SOCKEYE	12,500	2,492	-	-	-	-	12,500	2,492
SILVER OR COHO	64,800	8,159	-	-	-	-	64,800	8,159
TOTAL	434,600	48,427	-	-	-	-	434,600	48,427
REEF NETS:								
CHINOOK OR KING	129,800	16,219	-	-	-	-	129,800	16,219
CHUM OR KETA	181,100	24,084	-	-	-	-	181,100	24,084
PINK	3,183,100	318,309	-	-	-	-	3,183,100	318,309
RED OR SOCKEYE	475,300	95,067	-	-	-	-	475,300	95,067
SILVER OR COHO	250,500	31,559	-	-	-	-	250,500	31,559
TOTAL	4,219,800	485,238	-	-	-	-	4,219,800	485,238
DIP NETS:								
CHINOOK OR KING	-	-	-	-	228,100	38,097	228,100	38,097
CHUM OR KETA	-	-	-	-	1,800	142	1,800	142
RED OR SOCKEYE	-	-	-	-	4,400	888	4,400	888
TOTAL	-	-	-	-	234,300	39,127	234,300	39,127
GRAND TOTAL	65,646,400	8,354,388	6,425,700	1,358,535	4,519,300	737,349	76,591,400	10,450,272

GEAR AND SPECIES	OREGON					
	COLUMBIA RIVER		OREGON COAST		TOTAL	
	POUNDS	VALUE	POUNDS	VALUE	POUNDS	VALUE
HAUL SEINES:						
CHINOOK OR KING	948,500	$158,396	-	-	948,500	$158,396
CHUM OR KETA	29,900	2,389	-	-	29,900	2,389
RED OR SOCKEYE	900	187	-	-	900	187
SILVER OR COHO	112,400	15,067	-	-	112,400	15,067
TOTAL	1,091,700	176,039	-	-	1,091,700	176,039
GILL NETS:						
CHINOOK OR KING	5,656,900	944,692	338,600	$62,643	5,995,500	1,007,335
CHUM OR KETA	234,600	18,770	445,000	35,600	679,600	54,370
RED OR SOCKEYE	2,900	579	-	-	2,900	579
SILVER OR COHO	456,100	61,112	639,500	83,133	1,095,600	144,245
TOTAL	6,350,500	1,025,153	1,423,100	181,376	7,773,600	1,206,529
LINES:						
CHINOOK OR KING	223,900	60,229	1,136,900	244,427	1,360,800	304,656
SILVER OR COHO	163,400	24,673	1,126,700	145,678	1,290,100	170,351
TOTAL	387,300	84,902	2,263,600	390,105	2,650,900	475,007
POUND NETS:						
CHINOOK OR KING	398,500	66,543	-	-	398,500	66,543
CHUM OR KETA	17,300	1,386	-	-	17,300	1,386
RED OR SOCKEYE	900	177	-	-	900	177
SILVER OR COHO	104,800	14,046	-	-	104,800	14,046
TOTAL	521,500	82,152	-	-	521,500	82,152
DIP NETS:						
CHINOOK OR KING	790,100	131,950	-	-	790,100	131,950
RED OR SOCKEYE	8,100	1,628	-	-	8,100	1,628
SILVER OR COHO	1,600	209	-	-	1,600	209
TOTAL	799,800	133,787	-	-	799,800	133,787
GRAND TOTAL	9,150,800	1,502,033	3,686,700	571,481	12,837,500	2,073,514

(CONTINUED ON NEXT PAGE)

SALMON CATCH BY DISTRICTS AND GEAR, 1949 - Continued

GEAR AND SPECIES	CALIFORNIA								TOTAL	
	NORTHERN DISTRICT		SAN FRANCISCO DISTRICT		MONTEREY DISTRICT		SAN PEDRO DISTRICT			
	POUNDS	VALUE	POUNDS	VALUE	POUNDS	VALUE	POUNDS	VALUE	POUNDS	VALUE
GILL NETS: CHINOOK OR KING	-	-	899,100	$220,098	-	-	-	-	899,100	$220,098
TOTAL. . .	-	-	899,100	220,098	-	-	-	-	899,100	220,098
LINES: CHINOOK OR KING	2,601,400	$617,574	2,455,500	$552,498	468,700	$117,612	5,000	$1,521	5,530,600	1,289,205
TOTAL. . .	2,601,400	617,574	2,455,500	552,498	468,700	117,612	5,000	1,521	5,530,600	1,289,205
GRAND TOTAL	2,601,400	617,574	3,354,600	772,596	468,700	117,612	5,000	1,521	6,429,700	1,509,303

SUMMARY OF SALMON CATCH BY GEAR, 1949

STATE AND DISTRICT	PURSE SEINES	HAUL SEINES	GILL NETS	LINES
	POUNDS	POUNDS	POUNDS	POUNDS
ALASKA:				
SOUTHEASTERN	73,343,109	-	3,184,868	23,955,914
CENTRAL.	52,968,280	-	20,836,846	-
WESTERN.	1,033,219	-	43,763,045	-
TOTAL.	127,344,608	-	67,784,759	23,955,914
WASHINGTON:				
PUGET SOUND.	45,256,600	589,800	10,311,100	4,834,500
WASHINGTON COAST	-	-	3,026,900	3,398,800
COLUMBIA RIVER	-	-	3,245,500	1,039,500
TOTAL.	45,256,600	589,800	16,583,500	9,272,800
OREGON:				
COLUMBIA RIVER	-	1,091,700	6,350,500	387,300
OREGON COAST	-	-	1,423,100	2,263,600
TOTAL.	-	1,091,700	7,773,600	2,650,900
CALIFORNIA:				
NORTHERN DISTRICT.	-	-	-	2,601,400
SAN FRANCISCO DISTRICT . .	-	-	899,100	2,455,500
MONTEREY DISTRICT.	-	-	-	468,700
SAN PEDRO DISTRICT	-	-	-	5,000
TOTAL.	-	-	899,100	5,530,600
GRAND TOTAL.	172,601,208	1,681,500	93,040,959	41,410,214

STATE AND DISTRICT	POUND NETS	REEF NETS	DIP NETS	TOTAL
	POUNDS	POUNDS	POUNDS	POUNDS
ALASKA:				
SOUTHEASTERN	131,412,629	-	-	231,896,520
CENTRAL.	37,847,250	-	-	111,652,376
WESTERN.	-	-	-	44,796,264
TOTAL.	169,259,879	-	-	388,345,160
WASHINGTON:				
PUGET SOUND.	434,600	4,219,800	-	65,646,400
WASHINGTON COAST	-	-	-	6,425,700
COLUMBIA RIVER	-	-	234,300	4,519,300
TOTAL.	434,600	4,219,800	234,300	76,591,400
OREGON:				
COLUMBIA RIVER	521,500	-	799,800	9,150,800
OREGON COAST	-	-	-	3,686,700
TOTAL.	521,500	-	799,800	12,837,500
CALIFORNIA:				
NORTHERN DISTRICT.	-	-	-	2,601,400
SAN FRANCISCO DISTRICT . .	-	-	-	3,354,600
MONTEREY DISTRICT.	-	-	-	468,700
SAN PEDRO DISTRICT	-	-	-	5,000
TOTAL.	-	-	-	6,429,700
GRAND TOTAL.	170,215,979	4,219,800	1,034,100	484,203,760

SUMMARY OF SALMON CATCH BY DISTRICTS, 1949

SPECIES	ALASKA							
	SOUTHEASTERN		CENTRAL		WESTERN		TOTAL	
	POUNDS	VALUE	POUNDS	VALUE	POUNDS	VALUE	POUNDS	VALUE
CHINOOK OR KING. .	9,601,260	$1,786,799	2,581,950	$290,470	1,892,480	$141,936	14,075,700	$2,219,205
CHUM OR KETA . . .	23,154,752	1,591,889	20,256,680	759,625	3,322,568	132,903	46,734,000	2,484,417
PINK	175,682,704	16,470,253	53,266,700	3,062,835	200	5	228,949,604	19,533,093
RED OR SOCKEYE . .	2,938,794	391,839	28,888,098	3,129,544	39,102,000	2,085,440	70,928,892	5,606,823
SILVER OR COHO . .	20,519,010	2,321,004	6,658,938	480,923	479,016	17,032	27,656,964	2,818,959
TOTAL	231,896,520	22,561,784	111,652,376	7,723,397	44,796,264	2,377,316	388,345,160	32,662,497

SPECIES	WASHINGTON							
	PUGET SOUND		WASHINGTON COAST		COLUMBIA RIVER		TOTAL	
	POUNDS	VALUE	POUNDS	VALUE	POUNDS	VALUE	POUNDS	VALUE
CHINOOK OR KING. .	4,107,900	$997,546	2,000,000	$496,030	3,481,300	$613,912	9,589,200	$2,107,488
CHUM OR KETA . . .	4,290,800	582,996	658,800	52,046	263,200	21,056	5,212,800	656,098
PINK	44,196,700	4,419,659	17,500	1,744	600	56	44,214,800	4,421,459
RED OR SOCKEYE . .	6,164,600	1,232,930	869,900	265,311	11,100	2,223	7,045,600	1,500,464
SILVER OR COHO . .	6,886,400	1,121,257	2,879,500	543,404	763,100	100,102	10,529,000	1,764,763
TOTAL	65,646,400	8,354,388	6,425,700	1,358,535	4,519,300	737,349	76,591,400	10,450,272

SPECIES	OREGON					
	COLUMBIA RIVER		OREGON COAST		TOTAL	
	POUNDS	VALUE	POUNDS	VALUE	POUNDS	VALUE
CHINOOK OR KING. .	8,017,900	$1,361,810	1,475,500	$307,070	9,493,400	$1,668,880
CHUM OR KETA . . .	281,800	22,545	445,000	35,600	726,800	58,145
RED OR SOCKEYE . .	12,800	2,571	-		12,800	2,571
SILVER OR COHO . .	838,300	115,107	1,766,200	228,811	2,604,500	343,918
TOTAL	9,150,800	1,502,033	3,686,700	571,481	12,837,500	2,073,514

SPECIES	CALIFORNIA									
	NORTHERN DISTRICT		SAN FRANCISCO DISTRICT		MONTEREY DISTRICT		SAN PEDRO DISTRICT		TOTAL	
	POUNDS	VALUE	POUNDS	VALUE	POUNDS	VALUE	POUNDS	VALUE	POUNDS	VALUE
CHINOOK OR KING.	2,601,400	$617,574	3,354,600	$772,596	468,700	$117,612	5,000	$1,521	6,429,700	$1,509,303
TOTAL. . .	2,601,400	617,574	3,354,600	772,596	468,700	117,612	5,000	1,521	6,429,700	1,509,303

TUNA JIG

PACIFIC COAST TUNA FISHERY

Landings of tuna and tunalike fishes in the Pacific Coast States during 1949 totaled a record high of 332,068,900 pounds, valued at $53,851,900 to the fishermen. The catch exceeded the previous high established in 1948 by over 7 million pounds.

Prices paid for tuna during 1949 were not as high as the 1948 prices. The high and low prices paid per ton for the various species were as follows: yellowfin, $340 to $310; bluefin, $330 to $300; skipjack, $320 to $290; bonito, $235 to $195; and yellowtail, $225 to $185. Albacore prices were reduced from $400 per ton at the start of the season to less than $350 per ton in the latter part of the season. Albacore prices in 1948 ranged from $750 to $500.

Yellowfin was the most important species accounting for 57 percent of the total landings. Skipjack and albacore represented 24 and 16 percent respectively, with the balance consisting of bluefin and bonito.

SUMMARY OF PACIFIC TUNA CATCH, 1949

STATE AND DISTRICT	ALBACORE		BLUEFIN		BONITO	
	POUNDS	VALUE	POUNDS	VALUE	POUNDS	VALUE
			PURSE SEINES			
CALIFORNIA:						
SAN FRANCISCO DISTRICT. . . .	200	$24	1/222,700	$36,746	-	-
MONTEREY DISTRICT	106,700	16,750	7,800	1,714	-	-
SAN PEDRO DISTRICT:						
OFF CALIFORNIA.	15,400	2,870	2,201,500	357,521	59,800	$5,810
OFF LATIN AMERICA	25,900	18,022	1,824,200	296,248	1,575,700	153,002
TOTAL SAN PEDRO. . .	41,300	20,892	4,025,700	653,769	1,635,500	158,812
SAN DIEGO DISTRICT:						
OFF CALIFORNIA.	3,300	657	21,000	3,147	2,900	288
OFF LATIN AMERICA	64,100	12,626	29,900	4,487	24,600	2,468
TOTAL SAN DIEGO. . .	67,400	13,283	50,900	7,634	27,500	2,756
TOTAL CALIFORNIA. .	215,600	50,949	4,307,100	699,863	1,663,000	161,568
			LINES			
WASHINGTON:						
PUGET SOUND	943,800	$167,998	-	-	-	-
COASTAL	3,343,400	595,128	-	-	-	-
COLUMBIA RIVER.	146,700	26,255	-	-	-	-
TOTAL WASHINGTON. .	4,433,900	789,381	-	-	-	-
OREGON:						
COLUMBIA RIVER.	4,553,200	815,019	-	-	-	-
COASTAL	1,773,800	289,123	-	-	-	-
TOTAL OREGON. . . .	6,327,000	1,104,142	-	-	-	-
CALIFORNIA:						
NORTHERN DISTRICT	2,817,500	427,697	-	-	-	-
SAN FRANCISCO DISTRICT. . . .	1,504,900	231,008	-	-	-	-
MONTEREY DISTRICT	5,018,700	787,937	-	-	-	-
SAN PEDRO DISTRICT:						
OFF CALIFORNIA	4,008,500	727,011	37,000	$6,008	17,700	$1,719
OFF LATIN AMERICA	5,686,100	1,043,264	2,500	406	15,000	1,455
TOTAL SAN PEDRO . .	9,694,600	1,770,275	39,500	6,414	32,700	3,174
SAN DIEGO DISTRICT:						
OFF CALIFORNIA.	6,981,400	1,373,930	6,700	1,004	9,700	979
OFF LATIN AMERICA	17,800,800	3,503,197	36,100	5,421	114,400	11,500
TOTAL SAN DIEGO . .	24,782,200	4,877,127	42,800	6,425	124,100	12,479
TOTAL CALIFORNIA .	43,817,900	8,094,044	82,300	12,839	156,800	15,653
			GILL NETS			
CALIFORNIA:						
SAN PEDRO DISTRICT:						
OFF CALIFORNIA.	-	-	-	-	6,100	$ 587
OFF LATIN AMERICA	-	-	-	-	200	18
TOTAL SAN DIEGO. .	-	-	-	-	6,300	605
SAN DIEGO DISTRICT:						
OFF CALIFORNIA.	-	-	-	-	2,400	244
OFF LATIN AMERICA	-	-	-	-	400	43
TOTAL SAN DIEGO	-	-	-	-	2,800	287
TOTAL CALIFORNIA	-	-	-	-	9,100	892
			OTTER TRAWLS			
CALIFORNIA:						
SAN PEDRO DISTRICT:						
OFF CALIFORNIA.	-	-	-	-	600	68
GRAND TOTAL.	54,794,400	$10,038,516	4,389,400	$712,702	1,829,500	178,181

STATE AND DISTRICT	SKIPJACK		YELLOWFIN		TOTAL	
	POUNDS	VALUE	POUNDS	VALUE	POUNDS	VALUE
			PURSE SEINES - CONTINUED			
OREGON:						
COLUMBIA RIVER.	1/565,000	$62,709	1/2,409,300	$283,007	2,974,300	$345,716
CALIFORNIA:						
SAN FRANCISCO DISTRICT. . . .	-	-	-	-	222,900	36,770
MONTEREY DISTRICT	-	-	-	-	114,500	18,464
SAN PEDRO DISTRICT:						
OFF CALIFORNIA.	-	-	-	-	2,276,700	366,201
OFF LATIN AMERICA	3,511,200	512,983	23,256,500	3,781,501	30,193,500	4,761,756
TOTAL SAN PEDRO. . .	3,511,200	512,983	23,256,500	3,781,501	32,470,200	5,127,957

(CONTINUED ON NEXT PAGE)

SUMMARY OF PACIFIC TUNA CATCH, 1949 - Continued

STATE AND DISTRICT	PURSE SEINES - CONTINUED					
	SKIPJACK		YELLOWFIN		TOTAL	
	POUNDS	VALUE	POUNDS	VALUE	POUNDS	VALUE
CALIFORNIA - CONTINUED:						
SAN DIEGO DISTRICT:						
OFF CALIFORNIA	-	-	-	-	27,200	$4,092
OFF LATIN AMERICA	78,800	$11,772	877,400	$144,640	1,074,800	175,993
TOTAL SAN DIEGO. . .	78,800	11,772	877,400	144,640	1,102,000	180,085
TOTAL, CALIFORNIA. .	3,590,000	524,755	24,133,900	3,926,141	33,909,600	5,363,276
	LINES - CONTINUED					
WASHINGTON:						
PUGET SOUND.	-	-	-	-	943,800	167,998
COASTAL.	-	-	-	-	3,343,400	595,128
COLUMBIA RIVER	-	-	-	-	146,700	26,255
TOTAL WASHINGTON .	-	-	-	-	4,433,900	789,381
OREGON:						
COLUMBIA RIVER	1/1,376,800	206,518	1/3,161,800	524,861	9,091,800	1,546,398
COASTAL.	-	-	-	-	1,773,800	289,123
TOTAL OREGON. . . .	1,376,800	206,518	3,161,800	524,861	10,865,600	1,835,521
CALIFORNIA:						
NORTHERN DISTRICT.	-	-	-	-	2,817,500	427,697
SAN FRANCISCO DISTRICT . .	-	-	-	-	1,504,900	231,008
MONTEREY DISTRICT.	-	-	-	-	5,018,700	787,937
SAN PEDRO DISTRICT :						
OFF CALIFORNIA	15,300	2,232	4,500	728	4,083,000	737,698
OFF LATIN AMERICA. . . .	20,399,600	2,980,385	46,793,300	7,608,599	72,896,500	11,634,109
TOTAL SAN PEDRO. .	20,414,900	2,982,617	46,797,800	7,609,327	76,979,500	12,371,807
SAN DIEGO DISTRICT:						
OFF CALIFORNIA	11,400	1,710	5,400	885	7,014,600	1,378,508
OFF LATIN AMERICA. . . .	54,554,100	8,144,912	114,035,200	18,655,059	186,540,600	30,320,089
TOTAL SAN DIEGO. .	54,565,500	8,146,622	114,040,600	18,655,944	193,555,200	31,698,597
TOTAL CALIFORNIA .	74,980,400	11,129,239	160,838,400	26,265,271	279,875,800	45,517,045
	GILL NETS - CONTINUED					
CALIFORNIA:						
SAN PEDRO DISTRICT:						
OFF CALIFORNIA	-	-	-	-	6,100	587
OFF LATIN AMERICA. . . .	-	-	-	-	200	18
TOTAL SAN PEDRO .	-	-	-	-	6,300	605
SAN DIEGO DISTRICT:						
OFF CALIFORNIA	-	-	-	-	2,400	244
OFF LATIN AMERICA. . . .	-	-	-	-	400	43
TOTAL SAN DIEGO .	-	-	-	-	2,800	287
TOTAL CALIFORNIA.	-	-	-	-	9,100	892
	OTTER TRAWLS- CONTINUED					
CALIFORNIA:						
SAN PEDRO DISTRICT:						
OFF CALIFORNIA	-	-	-	-	600	68
GRAND TOTAL.	80,512,200	11,923,221	190,543,400	30,999,280	332,068,900	53,851,900

1/ CAUGHT IN WATERS OFF LATIN AMERICA.

TUNA·JIGS

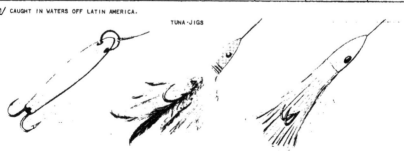

SUMMARY OF TUNA CATCH BY DISTRICTS, 1949

STATE AND DISTRICT	ALBACORE		BLUEFIN		BONITO	
	POUNDS	VALUE	POUNDS	VALUE	POUNDS	VALUE
WASHINGTON:						
PUGET SOUND.	943,800	$167,998	-	-	-	-
COASTAL.	3,343,400	595,128	-	-	-	-
COLUMBIA RIVER	146,700	26,255	-	-	-	-
TOTAL WASHINGTON . . .	4,433,900	789,381	-	-	-	-
OREGON:						
COLUMBIA RIVER	4,553,200	815,019	-	-	-	-
COASTAL.	1,773,800	289,123	-	-	-	-
TOTAL OREGON	6,327,000	1,104,142	-	-	-	-
CALIFORNIA:						
NORTHERN DISTRICT	2,817,500	427,697	-	-	-	-
SAN FRANCISCO DISTRICT	1,505,100	231,032	2/222,700	$36,746	-	-
MONTEREY DISTRICT.	5,125,400	804,687	7,800	1,714	-	-
SAN PEDRO DISTRICT:						
OFF CALIFORNIA	4,023,900	729,881	2,238,500	363,529	84,200	$8,184
OFF LATIN AMERICA.	5,712,000	1,061,286	1,826,700	296,654	1,590,900	154,475
TOTAL SAN PEDRO. . . .	9,735,900	1,791,167	4,065,200	660,183	1,675,100	162,659
SAN DIEGO DISTRICT:						
OFF CALIFORNIA	6,984,700	1,374,587	27,700	4,151	15,000	1,511
OFF LATIN AMERICA.	17,864,900	3,515,823	66,000	9,908	139,400	14,011
TOTAL SAN DIEGO. . . .	24,849,600	4,890,410	93,700	14,059	154,400	15,522
TOTAL CALIFORNIA . . .	44,033,500	8,144,993	4,389,400	712,702	1,829,500	178,181
GRAND TOTAL	54,794,400	10,038,516	4,389,400	712,702	1,829,500	178,181

STATE AND DISTRICT	SKIPJACK		YELLOWFIN		TOTAL	
	POUNDS	VALUE	POUNDS	VALUE	POUNDS	VALUE
WASHINGTON:						
PUGET SOUND.	-	-	-	-	943,800	$167,998
COASTAL	-	-	-	-	3,343,400	595,128
COLUMBIA RIVER	-	-	-	-	146,700	26,255
TOTAL WASHINGTON. . . .	-	-	-	-	4,433,900	789,381
OREGON:						
COLUMBIA RIVER	1/1,941,800	$269,227	1/5,571,100	$807,868	12,066,100	1,892,114
COASTAL.	-	-	-	-	1,773,800	289,123
TOTAL OREGON	1,941,800	269,227	5,571,100	807,868	13,839,900	2,181,237
CALIFORNIA:						
NORTHERN DISTRICT.	-	-	-	-	2,817,500	427,697
SAN FRANCISCO DISTRICT	-	-	-	-	1,727,800	267,778
MONTEREY DISTRICT.	-	-	-	-	5,133,200	806,401
SAN PEDRO DISTRICT:						
OFF CALIFORNIA	15,300	2,232	4,500	728	6,366,400	1,104,554
OFF LATIN AMERICA.	23,910,800	3,493,368	70,049,800	11,390,100	103,090,200	16,395,883
TOTAL SAN PEDRO . . .	23,926,100	3,495,600	70,054,300	11,390,828	109,456,600	17,500,437
SAN DIEGO DISTRICT:						
OFF CALIFORNIA	11,400	1,710	5,400	885	7,044,200	1,382,844
OFF LATIN AMERICA.	54,632,900	8,156,684	114,912,600	18,799,699	187,615,800	30,496,125
TOTAL SAN DIEGO . . .	54,644,300	8,158,394	114,918,000	18,800,584	194,660,000	31,878,969
TOTAL CALIFORNIA . .	78,570,400	11,653,994	184,972,300	30,191,412	313,795,100	50,881,282
GRAND TOTAL	80,512,200	11,923,221	190,543,400	30,999,280	332,068,900	53,851,900

WHALING

Only one firm, Maritime Industries, Inc.. which operated a shore station at Fields Landing, California, engaged in the whale fishery during 1949. A total of 49 whales was taken, consisting of 28 sperm, 11 finback, and 10 humpback whales. Two killer boats with a net tonnage totaling 311 tons, and having crews totaling 8 men carried out these operations.

SECTION 13.- STATISTICAL SURVEY PROCEDURE

This report is another in a series of annual statistical, reports containing data on the quantity and value of the commercial catch of fishery products and the numbers of persons and operating units engaged in the commercial fisheries of the United States and Alaska. The report has been prepared and published by the Branch of Commercial Fisheries, Fish and Wildlife Service, Department of the Interior, and is a continuation of a series inaugurated by its predecessor organizations in the Departments of Interior, Commerce, Commerce and Labor, and the United States Fish Commission.

In order that those who use the statistical data contained in this and previous reports may be informed as to the source of the figures and methods for their collection, it has been deemed advisable to outline, in moderate detail, the survey procedure followed. This procedure has been developed over a period of years, and changes in methods have been made at times when such changes have appeared to work toward general improvement. While the surveys in the several sections are not made in the same manner, owing to varying facilities and records in different states, an attempt has been made to make the data collected by various methods comparable with respect to the same year as well as over a period of years. Throughout the entire plan it has been the intention to coordinate State and Federal fishery statistical work so that there will be as little duplication of effort as possible.

SECTIONAL SURVEYS

Statistical surveys of the fisheries and fishery industries of the various sections of the United States occupy by far the greatest part of the time of the statistical personnel of the Branch. In the course of these surveys, the field representatives visit the individual fishing localities of the various States to collect statistics on the volume and value of the catch of fish and shellfish, employment in the fisheries, quantity of fishing gear, number and classification of fishing and transporting craft, and the volume and value of manufactured fishery products and byproducts. The various phases of these surveys are discussed in detail in the sections following.

History.--The first comprehensive statistical survey of the fisheries and fishery industries of the United States was made for the year 1880 by George Brown Goode, Assistant Director of the United States National Museum, and associates, with the co-operation of the Commissioner of Fisheries and the Superintendent of the Tenth Census. Data for specific fisheries, or restricted sections for years prior to 1880, also were collected in the early survey and recorded in Mr. Goode's reports. The survey for 1880, however did not include the Mississippi River and its tributaries. Periodic general surveys of a limited number of States of limited areas of the United States were made for various of the intervening years between 1880 and 1908 and from 1909 to 1928. A survey of the entire United States was made for 1908. The next general survey of the entire United States was not made until 1931, although complete data for all sections, excluding the Mississippi River and its Tributaries, were collected for 1929 and 1930. Complete data on the catch and operating units for these same sections were also collected for 1932. In the latter survey, however, lack of sufficient funds prohibited collection of data on the wholesale and manufacturing operations except those data collected as a part of the canned fishery products and byproducts survey. Various sections were surveyed during the years from 1933 to 1949, inclusive. Data on the wholesale and manufacturing industries were collected in all of the surveys from 1933 to 1940, inclusive. In the years since 1940, the lack of personnel and funds precluded the collection of data on wholesale and manufacturing firms except for those data collected as a part of the canned fishery products and byproducts surveys.

The chart on the following page indicates the years for which surveys have been made in the various sections. Figures for more recent years are available from the Service in bulletin form, but data for the earlier years are available only in the Fish Commission and Bureau of Fisheries printed reports. These reports are available for reference in the Department of the Interior library and in many public libraries. A bibliography of these reports will be found in Section 16 of this Digest.

SURVEYS OF THE FISHERIES OF THE UNITED STATES

Since the surveys of the fisheries have varied in completeness three legends have been used for the years shown in the chart to indicate whether complete, partial, or no surveys were conducted in the individual regions. The designation 'complete survey' has been used to indicate that basic operating unit, and catch data were obtained and that complete information was collected on employment in wholesale and manufacturing establishments and on the production of manufactured fishery products. The legend 'partial survey' usually indicates that operating unit and catch statistics were collected, but that no information was obtained on employment in wholesale and manufacturing establishments and that only partial data were obtained on the production of manufactured fishery products. In some instances the designation 'partial survey' is used for regions in which only catch statistics were collected. The legend 'no survey' indicates that a general canvass was not conducted to obtain operating unit, catch, employment in wholesale and manufacturing plants, and complete manufactured products data. Although the charts indicated that in certain regions no surveys were conducted some information may be available on the landings at certain important ports. Likewise information on the catch of certain species, such as menhaden, may be available as a result of information collected with the annual canned fish and byproducts survey. Data on the annual production of canned fishery products and byproducts have been collected for all regions since 1921, while information was obtained on the production of packaged fish for 1926 and annually since 1928.

A bibliography listing the various surveys made since 1880 and the publications in which the results were published appeared in Statistical Digest No. 21. A list of the statistical bulletins in the Current Fishery Statistics series published during 1949 may be found in Section 16 of the current digest.

Field Personnel.--The statistics contained in this volume have been collected by a group of trained marketing specialists which comprises a part of the permanent staff of the Branch of Commercial Fisheries of this Service.

Period Covered.--These specialists are assigned permanent field stations, generally in the principal port within their field, and travel from that station in conducting their various surveys. They collect statistics of fishery operations for the year preceding that in which they are working; and since their field work occupies the greater part of the year, it is usually at least a year from the end of the calendar year for which they are collecting data until the figures are published. The data usually are collected and published on a calendar year basis, although for some States they are on a fiscal year basis. Prior to 1930, statistics on the catch of oysters in the Atlantic and Gulf States were collected for the oyster season; that is, from September to April, inclusive. Beginning with 1930 and continuing to the present time, they have been collected on the basis of the calendar year.

Scope.--The scope of the coastal statistical surveys include canvasses of the commercial fisheries of the oceans and bays and of the coastal rivers as far inland as commercial fishing is important. This usually coincides with the range of commercial fishing for anadramous species. Statistics of the fisheries of the Mississippi River cover canvasses of the fisheries of the Mississippi River proper as well as all of its tributaries wherein commercial fishing for either fish, crustaceans, or mollusks is prosecuted. Statistics of the fisheries of the Great Lakes cover canvasses of the fisheries prosecuted in the lakes proper, adjacent bays, the International Lakes of northern Minnesota, and rivers which sustain a commercial fishery having outlets into these waters. Statistics on the fisheries of Florida include the commercial fisheries prosecuted in Lake Okeechobee. Surveys for statistics of the wholesale and manufacturing fishery industries cover such plants located in the coastal, river, and lake areas adjacent to the waters mentioned above.

Methods of Collection.--Several methods for the collection of fishery statistics are employed, each of which has been carefully studied to obtain the best results with the available personnel and funds. In most instances the field personnel obtain lists of the names of fishing vessels, names and numbers of motorboats, and names of owners of these craft from local custom officials. Also it usually is possible to obtain the names of licensed commercial fishermen, fishing craft and some statistics on the catch from State fishery agencies; from other State, county or city sources; or from private organizations.

With such preliminary records as are available for their guidance the field specialists visit each fishing community in their field unless these preliminary records are so complete that personal visits may be eliminated. If complete catch data are not available from central sources, wholesale dealers and manufacturers of fishery products are visited and data are obtained from them on their purchases of fishery products. While it is impossible for the few Service representatives available for this work to interview each fishermen in a given locality, the more important ones are visited, and a sufficient number of those of lesser importance are interviewed to obtain reliable information on their production, the number of fishing craft employed, the quantity of gear operated, and the number of persons employed as fishermen.

The state fishery agencies in a number of states have developed relatively complete statistical systems which greatly facilitate the Service's surveys in these states. In these states the Service only conducts such surveys as may be necessary to make the data comparable with that of other States.

As regards the fisheries of the Great Lakes and International lakes of Northern Minnesota, the Service obtains most of the catch statistics and usually the value of the catch direct from the records of the State fishery agencies. To obtain data on the number of fishermen, boats, vessels, and gear, the Service conducts such personal surveys among the fishermen as may be necessary to supplement the State records.

Service statistical personnel are stationed at Seattle, Washington, and San Pedro, California, who survey the fisheries of the Pacific Coast States. As a rule they obtain figures on the volume of the catch from the records of the State fishery departments. The value of the catch is derived from dealers' records. In Washington and Oregon the data for operating units in the offshore fisheries are obtained from the records of various fishery organizations as well as from records of the State department of fisheries. Statistics of the wholesale fishery industry for this section are obtained largely by personal interviews.

In the administration of the Alaska fisheries the Service obtains sworn statements concerning the activities of those prosecuting the fisheries in this area. These statements are compiled by the Alaska Branch of this Service and the summary data, by districts, are reproduced in this report.

Statistics on the volume of the catch of fish of the Great Lakes States usually are shown in weights as landed, which may be in the round or dressed condition. Statistics on the volume of the catch of fish taken in the remainder of the United States are shown in round weight.

The figures in the tables for shellfish represent the weight of the meats in the cases of univalve and bivalve mollusks and gastropods, and the round weight of crustaceans and such mollusks as squid and octopus.

Shore and vessel fisheries.--In general, statistics of the shore fisheries, as collected by the Service's representatives, include data on the number of casual and regular fishermen; number of motor and other fishing boats and accessory boats; type and quantity of gear used; and the volume, value, and method of capture of each species caught by boats (for our purpose craft of less than 5 net tons capacity are called 'boats') for each locality or group of localities. This method is not followed in some sections where the availability of data collected by the States fishery agencies obviates the necessity of detailed locality surveys.

Statistics of the vessel fisheries include data on the number of the crew, rig of vessels, net tonnage, kind and quantity of gear used, accessory boats carried, and volume, value, and method of capture of each species. For our purpose craft of 5 net tons capacity or more are called 'vessels'. As in the shore fisheries, the availability of figures collected by State fishery agencies may eliminate the necessity of our agents collecting these data for individual vessels.

Statistics of the quantity of gear operated indicate the maximum number of units fished at any one time during the year. Gear carried in reserve for replacement is not enumerated.

All persons engaged in commercial fishing operations are included as fishermen. For our purpose these have been divided into 'regular' and 'casual' fishermen. Regular fishermen are defined as those who receive more than one-half of their annual income from fishing; whereas casual fishermen are those whose principal business is something other than fishing, and who receive less than one-half of their annual compensation from fishing.

The catch of fish and shellfish is credited to the port where it is landed and the craft making the catch is credited to the locality where it landed the greatest portion of its catch during the year, except in the Pacific Coast States. Prior to 1949, craft in these states were credited to its home port unless it did not fish from that port during the year. In that case, it is credited to the locality where it landed the greatest portion of its catch. In 1949 each craft in the Pacific Coast States was credited to each State in which it landed fish during the year and a total exclusive of duplication is given for the entire Pacific Coast. Prior to the survey for 1942 it was the practice of the Service to credit the entire catch of a vessel to the principal port of landing, regardless of the actual point of landing. This policy was discontinued, however, since it quite often resulted in inconsistencies by presenting catches of certain fish in areas to which they are not common inasmuch as fishing vessels frequently operate in areas far removed from their principal fishing port. An outstanding example of this is the case of the Southern trawl fishery. In this fishery off the New Jersey, Maryland, Virginia, and North Carolina coasts, many fishing vessels from Massachusetts operate for 6 to 10 weeks during the winter season. Prior to the survey for 1942 the catch of these fish, principally common to these waters, was credited to Massachusetts. Under the present system the catch is credited to the southern port at which the major portion of their catch was landed.

Publication of Data.--Statistics of employment in the fisheries, craft and gear engaged, quantity and value of catch, and certain data on industries related to the fisheries are summarized according to the geographic division and published in bulletin form as soon as possible after the completion of each survey. Later, the figures, in more detail, are included in the annual reports of the Service entitled 'Fishery Statistics of the United States' and in 'Alaska Fishery and Fur-Seal Industries'.

Since 1928, data on the operating units (fishermen, fishing craft, and gear) and catch by counties for the Atlantic Coast and Gulf States have usually been included in the annual statistical reports 'Fishery Statistics of the United States' or its predecessor publication 'Fishery Industries of the United States.' However, funds were not available for the publication of county data for 1932 or for any year after 1938, except 1945. County data were collected for the areas in which surveys were conducted during those years, except in Maryland since 1942, and the data are on file in Washington, D. C. office of the Branch.

FISHING FOR MULLET

LOCAL AND SPECIAL SURVEYS

Landings at Certain Massachusetts Ports.--Detailed statistics are collected on the landings of aquatic products by individual fishing craft at Boston, Gloucester, New Bedford, Provincetown, and other Cape Cod ports. Service representatives are permanently stationed at each of these ports. They obtain daily figures on the quantity of fish landed by each fishing craft, the value of such fish landed, the date of departure and arrival of the craft, the gear used in their capture, and, except for ports located on Cape Cod, the grounds from which the fish were taken. The Branch of Fishery Biology and the Fishery Market News Service cooperate in the collection of these data.

Statistics on the landings at the above ports are released monthly and annually in bulletin form and detailed data are published in the annual statistical digests of the Branch. Products of American Fisheries received duty free at Boston and Gloucester from the treaty coasts of Newfoundland, Magdalen Islands, and Labrador, have not been included in the landings at these ports since 1938. Data on the landings at Boston and Gloucester have been collected annually since 1893. Some data are also available for these ports for earlier years. Information on landings at Provincetown and other Cape Cod ports has been collected annually since 1945, and at New Bedford since 1938.

Statistics on the landings of Fish at Seattle, Washington.--Data on the landings by the United States halibut fleet at this port are assembled by the Service from information collected by the International Fisheries Commission. Generally the halibut fleet is considered as consisting of those vessels belonging to members of the Fishing Vessel Owner's Association, Inc., which sell their fares through the Seattle Fish Exchange. This fleet originally fished almost exclusively for halibut. With the shortening of the halibut season, particularly in Area II, a portion of the fleet has fished for other species during the closed season for halibut, and has continued selling their fish through the Exchange. Data on other fishery products received by Seattle Wholesale Dealers, including receipts from Alaska and Canada, which appear in this report, are collected by the Service's Seattle representatives. Prior to 1944, receipts from Alaska and British Columbia were not included in the Seattle receipts published in the Statistical Digests. However, since October, 1938, these data were contained in the monthly and annual reports published by the Seattle Fishery Market News Office.

Shad and Alewife Fisheries.--Owing to the importance of the Hudson and Potomac Rivers in the production of shad, surveys for statistics of the catch, value of the catch, and operating units are made annually. On the Potomac River similar statistics are also obtained for the alewife fishery. Much of the data required for these surveys are available from the State fishery agencies.

Statistics of the annual shad and alewife fisheries are not published separately in bulletin form. However, a summary of the data is published in the annual Statistical Digest.

Statistics of the shad fishery of the Hudson River are available for 1896, 1897, 1898, 1901, 1904, 1910, and annually since 1915, while data for the shad fishery of the Potomac River are available for 1896, 1901, 1904, 1909, 1915, from 1919 to 1942, inclusive, and annually since 1944. Statistics of the alewife fishery of the Potomac River are available for 1896, 1909, 1915, 1919, to 1942, inclusive, and annually since 1944.

Pacific Halibut Fishery.--Statistics of the Pacific halibut fishery are obtained by the Service's personnel in Seattle, aided by Service representatives in Alaska, and the International Fisheries Commission. The fleet classification is that of the International Fisheries Commission, under which vessels that are listed by the Commission as having their home port in Alaska are included in the 'Alaska fleet', and all other vessels of United States registry landing at Seattle or ports in British Columbia or Alaska are included in the 'Washington fleet'. The catch is credited to the point where landed in the section 'Review of Certain Major Fisheries'. In the other sections of this report, all halibut is credited to the port where landed, except that all halibut landed by United States and Alaskan craft in British Columbia is credited to Alaska.

Monthly and annual statistical bulletins are available on this fishery, being published along with the statistics of the landings of fishery products at Seattle, Washington and detailed statistics are published in the annual statistical reports of the Branch. Statistics of the landings of halibut at Pacific Coast ports have been collected since 1925.

Canned Fishery Products and Byproducts.--Beginning in 1921, the Service has made annual surveys for statistics of the canned fishery products and byproducts industries of every section. These are begun the first week in January of each year for statistics of the production in the preceding year. The Service obtains by mail, so far as possible, the production of canned fishery products or byproducts from each plant in the United States engaged in this business. Where it is impossible to obtain reports by mail, the report is secured by personal visit by the Service's agents. The data obtained for canned fishery products include statistics on the yield and value of the production for each commodity by can sizes, case sizes, and trade classifications. The value shown for canned products and byproducts constitutes the gross amount received by the packer at the production point, no deductions being made for commissions or expenses. Statistics of the canned fishery products and byproducts produced in Alaska are received on the same statements obtained by the Alaska branch that include statistics of general fishery operations.

Annual statistical bulletins are issued on this trade, and detailed statistics of the output are published in the annual Statistical Digest. In addition to the data obtained on the output of these products annually since 1921, data also usually were obtained prior to 1921 for the years the various sections were surveyed.

Packaged Fish Trade.--Statistics of the annual production and value of fish packaged in the United States are obtained as a part of the survey for the statistics of the canned fishery products and byproducts industries. These data are released in bulletin form annually and later in more detailed and adjusted form in the annual Statistical Digest. Statistics of the production of packaged fish are available for 1926 and annually since 1928, except that no data was collected for the years 1941 to 1946, inclusive, in California.

Cold-Storage Holdings of Fish.--Information on the monthly freezings and holdings of fishery products is obtained from cold storage warehouses by mail and by Service employees in various cities of the country. Data are also obtained on the holdings of certain cured fish. Bulletins showing these statistics are issued monthly and annually.

Detailed cold-storage statistics also are published in the annual Statistical Digests issued by the Service. Information regarding cold-storage holdings of fishery products have been published since 1917 and data on quantities of fish frozen, for the years from 1920 to 1925, inclusive and annually since 1928.

Sponge Market, Tarpon Springs.--The major proportion of the output of sponges in Florida is sold on the Sponge Exchange at Tarpon Springs. The Service has obtained, from a representative of the Exchange, annual statistics of the quantity and value of the sponges sold by variety. Data on the quantity of sponges marketed by the Exchange is published in the Branch's annual Statistical Digest. Information regarding the transactions on the sponge exchange also are available in bulletin form for 1913, 1914, for the years since 1917.

Foreign Fishery Trade.--Statistics of the foreign fishery trade are obtained from compilations made by the Bureau of the Census, Department of Commerce. Statistics of all known fishery products imported or exported have been assembled and published annually since 1926 in the Branch's Statistical Digest. For earlier years, they are available in the reports of the Bureau of the Census, Bureau of Foreign and Domestic Commerce, the Bureau of Statistics, the Department of Commerce and Labor, or the Treasury Department.

PRACTICES AND TERMS

Certain practices and terms of importance used in the compilation of fishery statistics are explained below.

Days Absent.--In computing 'days absent' for vessels landing fares at the various ports, the day of arrival, but not the day of departure is included; thus a vessel leaving port on the 8th of the month and returning on the 15th of the month will be credited with 7 days absence. Prior to 1944, 'days absent' included both the day of departure and the day of arrival.

Operating Units.--Operating units as referred to in this document include persons engaged in the fisheries, and craft and gear employed in the fisheries.

Vessel.--The term 'vessel' refers to a craft having a capacity of 5 net tons or more.

Boat.--The term 'boat' refers to a craft having a capacity of less than 5 net tons.

Incidental Catch.--The term 'incidental catch' refers to the catch of certain species by a type of gear which ordinarily does not capture such species.

Percentages.--Percentages are usually shown as whole numbers. Fractions of percents are dropped if less than five-tenths, and the percentage is raised to the next higher integer if the fraction is greater than five-tenths. If the fraction is exactly five-tenths, the integer is raised or lowered to make it an even number.

Fish.--The term 'fish' as used in this report includes all species belonging to the class Pisces.

Shellfish, etc.--A shellfish is an aquatic invertebrate animal having a shell, such as a mollusk, or crustacean. However, in order to reduce the classifications appearing in the catch tables, all items not properly listed as 'Fish' or 'Whale Products' have been included under 'Shellfish, etc.' Accordingly, there is included under this classification turtles, frogs, sponges, sea weed, worms, etc.

Whale Products.--Since data are not available on the poundage of whales taken, statistics appearing in catch tables on the yield of these animals represent the weight of whale products produced such as meal, sperm oil, whale oil, etc. The values shown represent the amount received by the manufacturer for the products.

Converting.--Many of the figures shown in the statistical tables published herewith have been converted to thousands of pounds or dollars. In making these conversions the largest number from which a group of items is computed is raised or lowered to the nearest thousands place. The individual items are adjusted to conform to the total thus obtained.

Confidential data.--The statistical data collected by the Branch are confidential, and unless specific authorization is given, are not divulged in any manner except to employees of the Fish and Wildlife Service whose duties require this information. Statistics on the production of wholesale and manufacturing firms are published only for commodities or geographical areas where the production of three or more firms may be grouped, unless special permission is obtained from the firms involved to release the data.

CONVERSION FACTORS

It is the policy of the Service to show detailed catch figures of all products in pounds for the sake of uniformity and for purposes of comparison. This presents little difficulty in the case of fish since in very rare instances are fish reported in units of measure other than pounds. For shellfish, however, the units of measure may be bushels, sacks, barrels, thousands of shellfish, gallons of meat, etc. These many units make standardization difficult, and when combined with the wide variation in the requirements or definitions of some of these units in the various States the problem becomes even more complex.

All bivalve mollusks are reported in pounds of meats in the detailed catch tables presented in this report. In addition, there are included supplementary tables for most of the sections, which give data on the production in bushels. These supplementary tables also give the production of certain other shellfish, such as crabs, in number.

Oysters.--Probably the greatest problem in the presentation of fishery statistics in uniform units of measure is in the case of oysters. Usually the production of oysters on the Atlantic and Gulf coasts is reported to Service personnel in bushels; and prior to the data obtained for the year 1930 conversion from bushels to pounds of meats was effected on the basis of a uniform yield of 7 pounds of meats to the bushel. However, investigations have shown considerable variation from this figure. There follows a table which gives the measures used for oysters in the various States and the average yields per bushel. The statistical tables in this report are based on these average yields.

MEASURES AND YIELDS OF OYSTERS

STATE	CAPACITY OF STATE BUSHEL	VARIATION FROM U.S. STANDARD BUSHEL		MARKET OYSTERS	
				YIELD PER STATE BUSHEL	YIELD PER STANDARD BUSHEL
	CUBIC INCHES	CUBIC INCHES	PERCENT	POUNDS OF MEATS	POUNDS OF MEATS
MASSACHUSETTS	2,150.4	-	-	6.50	6.50
RHODE ISLAND.	2,150.4	-	-	7.00	7.00
CONNECTICUT	2,150.4	-	-	7.70	7.70
NEW YORK.	2,150.4	-	-	7.50	7.50
NEW JERSEY.	2,257.3	+ 106.9	+ 5.0	7.35	7.00
DELAWARE. . . ▸	2,257.3	+ 106.9	+ 5.0	6.30	6.00
MARYLAND.	2,800.7	+ 650.3	+ 30.3	6.15	4.72
VIRGINIA.	3,003.9	+ 853.5	+ 39.7	6.06	4.34
NORTH CAROLINA.	2,801.9	+ 651.5	+ 30.3	4.01	3.08
SOUTH CAROLINA.	4,071.5	+ 1,921.1	+ 89.3	4.96	2.62
GEORGIA	5,343.9	+ 3,193.5	+ 148.5	7.68	3.09
EAST COAST FLORIDA. . .	3,214.1	+ 1,063.7	+ 49.4	4.47	2.99
WEST COAST FLORIDA. . .	3,214.1	+ 1,063.7	+ 49.4	6.17	4.13
ALABAMA	2,826.2	+ 675.8	+ 31.4	6.37	4.85
MISSISSIPPI	2,826.2	+ 675.8	+ 31.4	4.91	3.74
LOUISIANA	2,148.4	- 2.0	- 0.1	3.88	3.88
TEXAS	2,700.0	+ 549.6	+ 25.6	5.20	4.14

NOTE:--DATA ON THE YIELDS FOR THE STATES OF NORTH CAROLINA, SOUTH CAROLINA, GEROGIA AND THE EAST COAST OF FLORIDA ARE FOR 1945. ALL OTHER ARE FOR 1949.

Other Mollusks.--The following table shows the conversion factors for various mollusks, other than oysters, used in this report.

AVERAGE YIELDS OF CERTAIN MOLLUSKS

POUNDS OF MEAT PER U.S. STANDARD BUSHEL

STATE	CLAMS, HARD		CLAMS, SOFT	CLAMS, SURF,	CLAMS, RAZOR	MUSSELS, SEA	PERIWINKLES AND COCKLES	SCALLOPS		CONCHS
	PUBLIC	PRIVATE						BAY	SEA	
MAINE	11.00	-	15.00	-	-	15.00	18.00	-	6.00	-
NEW HAMPSHIRE	-	-	15.00	-	-	-	-	-	-	-
MASSACHUSETTS	11.00	11.00	13.00	11.00	32.00	12.00	18.00	5.88	6.00	-
RHODE ISLAND.	1/ 12.00	-	20.00	12.00	-	12.00	18.00	6.00	-	-
CONNECTICUT	12.00	-	20.00	-	-	10.00	-	6.20	6.00	20.00
NEW YORK.	12.00	12.00	16.00	12.00	-	10.00	-	5.00	6.00	15.00
NEW JERSEY.	9.00	9.00	20.00	12.00	-	-	-	-	6.00	14.00
DELAWARE.	9.00	9.00	-	-	-	-	-	-	-	-
MARYLAND.	7.00	7.00	12.00	-	-	-	-	-	6.00	20.00
VIRGINIA.	7.00	7.00	-	-	-	-	-	-	6.00	20.05
NORTH CAROLINA. . . .	7.65	-	-	-	-	-	-	7.70	-	-
SOUTH CAROLINA. . . .	8.00	-	-	-	-	5.00	-	-	-	-
EAST COAST FLORIDA. .	8.05	-	-	-	-	-	-	5.06	-	17.00
WEST COAST FLORIDA. .	8.05	-	-	-	-	-	-	5.06	-	15.00

1/ INCLUDES OCEAN QUAHOG.
NOTE:--DATA ON YIELDS FOR NORTH CAROLINA, SOUTH CAROLINA, AND EAST COAST OF FLORIDA ARE FOR 1945. ALL OTHER DATA ARE FOR 1949.

Other Conversion Factors.--The principal other conversion factors that have been used in this report are as follows:

Crabs, blue, soft and peelers:

To convert number of crabs to weight in pounds in Delaware and New Jersey, divide by 4; in Maryland, by 3.03; in Virginia, by 3.01; and in Louisiana, by 2.94.

Crabs, blue, hard:

In Maryland, divide by 4.33; in Virginia, by 4.1; in Connecticut, by 4; in New Jersey and Delaware, by 3; in Alabama, by 2.40; in Louisiana, by 2.09; in Florida, West Coast, by 2.07; in Mississippi, by 2 and in Texas, by 1.74.

Crabs, rock:

In Maine, Massachusetts and Rhode Island, divide by 3.

Crabs, stone:

In Florida, West Coast, divide by 1.

Horseshoe crabs:

In New Jersey, multiply by 3.

Sponges, dried:

In Florida, convert number of bunches to weight in pounds as follows: large wool, multiply by 11; small wool, by 7; wool rags, by 9; yellow, by 4.25, and grass, by 4.166.

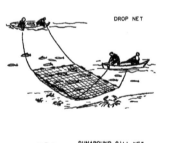

DROP NET

PARANZELLA NET

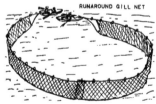

RUNAROUND GILL NET

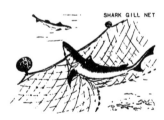

SHARK GILL NET

SECTION 14. GLOSSARY OF NAMES OF FISHERY PRODUCTS

In order to prevent misunderstanding in the use of common names employed in the tables and discussions, the following list of common and scientific names is given.

Common names as shown in Service reports	Other common names	Scientific names
FISH		
Alewife	Branch herring, big-eyed herring, river herring	Pomolobus pseudoharengus
	Blueback, glut herring, shad herring	Pomolobus aestivalis
Amberjack	Jack	Seriola species
Anchovy	....	Engraulis mordax
Angelfish	....	Pomacanthus species
		Holacanthus species
Anglerfish	Goosefish, allmouth, headfish, monkfish, bellyfish	Lophius piscatorius
Barracuda	....	Sphyraena species
Black bass	Smallmouth bass	Micropterus dolomieu
	Largemouth bass	Micropterus salmoides
Bluefish	Tailor, skipjack	Pomatomus saltatrix
Blue pike	Pike perch, hard pike, blue pickerel (Canada)	Stizostedion vitreum glaucum
Blue runner or hardtail	Runner	Caranx crysos
Bonito	See tuna and tunalike fishes	
Bowfin	Fresh-water dogfish, tchoupique, grindle	Amia calva
Buffalofish	Winter carp	Ictiobus species
Burbot	Lawyer, ling	Lota maculosa
Butterfish	....	Poronotus triacanthus
Cabezone	Marbled sculpin	Scorpaenichthys marmoratus
Cabio	Crab eater, coalfish, lemonfish, black bonito	Rachycentron canadus
Cabrilla	Rock bass	Epinephelus analogus
Carp	German carp, summer carp	Cyprinus carpio
Catfish and bullheads	....	Ameiurus species
		Ictalurus species
		Pilodictis olivaris
Chub	Longjaw, bluefin, blackfin (United States), tullibee (Canada)	All leucichthys except artedi (in Great Lakes)
Cigarfish	Scad	Decapterus punctatas
Cisco	Herring (Canada)	Leucichthys artedi (Lake Erie only)
Cod	Codfish	Gadus morrhua (Atlantic)
		Gadus macrocephalus (Pacific)
Corbina	California whiting, corvina, surffish	Menticirrhus undulatus
Crappie	White crappie, calico bass	Pomoxis annularis
	Black crappie	Pomoxis sparoides
Crevalle	Jack, jackfish	Caranx hippos
Croaker	Crocus, hardhead	Micropogon undulatus
Cunner	Chogset, blue perch, bergall	Tautogolabrus adspersus
Cusk	....	Brosme brosme
Dolly varden trout............	Salmon trout, bull trout	Salvelinus malma
Dolphin	....	Coryphaena hippurus
Drum:		
Black	Oyster cracker, oyster drum, sea drum	Pogonias cromis
Red	Channel bass, redfish, spotted bass.	Sciaenops ocellata
Eel:		
Common	....	Anguilla bostoniensis
Conger	....	Leptocephalus conger
Flounder:		
Gray sole	....	Glyptocephalus cynoglossus
Lemon sole	....	Pseudopleuronectes dignabilis
Yellowtail	Dab	Limanda ferruginea
Dab	Sea dab	Hippoglossoides platessoides

(Continued on next page)

Common names as shown in Service reports	Other common names	Scientific names
Flounder: - Continued		
Blackback	Winter flounder	*Pseudopleuronectes americanus*
Fluke	Summer flounder, gulf flounder, flounder	*Paralichthys* species
'Sole'	....	Pleuronectidae species and bothidae species
'California halibut'	....	*Paralichthys californicus*
Unclassified	....	Pleuronectidae and bothidae species
Flying fish	Boo hoo	*Cypselurus* species
Frigate mackerel	Boo hoo	*Auxis thazard*
Garfish	Gar, sea gar	*Lepisosteus* species
Gizzard shad	Nanny shad, mud shad, winter shad ..	*Dorosoma cepedianum*
Goldfish	Sand perch, gold perch	*Carassius auratus*
Goosefish	See anglerfish	
Grayfish	Dogfish .... / Spiny dog .... / Smooth dog	*Squalus suckleyi* (Pacific) / *Squalus acanthias* (Atlantic) / *Mustelus canis*
Grouper	'Sea bass'	*Epinephelus* species / *Mycteroperca* species
Grunt	Margate fish, sailors' choice	*Haemulon* species
Haddock	....	*Melanogrammus aeglefinus*
Hake:		
Red	Squirrel hake, ling, black hake, mud hake	*Urophycis chuss* (Atlantic)
White	Hake	*Urophycis tenuis* (Atlantic)
Pacific	Merluccio	*Merluccius productus* (Pacific)
Halibut	....	*Hippoglossus hippoglossus* (Atlantic) / *Hippoglossus stenolepis* (Pacific)
Hardhead	Sacramento rockfish	*Orthodon microlepidotus* (Pacific)
Harvestfish	Starfish, dollarfish, pappyfish, butterfish (N.C.)	*Peprilus alepidotus*
Herring:		
Lake	Herring	*Leucichthys artedi* (Great Lakes, except Erie)
Round	....	*Etrumeus sadina*
Sea	....	*Clupea harengus* (Atlantic) / *Clupea pallasii* (Pacific)
Hickory shad	Tailor shad, skip, autumnal herring	*Pomolobus mediocris*
Hogchoker	....	*Trinectes maculatus*
Hogfish	Capitaine, perro perro	*Lachnolaimus maximus*
Horse mackerel	Pacific (see jack mackerel) .... / Atlantic (see tuna, bluefin)	
Jack mackerel	Horse mackerel	*Trachurus symmetricus*
Jewfish	....	*Promicrops itaiara*
John dory	....	*Zenopsis ocellata*
Kingfish	Little roncador, croaker, tom cod ..	*Genyonemus lineatus*
King mackerel	Cero, kingfish	*Scomberomorus cavalla* / *Scomberomorus regalis*
King whiting or 'kingfish' ...	Whiting, sea mink, ground mullet ...	*Menticirrhus* species
Lake trout	....	*Cristivomer namaycush*
Lamprey	....	*Petromyzon marinus* (Atlantic) / *Entosphenus tridentatus* (Pacific)
Launce	Sand eel, lant, sand launce	*Ammodytes tobianus*
Lingcod	Cultus cod, blue cod, buffalo cod, ling	*Ophiodon elongatus*
Mackerel	....	*Scomber scombrus* (Atlantic) / *Pneumatophorus diego* (Pacific)
Marlin	....	*Makaira* species
Menhaden	Mossbunker, pogy, fatback	*Brevoortia* species
Minnow	....	Cyprinidae family

(Continued on next page)

Other names as shown in Service reports	Other common names	Scientific names
Mojarra	Sand perch, sand bream	Gerridae family
Mooneye	Toothed herring	Hiodon species
Moonfish		Vomer setipinnis / Selene vomer
Mullet	Jumping mullet, striped mullet, silver mullet	Mugil species
Mummichog	Mayfish, killifish	Fundulus species
Muttonfish	Mutton snapper	Lutianus analis
Ocean pout	Eelpout, sea pout	Macrozoarces anguillaris
Paddlefish	Spoonbill cat	Polyodon spathula
Perch	Surffish	Embiotocidae family (Pacific)
Permit		Trachinotus goodei
Pigfish	Hogfish (N. C.)	Orthopristis chrysopterus
Pike or pickerel	Great lakes pike	Esox reticulatus / Esox lucius
Pilchard	Sardine	Sardinops caerulea
Pinfish	Bream, salt-water bream	Lagodon rhomboides
Pollock	Boston bluefish	Pollachius virens
Pompano	Great pompano	Trachinotus species (Atlantic) / Palometa simillima (Pacific)
Porgy	See scup or porgy	
Quillback	Spearfish or skimfish	Carpiodes species
Ratfish		Hydrolagus colliei
Roach	Golden shiner	Notemigonus crysoleucas
Rock bass	Redeye, goggle-eye / Groupers, sand bass	Ambloplites rupestris (fresh-water) / Paralabrax nebulifer (Pacific)
Rockfish	Rock cod, snapper	Sebastodes species (Pacific)
Rosefish	Ocean perch, redfish, red perch	Sebastes marinus
Rudderfish	Blue bass, greenfish / Halfmoon	Girella nigricans / Medialuna californiensis
Sablefish	Black cod	Anoplopoma fimbria
Salmon:		
Atlantic		Salmo salar (Atlantic)
Pacific:		
Chinook or king	Tyee, spring	Oncorhynchus tschawytscha
Chum or keta	Fall, dog	Oncorhynchus keta
Pink	Humpback	Oncorhynchus gorbuscha
Red or sockeye	Blueback	Oncorhynchus nerka
Silver or coho		Oncorhynchus kisutch
Steelhead	See steelhead trout	
Sand perch	Yellowtail perch	Bairdiella chrysura
Sauger	Sand pike	Stizostedion canadense
Sawfish		Pristis pectinatus
Sculpin	Scorpionfish	Scorpaena guttata
Scup or porgy	Porgee, paugy, fair maid	Calamus or stenotomus species
Sea bass:		
Black	Black jewfish (Pacific) / Blackfish (Atlantic)	Stereolepis gigas / Centropristes striatus
White		Cynoscion nobilis (Pacific)
Sea catfish	Gafftopsail	Bagre marina
Sea robin		Prionotus species
Sea trout or weakfish:		
Gray	Gray trout, squeteague	Cynoscion regalis
Spotted	Spotted trout, speckled trout	Cynoscion nebulosus
White	White trout, sand trout	Cynoscion arenarius
Shad	American shad, white shad	Alosa sapidissima
Sharks		Carcharodon species; mustelus species, carcharhinus species; sphyrna species, lamna species; and others

(Continued on next page)

Other names as shown in Service reports	Other common names	Scientific names
Sheepshead:		
Fresh-water	Fresh-water drum, whitefish, gaspergou, gou	*Aplodinotus grunniens*
Salt-water	Redfish, fathead	*Archosargus* species (Atlantic) *Pimelometopon pulchrum* (Pacific)
Silver perch	See sand perch	
Silverside	Spearing	*Menidia* species
Skate	Ray, rajafish	*Raja* species
Skipper	Billfish	*Scomberesox saurus*
Smelt	....	*Osmerus mordax* (Atlantic and Great Lakes)
	....	Atherinidae and osmeridae species (Pacific)
	Eulachon	*Thaleichthys pacificus*
Snapper:		
Lane	Schoolmaster	*Lutianus synagris*
Mangrove	Gray snapper	*Lutianus griseus*
Red	....	*Lutianus blackfordii*
Snook	Robalo, sergeantfish, pike	*Centropomus undecimalis*
Spadefish	Porgy (N. C.), angelfish	*Chaetodipterus faber*
Spanish mackerel	Mackerel	*Scomberomorus maculatus*
Splittail	....	*Pogonichthys macrolepidotus*
Spot	Lafayette, goody	*Leiostomus xanthurus*
Squawfish	Sacramento pike	*Ptychocheilus grandis*
Squirrel hake	See hake, red	
Steelhead trout	Salmon trout	*Salmo gairdnerii*
Striped bass	Rockfish, rock	*Roccus saxatilis*
Sturgeon:		
Common	....	*Acipenser* species
Shovelnose	....	*Scaphirhynchus platorynchus*
Sucker	Fresh-water mullet, redfin, bayfish ...	Catostomidae species
Sunfish	Bream, perch, bluegill	Centrarchidae species
Surffish	See perch	
Swellfish	Puffer, swell toad, globefish, blowfish	*Sphoeroides maculatus*
Swordfish	....	*Xiphias gladius*
Tautog	Blackfish, oysterfish	*Tautoga onitis*
Tenpounder	Big-eyed herring, ladyfish	*Elops saurus*
Thimble-eyed mackerel	Chub mackerel, bullseye, mackerel	*Pneumatophorus colias*
Tilefish	....	*Lopholatilus chameleonticeps*
Tomcod	Frost fish	*Microgadus tomcod* (Atlantic) *Microgadus proximus* (Pacific)
Triggerfish	....	*Batistes capriscus*
Tripletail	Sunfish (N. C.) blackfish	*Lobotes surinamensis*
Tullibee	See chub	
Tuna and tunalike fishes:		
Albacore	Longfin tuna	*Germo alalunga*
Bluefin	....	*Thunnus saliens*
	Horse mackerel	*Thunnus thynnus*
	....	*Thunnus secundodorsalis*
Bonito	....	*Sarda sarda* (Atlantic) *Sarda chiliensis* (Pacific)
Little	Bonito, albacore, false albacore	*Euthynnus alleteratus*
Skipjack	Striped tuna	*Katsuwonus pelamis*
Yellowfin	....	*Neothunnus macropterus*
Turbot	Greenland halibut	*Reinhardius hippoglossoides* (off New England)
	American turbot, triggerfish	*Batistes carolinensis* (off Florida)

(Continued on next page)

Common names as shown in Service reports	Other common names	Scientific names
Wahoo	White lake bass	*Acanthocybium solandri*
White bass	White lake bass	*Roccus chrysops*
Whitebait	Small fry of several species	
Whitefish:		
Common		*Coregonus clupeaformis*
Menominee		*Prosopium quadrilaterale*
Ocean	Blanquillo	*Caulolatilus princeps*
White perch		*Morone americana.*
Whiting	Silver hake	*Merluccius bilinearis*
Wolffish	Catfish (New England)	*Anarhichas lupas*
Yellow perch	Ringed perch, perch	*Perca flavescens*
Yellow pike	Wall-eyed pike, pike perch, dore (Canadian)	*Stizostedion vitreum vitreum*
Yellowtail		*Ocyurus chrysurus* (Florida) / *Seriola dorsalis* (Pacific)
Yellowtail flounder	See flounder, yellowtail	
CRUSTACEANS		
Crabs:		
Blue:		
Hard	Hard-shell crab	*Callinectes sapidus*
Soft and peelers	Soft-shelled crab	*Callinectes sapidus*
Dungeness		*Cancer magister*
King	Alaska king crab	*Paralithodes camtschatica*
Rock		*Cancer irroratus* (New England) / *Cancer species* (California)
Stone		*Menippi mercenaria*
Crawfish:		
Fresh-water	Crayfish	*Cambarus species* (Atlantic) / *Astacus species* (Pacific)
Sea	See lobster, spiny	
Horseshoe crab	King crab	*Limulus species*
Lobster:		
Northern		*Homarus americanus* (Atlantic)
Spiny	Sea crawfish, rock lobster	*Panulirus argus* (Atlantic) / *Panulirus interruptus* (Pacific)
Shrimp	Prawn	*Penaeus setiferus* (South / *Penaeus duorarum* Atlantic / *Penaeus aztecus* and / *Xyphopeneus kroyeri* Gulf) / *Pandalus species* (Atlantic and Pacific) / *Pandalopsis species* (Pacific) / *Crangon species* (Pacific)
MOLLUSKS		
Abalone		*Halotis species*
Clam:		
Cockle		*Cardium corbis* (Pacific)
Coquina	Pompano shells	*Donax variabilis*
Hard	Butter / Little neck / Round clam, cherrystone, quahog, little neck	*Saxidomus nuttali* (Pacific) / *Paphia staminea* (Pacific) / *Venus mercenaria* (Atlantic) / *Venus mortoni* (Florida)
Pismo		*Tivela stultorum* (Pacific)
Razor		*Ensis species* (Atlantic) / *Siliqua patula* (Pacific)
Soft	Soft-shell clam, sand clam, nannynose, maninose	*Mya arenaria*
Surf	Skimmer	*Mactra solidissimo*

(Continued on next page)

GLOSSARY OF NAMES OF FISHERY PRODUCTS

Common names as shown in Service reports	Other common names	Scientific names
Conch	....	Strombus species / Busycon species
Limpet	....	Achea testitudinalis
Mussel:		
Sea	....	Mytilus californianus (Pacific) / Mytilus edulis (Atlantic)
Fresh-water	....	Quadrula species / Lampsilis species / Unio species / Symphynota species
Octopus	Devilfish	Octopus punctatus
Oyster:		
Eastern	Cove	Ostrea virginica
Pacific (introduced).........	Japanese	Ostrea gigas
Western	Olympia, native	Ostrea lurida
Periwinkle or cockle	....	Littorina species / Lunatia species
Scallop:		
Bay	....	Pecten irradians (Atlantic) / Pecten aequisulcatus (Pacific)
Sea	....	Pecten magellanicus
Squid	Inkfish, bone squid, tawtaw..........	Loligo opalescens (Pacific) / Loligo pealei (Atlantic)
OTHER		
Sea urchin	Sea eggs	Strongylocentratus drobachiensis
Starfish	....	Asteroidae class
Terrapin	Diamond-back terrapin	Malaclemys species
Turtle:		
Green	....	Chelonia mydas
Loggerhead	....	Caretta species
Hawksbill	....	Eretmochelys inbricata
Snapper	Hard-shell, alligator turtle	Chelydra serpentina / Macrochalys temmickii
Soft-shell	....	Trionyx species
Frogs	....	Rana species
Irish moss	....	Chrondrus crispus
Kelp	....	Macrocystis species, nereocystis species, pelagophycus species, alaria species
Rockweed	Seaweed	Laminaria species
Sponge:		
Glove	....	Spongia graminea / Euspongia officianalis
Grass	....	Hippospongia equina cerebriformis
Sheepswool	Wool	Hippospongia canaliculata gossypina
Yellow	....	Hippospongia equina elastica
Trepang	Sea cucumber	Cucumaris frondosia, Thyone briareus
Bloodworms	....	Terebillidae family
Sandworms	....	Nereis species

SECTION 15. - PICTORIAL SECTION

As many of the readers of this publication may not be familiar with all of the species of fish and shellfish, etc., taken commercially in the United States and Alaska, illustrations of many of the various species are included in the following pages. The descriptive material appearing with each species includes the areas in which they are taken commercially and does not constitute the extreme limits in which they occur. Similarly, the gear listed for each species do not represent the only types of apparatus by which these species are obtained, but represent those types of apparatus which are normally used in their capture. The gear do not necessarily appear in the order of their importance.

For more detailed information on the nomenclature of the fishery products listed below the reader is referred to Section 14 of this publication entitled, 'Glossary of Names of Fishery Products'.

ALEWIFE
RANGE - FLORIDA TO NEW ENGLAND
GEAR - POUND NETS, GILL NETS, WEIRS,
       DIP NETS, HAUL SEINES, .
       FLOATING TRAPS, FYKE NETS

ANGELFISH
RANGE - FLORIDA
GEAR - HAUL SEINES

BLACK BASS
RANGE - FRESH-WATER
GEAR - HAUL SEINES, FYKE NETS, POUND
       NETS, LINES

AMBERJACK
RANGE - FLORIDA
GEAR - HAND LINES, TROLL LINES

ANGLERFISH
RANGE - NEW JERSEY TO MASSACHUSETTS
GEAR - OTTER TRAWLS, POUND NETS

BARRACUDA, (PACIFIC)
RANGE - CALIFORNIA
GEAR - PURSE SEINES, SET LINES,
       HAND LINES, TROLL LINES,
       GILL AND TRAMMEL NETS.

BARRACUDA, (ATLANTIC)
RANGE - FLORIDA
GEAR - TROLL LINES, HAND LINES

BLUEFISH
RANGE - GULF OF MEXICO TO NEW
            ENGLAND
GEAR - HAUL SEINES, GILL NETS,
            POUND NETS, TROLL LINES
            PURSE SEINES

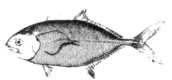

BLUERUNNER OR HARDTAIL
RANGE - GULF OF MEXICO
GEAR - HAUL SEINES, GILL NETS, POTS

BONITO, (ATLANTIC)
RANGE - NORTH CAROLINA TO MASSACHUSETTS
GEAR - POUND NETS, TROLL LINES, GILL NETS

BOWFIN
RANGE - FRESH-WATER
GEAR - HAUL SEINES, TRAP NETS,
            FYKE NETS

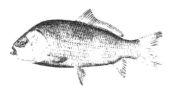

BUFFALOFISH
RANGE - FRESH-WATER
GEAR - HAUL SEINES, FYKE NETS,
            TRAMMEL NETS, TROT LINES

BURBOT
RANGE - GREAT LAKES
GEAR - GILL NETS, FYKE NETS, POUND
            NETS (TRAP NETS)

BUTTERFISH
RANGE - FLORIDA TO NEW ENGLAND
GEAR - POUND NETS, HAUL SEINES,
            OTTER TRAWLS

CABIO
RANGE - FLORIDA TO VIRGINIA
GEAR - HAND LINES, POUND NETS

CARP
RANGE - FRESH-WATER
FEAR - HAUL SEINES, GILL NETS, TRAP NETS,
            FYKE NETS, POUND NETS, TROT LINES

CATFISH
RANGE - FRESH-WATER
GEAR - HAUL SEINES, TROT LINES, POUND
            NETS, POTS, FYKE NETS

CHUB
RANGE - GREAT LAKES
GEAR - GILL NETS

CIGARFISH
RANGE - FLORIDA
GEAR - HAUL SEINES

COD
RANGE - VIRGINIA TO MAINE, WASHINGTON
           AND ALASKA
GEAR - OTTER TRAWLS, LINE TRAWLS,
          GILL NETS

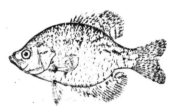

CRAPPIE
RANGE - FRESH-WATER LAKES
GEAR - HAUL SEINES, LINES, POTS

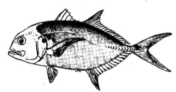

CREVALLE
RANGE - SOUTH ATLANTIC AND GULF STATES·
GEAR - HAUL SEINES, GILL NETS, LINES

CROAKER, (ATLANTIC)
RANGE - GULF OF MEXICO TO NEW YORK
GEAR - POUND NETS, OTTER TRAWLS,
          HAUL SEINES, GILL NETS

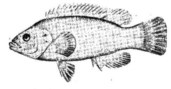

CUNNER
RANGE - NEW ENGLAND
GEAR - OTTER TRAWLS, HAND LINES

CUSK
RANGE - NEW ENGLAND
GEAR - OTTER TRAWLS, TRAWL LINES

DOLLY VARDEN TROUT
RANGE - PACIFIC COAST
GEAR - POUND NETS, GILL NETS, LINES

DOLPHIN
RANGE - FLORIDA TO NORTH CAROLINA
GEAR - TROLL LINES

DRUM, BLACK
RANGE - TEXAS TO NORTH CAROLINA
GEAR - HAUL SEINES, POUND NETS, LINES

DRUM, RED
RANGE - TEXAS - MARYLAND
GEAR - POUND NETS, HAUL SEINES,
        GILL NETS, LINES

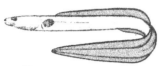

EEL, CONGER
RANGE - FLORIDA TO NEW ENGLAND
GEAR - OTTER TRAWLS

EEL, COMMON
RANGE - FLORIDA TO NEW ENGLAND AND
        IN MISSISSIPPI RIVER, LAKE
        ONTARIO
GEAR - POTS, SPEARS, POUND NETS

GRAY SOLE
RANGE - MASSACHUSETTS TO MAINE
GEAR - OTTER TRAWLS

LEMON SOLE
RANGE - NEW YORK TO MAINE
GEAR - OTTER TRAWLS

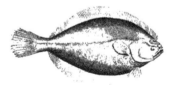

DAB
RANGE - MASSACHUSETTS TO NOVA SCOTIA
GEAR - OTTER TRAWLS, TRAWL LINES

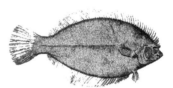

BLACKBACK OR WINTER FLOUNDER
RANGE - NORTH CAROLINA TO MAINE
GEAR - OTTER TRAWLS, POUND NETS,
        FYKE NETS, SPEARS, LINES

FLUKE
RANGE - TEXAS TO MASSACHUSETTS
GEAR - OTTER TRAWLS, SPEARS, LINES

FLYING FISH
RANGE - PACIFIC AND ATLANTIC
        OCEANS
GEAR - GILL NETS

FRIGATE MACKEREL
RANGE - MIDDLE ATLANTIC
GEAR - POUND NETS

GARFISH
RANGE - FRESH-WATER
GEAR - HAUL SEINES, LINES

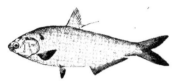

GIZZARD SHAD
RANGE - NORTH CAROLINA TO
        MARYLAND, GREAT LAKES
GEAR - HAUL SEINES, POUND NETS,
       GILL NETS

GOLDFISH
RANGE - LAKES AND RIVERS
GEAR - HAUL SEINES, TRAP NETS, FYKE
       NETS

GRAYFISH
RANGE - PACIFIC COAST STATES
GEAR - TRAWL LINES, OTTER TRAWLS,
       GILL NETS

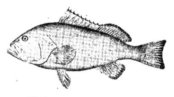

GROUPER
RANGE - TEXAS TO SOUTH CAROLINA
GEAR - HAND LINES, POTS

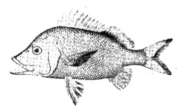

GRUNT
RANGE - FLORIDA
GEAR - POTS, GILL NETS, LINES

HADDOCK
RANGE - NEW ENGLAND STATES
GEAR - OTTER TRAWLS, GILL NETS
       LINE TRAWLS

HAKE, RED
RANGE - CHESAPEAKE BAY TO NEW ENGLAND
GEAR - GILL NETS, OTTER TRAWLS, LINE TRAWLS

HAKE, WHITE
RANGE - CHESAPEAKE BAY TO NEW
        ENGLAND
GEAR - GILL NETS, OTTER TRAWLS,
       LINE TRAWLS

HALIBUT
RANGE - PACIFIC COAST - NEW ENGLAND
GEAR - TRAWL LINES, OTTER TRAWLS

HARDHEAD
RANGE - CALIFORNIA
GEAR - FYKE NETS

HARVESTFISH OR "STARFISH"
RANGE - NORTH CAROLINA TO
CHESAPEAKE BAY
GEAR - HAUL SEINES, POUND NETS

HERRING, LAKE
RANGE - GREAT LAKES
GEAR - GILL NETS, HAUL SEINES,
POUND NETS, TRAP NETS

HERRING, SEA
RANGE - NEW JERSEY TO NEW ENGLAND
PACIFIC COAST STATES AND
ALASKA
GEAR - PURSE SEINES, WEIRS,
FLOATING TRAPS, STOP SEINES

HICKORY SHAD
RANGE - FLORIDA TO RHODE ISLAND
GEAR - POUND NETS, HAUL SEINES, GILL NETS
FLOATING TRAPS

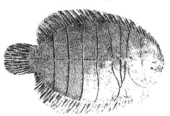

HOGCHOKER
RANGE - CHESAPEAKE BAY
GEAR - POUND NETS, HAUL SEINES

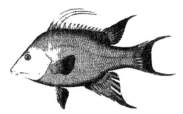

HOGFISH
RANGE - FLORIDA
GEAR - LINES

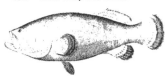

JEWFISH
RANGE - FLORIDA
GEAR - HAND LINES

954711 O - 51 - 20

KING MACKEREL
RANGE - TEXAS TO NEW YORK
GEAR - TROLL LINES, GILL NETS,
     HAND LINES

JOHN DORY
RANGE - MIDDLE ATLANTIC STATES
GEAR - OTTER TRAWLS

KING WHITING
RANGE - TEXAS TO MASSACHUSETTS
GEAR - OTTER TRAWLS, HAUL SEINES,
     POUND NETS

LAKE TROUT
RANGE - GREAT LAKES
GEAR - GILL NETS, LINES, POUND. NETS
     (TRAP NETS)

LAUNCE
RANGE - NEW ENGLAND
GEAR - HAUL SEINES

LAMPREY
RANGE - FRESH-WATER
GEAR - POTS, FYKE NETS

MACKEREL
RANGE - CHESAPEAKE BAY TO GULF OF
     ST. LAWRENCE, CALIFORNIA
GEAR - PURSE SEINES, GILL NETS,
     POUND NETS, FLOATING TRAPS,
     DIP NETS, LAMPARA NETS

LINGCOD
RANGE - CALIFORNIA TO ALASKA
GEAR - OTTER TRAWLS, TRAWL LINES,
     SET LINES, HAND LINES

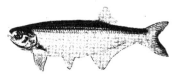

MOONEYE
RANGE - GREAT LAKES
GEAR - HAUL SEINES

MENHADEN
RANGE - GULF OF MEXICO TO NEW ENGLAND
GEAR - PURSE SEINES, POUND NETS

MOONFISH
RANGE - FLORIDA
GEAR - HAND LINES, HAUL SEINES

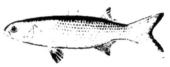

MULLET
RANGE - TEXAS TO NEW JERSEY
GEAR - GILL NETS, HAUL SEINES,
       POUND NETS, CAST NETS

OCEAN POUT
RANGE - NEW ENGLAND
GEAR - OTTER TRAWLS

PADDLEFISH
RANGE - GULF OF MEXICO, MISSISSIPPI
                      RIVER
GEAR - HAUL SEINES, TROT LINES

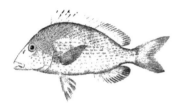

PIGFISH
RANGE - FLORIDA
GEAR - POTS, HAND LINES, GILL NETS

PIKE OR PICKEREL
RANGE - FRESH WATER
GEAR - TRAP NETS, FYKE NETS,
       GILL NETS, POUND NETS,
       HAND LINES

PILCHARD
RANGE - CALIFORNIA TO WASHINGTON
GEAR - PURSE SEINES, LAMPARA AND
       RING NETS, GILL NETS

PINFISH
RANGE - FLORIDA TO NORTH CAROLINA
GEAR - HAUL SEINES, GILL NETS

POLLOCK
RANGE - MIDDLE ATLANTIC AND NEW
               ENGLAND STATES
GEAR - TRAWL LINES, FLOATING TRAPS,
       POUND NETS, OTTER TRAWLS,
       GILL NETS

POMPANO
RANGE - TEXAS TO NORTH CAROLINA
GEAR - TRAMMEL NETS, HAUL SEINES,
       GILL NETS, HAND LINES

QUILLBACK
RANGE - FRESH-WATER
GEAR - HAUL SEINES, TROT LINES, FYKES

RATFISH
RANGE - WASHINGTON TO ALASKA
GEAR - BEAM TRAWLS, TRAWL LINES

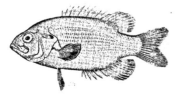

ROCK BASS
RANGE - GREAT LAKES
GEAR - TRAP NETS, FYKES,
HAUL SEINES, GILL NETS

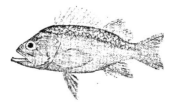

ROCKFISH
RANGE - CALIFORNIA TO ALASKA
GEAR - LINES, OTTER TRAWLS
PARANZELLA NETS, GILL NETS

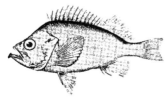

ROSEFISH
RANGE - NEW ENGLAND
GEAR - OTTER TRAWLS

RUDDERFISH
RANGE - CALIFORNIA
GEAR - LAMPARA AND RING NETS

SABLEFISH
RANGE - PACIFIC COAST STATES AND
ALASKA
GEAR - TRAWL LINES, OTTER TRAWLS

SALMON, RED OR SOCKEYE
RANGE - OREGON TO ALASKA
GEAR - GILL NETS, PURSE SEINES,
POUND NETS

SALMON, CHUM OR KETA
RANGE - OREGON TO ALASKA
GEAR - POUND NETS, PURSE SEINES,
GILL NETS, HAUL SEINES

SALMON, PINK
RANGE - WASHINGTON TO ALASKA
GEAR - PURSE SEINES, POUND NETS
GILL NETS

SALMON, SILVER OR COHO
RANGE - CALIFORNIA TO ALASKA
GEAR - HAUL SEINES, PURSE SEINES, GILL
       NETS, TROLL LINES, POUND NETS.

STEELHEAD TROUT
RANGE - OREGON TO ALASKA
GEAR.- HAUL SEINES, POUND NETS,
       GILL NETS, LINES, DIP NETS

SAUGER
RANGE - GREAT LAKES
GEAR - GILL NETS, HAUL SEINES, TRAP
       NETS, FYKE NETS

SCULPIN·
RANGE - PACIFIC COAST STATES AND
        ALASKA
GEAR - LINES, GILL NETS, POTS

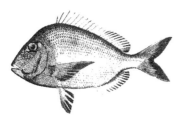

SCUP OR PORGY
RANGE - FLORIDA TO NEW ENGLAND
GEAR - OTTER TRAWLS, POUND NETS

SEA BASS
RANGE - FLORIDA TO NEW ENGLAND
GEAR - OTTER TRAWLS, HAND LINES, POTS

SEA CATFISH
RANGE - TEXAS TO CHESAPEAKE BAY
GEAR - OTTER TRAWLS, HAUL SEINES, HAND
       LINES

SEA TROUT OR WEAKFISH, GRAY
RANGE - FLORIDA TO MASSACHUSETTS
GEAR - OTTER TRAWLS, POUND NETS,
       PURSE SEINES, GILL NETS,
       HAUL SEINES

SEA TROUT OR WEAKFISH, SPOTTED
RANGE - MARYLAND TO TEXAS
GEAR - GILL NETS, TRAMMEL NETS,
       HAUL SEINES, POUND NETS,
       OTTER TRAWLS, HAND LINES

SEA TROUT OR WEAKFISH, WHITE
RANGE - GULF OF MEXICO
GEAR - GILL NETS, HAUL SEINES,
       HAND LINES

SEA ROBIN
RANGE - CHESAPEAKE BAY TO NEW ENGLAND
GEAR - POUND NETS, OTTER TRAWLS

SHARK
RANGE - ATLANTIC COAST, GULF,
PACIFIC COAST STATES
GEAR - TRAWL LINES, GILL NETS,
OTTER TRAWLS

SHEEPSHEAD, CALIFORNIA
RANGE - CALIFORNIA
GEAR - SET LINES, TRAMMEL NETS,

SILVERSIDES
RANGE - NEW YORK
GEAR - HAUL SEINES, OTHER TRAWLS

SKIPPER OR BILLFISH
RANGE - VIRGINIA TO NOVA SCOTIA
GEAR - POUND NETS, WEIRS

SKATE
RANGE - PACIFIC COAST, CHESAPEAKE
BAY TO NEW ENGLAND
GEAR - LINES, OTTER TRAWLS, POUND
NETS, HAUL SEINES

SHAD
RANGE - FLORIDA TO NEW ENGLAND
GEAR - GILL NETS, POUND NETS,
FYKE NETS, HAUL SEINES

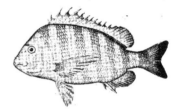

SHEEPSHEAD
RANGE - TEXAS TO CHESAPEAKE BAY
GEAR - HAND LINES, POTS

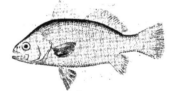

SILVER PERCH
RANGE - TEXAS TO NEW YORK
GEAR - HAUL SEINES, GILL NETS,
POUND NETS

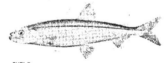

SMELT
RANGE - NEW YORK TO MAINE,
PACIFIC OCEAN, GREAT LAKES
GEAR - POUND NETS, DIP NETS, GILL NETS,
HAUL SEINES

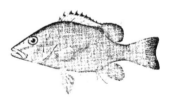

LANE SNAPPER
RANGE - FLORIDA
GEAR - HAND LINES

GRAY SNAPPER
RANGE - FLORIDA
GEAR - HAND LINES, GILL NETS

RED SNAPPER
RANGE - TEXAS TO FLORIDA
GEAR - HAND LINES

SNOOK
RANGE - TEXAS TO FLORIDA
GEAR - GILL NETS, HAND LINES,
       HAUL SEINES

SPANISH MACKEREL
RANGE - TEXAS TO VIRGINIA
GEAR - GILL NETS, LINES, HAUL
       SEINES

SPADEFISH
RANGE - FLORIDA
GEAR - GILL NETS, TRAMMEL NETS

SQUAWFISH
RANGE - CALIFORNIA
GEAR - FYKE NETS, GILL NETS

SPOT
RANGE - GULF OF MEXICO TO MIDDLE
        ATLANTIC STATES
GEAR - HAUL SEINES, GILL NETS, POUND
       NETS, OTTER TRAWLS

STRIPED BASS
RANGE - NORTH CAROLINA TO NEW
        ENGLAND, CALIFORNIA TO
        OREGON
GEAR - HAUL SEINES, GILL NETS, POUND
       NETS, HAND LINES, FYKE NETS

STURGEON
RANGE - COASTAL AND RIVER AREAS
GEAR - GILL NETS, LINES

STURGEON, SHOVELNOSE
RANGE - FRESH-WATER
GEAR - HAUL SEINES, LINES, POUND NETS

SUCKER
RANGE - FRESH-WATER
GEAR - POUND NETS, FYKE NETS, GILL
       NETS, HAUL SEINES, TRAP NETS

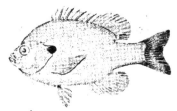

SUNFISH
RANGE - FRESH-WATER
GEAR - POTS, SEINES, TRAP NETS

SWELLFISH
RANGE - CHESAPEAKE BAY TO MIDDLE
ATLANTIC
GEAR - POUND NETS, HAUL SEINES,
OTTER TRAWLS

SWORDFISH
RANGE - NEW ENGLAND AND CALIFORNIA
GEAR - HARPOONS

TAUTOG
RANGE - CHESAPEAKE BAY TO NEW
ENGLAND
GEAR - POUND NETS, HAND LINES, POTS

TENPOUNDER
RANGE - FLORIDA
GEAR - HAUL SEINES

THIMBLE-EYED MACKEREL
RANGE - CHESAPEAKE BAY TO NEW ENGLAND
GEAR - POUND NETS, PURSE SEINES,
OTTER TRAWLS

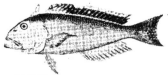

TILEFISH
RANGE - MIDDLE ATLANTIC AND NEW
ENGLAND STATES
GEAR - TRAWL LINES

TOMCOD
RANGE - PACIFIC COAST, MIDDLE
ATLANTIC AND NEW ENGLAND
STATES
GEAR - OTTER TRAWLS, DIP NETS

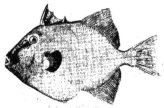

TRIGGERFISH
RANGE - FLORIDA
GEAR - HAND LINES

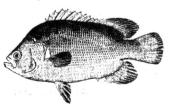

TRIPLETAIL
RANGE - FLORIDA
GEAR - HAUL SEINES, GILL NETS, LINES

TUNA,ALBACORE
RANGE - PACIFIC COAST
GEAR - LINES

TUNA,BLUEFIN
RANGE - CALIFORNIA,NEW JERSEY TO
            MAINE
GEAR - PURSE SEINES,LAMPARA NETS
        TROLL LINES,POUND NETS,
        HARPOONS

TUNA,LITTLE
RANGE - MASSACHUSETTS TO TEXAS
GEAR - POUND NETS, TROLL LINES
        OTTER TRAWLS

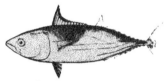

TUNA,SKIPJACK
RANGE - CALIFORNIA
GEAR - LINES,PURSE SEINES

WHITEFISH, MENOMINEE
RANGE - ALASKA, UPPER GREAT
        LAKES. TO NEW ENGLAND,
        IN LAKES
GEAR - GILL NETS, HAUL SEINES,
        TRAP NETS, POUND NETS

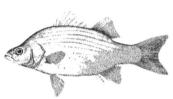

WHITE BASS
RANGE - GREAT LAKES
GEAR - TRAP NETS, FYKES,
        HAUL SEINES, POUND NETS

WHITE PERCH
RANGE - NORTH CAROLINA TO MAINE
GEAR - POUND NETS, FYKE NETS, HAUL
        SEINES

WHITEFISH, COMMON
RANGE - GREAT LAKES
GEAR - GILL NETS, POUND NETS, TRAP
        NETS

WOLFFISH
RANGE - MASSACHUSETTS AND MAINE
GEAR - OTTER TRAWLS, LINES TRAWLS

WHITING
RANGE - VIRGINIA TO MAINE
GEAR - OTTER TRAWLS, POUND NETS

YELLOW PERCH
RANGE - GREAT LAKES, OTHER LAKES
GEAR - GILL NETS, TRAP NETS, POUND
NETS, FYKE NETS

YELLOW PIKE
RANGE - GREAT LAKES
GEAR - POUND NETS, FYKE NETS, GILL
NETS, TRAP NETS

BLUE CRAB
RANGE - TEXAS TO RHODE ISLAND
GEAR - TROT LINES, POTS, FYKE NETS,
DIP NETS, SCRAPES, DREDGES

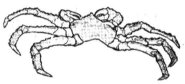

KING CRAB
RANGE - ALASKA
GEAR - TANGLE NETS, OTTER TRAWLS

DUNGENESS CRAB
RANGE - PACIFIC COAST STATES AND
ALASKA
GEAR - TRAPS

ROCK CRAB
RANGE - NEW ENGLAND
GEAR - POTS

STONE CRAB
RANGE - FLORIDA
GEAR - DIP NETS, CRAB POTS

HORSESHOE CRAB
RANGE - MARYLAND TO NEW YORK
GEAR - POUND NETS. WEIRS, BY HAND

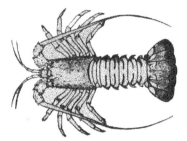

SEA CRAWFISH OR SPINY LOBSTER
RANGE - CALIFORNIA AND FLORIDA
GEAR - DIP NETS, POTS, HOOKS

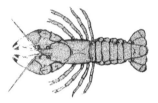

FRESH-WATER CRAWFISH
RANGE - RIVERS AND LAKES
GEAR - CRAWFISH (POTS)

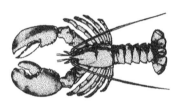

LOBSTER
RANGE - VIRGINIA TO MAINE
GEAR - POTS

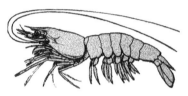

SHRIMP
RANGE - TEXAS TO NORTH CAROLINA,
        MAINE, CALIFORNIA,
        WASHINGTON, AND ALASKA
GEAR - SHRIMP TRAWLS

SOFT CLAM
RANGE - MIDDLE ATLANTIC TO
        NEW ENGLAND, PACIFIC
        COAST STATES
GEAR - FORKS, HOES, RAKES

RAZOR CLAM, PACIFIC
RANGE - OREGON, WASHINGTON AND
        ALASKA
GEAR - SHOVELS

HARD CLAM
RANGE - FLORIDA TO MAINE
GEAR - HOES, DREDGES, TONGS, RAKES
       HAND

LIMPET
RANGE - NEW YORK AND NEW ENGLAND
GEAR - DREDGES

LITTL -NECK CLAM
PANGEE- PACIFIC COAST
GEAR - SHOVELS

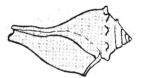

CONCH
RANGE - FLORIDA TO MAINE.
GEAR - SPONGE HOOKS, OTTER TRAWLS,
DREDGES, POTS

TREPANG
RANGE - WASHINGTON
GEAR - BEAM TRAWLS

BUTTER CLAM
RANGE - PACIFIC COAST
GEAR - SHOVELS

FRESH-WATER MUSSEL
RANGE - FRESH-WATER STREAMS
GEAR - CROWFOOT BARS, PICKS, HAND

OCEAN MUSSEL
RANGE - NORTH CAROLINA TO MAINE
GEAR - DREDGES, TONGS, RAKES, HAND

OYSTER
RANGE - TEXAS TO MASSACHUSETTS,
PACIFIC COAST STATES
GEAR - TONGS, DREDGES, RAKES, HAND

SQUID
RANGE - VIRGINIA TO MAINE,
CALIFORNIA AND
WASHINGTON
GEAR - LAMPARA NETS, GILL NETS
OTTER TRAWLS, POUND NETS

BAY SCALLOP
RANGE - FLORIDA TO MASSACHUSETTS,
WASHINGTON
GEAR - DREDGES, SCRAPES, PUSH NETS,
TONGS, RAKES

SEA SCALLOP
RANGE - NEW JERSEY TO MAINE
GEAR - DREDGES

STARFISH
RANGE - ATLANTIC AND PACIFIC COASTS
GEAR - HOOKS, SCRAPES, "MOPS"

TERRAPIN
RANGE – TEXAS TO NEW JERSEY
GEAR – HAUL SEINES, HAND

GREEN TURTLE
RANGE – FLORIDA
GEAR – GILL NETS, TANGLE NETS

LOGGERHEAD TURTLE
RANGE – FLORIDA TO NEW JERSEY
GEAR – GILL NETS

HAWKSBILL TURTLE
RANGE – GULF OF MEXICO AND ATLANTIC
        COAST TO NEW YORK
GEAR – HAND, TANGLE NETS, POUND NETS

FROG
RANGE – FRESH-WATER, MARSHES, PONDS
GEAR – SPEARS, GRABS

SOFT-SHELL TURTLE
RANGE – LAKES AND RIVERS
GEAR – HAUL SEINES, FYKE NETS,
       POTS

SPONGE
RANGE – FLORIDA TO WEST INDIES
GEAR – HOOKS, DIVING OUTFITS

IRISH MOSS
RANGE – NEW ENGLAND
GEAR – RAKES

STATISTICAL PUBLICATIONS SECTION 16.-

CURRENT FISHERIES STATISTICS

The following list of publications includes all reports issued in the Current Fishery
Statistics series during 1949,

C.F.S. No.	Title
447	Massachusetts Landings, August, 1948
448	Maine Landings, October, 1948
449	Fish Meal and Oil, December, 1948
450	Frozen Fish Report, January, 1949
451	Maine Landings, November, 1948
452	Massachusetts Landings, September, 1948
453	Frozen Fish Report, February, 1949
454	Massachusetts Landings, October, 1948
455	Fish Meal and Oil, January, 1949
456	Maine Landings, December, 1948
457	Frozen Fish Report, Annual, 1948
458	Maine Landings, By Months, Annual, 1948
459	Frozen Fish Report, March, 1949
460	Massachusetts Landings, November, 1948
461	Massachusetts Landings, December, 1948
462	Maine Landings, January, 1949
463	Fish Meal and Oil, February, 1949
464	Frozen Fish Report, April, 1949
465	Fish Meal and Oil, March, 1949
466	Massachusetts Landings, January, 1949
467	Maine Landings, February, 1949
468	Chesapeake Fisheries, Annual, 1946
469	New York Fisheries, Annual, 1946
470	Massachusetts Landings, February, 1949
471	Frozen Fish Report, May, 1949
472	Massachusetts Landings, By Ports, Annual, 1949
473	Maine Landings, March, 1949
474	Fish Meal and Oil, April, 1949
475	Massachusetts Landings, March, 1949
476	Imports and Exports, 1944 - 1948
477	Frozen Fish Report, June, 1949
478	Fish Meal and Oil, May, 1949
479	Maine Landings, April, 1949
480	New England Fisheries, Annual, 1946
481	Pacific Coast Fisheries, Annual, 1946
482	Massachusetts Landings, April, 1949
483	Frozen Fish Report, July, 1949
484	Maine Landings, By Counties, Annual, 1948
485	Maine Landings, May, 1949
486	Fish Meal and Oil, June, 1949
487	Fisheries of the United States and Alaska, 1946
488	Pacific Coast Fisheries, 1947
489	Frozen Fish Report, August, 1949
490	Massachusetts Landings, May, 1949
491	Maine Landings, June, 1949

(Continued on next page)

C.F.S. No.	Title
492	Packaged Fish, Annual, 1948
493	Fish Meal and Oil, July, 1949
494	Frozen Fish Report, September, 1949
495	Fish Meal and Oil, August, 1949
496	Maine Landings, July, 1949
497	Canned Fish and Byproducts, Annual, 1948
498	Massachusetts Landings, June, 1949
499	Frozen Fish Report, October, 1949
500	Massachusetts Landings, July, 1949
501	Maine Landings, August, 1949
502	Fish Meal and Oil, September, 1949
503	Texas Landings, September, 1949
504	Manufactured Fishery Products, Annual, 1946
505	Massachusetts Landings, Gear and Area, 1947
506	Massachusetts Landings, Gear and Area, 1948
507	Frozen Fish Report, November, 1949
508	Maine Landings, September, 1949
509	Texas Landings, October, 1949
510	Fish Meal and Oil, October, 1949
511	Frozen Fish Report, December, 1949
512	Maine Landings, October, 1949
513	Texas Landings, November, 1949
514	Massachusetts Landings, August, 1949

TUNA CLIPPER

U. S. GOVERNMENT PRINTING OFFICE : O—1952